Date Due

No 25 '31			

A LITERARY HISTORY OF RELIGIOUS THOUGHT IN FRANCE

The French book, of which this is the authorised translation, was published in 1916, under the title *Histoire Littéraire du Sentiment Religieux en France depuis la Fin des Guerres de Religion jusqu'à nos Jours:* II. *L'Invasion Mystique*, by Bloud et Gay, Paris.

Press Notices of Volume I

The Observer says: "Abbé Bremond's fascinating work has waited too long for an English version, but it could scarcely have a better than this given by K. L. Montgomery. . . . No French writer on literature since M. Jusserand has written so enticingly and with so wide a range of knowledge."

Evelyn Underhill in *The Spectator* says: "The main interest and value of M. Bremond's work . . . lies rather in his discovery and presentation of a crowd of forgotten saints and teachers who yet made a vital contribution to the spiritual history of their time; and his power of exhibiting them, not merely as 'historical' or 'literary' figures, but as living and experiencing souls. . . . It is the successful fulfilment of this aim, together with the richness and interest of the material drawn upon, and the author's literary genius, which combine to set the 'Histoire Littéraire' apart from all other works of the kind."

The Month says: "No one who is interested in the development of religious thought, not in France alone but in the whole Church, can afford to neglect the results of the learned author's immense industry and erudition."

A Literary History of Religious Thought in France

FROM THE WARS OF RELIGION DOWN TO OUR OWN TIMES

BY

HENRI BREMOND

VOL. II

THE COMING OF MYSTICISM

(1590–1620)

TRANSLATED BY K. L. MONTGOMERY

NEW YORK

THE MACMILLAN COMPANY

First published 1930

PRINTED IN GREAT BRITAIN

PREFACE

NO reader need be alarmed by this title. It is possible to take an interest in the following pages with their scenes and quotations without having sounded the depths of Mysticism. It is sufficient to know that the Mystic, while very human, enjoys the privilege of intimate and lofty intercourse with God. Those who may desire further illumination, and who have no time for specialized books, will find in the Appendix an instruction in catechetical form which I arranged for my own guidance, and in which I have summarized the general teaching of the theologians.

CONTENTS

CHAPTER I

THE SIXTEENTH CENTURY: THE TRADITION OF FRENCH MYSTICISM

I. WE must not imagine a New Jerusalem emerging radiant from chaos at the sound of the bells of S. Denis which announced to the world the abjuration of Henri IV. Autumn does not immediately succeed winter; a single day does not make a whole harvest of saints spring up from an exhausted earth. The sixteenth century claims most of the persons treated in the present volume. Nearly all were born and brought up—well brought up too—during the reigns of the Valois in a France where, despite many abuses, the purest spirit of Christianity yet flourished. Religious Orders were to be found which still kept their primitive austerity; the Carthusians, for example, more numerous than to-day and less far removed from the centres of action, maintained a firm front. After much tribulation the Victorines of Paris had returned to their former ideals; a trustworthy historian assures us that in their monastery between 1550 and 1600 "a fine revival of religious and intellectual life" was witnessed.[1] Those monasteries which, viewed from afar and as a whole, give the clearest impression of laxity yet had saints groaning in the dark, agonizing for reform. Capuchins, Jesuits, and new Orders burning with zeal and numbering men of exceptional merit, evangelized the length and breadth of France, towns and hamlets alike, combating the Protestants and teaching the elements of religion to the masses, but also, as is too often forgotten, directing the select few towards the summits of prayer. Take, for example, the quiet University of Pont-à-Mousson, founded in 1572, one of the strongholds of the Jesuits. About 1580 several of its students destined to rank among the leaders of the coming spiritual renaissance received the Divine spark—Pierre Fourier; the future reformer of the Premonstratensians, Servais de Lairuels; Didier de la Cour, the future reformer of

[1] Fourier-Bonnard, *Histoire de l'abbaye royale de S. Victor de Paris*, Paris, 1908. II. 57–70.

S. Vanne and initiator of the more famous reform of S. Maur; Didier's collaborator, Claude François; and, somewhat later, Philippe Thibaut, who was to reform the Carmelites and have Jean de Saint-Samson as his disciple.[1]

From the highest to the lowest rungs of the social ladder there were exemplary families in which the stock of national piety remained unimpaired. They were sometimes, often perhaps, the seed plot of the higher mysticism. In some cases precious details have come down to us. Claude Bernard, "the poor priest" (1588–1641), gave to the world his father's will, a touching document in which Jean-Pierre Camus recognized "those airs of Paradise which greet us in the Canticles."[2] Charles Bochart de Champigny, councillor of the *Parlement* of Paris under Charles IX and Henri III, was a kind of spiritual director to his young cousin, Madame Acarie. The children of such obscure and holy souls are perhaps their best witnesses. Of Bochart de Champigny and his wife (great-niece of Guillaume Briçonnet, Bishop of Meaux) were born that famous and saintly Capuchin, Honoré de Paris (1556–1624), his brother, also a Capuchin, and another brother, a Carthusian.[3] Nor must Père Denis Petau, who was born at Orleans in 1583 and joined the Jesuits in 1605, be forgotten. We know nothing about his father Jérôme or his mother, but of their children, "to say nothing of Denis, Jacques joined the Carthusians, François the Capuchins, Claude became Curé of Pithiviers, Étienne Canon of Orleans, and Marguerite took the veil in the Carmelite Order."[4] It is natural to suppose that a high supernatural level had been maintained in such circles.

What is really new, unique even, in the contribution made by the first half of the seventeenth century is not so much the fervour or even the number of its mystics as their radiating activity, their prestige and influence. We observe them arising suddenly from the obscurity

[1] Dom Didier Laurent, *Dom Didier de la Cour de la Vallée et la réforme des bénédictins de Lorraine*, Nancy, 1904, pp. 25–28; Eugène Martin, *Servais de Lairuels et la réforme des Prémontrés*, Nancy, 1893; Dom Vuillemin, *La Vie de Saint Pierre Fourier*, Paris, pp. 18 ff.; Abram, *Histoire de l'Université de Pont-à-Mousson* (Vol. V. of the *Documents inédits*, by P. Carayon).

[2] De Broqua, *Claude Bernard dit le Pauvre Prêtre*, Paris, 1914, p. 22.

[3] J. B. A. Boucher, *Vie de la bienheureuse Marie de l'Incarnation*, edition Bouix, Paris, 1873, p. 25; Mazelin, *Histoire du vénérable serviteur de Dieu, le P. Honoré de Paris*, Paris, 1882, pp. 1–10.

[4] Vital Chatellain, *Le Père Denis Petau*, Paris, 1884, p. 8.

which ordinarily shrouds them, to arrest popular attention and take the centre of the stage. They become heroic figures, uniting and grouping themselves, opening schools of holiness, inaugurating works destined long to endure, influencing the political machine, sharing in royal councils, and alternately helping and embarrassing the Ministers who treated them as powerful forces. Nothing similar had been seen in the preceding era, when the living water flowed from the same fount, but its murmur was not heard beyond the fences of the garden enclosed; when the timid branches of the same tree as yet offered only an uncertain shade, attracting none but the humblest birds of heaven.

It cannot be denied that the sixteenth century, and the opening years of the seventeenth, have been painted by most historians, sacred and secular, and notably by the first biographers of P. de Condren and Vincent de Paul, in the blackest of colours. They exaggerate, I am sure,[1] but in any case it concerns us little. From our rigorously limited point of view, we are not occupied with contemporary scandals, but solely with those who will always be a little flock—the elect.

Again, the comparative merits of the sixteenth and seventeenth centuries are not to be judged by the number of pious biographies produced in those periods. From the time of Louis XIII onwards

[1] "Even the name of priest had become a shame and a disgrace," wrote P. Amelote in his *Life of Père de Condren*; "wellnigh its sole use by the world was to express an ignoramus or a *debauché*. Intercourse with the class was considered disgraceful. Priests were only to be seen at markets or in some shop frequented by low artizans; their tonsure was effaced and they shunned wearing their habits, as affording matter for public raillery" (pp. 391-2). It has been already remarked in the previous volume that such charges could only have been true of the lowest ranks of the lower clergy. Among the professors of the Sorbonne and the *Curés* of Paris and other large towns there were eminent men such as we could hardly rival to-day, who did not frequent the market-place and could scarcely have been taken for ignoramuses. The admirable biographer of Vincent de Paul, Abelly, however, speaks in the same tone, and it is amazing that such an historian as the Abbé Maynard in his *Vie de Vincent de Paul* should have accepted both Abelly's text and certain contemporary testimonies on this point. Evidence such as this, M. de Calvet justly observes in his *Vincent de Paul* in the *Bibliothèque Française* (p. 31), assuredly has a value of its own, but cannot be taken literally. Generally speaking the pictures of the sixteenth century which frequently precede modern biographies of seventeenth-century saints are no more than oratorical generalisations; for instance, the introduction of *l'Histoire de la vénérable Marguerite du Saint-Sacrement*, by the Abbé Deberre (Paris, 1907). Through all time there have been pessimistic critics to declare with M. Bourdoise that "the age is very ill," or with Guy Patin that one had reached "the dregs of the centuries." Using these methods, what a sinister picture might one not draw of what have been called "the ages of faith"!

such books abound; a convent portress, a lackey, or a shoemaker, each has his or her chronicler. This is a touching but new departure,[1] for the preceding age had devoted itself to publications considered more important, or more reserved in tone. " God glorifies Himself," so it was then held, " by keeping hidden away from the knowledge of men, thousands of His faithful worshippers."[2] In the same way great crimes generally make more noise than great virtues. Everyone knows, or can find out, that the canons of Ste. Geneviève in Paris raised a veritable witches' sabbath when Père Faure undertook to reform them, but only by a miracle has the name of the pious priest, M. Roussel, been preserved, who, in the reign of Henri III, was wont to pass the whole day in prayer in that very church of Ste. Geneviève, only leaving his ecstasy there to betake himself to S. Étienne du Mont, " in order to hear the confessions of young scholars or certain devout ladies." " We and other students seeing him pass," relates Dr. André Duval, " used to exclaim, ' there goes that holy priest! ' One of us used to say that he wished to see how long his prayers at Ste. Geneviève would continue, but after long waiting he was compelled to leave the priest still on his knees."[3] Against the background of Time this figure stands out boldly, but many mystics and the majority of other fervent Christians remain unknown, only comparable to " those black emmets," to quote the Koran, " which in the black night crawl over black stones." God knows them, and sometimes their neighbours know them, but these, most frequently, neither can write nor wish to do so. Bibliography confirms our suspicions and conjectures on this point with astonishing emphasis. Without going into minute statistics it may be remarked that in France, between 1570 and 1615, were published and republished, either in Latin or French, nearly all the classics of the higher

[1] See Vol. I. ch. viii.

[2] *La Vie du R. P. D. Eustache de S. Paul*, Paris, 1646, preface.

[3] *La Vie admirable de la bienheureuse soeur Marie de l'Incarnation*, by M. André Duval, Paris, 1893, pp. 13, 14. This M. Roussel was that confessor from whom Pierre Acarie was wont to borrow spiritual books for his wife's reading. One of these books produced a profound impression on young Mme Acarie and was, in Duval's words, " the instrument of which God availed Himself to raise her to the height of her eminent sanctity." It is to this fortunate circumstance that we owe our knowledge of M. Roussel. On the reform of Ste. Geneviève, see Feret's work, *L'abbaye de Ste. Geneviève*, Paris, 1883, and more especially the long and interesting *Vie du R. P. Charles Faure Abbé de Ste. Geneviève de Paris*, Paris, 1698.

spiritual life, to say nothing of a host of other similar works of minor importance.[1]

II. A valuable book might be easily written upon the inner life of French Catholicism during this period of effervescence. It is not mine to write this book, but I should like at least to give a rapid sketch of the final chapter which shows how the mysticism of the sixteenth century prepared for that of the seventeenth and passed on the torch to it. With this in view I shall confine myself to a single province, preferring precise and living detail to the often unsatisfying generalities of a vast fresco looked at as a whole.

I might have chosen the south-west,[2] Quercy and two of our holy cities, Bordeaux and Toulouse, taking, for example, Montaigne's niece, the venerable Mère Jeanne de Lestonnac (1556–1640), and her fellow-worker, the Jesuit Jean de Bordes; or better still, the famous Jean de la Barrière, out of whose name contemporaries skilled in anagrams read, "*J'ai relevé Bernard*" ("I have raised up Bernard").

Jean de la Barrière "was born at Saint-Céri in the diocese of

[1] The propaganda of translating the mystics had been started by Lefèbvre d'Etaples long before. In 1558 a translation of the *Théologie germanique* appeared at Antwerp. For our period the following dates may suffice :—

1570. Denis the Carthusian.
1572. Grenada.
1574. Grenada.
1575. Grenada.
1577. Grenada.
1580. Catharine of Siena.
1586. Suso ; Stella.
1587. Tauler ; Alphonse of Madrid ; Denis the Carthusian.
1588. Avila.
1589. Avila.
1597. Catharine of Genoa.
1599. Catharine of Genoa ; Grenada.
1601. Life of Ste. Teresa.
1603. Angela of Foligno.
1615. Life of Balthazar Alvarez.

The complete list would be, I take it, four or five times longer. Among the translators, Chapuys and the Carthusians of Bourgfontaine are to be distinguished at least for the fecundity of their works. With the seventeenth century appeared a new worker, M. R. Gauthier, who published Ribadeneyra's *Fleurs des Saints* in 1609 and the *Vie d'Alvarez* in 1615. I say nothing of the Latin texts, translations of the pseudo-Dionysius or reprints of the Victorines and of Harphius, etc., any more than of the MS. booklets so widely circulated during this era.

[2] [The district actually chosen is the south-east, see below. *Tr.*]

Cahors, and early nominated as commendatory of the Cistercian Abbey of the Feuillants in the diocese of Rieux, six leagues from Toulouse. During the first years in which he held office he merely employed himself in receiving the revenues, studying, and leading a life of which the most that could be said was that it was free from scandals. Soon, however, touched by the grace of God, he resolved on being in reality what he was in name, true religious and true abbot." In order to prepare himself for the reform he contemplated, in 1573 he entered the Chartreuse of Paris, there passing four years in religious exercises and such extreme austerity that, denying himself even bread, he lived solely on vegetables. Next, he proposed that his Community should follow his example, but with small success, for, indignant and alarmed, after various intrigues, all forsook him to join other houses of the Order, and Jean remained alone in his Abbey. In a short while, however, novices arrived "and at this point the congregation of Notre Dame des Feuillants was inaugurated (1577). In a few years his monastery was filled by a hundred and fifty monks attracted by the reputation of his sanctity. The foundation of other branch houses followed, and the official recognition of the congregation by Sixtus V (1586, 1587). The rule was very severe—meat, wine, fish, and eggs being prohibited—and in other respects corresponded to its bill of fare. Food was taken kneeling, the monks slept on boards, rose at midnight, went barefoot, and practised a rigorous silence. . . . Soon women aspired to this life, asking to be united under the direction of Jean de la Barrière."[1] These were the first Feuillant nuns, with Marguerite de Polastron (1588) at their head. In 1599 Antoinette d'Orléans-Longueville took refuge among them and later, together with Père Joseph, founded the "Calvaire."

Henri III, who had already established—first at the Bois de Boulogne and later at Vincennes—the Hieronymites, religious whom he had known in Poland, looked favourably on the Feuillants and built for their reception a monastery in the Faubourg S.-Honoré, near the Tuileries Gardens. The removal of this colony was dramatic enough to impress the populace. The King had sent an escort of forty cavalry. "Never before in mortal memory had such a procession been seen. The sacred band, sixty in number, marched on foot for a hundred and fifty leagues, headed by a cross-bearer, the other monks

[1] *Vie de la Mère Antoinette d'Orléans*, by Petit, Paris 1880, pp. 22-4.

following in pairs marshalled by the saintly Abbé, the horsemen in front and behind and on the flanks guarding the devout company. The silence maintained was so perfect that all could listen to the spiritual readings of the Fathers as they paced soft-footed along the highway. . . . When they approached cities, market-towns or villages, ecclesiastics, laity, sometimes even a bishop, joined the procession. . . . Each morning the Abbot said Mass and either preached himself or directed the celebrated minor Feuillant, Dom Bernard, to take his place."[1]

Many Feuillants have played active parts in the history of France; among others, Eustache de Saint-Paul and two intimate friends of S. François de Sales, Dom Sans de Sainte-Catherine, and " Dom Jean de Saint-François, known to the world as Goulu." The last-named, one of the most original figures of his time, deserves special mention. He was the son of Nicholas Goulu, Regius Professor of Greek, and grandson on the maternal side of the great humanist Jean Daurat. In 1608 Jean himself translated the works of the pseudo-Dionysius and the following year the *Manuel* of Epictetus; later, in 1624, publishing the life of François de Sales, and in 1629 the famous *Lettres de Phyllarque*, aimed against Balzac; thus alternating between mysticism and the humanities with perfect balance.[2]

Jeanne de l'Estonnac and Jean de la Barrière would be amply sufficient to detain us in Languedoc; Paris, which will absorb our attention only too much in the sequel, would not be less interesting. But, as I see it, the most ardent centre of mystic activity towards the end of the sixteenth century is Comtat, that is Provence. In the foreground, Avignon, l'Isle-sur-Sorgue, Cavaillon, Saint-Remy, Arles, Les Baux, Aix-en-Provence; in the distance the dome of Milan, the Oratory of S. Philip Neri at Rome, and the Vatican, such is the vast and noble scenery of the history which must be summarized in a few pages. It is a scene motley and crowded as a romantic drama, filled with over a hundred figures—village shopkeepers and holy women, hermits, small *rentiers*, rich *bourgeois*, soldiers, young girls of the upper middle-class or of the nobility, bishops, cardinals—all caught in the same net of grace, working together at

1 *La Vie du R. P. Dom Eustache de Saint-Paul*, pp. 198–202.

2 Cf. *Œuvres de S. François de Sales*, XV. 77–8. Jean Goulu, born in 1576, and Sans de Sainte-Catherine both died in 1629.

great undertakings, planning and carrying out the same schemes as were soon to be attempted by the mystics of the Ile-de-France. It is impossible to give an impression of this seething life, difficult even to select among so many shadowy figures. They are too numerous for me to call them up. I could not range them all on the opposite bank, for behind the chief figures crowd a nameless mass—their masters, their disciples, their friends—a cloud of saints.

César de Bus stands out among the chief figures of the throng, although nearly equal to him is his cousin, Jean-Baptiste Romillon. Both were born in the Comtat, César at Cavaillon in 1544, Jean-Baptiste at l'Isle-sur-Sorgue in 1553. The family of de Bus, or de Buxis, were originally of Rome, migrating to France towards the middle of the fifteenth century. They were received at Court, César's eldest brother, Alexandre, being captain of the guard under Charles IX, and probably playing a modest part in the massacre of S. Bartholomew. The Romillons, although of good stock, attract less notice in the picture, but another cousin of both families, Louis Suffren, son of a Councillor of the *Parlement* of Provence, became the Jesuit confessor of Louis XIII.

César set out for Paris, where his brother offered him a splendid career, but, finding the novitiate of a courtier too tedious and rough, he returned to Cavaillon, where, from twenty to thirty, he was the life and soul of the gilded youth of the town. A couple of lines by one of his biographers paint him for us. "He loved company and was always welcomed . . . he dressed well, spent freely, composed little poems which, fostering the passions, were acceptable to those ruled by them. I shrink from chronicling this, but one must show the extent of the wound in order to give due honour to the hand which brought the cure. He was as tactful and felicitous in ending the quarrels of others, as in holding his own where necessity demanded."[1] His rhymed tragedies, which were played at Cavaillon, unfortunately have disappeared with the other poetical work, burnt by him after his conversion. This former Ronsardist, oddly enough, was to become one of the reformers of the pulpit. "His own discourses were ordinary and familiar in style, avoiding the dangerous rock of new and uncommon words, or superfluous ornament, however beautiful. . . . Once, long afterwards remembering an affected

[1] *La Vie du V. César de Bus*, by R. P. Pierre Dumas, Paris, 1703, p. 24.

turn in one of his harangues, he caused a lengthy manuscript to be searched through until the offending word could be struck out."[1] "Being at Cavaillon, in company with a religious who was a noted preacher, they heard certain verses recited at the entry of the Vice-Legate of Avignon, in which the word '*bouboullonnant*' was used. 'There's a tremendous word!' smiled the religious. 'You employ many such in the pulpit!' replied P. César, 'which are more so.'"[2] Cavaillon, more refined and elegant than it is to-day, and a rich suburb of the papal city, was, however, only a little town. Everyone knew everybody else; even in the humblest dwellings César de Bus and his brilliant follies were household words. The good folk recalled with affectionate sadness his angelic youth, when in the penitent's black cowl he was wont to decorate the chapels on Maundy Thursday or the street altars for the Corpus Christi procession; when he had looked forward to becoming a priest and Canon of Cavaillon. Paris had changed all that, but still the prodigal was the subject of prayers entreating God for his conversion. Active efforts were also made to bring such conversion about. Two saintly persons, a hatter and a peasant woman, undertook this mission and worked in concert towards this end. Humble instruments in truth, but free Provence has never known the feudal terror; she has always treated her nobility with a simple familiarity that does not preclude respect. The hatter, Louis Guyot, was in fact of fair social position, a distant cousin of his being Bishop of Riez; he himself, had he wished it, could easily have stepped into a benefice. His humility alone had prevented his entering the Church. For some time sacristan of the cathedral of Cavaillon, in the end he deemed even this too high for him, and opened a hatter's shop, which soon became a spiritual centre in the little town. He was venerated and loved, and his discourses were listened to gladly. He exhorted some to repentance, others to greater fervour of life. He prepared his neophytes in person "for general confessions, taking them on occasions in large numbers to Avignon to R. P. Péquet, of the Society of Jesus."

This last touch is interesting, for we have put our finger on the *liaison* which was then being effected spontaneously between the saints of every day—mystics of the soil, so to speak—and the agents

[1] *La Vie du R. P. César de Bus*, by P. J. Marcel, Paris, 1619, pp. 206–7.
[2] *Ibid.*, p. 415.

of the Counter-Reformation. This Père Péquet, long Rector of the College of Avignon and himself one of the most active workers in the religious renaissance, was director of César de Bus and Romillon, guiding them step by step with an exceptionally delicate and sure touch. To-day who knows so much as his name? It occurs only once in the great official history of the French Jesuits.[1]

The Bishop of Cavaillon, Monseigneur Pompée Roch, was the first to encourage the zeal of this lay missionary and to praise his great virtues. He also received and listened with sympathy to the good peasant woman whose dream it was to draw back César de Bus into the right path. Antoinette—we only know her by this name—"after her husband's death . . . being moved by divine inspiration to quit her cottage in the fields" came "to live in Cavaillon in order to work more effectively for César's conversion. Lest there should be any doubt in her mind about the purpose of her mission, God allowed her to be accompanied during her journey by a heavenly light. She established herself in a lodging opposite the de Bus mansion, where she soon got a familiar footing. . . . She . . . passed the greater part of the day in prayer . . . although attenuated, pallid, and almost reduced to a skeleton by her continued prayers and severe penances, when she spoke of the Mercy of God her face would flush crimson, as if glowing with interior fire. . . . When she spoke of the death . . . of the Divine Redeemer, she was wont to weep and mourn, as though she had been actually present at the sacrifice.

"Such zeal indeed inflamed her, that it was a saying she would have walked on naked swords . . . to carry out the Will of God. Her ardour led her to rebuke vice wherever she encountered it, and even took her to Orange to encourage and strengthen those Catholics . . . whose faith was wavering. She harangued the Protestants at a synod, and boldly prophesied . . . that the Mass would again be celebrated in that town."[2]

[1] *Histoire de la Compagnie de Jésus en France*, by P. H. Fouqueray, Paris, 1913, II. 69. Louis Guyot died in 1578.

[2] *Vie du vénérable César de Bus*, by M. l'Abbé Chamoux, Paris, 1864, pp. 36–38. This book, badly enough written and possessing graver faults, has at least the merit of faithfully epitomizing the excellent life of P. de Bus, by P. Marcel. The latter, published shortly after the death of the saint, is fully reliable, based as it is on traditions then known to contemporaries. The lengthy quarto of P. Dumas is less trustworthy.

She had no sooner penetrated to the heart of the citadel than the de Bus family welcomed her as a saint—gathered around her, even César, hastening to his pleasures, now and again pausing to listen to her. She went so far indeed as to remonstrate with him. He let her speak, with his Comtat good-humour, but replied only in jesting fashion. The siege was long, the pious soul often retiring discouraged, to be again cheered to the advance by Louis Guyot. At last they hit on a pathetically childish stratagem. Antoinette could not read, so, arming herself with a copy borrowed from Guyot of *Lives of the Saints*, she placed herself in César's way. " You who are so courteous and complaisant to everyone," she began, " will surely not be otherwise with me if I beg you to read me half a dozen lines of this book, or if that be too much, then three." César took the volume and read some sentences in a tone half bantering, half good-natured, handing it back then to the woman. " Now, monsieur," she cried, " how does that strike you? Do you not blush for your excesses—in comparing your life with that of the saints? Beware of death, death, judgment, judgment, hell, hell eternally! " She repeated the awe-inspiring words several times, her voice earnest, vehement, and full of fervour. César laughed at these eager apostrophes and sought his accustomed *rendezvous*. " So difficult is it," says the chronicler, " to loose the bands of evil habits."[1]

The day came when grace conquered. César docilely placed himself first under the direction of Antoinette and Louis Guyot, later, under that of the Jesuits at Avignon. He was not ordained priest till 1582, but from 1575 or 1576 we see him utterly devoted to God. His cousin, Romillon, followed in his footsteps, and before the sixteenth century closed, the two Provençals had founded a new Order, the *Congrégation de la Doctrine Chrétienne*, introduced the Ursulines into France, and laid the foundation of the French Oratory.

" In the Comté d'Avignon there is a river called the Sorgue, flowing from the fountain of Vaucluse, which a league further on encircles a small town called on that account *l'Isle* (the Island). This was the birthplace, in 1553, of Romillon. . . . His father Barthélemy, brought up in the bosom of the Church, had in a moment of hopelessness separated himself from it, shortly after his marriage with

[1] Chamoux, *ibid.*, pp. 44–5.

Catherine de Suffren. . . . The avarice of certain persons who falsely accused him of heresy for the sake of obtaining his possessions, contributed to his lapse, and as everything was then involved in the troubles of the civil wars, these greedy scoundrels found no difficulty in accomplishing their plans. . . . Reduced to necessity, he let himself be so blinded by his grief . . . (that he conceived) the unhappy idea of joining the heretics and taking refuge in one of their towns, hoping to find there shelter from his persecutors." But ill-luck followed him; he failed to regain his fortune and he lost his faith, as it turned out, for good and all. His son, like himself a zealous Calvinist, in early youth took service on that side. "What could be expected of a young man who bore arms in the cause of heresy but every kind of vice associated with youth, fostered by war, and authorized by error? We see him up to the age of twenty-six immersed in the debaucheries of youth, the violence of military life, and the blasphemies of heresy."

However, memories of his pious mother disturbed him and certain clumsy sermons revealed the weakness of the Reformers. He was much upset and, seeking for distraction, he took the first opportunity that offered, a friendly visit to his relative M. de Chateauneuf, lately returned from Paris. "He (Romillon) had difficulty in hiding his trouble during the first exchange of greetings, and presently his anxiety broke bounds. He needed some charitable hand to heal his spiritual wound, and this hand was stretched out by his good relative, Madame de Chateauneuf, who, observing his deep depression, enquired the reason of this change. Divining from a few broken words that he was overborne by grief, she decided to give him and advise him to read the Treatise on Prayer (*Traité de l'Oraison*), by R. P. Louis de Grenada, which her husband has brought her from Paris." Such details are full of savour and meaning, and make us see a France which the historians of the wars of religion do not seem to suspect—the young Huguenot soldier paying a country visit to Catholics, good M. de Chateauneuf bringing back from Paris a book of devotions for his wife, and the gentle Provençal dame, wise enough not to alienate her kinsman by a work of controversy, but kindly offering a book on prayer. Next we see Jean Baptiste Romillon studying the book with delight and "comparing it with the Institutes of Calvin." "Having read a page of the one he read a page of the other and at once asked himself which of the two books displayed more truth and more grace." Calvin came out second best, and Romillon publicly abjured his heresy before the Bishop of the diocese in the church of Cavaillon, in 1579.[1]

We may pause here to remark that the faithful disciple, friend, and successor of Romillon, Père Jacques de Rez (1577–1666), also comes to us from Calvinism. A native of Baux, " he was but thirteen years old when, being present one day at Mass, said by P. Romillon who then lived at Avignon, he saw several persons approaching the Holy Table. He was led to join them, either by supernatural drawing or by a child's thoughtlessness, and at the moment of receiving the Consecrated Host he experienced such longing for the Catholic religion that he rose from his place, followed the priest into the sacristy, and said smilingly though firmly: 'Sir, I would like to join your religion!' Père Romillon recognized him as the lad to whom he had just given Communion, and was much surprised at this announcement. He questioned him, learned that he was a Calvinist . . . which gave him qualms of conscience. However, he remarked in the youth the presence of something miraculous and divine . . . he began to instruct him . . . and after some months received his abjuration."[2] Long after when Pierre de Bérulle wished for information about the Oratory of Provence, Romillon sent Jacques de Rez to him.

III. Up to the time of his conversion, Romillon, when not at the wars, had lived at l'Isle with his parents, helping his father " in his business," but now he felt called to a different life and desired to become a priest. It was very late for a man who had received only a scanty education, but he possessed ability, a will of iron, and an unquestionable vocation. His director—director, too, of all the Comtat—Père Péquet, suggested to him " the college of Tournon, then enjoying an extraordinary reputation." He departed forthwith, " arrived at Tournon on May 15th, 1583, and paying no heed to the reasons, naturally suggested by his age, why he should avoid the shame of sitting in class with young urchins, set himself to acquire

[1] *La vie du Père Romillon*, by M. Bourguignon, Marseilles, 1649, pp. 1–13. This Life is well written and very accurate, Bourguignon having had good opportunities of learning about his hero from P. de Rez, who had been Romillon's intimate friend.

[2] *Recueil des vies de quelques prêtres de l'Oratoire*. P. Cloyseault, published by R. P. Ingold, Paris, 1882, II. 73–5.

the grammar and first elements of Latin, and to listen to the lessons of the sixth class. . . . Seated among more than two hundred small children, for the most part below seven years of age, while he was over thirty . . . his fellow-pupils called him 'Papa,' and made him endure daily a hundred mortifications." Thus he lived wretchedly enough, till the day when he was sufficiently advanced in his studies to take "a room of his own, where the fame of his virtue attracted immediately to his guidance a number of the youth of Tournon." At first he applied himself to philosophy, "but God, destining him to greater things and Himself teaching him the science of the saints, willed not that he should long apply himself to a study wholly subjugated to the knowledge of the world and of Nature. . . . He had no sooner begun to learn the principles of the science of Aristotle and Plato than he found himself compelled to give them up for those of Jesus Christ. The reason for the change was the action of the Bishop of Cavaillon, who, long acquainted with his virtues and his merit, conferred on him a Canonry of the Collegiate Church of l'Isle."[1] That is how things were done in the good old days. Romillon and César de Bus, too, learned theology by preparing their Catechisms and meditating on the Scriptures.

The fields around were indeed white to harvest, the bishops were prompt to receive such good workmen as offered to their hand. I do not find that any of them—Archbishops of Avignon or Aix, or Bishops of Cavaillon, Carpentras, or Arles—discouraged any of the innovations, sometimes bold enough, of César de Bus and Romillon. On the contrary, they encouraged the two saintly men, defending them against calumny, supporting them at Rome, and often taking an active part in their various foundations. Most of these Bishops were Italian, and through them the Counter-Reformation in France was united to the Mother Church, our French saints to those of Milan and of Rome. The Archbishop of Aix communicated to César de Bus many details about Carlo Borromeo, whom he had personally known and who had but recently died (1584). We find him sending the earliest biography of this eminent saint to his friend, and César replying: "I have received the history of him whose mortal life has, as I hold, been translated to a better one. I assure you, while reading it, I have been so carried away and fired with such

[1] Bourguignon, *ibid.*, pp. 34–44.

desire to go and do likewise, that I shall not give sleep to my eyes or rest to my days before I have satisfied this resolution of mine in some way."[1] Thus began among us the devotion destined speedily to become so popular and so fruitful. Tarugi, Archbishop of Avignon from 1593 to 1597, a patron of César and of Romillon, had been the intimate companion and right hand of Philip Neri, and had succeeded him in the government of the Oratory. So with many others. There was continual contact then between Italy and Provence, as there would soon be between Spain and France. In both directions the same spirit was at work. Rome was on the alert, helping forward this coming and going and facilitating these exchanges. Our founders obtained all the Bulls they required, without the least trouble.

L'Isle lies near Cavaillon, and the two cousins saw a good deal of each other. The same zeal animated them, they had the same objects of ambition, and were inspired by the same man, Père Péquet. The lines of their lives soon became so interwoven that it is difficult to distinguish the share borne by each in their common undertakings. With sufficient dissimilarity for each to be the complement of the other, they remained associated until the day when diversity of their call should separate them. César de Bus, of Italian stock, was a poet, had more initiative and imagination, and his saintliness has a more arresting quality; Romillon, a staid Provençal, possessed deeper penetration, a surer knowledge of men, and a firmer will, and could organize more solidly his contemplated undertakings. But History, always in a hurry and tending to simplification, a little feminine in character, retains by preference the figure that lends itself to legend. She was to remember César de Bus in blurred outlines, but to forget Romillon.

Canons both of them, they turned at once to the most urgent duty, the teaching of the Catechism to their flocks, grown-ups as well as children. This was a startling novelty in those days. Biographers speak of it under sonorous titles. "César de Bus discovers a new method of teaching Christian Doctrine," or again, "The discovery of the Greater Catechism is his." "This is his method, hitherto unknown," writes P. Marcel. "Beginning with an explanation of the Creed . . . he takes one article after another, deducing

[1] Marcel, *op. cit.*, p. 110.

three or four doctrines from each. At that time the principal folk in the town scarcely knew how to make their confessions, partly from the neglect of the pastors, partly from the irreligion fostered by war; the lower orders were ignorant of the necessary elements." Preachers there were, but too learned and lost in the clouds. "Now, however, forsaking all other public teaching, everyone hastened to this as the easiest, even the most profitable. . . . All sorts of people, great and small, learned and ignorant, went away instructed. . . . Both method and manner bore the stamp of an extreme but rich simplicity, faithful to the Primitive Church and in accordance with the Council of Trent; they were so successful in his hands that henceforward he substituted the arts of love for those of oratory, and gave himself entirely to them, distasteful though they might be to proud spirits."[1]

The method was, however, less miraculous than was supposed, for, following Canisius and many others, the Capuchins and Jesuits were already inculcating doctrine in much the same fashion. In the very town of P. de Bus, the Jesuit Philippe Chanan was actually employing such catechisings, among his disciples being our friend Romillon, sent there by P. Péquet. "He assisted with all possible assiduity," says Romillon's biographer, "at the catechisings of P. Philippe, in pursuance of his design to mould his own teaching upon it, sojourning at Cavaillon for the purpose. He carefully noted the priest's familiar ways and his method, the gentleness with which he treated the little children and the gravity which he resumed from time to time to obtain silence. He admired the skill with which he instructed those of ripe age, and even asked them questions, without their being confused or ashamed to answer. . . . Nor was he content with thus listening to the Father, but often privately conferred with him on the value and peculiarities of these methods of instruction and the possibility of extending his system to other towns. He likewise frequently discussed the matter with Mgr. de Cavaillon and with his saintly director (Péquet) and even[2] with M. de Bus, his close friend . . . until, instructed by the example and maxims of

[1] Marcel, *op. cit.*, pp. 125–8.

[2] This "even" is to my mind a bit of innocent malice on the part of Romillon's biographer, his naturally critical turn of mind being stimulated by enthusiasm for his own hero. He protests justly enough against the tradition which has exalted César de Bus at the expense of his collaborator Romillon and his inspirers, the Jesuits of Avignon.

Père Philippe, he resolved to return to l'Isle, and devote himself wholly to inculcating the method there."[1]

César, then, at Cavaillon and Romillon at l'Isle proclaimed "the Christian doctrine" with marvellous success. Recognition from without was not slow in coming, and together they conducted Missions in outlying regions, as far as the Cévennes. Young disciples joined them, and about 1593 the *Congrégation de la Doctrine Chrétienne* was founded at Avignon and soon spread into several provinces.

I cannot follow the destinies of these Catechist missionaries, but I must at least mention in a few words the innocent and providential difference of opinion that separated Romillon and César de Bus. To begin with, the brethren were bound by no vows; though living in Community they remained content with "the purely ecclesiastical state," as the Oratory of P. de Bérulle and S. Sulpice were to do later. In 1602, however, César de Bus, possibly yielding to pressure from some Father or other, desired to modify the rule of the Congregation on this essential point and proposed the change to his brethren. Some accepted it at once, but Romillon, "firmer than a rock in the spirit of priesthood and the purely ecclesiastical state, asked with all possible moderation whether the vows must be made in response to human persuasion or through inspiration of the Holy Spirit, and when he received no other answer save that he must obey or go, he said that he would not take a vow without having consulted God, and that he felt no inclination thereto. After saying this he went out, bathed in tears." Some of the Fathers were of his opinion, so that, though there was no open rupture, the existing situation could not continue. After lengthy negotiations it was settled "that Père de Bus and his following should remain masters in the House of Avignon, while Père Romillon with his disciples should establish themselves in that of Aix," preserving friendly relations with their former *confrères*.

There were now two little independent Societies. What would Romillon do "with his little community of twelve, which he had saved from storm in the Barque of S. Peter? He began by writing to all his acquaintance among representative men," among others addressing himself to Tarugi, recalled some years previously from

[1] Bourguignon, *op. cit.*, pp. 75–7.

Avignon to Rome to receive a Cardinal's hat. Tarugi "showed by his reply that he was entirely satisfied with Romillon's action and, it being clear that God had called him to the ranks of the secular clergy, to confirm him in his original design . . . the Cardinal sent him details of the Oratory at Rome and of the exercises there practised, further counselling him to model his little community on that of S. Philip, his master in the spiritual life, and to take the name of *l'Institut de l'Oratoire*. Bulls for the foundation in France would be easily obtained, as there were already several of the same congregation in Italy."[1] Thus little by little the House at Aix steadied itself, and soon was formally established by Paul V *ad instar Oratorii romani* (1615).

Shortly after, Père de Bérulle, meditating a similar project, put himself into communication with the Oratorians of Provence, and, in 1619, the Oratory of Romillon, embracing eleven houses, united itself with the Oratory of France. The step was desirable and doubtless necessary, but it leaves some slight matter for regret. No one admires more than I, Père de Bérulle, Père de Condren, and the first generations of the French Oratorians, yet I hold that those of Provence, as near to Rome as to Paris and formed by a direct disciple of Tarugi, approached more nearly the primitive spirit of Philip Neri. Less metaphysical, less lofty and eloquent, their simple fervour, their human touch, sometimes even their peculiarities, made for popularity, giving them over the minds of the people an influence usually lacking to the refined sons of Bérulle. They kept the accent of their native country and mingled with it something of the accent of "the Valli-

[1] Bourguignon, *op. cit.*, pp. 239–41. The biographers of César de Bus, and especially the latest, Chamoux, incline to blame Romillon entirely in this incident, yet by the most elementary laws of morals he is wholly justified. If, ten years after the foundation of the Society of Jesus, S. Ignatius had proposed the Carthusian Rule to his companions they assuredly would have had full right to take back their pledges. To quote Bourguignon (p. 240), Père Romillon "in his task of establishing Christian doctrine had but one thought, that of the perfection of the priesthood"; he begged his brethren "to reflect on those Papal Bulls" already establishing their congregation on lines laid down by Tarugi, "who had been promoter of the whole business." If his biographer is correct, César, then blind and infirm, apparently confided to Romillon that "he was not the author of the separation, but that his authority had been abused and his state of health taken advantage of" (*ibid.*, p. 241). Romillon, at that date superior of the *Doctrinaires* of Aix, having special fame as co-founder and by nature independent and enterprising, may possibly have offended Père Vigier, who was next to César in authority, and had the effective direction of the Society. Cf. the *Mémoires domestiques*, Batterel, Paris, 1902, I. 17 ff.

celle." The French Oratory was unlike the Roman, but it was thoroughly French and, prematurely, French after the style of *le grand siècle.* In the first chapters of its splendid chronicle, some of the companions of Romillon pass before us, P. de Rez, P. Jacques Merindol, P. Jean Jaubert, and others. Jaubert is said to "have been very like S. Philip Neri in figure, features, and methods of work."[1] He was wont to travel on a donkey through the countryside on evangelistic Missions. Another contemporary, P. Yvan, had an ardent devotion for the saintly founder whom he often called in caressing Italian "*Il mio padre Filippo*"; "not content with imitating the exterior virtues of this great saint, he endeavoured to copy his outward appearance, from his style of wearing a *soutane* to the way he wore his hair. When his beard was being trimmed he would hold the saint's portrait in his hand like a mirror, in order to express him better."[2] These are trifles, but all else is in keeping. Those who hold that lukewarmness and formalism as well as *ennui* are produced by uniformity, have an affection for these good men, guardians of a tradition. But gradually the original *naïveté* disappears; our Provençals acquired a Parisian manner. P. Yvan's compatriots, Mascaron and Massillon, brought no discredit upon the Oratory, but one wonders what would S. Philip have said had he heard them.[3]

IV. In the present chapter my design is not to paint the mystics at length and one by one. Belonging to the period of transition between the sixteenth and seventeenth centuries, these precursors of dawn scarcely belong to our period, while from another point of view we have few details of their interior life, nor does their apostolate immediately concern us here. I want only to stimulate the reader's imagination, to breathe into his ear the soft whisper of a rising tide, or rather the imperceptible rustle of a germinating harvest. When

[1] Cloyseault-Ingold, *op. cit.* II. 111. All the description of Jean Jaubert is very interesting. Cf. p. 73 ff. for a notice of P. de Rez.

[2] Cf. Bremond, *La Provence mystique*, Paris, 1908, p. 39.

[3] Before Romillon's day, Rollin-Ferrier had established at Notre Dame des Grâces, near Cotignac in the Var, an Oratorian community, having previously conferred thereupon with Philip Neri himself, in Rome somewhere about 1586. In this little Oratory, united with that of Bérulle in 1615, there was still living in 1608 an old priest, P. Paul, an odd character, but regarded by his disciple, P. Yvan, as one of the most eminent mystics of the period. The portrait of this curious personage, together with that of Antoine Yvan and Antoinette Martin, has been sketched in my *La Provence mystique*.

César de Bus and Romillon appeared a thousand sympathies were ready to support them, guides and followers were not wanting. If they stand out more than the others, the others are there. The same thing is to be observed in the history of the first Ursulines. They are shadows, nothing but shadows, but without speaking they tell us much about the supernatural world in which they moved, and the earth over which they passed.

In what follows I have been content to borrow from Bourguignon, a priest of Marseilles, Romillon's biographer. This contemporary of Guez de Balzac writes better than I and with an unction impossible to-day.

When Père Romillon had passed some months at Avignon during the first years of his ministry, God gave him

the direction of certain worthy maidens and . . . being divinely enlightened, he knew from the outset that God intended them neither for marriage nor for any existing Order in the kingdom, but for the salvation of their neighbours and especially for the instruction of their own sex. But, whether the time of such sacred harvest had not yet come, or the *Doctrine chrétienne* which the zealous priest had just established in l'Isle prevented him from attending to the matter, or, better, that God had given him the knowledge of their Vocation but had not yet revealed to him the steps they must take to follow it, it was not till 1594 that the Bride of the Lamb was adorned with this new glory, and the charitable priest . . . established a community of holy women for the education of the poor. . . . The opportunity God gave him was as follows:

In Avignon there was a servant, one Antoinette, native of Orange, whose father, for upholding his faith, had been killed by the heretic party. This girl dwelt with a lady of great virtue, and she herself lived so piously and devoutly that she was held to be a saint. As it is the property of good to generate goodness, and virtue is never so remarkable as in obscurity, another girl, Sibylle d'Olivier, daughter of a merchant in the town, profiting by the example and neighbourhood of the servant of God, contracted a holy friendship with her, imitating her in all her shining virtues, especially in her purity, for love of which she resolved to withdraw from the world and enter the convent of the religious of S. Clare. She had not, however, the requisite dowry, and God permitted for His greater glory that she should be rejected. . . . She joined herself therefore to the good Antoinette, and in her company continued to frequent the Sacraments and all exercises of piety for which they had opportunity.

A young lady, (attracted by their) angelic modesty and the joyful serenity of their faces, (sought) their acquaintance. By name Françoise de Bermond, she was daughter of a gentleman of Paris, the Treasurer-General of France, who had married in Avignon. To her force of character was chiefly due the establishment of the Ursulines; indeed, we may call her the foundress of this holy congregation, God bringing her and the saintly Romillon together for this work. . . . Mlle de Bermond was very attractive, physically as well as mentally, with all the graces of polite society, and her conversion took the town by storm. . . . (Many desired to follow her example, among others her sister) Catherine, and Jeanne, sister of Sibylle d'Olivier. These in their turn attracted others, so that these good maidens very soon found themselves, twenty-four in number, all united in the desire to serve God and have no more to do with the world. . . . They frequented the Sacraments and followed the exercises of the *Doctrine chrétienne*, helping the poor, visiting the sick, and practising all such works of piety as their age and sex permitted. But, as they had not all the same director, the same plans, or the same capability of executing them, owing to the difference of their conditions, some among them asked to be allowed to use the monastery of Ste. Praxède (an ancient Dominican cloister no longer inhabited), there to live by the rule of S. Benedict, S. Dominic, or S. Francis. . . . One of the leaders went so far as to speak on her own responsibility to Mgr. Grimaldi, Archbishop of Avignon. This prelate possessed rare wisdom and virtue, and told her in reply that what was lacking among the French *religieuses* was recollection, and that in Italy there were certain holy virgins who had taken simple vows without being enclosed, observing them with far more saintliness and exactitude, and who, while guarding the spirit of interior solitude and retreat, were of infinitely greater use in the salvation of those of their own sex. However, they failed to realize that there could be any mode of life possible to them save marriage or religion (that is, the religious life, of the old style with its tradition of enclosure and solemn vows) and all accordingly entered one or the other state, with the exception of the two sisters d'Olivier and the de Bermond ladies. . . . These, unable to choose either enclosure or marriage, remained with their parents, living apart from the world and practising acts of piety, waiting till God should make His Will for them known through their director, M. Romillon.

There was in the County of Avignon a young lady of the ancient and noble house of Mazan, only daughter of the Baron de Vaucluse, who, holding lightly all advantages of beauty, position and wealth . . . resolved to unite herself to the Heavenly Bridegroom, and consecrated to Him her chastity. Delicacy of constitution forbidding her the life of a religious community . . . she bound herself by a vow . . . before the Bishop of Carpentras, intending by this means to deprive her suitors of all hope, as also her kinsfolk, who agreed in opposing her retirement. The good bishop gave her much good counsel, explaining to her the manner of life of the Ursulines whom S. Carlo had established at Milan, and presenting her with their book of Constitutions, which he had brought from Ferrara, where this community was held in esteem.[1] Receiving it with much gratitude, the demoiselle forthwith placed it in the hands of M. Romillon . . . without whose advice she took no step that concerned her salvation. The holy priest received it from the virtuous young lady at her château of Mazan, and, transported to find in its pages what he had long sought, returned to Avignon, bearing, like another Moses, the tables of the law contained in the little volume.

Immediately on his arrival he imparted the good news to the four saintly maidens, who joyously volunteered to embrace this method of life; Françoise de Bermond with special joy, for she had already resolved to live with some others in a state of virginity without entering the religious life. . . . She had spoken of this project to sundry spiritual persons. . . . But P. Majorius (a Jesuit) . . . had always dissuaded her, asserting the desire to be but a temptation, and that it was essential for a young girl to have either a husband or the walls of a nunnery, so that she had not dared take any decisive step, until God pointed out both model and opportunity, and her purpose was confirmed by her good director, who now counselled her to lose no more time, but to establish her sister and the Oliviers at once at l'Isle as a first branch of the community. . . . P. Majorius, who was most opposed to the carrying out of the plan, meanwhile received orders from his General to leave Avignon and preside over a house of the Society in the Duchy of Milan, where the excellent work being carried on by the Ursulines led him to recognize the necessity of such a community, so that he advised Mlle Françoise de Bermond by letter to undertake what he had so often forbidden.

The new priest who came from Rome to succeed him as Superior of the Avignon house, a man of great judgement and piety, gave them the same counsel, so that, all being propitious to their enterprise, the girls left their homes to settle in the dwelling prepared for them in l'Isle, and began at once the work of instructing their own sex in the *Doctrine chrétienne*, while they waited for Romillon, who had sole

[1] The Ursulines had been founded at Brescia by Angèle Merici of Desenzano on L. Garda (1474–1540).

charge of their work, to draw up their Constitution and obtain a special Bull from the Pope for their establishment, and for that of other houses of the Order to be set up later throughout the kingdom.[1]

First l'Isle-sur-Sorgue, then Aix in Provence where Françoise de Bermond was soon to follow P. Romillon. These were the two cradles of the Ursulines, soon to spread over France with miraculous rapidity. What we have just related happened in the last years of the sixteenth century—a hundred years later, in 1699, we find three hundred houses of Ursulines in France.[2]

V. While new Orders thus came to the birth, many of the older ones were awakening after a too long slumber. Under Pope John XXII, Cardinal d'Albornos had founded in Avignon a house of Dominican nuns, and, as the title of his cardinalate was Ste. Praxède, he had conferred the saint's name upon this sisterhood (1347). Little by little the nunnery—once honoured, it is said, by a visit from S. Catherine of Siena—fell into decay, in 1587 numbering but five sisters, who by a brief of Sixtus V were dispersed in various convents of the town. A little later (1593) the empty building was by Archbishop Tarugi assigned to César de Bus and his first Fathers of the *Doctrine chrétienne*, who occupied it till 1598. Strangely enough, though doubtless explained by the utter decay of the old house, even before the sad end of Ste. Praxède, another community of Dominican nuns had been formed at Avignon, in which were two aged sisters from the famous convent of Prouille, Phillippe and Marguerite d'Arpajon, who during the religious wars in Languedoc had taken refuge with their relatives (1564). "And since after fourteen years spent in their family these devout nuns were weary of living in the world without the offices of their Order," the Archbishop of Avignon, Cardinal d'Armagnac, obtained for them the Benedictine Abbey of Saint-Jean-le-Vieux, "situated in this same town of Avignon, and containing but two sisters, the Abbess, Mme Romane de Jarente d'Ardaillon and another" (1577).

[1] Bourguignon, *op. cit.*, pp. 164–74.

[2] Bourguignon exaggerates slightly in saying that Romillon had "sole direction" of this work. César de Bus laboured also on the same lines, but in the main the honour is due to Romillon, and, doubtless in a greater degree, to Françoise de Bermond. She was born in 1572 and died in 1628. Her Life had been recently written, and there is much mention of her in the Lives of Mme Acarie and Mme de Sainte-Beuve. Cf. *La R. M. Françoise de Bermond et l'etablissement des ursulines en France*, Lyon (now Paris, Beauchesne), 1896.

These ladies consenting to the transformation, the ancient Benedictine Abbey became a Dominican Priory, and Mère Philippe the Superior of the tiny group, two sets of waifs and strays—a picturesque and touching foundation. Almost immediately the old tree put out new leaves. A number of young girls, children rather, appeared. Lucrèce de Peyrès and Anne de Jarente de Monclar, aged thirteen, with Jeanne de Bermond, aged eleven, sister of the foundress of the Ursulines, with others among whom the pestilence of 1580 claimed all too many victims. The aged sisters led the little flock tenderly. "As they were already old and the novices they had received were very young, they did not introduce them at first to the austerities of the Order," but when in 1591 Mère de Monclar was elected Prioress, "her first care was to set to work vigorously on the establishment of the full Dominican life and to make a happy start on the reform of her convent." Her adviser in this was the illustrious Provençal Dominican, Sebastien Michaelis (1543–1618), who was himself then preparing to reform the Preaching Friars. The reform of the Dominican sisterhood was, so to speak, effected from within; only the old Dominican cloister of Ste. Praxède was lacking, and that was given them in 1598.[1]

We must realize (writes a learned Dominican) that the monastery of Ste. Praxède fills a high, or rather an exceptional, place in the history of our second Order in France. Founded at the end of that sixteenth century so rich in works of piety, by nuns from our ancient house of Prouille where already they had passed forty years, this convent belonged at once to the past and the future. From the past it derived four centuries of tradition, and in the future it was to develop with an energy and fruitfulness rare in history. From Ste. Praxède indeed started that great religious movement which dominated the (Dominican) seventeenth century and in a few years enriched France with twenty-five houses of our Second Order."[2]

One of these foundations, the Convent of Langeac, we shall meet again in the following volume, where Mère Agnès and M. Olier await us. The Convent of Avignon itself was soon to welcome

[1] The Fathers of the *Doctrine chrétienne* received in exchange the house of Saint-Jean-le-Vieux now abandoned by the nuns. All these details have been borrowed from the charming work of R. P. Rousset, *Intérieur d'un cloître dominicain. Le Monastère de Sainte-Praxède à Avignon*, Lyon (now Paris, Beauchesne), 1876.

[2] Rousset, *op. cit.*, pp. viii–ix.

one of the most lovable of seventeenth-century mystics, Julienne Morell.

VI. Nicolas Rampalle, a small *rentier* of Saint-Remy in Provence, and his wife Dauphine Lanfrèze made little stir in the world, but happily the Life of one of their daughters, Jeanne de Jésus, founder of six Ursuline houses (1583–1636), was published. From this we learn that Nicolas and Dauphine, already very good people, " entirely dedicated themselves to devotion influenced " by two Jesuits, PP. Péquet and Balsamo, who conducted a Mission about the year 1580 " in the town of Saint-Remy." We are amused and interested to learn that, after some years, these humble mystics, " recognizing that at their age they had no time to lose, decided to leave Saint-Remy and live in the beautiful and devout city of Avignon, where they might more conveniently practise the exercises of the devout life, and at the same time educate their daughters better, and be near their only son, then studying in the school of the Jesuit fathers. This was decided in 1590 . . . and in 1593 they were received as inhabitants of the town by Letters Patent of the most eminent cardinal Mgr. Aquaviva, then legate." Settled in Avignon, their modest home, for they were not rich, became a veritable monastery. Rampalle " devoted himself to prayer and spiritual readings, gave charitable assistance to the poor . . . and used feet, hands, heart, wherever he thought he could serve God. Above all, he was extraordinarily austere in his life and treated his body with severity, living usually on bread and water . . . wearing nearly always . . . the *cilicium* or hairshirt, and often taking the discipline in secluded corners of his dwelling with such rigour that his children, who often heard the sound of blows, were dismayed and wept bitterly. One day he took his son to the cellar on the pretext of showing him some fruit and suddenly half-stripped himself and began to use the discipline. When the boy wept and cried distractedly he said: ' Learn, my child, to flee sin, for this is how God chastises it! ' " Dauphine also invented pious " instruments of mortification . . . the names of Jesus and hearts and crosses studded with sharp points," which she wore herself and with which she " furnished " her daughters, " saying that such were the jewels with which she would adorn them." Since their establishment in Avignon she and her husband " occupied separate beds . . . and lived in wedlock like the angels in Heaven." Whether

Nicolas died or not in 1602 we know not, but in that year Dauphine with two daughters and two nieces went to Arles, where they founded a community of Ursulines.[1]

As may be seen, we have been rapidly through one of the provinces only, and have hardly ever lost sight of Avignon and its beautiful ramparts. We have been taking a walk in Spring. It is too early in the year for leisurely conversations on the borders of clear fountains. Rather like diviners we have tried our hazel wand in all directions, we have made some soundings and then moved on to seek new sources. It is enough to have established that in one region, doubtless more or less resembling all the rest, the living waters of grace were flowing. Henceforward we can be sure that the various currents are fed by an underground reservoir, the mysticism of the humble and unlearned, such as Antoinette de Cavaillon, Antoinette d'Avignon, Sibylle d'Olivier, and certain elect families, the Bermonds and Rampalle, who kept the mystic tradition. Here are fountains ready to flow, and to join the mighty river which descends from the holy hills of Rome, Brescia and Milan. It needs but a few apostolic men, heralds of the Italian Counter-Reformation or native saints—the Cardinal Tarugi, Père Péquet, César de Bus, Romillon, Michaëlis—to pierce the already moistened soil, and a thousand impatient streamlets will hasten towards the river which will fertilize all France.

[1] *La vie de la Mère Jeanne de Jésus*, by R. P. Henri Albi, of the Society of Jesus, Lyon, 1640. The details given by the biographer are doubtless exact, having been furnished by the son of Nicolas and Dauphine, Antoine Rampalle, doctor of theology and proto-notary of the Holy See, to whom the book is dedicated. In youth the biographer himself had been professor of philosophy in the Trinité of Lyon (1622–4), having among his pupils J.-J. Olier. Cf. Monier, *Vie de J.-J. Olier*, Paris, 1914, I. 28.

CHAPTER II

MARIE DE VALENCE : PÈRE COTON AND THE KING'S TRUCE

§1. *Marie de Valence*

I. IN the majority of enterprises which, during the first half of the seventeenth century, directly or indirectly influenced the mystical conquest of our country, and notably in the Mission of Père Coton, with whom our history must begin, a woman's inspiration is to be discovered. In this constant phenomenon, this almost invariable law, there is nothing that need surprise or embarrass a thoughtful mind, still less a Christian one. Certainly Catholicism —the religion of authority, a hierarchy justly jealous of its rights and highly inimical to illuminism—not only reserves to itself the right to judge all the mystics, but also tends increasingly, in modern times, to limit the share of authority enjoyed by the Abbesses and women seers of the Middle Ages. But to inspire, even to direct, is not to govern. If the Church had regarded feminine initiative as contrary to her fundamental organization, she would not have permitted even a S. Teresa to preside over the reform of the Carmelites. She knows that "the wind bloweth where it listeth," and that women are peculiarly sensitive to that Divine touch which makes the mystic. Nor is she ignorant that, in the Divine plan, these higher graces must radiate upon the communion of the faithful, and upon the pastors themselves. It is for her to reconcile these ardent and luminous forces with the exclusive mission of governing and instructing souls which belongs to the hierarchy. This reconciliation is only a difficulty in the abstract, and when one tries to put exact definitions into the treaty. In practice, there is nothing simpler, and as soon as it is understood that at the first signal, however arbitrary, from one of the two parties, the other has only to be silent, there is no opportunity for conflict.

True mysticism indeed easily adjusts itself to the delicate *rôle* demanded in such circumstances. It is holy, and the voices it hears preach renunciation rather than assertion. It is feminine and knows the art of speech without words, of gently wearing down resistance and gaining its ends by imperceptible moves. Ignorant, possibly, the mystics may be, but those whom God chooses are never vulgar. Seeing in them so much wit, such vivid imagination, such exquisite sensitiveness, one concludes that there is a certain relation between their natural graces and the heavenly calling. Even when they are ignorant of the world their dexterity is admirable. M. Olier writes with a humble and confiding ingenuousness that forbids a smile:

I do not remember ever to have met a holy soul who has not assured me that she felt greater respect and affection for me than for anyone else. This was the case with Sœur Marie de Valence . . . Sœur Agnès (de Langeac) . . . and all those souls with whom God has placed me in touch. I do not say that all have felt for me equally great tenderness, but only that their tenderness was for me greater than for all others whom as yet they had seen.[1]

One cannot doubt the sincerity of these saintly women who spoke thus to M. Olier, but what they said to him they may possibly have said quite as sincerely to others, without the least suspicion of untruthfulness, for the most insignificant moments of these marvellous lives had always something unique about them. At any rate their gift of gentle but powerful persuasion is well illustrated by this piquant example. Such spirits can be trusted to turn the flank of difficulties caused by the clash of temperaments mentioned above.

With the exception of the very rare cases in which the mystic addresses her ecclesiastical superiors with a direct message from God, as did Catherine of Siena, her influence is exercised indirectly through her director or directors—for there are usually several of them—who are for her the official delegates of the Church. The rhythm of her relations with them, though varied in details, follows as a general rule the same sequence. Very often the mystic is under confessors inexpert in these high matters. In great distress she asks herself the real name of the spirit which threatens to take possession of her. Is it God Himself or the devil? Whether in her family or in the convent, opinions differ. Some prostrate themselves instantly, as the

[1] *Vie de M. Olier*, by M. Faillon, 4th Ed., Paris, 1873, II. 232.

Hebrews before Moses, before one who has seen God. Others are very suspicious and talk of cold water or of exorcism. But, however cruel they may be, these outside disturbances are only a gentle breeze compared with the storms within, the grievous doubts which assail the sufferer. The more insistent the inward call, the more she trembles, for the more advanced are the most humble. Finally her destined director comes, who first hesitates and examines the matter for himself, then with a decisive and calming gesture sweeps away vain fears and bids the mystic abandon herself to grace. In this first phase of his intervention the priest is only a priest, that is an authority, he directs, his charge has but to obey.

Soon, however, it is his own turn for an interior unrest, which insensibly modifies his attitude. Certainly he did not go to her with any idea of personal interest; he had no desire to be in any other relation to this soul than that of ambassador of God and the Church. But he cannot always so forget himself. I assume that he is, as he should be, at home in the spiritual world. Must not a mystic be, for him, one who in a manner strips and effaces herself in order to open the way wholly to the Wisdom and Power of God? Having received the spiritual confidences of this woman, will not the director sooner or later be led to requite them with his own? will he not stoop to refresh, instruct, fortify himself from the spring gushing out so near him? As for the mystic, when the director ceases to speak to her in the name of Divine authority, she perceives in him only a soul to succour, to raise heavenwards. She would repay the help she has received, associate him with her as intimately as possible, make him a participant in the Divine graces with which she is crowned. Do not tell her that henceforward she is the director—she has no pretensions that way—she knows how to adapt herself to the various phases of his character. Let him command and he finds her humbly submissive. But he is not always giving commands, his "Yes" and his "No" are soon said. His decisions once given, he is like other souls—uncertain and faltering. He behaves rather as a disciple than as a master. Why should she refuse the appeal of this new side of him? Not that she ever speaks with authority, her deep humility and self-emptying forbid that. She directs by telling her own experience and singing her song of praise. She stimulates, suggests, illumines—a gentle queen—not on a throne but on her knees.

M. Olier, writing on this subject, remarks:

Blessed be God, Who in all the crises of my life has raised up for me saintly souls . . . and has not only allowed them to have spiritual affinity with me, but has commanded them to offer me continually to Him, at the times of their closest union with the Divine goodness. O Great God, I am infinitely grateful to Thee for all these benefits, as also to these blessed souls who are so profoundly interested in my salvation. I thank Thee that Thou didst lead them . . . to make known to me the favours by which Thou hast loaded them, and that through them Thou hast revealed to me Thy treasures of liberality.[1]

Whether the woman be cultivated, or ignorant, great lady or peasant, once more this matters not in the least. "If I wished to go to Paris from Dammartin," said Fénelon, "and a peasant from the place offered to guide me, I should follow him and trust him, although he was only a peasant."[2] S. Teresa was of the same opinion. "Instead of being astonished," she wrote, "and considering these things impossible, let them know that to God all is possible, and humble themselves to think that His majesty is pleased to give more light to some good old woman than to them with all their knowledge."[3]

That this was the prevailing opinion in the period with which we deal, the story of Marie de Valence sufficiently demonstrates. She may fitly come first. Chronological order allows, the plan of our book demands, that she should head the saintly procession which is going to pass before us. Born about 1575, on the eve of the mystic movement of which we write, she died in 1648, when this celestial renaissance reached its height, and the threat of approaching decadence was already manifest. From another point of view we have, I believe, good reasons for devoting to this humble seer her right place in our opening chapter, in which we shall study the environment and the political conditions which, if they did not give rise to the movement, undoubtedly gave powerful support to it. For our mystics owe much to Henri IV, Henri IV to P. Coton, and P. Coton to Marie de Valence, as we shall see presently.

Disregarding these many and significant points of contact, Marie

[1] Faillon, *op. cit.*, I. 193.

[2] (Phelipeaux) *Relation de l'origine . . . de Quiétisme*, Paris, 1732, I. 44; cf. H. Bremond, *Apologie pour Fénelon*, p. 43.

[3] Bremond, *ibid.*, p. 44.

throws a vivid light on all the approaches, however secret, to our subject. She founded nothing nor did she belong to any community. She was a pure contemplative, so to speak Contemplation personified. She owed nothing to books either directly or indirectly, nor was she fashioned by any human master. A *Théodidacte* in the fullest sense of the word, when in 1599 P. Coton first encountered her, he found her open to all mystic influence, and doubtless learned more from her than she from him. These details are sufficient to indicate to us the interior resources and spiritual possibilities of France of that day towards the end of the sixteenth century. For Marie de Valence was not a unique prodigy, as we have already stated. Circumstances put her light on a candlestick, but many others burned brightly in such obscurity. Had P. Coton in 1599 not visited Valence, had Valence not been situated on the banks of the Rhône, had the Rhône not been one of the royal routes, how could the great ones of the world have known or sought after Sœur Marie, or would the Life of this *béguine* have been written " by the express order of the Queen Regent and printed by the command of Her Majesty "?

To the many other reasons attracting us to this mystic must be added the originality of her biographer, the Minim Louis de la Rivière. This monk, charmingly tender and frank, knew Marie intimately for thirty years, keenly observed her, laboured with all his soul to understand her, loved and venerated her with all his heart. He was not her director. This title and this mission he left to P. Coton and others; it would have overwhelmed him. He was her chaplain, her theologian, her confessor in ordinary, but above all he was her spiritual child. " She had always a tender affection for me," he writes, " and had much confidence in my simplicity." She chose for him a sister in the person of the devout Marguerite Chambaud, whom she kept by her side as confidante or secretary. " The two children," continues de la Rivière delightfully, " comprehended one another perfectly. Marie recognized it readily and generally with a good grace, though she would say that they did not tell her all their little secrets. They loved each other like brother and sister, with a holy and constant affection, for thirty-six years."[1]

Much as we in turn like Louis, we bear him a grudge for scru-

[1] *Histoire de la vie et mœurs de Marie Tessonier*, by R. P. L. de la Rivière, Lyon, 1650, p. 113. Cf. also *Marie de Valence*, by l'Abbé Trouillat, 3rd Ed., Paris-Valence, 1896.

pulously omitting all picturesque details in his book—the street, the house, doubtless the garden a few steps from the Rhône—which would have enabled us to reconstruct the tiny and delightful *béguinage*. We can, however, unravel thread by thread the little plots of Louis and Marguerite, their innocent intrigues meant to penetrate the deepest secrets of the saint, whom they find day by day dearer and more incomprehensible. Little is known of Marguerite Chambaud, but such is the constant attitude of Louis de la Rivière towards Marie de Valence, and it is not the least valuable feature in his abundant testimony.

Marie's least important words haunt and penetrate him. He is never certain of having understood them. He is always awaiting new miracles or unknown depths. Not that he lacks theology; on the contrary, with a theologian's laboriousness he succeeds in reconciling the living book which he spells out with the dead books he knows so well. He has a vivid and true impression that what Marie reveals of her visions is but dust compared with the infinite richness of the visions themselves. Yet he does not err through over-credulity. No, he passes through the crucible all that he hears, and without strain reconciles his critical spirit with his eager curiosity in regard to things divine.

One day, for instance, he perceives in a prayer composed by Marie an expression which makes him prick up his ears—" divine ambrosia," applied to the sacred Host.

When I questioned this servant of God (he writes) I did not pause over the beautiful and ardent phrases of which the prayer was composed, knowing from of old that she was familiar with them. Still, returning to the point a little later, I was curious to know whether she understood this word " ambrosia," feeling sure it must be strange to her. So I said: " Where did you get the phrase? " She answered that it had come into her mind with the others. " Do you know what ambrosia is? " I said. " I think so," she answered . . . " ambrosia is a food which imparts immortality to those who partake of it."[1]

Let us not be so foolish as to worry him by suggesting that Marie had heard the word in some sermon. He would reply, as he does somewhere:

[1] La Rivière, *op. cit.*, p. 169.

Pray, let us have a teachable mind and a humble heart. Let us incline ourselves with dove-like simplicity piously to believe all that may edify. Charity believeth all things, says the apostle, that is to say the soul that loves God will eagerly believe all good and will not easily persuade itself that anyone wishes to deceive it.[1]

This is not so badly said.

One last word of his about himself will complete the picture and show the profound seriousness of his friendship for Sœur Marie:

I frankly confess (he says) that, knowing her as I did, I do not recollect ever going to see her—and in thirty-eight years I went an infinity of times, if I may use the expression—without having made a short self-examination, so great was the awe that I felt for the celestial beam that lightened her soul.[2]

Marie de Valence was so called because she was born at Valence in Dauphiné and lived most of her life there; her real name was Marie Teyssonnier. Childhood and youth were unusual rather than unhappy, owing to the action of her parents—small shopkeepers who had embraced and then more or less abandoned Calvinism—and of her husband. Baptised in the Huguenot temple, she was forcibly betrothed to a Calvinist notary, Mathieu Pouchelon, who lived in an almost entirely Huguenot village, Baume-Cornillane. She was then thirteen, and they gave her two years' respite before packing her off to her new home. At Baume there was, it appears, neither priest nor church, and Marie, who was a Catholic, since her parents had become Catholics, but totally ignorant of these things, was chaperoned by a Huguenot of the place. So she went to the preaching like every one else, but once there she alone knelt down. It is touching to think that the whole of her little equipment of orthodoxy consisted of that gesture. It caused a scandal—" does not the minister pray for everyone? " they said. Louis de la Rivière makes but few allusions to the misty past, which no doubt Marie never recalled without sorrow. It is pretty certain, however, that, after three or four years of this strange life, she considered herself a Calvinist.

It was natural enough. I have known a young Frenchman totally denaturalized by six months in England. Nevertheless Marie vaguely recalled, and pined for the Mass: grace certainly was even

[1] La Rivière, *op. cit.*, pp. 166–7. [2] *Ibid.*, p. 331.

then at work in her, but as it might be in a child. She conceived "a strong desire to have a copy of the Four Gospels . . . although she knew neither how to read nor write, she was only satisfied when she had it near her, and once when she was seriously ill could only be soothed by having it day and night under her bolster, her head resting on it as on a pillow."[1]

The notary Pouchelon, her husband, would have made a good figure in the *Roman comique* or the *Capitaine Fracasse.* Louis de la Rivière, as was only to be expected, laid on his colours too thickly. A great drinker, hot-headed, a husband who would draw his knife on occasion, he sometimes terrorised the poor little thing, only to be disarmed in a moment. He loved her greatly and seems to have regarded her as a saint, or rather—this word not being in his vocabulary—as a dainty creature, far away from him and above him. When the physicians prescribed the air of Valence for the young wife whose health was being undermined by some unknown malady, he not only authorized the journey, but also the Mass for which on that occasion his wife asked. "Go to Mass whenever you like," he said, "I will go too!" She needed no second telling, for she was dying to go, but it is plain that her husband's Calvinism was not very fierce. After some time "he took a fancy to go to the wars" and "bore arms a couple of years." On his return he found Marie Catholic out and out. He submitted good-humouredly on her entreaties to be instructed by a Jesuit, who doubtless effected his conversion without being compelled to re-read Bellarmine's controversial works. It only remained for him to die a good Catholic, which he hastened to do. So much for the first miracle of Marie Teyssonnier, Widow Pouchelon, soon to be insensibly transformed into Marie de Valence. For the dates of these events it is useless to consult Louis de la Rivière; he either neglects or invents them. Pouchelon must have died shortly before or after 1595, Marie being then anything from twenty to twenty-five years of age. Her warrior-notary left her no fortune, but she had a little house in Valence, fairly respectable, one imagines, since later the Bishop allowed her to arrange a chapel in it and to have Mass said. With the exception of some rare journeys or pilgrimages to la Sainte-Baume, Lyons, Grenoble, she lived there till her death in 1648. Too delicate to gain her own livelihood, she

[1] La Rivière, *ibid.*, p. 18.

abandoned herself to Providence. The good souls of Valence afforded her some aid; "often when she was at church, without attracting her attention, they were wont to slip pieces of gold inside her Book of Hours."[1] This manna, however, was not sufficient, for subsequently M. Olier, with the approval of Père de Condren, relieved a situation which, in spite of the growing reputation of this mystic, was very precarious. "My director," he writes in his *Mémoires*, "considering it well that I should assign Marie de Valence a hundred livres yearly, which she had herself calculated should be sufficient for all her needs, I was only too happy to have the privilege."[2]

We are totally ignorant of the first steps taken by Marie on the mystic way, but one thing at least, and that very remarkable, is certain. In 1599, directly after she became a widow, this young woman, but yesterday converted to Catholicism, had already reached a critical point, where the soul, assailed by Divine visitations and more or less uneasy as to their origin, awaits, seeks, demands a guide to reassure her and command her, in the Name of God, no longer to resist grace. Who in 1599 had said to Marie that this guide had come? Who had conducted this novice to the confessional of P. Coton? The same instinct doubtless which eight years later would thrill Jeanne de Chantal with tremblings at the approach of François de Sales. At any rate Marie never had cause to regret this step of hers, and P. Coton still less. The Jesuit speedily recognized the rare integrity and the gifts of this woman who could not yet read, and bore within her the manifest tokens of Divine operation. Their first interview was short, but the contemplative vocation of Marie de Valence was fixed from that time forward. P. Coton was supple, large-minded, and scrupulous to respect the liberty of souls; he did not desire to make any change in the very simple and ingenuous plan of life which Marie without consciousness of choice had chosen. She retired neither from Valence nor from the world, but continued her obscure and tranquil manner of life where she was. Revealed only to an elect few, the humble and pure flame gradually burned itself out in the dark.

Nevertheless, there was another side. Though Marie never left Valence, she gradually, perhaps rather quickly, became known as the official "saint" of the district. Legend could not be busy with

[1] La Rivière, *ibid.*, p. 27. [2] Faillon, *ibid.*, I. 193.

one so vivid and sane, such an enemy to all affectation, reserved even towards the priests. Manifestly the Divine Presence in her must have shown through in an extraordinary way. A soft radiance streamed from her when she prayed. "Truly (as de la Rivière well remarks), the raptures of Marie always took place in perfect calm and tranquillity, in perfect contrition and modesty; there were no convulsions, tremblings or unbecoming poses."[1] From this moderation which she always maintained, even in involuntary movements, this decent grace, doubtless came the influence she always exercised on the *élite* of her time. Her light was not blinding. Supernatural enough to stir every one a little, it was not sufficiently so to upset anyone. The multitude venerated her, but without popular excitement, and this is possibly the reason why her name was so soon forgotten. Her message had a more direct appeal for souls that had a natural affinity with her, owing to their type of sanctity, their more refined culture, or even—and why not?—their natural good breeding. The France of those days, which seems from this distance a little garish, had a preference for the rarest flowers, such as Jeanne de Chantal, François de Sales, Madeleine de Saint-Joseph and Sœur Marie.

Marie's extreme refinement was once demonstrated in a characteristic incident.[2] She had a great devotion to Mary Magdalene. "This great saint often appeared to her. . . . Marie could hardly speak of her without an overflowing heart." It grieved her to the quick if preachers, whether in the pulpit or in familiar talk, with too little prudence or decorum, exaggerated her faults. "What need" (she would say) "to regret so poignantly the failings of this saint, or to expatiate upon them with unbecoming words, when God has passed His sponge over them?" Why reopen "so cruelly wounds which Our Lord has healed, and that too with words ugly in themselves and unbecoming on the lips of those who profess modesty and decorum? A certain preacher preaching a Lent course at Valence handled the Magdalene somewhat discourteously, and some of his audience remarked to Marie de Valence that the discourse had displeased them. 'Me, too!' she said simply. The criticism came to the ears of the preacher, who was not pleased with it. The following July it fell out that the reverend Father Bazan of our company

[1] La Rivière, *ibid.*, p. 287.

[2] See Vol. I. 302.

(Minim) preached on the feast of this saint and, ignorant of what had happened, said frankly that one ought to speak with reserve about her former frailties."[1] This act of reparation rejoiced Marie.

God save me from rash judgment, but I would not swear that all the clergy of Valence appreciated Sœur Marie. Either from excess of zeal or in the interests of their parties, many, both regulars and seculars, had sought admittance to her house and Marie in her weariness had been compelled to bar the door. All visitants to flowers are not honey-bees. Among these intruders it is interesting to note a Jansenist before his time who tried after his kind to "Augustinise" the spiritual child of P. Coton. "A certain religious visited her and propounded the thesis that there was none who could do his duty towards God."[2] Marie did not ask him to come again. As she never went out save to church, it was natural that the ecclesiastical world interested her. "She did not like" (Louis de la Rivière tells us) "preachers to take liberties with the scriptures."[3] She adored sermons, "running to them as to a fire," but disliked affectations, far-fetched allusions, or the blending of fables or profane stories with a discourse. In the highest mystics of this period, even in the gentlest of them, we often meet these temperate and independent judgments.

Little by little people from every quarter came to visit her, and, what is more curious, they came in groups. "At certain hours of the day numbers of persons, great and small, began to gather at her house. . . . We have indeed," continues La Rivière, "seen not only high-born dames and men of fashion, but also priests and ecclesiastics receive methods of devotion from her."[4] It is probable that, after the fashion of the time, she wrote or caused Marguerite Chambaud or Louis de la Rivière to write for her, forms of prayer, which she distributed to her visitors either for public recitation in her little oratory or for private use. She must have chosen her circle and guided it with much tact, since she succeeded in avoiding the serious annoyance often caused by such meetings of pious admirers. She does not seem to have been seriously troubled. She had her enemies, having unmasked certain false devotees and turned the cold shoulder to sundry clerics, who, as we shall see, took their revenge

[1] La Rivière, *ibid.*, pp. 67–9.
[2] *Ibid.*, p. 60.
[3] *Ibid.*, p. 298.
[4] *Ibid.*, p. 231.

after her death, but as long as she lived she was protected both by the devotion of the town and by her influential friendships, P. Coton among them. From near or far, by himself or through friends, P. Coton watched over her, and when the famous Jesuit died, more than twenty years before her, Marie de Valence, often the theme of his conversations at Court and with the spiritual leaders of the time, had come to be venerated throughout France.

The relations between Marie and P. Coton are very touching. After their first meeting in 1599 the priest never missed a chance of stopping at Valence, where we find him in 1600, 1601, 1603, 1618 and 1624. He wrote to her regularly in the intervals and had all her private papers sent him. But this was not enough ; he wished to have her at Paris near himself, " in order " (says de la Rivière) " to be better informed about her interior life. . . . To gain this end he set several persons of quality to work, the late Mme la Duchesse d'Aiguillon and the late Mme de la Fare. These ladies, to oblige P. Coton, did everything in their power to . . . take Marie in their coach and bring her to Paris,"[1] and, but for the intervention of the Bishop André de Leberon and other worthies, they would have succeeded. This would seem hardly in accordance with Coton's normal zeal for the spiritual affairs of his *Philothée*, since Marie's welfare did not require her to leave Valence, where she was in the safe hands of P. de la Rivière, her sub-director, who himself submitted wholly to P. Coton. It was for other ends that she was wanted in Paris, and indeed she was really needed. P. Coton did not forget that Marie had some time previously foretold the mission that he would have to discharge towards the King, and he remembered other illuminations and similar help received from God through this lowly woman. He would have liked to be able to consult her constantly, placed as he was in an infinitely difficult situation. Doubtless also he hoped to win or train by her help other souls in his care. Mystics were not lacking in Paris, and P. Coton was intimate with many, including Mme Acarie herself. But in his eyes none of these glorious ones surpassed the delicate flower which had first been revealed to him on the banks of the Rhône, and which he had revealed to the world, the timid charming countrywoman, linked to him, as it seemed, by Providence in close intimacy.

[1] La Rivière, *ibid.*, p. 102.

Since she would not go to Court, the Court came to her. While waiting for Louis XIII at Lyons after the siege of Montpellier, Marie de Médicis sent for the Saint of Valence. The Queen Mother had not chosen her ambassador at haphazard. Armand de Richelieu, Bishop of Luçon, presented himself at Marie's house, " where he discoursed with her for at least an hour by the clock, questioning and observing her keenly, and consulting her about some secret affairs needless to specify." In a word, he sounded her thoroughly. Did Marie know him by reputation or read him then and there? Anyhow, continues Louis de la Rivière, " she maintained a great reserve and took special care to prevent his knowing or even suspecting that she had extraordinary communications with God. She responded, however, so wisely and prudently as to satisfy him completely." Having thus got to know her, Richelieu discharged himself of his mission, and noticing that Marie received the Queen Mother's invitation with some distaste, " It is a case of *must*, madame! " said the Bishop. " Either at Lyons or Paris, you cannot help yourself! "[1] She chose Lyons, resolving to say nothing to the Queen but what the simplest Christian might say.

She had no turn for playing the saint; she would reserve her happy secrets for those who directed her, such as P. Coton, or for her young disciples Louis de la Rivière and M. Olier.

The latter, who belongs to the second spiritual generation of the seventeenth century, and whom we shall meet again in his proper place, had as yet taken only the first steps in the mystic way when he came into contact with Marie de Valence, and received illumination from her. She was then more than sixty, Jean-Jacques Olier was not yet thirty (1637 or 1638). Marie, whom we have seen so reserved before Richelieu, recognized at once the graces of this youthful priest and opened her heart to him unconstrainedly.

After the death of Sœur Agnès (he himself says) Our Lord gave me the friendship of Marie de Valence, who was more unreserved to me than to anyone since the death of her director, P. Coton, so that she was ready to reveal to me all the graces bestowed upon her since his death, besides telling me all that she had written down during his lifetime. She loves me like a mother.[2]

[1] La Rivière, *ibid.*, p. 276. [2] Faillon, *ibid.*, p. 192.

All such details about the passing on of the mystic torch seem to me vividly interesting; the parallel between the two "motherhoods" of Marie de Valence is equally significant. The same woman who predicted to P. Coton that he would one day be called to the King's side and had continually encouraged him in his mission, now, it seems, directed Jean-Jacques Olier to the sanctification of the secular priests, assuring him that God would do great things by his ministry. They saw each other again some six months before Marie's death. M. de Bretonvilliers, who accompanied M. Olier, relates the extraordinary impression made upon him by this visit.

Methought I saw an angel in Heaven (he writes) rather than a creature still living on earth; so filled with the Spirit of God did she appear, and such an impression did the charming modesty of her countenance, which had something supernatural about it, make on me, that even to-day, although many years have passed since we met, I am as much moved when I recall it as if I were still hearing her voice.

Some time afterwards M. Olier returned to Valence and, having prayed at his friend's tomb, repaired to the artist who had executed her portrait for him.

I found there (he says) something else to which doubtless this holy soul had guided me. For, apart from the portrait, in which I found no resemblance and was not greatly concerned, for I loved her spirit and the impress of grace in her more than her exterior, I noticed a large picture of a very vile tendency. Remonstrating forcibly with the artist, he agreed to all I asked and sold me the picture, which I forthwith cut in pieces, set fire to, and burnt in his presence.[1]

II. The spiritual activity of this unlearned woman can be studied in the meditations and reminiscences which she dictated to her astonished disciple, Louis de la Rivière. This activity is in accordance with the normal rhythm of mystic initiation, adapted by the Divine Master to a young unlettered imagination. Marie lingers later than most in the region of sense, so that it is easy to follow in her the process of progressive putting away of images and their sublimation, so to speak. She begins with S. Gertrude and ends with S. Teresa.

"God shows her a fair spiritual castle which represents the glorious

[1] Faillon, *ibid.*, II. 599. Cf. Letters of M. Olier, II. 61–2.

Virgin Mary"; or "she was made to see in a vision that the glorious Virgin was a fair garden of fruits"; or again, "she sees between her hands a vase filled with precious cordial and understands what it signifies."[1] Once "the Virtues, in the form of maidens," came and fêted her.

The first to come forward was called Love of God. . . . In the midst of her caresses she spoke in high praise of her sister Charity, or Love of One's Neighbour, whom she called with great honour and respect, inviting her to make her dwelling in the heart of this devout woman. Then the two together pronounced a panegyric on the third sister Patience, bidding her abide with Marie. Then all three with one accord began to sing the praises of the fourth sister, Humility, conjuring her also to lodge at this inn of the Faithful Heart. . . . And in a marvellous way she perceived these Virtues entering her soul, homing to her like bees to their hive or doves to their cote.[2]

A well-balanced and rigorous theology ruled over these Pre-Raphaelite imaginations. Her biographer gives a good example of the scruples she felt.

In the year 1614 one of our Order preached an Advent course at Valence. . . . His subject was the theological and moral virtues; his text was taken from the Acts, "*The Spirit said to Philip, Join thyself to this chariot.*" The preacher painted the Virtues in glorious array, borne on triumphal chariots moving on four mystic wheels, each of which had two horses and a charioteer. Our Marie took a singular pleasure in the description of these noble Virtues, although the Holy Spirit made her see them as incomparably more beautiful.[3]

However, the sermon had a slight defect which did not escape her criticism of our theologian. The preacher had "succeeded better" with the moral virtues than with the theological. Marie put everything right, pointing out in detail to her disciples how this charming and clever picture should be touched up. Do not such conversations suggest a Platonic Academy of the Renaissance? Were we wrong, in our first volume, when we attached so much importance to this Devout Humanism which the literature of devotion made so familiar, even among humble souls?

[1] La Rivière, *ibid.*, chaps. xxxiii, xxxiv, xxxix.
[2] *Ibid.*, p. 241. [3] *Ibid.*, p. 238.

Towards 1613, Marie, obeying a summons of her great friend, the Duchesse de Nevers, to Grenoble, halted at Voyron, the seat of the Sieur de la Buysse, another of her revering followers, who had set his heart on doing the honours of his garden, " one of the most beautiful in all Dauphiné." Louis de la Rivière, being among the company of seven or eight persons, noted eagerly the impressions of the saint taken for a walk amongst many new symbols. When La Buysse led Marie

through an open alley where the sun was very hot, he caused a parasol to be brought her, which she would have refused, but I bade her take it.

She obeyed, and her docility was forthwith rewarded by an ecstasy in which God was shown her " sheltering our souls from the heats of covetousness."[1]

As she walked round the garden she came to a place shaped like a grotto, where they diverted her with an artificial fountain which threw out jets of water in every direction by means of numerous pipes. Other pretty devices were found in the grotto—birds which seemed to twitter, a hermit ringing a bell, and many other inventions to surprise the visitor to the plashing fountain. Instantly she saw in spiritual vision Jesus Christ under the guise of a crystal fountain. . . .

From there they took her to see another fair fountain at the top of which there was a socket in which was placed a lighted candle. Then they touched certain springs and the water jetting out from under the socket took the form of a vase round the candle. . . . The water ceaselessly ascended and descended, always preserving a perfect oval with the flame within, and yet it was not put out. . . . Suddenly the Holy Spirit made her see in interior vision that the soul firmly based on Charity was such a masterpiece of God, setting forth at once both the living water of grace and the fire of Divine Love.[2]

All is mystical to the mystic, or all becomes so in a moment. " Where is He Whom my soul loveth? " is their constant cry, and the answer delays not. Marie gives us her own assurance in a writing which she dictated to Louis de la Rivière.

Seeing myself languishing and sick for love, what should I do save make straight for Thee, and what road should I take but that of asking everything I meet for Thee?

[1] La Rivière, *ibid.*, p. 264. [2] *Ibid.*, pp. 264–7.

Tell me, then, O Heavens, what way shall I take to find my Beloved, if not by rising high above the things of earth?

Tell me then, O waters, how shall I find my Beloved, if not by flowing softly by pure affections towards the source of my being? . . .

This exercise contains about three hundred and sixty questions and answers. . . . From this specimen the whole passage can easily be surmised.[1]

As all creatures are good to him who loves God, so the mystic spiritualizes all he sees in this world.

Our Lord (says de la Rivière) had given her a spiritual world, that is, He had made her see this great world spiritually, and all that was in it she so spiritualized that she saw nothing corporeal in it . . . the universe was supernaturally figured and imprinted in her understanding . . . she saw it always in her house or in the streets. The elements, the heavens, sun, moon and stars, everything in fact, was spiritualized to her, so that she clearly beheld in them the perfections of God. . . . For several years she lived in this fair and pleasant world, she made it the theme of her exercises, and continually drew from it subjects of devotion. Her memory was never overburdened nor her mind wearied by the constant attention she gave to so many and such varied objects. . . . After some years this vision of the world was taken from her.[2]

There is one defect in these delicate analyses. Louis de la Rivière does not make it clear that in this kind of sublimation the world of visions did not cease to appear real, sensible and concrete enough. It is incorrect to say that the eye of the saint "perceived nothing corporeal." The biographer unsuspectingly corrects himself in another place.

One day, being at prayer, she saw the heavens and the earth beautiful with the beauty bestowed on them by God before the Fall. . . . She beheld such exquisite qualities in the creatures, she saw them so gentle and benignant in imparting their influences and virtues to Man, that she marvelled. . . . Another time, God caused her to see many birds, some of rare plumage all-satisfying to the eye. For a long time the sight provided material for meditation and kept her in wonder before their Creator. . . . I remember that she called them *her* birds, and she readily owned that their plumage was unsurpassed for beauty. I remember, too, that she told us that if she paused

[1] La Rivière, *ibid.*, p. 260. [2] *Ibid.*, pp. 213–5.

even momentarily to dwell on their feathered beauty instead of deriving spiritual food and lessons from the sight, she had at once to pay the penalty of confusion and distress.

She loved these birds, distinguishing each from other, but she would not separate them from the spiritual objects that their beauty recalled and represented. She was only sensible of imperfection of " curiosity " when she forgot herself and contemplated the birds in and for themselves. She saw them as distinctly as the devout Encyclopædist whom we discussed in the first volume, but she saw them without "curiosity." Though subtly diverse, the two attitudes are akin and one leads to the other. It was to form souls on such lines as hers that the Binets and the Richêomes wrote. But Marie's own imagination had no need of such manuals of symbolism.

Many things shown to her (continues de la Rivière) were strange to us, and even the books made no mention of them that I know of. . . . God gave a special view of natural things to this His servant.[1]

Her deeper visions were equally precise and minute. To reveal to her the " high calling," which she had to fulfil, that is, the conversion and sanctification of special souls for whom she prayed and did penance, God one day made the whole world of human beings pass before her. " You would have said it was a procession passing gravely and modestly before you, an army defiling in good order with standards flying." The details of this lengthy pageant are curious. All conditions marched past, each in the precise rank assigned to it by the religious, political and social hierarchy. First the Pope, then Cardinals, nuncios, bishops, superiors of orders, kings, ambassadors, " all the dukes came together " . . . soldiers, lawyers, " doctors and surgeons separately," the *bourgeois*, shopkeepers, trades, villagers, and the common people. Then this multitude arranged in earthly order, which is vain and deceitful, breaks up, to reform presently, this time arranged according to the diversities of the interior life and of grace, first the sinners, then the converted, penitents, the innocent, the righteous, and lastly the saints.[2] Of these two processions, the second alone concerns the high design which the Holy Spirit was to unfold to Marie. The first was probably no more than a parade, intended to accustom the eye of the visionary to large numbers; having

[1] La Rivière, *ibid.*, pp. 303–4. [2] *Ibid.*, pp. 542–5.

seen in a bird's-eye view the human ant hill, Marie would be less likely to quail before her vast mission. Anyhow, when she had before her eyes all her contemporaries then alive, God made her recognize those souls which He meant to give her to win by her apostolate, fifty thousand sinners to convert, thirty thousand penitents to confirm in their resolution, fifteen thousand righteous, twelve thousand saints to aid and develop. These statistics may be voted wearisome by those who are ignorant of the importance that concrete signs, and especially numbers, have in the eyes of the mystics, yet all must admire the limitless ambitions and the glorious optimism which gave rise to such a spectacle. Twelve thousand saints linked to the prayers and sacrifices of one frail being! Marie's conception of Divine bounty and human possibilities was magnificent indeed.

In truth, such variety of images neither confused nor wearied Marie's powers of perception. All these symbols were wrought easily and harmoniously into a united whole. But in the end even she had to divest herself gradually of almost all the things of sense.

She enjoyed (Louis tells us) for the last two years of her life especially, a particular presence of God, pure and simple. We have often had long conversations, she and I, on this mode of Presence. The terms she used to explain her meaning were these: to see God, to see God in God, to see the creatures in God and oneself in God. She used these phrases simply and freely. But when I represented to her that it was not probable that she had seen the Divine Essence, humble and simple as she was she acquiesced and was content to believe that she had seen only a pure light, which to her figured the Divine Essence.[1]

But let her describe one of these ineffable experiences.

What I saw was without form or shape and nevertheless it was beautiful and pleasant to see. Without colour, it had the grace of all the colours. What I saw was not a Light like that of the sun or of the day, yet it shed a wonderful clarity, and from it proceeded all earthly and spiritual light. What I saw occupied no space, yet filled everything. It moved not, yet it animated and operated in all creation.[2]

These faltering, though sublime, accents will be heard on the lips of the other heroes of our book, varied according to the genius of each. We shall gradually get used to the ineffectiveness of these images

[1] La Rivière, *ibid.*, p. 437. [2] *Ibid.*, p. 285.

which clash and destroy one another in the dark, of these vain but splendid words which say nothing and yet would like to say everything. Let others weigh these testimonies, our task is simply to collect them.

When Marie de Valence died, on April 1, 1648, the mystic movement to the expansion of which this sainted friend of P. Coton had so largely contributed, reached its zenith, and henceforward began to decline. Even in the history of Louis de la Rivière, we hear the mutterings of the storm already brewing against the mystics. This book, written and published by order of Anne of Austria, appeared at Lyons in 1650. Among the authorities on whose backing he relies, the author especially mentions "the approbation of the Reverend Fathers of the Society of Jesus," of P. Georges de Rhodes and several others. The preface, although pacific in tone, is that of a man on guard, scrutinizing the horizon with disquiet.

With regard to the strange, incomprehensible and extraordinary things with which this history abounds, they may be read with confidence and without the least scruple, for all has been strained through a sieve. . . . I testify that the doctors . . . have not let me off any single page or line or even word. During seven months I had to read everything to them, line by line and word by word. They have sifted every word. . . . Never has the life of a saint, male or female, been more strictly examined.

These critics were of course favourable to Marie de Valence, but they thus held as it were a council of war to overthrow the plans of the enemy. And not without reason, for according to the report of the Abbé de Champvallon, the Clerical Assembly in their sitting of March 29, 1651, without disapproving of Marie personally, yet blamed severely the cult which Valence was beginning to have for her, as also Louis de la Rivière's biography. Unduly impressed by this decision, Picot, the classic historian of religion in France during the seventeenth century, has not ventured to praise her, but has relegated her in an obscure note to that questionable class of mystics whom one may venerate privately but hardly name without a blush.

It was, however, easy to see what happened in the case of this posthumous history of a mystic whom Rome had not censured and on whose side were François de Sales, Bérulle, Olier and Vincent de

Paul. The Bishop of Valence who denounced Louis de la Rivière's work to the Assembly of 1650–1651 was the same who in the Assembly of March 9, 1654, protested against the Bull condemning Jansenius, and demanded if S. Augustine were also to be condemned? "Marie," says the biographer of J.-J. Olier, appositely though perhaps with some exaggeration, "had P. Coton, a Jesuit, as her director; her Life had been approved by the Jesuits, who regarded her as one of the most eminent souls of her time, and the Bishop of Valence liked neither the Jesuits nor the doctrines for which they stood. He claimed not to have been consulted as to the publication of the Life, although the *imprimatur* asserts the contrary, and so he condemned alike the biography and the cult of the deceased."[1]

With regard to the cult, it is possible that Marie's devotees may well have been imprudent—it was a pretty mess in truth—but the book so painstakingly examined by experts could not be anything but orthodox. The learned Assembly, however, in a high-handed and unexpected manner pronounced it "filled with vain imaginations and absurd revelations!"[2] To score off the Jesuits, they would have said the same of S. Teresa! It is for the reader to decide between the piety, simple but shrewd and lofty, of Louis de la Rivière and the impertinence of his critics. In any case the pronouncement is valuable for the historian, as illustrating the contemptuous indifference affected by the latter half of the seventeenth century for all mystics; it reminds us that the religious divisions of France have not been unconcerned with the origin and diffusion of such sentiments, and enables us to appreciate better the immense service rendered to French Mysticism by the pacific policy of Henri IV and his friend P. Coton.

III. Certain circumstances have brought into high relief the visionary whom we have been discussing. Marie de Valence, providentially as it would seem, came across the path of P. Coton and guided the confessor of the King of France; among other disciples she also counted the worthy monk to whom we owe a charming book upon her. Otherwise, she has nothing exceptional to show us, nothing to make her stand out above many other mystics lost in the

[1] Faillon, *ibid.*, I. 206. Cf. a less severe note in Trouillat, *ibid.*, pp. xiv–xxx.

[2] *Actes, titres et mémoires concernant les affaires du clergé de France contenant ce qui a été fait depuis l'assemblée générale du clergé tenue à Paris les années* 1645–6, *avec ce qui s'est aussi passé ou obtenu pendant l'assemblée générale tenue en l'an* 1650–1, Paris, 1652, pp. 83–8.

crowd, of whom the greater number are known only to God. One day, relates her biographer,

A certain peasant woman came to see her, moved, so she asserted, by inspiration from on high. Her talk, though coarse and rustic, was yet seasoned with rare wisdom. . . . She may have been perhaps sixty years of age. . . . Her proper home was in a mountain village of the Die diocese, where all, save perhaps a half-dozen, were Huguenots. There was no priest, and Mass was said very rarely. This pious soul lived there as faithful Abraham among the heathen Chaldeans; giving herself to mental prayer, taught by Our Lord, for she had never had the slightest instruction in it. While reciting the *Pater* and the *Credo* she was wont to have admirable reflections and felt within her soul wholly celestial comfort. The beneficent Creator had bestowed upon her a supernatural light which guided her interior life and showed her marvels. Sometimes this light directed her to such and such a village . . . when the holy Mass was about to be said . . . and one day she was inspired to go and seek out a devout priest who lived far away from her. Her heavenly lamp led her to him. Having saluted him, "Sir," she said, "I am come hither in order that you may be pleased to impart to me that great blessing which God has given you, to bestow it upon us other poor sinners." By this great blessing she meant the power of absolution after confession of sins. She was wont to call Jesus Christ "Father," and our Lady "Mother" or "the beneficent Mother." Once, while discoursing with Sœur Marie on the Heavenly gifts she received, "We have within," quoth she, touching her forehead, "daylight, not the daylight which we see with our bodily eyes, but one by which I behold the Father, that is the Saviour, and the beneficent Mother."[1]

For this sacred page I would perhaps give all the rest of de la Rivière's book and many other lives too. And such instances are not very rare—I mention some, the record of which has been preserved. The Mère de Ponçonas, foundress of the Reformed Bernadines in Dauphiné, who was at Ponçonas (a little village of the *Mure mataisine* in the Grenoble diocese) in her childhood, mentions a little cowherd

so uncouth that at first she did not seem to know anything of God. She took her apart and began with goodwill to instruct her . . . This marvellous girl . . . bursting into tears and entreated to be taught how to finish her *Pater*, "for," said she in her mountain *patois*, "I

[1] La Rivière, *ibid.*, pp. 120–4.

don't know how to end. For near five years, when I've said the word *Pater* and think . . . that He is up there (pointing to the sky), that He is my Father, . . . I weep and remain all day in that state while I herd my cows."[1]

So Anne le Barbier, born about 1598 at Neuilly-l'Evesque near Caen,

keeping sheep in the fields, had already been drawn to a truly sublime way of prayer . . . having no other director than the Holy Spirit who worked things in her without her knowledge. . . . She gathered together the shepherdesses and other women of Neuilly and instructed them in the commandments of God and the Church.[2]

Here is pure sublimity, free, or nearly so, from all the petty secular detail often mixed up with the lives of our mystics, an example of which we find in this marvellous story, told by Père Amelote, biographer of Père de Condren.

A poor servant girl, Barbe, of an honest family in Compiègne, was from childhood touched by God and, like another Amos, filled with His light, as she kept her cows in the fields. From that time on she made spiritual communion, no other way being possible, and, with no other guidance than that of Jesus Christ, was led in the way of the Passion . . . It pleased God to lay upon her innocence the sins of others, and to continue in her the intentions of the Sacrifice of His Son. After Jesus Christ had thus directed her for fifteen years, He made known to her that He would give her a man for director to whom she must reveal the graces which she had received. God made an occasion for her to see this man in a very remarkable manner. A certain villain having been inspired by hell with the idea of conspiring against the King (Louis XIII), God, cherishing this great prince and watching over his safety, revealed the plot to this girl, who was then in service. He made her see all particulars and obliged her to reveal them. The obligation was so pressing that she persuaded her master and mistress to take her to Court, in order to warn the minister of the projected plot. Arrived at Paris, however, she was tongue-tied at sight of the great ones before whom she was brought, and her master nearly repented of the guarantees he had given for his serving-woman. In the end, taken in hand by M. le Cardinal de Bérulle

[1] *La vie de la Mère de Ponçonas* (1602–57) *institutrice de la congrégation des bérnardines réformées en Dauphiné*, Lyons, 1675, pp. 26–7.

[2] *Éloges des plusieurs personnes illustrés en piété de l'Ordre de S. Benoit*, Paris, 1679, II. 132–3. This book, to which we shall return later, is by Mère Jacqueline de Blémur.

and finding her soul in correspondence with his, she was enabled to tell him the whole story, and then to repeat it in the proper quarters. The conspirators were arrested, tried and condemned to death.

We must not forget in all this that P. Amelote, an eminently sober-minded and by no means credulous person, reports with scrupulous accuracy what he heard from the mouth of his intimate friend, the famous P. de Condren. When Barbe met the latter at Saint-Magloire she at once recognized that "this was the man who had been promised to her" and she "opened her heart to him."

Père Condren told me (continues Amelote) that he had never met one who had so much knowledge of Jesus Christ crucified. . . . She had so powerfully united herself with Jesus Christ's suffering and linked herself with Him as Victim for sins, that often for two or three hours at a stretch she seemed dead with anguish. At these times, she said, God made her taste sin, and no pain in the world was equal to that which she felt as she savoured its bitterness.[1]

What follows, coming from such a pen, is supremely important.

I could make a volume of the rare souls that this good Father knew. They came to him from all parts, and on his journeys God always directed him to the saints of the places through which he passed. He used to say that there were as many, though they were unknown, in our day as in the Early Church. He had seen many types of saints, and recognized that his own lamp burnt the more brightly by reason of their graces and God's guiding of them. In connection with his knowledge of so many saints, it is remarkable that in his youth he had desired this boon and God Who grants the prayer of those who fear Him had granted it to his prayers.[2]

[1] He adds some curious details. "The first time that I heard P. de Condren mention this soul I was still in ignorance of the ways of Divine grace. The respect in which I held him made me suspend my own judgement over the conversation, of which I should have thought nothing, had it come from other lips than his. But I became convinced that there were in very truth mysteries in the saints of which my theology had shown me nothing, at work among God's chosen, when he recounted to me a communication which this poor girl had made to him. God had laid upon her the duty of doing penance for a person living more than a hundred leagues from her, whom he had ascertained she could never have known. However, the impression which God had made in her soul of the state of this absent person was so strong that she was conscious of her sins and intentions and told the Father as a great secret that she committed such-and-such an offence. She went further, warning him that the person in question would come to Paris within the year and seek to deceive him, that she would tell him such-and-such falsehoods; that he would be on his guard; but that finally she would be converted and make a general confession to him. All which, improbable though it seemed, fell out exactly as Barbe had said." *La vie du Père Charles de Condren*, Paris, 1643, pp. 264–5.

[2] *Ibid.*, pp. 262, 266.

Let no one speak of illusion. The Condrens of the world know better than we that, for one authentic ecstasy, there are two or three counterfeits. We postpone to a subsequent chapter the summing up of what we have to say about this scourge, which after all is outside our subject. Do historians of secular literature trouble themselves with plagiarists or madmen? The false mystics prove the evidence of the true, in whom we know they inspire an instant and invincible repugnance. I could quote endless examples. Here is one which I borrow from the author of Mme Acarie's Life.

Nicole Tavernier of Rheims lived in Paris during the troubles of the *Ligue* and enjoyed the reputation of being a very holy maiden and a worker of miracles. She explained difficult passages of Scripture so as to astonish the most famous doctors. She had ecstasies, visions, revelations; predicted future events and warned the dying of sins left unconfessed; and what she said proved to be true. . . . A priest who had meant to consecrate a wafer for the Communion could not find the Host he intended for her, when the moment of Communion came; she asserted that an angel had brought it to her. Once when she was with Mme Acarie in the Capuchin Church at Meudon she disappeared for more than an hour. When she returned, that saintly woman asked what had become of her; she replied that she had been to Tours to dissuade some great nobles from a design injurious to religion.

She was consulted on all sides, the great ones of the realm begged her prayers, priests and religious esteemed her, no one as yet remarking in her . . . any imperfection. . . . She declared that, if men would repent of their sins, the public calamities would speedily cease. At her word throngs confessed and communicated; processions were ordered in various towns. She herself had one arranged in Paris, which was attended by the *Parlement*, other high courts, and a great concourse of citizens; Nicole even dared to tell the Bishop that, if this procession did not take place, he would die within the year.

Despite the popular confidence in this girl, neither Mme Acarie nor M. de Bérulle ever trusted her. Mme Acarie indeed from the outset declared that this soul was suffering from illusion; that the Devil was the author of all her visions, in his cunning consenting to lose a little in order to gain much; that ecstasies and raptures could take place in a sinner; that a spirit of darkness might have stolen the Host which had disappeared from the altar; that the journey to Tours had never been proved, but that it was not beyond the powers of the evil spirit; that this woman seemed absolutely devoid of the Spirit of God.

Let us neglect the explanations which she gives of these strange events. The fundamental and decisive reason is the last. In this doubtful character she has not recognized the Spirit of God.

So strongly did Mme Acarie persist in these opinions that people began to have doubts about the virtue of this girl; doubts changed to certainties when the Blessed one who had received her into her house tested her in various ways and convicted her of many lies.[1]

About the same time another person with whom we shall soon make acquaintance, Jean de Quintanadoine, warned by a friend, prioress of the Carmelites of Lisbon, unmasked an impostor who had excited the enthusiasm of all Portugal by claiming the Stigmata.

Having keenly observed the reluctance, under the guise of humility, of this nun to show her hands . . . he detected in a vain and light gesture which the girl unwarily used as she moved her hands . . . that the miracle was all pretence.

Although Quintanadoine was, as we shall see, one of the most simple of spiritual men, yet his divine candour gave him fine perception. He had indeed to do with a veritable conjurer, for this woman "proved to be artistically and ingeniously painted with wounds on hands, feet and sides," and could raise "her body from the ground by means of her shoes or pattens, which she wore very high, supported meanwhile on a stout stick . . . all this accompanied with a false radiance which she caused to shine round her by means of little earthen lamps concealed within her sleeves."[2]

Counterfeits or not, this borderland of ecstasy made no impression on our mystics. Rather a "celestial lamp," a diviner's instinct, led them straight to the obscure retreats inhabited by the friends of God. Amelote's beautiful phrase—"On his journeys, God always directed him to the saints of the places through which he passed"—may be applied not only to P. de Condren, but to all our mystics.

I am (writes Père Surin from Marenne in 1654) in a rural spot far from the great world and its fashions and all the civilization of human life. Nevertheless I must confess that in this little place is great

[1] *Vie de la B. Marie de l'Incarnation*, by J. B. A. Boucher, Paris, 1873, pp. 187–9.
[2] *Vie* (in MS.) *de M. de Bretigny*, by M. Champignol, pp. 40–3

treasure of grace, and I think that I have been divinely led hither, that I may be instructed in the greatness of God . . . not in myself, but in souls which He has marvellously enriched with His gifts, and in whom I can see, as through small chinks, the light of the Other Life.[1]

He then describes the sublime heights attained by two unknown mystics, compared with whom celebrated religious masters were but as novices. Twenty years earlier, he related to his director, P. Louis Lallemand, a similar experience.

I should like to tell you of the gracious adventure with which it pleased God to favour me on leaving Rouen, in that I met what I cannot prize enough, a rare and holy soul. In the coach I found myself beside a youth of some eighteen years, simple and even boorish in appearance and particularly in speech, ignorant of reading and writing, for he had spent his life in domestic service, with a priest, but filled with graces of every kind and with rare heavenly gifts the like of which I have never yet seen. Uninstructed by men in the interior life, he yet spoke so fluently, so subtly and with such weight as to surpass all that I have either read or heard. As soon as I discovered this treasure I took every possible occasion of talking to him in private. We took our meals apart and I talked solely with him; he when not conversing with me was continually at his prayers. . . .

His prayer is sublime. He began with ecstasies, but, he said, these were imperfections from which God had freed him.

With all this there was no presumption. He revealed himself as he was, perfectly frankly.

Reflecting on what he had said to me, he would fain have thrown himself at my feet in humiliation. . . .

I had to use all my tact to make him talk, affected to think little of him, and persuaded him that it was an obligation of charity to entertain me with good discourse, since I could not do all the talking. Presently he took fire and, losing himself, spoke, following the lead of the Holy Spirit that animated him. Directly I begged for his prayers he took alarm and drew into his shell, but as he is extremely simple and believes himself the least of all men, he has revealed more of himself than he suspects.

I cannot transcribe all this splendid letter, which is a veritable treatise on Mysticism. It descends from the heights to the valleys at times, always revealing some tender charm.

[1] *Lettres spirituelles du R. P. Surin*, Avignon, 1721, I. 116.

Our Lord had taught him not to take offence at anyone and always to excuse his neighbour. This he does in a twofold way; first, by the maxim that God leads souls in various ways . . . secondly, to attribute to everyone simplicity. . . . Once seeing a cavalier in a scarlet mantle, " My father," said he, " these good folk follow the inclination of pride and wear such bright colours to make themselves seen from afar and inspire fear by the appearance of fire and flame."

Pressed to say if he had never been instructed by a director,

he said, No; he had had no master but the Holy Spirit; if the Sacred Books should be lost, he could do without them, God Himself having taught him sufficient for salvation.[1]

Still less did he owe anything to the masters of the contemplative life. It is the same with all the mystics, learned or ignorant, God made them. It is good to recall this truth at the outset of a work in which the secondary human agency may at times threaten to absorb us. We shall study powerful religious organizations, traverse the schools, and scarce leave the world of books, but this must never make us forget the fundamental and exclusively divine experience from which all else radiates or the shining examples we have just given.

§2. *Père Coton and the King's Truce*

I. Père Coton belongs to us entirely. On the one hand, as friend, counsellor and collaborator of Henri IV he did more than anyone else to forward the Renaissance of Mysticism; on the other hand, by his direct influence on souls and his inner life, he stands out as one of its most eminent witnesses. Nowadays the latter aspect of his genius and grace is apt to be overlooked, but the mystics and saints of that time, who are alone competent to decide the matter, were not blind to it. On the morrow of the miserable intrigue which forced King Louis XIII to dismiss his confessor (1617), the future chancellor de Marillac, whom we shall discuss when the time comes, used a figure not more charming than just to describe the noble exile. " Père Coton leaves the Court as calmly, freely, and peaceably as one could desire, no more ruffled than a swan coming out of the water whose feathers are in no way wet." Louis de la Rivière, the spiritual son and biographer of Marie de Valence, with more

[1] Surin, *ibid.*, I. 1, 15.

precision but less happily, speaks in the same strain and relates a testimony even more important than his own.

This angel in the midst of the distractions of Court kept himself carefully in the Presence of God . . . with his left eye he looks upon the world to scorn it, with his right upon eternity to love it. One day the Sieur Gallemant, doctor of the Sorbonne and himself a great contemplative . . . remarked to me, speaking of Père Coton, that Père Coton was a very *interior* person and quite other than what some held him to be."[1]

So we, who live to-day under a monarch who is a sworn foe to fraud, I mean independent criticism, and are independent enough ourselves, will not waste time in discussing the many foolish things which have been written about this great man. Our task is not to defend P. Coton, but to paint as he actually was, and with all possible care, one of the essential figures in our vast canvas.

Like several contemporary mystics—Ste. Chantal for instance—Pierre Coton, a native of the Forez, born in 1654 (two years earlier than his compatriot Honoré d'Urfé) at Neronde, grew up in a circle which held the " Sainte Ligue " in heartiest detestation. Guichard Coton, his father, *seigneur* of Chenevoux, collaborator of Claude d'Urfé in the government of Forez, and, in later life, secretary of decrees to Queen Catherine, went even further, detesting with equal heartiness Huguenots and Jesuits alike, and bringing up his children to shun these twin plagues. Père Prat, the official biographer of Père Coton, deplores the second of these aversions, in which we are tempted rather to see the hand of Providence. It seems to us that the reflections which could not have failed to arise in his mind when he had become a fervent Jesuit, as he thought over the memories of childhood, must have paved the way for what may be fitly termed the *liberalism* of P. Coton. Assuredly no shred of the hostile sentiments of his father towards either ultramontanes or the Society of Jesus remained in him, but early in life he had been taught by the example of one dear to him that there are honest folk on both sides of the rampart. This lesson, by which he continually profited, gave him a certain flexibility which distinguished him from fanatics whether of left or right, a spirit of conciliating moderation highly disconcerting to his natural

[1] Cf. Prat, *Recherches historique et critiques sur la Compagnie de Jésus en France du temps du Père Coton*, Lyons, 1876, III. 760–7.

adversaries, which indeed at times made him more or less suspect in the eyes of his superiors and their friends.

His own disposition did not predestine him to play a part among the violent. A recluse, a book-lover, inclined to be timid, he possessed a sweetness and charm which his contemporaries recognized with one accord, though they sometimes attributed it to magic. In Huguenot eyes he was a "charmer," or "enchanter," two words which at that time had about them the odour of a witches' sabbath. In simple fact he had a very tender disposition, the grand air, good manners, and a most seductive voice. "He is," said Palma-Cayet, "so attractive and gracious that one could never weary of listening to him."[1] De la Rivière, who knew him well, describes him as "handsome of face and figure, dignified in bearing, gracious in speech, easy of access, condescending, gentle and friendly."[2]

Such he showed himself, from the outset of his apostolic career, in his frequent encounters with Protestant ministers. Whether he wrote against them or took part in those conferences then fashionable in which each side contradicted the other, reminding us of meetings of the Chamber to-day, he astonished, disconcerted, sometimes even gained over his adversaries by the human touch in his arguments. In doing this the young controversialist showed some originality, for we find ministers spreading the tidings of P. Coton's conversion to Calvinism, even Catholics uniting in lamentations over this infamy. Things went so far that the Jesuit had to defend himself publicly from the charge of treason, learning thus betimes that the peacemakers only "inherit the earth" at the price of painful humiliations. Yet had he abandoned himself to his natural *verve* he would certainly not have lacked in freshness or sharpness. Less truculent, and more delicate in intellect and heart, than the giants around him who dealt heresy smashing blows with their clubs and who at bottom were no worse than the author of the *Histoire des variations*, who could yet have been quite as deadly, Pierre Coton resembles in both respects the ingenuous and terrible Garasse, or, if one likes, one much greater than Garasse. It is one of the most amusing features of the religious literature of this epoch, that so many pious writers who have never read Rabelais and anathematise him, should, in style at least, depend on him.

[1] Prat, *ibid.*, II. 111.

[2] La Rivière, *ibid.*, p. 99.

Let the reader decide where Père Coton gets the description of the " redundant person " of Daniel Chamier, minister at Montélimar, guilty of inventing and circulating the *Histoire notable du P. Henry, jésuite*, " condemned at Antwerp to the stake for his lewd life." After having proved the inanity of this fable, Coton turns to Chamier's harangues on the intemperance of the monks.

Great Heaven, what do we see? The paunchy, heavy-jowled minister, served by his drab and surrounded by his brats, red cap on his head, seated at the head of a table loaded with tripe stewed in oil,[1] filling a large chair with his great breadth, vest unfastened, cuffs turned back to the elbow, chewing hard and helping himself with both hands, sweating, dribbling, greasily snuffling, sighing with deep bass sighs. . . .

I stop short, just in time. That which follows is of equal force, but on a " higher " note.

The minister frowning over a book, intoning a psalm, galloping from synod to synod at the expense of the *cause* ; the minister quarrelling, vituperating, rebelling, asserting what seems good to him in matters of faith; interpreting Scripture as it likes him; trumpeting his visions; the minister, in short, living ministerially, esteemed a holy Reformed pastor, a model of uprightness, provost of the newly arisen Church and buttress of the newly printed Gospel, while these poor wights of Capuchins, Minims, Carthusians, Jesuits, etc., are only good-for-noughts.[2]

Allowing for disgust only too well founded, one may admire at least the precision and glow of the graphic touches in such passionate sentences, characteristic traits of the writer. Almost in spite of himself, he seizes and vividly paints whatever is ridiculous in his adversaries. Take the theatrical prayers with which some ministers were wont to season their public controversial exercises.

The preacher in this place, whimpering, throws up and rolls his eyes, draws a breath from the bottom of his lungs or the depths of his hollow soul, waves his arms about as though personating a windmill, then suddenly lets them fall as though staggering under a blow, rather than crossing them.[3]

In another place he depicts a hectoring minister defying at his ease an absent enemy.

[1] Chamier's partiality for this dish had won him the nickname of "*tripier*" (Tripes).

[2] Prat, *ibid.*, I. 687–8.

[3] Prat, *ibid.*, I. 331.

You were seen . . . after my departure, strutting about the Place Saint-André, arms akimbo, the conquering hero; when an audience came within hail, you had a hit at the absent, with swelling cheeks you played the *quos ego*, always supposing it was with someone safe to do so; in short, you practised the proverb, *lepusculus barbam vellit leoni mortuo*, in complete forgetfulness of the sage counsel that Mgr. de Lesdiguières, always careful of your reputation, has so often given you, never before such an one to dare open your mouth, and that you should beware of intermeddling, that you were too often given to vaunt yourself, and that one glorious day you gained a battle for the Pope by presuming to dispute with M. Tholosain at S. Marcellin; that anything is better for you than the tongue in your mouth or the pen in your hand.

The fellow is dusted down in a masterly manner; Lesdiguières gave good advice in telling him to lie low. A little Latin does no harm. The next passage is more original and indeed more amusing.

This is the third time that he taxes me with extravagant (*cornus*) arguments and extravagant deductions, leaving me on the horns of a dilemma. He has horns on the brains: *scilicet ad sylvas et sua lustra redit.*[1]

I was obliged to give some idea of P. Coton's fighting pen, but this is not his ordinary tone. He did not flatter himself when he wrote on the cover of one of his books a motto from Proverbs: *Responsio mollis frangit iram* ("a soft answer turneth away wrath"), and he could reproach adversaries for undue warmth, without fearing that the compliment would be returned.

To inspire confidence, we must always do our utmost to preserve moderation and balance. He who is always sputtering, muttering, foaming, grinding his teeth, blusters and dribbles, nothing more.[2]

To feel his attractiveness and his style one need only study the pamphlet, spiritual, calm and loving, which he wrote to reassure Catholics as to his reported apostasy and to disillusion Huguenots of their vain hopes. It is addressed to the originator of the startling tidings, the pastor Chamier.

Ah, M. Chamier, so it is due to the modesty (in the sense of moderation) and gentleness I have practised, to the affection I bear you, to the charity which I conceive I owe you, that so great a discourtesy has been done as to cast the shadow upon me of what I detest

[1] Prat, *ibid.*, I. 325–9. [2] *Ibid.*, I. 534.

cane pejus et angue and abhor, both by grace and education, a world more than death itself. . . . Can you incite yourself thus lightly to laughter, at the risk of your salvation and the good name of those who wish you well, save only in your religion? This hope, you say, made you tremble with joy, but who instructed you to pasture thus on vanity, to feed on shadows and feast on falsehood? . . .

Why did you not hope at once that one fine morning I was about to become faun, satyr, werewolf, hippocentaur . . . or that coming down into Avignon I should throw myself into the Rhône . . . or that I should soon turn Mussulman? This it is to refuse belief to the things that are, and to strain oneself blind after those that are not.

It is true that I have sent you books; I acknowledge that I have talked to you with real affection: the books contained the answer to the Sieur de Plessis, . . . the other charge shows my zeal for your salvation, the affection inspired within me by your strange condition, that such affection might be the antidote to your faults and errors, that if possible I might save a soul dear to me. . . .

Ah, permit me to love you, though I hate your ideas, love you personally though I despise your practices, admire your qualities, yet blame your circumstances, rejoice in your natural gifts, and aspire that you may receive those supernatural.

After as before this incident, he would fain remain on friendly terms with the minister, although, as Chamier must first acknowledge, he was never involved in any treachery to the Church. This done,

. . . it is unreasonable to wonder that friendly relations should exist between a Jesuit and a minister, that is to say between an arch-Catholic and an arch-Huguenot, always provided that friendship takes its stand, not on faith, but on charity, in which I have the advantage, inasmuch as charity joined to the true faith surpasses charity which comes only by nature.

Such a theology of friendship may be slightly subtle, but is wholly charming; as a Catholic he loves doubly those whom he loves. He adds with delicious malice that, since the coming of Christ, Isaiah's prophecy must be fulfilled: *habitabit lupus cum agno et pardus cum haedo accubabit ; vitulus et ovis et leo simul morabuntur*.

We are brothers, not on the mother's side, for we have not the same Church as mother, but on the side of God, our Father and Saviour.[1]

[1] Prat, *ibid.*, pp. 411, 417. As Daniel Chamier does not occupy us directly, I will only quote a few lines of his, sounding strangely after this letter : "Great heavens," he writes, "what fury in this communication. I have never read anything more atrocious : this is not anger, but madness," and he winds up by comparing Père Coton to a mad dog (Prat, I. 418.)

But for the difference of the times, is not this the style of Anselm, or of Fénelon? It is plain, moreover, that, in writing thus, P. Coton but follows his nature, not merely politeness or charity. His temperament was one of moderation, disliking all extremes. The doctrinal moderation of Bossuet's books against the Protestants, especially that of his *Exposition*, has often been praised, but P. Coton published a work of the same kind at a time when such action demanded greater courage, and, as Bossuet would be later, so Coton was suspected of *minimisme*. Indeed, but for the support of the King of France and of Bellarmine, his work would, it is said, have been put on the Index. But the doctrinal side of the great controversialist is not our subject. We want only to establish relations with this illustrious peacemaker, and prepare the reader for Henri IV's choice of him as his associate in that policy of union and conciliation which, if it did not originate, at least marvellously promoted the mystic renaissance of France.

II. P. Coton, who was not charged with care of the royal conscience till after the death of the Curé Benoit in 1608, did not occupy at Court the position later accorded to the confessors of Louis XIV. All sorts of more or less diplomatic *rôles* indeed were his: preacher-in-ordinary to the King; official representative of the Holy See, at least during the nunciate of Ubaldini, who was shrewd enough to avail himself largely of his services; tutor to the Dauphin; casuist, director or catechist of the world at large—all these and many other functions were little by little added to the curious and delicate mission which had first launched him on these waters. Above all, he was there in the character of Jesuit, in fact, be it said frankly, as a hostage for the Society.

The history is well known. In 1595 a former pupil of the Jesuits had tried to assassinate the King, and the *Parlement* used this as an excuse to hang one Jesuit, Père Guignard, and banish the rest from the kingdom. A pyramid erected on the ruins of the house of Châtel and ornamented by the Protestant Joseph Scaliger with four frenzied inscriptions commemorated these acts, and symbolized concretely the sentiment prevailing in the *Parlement*, among the Reformed, and one party in the Sorbonne, towards the Society of Jesus. The son of Jeanne d'Albret on his side had no sympathy for the Jesuits. He had too much good sense and too long a memory to consider them solely responsible for the *Ligue*, but he believed them rather Roman than French, sold to Spain, and past-masters of regicide. This was enough for him. For these reasons he was afraid with a genuine fear, in the full sense of the word, of the Society. On the other hand, the Jesuits had warm and powerful friends. They were ubiquitous; towns and provinces contended for them, braving fearlessly the sentence of the *Parlement* of Paris. The King was petitioned and counter-petitioned on this subject; clear-sighted and uninfluenced by fanaticism, after ripe reflection he decided upon reconciliation. The political views leading him to this resolution (which would strike us of to-day less if so many governments since then had not shut their eyes to equally convincing evidence), are well set forth in a letter of Henri IV to James I, King of England.

The principal reason which prevents me from treating the Jesuits with the utmost rigour is that they are a corporate Order, and one so powerful to-day in Christendom, being composed of men of judgement and learning, who have acquired great credit and authority among the Catholics; so that, in persecuting them or driving them to despair of remaining in my kingdom, I should band against myself many superstitious spirits, and displease a great number of Catholics, giving them a pretext to rise against me and bring about fresh troubles in my said kingdom, even, it may be, to lend an ear to the enemies of the peace of the realm, abroad as well as at home.

He goes on to recall that several provinces continued to harbour them, in defiance of the law, and that, if he employed his authority against them, "there might possibly be resistance, injurious to *his* concerns." The amiable Macchiavellism which follows is not less sage.

I have likewise considered that, by leaving the said Jesuits some hope of being recalled and reinstated in my kingdom, I should create a diversion and prevent them from giving themselves entirely over to the ambitious will of the King of Spain, in respect of which I learn that I have not miscalculated. . . . With so much gained, I now desire to confine and regulate their power and undertakings within my own realm, so as to ensure their cheerful service and obedience in the future, and to restrain their opportunities to do me disservice, supposing they should have will thereto. This is why I am minded to make provision by wise ordinance, which being strictly observed, they shall not be able, should they desire it, to serve the said King of Spain or even the Pope to my prejudice.[1]

If the latest biographer of P. Coton is to be relied on, this valuable document does not reveal the true thought of the King of France. One must not take it literally. Desiring to humour James I, he used the only language a Protestant sovereign could understand. For himself, at the date when he wrote thus (August 15, 1603), he had entirely laid aside his former sectarian and partizan prejudices against the Jesuits; then and henceforward he was altogether won over to the Society. This ingenious interpretation seems to us impossible. P. Coton, I believe, would agree with us; he had so much trouble in driving from the royal head and heart the old suspicions which others actively cherished and which the smallest occasion would revive. It is true that, in his letter to the English King, Henri IV somewhat minimises the concessions he has already made to the Jesuits, as well as those he contemplates making in a future to be as long as possible. But he explains his reasons for the change of attitude with absolute frankness, speaking as he would to himself. His clear intention is first to prevent all the troubles which the continuation of measures of persecution might involve, then, by whatever means, to attach to himself a great Order and utilize it as other Catholic sovereigns had done. He is very suspicious, and means to keep a close watch over them even when he embraces them. As a politician, he means to distribute his favours a drop at a time, both to bind them to his service more closely and to lull by such slow methods the suspicions of the *Parlement*, the Sorbonne, and the Reformed. Such in 1603 was, and would long be, the attitude of Henri IV towards the Jesuits. It was a wholly political policy which P. Coton with great skill gradually transformed and softened. In 1603 Henri still doubts, uses artifice, plays a game of wits with them; by 1610 he has conceived a lasting affection for them.

The King and the Jesuit met for the first time at Fontainebleau on May 29, 1603. They were never to part again. P. Coton had just finished a course of sermons in the capital of Provence; he was then thirty-nine and had already been given to understand by supernatural warnings that a high mission awaited him and that he was a

[1] Prat, *ibid.*, II. 132–3.

chosen instrument of God for the triumph of the Society. He was, therefore, scarcely surprised on receiving a royal mandate to attend the Court. On the way he stopped at Valence for a glimpse of his saint. This man, who has been represented as an intriguer, started for the political arena with childlike confidence and faith. Marie de Valence promised him the heart of Henri, a prediction which was to be realized twice over and later was to comfort this loyal and tender servitor in his deep distress on receiving the dead heart of his prince, with a commission to bear it to the College de la Flèche.

Other eminent Jesuits, Louis Richeone and Ignace Armand, had already laid siege to the King, in whose mind the policy just sketched was already decided upon. It remained to put the tortuous and slow programme into operation. That he might get to know this mysterious Society thoroughly, Henri wished to have at hand a typical Jesuit, whom he could sound and question and examine at his leisure. This Jesuit would be thus living example, type, official agent, and hostage of his Order in one; let him but be caught out in concocting some treachery, and it would be all up with the Jesuits. From another point of view, if these men were equal to their reputation, a distinguished Jesuit would not only adorn the Court, but also in many ways be of service to the royal policy. With such considerations in view, Henri met halfway the proposal of the Generals to assign him P. Coton, whom he knew to be one of the first preachers in France and of whom Lesdiguières, a good judge, had told him "all imaginable good things." To test his eloquence and personality, Coton should have an audience of the King and preach before him. If the first impression were favourable, he would be retained.

So the two men looked into each other's eyes. The King was charming with his grand air of simplicity, his good-humour and his welcome. His reception, so an old and discreet Jesuit chronicler tells us, "begot in Père Coton's heart a tender affection for the person of this great monarch, such as one has for a friend rather than for a master. Henri, too, knew that, from that time on, his sentiments for P. Coton would be something deeper than the ordinary feelings of a sovereign for a good subject."[1]

Some days later Coton, having followed the Court to Paris, writes to one of his friends:

[1] P. d'Orléans, cited by P. Prat, *ibid.*, II. 109.

The King spoke to us several times at the Tuileries both before and after Mass, always with much goodwill, once especially conversing with us more than half an hour, in the presence of his principal courtiers and various Paris notabilities. . . . Before his departure he said to us, "Come to Saint-Germain and you shall see my Dauphin!"

His Majesty subsequently condescended to conduct us to some of his artificial grottoes and the exquisitely painted chapel which he has had built. On the morrow he made an appointment to shew us his fountains, where the waterworks are marvellous, surpassing, they say, those of Pratolino and Tivoli. On the jets spouting out unexpectedly, the King was so gracious to us as to take no note of anyone save Monseigneur the Prince and us, pointing out the places where we should be sheltered and pressing us against his royal person in narrow nooks.

Once I was in his presence with M. Duperron for more than two hours on end, discussing holy and instructive things, which proves that His Majesty is much interested in such subjects.[1]

Père Coton was not one to lose his head, but it is plain he was delighted with such graciousness which, as he rightly felt, augured favourably. On his side, the King found him much to his taste, but Henri IV was not the man to confide blindfold in anyone. In fact, it is known that more than once he was alarmed at the plots imputed to the suave Jesuit. Once indeed the latter seemed within an inch of destruction. A plot had been discovered, disclosed in time by accomplices for whom Coton was too slow! At first, half reassured by a calm denial, the King took fresh alarm at the appearance of a threatening black and lurid cloud; the elements were taking part in the game. Henri, who was at table, ate no more; unnerved, "he mechanically drew the dishes to him, then pushed them away." Silently observant for some time, Coton at last whispered in the royal ear that there was a very simple means to prevent all danger, his own arrest, since it was he whom they suspected. The guard was at hand, and he would make no resistance! That nothing should be wanting to this triumph of innocence, the story goes that the ominous cloud faded away at the same moment.

In this scene and others like it, which can easily be pictured, Henri's attitude is not so contemptible as one might imagine at first sight.

[1] Prat, *ibid.*, II. 114–5.

All his faults notwithstanding, he had a lofty soul, and to doubt the loyalty of one dear to him was anguish. If Coton turned traitor, on whom could he rely? Add to this the idea, ridiculous no doubt but excusable, that the prince, new to Church ways, had formed of religious obedience. Were there not two men in P. Coton, the Frenchman and the Jesuit? and was not the latter blindly submissive to the orders of a foreign Superior, Aquaviva, himself a slave of another power that might at any moment ally itself with Spain? Such considerations were more than was necessary to nourish the innate suspiciousness of the King and to render the principal task which P. Coton had to fulfil very thorny. During the first months after his arrival at Court, the question of the Jesuits was still hanging in the balance. As we have already seen, the King agreed in principle to their recall, but a thousand points still remained to be settled. Aquaviva and the Holy See, building on Henri's favourable mood, hoped for a measure of full liberty, a reinstatement pure and simple of the Order in France, which the King could not and certainly would not accord. The Jesuits might return, so much was settled, but only under certain conditions more or less paralysing and humiliating, that should keep them more straitly and perpetually than the other Orders in dependence on the royal power. Of all these conditions the most unacceptable, in the eyes of the General and the Pope, was the vow of fidelity to the King that the Jesuits would have to renew at the beginning of each year. After much discussion, Coton obtained the concession that this vow should only be demanded once from each member. Several other points were subsequently conceded to him, but when, on September 1, 1603, the famous Edict of Rouen was published, reopening France to the Jesuits, neither the Pope nor the chief authorities of the Order were satisfied. Coton, they held, had sinned by his excessive moderation, and forthwith they began a campaign to secure, by fair means or foul, the modification of the Edict.

P. Coton's diplomatic abilities, nobility, wise and pacific spirit, and sanctity now appeared in the most favourable light. To their honour, be it said, the majority of the French Jesuits were on his side. They loved their King and had full confidence in the verbal promises they had received from him, which led them to expect greater favours in a near future. They realised also the passionate resistance of their enemies. In a word, the Edict of Rouen filled them with joy. "To do or undertake nought against Our interests, the public peace and the tranquillity of Our realm"—the oath imposed cost them nothing.

P. Coton was more deeply affected than his brothers in France, for he had received formal blame from his General, and barely held his ground. Before taking any steps in the movement, the nuncio Buffalo, to whom the Secretary of State, Aldobrandini, had entrusted the delicate mission of requesting the King's modification or suppression of various clauses in the Edict, had confided his perplexities to P. Coton. It is impossible to read without pleasure and admiration the Jesuit's reply (although translated into modern French from the original Latin) addressed, through the medium of the nuncio, in reality to the General and the Pope. It is adroit, since it merely presents the mind of a third independent person—the King's Secretary of State; but it is touching and noble, for one reads between the lines that Coton thought exactly as did Villeroy.

All those of our friends whom I have consulted on the subject of the communication of your Illustrious Lordship informed me that it would be necessary to address oneself to M. de Villeroy, who alone could say whether it would be opportune to speak of the matter to the King, whether a possible modification of the Edict might be expected from Council, and finally what might be written to Rome. Accordingly last evening (October 29, 1603) I visited him very late at night. Having read the letter of the illustrious Cardinal Aldobrandini, he said to me that in his opinion this was not the moment to petition the King about this affair, he being irritated at learning that what had been approved at Venice and elsewhere had been disapproved of by the Roman Jesuits, possibly inspired by Spain. . . . He considered that something of the sort might be communicated to the illustrious Cardinal Aldobrandini and to our own Fathers.

As to the oath . . . that the King, in prescribing it, thought less of his interests than of ours: for it is necessary in order to confound the false reports maliciously spread against us among the public mind, to obtain the consent of the Parlement, . . . to take away any ground for the evil intentions which they would not fail to ascribe to us, if they saw us raising any difficulties on this point.

But why exact from the Jesuits an oath not exacted from other Orders? Partly because these latter, whether justly or unjustly, and although they had had among them full-blown leaguers, were never exiled from the kingdom; because pamphleteers had been more merciful to them; finally and above all because no special vows bound them to the Holy See, as their fourth vow binds the Jesuits. After some more equally lucid reasoning come these more stirring lines which, if I mistake not, are not from Villeroy:

If no other means of exercising our ministry in France remains, shall we not go back there with the law of the kingdom, in order to return with the law of Jesus Christ? Shall we not cede something of our special rights, or of the common rights of the religious, in order that the common rights of nature and man, of the Church and the Holy See, may be integrally maintained by these means throughout this vast realm? Since for the glory of God we are at times bidden to resume lay dress, to mingle in worldly merrymakings, why for the same motive should we not place in lay hands the expression of our loyalty to the King and the State?

Admirable priest, good Frenchman! That said, the Secretary of State can take the stage once more.

It seems to M. de Villeroy (continues P. Coton) that one should not cavil when there is no room for doubt of the good faith with which what is good and equitable is desired. Now it is certain that we do not desire to lend our services to France as much as the King desires to receive them; but we must rely on His Majesty and not refuse him our loyal homage. There will be no cause to fear either second thoughts or double meanings, provided that we do not wound him by raising all these difficulties, as if we wished to put our loyalty up for sale. This is at bottom, and expressed much in the same terms, the response of M. de Villeroy.

Villeroy had broad shoulders and was besides, in this affair, entirely one with the Jesuits; both understood the natural susceptibility of the King and his really generous intentions.

I will add here (concludes Coton) a trait which proves that one must not judge prematurely a prince so benevolent, so worthy of respect and regard. Only four days ago he asked me what the Italians thought of the edict of our reinstatement. "Sire," I replied, "all thank your Majesty, but some say that the child was hardly worth so painful a travail!" "Write to them," said the King, "that the mother is fruitful and will bring forth again!" In sooth, each day's fresh experience shows that he has intentions of according us new benefits.[1]

[1] Prat, *ibid.*, II. 171–5.

This document, written in haste by a man who instinctively sees only the highest motives, hardly lays sufficient stress upon the danger that the opposition at Rome to the Edict of Rouen threatened to become. At this date the fate of the Society in France and the friendly policy of the King towards the Holy See hung by a thread; whether it was understood or not at Rome, Henri IV, in signing the Edict of Rouen, had dealt a vigorous blow, bold, perilous perhaps, for the Roman side. In doing this he had taken great risks, so determined and strong was the Gallican and anti-Jesuit movement in France. Having committed himself so conspicuously, if neither the Pope nor the Jesuits were satisfied, the King, wounded to the quick in his feelings and crossed in his policy, would soon have dismissed friends even more importunate than they were compromising. Neither Coton nor Villeroy had any illusions on this point. "If you persist in your demands," wrote the latter to Aquaviva, "I apprehend misfortune for your Order, and even for the Catholic religion."[1] What was, therefore, Coton's consternation when a few days after writing the letter already quoted, which had not yet arrived at its destination, he received from his General, with new expressions of blame, the formal command to bring the question of the oath once more before the King! He had to obey. His soul died within him, for he was convinced that he was marching straight to his own disgrace, and, what was far worse, to the ruin of his work. The dignified and touching letter that he wrote a few days later to his General makes this forlorn hope live again for us in moving detail. Here also we follow the translation of the Latin text.

I was profoundly afflicted on reading the letter of your Paternity, (such is the mode of address to the General of the Jesuits) to perceive that this negotiation had not obtained the approbation of him whom I have always ardently desired to please in God. I have sought, as always, consolation in the Divine Will. What is there for me in Heaven and what upon earth do I desire but It? Your Paternity thinks that the affair might have been handled otherwise and have fallen out differently. Such is not the belief of those acquainted with this Court, the disposition of the King's Council, and the character of the Prince. I shall, however, act according to your Paternity's desires, as occasion serves.

He proceeds to explain that, on receiving Aquaviva's "orders," he

[1] Prat, *ibid.*, II. 184.

went to Villeroy, whom he found ill at ease, discontented, and repeating: "These Italians do not comprehend our affairs!" So also with M. Sillery. As for their intimate friend La Varenne, he had "turned cold" with fear, holding that the Jesuits were lost if anyone dared to send Aquaviva's letters to the King.

If it had depended on myself, I should certainly have prevented these letters ever being laid before the King, but it was my duty to submit my judgement and will to the judgement and will of your Paternity. Therefore, after commending the matter to the Lord, I assented to their being read to His Majesty. Scarcely had he heard them before he summoned me and, upon my presenting myself, "Your Fathers in Italy," he said with an air of irritation, "do not approve then of what we have decreed, although all others, save the Spaniards, do. They cannot endure this oath of fidelity—what does that signify?" I replied as pacifically as possible, bringing forward the strongest reasons I could conceive, but the King would none of them. "You deceive yourself," he cried, "they are either ill-disposed towards me or they err in judgement. For they do not see that by refusing this oath they tacitly avow themselves guilty of all with which you have been reproached hitherto. . . . You insist on bearing a stigma which I am trying to remove from you. . . . These foreigners are ignorant of French ways, and yet they would force all to view things from their standpoint. Well, since they refuse fidelity to me, I shall refuse trust to them. But since you hold my promise, choose you out twelve among those of the Order still in France, more I will not permit to remain with you and share your duties." It was thus, by reproaches, and other hard words, that the King testified his irritation to me. How I answered him, He alone knows Who never forsakes His own, and Whose favour the prayers and sacrifices of your Paternity had won for me. The King appeared calmed and dismissed me graciously.

Subsequently I accompanied him to Mass. There, as is customary with him, he questioned me as to the Invocation of the Blessed Virgin. Afterwards he would have me present while he ate, all the while proposing various problems for me to solve. As he showed such graciousness, I thought it my duty to profit by the occasion offered by God to destroy any remnants of resentment in his heart, and did my best accordingly. The Lord in His mercy aided me, for the King allowed the fears of your Paternity to be explained and they seemed to him reasonable. . . . He promised to reply in a fashion that will satisfy us all.[1]

[1] Prat, *ibid.*, II. 180–3.

This reply of the King of France to the Jesuit General still exists, royal truly in tone, but pacific and friendly. Notwithstanding the dangerous attempt of Aquaviva, things remained as on the morrow of the Edict of Rouen. The King did not modify any of the clauses, but he took "in good part" the observations of the General. He had at heart the reinstating of the Jesuits in his realm, and would not be content until he had conducted it to a happy conclusion. Consequently, he concluded,

I desire that you should confide yourselves to me, who have, besides good will towards you, a better knowledge than any other of how to conduct this business.[1]

His promises were to a large extent kept, but the story need not be further pursued. It was but natural that P. Coton should be better aware of the true sentiments of the King of France than the Italian religious or the Pope himself. It is not this clearness of perception that we are emphasizing, but the generous and conciliatory disposition of this great man, ready on his side to accept without haggling for himself and his brethren terms onerous and humiliating and seeming to contravene both "the particular rights of the Jesuits" and "the common rights of the religious."

III. Perhaps we have lingered too long on these memorable incidents which, sealing as it were a kind of treaty between the House of France and the Society of Jesus, belong properly rather to general French history than to the subject of this work. But it seemed a good opportunity to throw light, from a striking example, on a whole class of phenomena, common enough at that period, which perplex secular historians.

We find it difficult to understand, and to present as a convincing and edifying whole, the rich complexity of so many men of that time, who could turn with ease from lofty contemplation to terrestrial preoccupations, science, politics, government, or even the art of war. When Père Joseph examines as an expert the fortifications of La Rochelle, it is hard to recognize in him the founder of a religious Order exclusively vowed to piety, the author of a mass of spiritual writings, a master and a model of the interior life. In him I confess the antinomy touches its extreme limits. P. Coton, more human

[1] Prat, *ibid.*, II. 183–4.

and lovable in my opinion, or, better perhaps, less perplexing, than the famous Capuchin, helps us to understand the latter. For P. Coton publicity has no attraction; he is oftener to be met on pilgrimages than in the trenches, mixes as little as possible in business, and only becomes slightly interested, so I believe, in the project of the Spanish marriages. Whether it was good policy, in the interests of France or not, that a daughter of Henri IV should not marry the Prince of Wales or that the Dauphin should marry a Princess of Spain I know not, but rightly or wrongly, P. Coton settled the question in a *simpliste* manner, entirely guided by Catholic interests. Naturally P. Joseph himself was wont to reduce all to this point of view, but after analysis and complicated calculations. Willingly or unwillingly, however, Coton shone at Court and in the diplomatic world; whatever his personal tastes he frequently quitted his oratory for Villeroy's cabinet. Nevertheless is it not evident from the passages we have read above that, in the midst of his most tangled negotiations, this man moved in a celestial atmosphere, that what we term his liberalism was derived from motives, not merely upright and generous, but always saintly?

While the royal anger thunders about him, he shields himself with rapid and fervent prayer; he attributes the triumph of the reply, that he had sought to make meek and gently touching, to "the holy sacrifices," the Masses promised by Aquaviva. These are not mere phrases on his pen; he sees clearly the King's heart between the almighty hands of God, the angel of the realm, the angel of his Order, and his own guardian angel putting upon his lips the necessary words. We shall return to the subject of his interior life in which such thoughts were at home. For the present his actions occupy our attention. Imagine this religious reeling under the displeasure of his chiefs, on the morrow of a success which had cost him such long efforts and on which rested so many hopes. He knows, cannot but know, that the Pope and the General are mistaken; nevertheless he endeavours to alter his own judgement, to accept theirs, as he will endeavour, with what winning wiles, to render this error excusable, praiseworthy even, in the eyes of Henri IV. Loyal to his vow of obedience, he believes firmly that, in one way or another, even should he himself make shipwreck, all will be overruled for the best.

Henri IV did not assist as a mere onlooker at these great scenes, which, for reasons already given, seem to us pre-eminently religious. That in these matters his primary preoccupation was political we have already insisted. It was in his capacity of King-peacemaker, restorer of unity, that he imposed a truce on the parties which tore each other to pieces, and recalled the Jesuits; but also, as Leibnitz was to do later and by the same methods, he desired to work for the kingdom and "for the glory of God." We are not claiming that he was a mystic, but, on the other hand, neither his numerous mistresses nor the very practical views that had influenced his conversion to Catholicism affect the matter. The Roman Church, its dogmas, rites, and spirit, which he studied with a sort of affectionate curiosity, touched his heart. Once when he made his Communion on S. Martin's Day he was seen to weep for devotion. The nuncio who was present advised his government: "*martedi, giorno di San Martino, si communico con tanta devotione che piangeva.*"

One is the less astonished (comments Père Prat) when one recollects that, since his conference with Père Maldonat in 1572, Henri of Navarre had always had perfectly orthodox and lofty ideas on the Blessed Sacrament. Even though resentment, policy, and circumstances had united to draw him back towards the Protestant party, a religious system without the Holy Sacrifice would never appeal to him. The God of the Eucharist was in his eyes the soul, the centre, the reason, the essence of the true religion. He often avowed as much to his ministers, "I hold scrupulously," he said to them in 1584, "that without genuine belief that the Body of Our Lord is in the Sacrament, religion can be nothing but ceremony" (Palma-Cayet.) . . . He declared firmly, in the conferences that preceded his abjuration, that he had never had any doubt on this point. And, finally, the Eucharist was always that one of our dogmas which inspired him with most respect and veneration.[1]

Head of the Church externally, and, from this point of view, an incomparable head, he was also, although in his own way, Catholic internally.

In Père Coton he appreciated not merely the faithful friend and charming companion but also the priest and man of God. It has been mentioned that the Jesuit was not officially the royal confessor till after the death of the Curé Benoit, that is for a period of over

[1] Prat, *ibid.*, II. 188–9.

two years, from March 1608 to May 1610. This ministry inspired him with alarm, and with good reason.

Hitherto, a very charming virtue—so rare apparently that since the days of the Schoolmen no French name has been found for it, although names for its opposites abound—*epieikeia*, in a word, had sufficed to extricate him from the delicate situation in which the mad frolics of the King often involved him. Doubtless he had remonstrated with the culprit privately, but as priest, not confessor, so that the new responsibilities now descending upon him were often overwhelming. Immediately he entered on the charge he wrote to his General:

It is justifiable to apply *epieikeia* in most circumstances outside the confessional, but can it find place in the rigour and vigour of the sacrament of penance? And yet how many things are pardoned to princes! . . . I am terrified, in reading the ancient Fathers, to see what zeal they displayed. . . . It makes me tremble.[1]

That nothing should be wanting to his discomfort, he came to the office, as is well known, at a regrettable and ridiculously momentous epoch in Henri's life of gallantry. What he said and what he was to his penitent remains the secret of P. Coton and the King. There were ups and downs, and the confessor's authority was certainly less inefficient than one might fancy, glancing cursorily over the scandalous chronicle of these two sad years. "P. Coton," appositely remarks Louis de la Rivière, "if he did not always succeed in preventing all the evil he might have wished, at least prevented there being more."[2] The King had spasms of good sense and remorse, and moments of semi-courage. That was why it was possible to absolve him at the beginning of 1609, but the absolution must have been tremulously pronounced, the confessor's joy mixed with sorrow. Yet what could be done? P. Coton, excellent theologian as he was, lacked the rigidity of Port-Royal; himself full of grace, he believed in its miracles, and, better than we can do, he perceived distinctly the duty imposed by each new day. In January 1609 he wrote to his General, of course saying nothing that should not have been said:

Thanks to the benediction of the Sovereign Pontiff, to the grace of the jubilee and the prayers of your Paternity, the King has lately

[1] Prat, *ibid.*, III. 8. [2] *Op. cit.*, p. 99.

put his conscience in order. . . . He has formed fresh aspirations, intentions and resolves. May the Father of Lights, from Whom comes every perfect gift, grant that these good resolutions be fulfilled. They will be, I doubt not, at least in some measure, for either the penitent will amend, or the confessor will lay down so formidable an office. I waver between fear and hope.

Hope always revived in spite of all. In short, he remained. I think S. François de Sales would have done the same, and Bérulle, and many others. Would even M. de Saint-Cyran have departed? It is *permissible* to doubt it.

The influence of P. Coton at the Court did not confine itself solely to the royal conscience. Proud of the learning and saintliness of his friend, and very anxious to augment Jesuit prestige by means of him, and to undermine the ridiculous legends current about the Order, Henri IV pressed his confessor on everybody. He became the fashion. In despite of its frivolity the Court liked to hear religion talked of. "If one speaks of God in any place," wrote Père Coton, "they flock thither like bees to blossoms."[1] Our forefathers are disconcerting. For more than a century sermons were for them a treat, theology a fashionable pursuit. It is almost a truism that they knew their religion better than do we; yet there were certain epochs, and those not the least informed, when their ignorance was crying. The contemporaries of Henri IV, even those born Catholic, knew hardly anything of the Faith. The doctrinal scraps they had retained in their zealous brains were confused, and aggressive, so to speak, rather than nourishing. It is a great misfortune to learn the Catechism only *against* one's neighbour. Such men were apt to be better instructed in the dogmatic and moral abominations of Calvinism than in Catholic realities; naturally I except certain eminent laymen and the *élite* of the clergy, who had been formed by the discipline of the great Orders and by the old Sorbonne, an admirable schoolmistress who as yet has never been replaced.

The preceding volume has done justice to this shining *pleïade.* But just at the beginning of the seventeenth century this *élite* was coming down to the crowd by books, sermons, and the intercourse of daily life, in all of which P. Coton excelled. Public curiosity, stirred in some by a deeper emotion, was set in that direction; many

[1] Fouqueray, *Histoire de la Compagnie de Jésus en France*, II. 653.

desired knowledge for its own sake, many again in order to live better lives.

Even the libertines wanted to take part; in short, all the Court, transformed into a sort of theological academy, badgered P. Coton, who had his hands full with them. There is a document existing on this subject which, had it not been retouched by too elegant a pen, would have been of great value; as it is, it is very curious.

Returning from these conferences (relates P. Prat), P. Coton used to note down their subject, the objections raised, his counter-arguments, and the way in which he had developed his theme. He intended to collect these notes one day and make a book of them. He had never time to carry out the project, but his papers fell into the hands of P. Michel Boutauld, who for two years had enjoyed the privilege of intercourse with P. Coton; he compiled from them a work of religious philosophy, the intrinsic value of which is further enhanced by the beauty of its language, published under the felicitous title, *Le Théologien dans les conversations avec les gens du monde.*[1]

In these discussions neither the practical nor the theoretical difficulties of Christian morality were neglected. At a time when regicides were swarming, on the eve or the morrow of the Gunpowder Plot, the secrecy of the confessional was endlessly criticized before the brother of P. Garnett. Entrusted with a monstrous confession, had not the priest the right—was it not even his duty—to give timely warning to the police? Henri, naturally interested in such a question, had a theology of his own in this matter to which he tried to convert P. Coton. Another problem of the moment was: Could the Pope excommunicate the Sovereign? In Olympian detachment the theologians of the Roman College tranquilly argued the point, oblivious of the sometimes tragic anguish their speculations caused the French Jesuits, always spied on by the *Parlement*. At Court P. Coton found a graceful means of parrying this thrust by postponing the question until the day when a Nero should mount the throne of France.

Such controversies were a display of fencing, even more useless than they were irritating. The casuistical conferences usually were on a simpler note and more immediately practical, especially when the Queen or her ladies took part, as often happened. One day the Queen said to the ladies of her suite: "We must take P. Coton to

[1] Prat, *ibid.*, II. 599–600.

Notre-Dame de Liesse. He will tell us in what directions we are in danger of mortally offending God. Then when we fall into these offences we can remind one another of his warnings." P. Coton formed their consciences, and led to true sanctity those whom he saw capable of higher things; in a word, he introduced the loftier spirits of the Court to the devout life. No less tender and persuasive than François de Sales, he wrought for the same ends and by the same means as the Bishop of Geneva. We have a charming little book of his, *L'intérieure occupation d'une âme dévote*, which anticipated the *Introduction* by several years. Like the masterpiece, this sketch also is composed of letters written by the Jesuit to a great lady under his direction. We find in it "prayers and fugitive considerations, inspired by everyday occurrences." For instance:

when contemplating a garden or flower-bed, you exclaim: If this passing world is so beautiful, what will be that of immortality?[1] Seeing a flowery meadow: The fragrance of the Son of God and the Child of Mary is as that of a field on which Heaven has shed its benediction.[2]

Should one be tempted to admire "the beauty of certain buildings" overmuch, it is well to consider "that the bees think as much of their hive."

On smelling a bouquet, one might say: Such is the scent of my Jesus, my Beloved.

While using a fan: Divine Breath proceeding from the mouth of the Father and the Word, as from one principle, cools the ardours of our passions and all intemperate affection.

And on seeing the splendours of the Court, make a meditation and delight in this canticle:

Greater things have been told us of thee, O celestial Sion.
All this is no more than the sweepings of Heaven.
When shall we behold Thee in Thy splendour, O King of Glory?[3]

We must insist on it—whether we like it or not, and why should we not?—all this is history. Part of the Court lived, as it were, this little book of P. Coton's, or books more or less like it. We must not let other clanging noises drown the voice of these chimes of prayer, amidst all the other smoke let us see this incense rising.

[1] *L'intérieure occupation*, p. 129. [2] *Ibid.*, p. 130. [3] *Ibid.*, pp. 130-7.

IV. Innumerable links attached the devout souls, at whom we have been looking, to the more striking virtues then budding or even in full bloom in every quarter of France. It is not my intention to give here a summary description of this movement, since to describe it is the purpose of my whole work, but I must remind the reader in a few words of the way in which the royal policy facilitated the conquest of France by Mysticism. But he already knows it. All those holy persons, the moment they wanted to have an influence outside their cells, could do nothing without the King of France. Even if they wanted a cell, they needed him. For every kind of foundation undertaken during the reigns of Henri IV and his successor, the approbation and aid of the civil power were necessary. What was more irksome, in many cases the reforms of the old-established Orders demanded the same support. In truth even that might not have sufficed without the intervention of the great houses, the princes and the princesses of the blood, but it is known that these valued helpers very frequently modelled their generosity on the intentions and example of their sovereign. Henri IV's deliberate and active sympathy had been enlisted for all these designs. We have seen this prince at work in the matter of the reinstatement of the Jesuits. Many similar projects received from him the same support, for P. Coton, the adviser most listened to in these concerns, was too large-hearted to limit his solicitude to the Order which concerned him most nearly.

France, during this happy period, saw with her eyes and touched with her hands a miracle which surpassed all others, which partly explains them and makes them less surprising. The Catholics no longer vilified one another. They had sincerely accepted the peace-making policy of Henri IV and had signed the King's Truce. Laying aside their former polemics and rivalries, the admirable men whom we see at the head of the movement—Cardinals, Bishops, Doctors of the Sorbonne, Carthusians, Feuillants, Capuchins, Jesuits, and the rest—worked fraternally together hand in hand. That this was an actual fact will be shown by the sequel. Take, for example, the foundation of the French Carmel or the reform of the Benedictines of Montmartre. Seculars and regulars, monks and religious of every Order, mixed indiscriminately in the conferences where such bold projects were initiated, in the parlours and chapters where they were pursued. What priest claims the honour of having directed Mme Acarie? Bérulle, M. de Duval, Père Benoit de Canfeld, Dom Beaucousin, Père Coton; that is to say the Oratory, the Sorbonne, the Capuchins, the Carthusians, the Society of Jesus—one cannot give a definite answer. Each of these, and others too, had a share in supporting, inspiring, guiding this holy soul, no group can lay exclusive claim to her. Another example, still more striking, if possible, of this perfect harmony: contemplate the noble friendship which Pierre de Bérulle and Pierre Coton, Oratorian and Jesuit, had for one another; the devotion with which Bérulle defended the persecuted Jesuits, and the firm and courageous support given by Père Coton to the newly instituted Oratory.

In the early years of Louis XIII a proposal was submitted to Pope Paul IV from Paris to set up a Commission which, under pontifical authority, should pronounce on the thousand problems raised by the reform of the ancient Orders. At the head of this Commission were the Cardinals de la Rochefoucauld and de Retz with several bishops; then came two Benedictines; two Jesuits, Séguiran and Arnoux; a Capuchin, Honoré de Champigny; a Feuillant, Eustache de Saint-Paul (Asseline); an Oratorian, Bérulle: lastly some laymen, Marillac and Mathieu Molé.[1] Note the presence of the two Benedictines. The contemplated reform centred principally on their Order, they willingly consented that the representatives of new Orders should take part in delicate discussions.

The King's Truce lasted but a moment, at the longest no more than fifteen or twenty years. But it was long enough to settle the lines of future development, to lay the foundations of many holy lives and good works. Sweet peace presided over the mystic sowings of these years and their fruit cannot be measured. The accursed thorns were not to choke either the first harvest or the later reapings, in spite of the noise of renewed quarrellings.

The divine law regulating the number and varieties of mystic vocations must always remain a mystery. Why did the first half of the seventeenth century witness such prodigious multiplication of Contemplatives? At this epoch the mystics were everywhere, loved,

[1] The project of this Commission did not please Rome. By a brief of April 8, 1622, Gregory XV conferred on La Rochefoucauld, for six years, full and absolute powers to reform in France the Orders of S. Augustine, S. Benedict, Cluny, and Citeaux.

venerated, and, if not always obeyed, never disputed. The centuries pass, there are still mystics on French soil, as there will be always. But they are, or appear to be, few in number, scarcely known even to the *élite* of their country, or if their existence is recognized it is held in suspicion. Once more, the final cause of these phenomena remains God's secret, but we may reflect on parallel phenomena and similar oscillations in the same periods, which perhaps throw some light on the sudden change. We shall notice some of these coincidences as we proceed, but none will appear more significant than what we have just mentioned. For one sees that the atmosphere most favourable to the diffusion and flourishing of the mystic life is one of peace, by which I mean the peace which is far less disturbed by persecution from without than by dissensions within. The wild beasts of the Coliseum did not interrupt the ecstasies of S. Ignatius, but is it certain that the prayers of S. Jerome were not disturbed by the quarrels, right or wrong, which that terrible disputant picked with his brethren? *Extrema linea amare haud nihil est*, says Terence. A touch, even a passing shadow of love, can do its work; and the same is true of the contrary sentiments. Diluted a thousandfold, so as to be imperceptible to the heart that contains it, a drop of bitterness or suspicion does its work; in any case it is generally enough to clog or weaken the soul's ascent to God. It is enough to recall memories of the nuns of Port-Royal and the atmosphere of dreariness which spread over the combative half of the seventeenth century. The true century of Louis XIV, that which contained Bossuet and Fénelon, would doubtless have seen more mystic vocations if it had counted fewer family quarrels.

Of course it cannot be claimed that this truce of Henri IV suspended all interior dissensions or united all hearts. The jealous, the mischief-makers, the fanatics are always with us, agitating and vilifying. Party spirit never ceases its petty moves. If the old reasons for distrusting one's neighbour go out of fashion, new ones imperceptibly come along which to-morrow will be gospel. Need I mention that even in religious circles Père Coton's moderation was a stumbling-block ; cowardly flatterer, lukewarm Christian, always ready to sacrifice the rights of the Church—he was spared none of the usual violent language. For a pious formula, somewhat confused, but most orthodox, Bérulle became the prey of pamphleteers. A monk reviled

François de Sales from the pulpit. The list could be lengthened indefinitely, but at last, with the royal assistance, the discordant voices sank and the general harmony ceased to be broken. The masters of the hour understood one another; for an instant the City of God was not (or almost not) divided against itself; it allowed itself to be guided by the unanimity of the saints.

V. After all this the reader will not be surprised if we devote a special study to the interior life of P. Coton. From this point of view, which secular historians have wholly neglected, and which, more singular still, has never tempted the hagiographer, Coton seems to me no less curious and interesting than François de Sales himself. No, Coton need not shrink from this formidable comparison, which helps us to know both, and to define with more precision the religious characteristics of their times.

That the *forézien* Pierre Coton was more simply and genuinely French than the Bishop of Geneva cannot be doubted, but his piety, like that of François de Sales, received an Italian stamp under remarkable conditions. As a Jesuit novice at Arona, he had seen the dying Carlo Borromeo passing by (1584). From the shores of Lake Maggiore he had gone to Loretto as a true pilgrim, that is, on foot and without money. At Rome he had had Louis de Gonzaga for fellow-student, Bellarmine for director, Vasquez for professor, and certain aged Jesuits who had known S. Ignatius for models.

As regards theological and spiritual formation, François de Sales and Pierre Coton resembled each other like brothers. They held the same doctrine upon grace; they were equally the antipodes of that temper, as old as the world, soon to be called the spirit of Jansenism. The same wisdom arms them against visionaries, and proud or chimerically spiritual persons. On the other hand, they ask nothing better than to bring all their learning into submission before the saintly souls who know more than books, since God Himself teaches them. (Coton perhaps appears on this point, if not less prudent, at least more hasty, more eager, than François de Sales.) Finally, and above all, they are marvellously well balanced and harmonize with ease the sometimes apparently conflicting demands of the devout life and the life of Mysticism proper. Their prayers are very active and call into play all the powers of the soul; full of images, they breathe all the naïve tenderness of mediæval piety, but this flowery abundance neither absorbs nor satisfies them. They have not reached, it seems, the heights of contemplation, but they profess and live the doctrine of pure love, source and bourne of all true Mysticism. Each is equally apt also in introducing the simple faithful to the devout life, in comprehending, sustaining, and even following those elect souls who attain the divine union by darker and more arid paths. Their fundamental originality is perhaps to be found in this equilibrium and sense of harmony, which their most eminent successors, a Fénelon, for example, did not always achieve. The "pure love" of the Bishop of Cambray is the same as animates Coton and François de Sales, but Fénelon too much gives the impression of isolating it from everyday piety; he mixes with it something wilful, strained, complex. Contrast the spontaneity, ease, familiarity with the sublime in the *Traité* of François de Sales and the sermons of P. Coton.

P. Coton wrote much on spiritual subjects. I have already quoted his *Intérieure occupation*, and other collections of the time contain many prayers which bear his name. But best of all are the beautiful sermons which he published himself long after they were preached, stripping them of much of their oratorical ornament and presenting them simply as a collection of Meditations. In truth, religious psychologists distrust eloquence, and of all the documents submitted to their analysis, sermons are among the most equivocal and deceptive. If we took them all as autobiographical testimony we should have to canonize half the world. Bossuet would surpass the saints. Nevertheless there are sermons that carry conviction, and those of P. Coton are among them, if I have read them aright.

By publishing them as Meditations, Coton restored them to their original form. It seems to me certain that before being preached they had been *prayed*, if the expression is not too extravagant. They follow the method and keep the personal note of those interviews with God, to which the Jesuit abandoned himself in his cell before ascending the pulpit, thus conforming himself, with as much exactitude as suppleness, to the instructions in the *Exercises* of S. Ignatius. P. Coton's sermons are indeed no more than a commentary, very original and very much alive, on that little book on which the Jesuits mould their interior life. It is amusing to see a brother of Coton, Gisbert, in his *Histoire critique de la chaire française*, shutting his eyes to escape the obvious, and finding comical a certain page of the

Sermons which reproduces, point by point, the famous meditation of S. Ignatius on *The Two Standards.* To us, who no doubt have less taste than the refined critic, the page appears nevertheless of singular attraction and sombre beauty, doubly curious for the light it throws on the preacher's religious imagination and the individual needs of the audience.

I represent to myself Lucifer, prince of wretched demons, in the midst of the field of Babylon, seated on a red-hot throne of fire, himself darkly aglow and smoking in every pore of a frame more horrible than the most lurid imagination could paint.

I hear how he calls unto him divers demons, in especial Leviathan, tempter to pride; Baalberit, inflamer to anger; Beelzebub, instiller of envy; Mammon with the bait of cupidity; Asmodeus, demon of lust; Beelpheger, inciter to gluttony; Baalin and Astaroth, parents of sloth, and after these a swarm of impure spirits to whom he thus speaks: "My desire is to reduce to my obedience all Christian souls . . . till . . . none shall dare raise the crucifix. Up then, my warriors, mighty by malice, powerful in audacity, speed me through Italy, Germany, Spain, Gaul, the British Isles! Pass over the Mediterranean, get to work in Greece and wherever else the Galilean is invoked. Embroil their belief and embarrass their creed by a variety of sects and pretended Churches all claiming the titles of Illuminated, Reformed, Sanctified. Confuse the true with the uncertain, leave not one who is not aware of doubts and consequently out of the circle of the True Faith. Rouse jealousy against the Apostolic See, under the pretext of the spiritual power that the Son of Mary lavished upon Peter; make it believed that, to be a statesman, one must not trouble oneself with religion, that, to be a good Frenchman, one must be neither Spaniard nor Papist. You have ruined France under pretext of religion, now ruin religion under pretext of the State. Should some religious dare to speak against you, some blackbeetle or flagellant fanatic oppose you, decry me this vermin, exterminate me this offal, insult, slander, terrify. Give them leisure neither to breathe nor live; render me them so contemptible that there will be dishonour in maintaining them, loving them, showing them kindness."

Although he cites this passage as a specimen of enormity, the modest Gisbert has nevertheless cut out some words which pained him too much, but which are here restored. Lucifer's discourse continues, for it is necessary that every one of the audience be warned against his individual temptations.

As for devotees . . . (who would) live in God's presence serene and at peace, fill them with scruples, anxieties, perplexities, melancholy. Is a soul desirous of purity, never begin with offering it gross temptations, but rather render it mercenary in its devotions, desirous of consolations, sensuous in its ardour, then plunge it into dryness and aridity of spirit, so that it may turn to the consolations of the creature, agreeable companions, worldly books, the tragic histories of *Astrée* and *Armide*. Make them believe that they mean no harm, but only to learn to talk, answer and write. Presently awaken in them the memory of such readings, then frame conceptions similar to the memory, excite their curiosity to understand the mysteries of marriage, tickle gently their sensuality, tend the spark till it takes fire. . . . Forget not to make confession odious, and to decry by every means in your power the confessors. Further, spare not the wheat, wines, fruits, fly from sea to sea, awake the tempest, provoke duels, and wherever ye find such forbidden by edict, revive assassinations, that men's reflections thereupon may serve to restore duels.

The peroration following, in which, be it remarked, we hear an echo of Corneille, is that of no mean orator. This Satan perhaps might lack taste, but he knew French. These are his final words to his infernal troops:

Forth then, valiant spirits, speed, *run, fly to avenge us* on Him Who has doomed us to such horrible torments, and since His punishments are everlasting, be your offences everlasting; since He makes war on us without hope of truce, make war on Him incessantly, perpetually, ruthlessly, O Eternity, thou shrine of hate![1]

Does it not seem, so Gisbert concludes his criticism, as if Père Coton had seen all these devils, heard the harangue of their chief? "I am almost tempted to believe that he held an assembly like that which he has just depicted so vividly."[2] The good Father makes merry, but he may spare his laughter. Certainly, like S. Ignatius, and Christ Himself, Père Coton realizes with startling vividness the actors and scenes of the world invisible, which was to him as much present as the visible world, and on the whole more real. It was the same with his contemporaries, the King among them. Devils in flesh and bone, as one may say, caused them more nightmares than they did P. Coton. He was not slow to paint the Personage himself

[1] *Sermons sur les principales et plus difficiles matières de la foi*, preached by R. P. Pierre Coton, and edited by him in the form of Meditations, Paris, 1617, pp. 134–5.

[2] *Revue Bourdaloue*, 1902, p. 369.

as large as life. He invites us to "make an image of him" "as horrible" as we can, but as regards himself he does not take the trouble. Eager to hear Lucifer speak, he does not try to visualize him. It is a remnant of the pious realism of the Middle Ages, but already largely modernized, spiritualized, I should say. It is a great improvement. Notice how in the page just quoted Lucifer himself invites us, ever so indirectly, to have little fear of the harm he may work us. "Fill them," he says to the subtle demons whom he sends to conquer devout souls, "fill them with scruples, anxieties, perplexities, melancholy, make them mercenary in their devotions." "Mercenary"—a far-reaching idea, and one which nearly a century later Bossuet was to find scandalous. To act in a mercenary spirit, as opposed to a filial one, is, say the mystics, to act with too absorbing an anticipation of recompense or chastisement, of heaven or hell. Is it not remarkable that, nearly a century before the Quietist controversy, such instruction should have been given, not in a book for the use of the initiated, but from the pulpit? The fundamental truths of that mystic life with which he himself was so deeply penetrated, P. Coton had no fear of expounding to the simple faithful. We shall show this presently by some striking quotations.

In this invisible world, which the Jesuit realized so intensely, good angels bulk much more largely than evil ones. To give the source of his extraordinary devotion to the Blessed Ones—whether his family or the Jesuits in France or Italy—would require a knowledge of the history of the sixteenth century piety which I do not possess.[1] However, in the period that now concerns us, I know of no one who lived so intimately and unbrokenly in the companionship of the good angels as Père Coton.

I am not surprised (remarks Louis de la Rivière, the habitual confidant of Marie de Valence, on this point) that living the angelic life down here as he did . . . the angels should sometimes have complimented him with their presence. One thing is certain, that on his return from Rome he declared to Sœur Marie that, while celebrating in the

[1] Unless I am mistaken, this devotion to the angels, as P. Coton understands it, is a characteristic feature of the Renaissance. The reading of the pseudo-Dionysius will have brought it into vogue. The devotion will be found in its full development in a book, little known but extremely valuable, the *Memorial* of a Savoyard, the blessed Père Lefèvre, one of the first disciples of S. Ignatius. The decadence (or as some may prefer to say, the modern transformations) of this devotion is an interesting study.

holy chapel of Our Lady of Loretto, his good angel appeared to him, in company with those of the said Sœur Marie and the Demoiselle Marguerite Chambaud. He was also on familiar terms with the tutelary Angel of France.[1]

To render their presence and their power more convincing to himself, Coton with a delightfully human logic comments on the various sensations which the presence and the power of devils cause in most of his contemporaries.

When magicians unite their wicked will to those of demons they often have power to injure and Satan affects by them an infinity of woes under cover of powders, unguents, charms, virgin parchments, and other instruments of accursed doings. Why then should I not believe that the holy angels will assist me and my neighbours, when I unite my will to theirs, and they and I unite our will to God's? Are they not as mighty for good as these others for ill?[2]

To unite his will to that of the angels—is not this idea of counter-magic and wholly spiritual spells very happy? The angels are at once living images and instruments of that "prevenient grace" which the Jesuits did not indeed invent, but on which their theology perhaps led them to lay more stress.

It is needful to recognize angelic intervention even in trivial matters, but still more so in those which may influence our whole lives; thus S. Gregory Thaumaturgus thanked his good angel for his having had Origen as his tutor.[3]

Or again and better:

How shall I speak of the comings and goings (of the angels) from God to us, from us to God, stimulating here, calming there; carrying requests, bringing back gifts? How many inspirations, secret movings, benignant influences, interior and exterior aidings, how many angelic ideas, ruses and stratagems of Love.[4]

Whether or not Bossuet, before composing his magnificent sermon on guardian angels, had read this passage I do not know, but his angels seem to me more aloof, less fraternal, than those of Père Coton, who meets them wherever he goes.

We are not merely indebted to our good own angels, but also to those of our parents and especially of our mothers, who would sink

[1] *Histoire de la vie et mœurs de Marie Tessonier*, p. 99. [2] *Sermons*, pp. 112–3.
[3] *Ibid.*, p. 132. [4] *L'intérieure occupation*, p. 46.

a thousand times without the support of their guardian angel. According to Tertullian, the little limbs are moulded in the mother's womb by the angels, performing what they term "*divin office*" in place of the various Lucinas which pagan superstition supposed to preside over the conception, pregnancy and delivery of women.[1]

Two angels for the meanest cradle; what will be required to preside over the destiny of the world-rulers?

The public actions of the great are never small. . . . Thus in Eternal Wisdom (O my God), hast Thou put the kings and sovereigns of the earth under the protection and special conduct of the archangels. The demons their adversaries are equally exalted in their kingdom.[2]

What a place the archangel and arch-demon of the King of France must have held in the thoughts and life of P. Coton! But nearest of all, the dearest friend, is his own guardian.

Governor of my life, escort of my pilgrimage, torch-bearer of my understanding, preceptor of my soul . . .[3]

There is no stopping him when he begins his litanies.

Thus I come to you, faithful friend, sweet comrade, kindly teacher. . . . True explorer of the Promised Land, encourage us to the conquest of our own Country. You are the governors of our life, the escorts of our pilgrimage, the pilots of our navigation, the lighthouses of our course . . . the catechists who purge our understandings, the captains marching before us to battle, in a word, the closest friends that we have on earth.[4]

Those interested in style will have remarked these long strings of appositions and epithets, a fashion, which, until suppressed by Balzac and Vaugelas, was a favourite literary habit of those days, used effectively by no less a one than Rabelais. Besides being dear to our old writers, it was especially used by the Church, lending itself, so it seems, to the various movements of prayer much better than the regular period. P. Coton used it constantly and took much pleasure in it, the humanist in him, rich in literary associations, and the man of God being equally satisfied by it. Let me give an example of the graceful rhythm he obtained by alternating the period and the litany.

[1] *L'intérieure occupation*, p. 44.
[2] *Ibid.*, p. 118
[3] *Ibid.*, p. 44.
[4] *Sermons*, pp. 141–2.

O Mother, Queen of Heaven, Empress of the world, purest of the pure, holiest of the holy, by the womb which bore my Redeemer and the paps which He has sucked, I adjure thee, O Immaculate, and supplicate thee, most loving that is or ever shall be among all creatures, that thou wilt be pleased to obtain for me this grace. . . . And ye, most happy souls, with right of citizenship in the Celestial Jerusalem, seated at the table of the Great King, nourish us with the crumbs of your divine repasts. Spouses of the great Ahasuerus, this earth was the scene of your marriage-contract, cast then your gracious eyes upon us, making us participants in your benign influences; reapers of the Celestial Boaz, leave some ears for those who glean after you; faithful explorers of the Promised Land, as you hold the grapes in your hands, distil some drop upon us; doves roosting on the Tree of Life, deliver us from the black infernal guard, from harpies and birds of prey that but seek to rend our souls; spotless lambs pasturing on Mount Sion, care for the sheep wandering in the deserts of this world. . . . And you, O Divine Solomon, who raised the temple of your glory in the Lebanon of this world, preserve us to furnish one day materials for heavenly Sion. As the hammer was never heard in the structure of your house, so suffer not the passions and persecutions of this life to strike upon the chosen stones, destined for so august an edifice.[1]

A sweet familiarity, " the childlike spirit," animates this picturesque and spontaneous prayer. In another passage, predestination itself, that inevitable dogma which was soon to hypnotise unto despair so many ill-instructed souls, only inspires P. Coton with sentiments of joy and filial surrender.

Any anxiety which I might feel from not knowing what will happen to me when this poor mortal life is over is entirely done away with, when I recall, O God of my soul, the Love that it pleases Thee to have for us, what Thy Son is to us and what through Him we are to Thee! . . . Did my predestination depend on myself, I should consider it assured on account of the natural affection I bear towards myself. Now that which Thou bearest for me is supernatural, divine, infinite, and consequently as far above mine as the sky above the earth. . . . How happy then am I to fall into such good hands instead of into my own, and to know my salvation committed to Him Who loves me infinitely more than I love myself.[2]

This is no sentimental effusion. P. Coton was a man of strong intellect and virile heart. Occasionally, it may be, he lacks taste, but

[1] *Sermons*, pp. 166–8. [2] *Ibid*, pp. 232–3.

we never find sentimentality or weakness in him. Tender and human as he is, it is from no consideration of his own petty personal interests, but from zeal for the Divine Perfection, that he refuses to make Christian piety a thing of terror. His own idea of God is indeed so august that it would crush a soul less profoundly and joyously religious. The mystic life, as he understood and practised it, is a burnt offering; the Christian a sacrificer in the fullest sense of the word. I would, he says to God,

love thee so ardently as to be consumed by that love . . . till nothing of me remains in me, save only the hideous memory of my past former and miserable state, which may serve as fuel to that fire of love and keep alight continually the brazier of Thy charity.[1]

He could wish the whole universe might share his experience and pass through these mystic flames which respect all forms of creation, consuming but evil and chaos. Bearing on this, we find a formula of prayer in the *Intérieure occupation* which seems to me of a rare magnificence.

Heretofore has much honour been paid to the great of the earth . . . incense burnt before idols, fleshly beauty adored. O God of my soul, I take all such thoughts, words, acts, profane passions, and with all the extent of my being, all the force of my will, do what in me lies to cleanse them from evil and offer them, together with Thy creatures, to Thee, Author of all.[2]

Can a vaster, more magnificent sacrifice be imagined than the pyres of all idolatries past and present, those which adored false gods and those which deified the creature, purified of the sacrilegious elements? It is a striking example of the lofty speculations and deep religious feeling, which Bérulle raised to honour about the same time, and in which Condren and M. Olier were soon to excel. I could collect many similar beautiful passages from the works of Père Coton, but I hasten on to that in which, in my opinion, his supreme originality consists, his doctrine of the Love of God. "(God) considers Love as good in itself when it has no expectation of reward."[3] When P. Coton writes like this it is nothing to his credit. All the theologians, Bossuet with the rest in his better moments, admit that it is possible and praiseworthy to love God in Himself, for the simple reason that He is

[1] *Sermons*, pp. 63–4. [2] *L'intérieure occupation*, p. 3. [3] *Sermons*, p. 341.

lovable. But many seem to believe that such love as this is above ordinary power, and that only the great saints are capable of it. For them, pure love: for ordinary Christians the fear of hell, expectation of a hundredfold reward promised in this world, desire of Heaven. P. Coton, on the contrary, will have none of this division, this compromise, either for himself or for others. Pure love seems to him not only the most needful but almost the simplest Christian virtue. Whether in writing or preaching, he continually reverts to this idea. Not that he teaches it *ex professo*, as if there was room for the smallest doubt upon a self-evident truth; rather, he makes acts of love before those who hear or read him, and, by his example, teaches other souls to practise it. This, I think, is an extraordinary sight. I should not use such language if we were considering a fanatic, a dreamer, a Father of the desert. But it is P. Coton whom we know so well. The religious Order which moulded him and judged him worthy of delicate diplomatic missions has not a reputation for encouraging visionaries. This friend of Henri IV is wise and moderate; he has received thousands of confidences in the confessional and knows human frailty thoroughly. Yet this man addresses the Court or an ordinary congregation as he might Carmelite nuns, proposing to all, without distinction or reserves, the very doctrine which nearly a hundred years later would appear supremely ridiculous to the wisdom of the world, and against which the flower and genius of the Gallican Church would range itself in full armour. Could anything be stranger and at the same time more of a revelation? Since P. Coton is no eccentric, and in his day numbers of French men and women were teaching or, better still, were living out these sublime truths, are we not justified in hailing this marvellous epoch of our history as the Golden Age of French Mysticism?

It has been already remarked that P. Coton's theology is more exact and cautious than that of Fénelon. It enshrines the great mystic principle with necessary explanations and restrictions. Thus he admits that

there is no man so holy and perfect upon earth as not to require at times once more to become a child and again serve his apprenticeship, drawing profit from the terrors of hell and the hopes of heaven.[1]

[1] *Sermons*, p. 353.

True, but the concession is as parsimonious as possible, and does not prevent P. Coton from denouncing in round terms what he, before Fénelon, called " the mercenary spirit," as paralysing the normal upward flight of the devout life. Be it due to nature or grace, doubtless both, he is never absorbed in the contemplation of himself or in cares for his own interests. Having small tenderness for the " frail Narcissus " who passes his time before a mirror, he would surely have been " much grieved that any single soul should be thinking of itself."[1] He troubles so little about himself that he has great difficulty, I will not say in excusing, but in comprehending self-love. Hear him speak

of men and women who seek themselves in all things, (and who) will stir no step, say no word, that is not for their own interest, that is to say that gives them neither pleasure, honour nor profit. Their devotions are but so many satisfactions of self-love; all their sorrows, joys, reflections, interior emotions centre round themselves; in short no matter where they go they never leave themselves behind.[2]

He is astonished at this weakness, which others call universal; he is even amused at it and uses bantering words.

From another point of view the reflections and the most innocent thoughts of self-love seem to him to contradict the natural movement of true prayer. He explains this delightfully in his own limpid, learned and profound way.

S. Antony the Great, a great expert in such matters, said in reference to Cassian that prayer cannot be called perfect when he who prays is conscious of praying; when prayer is perfect it so ravishes the spirit heavenwards that it thinks of nothing and remembers nothing save God with Whom it converses. The Roman orator, on a subject unlike this one, has left it in writing that he would not consider that eloquence which left the audience at leisure to remark that it was well said. Another along the same line of thought declares that sorrow capable of expressing itself in words cannot be called sorrow.[3]

This psychology, carried a little further, would greatly illumine a question over which much ink has flowed, resolving indirectly the fundamental sophism of La Rochefoucauld, and reassuring those pious souls who believe themselves too self-centred and " mercenary " ever to attain perfect love. In any case, the most exquisite and

[1] *Sermons*, p. 108. [2] *Ibid.*, pp. 107–8. [3] *Ibid.*, p. 391.

charmingly ingenious descriptions of pure love spring spontaneously from P. Coton's pen in such abundance, with such freshness, and expressed in such natural poetry as to express the habitual outlook of this lofty heart. He says to God, for example:

I thank Thee for what Thou art in Thyself, the greatest good that I could have or hope for.[1]

Or again:

The greatest happiness for me is that Thou art happy in Thyself, owing nought to any, that all depends on Thee, Thou dependest on none!

And so he continues, making the articles of the Athanasian Creed sound like joybells. Finally he concludes his canticle thus:

O, how indebted am I to Thee for that Thou art so wholly perfect that Thy Glory is neither diminished by all the maledictions of the reprobate nor increased by the praises of the elect!

And for as much that Thou fillest the heaven and the earth and in essence art in all creatures, I adore and recognize Thee in all.

I reverence Thee as being in the elements, in the life of the body, in the forms of the vegetable kingdom.

Thou art All and Sole, I have to do only with Thee. Art Thou but pleased, all is well!

Can adoration go further? For me, said Newman, " my Maker and I, His creature, were the two beings, luminously such, in *rerum natura*." I never read this phrase, sublime though it perhaps is, without a stricture at heart. He, Newman, then is someone before God, but we, fellow-creatures, are nothing before Newman! I like the " Thou art All " of Père Coton much better.

His contrition speaks the same language.

It is not so much to escape the penalty due to my iniquity that I ask this pardon, as to remove from before Thine eyes as best I may all that is displeasing to Thee.[2]

His intimacy with the world invisible breathes the same pure love. " I feel myself so greatly his debtor for his loyalty to Thee," he says to God of the Archangel Michael, and addressing the saints—

Thrice, fourfold, happy souls who are before God! I rejoice as much and more for what ye are than I lament for what I am. . . . The

[1] *L'intérieure occupation*, p. 4.

[2] *Sermons*, p. 278.

reason thereof is clear, for ye honour our common Saviour more than I dishonour Him; your purity is greater than my impurity, ye are more just than I am unjust, more happy than I am miserable, and therefore with all my strength I thank Him who has dowered you with happiness, blessing Him endlessly that the least among you causes Him more glory than the greatest sinners in the world can cause Him dishonour.[1]

Let us remember that these and dozens of similar prayers P. Coton expects the rank and file of the faithful to use. Just what we should expect in him. The sublime sentiments, which others would reserve for the most advanced mystics, he boldly puts on the lips even of those who have no more hope. Towards the close of a meditation on the Judgement, P. Coton imagines the damned coming to hear their doom and, in the flying moments which remain to them before they disappear, bidding farewell to earth and heaven.

Adieu, since so it must be, adieu, Son of Mary! Adieu, love of heaven and of earth. Adieu to delights of the world, adieu, Jesus! . . . Spotless Dove, Refuge of the miserable!

Though we are what we are, and beyond all hope, Thou ceasest not to be Thyself!

But ye, O our good angels, with what tone, accent, voice shall we salute you? . . . Ah, how oft have we displeased you. . . . In vain, O good guardians, have ye taken all these pains! May the great God, by Whose Commandment and for love of Whom ye did all these things, reward and requite your love! Adieu—O cruel word—our guardians, our protectors! . . . Here come ravishing wolves, roaring lions, with open jaws, sharpened teeth, talons outspread. . . . Adieu, fathers, mothers. . . . Adieu, happy souls. Ascend, happy company, live, reign, praise our God for yourselves and for us! [2]

In the throng of saints ascending at that instant towards the Right Hand of the Father, none perhaps in life had ever put up a prayer so disinterested. For some seconds the accursed rise to the heights of pure love. Though they may not say it in words, their whole attitude expresses "Thou art All . . . if Thou art pleased, all is well." I realize that this is only an oratorical flight, but such conceptions reveal the greatness of soul, the holiness of him who formed them, the man who, nerving himself one day to the hardest sacrifice, said to himself:

[1] *Sermons*, p. 163. [2] *Ibid.*, pp. 760–71.

Let us go to Him, O my soul, with giant strides! [1]

Yes, they were giants, he and many others still to come, but lovable giants, simple and human. Good-humour and tenderness soften in them any asperity of heroism, although heroism, or rather the Christian magnanimity defined so proudly by P. Coton and of which his whole life is an example, must needs dominate.

The spiritual man, although speaking, acting, working in public, fixes his gaze on none save the King of heaven and earth there truly present, in comparison with Whom all monarchs and potentates of this world are but flimsy rags. Should he endeavour to please anyone, it is God; should he fear to displease, it is God also; he will take no heed of men, save only because God wills that he should try to make himself agreeable to them for their good. And doing this, he attains so high that he can tread under foot the things of this world. [2]

VI. Since we have chosen P. Coton as one of the most representative of the saintly men of his time, it is necessary to say something of the attitude which he had often occasion to assume towards those extraordinary manifestations which seem more or less associated, although not invariably so, with the mystic life. It is difficult to decide whether these phenomena, at that period so common, demand of the priest compelled to pronounce on them, more prudence or respect. He is a bad director who, shrugging his shoulders, believes that he can explain everything either by trickery on the part of the subject or by diabolic intervention—the anti-mystics of P. Coton's day had no other alternative—or by nervous disturbances, like the anti-mystics of to-day. P. Coton had wholly different ideas. Persuaded, after many experiences, that the Arm of God is not shortened, he never showed himself slow to believe the marvels, either exterior or interior, of the Divine Union. The perceptible signs of this all-powerful influence on souls interested and touched him deeply. He sought with confiding eagerness the society of those privileged beings, on whose brows he descried the radiance reflected from the Light Divine. We have seen him the most eager of those around Marie de Valence, and shall meet him later among the intimates of Mme Acarie; he was well acquainted with Jeanne de Matel at Roanne, Anne de Xaintonge at Dôle, Madame de Sainte-

[1] *Sermons*, p. 252. [2] *Ibid.*, p. 447.

Beuve at Paris. Yet, by nature cautious and distrustful of himself, he was no more credulous than the wisest of his time. Characteristic touches in his life as director and exorcist show him in these two aspects. The Cardinal of Lorraine (relates Père d'Orléans in his picturesque and graphic style),

believing himself bewitched, had summoned from Milan to Nancy a certain Père Michel (*a certain* is rather good!), General of the Order of S. Ambrose, reputed to have a particular gift for exorcising demons and freeing the bewitched. The prince felt himself relieved, and attributed this to the virtue of the General, which brought the doctor and perhaps also the disease into fashion. Sundry people of quality at the Court of France, imagining themselves to be thus attacked, besought the Queen to request that the General should take Paris on his road back to Italy, which she accordingly did. On the Father's arrival a young girl of Picardy, Adrienne Dufresne, genuinely possessed by a most malignant devil, was brought before him, and he had already held out some hopes of curing her, when he was recalled to Italy on important business of his Order. Before leaving he besought the Queen, who had sometimes attended his exorcisms, not to allow the unhappy girl to be abandoned helpless before the cruelty of her wicked visitor.

When the Queen took P. Coton with her, she noticed that the demon had more aversion to him than to the others and feared him more. So she thought of him to continue the work of charity. She proposed it to him, but met with such resistance that, believing that royal authority alone in a matter of this kind would not move him to fulfil her wishes, she persuaded the Bishop of Paris to issue a formal command. The servant of God shrank from exercising so delicate a mission, especially for people who never pardoned a false step, but he bowed to episcopal authority, for which he had always a great respect.

As a first step, he applied himself to demonstrate the possession, to convince the heretics. . . . As then he wrought mightily against the demon, the demon threatened to proceed against him in turn, and in no long time the effect of his menaces was seen. For when it became known that, to make evident the fact of the possession, the Father had interrogated the evil creature, wicked-minded people presumed to circulate first a letter, then some longer writings containing unfitting questions which the servant of God was supposed to have put or to be about to put to the evil spirit. Of all the persecutions ever loosed against this servant of God, this was the most cruel and the hardest to bear.[1]

[1] Père d'Orléans, quoted by Père Prat, *ibid.*, II. 411–3.

It is needless to enter into details of these vexatious attacks or even to pursue the history of Adrienne's "possession"; attacks of this kind were so frequent and violent in the seventeenth century that we shall have to devote a special chapter to them. One thing only, in the present narrative, has a direct and immediate interest for us. I mean the sentiments of pity, veneration, almost envy, which this unfortunate and truly holy woman inspired in P. Coton. It is an acknowledged truth that, in many cases of Mysticism, the divine and the demoniac appear to dispute possession, and in Adrienne Dufresne, if the lower faculties and the senses were at times under diabolic sway, yet the apex of the soul enjoyed at the same time union with the Divine. Such at least was P. Coton's opinion, as "a holy priest named Sellier, Curé of Hauteville in Normandy," himself the ordinary director of Adrienne, testified in remarkable terms.

This good ecclesiastic left P. Coton in no respect ignorant of the state of this soul or of his management of it, and, as often as he came to Paris, he took opportunity of conversing with him on a subject interesting to them both. Subsequently, he made an authenticated deposition to the effect that P. Coton, listening one day to his descriptions of the lamentable state into which this suffering soul had been brought, being touched with compassion, cried out, "*O altitudo divitiarum sapientiæ et scientiæ Dei!*" and, abundant tears taking from him power of words, he remained a long while in silence. Then, with an effort recovering himself, "O my brother," said he, "how wonderful is Providence in the direction of souls! . . . Never, I beseech you, abandon the care of her placed in your hands. . . . I look upon my acquaintance with her as one of the greatest graces ever bestowed on me by God. No soul has ever drawn me more powerfully to Him than she. Her conversation has done me more good than all the good books I have ever read, nor have I found any approaching her perfection. . . . God wills to use her, and the state in which He has placed her from the age of two years, for the conversion of a great many heretics and a host of Catholics. By means of her, to my knowledge, more than five hundred Huguenots have been reconciled to the Church, and more than ten thousand first confessions have been made, as the evil spirit which possesses her has been forced to avow." The King, adds Père d'Orléans, was aware how highly Père Coton esteemed the virtue of this servant of God, and the King's cognisance of the fact made it widely known.[1]

[1] Cf. Prat, *ibid.*, pp. 422–5.

The reader will probably find matter for thought in this testimony. The question is not whether Père Coton was mistaken in so highly estimating the woman's virtue. Nowadays especially, we find it hard to assess sanctity, and the question is unimportant. But it is truly significant to note the extraordinary value that a man of the calibre of P. Coton attached to his relations with a soul united to God, as he was convinced in a special degree. A pupil of the famous Vasquez, and himself a good theologian and possessor of almost encyclopædic knowledge, the Jesuit would give all he knew and all that books could teach him for a few hours' conversation with a saint. In the eyes of scholars this is important testimony; but the crowd has to be considered too. The sight of Adrienne, a visible proof of invisible realities, did more for the conversion of Protestants and Catholics alike than all the sermons and controversial books. The supernatural has a universal appeal. Even some so-called sceptics desire to come into contact with it.

With this temperament, the anxious joy and sweet, holy awe of P. Coton may be imagined, when he had reason to believe on irrefragable proofs that his own family was selected to render similar shining testimony to God. One of his sisters, Jeanne-Marie Coton, married to Guillaume de la Chaize, *seigneur* of Aix (so Père d'Orléan tells us)

received in truth so great an abundance of graces and communications so extraordinary that her usual directors, in the place where she lived, found themselves often in the same difficulties as those of S. Teresa. So apparent was the working of God in her and so frequent were her ecstasies as to be recognized by all. The people venerated her as a saint. [So did her husband.] But her confessors feared the mingling of some demonic influence, some subtle illusion.

P. Coton was summoned. He had already known other ecstatics at close quarters, but this case must have been doubly affecting. In any case he had to test her with double caution. But there was nothing to be afraid of; the demon had no hand in this affair. Nevertheless, M. de Bérulle towards this time being in the neighbourhood of Forez (1614), Père Coton requested him to see Mme d'Aix, and wrote to his brother-in-law the following interesting and admirable letter.[1]

[1] We owe this precious letter to Père d'Orléans who, having examined personally the original, judged it worthy "of being quoted at length." The copy, however, does not inspire me with absolute confidence. A letter of 1688 resisting the temptation to *Balzacise* the originals would be a miracle. This, however, is a matter for literary critics, the retouches only concerning the rhythm and other details of style.

I am in truth grateful to you, monsieur . . . in that you have compassion for my sister's corporeal infirmities and that you permit her those spiritual exercises without which she could not live. As far as we know, the work is of God both essentially and in the principal circumstances. Yet one might be inclined to fear some illusion of the Evil One, transfigured into an angel of light, although the intimate union which she has with the God of Truth, the splendours that accompany the effusion of the Holy Spirit in her soul, her humility and implacable hatred of herself, the blind obedience she renders to her directors and confessors, are guarantees to us of her behaviour.

Here the brother in Coton slips in a charming word.

Formerly I feared for her rather weakness of nature than the wiles of the demon, but seeing what has passed and is yet passing in her, together with her sole desire to please God, I cannot doubt that divine power has operated in her soul according to what we see in her body, and even more than we can see. Nevertheless, since in extraordinary matters it behoves us to take extraordinary precautions, I advise and entreat you with all my might to take my sister, in company of her confessor M. de la Mure, to whom I shall write, to Roanne, about June 8, to consult a celebrated personage who will be passing through there. This is one M. de Bérulle, General of the Congregation of the Oratory in France, and Superior of all the Carmelite monasteries. He has, among other rare qualities, the gift of discerning spirits, and has successfully conducted a case similar to my sister's.[1]

The letter goes on with less interesting counsels. I should like to show the letter to a novelist I know. For how can one avoid smiling at the idea of the *seigneur* d'Aix, full of admiration no doubt but already slightly embarrassed by the ecstasies of his wife, and the theological consultations to which they had given occasion, now obliged to confer with Bérulle, who in turn will call in the Jesuits of Montbrison? No help for it; glory, even that of the saints, must sometimes be paid for. As for Jeanne-Marie Coton, she lived to become a widow and to make trial of the new Order founded by François de Sales and Jeanne de Chantal, but finally, on the advice of P. Coton, she quietly returned to Roanne where, both before and after her death, she was venerated as a saint and miracle-worker. One of her sons, François d'Aix, became a distinguished Jesuit, while a grandson, a Jesuit also,

[1] Cf. Père Prat, *ibid.*, IV. 7–10.

François de la Chaize, continued her fame. The celebrated confessor of Louis XIV was the great-nephew of the confessor of Henri IV and Louis XIII.

As we never intended to write a formal history of Père Coton but only to explain his spirit, analyse his interior life and define the part he played in the religious movement of his time, a few lines must suffice for the last stages of his career. On quitting the Court in 1619 he took up for some time his former office of preacher. In 1620 he was nominated Rector of the College of Bordeaux, where he renewed acquaintance with and soon witnessed the death of his old friend Père Richeome. In 1622 he became Provincial of Aquitaine; then, towards the end of 1624, of Paris. In these functions trials awaited him, less directly personal but more painful than any of his previous experiences. With Henri IV dead, the Paris *Parlement* reckoned on its speedy revenge on the Jesuits, and, with Richelieu wavering between the two parties, the slightest indiscretion might in a few days ruin the lifework of Père Coton. Such indiscretion was not long wanting. The theses of the Italian Jesuit Santarelli upon the pontifical power furnished the *Parlement* with the looked-for occasion. Père Garasse has recorded in a fine work, which appears worthy of credence, these events, reflecting little glory on French justice, which exhausted Père Coton's last reserves of strength and seem to have precipitated his end. The noble veteran died on March 19, 1626.

Paris loved the loyal friend of the late King and venerated him as a saint.

We were alarmed (says Garasse) at the concourse of people thronging the house of the Order[1] towards ten that Thursday, March 19, when we returned from our preaching. I can say without exaggeration that two-thirds of Paris visited the body of the holy man,

exposed at first in a chapel, but perforce later carried to a sacristy, as larger and more suited to the throngs. There,

from midday to seven o'clock in the evening was the greatest crowd ever seen in mortal memory in Paris. One saw doors and windows taken from their hinges, presses broken as if they had been pillaged, under the irresistible waves, not only of the common folk but of lords

[1] To-day the *Lycée Charlemagne.*

and ladies, who overflowed our three courtyards, the sacristy, and a good part of our garden.

That same evening was Coton buried at the foot of the High Altar, after absolution given by the Archbishop of Paris; some days subsequently Richelieu came in great pomp to celebrate a pontificial Mass and pray over the tomb of Pierre Coton.

The Jesuits were saved. We shall often meet them again in the following pages. Already a younger generation—Louis Lallemand, Jean Rigoleuc, Joseph Surin and many more—were walking, or preparing to walk, in the spiritual footsteps of Père Coton. They will go further and mount higher than he, but in a history in which they will take such a place, it was fitting that the special work of their glorious precursor should be warmly appreciated.

CHAPTER III

BENOIT DE CANFELD: PÈRE JOSEPH AND THE SERAPHIC TRADITION

I. IT may be well to remark here once and for all that when in the following pages we mention without further definition the "New Orders" which took an active part in the movement described, we shall mean the Jesuits certainly, but also the Franciscan Capuchins, that fresh shoot put forth by the old Franciscan Order at the dawn of the Counter-Reformation. At first sight, and for reasons that every reader will appreciate, this bringing of them together may seem strange. It would be even more astounding, did it not throw into bold relief the profound and miraculous unity of a Renaissance in which so many diverse minds were engaged, and which consequently was not the work or special glory either of Capuchins or Jesuits, or indeed of anyone but Him Who makes the most dissimilar instruments work together for one end. Let us guard against laying too much stress on contrasts which amuse or disturb the imagination more than they affect the intellect. From the point of view imperative here, Capuchins and Jesuits only represent different aspects of one and the same power, to wit, that mysterious, massive, irresistible impulse which, even before the Council of Trent, urged modern Catholicism, not primarily to the reform of some secular abuses, but rather to a more intense practice of interior prayer under all its forms. With equal ardour, although with different methods, Jesuits and Capuchins preached prayer to all, laity as well as religious, presenting it as the essential pivot of the true Christian life, and writing numberless books to facilitate the practice. Thus they paved the way for those higher and specially mystical graces which do not depend on human action, but which in the Divine scheme, according to S. Teresa and almost all the contemplatives, are the crown and normal completion of patient and fervent meditation.

It is also to be observed that, in the coming controversy which was to convulse the Christian world and reveal the depths of souls, Capuchins and Jesuits ranged themselves spontaneously on the same side. Have we not seen the History of Christian Humanism open with the portrait of a Jesuit and close with that of a Capuchin? From the outset Yves de Paris and several of his brethren were up in arms against the *Fréquente communion* of the great Arnauld, nor did the Capuchins, as a whole, ever testify the least sympathy for the Jansenist Cause. Since then I do not think that the *Entente cordiale* of the two Orders has ever in the long course of its history been troubled by serious conflicts. Perhaps tender affection has been absent, but a rational friendship exists, the roots of which, hidden underground, retain their life. Whether in the theological and philosophical work of the leading Jesuits, Scotus would have found an echo of his most inward thought is a question I cannot answer, but that the *Spiritual Exercises* of S. Ignatius in many points continue the Franciscan tradition cannot be doubted. In other respects the older of the two Orders owes nothing, or borrows nothing, from the younger.[1] In all that concerns the discipline of the interior life, the Capuchins retain the mediæval method, that of SS. Bernard and Bonaventura, the *Meditationes vitæ Jesu Christi* and the *Stimulus Amoris*. Franciscan spirituality appears more a matter of the affections, the Jesuit more a matter of the intellect and will. The former, perhaps, is freer, more genial, the latter more constrained and rigid; the one in fact more simply open to the mystic gifts, the other more fearful, more on guard against illusions, more resigned to the silence of God, aiming less at attaining the sweetness of contemplation than at casting off the old man. As has been well said, the sons of S. Ignatius offer "to the immense majority of the ordinarily instructed faithful, a method of clear, practical and sane piety, a series of exercises occupying the whole soul and calling into play all the faculties, so that their right balance is maintained. . . . The favourite method of the Jesuits, as familiar to them in theory as in practice, is meditation of the active and discursive type which is always certain of its ground,"[2] in a word, rather ascetic than mystic in the strict sense. The criticism is justified, but too much stress must not be laid on it. Neither the

[1] There were naturally exceptions, Père Joseph for example.

[2] H. Joly, *Sainte Thérèse* (*Les Saints*), p. 214, cited with approval by Père Brou, S.J., in his article "La Compagnie de Jésus," *Revue de philosophie*, May–June, 1913, p. 456.

author of the *Spiritual Exercises* nor the great minds of the Society have ever approved of the mechanical, inquisitorial, bourgeois interpretation given to the *Exercises* by short-sighted commentators; Ignatius, far from desiring to chain the soul by trivial rules, insists that it "should remain tranquil, peaceful, ready to submit to the working of God." Would Francis of Assisi himself have said otherwise? Again:

all meditation in which the understanding labours, wearies the body. There are other suitable methods, which are calming, lulling the understanding, not straining the lesser faculties of the soul and working without exterior or interior tension.

The characteristic of our devotion,

said a Jesuit who had been in a position to collect the traditions of his Order, shortly after the death of S. Ignatius,

is to keep free of a hard-and-fast rule, which is only good for beginners. . . . To sum up, there is but one master of Prayer, the Holy Spirit.

Finally,

we have in this matter the official pronouncement of the Society in a letter of the General, Claude Aquaviva. "The religious who have exercised themselves in meditation and by long use have acquired facility in prayer, have no need to be assigned either a fixed subject for meditation or a special method. The Spirit of the Lord goes on His way without leading-strings (*laxissimis habenis*). There are many ways by which He illuminates souls and attaches them closely to Himself, but there is no bridle for Him, no fixed boundaries. . . . Therefore, while manifesting severity to false contemplatives, we must profit by the constant experience of saintly Fathers, and not forbid contemplation to our people; for, if there is one thing attested and proved by the holy Fathers, it is that true and perfect contemplation is more powerful and efficacious than any other method of devotion to break and crush the pride of man."

All this is a true statement, yet S. Ignatius, of whom it was said that "the superlative was unknown to him," did not hesitate to say that "of a hundred people initiated in prayer (opposed here to meditation properly so-called) ninety are in illusion." The Father who reports this adds, "And I wonder he did not say ninety-nine." In detail he defined the danger for such souls as obstinacy, self-sufficiency, the temptation of wishing to lead others in their own special paths. He had the subject at heart, making it the object of a special rule. "Let them instruct (the young religious) to arm themselves by prayer against the illusions of the devil." And with a significant insistence, when he was asked concerning the higher forms of prayer, he harked back to mortification,[1] well aware that actual meditation, as he expounds it in his book, would be for many an ascetic exercise and veritable mortification.

Franciscan spirituality, on its part, does not encourage indolence or sham mysticism or self-sufficiency; but it would allow more assurance, greater spontaneity to the interior life. It prefers the unconstrained joy of the children of God to too exacting self-examinations; it believes that, even with beginners, the Spirit of the Lord may be left to go on His way without leading-strings. It does not regard mystic graces as rare experiences, but it speaks but little of them; it desires them as a child desires to grow or a flower to open, but it awaits without excitement the divine hour for the blessed flowering. With S. Teresa and the majority of the mystics it holds that a life of prayer and meditation "leads to contemplation and to the prayer of quiet recollection as its natural end." As a plain historian I need not decide between these two ways; but I must note that both are approved by the Church and that both are justified by their fruits.[2]

Founded in 1524, the Minor Capuchins had been introduced from Italy into France by Catherine de Médicis in 1574, and were speedily to be found in the principal towns of the kingdom. France had cordially welcomed these colonies, at first composed of none but Italian religious. Crowds haunted their chapels. "Two things especially attracted them," says the historian of the monastery of Toulouse.

One was our simple and sombre manner of chanting the office . . . the other the bareness and cleanliness of chapel and altar, the latter

[1] The above quotations are taken from Père Brou, *loc. cit.* In spite of slightly paradoxical tendencies, for it professes to show S. Ignatius as "a master of liberty," this learned, keen and exceedingly moderate article contains some of the best pages ever written on this difficult subject.

[2] Père Ubald d'Alençon, *De la méthode traditionelle de l'oraison au moyen âge. Études franciscaines*, XXIX. 314; Abbé Jean Delacroix, *Ascétique et mystique*, Paris, 1912. Cf. also the very valuable pamphlet of Père Ubald d'Alençon, *L'Âme franciscaine*, Paris, 1913, and the same author's translation of *Stimulus Amoris*, Paris, 1900.

being garnished with flowers, a practice unknown in this country.[1]

Recruits were easily enlisted from the best families of France.

"The Angels," Père Joseph would soon cry, "like nought better than to see Christians take the livery of this Babe of Bethlehem, arrayed in rags. . . . Nothing pleases them more than to see noble minds thronging in this garb to be pages of honour to the true David."[2] The simplicity, the occasional grotesqueness of their dress and of their talk, must not mislead us; the first French Capuchins numbered in their ranks almost as many humanists and perhaps more of the nobility than the Jesuits. Notwithstanding the *Ligue* and its memories, these religious must not be painted in too lurid colours; there were fully developed fanatics among them, but the mass of the Order appears very human. When it was a question of sending missionaries to the Huguenots of Vigan, "His Majesty," writes Père Joseph, "desired to employ our Order especially, knowing that many in that district desired them, and that usually they are received by the Huguenots with less aversion than some others." There are pretty anecdotes vividly depicting this mutual tolerance and budding friendship. When, for instance, in 1609 the Capuchins came to take possession of the monastery offered them at Montpellier, the Chevalier de Montmorency, natural son of the Constable, and another gentleman placed themselves sword in hand on each side of the Superior, Père Jacques d'Auch, ready to defend the religious against the anger of the crowd. The last street to be traversed before reaching the convent "was full of armed men, which when Père Jacques d'Auch perceived, he prayed the Chevalier de Montmorency and the other either to leave them or to sheathe their swords, the Cross being sufficient weapon. As the nobles refused, he stood still. The Bishop (Fenouillet, friend of François de Sales) intervened and insisted on their withdrawal."

Some time later the rebels again had the upper hand and the Capuchins had to fly in haste; but by good fortune, continues the historian, "three of our neighbours, although Huguenots, had conceived an affection for us, and our relations with them were most cordial. One

[1] *Toulouse chrétienne, Historie des Capuchins* . . ., by P. Apollinaire de Valence, Toulouse, 1897, I. 7.

[2] *Méthode d'oraison du Père Joseph du Tremblay.* Le Mans, 1897, pp. xxiv–xxv.

of them hid the church-bell in his house, another received our books, and a third took charge of the Chalice and the fittings of the sacristy."[1]

The more documents are studied, the deeper is the conviction that their right place in the history of the religious renaissance has never been assigned to the Capuchins. In zeal and success I am certain that they were second to none, and yet they are known to but few. The fault lies primarily with themselves; until our own time they have too much neglected to uphold the glories and bring into notice the deeds of their Order.[2] What care have they taken of their great humanists, Yves de Paris and Zacharie de Lisieux? Where have they defended their incomparable mystic, Benoit de Canfeld, against suspicions worse than oblivion? Also, why not confess that their history not only dazzles but bewilders us? A fatality, so to speak, dooms this Order to oddity. Two of their Fathers, not perhaps the leaders, but the most famous and captivating, we find disconcerting. I shall speak presently of Père Joseph, but first a word about Ange de Joyeuse.

II. He appeals to us more than one would think.

> Paris saw his changes, first the world seemed naught,
> He passed from it to cloister, from the cloister to the court;
> Vicious man of pleasure, penitent who burns,
> The cuirass and the hairshirt by him were worn by turns.
> Arising from the altars where he has wept by night,
> He speeds him to the Leaguers to foster bitter fight;
> And into France's bosom is plungéd that same sword,
> Which he had consecrated to the service of the Lord.[3]

Henri, Comte de Bouchage, was the son of Guillaume de Joyeuse, the King's lieutenant-general in Languedoc, and his wife, Marie de Batarnay. We cannot say how far the weakness of youth may have led him; but doubtless he was less "vicious" than Voltaire would have us believe. He was, I believe, the most gracious and attractive, the jewel, of the Joyeuse family, and that is saying much. An old

[1] Apollinaire de Valence, *ibid.*, pp. 75–87.

[2] Some scholars of the first rank, Pères Edouard and Ubald d'Alençon, for instance, are repairing the breach to-day; excellent work is being published by the review, *Études franciscaines.* But one understands that the primary enthusiasm of Franciscan scholars is for the first centuries of their Order.

[3] *La Henriade.* Chant IV.

chronicle recently discovered, delicious in its frank human touch, shows the extent to which he was idolized in his home. He was already a Capuchin when the following incident took place. He was finishing his theological studies at Venice, and the General of the Capuchins, Jérôme de Polizzi, summoned him to Genoa, to send him into Provence. One of his brothers, the Cardinal de Joyeuse, was in Italy at the moment, on the point of returning to France after the election of Innocent IX (October 1591). Père Ange, relates the secretary of Père Jérôme de Polizzi,

had come to Sestri to see the General. After some days' rest, he departed early one morning to go by sea to Savona, there to continue his journey. That same day the Cardinal arrived post-haste, knowing his brother was at Genoa and desirous not to lose the chance of meeting. . . . His distress, when he learnt that P. Ange had departed that morning, can be imagined; he lamented to the Father General "Then I shall not see him? What can I do? is there no remedy?" P. Jérôme did not know how to console him, so I came to the rescue. "Monseigneur," said I, "there is a way; let your Eminence use the means at your disposal to have P. Ange overtaken on the morrow and he will return." "Do you think so?" said the Cardinal. "Certainly, if he sees it is a matter of obedience, which the Father General will not refuse you."

At once they began to look for a boat, and the obedience was written, commanding P. Ange to return immediately on account of his brother's arrival. The Cardinal transmitted it himself to the *patron* (captain) of the boat, bidding him to do his utmost and promising him a good *pourboire* if he brought back his brother. He departed forthwith and returned on the morrow with P. Ange. When the Cardinal was informed that the barque was in sight he hastened to the seashore to wave joyful signals to his brother; but his impatience to embrace him was so great that, not waiting till the sailors had carried him to land, he rushed into the water, wetting not only his feet but *all* the hem of his red soutane. When his brother was on shore he kissed him many times, murmuring fondly, "P. Ange, my beloved brother; P. Ange, brother mine!"

Then turning to me (for, the General being confined to bed, I had accompanied the Cardinal) he said: "Father, how well my brother looks, what care you must have taken of him!" "Truly, Monseigneur, we give him cabbage, onions and boiled beans. It is the bread of grace of which the Lord is not sparing to him, the joy of being a religious and peace of soul that give him this splendid appearance." Then the Cardinal told me that, although there were six or seven in the family, their mother preoccupied herself wholly with P. Ange, whose digestion was so delicate as to tax all her resources to find suitable nourishment for him. After several days together, the brothers then departed for their respective destinations.[1]

Everyone loved Ange de Joyeuse—his mother, his brothers, the King of France, the Capuchin Fathers, the people of Languedoc—the hereditary fief and kingdom of the family—the congregations of our churches, the monasteries to whom he preached reform.

Some years previous to this charming encounter on the shores of the Genoese Riviera, he who was one day to be known as Père Ange began a brilliant career at Court. Witty and brave, brother of the Admiral Anne de Joyeuse, and brother-in-law of the Duke d'Epernon by his marriage with Catherine de Nogaret de la Valette, his prospects were brilliant in view of his own personality, the growing prestige of his family and the friendship of royalty. The young man appeared equally in love with his rosy future and with another very different world. Paris, and still more perhaps the Court of Henri III, were studying with stupefaction the Capuchins who had recently entered in possession of their convent in the Rue S.-Honoré, and who constrained " the most obdurate spirits to devotion merely by the austerity shown in their habit."

One day the Comte de Bouchage (Henri de Joyeuse) returning to town in the royal coach, for the King would seldom move without him, beheld by chance, or rather by a special Divine providence, two Capuchins, wallet on back, passing by. His eyes followed them long as if he were filled with ardent desire. The King, seeing him grow suddenly pensive, his eyes fixed on the religious, divined that he had them as much in his heart as in his eyes.[2]

He joined the Capuchins in September 1587, some few days after his wife's death, being then twenty-four years of age. " Henri III," we are told, " almost fell in a swoon," when he beheld his everyday companion " in this habit, head shaven, feet bare."[3] A pamphlet by Cardinal Duperron, entitled *L'Adieu au monde de M. de Joyeuse entrant en religion*, gives us the feeling of Court and town at the event,

[1] Edouard d'Alençon, *Pages inédites de la vie du Père Ange de Joyeuse*. *Études franciscaines*, Aug., 1913, pp. 138–9.

[2] *La Vie du R. P. Ange de Joyeuse*, by M. Jacques Brousse, Paris, 1621, pp. 59–60.

[3] Brousse, *ibid.*, p. 96.

but none questioned the entire sincerity of this act of heroism and the fervour of the handsome novice.

The works, ancient and modern, written about Fr. Ange contain more romance than history.[1] This is especially true of the most popular of these, the *Courtisan prédestiné*, of Sieur Jean de Callières. For instance, we are told that from the moment of Fr. Ange's entrance within convent walls, the King and the house of Joyeuse resolved on employing all means, even force, to carry off the fugitive. The reality is more simple and more touching. Addressing himself to the Provincial of the Capuchins, Bernard d'Osimo, Henry III only asked, and that humbly enough, one thing, that the novice should not be sent away from the capital.

My Father (he writes in October 1587), I rejoice that you have arrived in good health at your convent. May God keep you thus. I know that you love me, and am under infinite obligation to you, but, to increase such obligation indefinitely, and if you would please me mightily, I am sure you will not refuse a simple request that Frère Ange, whom I love as myself or my own child, may not stir from the convent at Paris. I entreat you with all my heart to give me this great joy, that I may still see him and commend myself to his prayers and to yours, the which I do now; for at least, though I have lost him near me, I yet esteem him fortunate in having entered the service of our good and great Master, and I shall have the happiness of seeing him in this holy place working out his salvation and aiding mine by his intercessions before God and His holy Mother. You, my Father, will prolong my days in granting this boon, and in truth you will be happy in having him with you, my Father, and he happy to have chosen this blessed and secure way. If I might have the pleasure of seeing you, it would rejoice me; from now till Monday I sojourn here, at Pluviers (Pithiviers); you can get here in two or three days, which brings us to Sunday, I will give you fair lodging for a day or two, and you will be able to give news of me on your return to Frère Ange. I will tell you of a place where I think of founding a Capuchin convent, which you can inspect, it is at Blois. God keep you. Recommend me to all the worthy brethren.—HENRY.

These poor last Valois! As one reads these charming lines from a very Christian king and spoiled child, the indulgence shown him by

[1] The remark is borrowed from Père Edouard d'Alençon, who certainly does not mean to have a hit at the first chapters of P. Apollinaire de Valence. Cf. *Toulouse chrétienne*, II.

the holiest personages of the epoch becomes comprehensible. As for Frère Ange, " Vicious . . . courtier," this is how Henri writes to him:

Jesus Maria.

My son and friend, I desire, as you know, to work out my salvation in the world, for I hold that this can be done in every place, however difficult. Therefore I would fain learn about the Third Order of S. Francis. As you have been in the world and now have taken the way of holiness in giving yourself to our good God, you know well how it is possible, as I said, to work out one's salvation in this world, by detesting sin and embracing virtue. Therefore I pray you with all my heart to send me your special advice, together with a rule that I should follow. A Dieu.[1]

After some years of solitude and fervour Frère Ange suddenly reappeared on the stage of the world. As we have seen, in 1592 his General sent him into Provence, on, to use modern terms, a mission no less political than religious; such distinctions, however, scarcely struck the minds of that time. The *Ligue*, half crushed, threatened to break up altogether. This was an effort to circumscribe the conflagration and lessen, as far as possible, the triumph of the King of Navarre, and, with that end in view, we are told, " to form a kind of federation which, while giving independence to each of the (Southern) provinces, should yet unite them under Papal protection." *Ligueur* to the backbone, brother-in-law of the Governor of Provence, brother of the Governor of Languedoc, kin to the Lyonnais Governor, Charles Emanuel of Savoy, Frère Ange was charged or charged himself—both perhaps—with these diplomatic negotiations. At the end of several months he had convinced himself that the project was destined to failure, but meanwhile the young Capuchin had gradually recovered the *éclat* that was his before taking the habit. In spite of five years of " the hairshirt," " the cuirass " still sat well upon him.

In October 1592 the Governor of Languedoc, Scipion de Joyeuse, surprised and defeated by the royal troops, met his death by drowning in the Tarn. He was the last of the Joyeuses, at least the last leader of fighting men, for the eldest and the fifth had been killed at Coutras, the second was a cardinal, and the third a Capuchin. Since, at all costs, a Joyeuse chief was desired, the choice must lie between the

[1] These valuable letters were discovered and published by Père E. d'Alençon. Cf. *Pages inédites*, loc. cit., pp. 126–7.

Cardinal and the Capuchin. The choice was not doubtful. Endless discussions first, then supplications of "all the common people, in their thousands surrounding the cloister and overflowing the garden crying piteously and insistently, 'We want Frère Ange the Capuchin for our Governor!' even adding threats of burning down the monastery and carrying him off by force."[1] The higher theologians were called into consultations; both Baronius and Bellarmine approved; Rome offered the necessary dispensations; Ange finally yielded. "On the morrow he appeared clad in black to symbolize inward mourning, Monseigneur the Cardinal, his brother, Archbishop of Toulouse, having girded on his sword." The *Chanson de Roland* has nothing more sublime or sweet than this last touch. The Turpin of 1592 refuses to fight, but joyously passes on the sword to his brother the monk, and never has that brother seemed to him so splendid.

The voice of the people, *vox Dei*, acclaimed the new leader.

> To say that in all these acclamations, his heart was there, would be, I hold, untrue, it was in God . . . no sooner had he taken the sword, effaced the tonsure, and slightly clipped his beard than, receiving the nobility hastening to greet him, he welcomed each according to his rank and quality, with so brave and finished a bearing that it was as if he had never entered the cloister, save perhaps for a certain sweetness of the religious, that tempered the dignity demanded by his position as captain and Governor. . . . As he walked after his bodyguard among the nobility, an unusual thing was observed, which pleased everyone. He wore the White Cross of Malta on his breast, the Pope having exchanged his vows as a Friar Minor for that of the Order of S. John of Jerusalem.[2]

We will follow him no further into a world affording no food for our search after things mystic. His exile from the Franciscan paradise lasted for seven years (1592–1599), but it was less hard to support than the panegyrists of Frère Ange would have us believe. They assure us ingenuously that "in the army it is most unlikely that he had the opportunity to lay aside the cuirass in order to take the discipline, as some imagine." No, "the hairshirt" is not so difficult to conceal, and as for the discipline, it is easy enough, does one so desire, to find a retired corner for it. Let us rather candidly avow

[1] Brousse, *ibid.*, pp. 138–9. Cf. *Toulouse chrétienne*, by P. Apollinaire.

[2] Brousse, *ibid.*, pp. 140–2.

that Frère Ange has vanished, and in his place stands the most honest *ligueur* that ever was, Henri de Joyeuse, *Honi soit qui mal y pense !* Nor did the former Capuchin appear at all in haste to end his vacation. The *Ligue* having ceased to be, he made his peace with Henri IV, who received him with open arms and restored to him all his former titles; he sought for his daughter an establishment worthy of the Joyeuses;[1] in short, he made hay while the sun shone. After all, his situation was canonically regular; nothing impelled him to a fresh act of heroism, harder than the first for a man no longer young, who had just passed through such sensational experience. Yet his friends were on the watch—let us say our friends, for we shall meet them constantly in our history—the headquarters staff of the Paris mystics, who after the *Ligue* came to an end had their generals, lists of officers, and plans of campaign. Henri de Joyeuse was under the direction of the famous Carthusian Dom Beaucousin, and he still saw his former comrade Père Benoit de Canfeld, of whose unique achievements we shall hear presently. Each of these, in his own way, impelled him in the same direction; Beaucousin with his wise and gentle insistence, Canfeld, the ecstatic soon to court martyrdom, with brotherly and noble severity. We have one of the latter's letters " to the Père Ange de Joyeuse, during the time of his return to the world."

How inexpressibly strong, O dearest brother in Jesus Christ, must be the bond of love between those born, not of a carnal but of a spiritual mother—divine, seraphic, and radiant—the Religion of S. Francis.

Thence he descends to details:

Where is the unitive and ecstatic life . . . the coarse habit, the thick cord, the patched mantle and sandals? Where the fasts, the discipline, the meals of bread and water? where the practices of humility, kissing the ground, sweeping the house? . . . Is the mirror of France tarnished . . . has the valiant captain of the Friars Minor fled from the battle . . . Has the child of S. Francis and seraphic Religion been killed? Is Frère Ange dead? I weep for you, O my brother Jonathan . . .

Let him not say that he will do

[1] His only daughter Catherine, who had been eighteen months old when her father had entered the Capuchin Order, was married first to Henri de Bourbon, Duc de Montpensier, and after his death to Charles de Lorraine, Duc de Guise. Her only daughter was Marie de Bourbon.

much good by slaying heretics with the sword. I say you will slay more of them with prayer.

Besides, he belongs to S. Francis, no casuist can disprove this truth.

And as for my calling you on the outside of this letter de Joyeuse, and on the inside my brother, it need cause you no astonishment, for only outside and on the exterior you are you, Duc de Joyeuse, but within and in all things interior Frère Ange; and not only should you be this, but also you cannot be ought else, even with a papal dispensation.[1]

So he became once more Frère Ange, took again the heavy cord and the patched habit, began again " the unitive and ecstatic life." That was in 1599; the dying century—and what a century!—bequeathed to the seventeenth this memorable example. That other League, our League, the unstained one of the mystics, now begins its triumphs. Ange de Joyeuse was one of its first soldiers. Benoit de Canfeld on leaving Paris was to entrust to him the reform of Montmartre, as we shall see in its place; he had the right to preach sacrifice. Round that noble brow the reflection from the abandoned cuirass glowed like an aureole. Strange career of the soldier-monk, whose last hour brings with it the echoes of the battlefield. Returning from Rome to France, Ange de Joyeuse died at Rivoli, September 28, 1608.

III. I might treat of many other leading figures in this first generation of Capuchins, for example, Père Honoré Bochart de Champigny, who seconded several of the great reforming Abbesses;[2] or again that Père Archange of Pembroke, for long (1609–1620) the favourite director of " the little Abbess " of Port-Royal, whose sane and kindly wisdom has been lauded by Sainte-Beuve;[3] but it is best to come straight to him who outdistanced them all by the splendour of his mystic genius and the extent of his influence.

William Filch, soon to be known as Benoit de Canfeld, was born at Canfeld in Essex during the early part of the reign of Elizabeth.

[1] Brousse, *ibid.*, pp. 685–703.

[2] Cf. *Histoire de V. S. de Dieu, le Père Honoré de Paris*, by the Abbé Mazelin, Paris, 1882.

[3] Cf. *Port-Royal*, I. 177–81, and especially *Les Frères mineurs et les débuts de la réforme à Port Royal des Champs . . . documents inédites publiés*, by Père Ubald d'Alençon.

Rich enough for independence, he spent, as he himself confesses, a very dissipated youth.

Alas! (he cries somewhere) how long was I an idler, a gamester, a looker-on at comedies; how often did I lounge in desecrated St. Paul's; what a frequenter of the schools, not of learning, but of fencing and dancing.

Converted by the reading of a pious book, he crossed the Channel and came to Douai to be thoroughly initiated into Catholic life. No disillusion awaited him on French soil. He has summed up his impressions in a long and beautiful autobiographical prayer.

We arrived at the desired haven, namely, a Catholic country, where for the first time I saw the majesty, beauty, and magnificence of Thy Church, and with what joy and satisfaction I remarked . . . the order reigning in this Church militant and celestial hierarchy, from the Pope at the head . . . down to the secular clergy.

This French Catholicism which roused him to enthusiasm has been represented to us by many historians, religious writers even more than others, as fallen into the uttermost decadence. In order to exalt the Reformers of the seventeenth century, the ruin which they had to repair has been exaggerated. We shall often have occasion to entertain doubts on this head. Canfeld indeed came from a country seething in chaos from successive religious revolutions; were the ancient Church in France but a wreck, there would be still much about her to enchant the eyes, heart and thoughts of a neophyte. But what are we to say when the same remarks, with even greater surprise, are made by the Spanish nuns who came to France to found the French Carmel? They fancied themselves journeying towards Babylon; and found in the Paris of 1605 almost the holy Sion.

When I beheld (Canfeld continues) the lofty and magnificent buildings of Thy temples, the great and spacious monasteries, beautiful within and without with sculpture, paintings, exquisite carvings, I could think of nothing but the gravity and majesty of Thy holy Church. . . . With Thy psalmist, Lord, I have loved the adorning and fair beauty of Thy house. In such great and glorious structures I could not but see the piety and devotion which the Catholic faith produces.

The glorious services of Thy Church to my mind embellish and magnify the whole. For, beholding the great solemnity of the Mass, celebrated by priests, deacons, sub-deacons, acolytes, each with the ornaments of his rank and each performing his own office; beholding the dressed altar glittering with candles and encircled by the choir; beholding the devotion and piety with which they censed it with goodly fragrance, and the great and solemn processions of thronging worshippers with torches, candles and numberless tapers; the choir filled with priests, clerks and choristers clothed in white in their stalls . . . beholding, I say, all these things, I could not but see as in a mirror, with strange and transcendent devotion, the beauty, splendour and majesty of Holy Church.

Chateaubriand or Walter Scott had not yet written. But these are the sentiments which, two and a half centuries later, would accelerate the conversion and gladden the sacrifice of Newman, Faber, and many another. The music of our churches transported him even more.

Above all, my Lord, what rapture when I heard the ineffable melodies, the incomparable and divine harmony of the well-tuned organs and the sweet voices which sang together in church . . . my heart trembled with joy and merriment, even while the sweetness distilled itself into the depths of a heart overflowing with fervour, wrenching my thoughts from earth to fix them on heaven. . . . I could scarce listen to such harmonies without great tears falling from my eyes. . . . These voices flowed into my heart and the knowledge and recollection of celestial things came gently into my heart, flowing as it were through a channel. When the organ played and the choir chanted antiphonally, the organs up aloft seemed to me like the celestial choir . . . the pipes like voices of angels ranged in order . . . who, having compassion on us, had descended into Thy church . . . to console us, invite us to Paradise, to join their divine praises with ours. The choir of choristers represented the Christian people who . . . hearing (the angels) respond by lifting up voice and soul, in token that they are ready to leave the earth and unite with the ranks in Paradise.[1]

We have already pointed out that the devout and the mystic lives are distinct. Let us own, however, that the devotion of this master of a whole generation of mystics was as poetic, tender, and loving as that of François de Sales himself. A significant anecdote, related, a little touched up perhaps, by Canfeld's biographer, may find a place here.

Being once sent to Andely there to sojourn, he saw on entering the chapel nearest the church door that there was no picture over the

[1] Brousse, *ibid.*, pp. 517–24.

altar. Filled with dismay, for, whatever heretics may say, pictures are the best books not only for the unlearned but even for the most advanced, he requested that some colours should be procured, and, although he had never touched brush or pencil, produced a picture of Our Lady, representing therein all those symbols and hieroglyphics by which are exalted the virtues of this Queen of Heaven.[1]

Canfeld took the Capuchin habit at Paris in 1586, but few details exist of his religious life. We only know that he must have remained a considerable time in the capital. When he was a novice his long ecstasies alarmed the monks of his monastery. They fancied him either ill or a victim of some diabolic wile. In one such rapture lasting two days,

the doctors, who very often do not have recourse to God so long as they can find a natural remedy, ordered freshly killed pigeons to be placed . . . on his head . . . they pricked his legs and thighs with great pins,[2]

but without succeeding in rousing him. Finally they became thoroughly convinced of the grace that was accorded him.

He tried hard to return to England, but Elizabeth's agents were too vigilant; he was arrested and put in prison. Liberated at the instance of Henri IV, he returned to Paris, there to die in 1611. Completely forgotten to-day, it is somewhat difficult to realize the importance of his influence ; nevertheless all that his panegyrists say of him falls short of the truth.

The sublimity of his doctrine has been recognized and valued in the cloisters . . . and God alone knows the number of religious, both men and women, who, through his writings or his words, have been guided to loftiest heights of perfection.[3]

Master of the masters themselves, of Bérulle, Madame Acarie, Marie de Beauvillier and many others, he, in my opinion, more than anyone else gave our religious renaissance this clearly mystical character which we see already stamping it and which was to last for the next fifty years.

Canfeld's literary output is difficult to trace, for of the books attributed to him none but manuscript copies were ever circulated. This indeed was his method and was also that of his time. He used to lend to those under his direction written sheets suitable to their

[1] Brousse, *ibid.*, pp. 648–9. [2] *Ibid.*, p. 573. [3] *Ibid.*, p. 593.

needs. Copies of these were made at once and distributed without discretion and often against the express wishes of the author. In a letter to one of his Capuchin friends, Canfeld complains bitterly of this abuse, declaring that he will appeal to authority to put a stop to it. Certain "jealous" persons spoke "in a sinister way" of these writings, and, "to destroy the taste for such in souls," secretly circulated versions of their own. The chief work of Canfeld is in any case the small book that became known in the last years of his life, entitled *Règle de perfection réduite au seul point de la volonté divine*, a work for us of capital importance, since it served as manual to two or three generations of mystics.

It is a beautiful book, glowing and luminous, and I find its great success easily explicable. Certain modern critics profess to find it obscure, on what grounds I cannot say—they agree in praising other books far more obscure. They quote against him the authority of François de Sales who allowed the Visitandines to read the first two parts of the *Règle de perfection*, but preferred the third to be left unread.

Allow the reading of the *Volonté de Dieu* (probably the *Règle de perfection*) as far as the last part, which, being not very intelligible, is liable to be misunderstood.[1]

This was wise advice with which Benoit de Canfeld himself would have wholly agreed.

I desire and advise (says he expressly) that no one enter on the third part unless he or she be adjudged capable, not by himself, but by his superior, confessor, or director, of profiting by it. If such delay should seem to retard any such soul, let him regard it as the Will of God . . . and assuredly he will thus advance farther and be raised to greater heights by the Divine Will (manifested through his superiors) than by means of the reading of this third part. I can speak no more strongly to prevent those unfitted for this treatise from meddling with it.

Such precautions once taken, had he not the right to let himself go?

It would not be equitable (he says again) that souls more mature should be deprived of solid meat because milk is best suited for babes,

[1] *Œuvres de S. François de Sales*, IV. ix. Cf. Père Poulain, *Les grâces d'oraison*, 5th ed., p. 592. The view of Canfeld's spirituality to be developed is happily entirely in accordance with that propounded by Père Ubald d'Alençon in his recent lectures at the Catholic Institute of Paris (January–March, 1916).

nor that a philosopher should be debarred from his philosophical tomes, under colour of the grammarian's not comprehending them.[1] I do not think, however, that even in this reserved portion of his book Canfeld studies the more exceptional states of the mystic life; he does not adventure himself in such lofty flights as his contemporary Jean de Saint-Samson or S. John of the Cross. But his peculiar turn of mind may surprise and even weary a reader. Himself a subtle theologian, he at times pursues his psychological analyses with too liberal a curiosity; as a logician, he loves fine systematic sharp-edged symmetries. It is the speculative thinker in him rather than the mystic that some may find complicated, although he always expresses himself with marvellous lucidity. To this is joined the imagination of a poet and a florid style. One thing prevents his being a great writer: he is a man of mixed speech, oscillating between English, French and Latin. Nevertheless he enraptured his contemporaries, even the more ignorant. It was Benoit de Canfeld's book which led the humble Provençal shepherd lad (one day to call himself Père Yvan) to the interior life. As for the learned, it is enough to say that eight doctors of the Sorbonne publicly approved the *Règle de perfection*, among them two authorities of the first order, André Duval and the Carthusian Beaucousin; there were also other highly respectable testimonies—Madame Acarie, Père Joseph, and the Capuchin General who in 1621 ordered the publication of a new edition. It may be possible to find in the *Règle de perfection*, as in most of the mystical works brought out before the condemnation of Molinos, certain faulty expressions, but anyone who taxed him with Quietism would show a lack of acquaintance with the most elementary rules of criticism, to say nothing of those of truth and good taste. The whole book, so to speak, breathes anti-Molinosism.[2]

Sundry spiritual experts of the *grand siècle* made the interior life consist in the practice of one single fundamental virtue, a pedagogic method which is suited to certain minds and for beginners obviates

[1] *La règle*, pp. 273–4.

[2] Assuredly R. P. Poulain could not have read Canfeld or even known him when he placed the author of the *Règle de perfection* at the head of his list of "Quietist Authors" (*Grâces d'oraison*, 5th ed., p. 592). Certainly one of the many editions, or, to speak more correctly, one of the *translations* of Canfeld, was placed on the Index of 1689, that is to say immediately after the condemnation of Molinos. But a certain book of Père Surin suffered a like fate, and that famous mystic does not figure beside Canfeld in Père Poulain's list. Moreover, the numerous citations following will remove the slightest doubt on this subject.

alike intellectual fatigue and the moral depression generally induced by a too elaborate programme. The stupid and the lukewarm can misuse anything, but a man of good will and good sense, well aware that the kingdom of heaven suffereth violence, will never expect to arrive in a day, without effort and once for all, at the heights of perfection. The virtues form a unity, helping and generating one the other; he who with a generous spirit practises one, will perforce be led on to practise the rest. "Love and do what thou wilt," said S. Augustine. Christ's reply to the young man desirous of doing good is scarcely longer. For Benoit de Canfeld, as later for the Jesuit Caussade, the cardinal virtue comprehending all else is surrender—active and heroic surrender—to the Divine Will. *Règle de perfection réduite au seul point de la volonté divine*, such is his 'short-cut,' his golden key; an attractive, soothing and stimulating summary, but one which permits no forgetfulness of any duty. To do "from the sole motive of pleasing God, all one is aware that God desires, commands, counsels, and inspires," is not this true perfection?[1]

This book, writes one of Canfeld's admirers, Dom Beaucousin,

is suited to the capacity of all pious and religious souls, whether beginners or those of riper experience or the already perfect, if only they enter, as did Esther before Ahasuerus, in due order through each door as it opens.

Each will find in it counsels fitted for him, which, faithfully followed, will lead him step by step through the stages of the interior life. The *Règle* is not solely, as some seem to believe, a summary of mystical theology, it is first and foremost a manual of Christian asceticism; Canfeld's conviction being that such asceticism prepares for and lures the soul to the heights of perfection.

IV. The first editions of the *Règle* contained a beautiful synthetic frontispiece, drawn, or at least designed, by the author himself, who thus describes and explains it:

[1] Cf. on this subject the somewhat curt remarks of Père Poulain (*loc. cit.*, pp. 502–3). In Canfeld's very title he scents Quietism. Is it then so dangerous a paradox to declare that the whole duty of a Christian is "to will what God wills"? Yet what does the "*Veni, sequere me*" of the Gospel mean? Without having so much as read Canfield, the Rev. Father is apparently convinced that that master considered it sufficient to await with open mouth the divine inspirations, as if the Will of God were not clearly and in a hundred ways indicated to each of us at almost every step.

This image of the sun represents the Will of God, and the faces placed in it (the sun), the souls living therein (the divine Will). . . . These faces are ranged in three circles, showing the three degrees of Divine Will: the first, souls of the active life; the second, contemplatives; the third those who have attained.

And while around the first rank are many tools of manual labour (pincers and hammers) denoting the active life; and in the third is *Iehoüa*; in the intermediate circle there is nothing, to signify that in the contemplative life, there is neither speculation nor practice, but solely following the indication of the Will of God. The tools of the first rank are earthly and in obscurity, seeing that works of themselves are full of darkness. Yet these tools are touched and enlightened by the rays of the sun, as works are illuminated and glorified by the Will of God.

The shining of this Divine Will is seen but little on the faces of the first rank; more clearly upon the second, but in full splendour on the third. The first circle are the most clearly delineated; the second, less; the third, scarce at all; which conveys that the souls of the first order are much occupied with self; the second, less with self and more with God; while the third are almost wholly absorbed into God and His Absolute Will. All these figures or countenances have their eyes fastened on Divine Will.

We have lost the understanding and appreciation of those symbolical compositions which our forefathers liked to put on the front pages of their books. It is to be regretted, for these frontispieces, which readily fixed the abstract doctrine of a long treatise in the mind, imagination and memory of the simple, served also as a touchstone, and, if necessary, a corrective of the doctrine itself. Had Jansenius commissioned a Flemish painter to illustrate the *Augustinus*, Port-Royal would certainly have recoiled in horror from a system which, from want of imagination, it never fully realized. Do they speak of the Quietism of Canfeld? Look at these tools of the active life, these pincers and hammers "touched by the rays of the sun." This image shows us that, despite the twilight encompassing it, the humble active life of the beginner is not opposed to the contemplative quietude of the perfect. The better the soul fulfils the duties of her station, the nearer she approaches the sun, the higher she arises towards the mystical repose which, far from weakening, rather inspires to fresh flight. Let us beware of despising these tools, or, in other words, the rudimentary works of our powers, but let us not be satisfied, or boast of so meagre an outfit. Let us not, misled by vain fears or by a vanity still more absurd, refuse to mount higher, for otherwise we fall into the error

of those who, too much given to the ministry of Martha, refuse to choose with Mary the better part . . . which we do not understand to mean merely the activity of the exterior life, but also and principally the activity of the interior, consisting in acts of understanding and will. For some, finding themselves drawn as it were from the active life with its accustomed acts of consideration, meditation, and aspiration, and as it were constrained by this strait rule to concentrate all the forces of their mind upon this sole Will of God, and there abide (in which consists contemplation pure and absolute), scarce know where they are or how they should proceed, and so turn away and reject contemplation pure and bare, holding that the spiritual exercises of the soul are profitless and delusive, unaccompanied by their accustomed acts and exercise of the mind.

They had a place at the board of slaves; they might have been admitted to the Royal Banquet, but, fearing to die of hunger, have clung to their miserable pittance.

To remedy this error and reduce these superfluous acts, primarily those of the understanding (one must), know that interior life is not perfected nor is true contemplation acquired by such discourses and speculations, which are acts of the understanding; but by fervour, love and affection, which are acts of the will: for by no intellectual speculation can God be possessed or enjoyed, but solely by the love of Him. . . . (As says Dionysius) "The hidden darkness of God, which He calls abundance of light, is beyond all revelation and hidden from all knowledge. And if there be any who beholding God know that he beholds Him, such a one has not seen God, but something that appertains to Him." For intellectual speculation would fain adapt God, the All-Powerful, Infinite, Incomprehensible, to our petty capacity; while the will, on the contrary, acting by love, seeks to adapt itself in some degree to the infinity and almightiness of God. . . . Such intellectual speculation is a human thing, causing us to dwell in ourselves, but the Will of God is a divine thing, raising and drawing us out of ourselves, transforming us into the Divine. Therefore it is manifest that such speculations and exercises of the mind are not perfection, nor true contemplation, which consists in such a vision of God as this mortality permits, to which all speculation is a hindrance.

For this reason the Holy Spirit admonishes the Spouse in Canticles, when He says: *Averte oculos tuos a me*, turn away thine eyes from Me, that is from curious reflection or speculation . . . *quia ipsi me avolare fecerunt*, lest they make Me flee from thee, that is from thy view, which, obscured by such reflection, cannot gaze on Me.

The same thing is taught mystically by the angel who caused Jacob to halt upon his thigh. . . . These two powers of the soul resemble two horses yoked to a chariot, of which one is slow and the other swift, the will being so slow through lack of love that it can scarce go, and the understanding so winged by curiosity that it would fain run always, so that the one has need of spur and the other of bridle.[1]

And this same will strips itself also in contemplation, not of essential energy—for there is nothing better in man and it is the ground of man—but of that conscious effervescence which is not love herself. It is an imperfection to desire overmuch the sweetnesses of prayer and to prefer them to the apparent and crucifying dryness of the Mystic Union. There are some who cannot rest without some consciousness of union, and thence arises it that they live continually in poverty of soul. In vain the Holy Spirit stirs them to some generous sally " beyond the home-fields of nature ";

sense impedes them, desiring not to be weaned from the breast of sensible consolations, like a beast always open-mouthed for its pasture, neighing for its oats, never desisting until its appetite has trodden underfoot the awakened impulse.[2]

They would seek God, feel Him on the surface of the soul; " they do not see that they have (already) That which they seek." Why desire Him " as though He were absent? " Instead of desiring " One absent," one must " enjoy Him as present."[3] How sadly hoodwinked is the soul that does not realize

her Bridegroom as truly present as herself, more so indeed, more within her than she is in herself, more her than herself, but as though in Paradise or far removed elsewhere.[4]

There, within ourselves, is consummated the Mystic Union, far above the obscure region agitated by rational intelligence or sentiment. In these changeless depths " the Spirit approaches so close to the soul that she perceives His very shadow."[5]

[1] *La règle*, 1st Part, Chap. XVIII. [2] *Ibid.*, III. Chap. X. [3] *Ibid.*
[4] *Ibid.*, III. Chap. IV. [5] *Ibid.*, III. Chap. V.

O what immense beauty irradiates this vision in which the Divine Smile of Love is perceived by the soul.

Here she extends her fair frank arms to embrace and hold fast her Bridegroom, but by Him is more closely embraced and held fast; she would strain the capacity of her spirit to bridge the depth, and finds herself rather blissfully swallowed up therein.[1]

But what is all this but activity! "Essential will," says one of Canfeld's editors,

has a way of working which seems purely passive, in which the soul appears to do nothing and God all; enough for her to receive His seal; the more so that the light of the gift of Wisdom illuminating the soul in this supernatural state is so clear, her love to God so spiritual, His operation so delicate, that it is as if she had no sensible knowledge, or love of God, nor any tangible sensation. So we must understand our author when he says in his Third Part that the soul, being purely passive, works no more by any faculty; no more, that is, in a bodily and perceptible manner, although never has she been so enlightened (and therefore so active), and she has never loved God with more ardour than in this passive state, in which the energizing force is so great that she herself can give no account of the vehemence of the working or of the reflections induced thereby, and so cannot form a distinct knowledge of it.[2]

Canfeld says all that in two lines.

One works more the more one is idle and less the less one is idle.[3]

Yet that this attitude by no means encourages the indolent inactivity of false mystics, Canfeld is never weary of repeating:

Mark well that we do not mean when we say we must not turn back to the exterior will—that of which the Divine Operation has suspended the material and perceptible workings—that one should despise or omit exterior works. Rather we mean that by the above methods they are spiritualized, transformed even as they are performed.[4]

In other words, the contemplative does not lay aside the ordinary virtues as, for example, penitence; he uses the discipline like any neophyte, but the "material" and "perceptible" part of this exercise

[1] *La règle*, III, Chap. VII.

[2] Preface to the edition of 1696.

[3] *La règle*, III. Chap. XIV.

[4] *Ibid.*, III. Chap. XIII. Cf. also Chap. XIV, a beautiful comparison between good and bad inactivity.

does not occupy, still less absorb, him. The most outward action, directed by an advanced mystic, becomes itself in a manner mystic. If so much is true of outward actions, how much more must it be of the ordinary exercise of our spiritual faculties?

Here is true life, at once active and contemplative, not separate, as some imagine, but united in one moment, so that the active life of such a one is also contemplative; his exterior works, interior; his corporeal, spiritual; his temporal, eternal; making thus *utraque unum*, out of two things one.[1]

This is the essential difference between servants of the spirit and those of the letter, between the true Christian and the Pharisee. The latter exalts the letter till he forgets the spirit; the former, while remaining loyal to the letter, yet spiritualizes it, and thus in a manner "annihilates" it. It is difficult for the spectator to understand the full meaning of this subtle dissociation, but we can feel that it exists, and that but for our thick-headedness we should comprehend it better.

Where many make a mistake is that, being commanded to do something, they murmur and excuse themselves, under pretext of being intent on what is spiritual, missing thus what they profess to seek, namely, God Who is all in work, and causing a threefold obstacle and darkness: first, the work itself; second, the fear of doing it; third, their own will and failure to obey.

When the soul gives herself over to introspection (on entering the Mystic Way), she flees from, and nourishes a certain fear of, exterior things, but the more she fears and shrinks from them the more their images are impressed upon her. Further, she gives them the place of God, Who should be found in all places, so that His very Presence makes all else vanish, whereas she gives so much place to these things that their presence makes God disappear.[2]

Therefore and for the same reason—for, as I have already said, we have to do with a metaphysician who never loses sight of that which is the keystone of his system—the contemplative must not yield to the unfortunately common temptation, which lures him to neglect the Word made flesh in order to lose himself more absolutely in the Divine Essence. The fundamental chapter of the Third Part of the

[1] *La règle*, III. Chap. VII.

[2] *Ibid.*, III. Chap. XIII. After these decisive quotations, I consider myself justified in repeating that whoever accuses Canfeld of Quietism cannot be acquainted with his writings.

Règle—reserved for the most advanced mystics—is entitled: *Qu'il faut toujours pratiquer et contempler la Passion de Notre Seigneur.*

The red thread bound by Rahab in the casement of her dwelling, teaches us that God wills us to place the red Blood of His Passion in the casement of our interior dwelling-place, that is to say our understanding, that our contemplation and meditation may be continually upon it.[1]

" Continually," even when a soul has attained those heights which dominate from afar created images, even the holiest. Then God Himself seems to summon the soul to contemplate only Divinity, but the soul clings to the Gospel scenes of the Passion. *Dimitte me*, Christ says to her, *aurora est*—cease to touch My human nature, for thou seest true day dawning, My Divinity. But the soul responds: *non dimittam te*, I will not leave Thee.[2] And that, I mean, to cling close to the God-man, is essential, because not only Christianity, but the highest contemplation itself is won thus.

Here we have the great principle safeguarding us alike from Quietism and Pantheism: God everywhere in all His Fullness of Being, so that " His Presence must absorb " the lower essences; which nevertheless retain their proper substance. So it is possible for the mystic to remain loyal to the letter of asceticism, yet spiritualizing, *annihilating* its exercises " even while performing them "; the same principle is apparent in our own union with the Incarnate Word. " The light of faith annihilates the images " the sight of which we should not wish even ecstasy itself to deprive us.

Though we have the representation of a crucifix . . . the immensity of faith absorbs and annihilates it.[3]

If philosophers would read these passages over again they would find them sublime, with that limpid yet profound sublimity which seems to throw a sudden illumination on the paths of mystery. To comment on such divine metaphysics would be beyond my strength and not in place here. It must suffice me to have called attention to the splendour and strength of this small book, on which so many mystics have fashioned themselves, among others that singular per-

[1] *La règle*, III. Chap. XVI. [2] *Ibid.*, III. Chap. XX.
[3] *Ibid.*, III. Chap. XVII.

sonality whose appearance here may seem surprising, *his gray Eminence*, Père Joseph.[1]

V. We know already, but Canfeld has told us again and given the final reason for it, that between the contemplative life and the exterior works there is no opposition, but, on the contrary, close union and secret harmonies. On the one hand the mystical flame marvellously exalts the powers of man, even the natural ones; on the other, it consumes and " annihilates " the impurities of action. Nevertheless when human activity applies itself to certain objects, moves at ease in certain surroundings, when it has no scruple as to the means to attain its end, and, in short, is marked by certain violent characteristics, we find it difficult to connect such activity with the pure fire of Mysticism. This would seem to be illustrated by the case of Père Joseph, the confidant, counsellor, agent and, as the Greeks would say, " dæmon " of Cardinal Richelieu. Was his policy that of a saint? As a whole he certainly wished it so to be and probably

[1] *Le Père Joseph et Richelieu*, the definitive and classic work of M. Fagniez on the political career of Père Joseph, is universally known. M. le Chanoine Dedouvres has for twenty years been preparing the *Vie du Père Joseph*, and has published in the *Revue des Facultés catholiques de l'Ouest*, or else in the *Études franciscaines*, the first chapters of this great work. M. Dedouvres, who knows every branch of this vast and little-known subject, cherishes for Père Joseph an unreserved admiration, in which we hope one day to join wholeheartedly. I will briefly recall the *curriculum vitæ* of the famous Capuchin during the period which concerns us. François Leclerc du Tremblay, Baron de Maffliers, was born in Paris on November 4, 1577, his father being Jean Leclerc, President of Petitions and later French Ambassador to Venice; while his mother was Marie de Lafayette, in her youth a Calvinist. François received a humanistic and brilliant education in Greek, Latin, law, philosophy, fortification, mathematics, Italian, English, Spanish, and Hebrew. When quite young he spoke in Latin for an hour " in a grave assembly of gentlemen gathered together for the funeral service of Ronsard." (This could not have been the first funeral service of 1585; but Ronsard was thus honoured by at least three of our devout humanists, Du Perron, Garasse, and Père Joseph.) In 1595 he departed for Italy and made a long stay at Padua, where Peiresc was likewise at the time. He returned to France by a lengthy route (Trent, Nuremberg, Augsburg, Strasbourg), was present at the siege of Amiens in 1597, and soon after went to England with the Ambassador, Hurault de Maisse. "In 1597 Shakespeare produced several of his great dramas. . . . Hurault relates in his memoirs that he saw *Hamlet* performed before the Court; the Baron de Maffliers must have seen it also." *Alas, poor Yorick!* what a good meditation for a future missioner! In 1598 we find him back in France and, like nearly all these mystics, in the little world of Bérulle-Acarie. Intimate with Bérulle, he had for directors André Duval and Benoit de Canfeld. In 1599 he became a Capuchin, and speedily lecturer of philosophy, novice-master, great preacher and co-founder with Antoinette d'Orléans of the *Congregation du Calvaire*. About 1613 he began to gravitate towards the orbit of Richelieu, and became insensibly the intimate auxiliary of the great man. See especially Dedouvres, *Un chapitre de la Vie du Père Joseph, le Baron de Maffliers*, Angers, 1906; and *Le Père Joseph . . . ses charges, ses prédications de 1604 à 1613*, Angers, 1915.

regarded it as such, but did he discern with perfect accuracy the true spirit that guided him? For us, Richelieu himself is less of a problem; he feared hell and loved theology, he was not indifferent towards the things of God, but his kingdom was of this world. Père Joseph, on the contrary, never retracted the holy ambitions of his Capuchin youth, never forgot the sublime teachings of his masters, Francis of Assisi, the Areopagite, Harphius, and Benoit de Canfeld. This diplomat of the old régime, versed in all the tricks of his trade, still knows how to remain the herald of Divine Love, still keeps the simplicity of the childlike mind. This Under-Secretary of State, overwhelmed with secular cares and strange commissions, yet practises the prayer of Quiet. He always remains a mystic, according to his panegyrists; I accept their assurance. Surely, though, he is a mystic *in partibus infidelium*, veiled in clouds which require vision more penetrating than mine to pierce. Please take these last words literally, as a confession of incapacity. From the day on which the political life of Père Joseph begins seriously I am lost in the depths of this extraordinary man. I understand the first part of his life better and love it more; he has left a doubly moving memorial of it in one of the most beautiful books of our religious literature, *l'Introduction à la vie spirituelle par une facile méthode d'oraison.*

According to M. Dedouvres, this book, which was not published till 1616, must have been written in 1613–14, that is, during the memorable years when Père Joseph finally gave himself completely over to Richelieu. I should like to believe that eight or nine years previously, manuscript copies of the *Introduction* were already in circulation among the Capuchins or other religious houses, and in 1614 Père Joseph did no more than publish the lessons he gave in 1604 or 1605 to the Capuchin novices of Meudon. For, at thirty as at fifty, P. Joseph, whether speaking or writing, seems always vehement and oracular, but the older he grows the more a mysterious bitterness threatens to destroy the old invincible enthusiasm. The *Introduction* is a work of marvellous youth and strange joyousness. Actually we know it already: it is the *Règle* of Benoit de Canfeld, but written afresh in the intoxication of discovery and triumph, by a born writer, or rather by a cornet of the King of kings, to the music of drums.[1] Read, or rather hear, the following:

[1] How could M. Dedouvres have written that in the *Introduction* of P. Joseph "the mystics—S. Teresa, Père Benoit de Canfeld, Tauler, Ruysbroek, Harphius, S. Denis—are

If the true Friars Minor, whose habit recalls the colour and harshness of the eagle, grey and with feathers awry, can conserve the royalty and pre-eminence of their spiritual life, then will their day be glorious; the men clothed with sackcloth will be in the van of that splendid flight of eagles, they will speed on strong wings from their solitudes to preach the glory of God among the fiercest foes; like the eagle, that royal bird, they will bear in their mouths the flaming brand, as is foretold in the latter days of those two valiant leaders of the Christian armies, of great Elijah and unspotted Enoch.[1]

He depicts himself, when he pictures the novice-master raising each of the souls confided to him "to the sublimity of seraphic perfection."

When dominating the soul with authority, as from on high, he wheels and flies overhead in the flaming chariot of instruction, and bestows the habit and cloak which he had given at the entrance to the noviciate, no longer of common stuff in the form of a sorry hair-shirt as was the mantle of Elijah when he let it fall upon Elisha; but now at the time of profession he offers it as a garb of pure gold purged in the fire, dyed anew and shining with a splendour of sanctity in the flames surrounding his triumphal car.[2]

M. Dedouvres likes to compare Père Joseph with Bossuet. Possibly, but surely a Franciscan and seraphic Bossuet, who has not read the elder Balzac and who has forgotten his Terence. They are both eagles, but he with "feathers awry" has, it may be, a bolder glance towards the sun and his flight soars further into the regions of lightning. As for Bossuet, it is enough to have read a couple of pages of the *Introduction* to expect and dread this parallel, which reveals to us one of the pet weaknesses of Père Joseph. He is an orator too. Had he been more directly and profoundly mystical he would perhaps have spoken less brilliantly concerning the supreme mystery

praised but very little exploited"? (*Un précurseur de Bossuet, le Père Joseph écrivain.* Angers, 1898, p. 14.) The evidence is to the contrary. It is *à priori* knowledge that P. Joseph did not invent that science of mysticism which in his day had arrived at the summit of its development. Moreover, the inspiration of Canfeld is manifest from the first chapter of the *Traité de l'oraison.* "Brief formula and foundation of the *Méthode d'Oraison* under the metaphor of the sun." Cf. above pp. 118–9.

[1] *Méthode d'oraison de Père Joseph du Tremblay*, edited and annotated by Père Apollinaire de Valence (Le Mans, 1897). I quote throughout from this excellent reprint of the *Introduction*, although I fail to understand why Père Apollinaire should have simplified the title. The two or three ancient editions are very rare, but old and new editions alike have had small effect.

[2] *Méthode*, pp. 44–5.

which is consummated at the centre of the soul, far from the glittering zone where beautiful thoughts are ranged in order and periods elaborated. He certainly knows by personal experience the first steps of that ineffable life, but when he would venture on the heights, only by his genius does he seem to advance further than we can go ourselves.

He is a genius stern rather than tender, impassioned almost without intermission. We shall see him at times in his prophetic chariot sailing towards the stars. When he stoops to the low level of mankind he is no less arresting. Our vocation, he declares,

being for eagles, for seraphim even, yet some continue to plod along like oxen, and when, instead of immolating one's beasts (the lower nature), they nourish them with all care . . . such novices deserve to be sent back to munch hay in the manger of the world.[1]

Some, still steeped in the mire of an imperfect life, go on, like the frogs, sporting on green grass in the sunshine; that is to say, notwithstanding the impurity of their irreligion, and while they squat in the mud of their venial affections, they console themselves with the hope that God will be kind to them, a hope inspired rather by a gay optimism than by filial confidence. Now true servants of God regard all impure pleasures and creaturely quests as the depths of an ancient cistern defiled with slime, whence the pure water has long since flowed away.[2]

He has a humanist's scruples, but if he elaborates his metaphors it is because the images he uses have impressed themselves so deeply on him. François de Sales' more diversified and less intense mind was amused by these "frogs"; they merely disgusted Père Joseph, recalling to him the shallow optimism of the falsely devout, who, happy in a good digestion, thinks that everything is for the best in this world and the next.

His images are always pregnant with meaning.

Self-love, instructed by Satan the Arrogant in the school of indolent Nature, persuades some to believe that they are already entered into the chamber of the Bridegroom and admitted to the chaste repose of the nuptial couch. So, their heads swollen with pride and laziness, he lulls them to sleep in the stable of vain sentiments, wallowing on the dungheap of corrupt inclinations, while he makes them imagine that they are in the gilded chamber of the Unitive Life.[3]

[1] *Méthode*, p. 34. [2] *Ibid.*, pp. 374–5. [3] *Ibid.*, pp. 95–6.

Again, speaking of quietude in its first stages—"a dish of strawberries and cream"—which may well in truth prelude the mystic call, but often is no more than "a light touch of sensible consolation," we see, says he, that "the so-called touch" deserved no attention,

for it is of short duration and leaves the soul satiated, disinclined to go forward, and grown greedy for distractions; it shows that Nature having made her little meal and, like a snail, being nourished in her own shell by her own froth, and having pushed out her feeble horns of the mind with their blunted ends, retires into herself with no further appetite for advance in the strait path of prayer, acquisition of truth and true love.[1]

So long as he drives home his point he is not afraid of homeliness; he passes from the loftiest images to the most trivial, with the indifference of the true gentleman and true poet. Some, he says, waste all the time of prayer in scrupulously examining their consciences,

as a young giddy girl, who holds it sufficient adornment for her wedding-day, to amuse herself by dressing her nails; as if prayer solely consisted in cleaning oneself and shaking trivial grains of dust away. God certainly commands the soul, by His prophet, to cleanse and dust itself, but in the same text He desires that it should carry itself majestically and with royal bearing, attired in the habiliments of glory, which signifies that in prayer . . . we must not employ ourselves so much in scrubbing our faces, which often is but a smearing of them anew, increasing the wound by scratching it. . . . Not that it is not necessary to know and correct our faults, for (to neglect this) would be to induce ringworm and to let the scalp rot under a fine head-dress, but there is a season for all things.[2]

But Père Joseph as a writer would lead us farther than we would go; hitherto the study of him under this aspect has been too much neglected. Even upon a subject entirely mystical, he promises the non-religious reader considerable pleasure.

[1] *Méthode*, pp. 116–7.

[2] Cf. Dedouvres: *Un précurseur de Bossuet: le Père Joseph écrivain* . . . Angers, 1898. This is not more than a clever sketch from a particular point of view. The true object of M. Dedouvres is to place the works of Père Joseph among "the sources whence the eagle of Meaux deigned to draw." His proofs are not convincing. Two orators, both drawing continual inspiration from the Sacred Writings, must often present the same ideas under the same images. Besides, Bossuet had little taste for contemporary writers, and (save for a few Oratorians) still less for the mystics. Had he read and esteemed Père Joseph he would not have mocked at Harphius, and he would not have found the ordinary expressions of the mystics so bizarre.

VI. Although constantly drawing inspiration from Benoit de Canfeld and the old masters, Père Joseph modifies the Franciscan line of thought to some extent. Like most of the spiritual writers of his day, he passed through the school of S. Ignatius, deriving thence, no doubt, the idea of subjecting the freedom of the past to a more rigorous discipline, of making meditation an "art," a methodical exercise. Besides, he had become accustomed at an early date to the more or less similar methods which make either the orator, philosopher, strategist, or the bureaucrat. The religious world in which he had grown up was beginning to attach much importance to these questions of method. As has already been said, the men of the Counter-Reformation preached unanimously and insistently the return to the interior life, in plain words, the practice of prayer, an entire novelty to the devout laity and even to many of the religious—a novelty and, as it seemed, complicated at that. Before seriously engaging in such an enterprise a detailed itinerary was wanted, an *organon*, rules clear, precise and within the compass of everyone, recipes—in a word, a *method*. This explains in great part, be it remarked in passing, the immense success then enjoyed by the Jesuits. In the little book bequeathed to them by their founder they had a method ready to hand, and so admirably suited to the needs of the greater number, that it was speedily brought into use almost everywhere and even in the Benedictine abbeys, those strongholds of old-time devotion. Younger and more independent, the *Frères Mineurs* had no difficulty in reconciling the Seraphic Tradition with the demands of the new spirit. Studied from this point of view, the *Méthode d'oraison* arranged by Père Joseph for his Capuchin novices is highly interesting. It is very nearly the same as the Ignatian gymnastic, but practised in the expectation of the mystic gift.

Père Joseph drags us from the grotto of Manresa to raise us with him to Mount Alverno. His analyses are perhaps carried too far, the programme is too detailed, there is too much scholasticism, too many divisions and sub-divisions, there is the slightly pedantic stamp of the former lecturer in philosophy, but these few defects only throw into relief the excellence of the method, one of the most stimulating, seductive, and perhaps even one of the simplest that I know. As to the slight flaws indicated, they are overlooked in the splendour of the author's design, the fire of his style, and the sublimity of his aim. But we must allow that the method is not for ordinary mortals.[1]

It may be said that such teaching exceeds the capability of novices. Yes, if they were not Capuchin novices, to whom the Novice-master could say, like Samuel to Saul, when the latter was still an ass-driver, running after his father's she-asses: "To whom should belong the richest treasures of the Apostolic spirit and all the goods of the true Israelites, if not to thee and thy father's house?"[2]

The meditation of spiritual experts is not that of philosophers. Knowledge for the sake of knowledge does not suffice for it; mere satisfying of the spirit is never its end, but it always turns to love. On this point S. Ignatius is at one with Père Joseph, but the method of the latter limits far more strictly the part of the intellect, scarcely allotting it a third or at most half of the time dedicated to devotion. However, having narrowed the field for imagination and intellect, the Capuchin prescribes a more intense activity. Equilibrium being thus established, it can be maintained without paradox that the more intellectual of the two masters is not the Jesuit. Even in his prayers Père Joseph lets us see him as he is revealed by the rest of

[1] It is impossible here to enter upon a technical examination of this method, a brief summary must suffice. Three parts: preparation, meditation, affection. This recalls roughly the Ignatian division, of preludes, meditation, and colloquies; but on entering into details, many and profound differences become apparent.

(1) *Preparation.* Four acts: sincere intention, profound humiliation, consideration of the subject, repudiation of distractions. Herein one recognizes the Ignatian *preludes*, which, however, gain nothing, but rather lose, by being set out in this manner. Nevertheless few commentators on the *Exercises* have explained them with so much unction and force as Père Joseph (*Méthode*, pp. 73–4). Also Père Joseph appears to allot to this first part more time than did S. Ignatius.

(2) *Meditation*, that is to say application of the intellectual faculties (imagination, memory, intelligence) to a given subject. Instead of the divisions into heads of S. Ignatius, here there are four acts: (1) knowledge of God, prototype of that particular perfection under consideration; (2) knowledge of self; (3) knowledge of the operations or sufferings of the Saviour; (4) knowledge of the aim for which the Saviour worked and suffered. Here there seems to be a reminiscence of the famous *Contemplatio ad Amorem* which terminates the *Exercises*, and less clearly, of the meditation of the *Règne*. But it is significant that Père Joseph prescribed these four considerations from the outset for each of his exercises. According to him, meditation should occupy scarcely more than a quarter of the allotted time; twenty minutes out of an hour of prayer. This again is curious.

(3) *Affection.* Four acts again: (1) the offering—once more manifestly derived from the *Suscipe* that terminates the *Contemplatio ad Amorem*; (2) the demand; (3) imitation; (4) union. This last has three degrees which lead insensibly to the higher quietude of the mystics. Some excellent pages on this method are to be found in the *Vie de la Mère Marie Antoinette d'Orléans*, by M. l'Abbé Petit, Paris, 1879, Introduction, pp. 54–73.

[2] *Méthode*, p. 19.

his life, a philosopher by training and inclination alike, a humanist, an orator, a man of great projects, and in all his undertakings bubbling over with energy. Here, for example, is the charmingly vivid sketch of a meditation on the Infancy of Christ. The author begins by a warning against the temptation of a too restless activity. He demands nothing from us but " some acts of lively and vigilant faith." He has no wish that the soul should impress

> on the imagination, as with hammerstrokes, all the corporeal circumstances of this scene, in such measure that it is dissatisfied if it be not sensibly filled with consolation and admiration at each detail, winding with the Mother the swaddling clothes round the tender flesh of the Child, kindling the fire with Joseph, and, emboldened by the boldness and the privilege of the ox and the ass, warming Him with the breath of adoring kisses, and leaping with joy among the shepherds. In short, it is not necessary, for realization of all the lovely following of Bethlehem, to force upon the brain pictures in such sharp relief that they might have been hammered on an anvil, at cost of heavy mental effort.

This is perhaps a criticism of S. Ignatius or of some commentator on the *Exercises spirituels.* All he wants is a lively faith, without too much curiosity as regards seeing and feeling. Indeed,

> when our sentiment and human reason concentrate (upon a mystery) it is as if one tried at night, with a great bundle of damp straw, to inspect a beautiful picture: the smoke of such wavering and scanty illumination would obscure the greater part, even perhaps darken the painting. The glimmer is soon gone and in the end, to avoid burned hands, one must leave go and let the straw fall to the ground. My meaning is that fleshly knowledge, mere intellectual speculation on divers mysteries, causes much smoke and little light, nay, takes even away something of the splendour of these mysteries, makes them appear smoked to us, soon comes to an end, and is often extinguished by a variety of distractions. And even should our straw burn and remain lit to the end, yet in most cases it finishes in so many errors, vain speculations, and possibly unbeliefs and erroneous convictions, that one must needs drop it, as one would a dangerous fire.

He certainly has the knack of picturesque and pregnant allegory, at times even surpassing S. François de Sales himself. All that he has just said is absolutely well-balanced, but, when it comes to practice, he forgets his own lessons. Take, for instance, his instructions how to foster the act of lively and simple faith which he prescribes.

For better comprehension (he is still speaking of the mystery of the Crib) I should proceed to consider three things, which we may explain to ourselves by the following comparison of a picture.

Let us suppose that it is the finding of Moses in the reed coffer, on the bank of the Nile. On one side Pharaoh's daughter, on the other the mother and sister of the abandoned foundling, contemplate it with pleasure. In order to acquit myself fitly of the honour of beholding the portrait of so high a personage, I should see in it three things.

In other words, he proceeds to do—and with what animation—precisely what he has warned us against doing.

First, the little Moses shut up in his swaying bed near the bank—so much for the body of the scene; but for the body there must be a soul within and fair garments without. Then secondly, the fair robes and accoutrements of the picture are formed by the landscape and the accessories of the various figures, furnishing appropriate setting for the main subject. . . . For instance—

(Here we are, and in no danger of glossing over it)

I behold this ark—the cradle of that great Moses who will conduct many thousands of people dryshod through the sea—caught in the reeds and in peril of being swallowed up by this muddy slime, of being devoured by crocodiles and other serpents, inhabitants of the Egyptian stream. I behold the Princess walking abroad to take the air on the river bank, nay, rather conducted thither by divine providence, to give air and breath to the innocent prisoner stifled in the basket. I can see her touched with pity at the child's cries, but more clearly still, I see his sweet sister Miriam, transfixed between hope and fear—hope that this lady, with the tenderness of her sex, may be moved by compassion, half paralysed with fear lest this Egyptian be still barbarous at heart. . . . So much for the accoutrements and robes of this picture.

Thirdly, comes the spirit, the soul, invisible yet conceivable. From the waving reeds, from the bodily presentment, I lift my thoughts to the truth. Not only do I figure to myself, either the canvas representation, or the actual body of Moses present and living, as I might that of the infant Romulus cradled in a like ark or rushes and exposed to fortune; but by the graving-tool of faith, as Holy Scripture enables me, I engrave in my mind the outlines and traits of that rare and celestial spirit, the friend of God, with open face holding in his hand the keys of nature, like a good steward and *major-domo* of the house of God; who grasps the rod in his fist and with a single imperious movement puts to flight the waves of the sea, calls forth waters from the barren rocks, sets the angels to kneading manna in the air, wheeling above the heads of the Hebrews, in the pillar of smoke, as it were a portable oven to bake their celestial bread, furnishing them, moreover, in that same column with a screen against the ardent heats of the sun. . . .

Then ascribing to God all the rays of the heroic virtues of Moses, as to their sun, they serve three purposes for me: first, to recognize fully the greatness of this prophet before God; secondly, to see my own littleness in comparison with him; and thirdly, by my applying this full light on the circumstances described in the picture of the finding of Moses, they will become wholly illuminated anew for me, as by a lightning-flash of divinity, darting from the spirit of Moses over his infancy and the accompanying story.

Now, returning to our Crib, let us behold in it, as in a picture, these three (same) things. . . .[1]

Here we note a twofold activity, first visualization; secondly, the work of spiritualization, so to speak. The artist first, then the philosopher and theologian, and to the artist, whatever he may say, Père Joseph gives a free hand. Thus he shows us somewhere the Virgin "lodged in a grotto at Nazareth, hollowed in the rock with never a window, such as one sees on the banks of the Loire, where fishers and humble folk dwell."[2] Yet all this is a flight of fancy, to penetrate still more deeply "the spirit and soul" of the mysteries. From "the little Romulus" in his "coffer of reeds," from "the crocodiles" and "the Egyptian stream," he rises insensibly first to the heroic virtues of Moses, then to the Divine Sun of Whom these virtues are but the rays; or again from the little Moses to the Child Jesus, the way embracing the whole history of the people of God and the Gospels themselves. Certainly he cannot be accused of reducing the intellectual powers of the contemplative to inactivity; rather is there danger of his overtaxing them.

All this, however, to Père Joseph is but the prelude—short enough relatively—of actual prayer. Such intellectual exercises have no other aim than to guide and stimulate the affections of the will; these affections themselves, gaining in calm as they deepen, must

[1] *Méthode*, pp. 180–4. [2] *Les dix jours*, p. 197.

logically culminate in quietude, the Mystic Union. By this mystical orientation the method of Père Joseph is clearly differentiated from that of S. Ignatius, and rejoins the Franciscan tradition.

From its beginnings in prayer, the gates of the mystic life are thrown open to the Capuchin novice. If it is asserted that he may only practise this life after the two others (purgative and illuminative),

I deny it absolutely (declares Père Joseph), for that would be contrary to the primary principle which demands that God should from the first be loved with all our forces, that every storey of our palace should be thrown open to Him as the absolute lord, Who receives all the keys together. But it must be said that it is necessary to practise walking in these three ways, not one after another, but one more than another, according to the type of soul concerned.

Whatever his condition, it is imperative for each to know in the wildest tempest how to raise his eyes to the sovereign Good, as towards a clear light shining on him from afar, to Whom he tries to aspire by this act of Union, not aspiring to the privilege of the perfect, not with full sail set and in the open sea of total abandonment of ordinary methods, as do greater ships; but as coasting along familiar shores, making headway without casting aside meditation and the other acts prescribed by the Method, which is the guide to Union.[1]

This statement is of extreme importance. Not that I ascribe to Père Joseph the pre-eminent authority of a John of the Cross, or the almost infallible wisdom of a François de Sales. On the contrary, I think he knows the final secrets of Mysticism only through books, and that, from another standpoint, his intellect is powerful rather than discriminating. But he represents the most venerable tradition; he says nothing that he has not tested on a number of young souls. Further, of all the spiritual writers of his day Richelieu's helper is assuredly the least suspect as regards illusion in these matters. Highly intellectual, keen and, I add, very suspicious, he nosed out false mystics in all directions. France would not have had prisons enough for the Quietists multiplying in his imagination all over the kingdom, as we shall see presently. Nevertheless, unwearyingly and with unshaken conviction, he reiterates such principles as these:

To allow beginners a certain access to (mystic) union cannot fairly be considered blameworthy. We must not hold them continually under the iron rod of the active life, which would be to treat them

[1] *Méthode*, pp. 105–6.

like children of high rank confined in college under a severe pedagogue, who will never let them see their friends. Such rigour may at times be a necessary evil, to prevent a greater, if the youths are tempted to debauchery, or if the luxury of home made them refuse to leave it and return to school.

He is always happy in his allegory. Two strokes, and the whole of Quietism is defined. But even so, he continues,

such slavish captivity will never cease to be an evil which may perhaps make them stupid and ignorant, of a pedantic and schoolboyish disposition, unfitting them for the activities and social intercourse proper to their degree.

These last four lines are of pure gold and of universal currency. It is easy to forget that, if the propaganda of Mysticism is not always free from danger, the zeal of anti-mystics may be as harmful. They are dull and clumsy tutors, who, to safeguard their pupils from the seductions of romanticism, teach them nothing further than spelling. Innocent tyrants, but like the man of the Temple who wanted to turn Louis XVII into a clodhopper. Obsessed by the spectre of Quietism, their narrow, grovelling prudence enervates and stifles elect souls, disgusts them with the interior life, sometimes even impels them to scepticism. I do not say this on my own authority.

Truly, without this interior union, the yoke of the Christian school is hard; how much more that of the austere religions which are limited, like Judaism, to mere ceremonies and exterior penances. Now God does not pour His sacred oil on the feet and lower extremities of the soul, but, as at the sacring of kings and high priests, on the head, that it may flow down over all. The director who without special cause is afraid to instruct the neophyte in some measure in the Act of Union, resembles one who should dread uncovering the head of a child called to the crown, but would keep it always hooded, lest it should be chilled. Yet for lack of his anointing, the affairs of his kingdom may go badly. In like manner the soul not taught to reign over her inclinations by the action of grace—so abundantly received in the act of union, when the spiritual sceptre that gives authority over feelings is placed in her hand—often, as time goes on, finds her natural passions so embroiled and her interior life so confused that it is hard to re-establish order. Then, losing courage and shrinking from the pains needed to attain the tranquillity of the unitive life, the soul acts as did poor Mephibosheth, royal child of the house of Saul but a cripple and a man of small courage, who preferred rather to live at ease as a private individual than to attempt to maintain his rights and prevail against his mighty foes.[1]

Directors who do not wish for mystics, or who wish for as few as possible, beware, you will add to the number of unbelievers! For many a one to renounce, from inclination or constraint, this higher life, this royal gift, is to renounce the supernatural and all grace. Fénelon may shock or amuse you; as you like—but take from him his doctrine of pure love, and you will turn him into a second Bayle, more seductive and more dangerous.

Logical even with himself, Père Joseph minutely describes the mystic union, in this little book which is after all nothing more than a manual for novices. This forms the longest part of the *Introduction*, and, if not the most illuminating part, is at least the finest. If François de Sales, soon to treat of the same subject in the *Traité de l'amour de Dieu*, dazzles and delights us less, he enlightens and persuades us more, for in these ineffable matters there is no oratorical fire without smoke. No true mystic would hesitate between these two books, yet the panting lyricism of Père Joseph has a beauty of its own.[2]

God deigns to enter into us and makes us enter into Him by a mutual immersion, a reciprocal absorption; which is expressed in Holy Scripture by the command to open the mouth and He will fill it. This expansion means that the soul, in this degree of union (the first), should stretch all the fullness of its desire and enlarge the capacity of its free will, that is to say, produce acts of the purest and greatest love that it can conceive.

The definition is doubtless clearer to the author himself than to the majority of his readers. The orator must come to the aid of the theologian, the impotent analyst.

And it is not sufficient to open the mouth in everyday wise, as for such ordinary actions as eating, speaking, breathing; rather must it be after the manner of him who long and violently pursuing some madly desired quarry, stops at last out of breath, with open mouth and feeling his heart beating, as though he were about to die.

[1] *Méthode*, pp. 398–402.

[2] "May I venture here to parallel two works of widely different fate," asks M. Dedouvres, "and shall I be believed when I say that two books, of which one from the first moment of publication was circulated throughout Europe, and the other has had to wait wellnigh three hundred years to pass beyond the convent thresholds . . . have merits, if not in common, at least equivalent, and, by their differing qualities, lay equal claim to attention and esteem? Such is nevertheless my conviction." (*Revue des Facultés catholiques de l'Ouest*, Oct., 1897.)

Some yield their will to God, to eat, that is to receive some interior sweetness; others, to speak, and derive matter for discourses; but others again, to breathe, to relax and refresh their spirit, stifled in the pursuit of the cares of this world.

All this is not to love God perfectly. One must expel the life of self-love with great gasps, holding nature at bay, and, at the end of a stern chase after perfection, breathe out and as it were, merge self mouth to mouth in God, fusing all one's will in His. For, at the finish of this course, He awaits us with open arms, to receive the soul running after Him out of self, and through the royal doors of His lips receiving it with all fair courtesy and gracious kisses of peace, suffers it to enter into the cabinet of His Heart.

So Scripture in the Hebrew tells us that Moses died upon the lips of God; for, after having pursued for a lifetime the quest of his Lord's glory, after having so oft spoken to Him face to face, not so much by the sight of his eyes as by the free interchange of hearts, after so many seas, deserts and mountains crossed, he expires, yields up the ghost, dies of the kisses from the lips of God.

O sacred Pyx of thrice blessed lassitudes! O Treasure-house of Divine repose, apportioned to the proportions of our soul, since God opens to it in measure as it desires to open unto Him. . . .[1]

Is it my fault or his, if the author seems longwinded? No matter; he fulfils his humble mission, which here is to excite in us the desire of the promised land. He himself has passed the first defences which separate us from marvellous country; but his personal mystic experiences are conducted in his own manner, strategically, as on a crusade, and, if I may risk the expression, beating the drum. Even Quietude for him is emotional and militant. Read, for instance, the palpitating and sublime instruction on The Second Degree of Union. That gives the true P. Joseph at his best.

David, engulfed in tempest and as it were embedded in the mire, ceases not to be devoured with zeal for the house of God; he stretches forth the hand of his aspirations to build the walls of Sion, to restore the honour of the Church and compress in his spiritual embrace heaven, earth, seas, and all time to come, to constrain them to render acts of thanksgiving to his Lord.

O arms wider than the heavens which contain beneath their rounded arches, not only all the centuries destined to roll, but also the generations of the creatures appertaining thereto! The desire of a soul jealous for God's honour contains and environs all blessed

[1] *Méthode*, pp. 355-7.

spirits during all time, delights itself in their felicity, honours the saints of heaven, seeks comfort for all in purgatory, and cherishes close intimacy with the faithful yet upon this earth. Who can assign it limits, since itself embraces God? It rejoices in His glory, and although it beholds the limits of its aspirations far surpassed, yet it forthwith desires greater.

The arms of such a soul grow each day, as those of an infant stretch out to cling round the neck of its mother. God holds thus His children and true servants clinging around His neck, caresses them like a tender mother, carries them at the breast, bears them on His knees, lets them see the infinity of His arms, invites them to measure theirs against the power of His mighty Hand, in order that they should be encouraged to bring by armsful, from the four corners of the earth, millions of souls in choicest gift . . .

Thus, in this Second Degree of Union, the soul sets itself with all its powers to work for God in tasks of obedience, holy example, and love. With Moses, it extends its arms and puts to flight serried ranks of atheists, heretics, infidels and all the other adversaries which Satan puts in the field against the Church.[1]

A poor enough explanation of the Mystic Union, which, though it certainly does not make zeal of little account, must not be confounded with it. On one side, the centre of the soul, the annihilation of human acts; on the other, the arms, always and ever the arms! Yet once more no matter; they are the arms of a giant. "O arms wider than the heavens!" How small must Richelieu, so fascinating to him at other times, have often appeared to Père Joseph!

VII. This last reflection leaves us on the brink of the great problem which I formulated at the outset but which I shall not try to solve. During the long years when Europe hung upon his name, continually associated with that of the Great Cardinal, what was Père Joseph's private judgement upon himself? Did he, when in the livery of another master, then and always consider himself the disciple of Canfeld? In his prayers, always ardent, did it never happen to him to hear the words of a Greater than Richelieu: *Martha, Martha, sollicita es et turbaris erga plurima*, or to meditate on the reply once made to a prophet: "The Lord was not in the earthquake, nor in the fire, nor the tempest"? I cast no doubt on either the solidity of his virtue or the fervour of his zeal; the difficulty is more

[1] *Méthode*, pp. 365–7.

delicate, and does not concern his sincerity. The moralist subtle enough to tackle this problem would doubtless find some clues in the numberless documents kept in the archives of the *Calvaire*.

Of all the achievements of Père Joseph (writes M. Dedouvres) that which adds brightest lustre to his zeal and his religious spirit, for which he laboured most and produced his most spiritual writings, is the congregation of Benedictine nuns of *Notre Dame du Calvaire*, otherwise known as *Filles du Calvaire*. This community was an outcome of the Reform of the great Order of Fontevrault, and was established at Poitiers on October 25, 1617, by Père Joseph, with the collaboration of Madame Antoinette d'Orléans, daughter of Léonor d'Orléans, Duc de Longueville, and his wife Marie de Bourbon. Madame d'Orléans, however, dying on April 25, 1618, six months after the foundation of the *Calvaire*, Père Joseph had to continue their joint enterprise alone.[1]

Here let me digress. Of Antoinette d'Orléans herself I do not intend to speak, for lack of space, but as in this volume the two families from which this princess sprang will be encountered a score of times, it may be well to recall in a few words the genealogy of two of our fiefs or clans of Mysticism. Antoinette d'Orléans was by birth a Longueville and by marriage a Gondi. Note the great names. Her father, Léonor d'Orléans, the Duc de Longueville, was descended from Charles V of France through Jean d'Orléans, the Bastard of Dunois, Comte de Longueville. Marie de Bourbon, Duchess de Longueville, was herself descended from S. Louis, and of the six children by this marriage, several play their parts in French history.

First of these is Henri d'Orléans, the then Duc de Longueville, whose son, another Henri, married a sister of the Great Condé, the Duchesse de Longueville of the Fronde, of Port-Royal, of M. Cousin. Then comes François, whose wife Anne de Caumont figures among the saints of the time of Louis XIII; next, Catherine, demoiselle de Longueville (†1638), foundress of the first French Carmel, with the aid of her devout sister Marguerite d'Estouteville; finally Antoinette herself, and Éléonore de Matignon, whose daughter was a nun of the *Calvaire*.

Antoinette introduces us into another world, less royal, but no less remarkable, and with no lack of saints. She married Charles de

[1] *Le Père Joseph et le Sacré-Cœur*, Angers, 1899, pp. 14–15.

Gondi, Marquis de Belle-Ile, son of Albert de Gondi, Duc de Retz, Marshal of France, and nephew of Pierre, Cardinal de Gondi, Bishop of Paris, who died in 1616. Charles de Gondi had three brothers, all interesting, and a sister no less so, known to us as the admirable Marquise de Maignelais; the brothers were Henri de Gondi, Bishop of Paris, Cardinal de Retz, who died in 1622; Philippe Emmanuel de Gondi, superintendent of galleys, who installed S. Vincent de Paul in his own house and died a priest of the Oratory (his son was Jean-François-Paul, Cardinal de Retz, coadjutor of Paris); finally Jean-François de Gondi, who before his death in 1654 saw the Bishopric of Paris become an Archbishopric, and who had for coadjutor his very illustrious nephew, a man with no inclination towards Mysticism. Antoinette, foundress of the *Calvaire*, was therefore sister of the Princess de Longueville, foundress of Carmel, sister-in-law of the Marquise de Maignelais, and aunt of Cardinal de Retz.[1]

To return to the *Calvaire*. This community offers another example of those happy *modernizations* which were then being attempted everywhere. Instead of a superstitious adherence to a rigid and fatally sterile *primitivism*, the reformers of the Orders sought and found with ease a harmonious adjusting of the customs of the past to the holy aspirations of the present. As Père Joseph learned from S. Ignatius, so the rules of the Daughters of the *Calvaire* were inspired equally by the spirit of S. Francis of the Stigmata and by that of S. Benedict; a happy conjunction which leaves intact all that is best in the Benedictine tradition. "I have remarked," writes an unimpeachable authority, the famous Grégoire Tarisse, Général de Saint-Maur, "that no child of S. Benedict in France ever entered better into his spirit than he to whom God Himself communicated it, namely, Père Joseph."[2] And that nothing should be lacking to this large-minded and generous eclecticism, he even avows that this Capuchin, in his exhortations to the Benedictines of the *Calvaire*, preached insistently and with prophetic clearness, that

[1] The two families speedily died out. Of the two sons of the Duchesse de Longueville, Jean-Louis d'Orléans, a priest, died in 1654; his brother Charles-Paris, Duc de Longueville and elected King of Poland, being killed at the passage of the Rhine in 1672, leaving no children. As for the Gondi, the last representative of the family was a great-granddaughter of Antoinette, by name Marie-Catherine, who died Superior-General of the *Calvaire* in 1716.

[2] Dedouvres, *Le Père Joseph et le Sacré-Cœur*, p. 19.

devotion to the Sacred Heart which a century later would be denounced as a Jesuit innovation, and against which would be instinctively ranged the "primitivism" of Port-Royal.[1] "What passes credence," adds Père Tarisse,

is that the time usually occupied in relaxation and amusement by those in heavy employments of State, Père Joseph used for more seclusion and for giving spiritual conferences to the good nuns of the *Calvaire*, which he did with so much fervour, illumination and high mystic teaching that the most learned contemplatives with careful preparation could never have equalled him in lucidity and ease, however prolonged their studies. One could never have believed that a mind oppressed by cares so alien, even contrary to devotion, could have accomplished such results, needing neither time nor other preparation, nothing save mere change of *milieu.*[2]

It was truly a miracle of united fervour and genius.

For his Daughters, M. Dedouvres informs us, Père Joseph composed

divers short *Traités, Constitutions, Exercises spirituels*, la *Vocation des religieuses de la première règle de Saint Benoit ;* also at least a part of the *Histoire de Madame Antoinette d'Orléans ;* and finally—I reckon only those still preserved—more than eleven hundred letters of direction and four hundred exhortations. Altogether his output, if it were printed *in toto*, would run to not less than thirty octavo volumes, each of five hundred pages.[3]

A fragment of this immense work, doubtless never to be published as a whole, has recently been printed—the retreat of the *Dix Jours*—preached in 1635, three years before Père Joseph's death, for the *Calvaire* nuns of one of the Paris houses. It is a singular work, strong and sublime in parts, but in others confused, unequal, crabbed, inferior in all points to the *Introduction.* In a word, it is a disappointment! It is now 1635. He has changed greatly from his triumphant youth; has grown sad and disillusioned, even bitter; criticising other religious communities with morose candour; not altogether sure of his own Daughters. "I tell you," he cries often, "that there are few who follow the spirit of the *Calvaire.*"[4] He feels

[1] Dedouvres, *ibid.* In this precious *brochure* M. Dedouvres has brought together a considerable number of quotations which show decisively that Père Joseph must be ranked among the most direct forerunners of Marguerite-Marie.

[2] *Ibid.*, p. 19.

[3] *Ibid.*, pp. 17, 18.

[4] The *Dix Jours*, p. 411.

around him jealousies, ambitions, certain intrigues. "There are many who wish to meddle, to put the sickle in to the harvest of others." He has a grudge not only against the Quietists, but one would say against nearly all the devout of the day; if he praises S. Paul with the fine enthusiasm of old, it is to add immediately, "But I know not where else such spiritual lights are to be sought, or what alembic of the spirit may be found in order to follow his example."[1] He is dissatisfied with himself.

I know from myself who, in punishment of my shortcomings and for having misused the time allotted to me, have now no leisure to think of the interior life, being always distracted by multitudinous occupations, the evil of not being united with God, of not surrendering the soul to the spirit of Jesus, that He may guide it according to His Will; and how necessary it is for that, to be in the company of the good, where each may strengthen and support the other.

All the saints say the same, perhaps someone remarks. Well, let none imagine that I am putting Père Joseph on the stool of repentance and letting his confession condemn him. It is only a question of becoming acquainted with him, of pitying him, and perhaps of loving him all the more.

When I reflect on that and see how I and the majority of creatures live, I believe that this world is a fable and that we have all lost our reason, and differ only in a few externals from the pagans and the Turk. Were not the Church pure and the early spirit yet within some few souls, I believe that God would consume all the universe, antedating the Final Judgement, or else that He would create a new world.[2]

The crusade against the Crescent had been one of the enthusiasms of his whole life, and now, "not having lived in good company," he is tempted to see no difference between the Christian and the Turk! Could there be a sadder reversal?

But I will not conclude with this cry of anguish. Père Joseph deserves another epitaph from us, that marvellous paragraph which he wrote in the first days of his Franciscan gaiety, in the noviciate at Meudon, far from Richelieu!

As, when the Seraphim thundered on high the Thrice Holy, the hinges of the Temple trembled as though about to open of themselves,

[1] The *Dix Jours*, p. 299. [2] *Ibid.*, pp. 299, 300.

so when seraphic souls, wheresoever they may be, bow before God, their faces covered in the devotion of their retreat, their wings unfurled in readiness to bear to men the flaming messages of Divine Love; then will Christians, each in his appointed condition, be moved to serve our common King, according to the prophecy received by S. Francis from His lips, that the state of the Church will be happy when the Franciscans acquit themselves of their duty.[1]

[1] *Méthode*, p. xxv. I can only cite here the more famous upholders of Franciscan tradition during this period, but there were others, for example, Père Simon of Bourg-en-Bresse, who, in his *Saintes élévations de l'âme à Dieu par tous les degrés d'oraison* (Avignon, 1657), reiterates the teaching of Benoit de Canfeld. Père Simon had also another master, Père Archange Ripault, who, he mentions, "has worthily written on this matter." (This Père Ripault we have already met in a romance of Camus.) Simon is convinced that God calls the greater number to the mystic life. "The trouble is that the majority of preachers, doctors, confessors, and directors entirely ignore these divine things, at least in practice and experience . . . despising, depreciating and calumniating them, and withdrawing souls from them" (p. 38). "And yet these things are not ineffable or out of the way, save in erroneous opinion or rather through the indolence and corruption of our vicious nature; nor do they demand lofty speculations, but consist altogether of love, so that surely they are for all and particularly for the most simple, and truly require nought save a good, true, sincere and ardent will. . . . It is then but abuse and ignorance not to dare to aspire to these things from fear of Satan's illusions and snares, for the dangers of the ocean and its pirates do not affright avaricious merchants from navigation and the rich marts of the Indies" (pp. 34–5).

CHAPTER IV

MADAME ACARIE AND THE CARMELITES

1. *Madame Acarie*

MADAME ACARIE, or, to call her by the style of her times, Mademoiselle Acarie, or by her name in religion and as beatified, Marie de l'Incarnation, is assuredly the most important person with whom this volume deals. François de Sales himself must yield her precedence, if only that his Annecy was not yet part of France and is not Paris, although this of course is to be understood solely in reference to the personal influence that Madame Acarie, who wrote nothing, exercised during her life. The activity of this woman, an invalid and an ecstatic, who died at fifty-two, was miraculous. To her is due the introduction into France of the Carmelite Order founded by S. Teresa, which at her death already numbered seventeen houses on French soil; as much as and even more than Mme de Sainte-Beuve, she laboured to develop the Ursulines; the reform of the Benedictine Abbeys owes her much, and countless other works also occupied her; lastly, she knew, grouped, stimulated and directed wellnigh all the leading religious spirits of her day. It is not too much to say that, of all the spiritual hearths kindled in the reign of Henri IV, none burned more brightly or equalled in intensity that of the Hôtel Acarie.

Yet this glory has departed, our Carmelites and some few pious souls alone keep its memory alive. On the testimony of a trustworthy witness, the Abbé Boucher, who in 1800 brought out a new Life of Mme Acarie, "this saintly woman . . . was scarcely remembered," when, towards the end of the eighteenth century, the Church beatified her. Things have not changed much since then, despite the efforts of Mgr. Dupanloup, the biographer of Bérulle, the Abbé Houssaye, the translator of S. Teresa, P. Bouix, and sundry others. "The life of Mme Acarie has been somewhat forgotten," wrote Cardinal

Richard in 1893, and the polite euphemism scarcely veils a too evident fact. Who can explain the posthumous history of the saints? A vast current of devotion to-day, for instance, flows towards the tomb of a young Carmelite, recently dead, scarcely known during her lifetime, but whose beatification seems probable.[1] Yet will Catholics of the twenty-first century know aught of the name of Sœur Thérèse de l'Enfant Jésus? Will the quiet stream of the Sâone, tranquil to-day as in the day when the feet of Roman legions forded it—*incredibili lenitate*—three centuries hence still see innumerable pilgrims crossing to the shrine of the Curé d'Ars?

The pages that follow will hardly resuscitate Madame Acarie. For my part, I fail to see her. She was one of those perfect beings that are the despair of artists. Her own contemporaries could not depict her as they knew her. "She had the gift, no small one, of impressing souls seriously," wrote her first biographer.[2] For indeed, when one was with this woman, one did not consider whether she were lovable, did not love her, but remained wonder-struck at the light of an almost absolute perfection. Yet one must not imagine a morose and rigid virtue. "Her conversation was affable and frank, gay rather than sad; she was accessible, sweet and modest, making it easy for souls to unbosom themselves."[3] None could be humbler or simpler. She did not lack either vivacity—for she was naturally eager—or grace, although, perhaps—we emphasize our "perhaps"—she may not have had the bloom of imagination or of wit. To speak of her charm would be inappropriate. Her presence inspires a sentiment, much deeper than respect, for which the French language has no name;—*awe* is the word used by the English, doubtless more familiar than we with such feelings. Even this word, when applied to Madame Acarie, needs to be made lighter, more tender. Among the nuns who went to consult her after she had become a Carmelite, "there was one who dared not address her, because she had seen her so honoured in the world and so serious in speech, and could only murmur, 'Sister, I cannot speak to you, I am too afraid of you; I came here only because our Mother desired it.'"[4] This was not ordinary timidity, but, I repeat, a sentiment entirely religious

[1] [She was beatified 1922, canonized 1925. Tr.]

[2] Duval, *La vie admirable de . . . Mlle Acarie*, Paris, 1893, p. 63.

[3] *Ibid.*, p. 13.

[4] *Ibid.*, p. 283.

which will help us more than anything else to define Madame Acarie and her prodigious influence. No more need be said before tackling this chapter, as formidable as it is fascinating. Of the three saints that stand out among the greatest, born in the last years of this extraordinary sixteenth century in France, Barbe Acarie (1566), Jeanne de Chantal (1572), Marguerite d'Arbouze (1580)[1], the two latter appear less far removed from us and more attractive. Less enthusiastic than the Baronne de Chantal, less many-sided and sensitive, on the other hand Madame Acarie does not transport us into the Middle Ages like Marguerite d'Arbouze, whose whole history is poetry. The Golden Legend could not have contained this woman in whom the incomprehensible gravity of holiness shines with almost unique glory.

Three years after the death of the saint, already beatified by the popular voice, Dr. André Duval published her Life (1621), which in 1627 had run into seven editions and, translated into many languages, was soon spread throughout Europe. A book of the first class, later biographers, the excellent Boucher, for instance, have done little more than transcribe it with some amplifications. Since, by some inexplicable oversight, the work was not given to the only writer capable of accomplishing it perfectly, I mean Mlle de Fontaines (Madeleine de Saint-Joseph), the next best for the task was Duval. Michel de Marillac, heavier perhaps and of less colour, had been at first approached, but had refused out of humility, and confined himself to writing out the memoirs which Duval, I think, reproduced without alteration.

By good fortune the indefatigable Père Binet, himself an intimate friend of Madame Acarie, did not put himself forward, thus sparing this delicate memoir more than one misfortune. He collaborated, it is true, with Duval, but, his professional honour not being in question, he laid aside for a time his florid verbiage. Several others, notably the daughters of Madame Acarie, likewise confided their recollections and impressions to Duval, who worked up these various testimonies into a successful book. Duval is not a great writer, but his fine French is nevertheless remarkable for its ease, breadth and sureness of touch. One can never admire too much these men of

[1] I do not mention here Mlle de Fontaines-Maran, as great certainly, but whose name is less known.

the old Sorbonne, they knew so much and never lacked words to express their knowledge. Duval is Theology incarnate; he never lays aside his doctor's robe, which, however, is not stiff and falls into fine folds. The model which occupies him does not distract him from his contemplation of first principles, and the vast general views sketched at the opening of his chapters give to his work, in other respects flexible enough, a singular force and majesty. For instance, before relating how Madame Acarie "carried herself towards her neighbour" and "the great fruit she bore in regard to that," "there are," he tells us, "many who are all that can be desired in private life, but few who converse fittingly in public. To be a good man and a good citizen are two different things; one is concerned with the man in himself, the other with his public dealings; many have suffered loss by intercourse with the neighbours who have been thought angels, before meeting in the flesh."[1] Again, writing on the saint's ecstasies: "We do not range ravishments and ecstasies among the number of beneficent graces, because they are to be found among evil-doers as among men of goodwill and of virtue. Some Platonist philosophers even have made them matters of experiment, by means of a strong and vehement concentration of their minds upon some object, and by the deceits of the malignant spirit, which led several of them (*several*, not *all*—in 1621—this view is significant!) to seduce others by wonder at these extraordinary manifestations."[2] Again, he speaks with vivid energy of "the emotion of the inferior appetite towards God," of this animal part of men which is "the seat of sensible devotion," which must be "seriously regulated and controlled."[3] A professional controversialist, he does not neglect the converting value of the life-story that he tells. If the virtues of this Frenchwoman of to-day were not published, he writes, France would fall below "other nations which in this century have been favoured by Heaven in the matter of illustrious saints, and France is seemingly more interested in that matter than the rest of Christendom seeing that she has in many places such a number of heretics; presumably, reading this Life, they will be confounded, seeing none among themselves honoured with great miracles, as she of whom we write has been honoured."[4]

[1] Duval, *ibid.*, Chap. IV. p. 58.
[2] *Ibid.*, p. 507.
[3] *Ibid.*, pp. 485–6.
[4] *Ibid.*, p. xxii.

Yet there is no exaggeration. I do not know how he manages, grave and restrained as he is, never to appear cold. "That which completely inflamed her," he says of the saint, "set her soul on fire, *if one may use the expression*, was the Holy Sacrament."[1] He considers daring an image which to us to-day is obvious. Nevertheless he employs it, heightening its effect by his very hesitation. But why specify details which the reader will soon notice for himself? One more masterpiece in a religious literature so rich as ours is scarcely worth stopping for. But this is more than a masterpiece. The surprising thing is to see the whole Sorbonne, in the person of its most illustrious representative, setting the seal of its approval publicly and solemnly on the triumph of Mysticism. A fine page of the Notice to the Reader deserves careful attention.

Even without these reasons (just cited) I should have held it advisable to make this admirable Life known to our age, although, as far as I am personally concerned, I was for some time withheld from putting my hand thereto, not considering myself equal to do it worthily, since it seemed to me that I had not the requisite experience of the extraordinary things to be read herein in almost every chapter, and consequently I could not describe them fitly. Moreover, one must be a saint to write the lives of saints. . . . Nevertheless, as it is not imperative that the trumpeters who inspire knights to battle should themselves be of like courage (*athletæ suis incitatoribus fortiores sunt*) so neither is it requisite that those who write the biographies of persons illustrious in saintliness and perfection should themselves be as holy and perfect; it is enough if they desire perfection and are chafed that they have it not; by this temper they are fitted to speak and write.[2]

It must not be concluded from this touching avowal that the author did not know at least the lowest degrees of mystic union; but in any case Duval, measured against Madame Acarie, was certainly but a novice. Besides, he was slow to believe and was persuaded, like his great friends the Jesuits, that "there are few souls attracted towards God in extraordinary ways."[3] Essentially a scholar, eager in his work and husbanding his time, the slightest distraction irritated him. "There is nothing more disconcerting," he says somewhere, "or which distracts attention more effectually, than the carillon of bells."[4] How gallantly nevertheless he quitted his books, deserting his echoing

[1] Duval, *ibid.*, p. 476.
[2] *Ibid.*, pp. xxii–xxiii.
[3] *Ibid.*, p. 494.
[4] *Ibid.*, p. 471.

but secluded retreat on the hill of S. Geneviève, to face the traffic as far as the Rue des Juifs and the Hôtel Acarie; how gallantly he set out later for Amiens or Pontoise eager to contemplate once more that which books may describe but which they cannot show, the ecstasies of a saint. He was not on terms of close intimacy with Madame Acarie, and she told him, so it seems, hardly anything of the sublime secret that she cherished within. No matter! The secret in some degree shone in her face—a distant and silent revelation, but enough to enrapture Dr. Duval.

Barbe Avrillot, to give the saint her maiden name, was born in Paris on February 1, 1566, probably in the Rue des Mauvais-Garçons. "Nicolas Avrillot, her father, *seigneur* de Champlâtreux near Luzarches, financier to the Chamber of Paris and Chancellor of the Queen of Navarre (Marguerite rather than Jeanne), was an excellent man, strongly attached to the Catholic faith, for him, as for many others, a motive for entering the *Ligue*. He was ruined by it, and after the death of his wife became a priest,"[1] as did the father of another noted Carmelite, M. de Fontaines-Maran, and at a later date the father of Bossuet. Her mother, of a good Parisian family older than that of her husband, was Marie Luillier. On the mother's side Barbe was a cousin of Mme de Sainte-Beuve (Madeleine Luillier) and (in another generation) of the Père Honoré de Champigny already met with in these pages. From the little we are told of the saint's parents, I imagine that she grew up in a rather gloomy atmosphere. Her mother seems to have been harsh, even violent; her father, better possibly, yet stiff and repelling; Barbe herself timid and frightened. Her father always alarmed her, as we shall see her husband doing later, and it is indeed astonishing that a nature so long under constraint should have kept latent so much initiative and courage. As a child, she was never really herself except when near one of her aunts, in a convent of strict obedience to which she had been sent; it was a delightful house, which she frequently visited in years to come and desired to see once more before quitting the world.[2] There

[1] Boucher, *ibid.*, p. 5.

[2] She made her first Communion at twelve years of age. Duval sees in this an instance of her precocious saintliness, "for," says he, "in these days folk did not frequently communicate, neither brought they the children so early" (p. 4). It may be observed that the habit of belated first Communions did not, as is sometimes asserted, come from the Jansenists. When Jansenius was born (1585) Barbe was already married.

assuredly the first ideas of vocation came to her; she wished to be a religious of the Hôtel Dieu in Paris, Duval tells us, to serve the poor "who assemble there in such numbers that the smell is very trying."[1] "But her mother did not agree," she was determined to marry off her only child, willing or unwilling. So she was married as soon as possible. At sixteen and a half Barbe became "Mademoiselle Acarie" (August 24, 1582).

"King's councillor and master-in-ordinary of the Chamber of Finance of Paris," like his father-in-law Avrillot and several of the Luillier family, Pierre Acarie had played his part in general history, having been one of the forty Parisians who had formed the council of the "valiant Prince d'Aumale," and with this chief had suffered a fairly long exile after the victory of Henri IV. He was nicknamed the lackey of the *Ligue*, if Maimbourg is to be believed, but the latter was no lover of Councillor Acarie and reproached him tartly for his poor imitation of his wife's virtues. We can put up with the sobriquet the more easily, since in my opinion the biographers of Madame Acarie have painted him too kindly. His legend has gone on growing and receiving embellishment from honest Duval, who gives as much praise as he can, down to indulgent Boucher, who graces him with nearly all the virtues. He will be less attractive to readers who have met hundreds of Parisian husbands of his type—hotheaded, fantastic, indolent, teasing, passing from coarse laughter to anger with disconcerting rapidity, by turns the delight and terror of their neighbours, in other respects remaining good, kind-hearted Christians.

In his frequent accesses of violence the Jesuit Père Commolet alone could bring him to reason. On one occasion, Duval relates, Madame Acarie was pressingly wanted at Pontoise, on the business of a newly founded monastery, "but in spite of sundry letters summoning her, she could not gain her husband's permission for her journey. . . . Père de Bérulle, knowing well how concessions were to be extracted from his cousin, M. Acarie, advised me to resort to the reverend father Commolet, who had a great influence on him. I found this good Father, who spoke to him, and the permission was forthwith granted."[2] He was somewhat given to the pleasures of the table, and rebelled against the physicians who wanted to diet him; his wife not venturing to contest the point, "by reason of her too

[1] Duval, *ibid.*, p. 7.

[2] Duval, *ibid.*, p. 34.

great respect for him, sent a message to Père Commolet to come and see him, and the invalid instantly deferred to the remonstrances of this good Father."[1] "Too great respect" is a way of expressing it. Duval in another passage is more outspoken and compares her to "a child fearing the rod and trembling before its master."[2] Frère Edmond de Messa, who had belonged to the Acarie household before entering the Oratoire, says: "that several times (his mistress), returning home with him from town or her devotions, had trembled with fear lest her husband should be vexed."[3] No doubt he enjoyed this attitude, though sometimes he pretended to desire "that she were not so cautious and so respectful with him."[4]

He comes into our narrative in an amusing story, which is memorable. One day, towards the sixth year of their marriage, Pierre Acarie surprised his young wife absorbed in reading the Romance of *Amadis*, lent her by a friend. Other romances were on the table, and a scene followed, doubtless both lover-like and uproarious. He did not approve of romances, at least for his wife. But being good-natured and not wishing to discourage the taste for reading which he had just discovered in her, he betook himself to his confessor, M. Roussel, the saintly priest of Saint-Etienne-du-Mont, and returned laden with volumes of piety. The pile exhausted, M. Roussel himself replaced the books with others, marking the most beautiful passages in pencil. Having arranged everything, sure of his wife's obedience, and with no misgivings as to his wife's virtue, Pierre Acarie chased back to his friends of the holy *Ligue* to rage with them against the politics of Henri III. He made the move, God directed him, and rendered him an agent in His high designs.

It is certain that those pious works, recommended, even imposed, by M. Acarie on his young wife, determined with startling suddenness her mystical vocation. Duval touches on this memorable crisis with masterly simplicity. She received these books and read them willingly, as much out of obedience to her husband and the good confessor as for her own pleasure. The worthy priest one day brought her a book, I do not know the author (how provoking!) which he praised highly, showing her this sentence—*trop est avare à qui Dieu ne suffit*. These words transformed her, so powerfully and instantaneously, that you could have said God had struck her with a

[1] Duval, *ibid.*, p. 35. [2] *Ibid.*, p. 33. [3] *Ibid.*, p. 34. [4] *Ibid.*, p. 31.

thunderbolt—she appeared turned inside out. She was as if completely changed, not only in her affections, which were no longer the same, but also in that she seemed to have a new soul, a new heart, a new understanding, walking, hearing, seeing, talking differently—so powerful was the divine stroke that came upon her then, to last all her life. She was often obliged to shut herself in her chamber, as much to hide the lofty impulses at work in her as to calm herself; there she would pace rapidly to and fro, rub her hands and arms, or set herself to some disagreeable task. . . . Sometimes she would play on the spinet, in which she was skilled, not, as we read of some saints, to draw down the divine upon her, but rather to hinder such visitation and to distract herself. And often all this was not sufficient to arrest the course of these ecstasies, which consumed and wasted her as slow fire.[1]

Boucher, usually very exact in his dates, fixes 1588 as approximately that of these first ecstasies. Madame Acarie was then twenty-two, and her first three children were already born (1584, 1585, 1587). Three more were to come later (1589, 1590, 1592), all healthy children. The mother was fresh, active and gay, never known to be ill. "She had a rosy complexion," so bright that when the doctors were consulted about these extraordinary happenings, they bled her a score of times, "thinking that she had too much blood." It does not appear that the books lent her were mystical in the technical sense, to judge from the short sentence that most certainly made most impression on her and to the end of her life was always in her mind, *trop est avare à qui Dieu ne suffit*. She was, besides, herself so strange to such emotions, and found in those around, and even in her confessors, so little light or encouragement on this subject, that she remained for five years in ignorance whence it came before "knowing what to think of the continual ecstasies and ravishments befalling her."[2]

To add to her bewilderment, crises were apt to be awkward. Wherever she might be, especially in churches, the moment she composed herself to devotion she was liable to be prostrated by these violent attacks. One Sunday morning, for instance, she went to High Mass in her parish church of Saint-Gervais and took her usual place in the Acarie chapel, near the lady chapel. Morning passed,

[1] Duval, *ibid.*, pp. 21–2. [2] *Ibid.*, pp. 24–5.

and evening came, without her returning home. At nightfall, all other places having been searched in vain, she was found at last in the chapel " in an ecstasy, like one dead." When she came to herself she asked whether the Mass was finished. Another time, " walking in procession among the other matrons and girls of the parish, she felt so strange and sudden a pang of divine love that her heart seemed to be cleft asunder and she uttered so piercing a cry that none knew what to say. Such happenings were frequent, even before her mother-in-law," adds Duval with his usual candour and with perfect seriousness.[1] Most of these ecstasies were accompanied by keen sufferings, to which were soon to be added the pangs of clearly marked stigmata.[2] With all her efforts at self-control, often using most energetic means, she could not always keep " herself from crying out." One example will show how painful the sight of these crises must have been. When, long afterwards, Madame Acarie took the Carmelite habit, her superiors decided that the ceremony should take place very early, not wishing the people of Amiens to witness one of the painful raptures which was certain to occur and which probably would have been misunderstood. The discreet arrangement reminds us that the spiritual experts of those times held much the same view of these complex phenomena as we do to-day. " We must beware of sharing the popular belief," wrote recently the famous theologian, Père L. de Grandmaison, " that these ecstatic phenomena constitute the essential part of the mystic state and call for admiration; they are but the concomitants, the consequences, the price thereof. They are due to the weakness and imperfection, the insufficient spiritualization of the human instrument, and they diminish with its progress. (During the last years of her life Madame Acarie grew much calmer in her ecstasies.) Ecstasy, I use the term strictly for the phenomena of inhibition, temporarary unconsciousness, is neither an honour nor

[1] Duval, *ibid.*, p. 24.

[2] Concerning the stigmata of Madame Acarie we have the formal testimony of Père Coton (Boucher, pp. 554–5), who with Bérulle alone shared the secret. It appears certain that her stigmatization was less apparent than that of many others. In her humility she was wont as far as possible to hide her hands. As for her feet, she could easily disarm suspicion there, having three times broken her leg and only walking on crutches. Duval, although distinctly affirming the fact, does so very guardedly, in view of the decree of Sixtus IV forbidding, under pain of excommunication, attribution of the stigmata to any save Francis of Assisi. Benedict III, justifying himself by the works of the future Benedict IV, somewhat relaxed this decree.

a virtue; it is a tribute paid by the mystics to their human nature. It is also to be remembered that it can be imitated, or, perhaps I may rather say, produced by all kinds of causes."[1] Needless to say, therefore, the ecstasies of Madame Acarie, in the medical sense of the word, are not especially interesting to us, save in the measure in which, in one way or another, they are connected with the genuine mystic graces with which this soul was filled. But I am sure that more than one reader finds his attention flagging in his curiosity to come back to the picturesque side of our story and to hear what Pierre Acarie thought, when having played his part in the affairs of the *Ligue*, he returned home and found his wife in ecstasy!

Whether it be due to forgetfulness on the part of the biographers, or because stupefaction and uneasiness overwhelmed the poor man at first, Pierre Acarie hardly appears on the scene when the first attacks came. We only hear of his mother, hitherto very fond and proud of her daughter-in-law, who goes about repeating, "What ails my daughter? I do not know her; my satisfaction with her has not lasted long." She it is who knows her own mind and insists on the visits of physicians, in spite of the patient's objections. When it was established that the doctors knew no more than anyone else and rather worsened matters by their endless bleedings, the household relapsed into bewilderment and terror until the day that Père Benoit de Canfeld, the great mystic authority of the day, temporarily relieved them, affirming without hesitation that "all came from God," and that the young woman must yield herself, unaffrighted and without resistance, to the Divine working.[2] This decision of Père Benoit was apparently given about 1593, and it ended five years of anguish, as we have already remarked, not without surprise. It is indeed strange that so long a time elapsed before they saw daylight in this matter, which would, I believe, have appeared less mysterious in a more modest *milieu*. Some years later manifestations of this kind, occurring among the nobility or higher *bourgeoisie*, aroused far less attention.[3] It may

[1] *La religion personnelle, Études*, May 5, 1913, pp. 328–39.

[2] Duval, *ibid.*, p. 26.

[3] Although the little work of criticism here summarized rests on the chronology of Boucher, generally reliable, I am tempted to advance the date of the meeting with Benoit de Canfeld to 1591 or 1592, instead of 1593, or else to delay the date of the first crisis (1589, or even 1590, instead of 1588). A curious remark of Duval may be added here: "Far from these austerities and violent seizures wasting her strength, she became daily fatter and more highly coloured" (p. 83).

be also that either the particular symptoms of these crises, or the constraints which Madame Acarie imposed on herself to avoid the ecstasies and hide them from the public, complicated the problem, but whatever else it did, the pronouncement of Père Benoit restored his former part to Pierre Acarie. Once more he takes the stage, to its confusion.

On hearing the good news, his first act was to run to the Jesuits, to get the Capuchin's verdict confirmed or at least explained. Then, "having recognized," writes Duval quite gravely, "whether through the Capuchin or the Jesuit Père Innocent, his confessor, that what was passing in his wife was of God, and by extraordinary graces she was being raised to a sublime degree of devotion, he betook himself to the study of spiritual books, thinking by these means to assist and console her. Among other things, he had translated for her the book of Angela of Foligno, who seemed to have been led by the same way; but she read nought thereof nor could ever do so, because such reading distracted her from her inner life and hindered the divine irradiations and succours, as she told her familiar friends on several occasions."[1] Once more the husband was amazed, and he changed his tactics. The fly was desirous of stopping the coach that presumed to make progress without him. "M. Acarie then, seeing that his carefully chosen books, especially that of Angela of Foligno, were of no use to his wife, because she did not read them, could not understand this sort of devotion. So he began then to cross her in many ways, and to tell her that many ladies much esteemed in the town did not practise her methods, which he systematically called scruples, and sometimes sheer suggestions of the Enemy. He carried his complaints to the preachers of their parish, representing his wife's devotions as scruples which caused her to neglect her house, himself and her children. They believed him, because he was in good repute (and because many priests are always ready to believe anything said against the mystics) and indeed he was an honest man. When a preacher promised to speak against such modes of devotion . . . he would command his wife and her maids to attend the sermon." To proclaim his conjugal difficulties publicly in the sacristy of Saint-Gervais, and

[1] Duval, *ibid.*, pp. 26–7. This consultation with Père Innocent fixes one of those essential dates about which the old biographers rarely trouble themselves. The expulsion of the Jesuits took place at the close of 1594, soon after Châtel's attempt (Dec. 24).

make the domestics witnesses of the public embarrassment of their mistress, argued a low-bred nature. "The preachers," continues Duval, "did not fail to reprove those women who, under cover of devotion, did not fulfil their appointed duties to husband or house, entering sometimes into such details that the servants could not fail to guess that their lord had carried tales to the preacher, and on the way home they said to our saint, 'What could Monsieur have said to the good Father to make him preach like that?' She smiled and only said, 'He must say what he likes, it will blow over.'" To be caricatured thus from the pulpit, and by preachers in the days of the *Ligue*, was sufficiently trying, but the clergy of Saint-Gervais found a way of wounding this innocent woman yet more cruelly: "A priest, to whom M. Acarie had made these charges against his wife, passed her over in giving the Holy Communion, but she never complained."[1] We find it hard to realize the coarseness of those times and the gratitude which modern Frenchwomen owe to their sisters the mystics of days gone by, at least as much as to the Hôtel de Rambouillet. But the question here is hardly one of delicacy. The worthy Acarie, whom some would represent as quite a good sort, is far less excusable than some think. It was permissible that he should sometimes feel inconvenienced by the strange situation in which Providence had placed him, that he should even, if he wanted to, amuse his clerical friends by a couplet of his composition on the surprises of marriage. But he had no business to assert, as he did, that everything was at sixes and sevens in his house since his wife began to have ecstasies. Of these two the ecstatic, that is, in his phraseology, the lazy good-for-nothing, is not the one he thinks. If anyone in his household cuts a sorry figure it is not, as will soon be shown, Madame Acarie.

II. For, though an ecstatic, enduring the stigmata, and soon by a sad accident reduced to walk only on crutches, Madame Acarie appears invariably admirable in intelligence as in piety; she performed all the duties of her position and the multitude of good works she set on foot, without ever allowing her private affairs to suffer from her preoccupations. We have already seen her, before her earliest experiences in Mysticism, going out hastily from Mass at the very moment of approaching the Altar, in order not to delay for an instant her

[1] Boucher, *ibid.*, p. 46.

husband's *petit déjeuner ;* and how she was never seen neglecting her duty as wife, mother, or mistress of the house, to take refuge in comfortable and listless quietism. Duval, who does not wish to be hard on the husband, writes: " As M. Acarie did not wish to trouble himself about domestic affairs, it was she who bore the burden, not only of daily business, but of all that concerned the children, boys as well as girls, and the numerous male and female domestics. So well did she superintend everything that order reigned down to the most minute details."[1]

Far from rendering her the least aid, her husband made her task heavier. Exacting, quarrelsome, interfering—that could be borne—but in a score of ways he complicated his wife's task. In spite of his usual reserve and abstract mode of writing, Duval makes us see clearly enough some of the daily difficulties. " She wished," he tells us, " his children and servants always to treat him (M. Acarie) with great respect. But this good gentleman, being of an easy temper and jovial disposition, was familiar with all, even with the servants and others who should have respected him. She feared that they might take advantage of this, and kept a firm hand, never permitting any liberty, however small ! "[2] Without her, he would never have been able to make himself obeyed either by the servants or by his children, the boys at least, one or two of whom seem to me to have been tiresome. To finish the picture, Pierre Acarie jovially dissipated an immense fortune, giving liberally to his friends of the *Ligue* and to other good works. Just when he was " subjecting," to use Duval's word, his wife to the preachers, he was doing his best to reduce her and their six children to poverty. Well-intentioned, I am convinced, but devoid of brains, he was duped by sharpers who nearly succeeded in making him lose more than his money. For the end of the *Ligue* found him, not merely loaded with debts, but on the edge of a worse catastrophe only vaguely hinted at, which his gallant wife must have had much trouble to hush up. His exile in 1594 came at a lucky moment for him and his, permitting Madame Acarie to intervene in this troublesome business which had hitherto been carefully concealed from her. The pleasant conditions of the exile were due, we are told, to the esteem which Henri IV had for Madame Acarie, or rather, I should say, to the political insignificance of the person concerned.

[1] Duval, *ibid.*, p. 346. [2] *Ibid.*, p. 35.

The King did not banish him from the country, but merely kept him at a distance from Paris. Eccentric as usual in his decisions, he chose for his retreat the Carthusian house of Bourgfontaine near Villers-Cotterets, taking with him the curé of Saint-Germain de l'Auxerrois, M. Cueilly, an adherent of the *Ligue*, but not exactly a champion. We are told that M. Acarie greatly edified his hosts. He had distraction enough, being one day carried off by a band of robbers. M. Cueilly was so alarmed that he forthwith fled to Italy. Madame Acarie, despite her poverty, contrived to scrape up enough to pay her husband's ransom, and took the opportunity to entreat the King to mitigate the punishment. The exile was allowed to come near Paris and live at first on his estates at Luzarches, then at Ivry, where he was still, it seems, in 1598. I do not know the precise date of his return to Paris, but for our purpose the important fact is that the separation of husband and wife lasted at least four years. This temporary widowhood, which evidently meant deep distress to Mme Acarie, could not fail to cause interesting developments in her destiny and character.

I believe that these years of perfect independence were useful to her, enabling her to become fully conscious of her gifts and her apostolic mission, and rendering it easier to exercise her influence on all around. Certainly she never lacked energy, as is proved by her managing a difficult husband for twelve years and governing a large household. Timid though she was, she knew how to take command. Either willingly or by constraint, all had to yield to her. Thus, during the frightful siege of 1590, she compelled her mother-in-law to share with the poor the wheat which that prudent housewife had hoarded. She actually threatened to report her to the magistrates in charge of the distribution of food. But she did not like putting herself forward, and the timid deference that she showed to her husband often paralysed her zealous inspirations. Once her own mistress, she altered completely and asserted herself in public as never before. It was necessary if she was to restore the fortunes of her house. On the morrow of her husband's departure the bailiffs had pounced on her. "A Minim Father told me," says Duval, "that one day he went to see the blessed one and while she was at dinner he saw the bailiffs come in and seize everything in her house, down to the dishes on the table and even the plate in front of her. . . . After this distraint she could not say that anything belonged to her, but yet saw herself responsible for a husband and six children, besides her father (a victim of the *Ligue*). Worse still, she had to make headway against many ill-wishers who cherished various animosities against her husband, whom in his absence they accused of much that might have made both lose honour, life, and goods."[1] These last words remind us of the little historical mystery, which I mentioned just now, and which I must leave to the skill of Archivists—it is hard to believe that the charge which was the subject of endless documents has disappeared entirely from the records. Duval does not magnify the episode, rather he slurs it over, either from feelings of natural delicacy or not to annoy the children of Pierre Acarie, who were still alive when the Life of their mother appeared. The hot-headed man must have been guilty of some act of great imprudence. Though innocent, appearances were certainly against him. However, our ecstatic, with no preparation for taking the initiative in such things, was found equal to a task as burdensome as it was complicated. It was against her principles as regards education of children, but, to devote herself entirely to this pressing duty, she began by " getting rid of all her children," even the girls, the youngest of whom was not yet three. " Then," continued Duval, " she could apply herself wholly to the matter in hand, going in person to plead before the judges, who often made her wait till the moon rose " out in the street. She made good use of the time, by instructing the girls who accompanied her in prayer, the virtues, or some point of the interior life.[2] I say nothing of the affronts she had to endure. She was considered mad, and her former friends deserted her. " One day, being in want of bread, she took with her some jewels which still remained and went to a relative, intending to borrow money from him and leave the jewels as security." Instead of money she was advised " to bind her children to a shoemaker." " My mother," says her eldest daughter, " had listened calmly to all but the last word, nor did she even then reproach her relation for his refusal, merely remarking that she did not think her children fitted by birth for the trade he indicated."[3] " Not only did she plead before the judges," Duval goes on, " but she drew up most of her case herself, working sometimes all through the night, arranging the facts of the defence so

[1] Duval, *ibid.*, p. 77. [2] *Ibid.*, p. 78. [3] Boucher, *ibid.*, pp. 50–1.

clearly that the advocates, much astonished, could find nothing either to expand or abridge, astonished at the lucidity of her intellect. Finally her pleadings and clever management freed her affairs from confusion, delivered her husband from his enemies' machinations, and restored the house so nearly ruined."[1] Such were the first attempts of this clear and practical genius, destined soon to revive, organize and support so many good works. Blessed be the debts and the other follies of Pierre Acarie! Thanks to them, his wife was trained in bold resourcefulness, initiative and patience, in short in all the human virtues needful to accomplish her divine task. Lest the reader, having given the husband more pity than he deserves, should get alarmed about the fate of the family, we hasten to show that the children of Mme Acarie did not suffer either from the ecstasies or the zeal of their mother.

About Mme Acarie as an educator we have the most trustworthy information, that of her three daughters who confided their reminiscences of childhood first to M. Duval, and later to the commissioners in the process of Beatification. Themselves Carmelites, as their mother had been, these ladies have a natural tendency to praise the education which they received from a saint, even the discipline which must have sometimes seemed severe in their tender years. But such idealizations are easily detected and allowed for; I am assured that French boys and girls of that period had cause to envy the young Acaries. This side of the saint's character, like the other sides, is the more original in that it is not only rare, at that epoch especially, but spontaneous. Her parents had only given her examples of what not to do, and her husband's interventions in the nursery merely caused confusion. She was not one to learn from books, and, though of high station, she knew nothing save what she was taught by her natural wit, good-heartedness, and divine grace. I have already said that she endeavoured to keep her children as much as possible with her. To show the care that she took of them when they were little, Duval tells two stories which he considered significant, for the picturesque for its own sake did not attract this grave doctor.

She sent her eldest son to Saint-Louis, the "profession" house of the Jesuits (the child was ten years old when they were expelled)

[1] Duval, *ibid.*, p. 79.

where he . . . was taught (the Catechism). It happened that the master wanted to show off his little catechumens, all of course baptized. Our lady's son was chosen to carry the banner. She had a fine one made for him of crimson silk, on which was represented Our Lord calling the children to him, and made him walk thus equipped through the city at the head of his little companions, to encourage him to learn Christian doctrine thoroughly. . . .

It happened about that time that M. Guincestre in one of his sermons at Saint-Gervais spoke against the parents who neglected to have their children taught the Catechism, saying: " If I say to a child, Come, my boy, tell me what faith is? " Mme Acarie's stepmother had one of her children in her arms, still at the bib stage. Thinking that the preacher was speaking to him, he began to say out loud: " Faith is a gift of God," and would have finished the definition if his grandmother, seeing everybody looking at the child, had not stopped his mouth.[1]

To appreciate the anecdote fully, it must be remembered that, on the morrow of the massacre of the Duc de Guise, this same Guincestre, a fiery *Ligueur*, had made all his hearers, including the Chief President de Harley, whom he addressed personally, swear to do all in their power to avenge their martyr. He must have known Pierre Acarie well, and the coincidence may perhaps give us the name of one of the preachers who rebuked the maternal and conjugal deficiencies of Mme Acarie from the pulpit of Saint-Gervais.

" She accustomed them to come and tell her their thoughts, and listened to them with patient attention,"[2] training them to be frank and open. But she had no need of confidences in order to know her children. They " felt that she penetrated to the depths of their soul by a simple look."[3] " One of the faults that displeased her most was a lie, however trivial, and her love of truth was such that she was implacable to faults which infringed it, saying often to her daughters: ' If you upset and disorder everything in the house I will gladly pardon you, if you own up when asked. But I will not pardon the smallest lie. If you were as tall as the rafters '—she herself was small—' I would hire women to hold you down rather than let one lie pass without chastisement, and the whole world would not make me pardon you.' "[4]

[1] Duval, *ibid.*, p. 39. [2] *Ibid.*, p. 44.
[3] *Ibid.*, p. 45. [4] *Ibid.*, p. 50.

One seems to hear her, see her even, and I believe her daughters did not alter a single word of this little discourse that they never forgot. " If you were as tall as the rafters I would hire women to hold you down." History becomes impossible, if one believes Dr. Duval capable of inventing such fine details.

When her daughters had been guilty of a fault " deserving chastisement," she would send them to fetch the rod; if they were still in a passion or wished to make excuses, the saint did not chastise them at once but waited till they were calm and God had put into their soul a true and sincere knowledge of their fault. Then she chastised them, as they deserved, telling them to kneel during the chastisement and say the *Pater* or *Ave Maria*, and afterwards making them even kiss the rod and thank it for the good it had done them.[1] Between the rod and the more primitive and sudden violence in vogue among us to-day I am not prepared to choose, but the important point is, what is nearly always forgotten, and what Mme Acarie recalls to us, that one should never touch a child at the moment of its fault and when it is still in a passion. She combated vanity in the hearts of her children by ways difficult for us to appreciate, but which throw sidelights on the manners of that time.

She desired everyone in her household to call her daughters by their Christian names with no prefix of " mademoiselle." She forbade the prefix absolutely to the servants and prayed visitors not to use it. She kept the rule always in regard to her eldest daughter, not allowing her to be called anything but Marie, when she was seventeen or eighteen. . . . For the same reason she wished her girls to speak gently and humbly to serving-men and women, though it were only a lackey, so that they never dared to say " Do this or that," but " Pray " or " Please," and the lackey had orders not to obey without this. . . . She was likewise wont to enforce sundry acts of mortification and humiliation, such as asking pardon and kissing the feet of those who had seen them offend, and whatever inspired special repugnance in the girls, that she insisted on the more. Thus she commanded her eldest daughter (more proud and difficult than the others) to sweep the stairs and perform other menial or even revolting offices. And seeing that she looked out for a time when there was no one in the house . . . she reproved her sharply and made her sweep in front of everyone.[2]

[1] Duval, *ibid.*, p. 49.

[2] *Ibid.*, p. 43.

She pursued the same discipline to inculcate obedience, and her daughters had to be "always ready to do or leave off doing without showing any ill-humour." The eldest, setting off one day for a pleasure party, was made by her mother "to descend from the coach and take off her things, which, when she had obeyed contentedly and calmly, she was told to get into the coach again."[1]

Now what does the reader make of all this? For my part, I hesitate either to praise unreservedly or to blame these ascetic exercises. Some of them, indeed, smack of the convent. But what asceticism does not, more or less? One thing is necessary, to tame the child without breaking him, to humanize him without blighting him. Mme Acarie had much tact, knew all about her children; she proportioned their tasks to their strength with watchful care; finally, she knew better than we exactly what suited them. We know too that she had a horror of driving them to the convent. "If I had a hundred children," she said, "and had no resources to set them up in life, I should not wish to make a single one enter religion." "She wept bitterly one day after one of her daughters had entered religion, fearing that she had merely done this on the advice of a friend."[2] "My mother," says her eldest daughter, "always dressed us very *properly* (we know the old sense of the word), though avoiding vanity, and she often told us to hold ourselves up. When a lady of our acquaintance seemed surprised at her attention to these points, she replied wisely: 'I bring up my children so that they can follow their vocation in whatever state Providence calls them: if they enter the religious state, *I do not wish any physical defect to serve as a motive for their step.*'"[3] Such sentiments were not common at the end of the sixteenth century and, indeed, are not to be expected so early. Rarer still, perhaps, is the spectacle of a mother so much occupied with the education of her children. That in this matter she had been at times too exacting, especially towards her eldest daughter, Mme Acarie recognized herself later. When they were both Carmelites, the daughter would amuse herself by teasing her mother gently on the subject, talking "in recreation of what she had done to mortify her in her childhood. The saint in her great simplicity seemed to be

[1] Duval, *ibid.*, p. 43. [2] Boucher, *ibid.*, p. 108. [3] *Ibid.*, pp. 107–8.

ashamed and would only say: 'I did you much harm, it was very wrong of me.'"[1]

"She was very gentle with us," says the same daughter, "but mingled with her gentleness was so solemn and imposing a seriousness that it seemed impossible not to do what she wanted." The younger daughter Marguerite (sweetest of the family) for her part writes: "She was always anxious to keep me humble, but did it so charmingly that I never resented the lesson thus given to my love of self. When obliged to punish me, she did it so that it never occurred to me that she was correcting me unreasonably and the correction never made me angry with her."[2] We may add that when they were very young she bought them "spillikins, draughts and other toys." Even when she was "lost in the depths of God," says Duval expressly, "she would show her children how to play, saying that youth ought not to be cramped, and that this blunted the intelligence. Again, when one of her daughters, aged twelve, looked too virtuous or was too serious, she would reprove her, looking on this in the light of premature fruit which drops off at once."[3]

[1] Duval, *ibid.*, p. 431. [2] Boucher, *ibid.*, pp. 110–11.

[3] Duval, *ibid.*, p. 44. When we come to the beginnings of the French Carmelite Order, we shall meet the daughters of Mme Acarie again, or at least the second and most famous, Marguerite du Saint-Sacrament, who, according to the Marquise de Maignelais, surpassed even her mother in holiness; she appears to me very attractive. One would like to know something of the sons, but Duval and early Acarie tradition seem resolved to ignore them. One suspects here a little mystery worth exploring, if, as I am led to believe, their misfortune was that they were sons of their father. Nevertheless Pierre, the second, at least was irreproachable and, according to Boucher, "highly illumined." "After finishing his (Navarre) college course, he joined the Jesuits, but quitted them before his mother's decease," M. de Marillac and Père Coton having procured him a good Priory on his return to the world, although they had had to do battle with the scruples of Mme Acarie, who was always severe on the matter of ecclesiastical benefices. High in favour with the Archbishop of Rouen, Harley de Champvallon (the first of the name), we find Pierre in 1622 busy with the beatification of his mother and in 1629 deputy of the Rouen clergy in the Estates of Normandy. "He had many books, which he bequeathed to the chapter of Rouen Cathedral, on condition that they should allow the public free access to them. . . . After his death the canons dined in common in his library annually on the Day of the Ascension, and during the grace at the end of the meal prayed for *the repose of the soul of M. Pierre Acarie who founded this library*." It is interesting and touching thus to find in the Golden Legend of bibliophiles the son of a great saint, herself so absorbed in God that she had found the reading of books of devotion impossible after her first ecstasy. Pierre Acarie inherited his taste from his father, who, when he had burnt his wife's romances, had the religious works he put in their place magnificently bound. Archdeacon of Eu, and official and theologian of Rouen, the bibliophile canon died in 1637 aged fifty-one.

His younger brother Jean, born in 1589, had a more varied and troublous career, having probably inherited his father's freakish disposition. Furnished at first like Pierre with a fat

These children who played at spillikins by the side of a mother lost in ecstasy, this mother who interrupted her ecstasies to join in her children's games—such is a picture of the true mystic reconciling heaven and earth, answering with equal readiness every voice that calls, the humblest as well as the most sublime. One would have thought that the continual cares of a household to be ruled and restored to prosperity, and of bringing up a numerous family, would have been sufficient for the activity of this woman who had had to struggle with God Himself, if she was to have head and hands free to accomplish her duties. But of all the works of religion and charity which began in Paris in the reign of Henri IV, I know none to which Mme Acarie grudged her help, though she had not been responsible for starting it.

III. In Duval's book there is a scene without words so beautiful, moving and pathetic, that it might have come from the Gospels. Mme Acarie went to Rouen to found a Carmelite house, Duval accompanying her. "When we arrived on Mont Ste.-Catherine," he says, "from which all the town of Rouen is to be seen, I stopped the coach in order that she might enjoy the prospect. She looked at it because I so wished it, and seeing it so large and thronged, and the harbour so full of shipping, she was inwardly touched, remaining for some time without speaking or even moving."[1] Such rapt emotion of love, pity and sympathy must recall the Divine plaint, "O Jerusalem, Jerusalem . . . if thou hadst known. . . ."

Mme Acarie gave herself freely to all in need, never approaching her neighbour with "a mind preoccupied." "Once, shortly after her marriage, a workman in their employment fell ill and begged

Priory, he exchanged—we know not when or how—the cassock for the cuirass, although he could scarcely have been in Orders at the time. His conduct greatly disquieted his mother, although in 1617 the Bishop of Verdun was lodging with the young officer. A little later we lose sight of him on the other side of the Rhine. He went off to Germany, married there, and probably never returned to France. He was the first of a race of soldiers. "His eldest grandson became aide-de-camp to Prince Xavier of Saxony, brother of the Dauphiné mother of Louis XVI, and was killed by a cannon-shot while summoning a *château* to surrender." One of the nephews of this descendant was still living at Strasburg towards the close of the eighteenth century, when his ancestress was beatified by Pius VI.

As the eldest son of Mme Acarie had had no children, the Acaries of Alsace were the sole direct descendants of the blessed one. They were very proud of the fact, and kept up relations at more or less frequent intervals with the Carmelites of France. Cf. Boucher, *ibid.*, pp. 113–4.

[1] Duval, *ibid.*, p. 173.

some help of her. She gave it, but thought of the inconvenience his illness would cause her household."[1] She wept bitterly at the selfish consideration, reproaching herself deeply. Neither kindness nor disinterestedness is rare among true saints, but the apostolic charity and activity of Mme Acarie present an uncommon type. Her zeal depended in some manner on her life of contemplation, the grace drawn therefrom directed and guided her always, and the good works were the outcome of the ecstasies. This is not far-fetched or exaggerated language or the subtleties of a panegyrist. Duval, to whom we owe this analysis, had studied Mme Acarie not only with a professional interest in souls, but also as a theologian and competent authority. We can trust this judgement. "Assuredly," he writes, "her soul was enlightened by some special ray of the Divine, bestowing on her unerring judgement in things earthly as well as heavenly. In good truth she once was favoured by God with a marvellous glimpse into His Providence over men, which lasted for three days, during which she saw, heard, or thought of nought but the incomprehensible way in which God governs all things . . . (and as this Divine governing embraces all things) we saw her advising on highly spiritual matters, and immediately afterwards abasing herself to direct bodily exigencies and temporal affairs."[2]

As a result of this state of mind, which was fundamental, "she never willingly applied herself to any mundane business without first perceiving an inward prompting thereto."[3] If there was no voice she would not move without a direct order from her confessor. It is even more significant that "she hardly ever engaged in discussion with anyone, at least on business of importance, unless she was entirely recollected and conscious of God's presence: so that, if this inward sight was not clear, she would break off, not seeming to know where she was, caring nothing for what those with whom she was speaking might think."[4] Dom Sans de Sainte-Catherine makes the same remark: "In speaking, if she perceived that she had said anything unnecessary or badly expressed, that is to say without recollection, she would stop short in her sentence, leaving it unfinished, though she might be speaking to people of high rank and the matter itself was trivial."[5] We see her the same in her innumerable labours—

[1] Duval, *ibid.*, pp. 59–60. [2] *Ibid.*, p. 59. [3] *Ibid.*, p. 60.
[4] *Ibid.*, pp. 60–1. [5] *Ibid.*, p. 61.

energetic and lively, yet always turned inward, her inward senses alert for the slightest sign or silence of her invisible guide. This is the secret of her extraordinary prestige: all who approached her were impressed with the clear assurance of coming very close to God Himself.

This bird's-eye view, which enables us to fit Mme Acarie's external activities into the framework of our book, must suffice. The details of such a Chapter might be piled up indefinitely; besides, I do not possess the necessary erudition. We hear, for instance, of her constantly visiting the neighbouring hospitals of Saint-Gervais and the Hôtel Dieu, near the Rue des Juifs, so that " she revived among ladies of quality the custom that had long ago died out, of visiting the hospitals and nursing the sick there."[1] This statement, however, must be accepted with caution, for I am not sure that French great ladies of the sixteenth century had entirely deserted the hospitals, or, if so, that Mme Acarie was the first to revive this splendid tradition. Such historical problems would take us too far afield, and if we began on them how should we justify our later condensation of what we have to say about Vincent de Paul and the Filles de la Charité into a few hasty pages?

Mme Acarie was a noted " converter." " M. Gauthier, who from being Advocate-General of the High Council became Councillor of State, and who was very intimate with the Saint, attested on oath (during the process of beatification) that more than ten thousand conversions were traceable to her."[2] Clearly we must abjure the long investigations necessary, first to verify these astonishing figures, then to bring to life this multitude of souls in distress to whom Mme Acarie brought peace. All Paris resorted to her and in a sense she kept its conscience. On this point we have the sure testimony of the first Parisian of his day. " One day," says Duval, who had the story at first hand, " evil-disposed people having spread abroad in Paris a malicious report touching the King, he upon his return from Fontainebleau sent Père Coton to assure her of the falseness of the rumour, for that he held her in such high esteem that it sufficed him if the saint did not give credit to the calumny."[3] True enough, no doubt, but Henry IV, clever even in his most spontaneous impulses, was glad enough to keep the good opinion of this woman, who was

[1] Boucher, *ibid.*, p. 131. [2] *Ibid.*, p. 134. [3] Duval, *ibid.*, pp. 549–50.

one of the powers of his capital. Other times, other preoccupations in rulers: a little less than two centuries after Père Coton's semi-diplomatic visit to Mme Acarie, Napoleon tried to make it up with Mme de Staël.

Like the story of Christian charity and converted sinners in the seventeenth century, that of the teaching communities is also outside our scope. So we shall speak later of the first French Ursulines only in so far as they played a part in the more intimate movement which concerns us here. Still we must not forget that the most flourishing branch, the Ursulines of Mme de Sainte-Beuve, might with equal right have been called the Ursulines of Mme Acarie. For to her was due the idea of this foundation, which according to Duval was regarded by " several great personages " as " impossible and useless." It was she who decided her cousin, Mme de Sainte-Beuve, to undertake it; she who selected and moulded the first recruits. " She was," Duval declares, " the principal, nay, I will say the primary, instrument used by God to establish these Ursulines . . . God having put into her soul such desire for it that she could not rest till this good work was in train." In truth, adds the same writer, whose testimonies have the added weight of having been addressed to the saint's own contemporaries, " in her day nothing notable for the glory of God was undertaken without her being told of it beforehand and giving advice."[1]

But among all these works there is one to which all else was subordinate, and which wholly belongs to our subject, the spiritual activity of Mme Acarie and that mystic influence, contagion as it were, which for more than thirty years radiated from her. It has been said at the outset of this Chapter that she awakened seriousness in all who approached her. It is time to complete, or rather explain, this pregnant assertion, and to recollect that Mysticism is after all but Christian seriousness raised to the highest degree. God alone makes the saint and the mystic, but His call to those whom He has chosen is sometimes almost imperceptible. Many do not hear it or dare not hear it; whether from weakness or ill-conceived humility or prudence, they paralyse, even stifle, grace. But—and this is the great Divine Law ruling most supernatural ascents—the words, or it may be no more than the sight, of a soul truly holy and manifestly

[1] Duval, *ibid.*, p. 218.

possessed of God, reveal their own latent gift to these timid, hesitating elect who do not know themselves. Before this living picture suddenly presented to their gaze, fascinated and encouraged at the same time, they are doubtless too modest to echo the famous cry of awakening genius, *ed' anch' io*, but none the less their vocation is fixed by the decisive meeting, and they set forth with resolute step upon the path which the night before seemed to them impassable, terrifying. Such is the true history of many Christians, men and women, and especially priests, in whom Mme Acarie "liberated grace," to borrow the splendid phrase applied to Cardinal de Bérulle, but equally suitable to the mission of this extraordinary woman. In truth the mystics of all ages have exercised the same kind of influence, but in her there is a particular character, the arresting originality of which it will be easier to understand after a rapid survey of her mystic life.

IV. Père Binet, one of the best of judges, seeing he is the least prejudiced in favour of the mystics, and, though a holy man, could be sharp, critical and even malicious, writes in the following terms on the supernatural gifts of Mme Acarie.

I have never known anyone in whom was more clearly to be seen what S. Denis calls *divina patiens*, that is to say, she was passive rather than active (we shall soon have to define this more accurately and qualify it a little); being continually illuminated with much light and abundant heavenly favours and having God so present to her soul, that had she not practised some distraction, she would often have fallen into ecstasy and been transported out of herself.[1]

The approach of this blessed one to God in prayer was *in modum fulguris coruscantis*, not solely on account of the warmth and ardour with which she applied herself, but also because, from her great inwardness and familiarity with God, her countenance, like that of Moses, was wont to become wholly luminous. . . . If interrupted while speaking on affairs of business or good works she was instantly silent, and forthwith concentrated herself so eagerly upon God that she would forget what she had been saying just before and had to be helped to remember. . . . I have seen this happen many times while I talked with her.[2] . . . Sometimes looking up to heaven she could hardly speak. She would say, "Let us talk of that," but she could not complete her sentence and was forced to show by signs the joy with which her soul was filled.[3]

[1] Duval, *ibid.*, p. 556. [2] *Ibid.*, pp. 497–8. [3] *Ibid.*, p. 473.

Such sudden and irresistible drawings made vocal prayer extremely difficult to her. " I have seen her," goes on Duval, " when I was walking in the fields with her, begin the Rosary with her eldest daughter, and be unable to say the first *ave* without immediately becoming rapt, so intense was her interior recollection. Her daughter was in no way surprised, being well accustomed to this; she whispered two or three of the words that followed, but finding her still oblivious finished the prayers alone. For this reason her confessors found it difficult to give her any penance, and often merely prescribed these two words, ' Jesus, Mary! ' or a charitable gift, or prostrating herself on the ground."[1]

Devotional reading was no more possible to her than vocal prayer. " At the first attempt her spirit would soar to God and become absorbed." Though a book had been " the first cause of her attraction," yet, " as when the arch is completed, the scaffolding is thrown down, so this soul, having been raised by God to the heights of prayer, had no more need of books . . . it sufficed her to seek Him in the depths of her soul. And although many devout people, regulars as well as seculars, presented her with certain exercises or spiritual books of the day, especially those dealing with the higher life of the soul, she never did or could read them, and might have said with S. Paul that those who seemed to be somewhat in the Church had taught her nothing, but she had learned all from God. That Book," continues the great reader André Duval, " never hurt her eyes, she could read therein at darkest midnight as at clearest noon, and it was with her always. . . . Towards the end of her life, however, she began to read certain spiritual works, as a distraction from the overpowering Divine influence which was then hers. Among these books, the most important were the *Chemin de la perfection* of the holy Mère Thérèse de Jésus, the *Points d'Humilité* and the *Combat Spirituel*, the last being a special favourite of hers." So it was of her friend François de Sales, whose own works she had perhaps never opened, or at least never finished. We note that, when not able to read herself, she would " listen to her daughters or others reading aloud."[2] Curiously enough the human voice could postpone, even avert, the divine assaults. More curious still are the various stages described by Duval, an acute observer: first, a book causes the initial

[1] Duval, *ibid.*, p. 495.

[2] *Ibid.*, pp. 491–4.

ecstasy; then all books are rendered impossible by the ecstasies which a single line threatened to precipitate; lastly, towards the end of life, the ecstasies become so absorbing that distraction was sought by devotional reading.

Far from diminishing her activity (as often, at least to outward seeming, is the case), or rather, let us say, far from reducing her to activities so deep and elemental as to resemble immobility and pure passivity, the ecstasies of Mme Acarie rendered her more " fertile " —her own word—" in conceptions," sentiments and images. For this we need only examine the inadequate but illuminating account which she herself gives of one of her long ecstasies.

Accidentally casting my bodily eye upon a crucifix (she writes to her director Bérulle in one of the too few letters of hers preserved to us), *the soul*[1] was so suddenly and sharply touched that *I* could no longer even look upon it outwardly, but beheld it interiorly. *I* was amazed to see the Second Person of the Most Holy Trinity served in this wise for *my* sins and those of mankind. *It* would be quite impossible for me to describe what passed *within*, particularly the excellence and dignity of this Second Person. This realization was so vivid and so clear that *she* could not comprehend how, having many other means to redeem the world, He had deigned to abase aught so worthy and precious; till it pleased the same Lord to comfort the anguish in which *she* fell (and *I believe* that, if it had lasted longer, *she* could not have borne it) by enlightening *her* so particularly, efficaciously and clearly, that *she* could no longer doubt that it was He Himself Who dawned through these shadows of death, teaching *her* as a good father would his child or a master his disciple. What is inwardly experienced cannot be spoken or expressed. *I* remember well that *the soul* admired His Wisdom, His Goodness, and particularly the excess of His Love towards mankind. Joy and sorrow together wrought diversely and rendered the soul fertile in conception. What did *she* not say to the Lord so surely present with her? What needs did *she* forget? What desires, aspirations, thanksgivings! Oh, how *she* entreated the efficacy of what He had done for our salvation! . . . Those dolours in hands and feet (the stigmata)

[1] Either to throw indiscreet curiosity off the track by an innocent precaution, or to follow the convent practice which proscribes "I" and replaces it by "we" or by the indirect style, Mme Acarie attempts to disappear from her own letters. But her natural vivacity often betrays her and she reverts to a "me" which is very charming on her pen. A similar confusion and awkwardness is often to be met among religious mystics. In the text I have italicised these obscurities, which also perhaps denote in the mystics a certain tendency to strip themselves even of their own souls.

which *we* have suffered for so many years, were rendered sweet, although poignant. . . . In short, *I* cannot say how it was with me; it lasted during the morning devotions, about four or five hours.[1]

Bossuet himself could not have suspected of Quietism an ecstasy so active and " fertile " as that of this matter-of-fact recital, in which the reader will have remarked the life-like appropriateness of spirit, and even of wording, which is certainly unstudied. If the seer fails to describe what passed within her it is from superabundance, not lack, of light. We have already seen, for she omits nothing essential, that in her the whole human being (conceptions, images, sentiments, sensations even) acts, suffers, palpitates in true harmony under the divine Touch, the pains of the stigmata becoming at once more poignant and more sweet as the spirit is flooded with a more dazzling " clarity." We know too that this activity was betrayed outwardly and that Mme Acarie frequently spoke her ecstasies, if we may so express it. In her moments of deepest recollection unconsciously " she ceased not to speak in words, sometimes to God, sometimes against herself." And when her lips were silent, her " luminous " countenance spoke for her.[2]

[1] Boucher, *ibid.*, pp. 517–9.

[2] *Ibid.* It may be allowed to add here in a note, for the benefit of theologians and *savants*, the very interesting report of one of the confessors of Mme Acarie, M. Fontaine, who supported her in her last illness till the arrival of M. Duval. It has already been said that her ecstasies were often accompanied by exterior phenomena, exhausting for her and painful for many of those witnessing them, which, far from proving by themselves the Divine action, merely render the weakness of mortal flesh more visible. The premonitory symptoms of a crisis of this nature can be traced in the prayer just analysed, in which Mme Acarie herself tells us that, if the anguish into which the thought of the plan of Redemption plunged her " had lasted longer, she could not have borne it." There may have been, at least in this instance, some connection between the ecstatic crisis and the devout activity described above. At least M. Fontaine believed that he could detect a similar connection in the phenomena produced during the last weeks of Mme Acarie's life. To quote M. Duval, who arrived on the very day of her death: " About half-past four violent convulsions seized her, succeeding one another with scarce an interval. . . . Arriving at Portoise at half-past five, I found the watching nuns dismayed . . . the invalid in strong convulsions. I said to the physician, ' This is an extraordinary attack!' but he told me that she had had others as violent, they were not fatal. . . . M. Fontaine, the confessor, likewise remarked that she had recovered from other attacks equally severe. ' She appears unconscious to you,' said he, ' but she is in reality inwardly occupied with God. *This kind of occupation, when it is general, does her no harm, but when in the midst of it there supervenes a vision of the Humanity of Our Lord or one of the Blessed Virgin or of some saint, her spirit leaves off contemplation and general attention, and the disturbance communicates itself to the body*, although she thereby receives some inward relief." (Duval, pp. 312–3.) Fontaine means that the physical suffering somewhat alleviated the inward pangs caused by vision. The alleviation does not imply

After what has been said, it is only natural to use the fertility and burning richness of these ecstasies to explain the mystic influence, the extent and depth of which we are presently to describe. Like a Gertrude, a Teresa, a Marguerite d'Arbouze, Mme Acarie might have attracted and moulded her many disciples by communicating to them the heavenly light so richly bestowed on herself. But, on the contrary, of all the great mystics I know none more reserved, and that to my mind is the most original feature of her marvellous history.

" She was once asked," remarks Duval, " why, with all her experience, she did not write on the interior life. She replied that she had at the beginning attempted something of the kind, but, feeling the poverty of her words, had burned her pages. To speak of God ' one must forget oneself.' ' For,' she said, ' as soon as I become conscious how high are the things of God and that my words come from so mean and diseased a dwelling, all that I say seems so worthless that I cannot abide it.' So at times when speaking of God with very great fervour and communicating sublime things, as soon as she perceived what she was saying, she would stop short! "[1] Her humility, even more than the inadequacy of words, stopped her mouth. " I do not think," says Père Binet, " that anyone but herself could speak satisfactorily of Sœur Marie de l'Incarnation; so profound and firm a humility screened the *sancta sanctorum* of her soul . . . in such wise that in my belief even the wisest hardly knew her."[2] " Of her extraordinary graces," writes Duval, " it was almost impossible to know anything, save when she was unconscious."[3] Directly she returned to everyday consciousness she discouraged curiosity mercilessly, even in her most intimate friends. I believe she spoke freely only to three of her confessors, Benoit de Canfeld, Cardinal de Bérulle and Père Coton, especially, I gather, to the last named.

With all the rest she practised reserve, even perhaps with the Carthusian Dom Beaucousin, who from Canfeld's departure to 1602, when he too left, was her director, and certainly with Duval himself,

that the soul withdraws from " this contemplation and general attention." This passage is doubly valuable, and reminds us that we must not judge the graces of devotion bestowed upon Mme Acarie by such a passage as has been quoted above, which makes no mention of this " general occupation." It is difficult to judge which of these two states was the more frequent with her.

[1] Duval, *ibid.*, pp. 363–4. [2] *Ibid.*, p. 555. [3] *Ibid.*, p. 381.

who was her director intermittently during long years and became ever dearer to her. How then could passing strangers expect to fare? " A religious once," writes Duval, " said some words to her regarding the sublimity of her devotion. She replied promptly: 'Father, I should be well content if I could live in the fear of God, and the keeping of His commandments, capable of telling my beads properly' (this was a pretty subterfuge and quite sincere, for her ecstasies frequently hindered her from telling her beads). 'What more can a married woman do with a household and children to manage?' " Better received, as certainly he deserved to be, Dom Sans de Sainte-Catherine, whom she saw much of and esteemed highly, advanced hardly any further into her confidence. Even with him she ceased abruptly to speak of " sublime things . . . as soon as she caught herself doing so." " She preferred," adds Duval, " to be thought foolish and distraught in her conversation than illumined by a divine and celestial light."[1] Her inflexible will in this matter must have imposed itself on all, so that none of those to whom she owed obedience ever insisted on her writing an account of her ecstasies and visions, in accordance with the general practice—perhaps too general. Would S. François de Sales have been more successful than the rest? He seems to have thought so, but at any rate she said nothing to him, as he himself tells us after her death:

She was an eminent servant of God, and I heard her confession many times, almost regularly for six months (in 1602) and notably in her illnesses of that time. Oh, what a loss was mine, not to have profited by her holy conversation, for she would willingly have communicated her whole soul to me, but the infinite respect I had for her held me back from questioning her.[2]

The phrase " infinite respect," used by such a pen, is worth a hundred portraits, and happily the saint himself develops the theme. Some months before his death, one of the first biographers of François de Sales, Dom Jean de Saint-François, tells us:

I asked him if he had any special knowledge of the extraordinary graces communicated by God to that holy lady (Mme Acarie), of which her biographers (Duval) had written? He answered frankly " No," for at his first meeting with this holy soul she had inspired him

[1] Duval, *ibid.*, p. 387. [2] Cf. Boucher, *ibid.*, p. 147.

with such great respect that he had never had the courage to enquire concerning what took place within her, and he never sought to know more than what she had felt herself moved to tell him, without any prompting. Indeed, said he, she was ever given to speak more of her shortcomings than of her graces, and I ever regarded her not as a penitent, but as a vessel wholly consecrated by the Spirit to His uses.[1]

This is valuable testimony and gives food for much reflection. No doubt fully aware already of the sublime graces of which Mme Acarie was the recipient, François de Sales had for six months heard the confessions of this already famous ecstatic; outside the confessional he had met her on a number of occasions, yet he always restrained himself from saying a word which might have led to intimate confidences, or (as he must have known) to a fresh ecstasy. If in their relations with other mystics of the time, true or false, all directors had practised such reserve, and shown themselves as little curious as the Bishop of Geneva, many abuses would have been nipped in the bud, and the final victory of the anti-mystics would have been delayed, possibly prevented altogether. Not that I feel any great sympathy for these gentlemen, but, sure enough, a host of unwise chatterboxes and simpletons made things easy for them.

Obviously François de Sales was not the man to doubt the true raptures of a true saint, although as Bishop of a distant diocese and only occasionally hearing Mme Acarie's confessions he was content with characteristic delicacy to play a minor part in the circle of the great Parisian mystic. But far from blaming her special friends, Coton, Bérulle, Binet, Duval, Beaucousin, Sans de Sainte-Catherine and others—whom he knew to be eagerly watching Mme Acarie in her ecstasies, trying to lay hold of at least some fragments of the divine secrets—he envied them. This devout eagerness of so many illustrious and representative men concerns us very particularly; let us proceed to examine one striking illustration of it.

André Duval—that is, let us not forget, the whole Sorbonne, not in the least credulous, and highly scholastic—had never probably studied ecstasy save in his peaceful library, when towards 1595 or 1596 the disturbing reality of such phenomena was revealed to him in the person of Mme Acarie.

[1] Cf. Boucher, *ibid.*, p. 148.

Visiting her once in the lodging of Mlle de Bérulle (he records), to which she had withdrawn during her husband's absence, I found her on the bed in such contortions and uneasiness that I thought she was in extremity and asked the maid watching her if the doctor should not be sent for. Nevertheless in this great uneasiness[1] her face was radiant as the sun, which astonished me much, although I said nothing to the girl. In the evening I reported to M. de la Rue her confessor, a learned man, the state in which I had found her about three o'clock. He replied, "I have just seen her, she is very well and quite as usual." I was still more amazed, but began to understand that what I had witnessed was not illness but intensity of effort which God imposed on her.[2]

Gradually a holy curiosity succeeded to the first surprise in the mind of the good scholar, and he was never tired of studying her.

I saw her on one occasion (he goes on to say) in a church, where a most solemn procession was being prepared for, everyone anxious to receive it suitably and moving about noisily on all sides of her; I watched her for a long time, but could not observe the least movement in her. . . . S. Antony once complained of the rising sun, because, by the multitude of the objects it disclosed, it hindered the union of his spirit with God, but this blessed one would not have been hindered.[3]

How amazed was this scholar, used to the silence of the library, when he beheld Mme Acarie so transported by "the chiming of church bells" that "she would lose the use of her senses, being sometimes constrained to stop her ears."[4]

I have never communicated her (he pursues), though I have often done so, without seeing her rapt. . . . I have often thought, when I came to her and saw her so wholly withdrawn, that I should have to give a touch to warn her of her turn; nevertheless when her turn came she would open her lips as if her good angel had reminded her. . . . M. Gallot the theologian, however, has told me that when communicating her he was sometimes compelled to touch her with his finger to make her open her mouth.[5]

M. Duval, Regius Professor, M. de la Rue and M. Gallot, both Doctors of Divinity—the Sorbonne is indeed interested in her;

[1] (*Inquiètudes*); the abstract term is delicate, but hardly conveys the true character of this "uneasiness" which made Duval think the mystic was about to die.

[2] Duval, *ibid.*, pp. 83–4.

[3] *Ibid.*, p. 471.

[4] *Ibid.*, p. 471.

[5] *Ibid.*, pp. 476–7.

eager and curious, yes, but much more discreet than might have been expected. Duval, far from seeking to multiply these precious experiences, would have liked to hinder them.

I remember (he writes) one day saying to the blessed one that Sœur Angélique de la Trinité, daughter of the Marshal de Brissac, had asked me the meaning of these words of Scripture: "God must be served in righteousness and in truth," and I told her the explanation I had given. She said: "There is yet another which I will tell you if you wish." As she began to tell me I perceived that she was entering into a state of interior recollection in which she would lose the use of her senses, and I feared, as she was only just recovered from sickness . . . this might cause a relapse. I stopped her then, and forbade her to continue . . . but have since much regretted that I did not let her speak; had I done so we should have now been profiting by her beautiful exposition.[1]

Similar incidents are to be found on almost every page of Duval's book, I will quote only one more, the most beautiful and significant of all. One day he visited the Carmel at Amiens where Mme Acarie, now Sœur Marie of the Incarnation, had been professed, but which she was about to quit for Pontoise.

Passing through the cloisters at first I did not see Sister Marie of the Incarnation, who was at the foot of the steps leading to the cloisters, because I was examining the stained glass in which was depicted the life of Blessed Mother Teresa. He who accompanied me, however, drew my attention to her, I turned round, but did not at first recognize her, so radiant and absolutely dazzling did her face appear to me. Although I had seen her a million of times in the world, I nevertheless said to my informant: "I should never have recognized her if you had not told me." I had never before seen her thus; and this view of her has remained so strongly imprinted on my mind that I never think of her without forthwith beholding that scene in the cloister at Amiens.[2]

Again, it is not a poet who is speaking, but a doctor of the Sorbonne. When Duval recalls the face of his friend it is luminous. A Jesuit, as typical a Jesuit as Père Binet, saw her the same. As for the Chancellor de Marillac, "his veneration for her was so great that almost always an extraordinary feeling arose in him when he approached her or even when his carriage turned into the street where she lived."[3]

[1] Duval, *ibid.*, pp. 322–3. [2] *Ibid.*, pp. 272–3. [3] Boucher, *ibid.*, p. 159.

Another gift, less dazzling, but appearing no less marvellous to Duval himself, added to the prestige of Mme Acarie and brought her numerous disciples. This mystic, so humble about her special graces and desirous to check curiosity on the subject, excelled in spiritual direction. She had, " in a sublime degree," what is termed the " discernment of spirits," that faculty of supernatural criticism which " by interior and penetrating sight . . . sees into the depth of the soul and recognizes the spring of its movements."[1] She had scope for this gift, for mystics, alike true or false, began to appear on all sides, especially in the capital, and the confessors, surprised by this sudden invasion, had not yet learnt, as they did later, how to steer dexterously between the two reefs, equally fatal, of credulity and scepticism. Grave and reverend signiors lauded to the skies adventuresses and hysterical subjects; others, no less imprudently, discouraged certain souls truly called to the mystic union, whose grace surpassed their own. How did Mme Acarie, herself so humble and discreet, come to be so promptly accepted as one of the greatest authorities in these delicate matters? The problem will appear less difficult to solve if one remembers the number of eminent priests who visited her and were justly reckoned the arbiters of the world of Mysticism. Most of them had come to her house first to help her in the organization of various charitable and religious undertakings. Insensibly they were drawn to consult her on their own needs and those of the souls whose mystic vocations were in question. This happened of itself, if one may dare to say so, and without Mme Acarie's being put on her guard.

One day (Duval tells us), before her and Père Coton, two souls were spoken of as very devout and of such admirable reputation that they were ranked above some who for a long time had been known as saints. When the visitors had gone and Père Coton remained alone, Mme Acarie remarked, " Had I the direction of those two souls I should probe them from top to bottom. Self-love, secret curiosity and spiritual sensuality inspire them to do most of what is so much admired and esteemed in them." She added that she would not have cared to say this to anyone else, but she had to tell him, because he could help them.[2]

This anecdote comes direct from Père Coton, who himself seems

[1] Duval, *ibid.*, pp. 331–2. [2] *Ibid.*, p. 333.

to have shared the common belief in these two visionaries, and who in the sequel acknowledged that Mme Acarie alone had judged them aright; it is very instructive, for it brings before us a whole society of eager, anxious, rather credulous people. Many similar incidents speedily established the peculiar influence of this woman over a multitude of priests all alike pious, wise and powerful, Jesuits like Binet, Jacquinet, and Coton; Feuillants like Sans de Sainte-Catherine and Asseline; Oratorians like Bérulle; or seculars like Duval. All these men when consulted by friends or disciples in their turn asked the opinion of Mme Acarie or, a simpler course, passed on to her direction those whom they found too much for them. "One well-versed in spiritual things" said to the most perplexing of his penitents: "I should like to send you for a month to school with Mme Acarie, in order to satisfy myself as to your manner of praying."[1]

I do not mean to start a discussion with those who, whether rightly or wrongly, would resent the intervention of this woman in the interior life of the Church. I have already treated the question in relation to Marie de Valence and, if I had to treat it every time the matter crops up in this history, my book would never end. In the abstract, the problem indeed is insoluble and unmeaning, for abstract woman, like abstract priest, has never yet appeared in the land of the living. In the concrete, however, it is plain sailing. Mme Acarie then stands before us, with exquisite tact, penetration and modesty, to say nothing of the graces that illuminated her. She is a woman, I know, and so lacking all official jurisdiction. In the confessional the most ignorant, coarse and corrupt of priests exercises a power no scrap of which belongs to her; he can by one inconclusive decision set all hers aside; if he even command her to resist the divine spirit that animates her, she is bound to submit, to obey as far as in her lies. To reserve to mystics alone the judging of mystics, is to establish illuminism and to deny the Church. History teems with such duels between the divine authority of the priest and the divine inspiration of the mystic, in which order always demands that the second should yield to the first, and God to God Himself. But here there is no question of authority in the strict sense. If Père Coton found himself in difficulties regarding the dubious visions of one of his penitents, why should he not submit the difficult case to the judgement of a

[1] Boucher, *ibid.*, p. 145.

woman whom he knew to be very clear-sighted and holy? If Michel de Marillac hesitated before abandoning himself to the obscure leadings which seemed to summon him to a path of loftier devotion, why should he not take counsel with a woman who had experience in just such ways and bore upon her very brow a reflection as of God? As for Mme Acarie herself, why should she refuse to those who came to her the few clear, simple words that would decide their sainthood, possibly even their salvation?

But too much stress must not be laid on this word direction. *Ars artium regimen animarum*—the government of souls is the art of arts—is a maxim written on the first page of manuals of direction. No doubt, but this difficult art can be reduced to simplicity, no books can teach it to those who were not born with it. Is it really an art? is it not rather a sort of spiritual instinct, or if one likes it better, a grace, or perhaps both together? " Lord, Thou hast told my soul," sings the poet. But to tell our soul is what we require of a director. Shall a man alone be able to render this service, and the quick intuitions of a woman's intelligence and heart be unequal to it? To these natural gifts of divining sympathy, of which it appears man has no monopoly, must be added in the case of a great mystic like Mme Acarie personal experience of sublimest mysteries, a sharpened sense, so to speak, of Divine Presence and Influence. What more could be wanted?

> The blessed one (writes Boucher) revealed to divers persons the secret thoughts of their spirit, better than could they themselves. . . . She laid bare to Père Coton the state of his soul in regard to several important points, and he owned that her pronouncements had been very useful to him and that he had felt their benefit for a long time. So with Père Binet, Provincial of the Jesuits, who says: " What she told me was known to God alone; she showed me all the consequences which the business might entail, and nothing could have been truer."[1]

What is all this but direction, simple and without a shade of presumption, but highly successful, since such directors congratulated themselves upon having received and obeyed it?

What age should a woman be before exercising such delicate functions? I cannot say, nor do I think the reader's mind will be

[1] Boucher, *ibid.*, p. 190.

troubled with so superfluous a question. A saint has no age. At twenty-five she commands no less respect than when she has white hair. It is slightly vexing to see the uneasiness on this subject displayed by some of Mme Acarie's friends and even by the most learned of her biographers, M. Boucher, although he has the excuse of writing at the end of the eighteenth century. We have moved on since then, and decent folk to-day, whether believers or not, require no proof of the perfect innocence of these *liaisons spirituelles* so constantly occurring in the lives of the saints. However, we shall all understand Mme Acarie and her circle better if we have the help of concrete examples, two of which will now be given.

Mlle d'Abra de Raconis, converted from Protestantism by Père de Bérulle, tells the first story.

When M. de Bérulle learned that Père Benoit de Canfeld, under whose direction he had put me . . . was going to England . . . he was kind enough to place me in the care of Mme Acarie. This pious lady, in order to let me profit by her kindness, received me into her house, where M. de Bérulle often came. I have never seen anything so admirable as the conversation of those two holy souls. Oh, how pure it was, although so frequent, for, in six or seven years, I do not think there was a single day, when both were in Paris, that they did not see each other. As both were busy with important works of piety and charity (especially the founding of the French Carmel) very frequent meetings were necessary, apart from the fact that, as regards Mme Acarie's interior life, he was her director and usual confessor, as soon as he was priested. Nevertheless, in this close intercourse I never remarked a familiar word on the part of either. Their bearing was as distant as if they had never before met, nor was their conversation in the least familiar.[1]

The intimacy between M. de Marillac and Mme Acarie (says Boucher again) was also very holy. It did not begin till July 1602, shortly before the registration of Letters Patent authorizing the establishment of the Carmelites (Marillac, as we shall see, was actively interested in this matter). . . . Certainly before this period M. de Marillac had not been an entire stranger to Mme Acarie; he had been a fellow-student at the college of Navarre with her husband, and he dwelt in the same quarter as she did. The saint often met him at church or in various houses, and thought she saw in him a disposition to attempt the heights of holiness; it was this that had

[1] Boucher, *ibid.*, p. 150.

inspired in her the desire for intimate friendship (in 1602 they were both still young). Words can hardly describe the seriousness of their interviews, the reserve of their communications, the precautions of the intimacy during the twelve years that passed before Mme Acarie entered religion. Although seeing each other for more than an hour almost every second day, they never permitted themselves any of those words, laughs and gestures that friends commonly admit without overstepping the bounds of innocent familiarity. M. de Marillac himself testifies to this, adding: " On her side all was virtue and grace: on mine the workings of grace reflected from her."[1]

This expression, which says so much so well, is, however, less suggestive than the simple description in the reminiscences of François de Sales, which we have already quoted. Notwithstanding his calm and silent dignity a certain vivacity of manner was natural to him. The first time he saw the Baronne de Chantal he waged war politely against the modest luxury of the young widow. Mme Acarie, however, appears to have made a greater impression on him. If we were not discussing a saint, and one of great simplicity, we might almost say that she frightened him a little. The exact shade of his sentiments towards her is a rarer state of mind than this and does honour to both. Like Bérulle, Coton, Binet, Marillac, and all the rest, François de Sales had to bow before the holiness of this woman. " She would gladly have shared all her soul with me," he writes, " but the unbounded respect I bore her prevented me from enquiring further."

France was then entering upon one of those periods I will not say of transition, for all periods are that, but of religious fermentation in which the most unforeseen and audacious departures are taken, without surprising or even annoying anyone. It might well have been that scrupulous regard for questions of privilege, custom, and tradition might retard a movement, at first timid and uncertain, yet full of promise and evident in all directions and in all classes. Advance had to be rapid; it was necessary to strike while the iron was hot, to sustain, disentangle and fortify the confused aspirations which inspired large numbers towards holiness, to bring together the well-disposed, at present out of touch with one another, to revive old organizations and create others more suited to the needs of the moment, finally,

[1] Boucher, *ibid.*, pp. 152–9.

to unmask the humbugs and repress the scatterbrains always to be found in such a movement. We have already met, and shall meet again, the leaders flung up by this great campaign. They were firebrands and incomparable as disciplinarians; for the most part men—religious, priests, even laity—marvellously united in the common task, for which they had no other authority than their zeal or their genius. The majority of bishops had the wisdom to give them a free hand. Christian France under Henri IV resembled a part of the mission-field in the first years of advance. The essential discipline was certainly not wanting, but many details were left to circumstances. Professional canonists would assuredly have raised their hands to Heaven had they been consulted over every step that had to be taken. Rome watched the moment very closely and gave these good workmen, whom she trusted thoroughly, a kind of blank cheque. For instance, she charged Cardinal de la Rochefoucauld to do all that was necessary for the reform of the Benedictines, the marvellous story of which we shall relate shortly. Had they held by the letter of the law, the natural heads of the Order would have refused to allow Jesuits, Capuchins, Feuillants, and other reformers to enter their abbeys. In ordinary times the possessors of ancient Customary rights, relying on the prescription of centuries, would have started interminable disputes which would have dragged out till the days of Louis XVI. Thanks to the support of the Court and the bishops the new foundations were settled with equal expedition. In vain did the *parlements*, defenders of the majesty of the law, raise a commotion. While the registrar was still fumbling among his useless documents, a new convent had sprung out of the earth, and the matins-bell informed the President and his councillors that they were beaten before the battle had begun. They might have been reassured. The decks were not to remain cleared for action long, but meanwhile we must be surprised at nothing, not even at the greatest miracle in a time full of miracles—Mme Acarie.

She applied herself primarily (writes Duval) to the reform of certain convents of nuns, and although ordinarily women religious do not willingly defer to married women, at least in matters regarding their interior life, yet God had bestowed upon her for that purpose such special grace, and she behaved with such humility and tact, that they made no difficulty in opening their hearts to her wholly and declaring their inmost thoughts to her. Though there are very many convents in Paris and the environs, she went everywhere, stimulating some to a better life and the conquest of their desires, prompting others to undertake the reform of their houses. When the Abbess of Montmartre adopted the enclosed rule with her daughters, and made a promising beginning in the reform of her house, Mme Acarie went to console and fortify her, giving special attention to certain good women more drawn than the others to the interior life.[1]

All the words tell in this passage, especially the concluding lines. The reform of the Benedictine abbeys was, as will be shown, a mystic movement in the true sense of the word, and when we come to study the mystics of Montmartre we shall not forget that Mme Acarie had passed that way.

When the troubles ceased (continues Duval) she visited more distant convents, for instance that of Saint-Étienne-lez-Soissons. She saw the Abbess, assisted her with her counsels, addressed the greater part of the nuns, and so strengthened the goodwill already present in this foundation that its reform served as an example to many others of the Order. She also was wont to visit the Charme (an abbey), of the Order of Fontevrault, and arranged that several worthy sisters should enter it. This convent was under a virtuous prioress, Mme Drouin, who was entirely guided by the counsel of the saint, and it attained such perfection as to be esteemed one of the most advanced of the Order.

Her charity was not confined to the religious, but extended itself to several communities of secular women which were then growing up, to live under obedience, for the practice of a holy life and to instruct little girls in the fear of God and in the knowledge suited to their sex. Learning that the theologian M. Gallemant had founded such a community in the town of Aumale, she went to visit it, making a sojourn of some days. . . . She went likewise to Pontoise, where the same M. Gallemant, during a Lenten course of sermons, had established a similar house, but its members being new to everything regarding community-life, there was some fear that the whole would end in smoke. The saint came there and during one whole night, which she passed without sleep, spoke to each individually, with such success that they took courage and resolved to persevere in spite of their difficulties. The result is that this small community has given birth to two flourishing convents of Carmelites and Ursulines to-day established in that town.

[1] Duval, *ibid.*, pp. 102–3.

The great work of the Ursulines and Carmelites was beginning. Another twenty years and they covered all France. In proportion as they belong to our subject justice will be done to them; but in spite of their achievements the historian lingers with perhaps even more curiosity on the short-lived groups which prepared in obscurity for the full development of these magnificent enterprises. Who to-day gives a thought to the *béguinages* of Aumale and Pontoise, in which "secular ladies" lived in common, devoting themselves to the practice of a holy life and "the instruction of little girls," not only "in the fear of God," but also "in the knowledge suited to their sex"? The large heart and prophetic genius of Mme Acarie had realized the importance of these humble beginnings and noble anticipations of what was coming. In her own Paris she followed these groupings closely.

Beside the women who lived in community (continues Duval) there were others who lived in their own houses, or two or three together, under the direction of Mme Acarie. After the King entered Paris these ladies began to wear a hood abroad, as much in order to have a modest and devout walking dress as to avoid seeing and being seen. So common did the practice become in Paris that hardly a maid or a wife was to be seen in the streets except in a hood. This had its inconveniences, for some women adopted the garb of the devout and wore a hood to avoid recognition. Mme Acarie, therefore, with the aid of Mme Du Jardin, a lady of good reputation, commanded these women to lay aside their hoods and to go about dressed in ordinary clothes, but modestly and simply, with the result that the abuse ceased forthwith. When these devout ladies did not all behave as was expected of them, some practising exaggeration in their devotions, others falling off in fervour, the saint used wisdom and admirable tact to moderate the fervour of the former and to stir up the sloth of the latter.[1]

Such pretty details justify the term used above, when we spoke of the "religious fermentation" of this time. Clearly we have not exaggerated either the activity or the influence of Mme Acarie. Obviously—and it is well to be reminded of it by Duval—she was not the only woman in the van of this movement, but she was a kind of lieutenant-general over devout Paris. A sign from her, and the hoods, numerous enough to bewilder Duval in the streets of Paris,

[1] Duval, *ibid.*, pp. 107–8.

all disappeared. Note the cleverness of her *coup d'état*. Suppression of the hoods discouraged the simpletons who wore them in order to play at sanctity and make themselves notorious. It was a form of licence which no longer troubles us, but under one form or another it continually recurred during the seventeenth century, sharpening the malice of the anti-mystics, and leading astray or compromising the truly devout.

We have already seen that Mlle de Raconis was a guest at Mme Acarie's; she had been recently converted to Catholicism, and Bérulle entrusted her to the saint's direction after the departure of Père Benoit de Canfeld about 1599. The same motive brought other boarders to this vast house. The hospitable customs of the day made such proceedings a matter of course. Before long these passing visitors were quite naturally succeeded by a more stable and semi-official community destined to become famous under the name of the *Congrégation de Sainte-Geneviève*.

While Spain and Rome were still considering the question of the foundation (of the French Carmel) Mme Acarie . . . with the consent of the husband (recently returned from exile) assembled in her house a certain number of her own sex who felt themselves called to be Carmelites. They had conceived the idea from reading the lately published works of S. Teresa, and as the steps being taken in France to establish Carmelite religious could not remain secret, they requested admission. The ecclesiastics (Bérulle, Duval, Gallemant) who had been designed as superiors of the Order, were well pleased to have tried persons ready to their hand when the Spanish Carmelites should arrive in France. Knowing the aptitude of Mme Acarie for guiding souls, they commissioned her to examine the vocation of such women as should present themselves, and to train them according to the Rule to which they aspired.

Such was the origin of that little community of Ste.-Geneviève, which rendered precious service to the budding Order. The difficulties which would have been caused by the choice of members were avoided; the weakening and even ruin, which the precipitate departure of the Spanish Carmelites for Flanders might otherwise have entailed, was prevented; the Order was filled with excellent nuns, many of them destined in their turn to become foundresses of the houses soon to spring up throughout France; and the Ursulines were provided with their first recruits. . . . (At first) only twelve postulants were received in the young community, but the number was speedily increased, and, during the six or seven years for which it lasted, a great many were trained there; twenty-six of them took the religious habit in the first year of the foundation of Carmel.[1]

This page—it might have been written more thrillingly, for it tells a unique tale—should have been graven in marble in the Church of Saint-Gervais, the parish of Mme Acarie. We shall come at last to the story of the first French Carmelites and all will agree that we can picture nothing more beautiful. But one can never exaggerate in speaking of the works of Mme Acarie. This congregation which she founded and governed was more than a preparation for the Carmel. Other Orders, and notably the Ursulines, owed to it many of their most eminent members. Here again the whole proceeding was paradoxical, for this woman, who lived with her husband and continued to educate her children, had no particle of that authority given by the Church to Abbesses and other superiors. And in admiring her, let us also admire the wise and large-minded prelate who allowed her so free a hand, Henri de Gondi, first Cardinal de Retz, and Bishop of Paris from 1598 to 1622.

There is nothing more delicate in the government of a religious house than the admission or refusal of candidates. Mme Acarie had here very decided ideas and an extraordinary sureness of vision. She did not settle things by herself, but her impressions were never resisted. Boucher relates that " she caused the rejection of a young lady in whom they (Bérulle or the others) thought they saw the fitting qualities for the religious life, and who would have brought a considerable dowry. ' If it depended upon me,' said she to M. Duval, ' I should not for all the world receive her. She is one of those characters who, by prudence and complaisance, not by grace, avoid committing faults.' "

" The blessed one opposed the reception of another young lady whose father was an excellent man who had suffered much during the civil wars. M. Duval, who thought the young lady was called to the religious life, requested her admission (also) on the ground of her father's merit, but Mme Acarie . . . knew her better. ' The girl is not frank,' she said; ' her lips are not in agreement with her heart . . .' Frankness was to her so important that she urged the superiors to receive a lady who, aware of sundry imperfections in

[1] Boucher, *ibid.*, pp. 230–5.

herself, dared not ask to be received. 'Her spirit,' said the saint, 'is simple and open, that is what is needed in a religious.'

"On another occasion two candidates were brought; one was weak in well-doing and tormented by inward anguish, while the other enjoyed a quiet conscience and shewed much disposition for the religious life. 'This latter may advance in virtue,' said Mme Acarie, 'but will make no progress in the interior ways, she has reached the point where God wills her to remain. With the other it is different, she will advance through falls and recoveries.' . . .

"Worldly considerations counted for nothing with this holy woman. A young widow, recommended by worthy ecclesiastics, was ready to offer ten thousand crowns of dowry towards the building of the first Carmel. At the first interview, Mme Acarie saw that she had no vocation. . . . 'I trouble myself not at all,' she said, 'about the money needed for the material building, but solely about the living stones which shall build up the spiritual edifice. Did I know of a soul fitted for this last, I should be ready to give all the gold of the universe to buy it; or to give as much to exclude one not fitted. . . .'

"A priest who heard the confessions of the little community complained sometimes that Mme Acarie made the reception of recruits very difficult. She said to M. Duval, speaking of this ecclesiastic, 'He has virtue, but being good himself he thinks that everyone is like him, and he believes too easily everything said to him . . . one must search the deeps of the heart and see whether God is there, or at least whether He will be there, when the soul is prepared by religion.'"[1]

"Whether God is, or will be there!" These are words which throw a light on more than the mystic life. Nothing more decisive will be found in the twenty volumes of François de Sales. When we hear such words we feel sure that the first French Carmelites, chosen, tested, moulded by this woman, will be worthy of her.

She seems so great, surrounded by these theologians and novices, that it is an awkward interruption when the player of an unimportant part takes the stage again. Long years of exile and silence have made him still more petulant. But the more sublime our story becomes the more we need to show its reality, by putting it on a background

[1] Boucher, *ibid.*, pp. 238–40.

by no means sublime—*bourgeois* Paris. Pierre Acarie, returning to his Penates, found all transformed, the *salon* almost a convent parlour. At first he hardly knew what to think of the change and of the heights to which his wife had attained. "He was perplexed," writes Duval, "by the fact that a great number of people of every description, great and small, men, women and girls, religious and secular, came to his house to speak to his wife, and letters came to her from every quarter. Nevertheless he accepted the situation and was at bottom content, and would not have wished things otherwise."[1] For a Regius Professor of Theology that is very acute. But as he was likely to be read by the children of M. Acarie he could not say all. Boucher takes up the tale. "M. Acarie often looked with a displeased eye on the number of persons . . . attracted by his wife's reputation . . . he ordered his domestics to refuse them admission, or if they gained it, he said disagreeable things to them. . . . As he remarked to an ecclesiastic of his acquaintance: 'It is uncommonly inconvenient to have such a saintly wife and one so skilled in giving advice.'"[2] I sympathize with him, but just when we are inclined to take his part the clumsy fellow manages to irritate us. Interested in everything, including Mysticism, with a word to say about everything, he would have liked to assist at these pious conferences. When they forgot to ask him, and scruples perhaps prevented his listening at the door, he consoled himself by rummaging among his wife's papers. Duval tells us this, and betrays but slight indignation. "As the letters received by the blessed one were affairs of conscience, and not therefore to be divulged, she practised considerable dexterity in concealing them from him, he being somewhat inquisitive; sometimes she was unable to do this, and then she had recourse to prudent dissimulation."[3]

He was more favourable towards the future religious gathered beneath his roof. They did not spend the whole day in prayer or closeted with Mme Acarie. They had impressive names and more than enough wit to keep the good man entertained. They found out his weak side. As there was no peace when he was about, each would take it in turn to sacrifice herself, either taking him for a walk or getting him into a corner of the house and making him tell his

[1] Duval, *ibid.*, p. 32. [2] Boucher, *ibid.*, p. 91.
[3] Duval, *ibid.*, p. 32.

doughty deeds in the times of the *Ligue*. The Marquise de Bréauté, among others, could turn him round her little finger. Though she had not yet definitely left her *hôtel*, she came to Mme Acarie's house almost every day. When the husband threatened a fresh scene, Boucher tells us "the good Marquise, to coax him out of his bad temper, would invite him to drive in her coach, so that he, charmed by her complaisance, often remarked to his wife, 'I trust that at least you will not turn this charming Marquise into a Carmelite!'"[1] Needless to say his trust was misplaced. His frivolity was not less disagreeable than his ill-humour. "He loves laughter; often, wearying of the seriousness of the atmosphere in this quasi-noviciate, he would break in upon the exercises under pretext of seeing that the novices lacked nothing." The biographer, desirous, as he tells us in his tranquil fashion, of delineating for us "the humour of M. Acarie and how it upset the exercises of the little community," adds an anecdote that does not lack piquancy. "One of the novices, by name Lejeune, of Troyes, with a pretty face, fancied she must laugh and even frolic and dance with him in order not to put him out; so that M. Acarie said to his wife, 'All your *dévotes* are so stiff, my little Troyenne alone is sensible!' The saint answered him nothing, but she took the young postulant aside and reproached her for her excessive complaisance, whereupon the latter naïvely explained the difficulty of behaving otherwise: 'Madame, what can I do? M. Acarie is my host and I cannot gainsay him!'"[2] The pretty Troyenne developed into an excellent Carmelite.

It must not be concluded that Acarie had no other defects than alternate fits of violence and levity. A good man in ordinary circumstances, here he was intolerable. So they had to leave him and seek quieter residence for the little community. The Duchesse de Longueville to this end bought a dwelling on the Place Sainte-Geneviève which gave its name to this society, which never actually became a sisterhood, for the members wore secular garb and took no vows. The house was closed in 1607. "All those women who appeared to have a vocation to Carmel entered the convents" recently established, while others "who, without a vocation to be Carmelites, yet felt themselves called to the religious life," furnished recruits for the first Ursulines under Mme de Sainte-Beuve. The success of the original

[1] Boucher, *ibid.*, p. 317.

[2] *Ibid.*, pp. 235–6.

experiment led to its being perpetuated in a manner among the Carmelites themselves, Mme Acarie persuading the Superiors of the Order "to rule that for the future the habit should only be given to postulants" after three months' probation. "Her aim was to enable the nuns to have closer knowledge of the vocation, character, and health of those who presented themselves, and to send away with more privacy those that were rejected. She thought that postulants and novices could not be tested too searchingly, and that one of the greatest mistakes that could be made in convents—a mistake which soon robs them of their fervour—was to accept recruits too readily."[1] Most of the great mystics are like that. If only we get to know them, we find them divinely wise. The great glory of Mme Acarie is, not merely to have founded the French Carmel, but to have founded the Order on such principles. She chose and formed Mlle de Fontaines, the Marquise de Bréauté, and others to be mentioned later, yet is she not to be admired just as much for the throng of young girls whom, in spite of the entreaties of Bérulle, Duval or Gallemant, she sent back to the world, and whose mediocrity and shortcomings would have clouded the pure ray of the French Carmel? After the death of her husband in 1613 Mme Acarie herself joined the Carmelites, though only as a lay sister. She was sent first to the Carmelites of Amiens, then to those of Pontoise, where she died in 1618. At the urgent request of Louis XVI, Louise of France and the Gallican Church, she was beatified in 1791.

These pages, too long, yet too short and dry, have endeavoured to bring out the distinctive features of this remarkable woman, the greatest religious force, it seems to me, of even her times. Am I wrong in thus setting her greatness above that of so many others? The historian may not always succeed in making his readers share the clear and vivid impression he has formed as to the true character and respective importance of his different characters. In politics and even literature the difficulty appears less great. A Joan of Arc, a Richelieu, a Ronsard, a Shakespeare may make different appeal to different understandings, but no one will dispute the sovereign place they occupy each in his own department. But when the problem is one of moral, religious or mystic excellence it becomes much more delicate, and still more complicated if the influence in question died,

[1] Boucher, *ibid.*, pp. 354–5.

so to speak, with him who first exercised it and its first disciples. What a shadowy idea we should have framed of the influence of Socrates had Plato himself written only in his own name! Mme Acarie wrote nothing, and in my opinion if she had, her writings would not have shown us the real woman. Not that we mean to say she was more saintly than the spiritual leaders of her time, that would be a stupid assertion, nor may she be ranked higher than her masters. Canfeld saw in her a second and even more admirable Catherine of Genoa. He had the right to speak, for he knew what three men only—himself, Coton and Bérulle—could have known. We may not make comparisons like this.

One thing alone is clear and should be sufficient for us: the contemporaries of Mme Acarie found in her a living type of that sublime life towards which so many souls of the time felt themselves vaguely called. Her ecstasies were but signs, as a light hung out for travellers seeking their way at night. Their attention was caught at first by such extraordinary phenomena, but they soon learned from her truths far simpler and of quite different import. Her message consisted of a sentence from the Gospel, the full sense of which only mystics realize, "The kingdom of God is within you." "One must," she said, "penetrate to the depths of the soul, and see if God is, or will be there." She meant most certainly that more intimate Presence of God which is the whole of the mystic life. Thus when deciding about the vocation of a very virtuous girl she said: "She will advance far in virtue, but make no progress in the interior ways." She did not hold that everyone was called to attempt such ways, but she knew that many timid people do not know the grace God gives them or fear to abandon themselves to it. She helped everyone, but especially these timid souls, and, as she had a horror of all subtlety, over-refining and, still more, affectation in these matters, and was herself divinely simple in the grace bestowed upon her, she found it easier than others to show that the heights of Mysticism are reached by way of the utmost simplicity.

I ask pardon for repeating the keyword simplicity so often. There is none more appropriate to the beginnings of the religious movement which we are trying to describe. At the end of the present volume we shall come to François de Sales, the great exponent of Mysticism reduced to its essential and wholesome simplicity, but Mme Acarie was at once his inspirer and the perfected model. Both alike were quick to make decisions and break down established customs, both alike were wise, but they differed in their modes of teaching, as in their gifts and position in the Church, yet they taught the same doctrine. The *Traité de l'Amour de Dieu* establishes, defends, propagates, with the authority of the theologian and the pontiff, what, long before the book was published, all could read, many had read, in the living book of Mme Acarie. All that generation, great and small alike, resembled these two more or less. After them, and during the first half of the seventeenth century, the movement continued to extend and develop, but also to grow complicated until the time when we seem to see in the very complications symptoms or menaces of approaching dissolution. The first period, represented by the two great names brought together here, is possibly less striking than the other two; perhaps it contains fewer geniuses, as the world reckons genius, but perhaps also it is purer. It reasons, analyses itself, dogmatises, refines less. It is mystic almost without knowing it, like a bird that does not reflect, I am a bird. Such wholesome simplicity was to fade all too soon. Incomparable splendours succeed this golden age: after Père Coton, Père Surin; after Marillac, M. de Bernières; after Duval, Père de Condren and M. Olier; after Mme Acarie, another Marie of the Incarnation, Mme Martin. I do not forget these brilliant lights, but I pass on to the third generation that were to follow them. Behind Mme Acarie and Mme Martin looms a lofty, seductive, sinister figure—Mme Guyon. I have no wish to be hard on the noble woman who wished to resuscitate under Louis XIV the wonders of Mysticism belonging to the time of Henri IV and Louis XIII, nor am I one of those who hold Fénelon to have been an evil genius. He came too late into a century grown old and which over long had been laughing at mystics. Had he been a contemporary, friend and disciple of Mme Acarie, Fénelon might not have written the *Maximes des Saints:* but would there have been anything to prevent his writing the *Traité de l'Amour de Dieu*?[1]

[1] What has been written of the influence of Mme Acarie strictly speaking applies only to our first period; Bérulle, living or dead, seems to me the predominating figure of the second.

2. *Jean de Quintanadoine of Brittany*

The changes in the curiosity, taste and historic sense of the public are indeed strange. Some fifty years ago a writer of merit, the Abbé Houssaye, undertook to describe in his Life of the Cardinal de Bérulle the origins of the French Carmel. In every line of the documents at his disposal he is confronted by one of those figures which any historian of to-day would find interesting, one of those beings who make us *sentir notre sujet*, as d'Aurevilly used to say. This personage leaves the Abbé Houssaye cold; his originality provokes no smile, he plays a leading part and is regarded as an obscure and insignificant super. As to studying him, making discoveries about him, there is no idea of such a thing. For the Abbé, the hero of this history is Pierre de Bérulle; for us, it is first Mme Acarie, and immediately after her Jean de Quintanadoine. Which is right? The reader must decide; the question is not unimportant. In attributing the first place to Pierre de Bérulle, Houssaye is supporting a theory, highly attractive, no doubt, but to our mind more than doubtful.[1] He represents the Carmel as wholly Bérullian and specifically French, in fact another Oratory. According to him, the message of those early Carmelites was no doubt the message of S. Teresa, but retouched, adapted to our national exigencies and to the individual tone of Bérulle, as much later the genius of Shakespeare was acclimatized among us by Ducis or the romanticists. Such an interpretation has far-reaching results, threatening to disturb a unique bit of history; if our Carmelites were no more than *bérulliennes*, they would interest me little; we should be better employed in learning to know Bérulle himself and his great disciples. For God forbid that I should belittle the founder of the Oratory. Bérulle is a world in himself, which we shall explore later, admiring without reserve the man who formed Condren, Vincent de Paul, M. Olier, Bossuet himself. But the spirit of Bérulle differs from that spirit of S. Teresa, simpler, more human, more mystic, more universal, which the early Carmelites

[1] For the Abbé Houssaye and all the historical and canonical problems raised by the most complicated history of the origins of the French Carmel, I refer continually to the *Mémoire sur la fondation, le gouvernement et l'observance des carmelites dechaussées, publié par les soins des carmélites du premier monastère de Paris*, Rheims, 1894. This excellent work is not on sale in the ordinary way, but the Carmelites willingly send a copy to those who desire to make a serious study of Carmel.

introduced to France. Many of these owed much to Bérulle who formed them with a master hand, yet he but quickened in them the seed sown by another, and those who received most from him remained before all daughters of S. Teresa. Whether Spanish or French matters little. The higher Mysticism knows no frontiers; France opened as eagerly as Spain to the great reformer. Though it took root on French soil, Carmel remained Carmel, nothing more and nothing less. We must retract the words written above: the outstanding hero of the following history is S. Teresa conquering France. Jean de Quintanadoine was, under Providence, the instrument of this conquest, an insignificant, obscure, awkward man, but obstinate and indomitable. His very littleness exalts him in my eyes. The dream of introducing S. Teresa into France fascinated and absorbed him, he existed for nothing else. He never distracts us from S. Teresa as the intensely individual Bérulle could not fail to do. We see in him one of the faithful servants found in children's stories, a wholly disinterested fellow, obstinate, devoted, who, in the end, manages to win a kingdom for his master. To show him as I see him I should need the novelist's art. An eighteenth-century Jesuit, Père de Beauvais, wrote a good Life of him, but with an epic solemnity which magnifies him unduly and renders him banal. An unpublished biography by one of Jean de Quintanadoine's friends, M. Champagnot, and the admirable chronicles of Carmel depict him with more simplicity and more truth. These minutely accurate documents have a vein of humour for the modern reader which I shall not attempt to conceal. The joyous history of Carmel must not be written with too Jansenist a pen. The Spanish Carmelites brought into France by Quintanadoine may not have packed the tambourine of S. Teresa in their baggage, but they certainly did not leave behind the fresh gaiety of their mother. Quintanadoine in his lifetime must more than once have amused them; even to-day when his name is spoken in the parlour of some Carmel, one imagines smiles and flashes of dainty malice behind the grille. Too heavy a hand in the historian of Quintanadoine would not be in keeping.

The Quintanadueñas came from Seville. The ancestor of our hero, Jean de Quintanadueñas, *seigneur* of Brétigny-sur-Brionne, belonged to "that Spanish colony which, in the sixteenth century, gradually established itself among the people of Normandy." That

Normandy was destined to become one of the chief centres of the Renaissance of Mysticism, an honour at first sight rather surprising, is due in a measure to this Spanish immigration. Fernand, eldest son of the first Jean, served "brilliantly in the army of Charles IX, married in 1552 a rich heiress of Roumois, Catherine Cavelier de Villequier, laid down his sword and settled at Rouen," in the street of S. Étienne-des-Tonneliers, where was born, on July 6, 1555, the future founder of the French Carmel. Our predecessors had a taste for levelling. For them Jean, whom the Spanish Carmelites called Don Juan and most of his contemporaries M. de Quintanadoine, is merely M. de Brétigny. M. Houssaye gives him no other name, disdaining the fine sonorous syllables that recall the origin and explain the mission of this compatriot of S. Teresa. One of the sisters of Fernand was maid-of-honour to Eleanor of Austria, second wife to Francis I, another and younger sister married Robert de Hanyvel or Hannivel and had for daughter the famous Carmelite Marie d'Hannivel (Marie de la Trinité), one of the foundresses of the Carmel at Dijon, where she received, loved, and formed the Baronne de Chantal.[1]

Jean de Quintanadoine's introduction to religion was purely Spanish. As a child he was sent to one of his uncles in Seville, there to remain for nearly ten years. On his return to Normandy he began before long the principal business of his life, continually signing bills of exchange. His father, a very good man and refusing his son nothing, had great wealth, and Jean himself had a considerable private fortune which he devoted at an early date to the service of the poor and of the Church. We may compare him to the rich manufacturers who to-day build splendid monasteries such as Maredsous, or support propaganda like the publications of the Rue Bayard. Quintanadoine had a passion for giving; his papers—he burnt nothing—afford touching instances of his charity, begging letters or letters of thanks addressed to him, even when he was no more than twenty. In 1577 friends from Antwerp told him of the misery of a young Flemish widow with a large family, whose virtue was menaced. A cheque was sent at once, and in reply came a noble letter which Quintanadoine carefully filed. About the same date one of his Spanish

[1] Most of these details are derived from a study of M. Paul Baudry: *Les religieuses carmélites à Rouen, documents inédite*, Rouen, 1879.

friends was wandering up and down Italy for amusement and plunging into vice. When his money ran out this scatterbrain appealed to his friend Quintanadoine, who replied by frequent letters " full of sane advice and holy warnings, to which he added from time to time remittances."[1] This was Quintanadoine's way, and though somewhat odd it succeeded, for on returning from Italy the young man became a Carthusian. But the years passed and a serious problem, destined to trouble Quintanadoine for a long while, presented itself: What should he do with his life? Humble by nature and but poorly educated, he shrank from the priesthood, and although strongly drawn towards the religious life, his health was too delicate for the work of a lay brother. On the other hand, his father was urging him to marry. Jean would not say no, but his assent was half-hearted. Slow, methodical, and always requiring to help out his thoughts by his pen, he began to write in his diary his ideal of the perfect wife, " where he specified the qualities of the woman whom he would marry, in whom he demanded nearly all the virtues of one who had reached perfection "—an innocent expedient to gain time. He made himself ill by his mental agonies. " The doctors say it is melancholy," he writes to a relation, " and they are not far wrong." It was a lucky illness, lasting just as long as was necessary to save him from the proposed marriage. Not that this chapter was finished—nothing happened quickly in this hesitating life. Worthy Fernand de Quintanadoine had no desire to force his big timid boy, so he sent him to Spain in search of distraction and health, the journey combining pleasure and business, for Jean had to conduct the sale of considerable property still possessed there by his family. " It was by these commonplace paths that Providence carried out its merciful designs for its servant " and for France. According to the Divine plan, as yet unsuspected, he set out " to taste the fruits of the garden of the great saint, Teresa, and to transplant therefrom some of the rarest and most exquisite plants to French soil, whence the perfume of their flowers and sweetness of their fruits were wafted so ravishingly that not only the whole

[1] *Vie inédite de Jean de Quintanadoine*, by M. Champagnot, p. 14. I quote this precious document from a copy, dating from the second half of the seventeenth century, preserved at the first Carmel of Paris (now in exile at Brussels). The copy seems trustworthy. It has been made with scrupulous accuracy and the copyist has not shrunk from using certain words which I cannot reproduce.

kingdom, but also Flanders, Burgundy and other neighbouring countries were desirous of possessing this boon."[1]

I have already said that Jean took his time over everything; his journey lasted four years (1582–6). He no sooner arrived at Seville than he formed an intimacy with a devout young man, Don Pedro de Tholosa, who invited him one day to accompany him to the Carmelites. Jean, it would appear, had never heard of S. Teresa, and "from what he knew of the disorders prevailing in certain Spanish communities, feared to set foot in such establishments." "Every nun," so Champagnot explains, to justify this repugnance, "had at that time a soul-friend, whose devotion took the form of frequent visits and long and useless discourse, accompanied by the exchange of little gifts." But no one I know has long resisted the charm of the Carmelites, and from his first interview with the Seville prioress, Marie de Saint-Joseph, Jean was gained over for good. "He felt born within him an enthusiasm for the propagation of this new Order . . . and knew no satisfaction save in the Church of the Daughters of S. Teresa. . . . He went there every afternoon and spent several hours in prayer. The silence and recollectedness prevailing in the church, only interrupted by slow and tender chanting, caused him to weep and stirred up ardent desires for the execution of the great project with which grace had inspired him. . . . He wished to learn more precisely in what the reforms of S. Teresa consisted," and the Prioress afforded him all facilities by introducing him to Père Jerome Gratian, first Provincial of the Discalced Carmelites. This was a man of great merit, illustrious birth, deep learning, and consummate experience of the ways of God. After passing his early life in the Court of Philip II, King of Spain, he had renounced the most flattering worldly prospects to embrace the reform of S. Teresa, to which he added lustre by his graces and virtues. It was to this holy religious that M. de Brétigny went to learn all that could enable him to form a just appreciation of the new Order. What Jean de Quintanadoine did, he did thoroughly. For three months he passed long hours of each day among the novices of Père Gratian, living their life and sharing their exercises, although for the rest of

[1] Champagnot, *ibid.*, pp. 21, 22; Beauvais, *La Vie de M. de Brétigny*, Paris, 1747, p. 38. I quote alternately from these two sources, although Père de Beauvais has merely modernised earlier work.

the day he was a gentleman at large, provisionally decided on marriage. In the last years of his life he would often recall the ardent memories of that time for the benefit of his friend Champagnot. "Of such experiences," the latter writes, "I will record one as sample of the rest. He told me that in these retreats he had often seen the novice-master (Gratian) holding a crucifix on high, exclaiming, *qui en quiere morir por Cristo?* . . . that is to say . . . not merely to die for Jesus Christ if the occasion should present itself, but at once to accept and suffer some sharp mortification. . . . Scarce would he finish speaking when, as with one voice, all those novices, ardent as cherubim, would vie in crying out: 'I! I!' . . . and the venerable priest, dwelling on these recollections, would glow with an equal fire."[1] After such experience we can understand that the world held no temptations for him. One of his favourite practices was to seek out Seville courtesans with his pockets full of money, "and make a pact with those miserable ones to give them so much each day if they would keep from sin." The Aunt with whom he sojourned, seeing him beggaring himself by such charity, made many a scene. "'Keep your money for your children!' she would cry with abusive language, wishing him fifty of them."[2]

A few months had turned this slow and deliberate young layman into the passionate admirer, the agent and slave of Carmel. When Portugal asked for some sisters of the Teresian reform, Quintanadoine, "in spite of his youth, was commissioned to go to Lisbon and to make all arrangements for the holy work." He was successful, and it was he again who, with a guard of ten gendarmes, escorted from Seville to Lisbon the Mother Marie de Saint-Joseph and the other Carmelites chosen for this foundation; he too who installed them in the new dwelling and watched over all their needs. He was one of those delightfully good and humble people whose devotion is accepted as the most natural thing in the world. At this period his zeal for the Daughters of Teresa nearly led him overseas. He learned at Lisbon "that an *infanta*, daughter of the King of the Congo, in Guinea, had seen an image of the Holy Virgin robed as a Carmelite and desired to know what it meant," and, her curiosity being satisfied, had con-

[1] Champagnot, *ibid.*, pp. 28–9; Beauvais, *ibid.*, pp. 46–7.
[2] *Ibid.*, p. 32.

ceived "a great desire to join this Order,"[1] so she herself wrote to Mother Marie de Saint-Joseph, requesting that a band of Carmelites might be sent to her. It was a time when the legendary was real and nothing seemed too good to be true. Marie de Saint-Joseph assented. And to whom should she turn if not to Quintanadoine for help in executing the project? But "when he was on the point of crossing to Africa with three religious of the Reform . . . he had the pain of learning that unforeseen events had dashed all their hopes." The missionaries over there had no longer access to the palace or to the princess. They had been cruelly deceived and were to have many more disappointments. But Quintanadoine never admitted defeat; long after we shall see him preparing with imperturbable confidence for his voyage to the Congo.

How could the idea of introducing Carmel into France have failed to occur to him? and how could Mother Marie de Saint-Joseph have failed to receive so magnificent a prospect with rapture? "I would rather go to France than to any other place!" she wrote later, ever faithful, in this respect as in all others, to the spirit of the great reformer, for when S. Teresa undertook the task of reform she had "specially in view the salvation of France." "Having learnt," she says in her *Chemin de la perfection*, "of the blows delivered at the Catholic faith in France, . . . my soul was racked with sorrow, seeing that the adorable Master had so many foes, so few friends. I wished that his friends at least should be utterly devoted to him, and I resolved to do the utmost that in me lay." If this rings strangely in our ears we must realize the true meaning of these generous souls. France for them spelt almost certain martyrdom; they imagined scarce any there save Protestants and executioners, and aspired to save France by sacrificing themselves for us.

Quintanadoine soon came to an agreement with the sisters and "departed from Seville to propose this great project to the Carmelite Fathers of the Reform, just then assembled at Pastrana in New Castille. He explained to them the desire which God had put in his heart to procure for his country the establishment of their Reform, together with his motives and the means at his command for that

[1] I quote the original narrative of Champagnot. It is curious to remark the free translation of the text given by Père de Beauvais: "They presented her (the Infanta) with several devotional pictures . . . among them certain representing *the saints* habited like Daughters of Teresa" (p. 59).

end. The Fathers thanked God for the holy purpose that inspired his generous heart, and gave him full powers to act as he thought best for the success of the enterprise; every one of them signed the Commission for which he asked. S. John of the Cross was among those presiding at this venerable assembly. . . . After giving him his commission they represented that it would be advisable to procure permission for them to settle in France first, as then they would be in a position to aid the nuns of the Reform who, without such assistance, might upon arrival find themselves in difficulties. M. de Brétigny deferred to the Fathers' proposal, returned to Seville, arranged his family affairs and . . . set out for France.

"Passing through Madrid, he confided his project to M. de Longlée, the French ambassador, who was delighted and gave him letters of recommendation to the Court, and subsequently wrote to him at Burgos where he had broken his journey. The contents of the letter were worthy of the minister of the Most Christian King. 'I herewith return the memoirs you entrusted to me regarding the reform set on foot by Mother Teresa of Jesus, together with the copy of a letter written by me to the King upon the subject. You will see how sincerely I enter into your views and how much I desire to serve you therein. At Madrid, November 2, 1586, Longlée.'"

These were strange times, when ambassadors of the Most Christian King wrote such letters! Nor were they empty promises. Furnishing proofs to Henri III "of his zeal for the service of His Majesty," Longlée "includes among his good offices in Spain his ardour in helping to despatch to France a new community of nuns, the most fitted to draw down the benediction of God on this kingdom and to diffuse an edification which can restore order in other communities fallen from their first fervour."[1] As one sees, the enterprise appears to him reasonable and possible; as little as Quintanadoine did he foresee the obstacles that for twenty years would hinder it. He had taken the scheme of the young layman very seriously, just as the leading Carmelite nuns had done and the great Chapter of the Carmel. Quintanadoine must have been more influential than one would imagine from the slight attention given him by the historians of the French Carmelites. He did not have the diplomatic agility later to be displayed by Bérulle, any more than he had the eminent wisdom

[1] Beauvais, pp. 64–8.

of Mme Acarie. He was very humble and gladly effaced himself in favour of those who were one day to complete his work. He appears to us zealous and tenacious rather than a genius, but none the less we must not underrate him.

We leave Spain and return with him to Normandy, knowing that neither delays nor disappointments will choke the French seed sown by him in his various Spanish cloisters.

I wish (writes a Spanish Carmelite to him) that you could have been in this convent lately and seen a vessel with crimson ensign, with sails and drum, with the device " Who will embark for France ? " You would have beheld many sisters running together, embracing the Cross and declaring their desire to die for the defence of the Faith; then up came others with staves and knives, laying about them as though they would fain stretch all dead before them. Such rehearsals, though in sport, proceed none the less from heartfelt desires.

It was thus that they represented France in these picturesque and innocent diversions of theirs.

This sinner Marie (writes Marie de Saint-Joseph to him in her turn) is quite prepared to depart for France. I write you this letter in French with the help of Mother Catherine du Saint-Esprit, who is my mistress in this tongue and who greatly rejoices that our Reverend Father has promised that, if we go to France, she shall come with us as interpreter; for she knows French, Spanish, and Flemish well.

And Quintanadoine replies:

The Lord begins to accomplish the desire of His poor servant. I had besought His Majesty that it might please Him to be glorified, blessed and praised in the French tongue by souls of your Order.[1]

II. Back in Normandy, where he remained for six years (1586-1592), Quintanadoine found himself once more at grips with the insoluble problem which had once made him ill, but which his activities in Spain had made him forget—marriage or the priesthood? His father entreating him to decide, he said that he was ready to do his will, in other words, to marry, " but added that he besought him to be allowed to confer in France and Spain with certain worthy

[1] Champagnot, pp. 51, 52, 55. Quintanadoine's reply is dated Oct. 11, 1586.

persons whose views he would follow blindly." It is amusing to hear that, with the exception of his Carmelites, all his councillors, even Jerome Gratian himself, plumped for marriage. "When I consider," wrote Gratian to him, "the state of affairs in France, I think that a married man, fervent and devout, can do much good, rearing a family in piety, and affording a refuge for those called to the office of apostles."[1] He declared himself ready to marry; but there the matter rested.

Despite the numerous good works that claimed all his time and wealth, "it was at this date that his devotion suggested to him that he should make an experiment in the apostolic life. Without exercising the ministry of the word, he endeavoured to fulfil one of its most important functions, setting himself to draw up for certain people who consulted him a series of spiritual counsels suited to their various conditions. In this he was singularly successful and made up for the excessive timidity that hampered him in spiritual intercourse by word of mouth.

"He made a rule never to pass a day without engaging in this good work, which was as dear to him as any other of his exercises. Several of these instructive letters have been preserved; they are full of discernment, they breathe in every line the spirit of God. Ecclesiastics and religious, those consecrated to God and those living in the world, all alike addressed themselves to the saintly young man and found in his counsels the help most fitted to their needs."[2] Strictly speaking, his were hardly spiritual letters, but rather pious notes, short meditations, and "a certain kind of dialogue between God and some saint or other." "I find that these little papers speak straight to my heart," wrote one Carmelite to him, and another:

Shortly before I departed from Seville, I received some of your letters, which I read, but left one for another time. But when about to set out, which I longed to do, being distressed by the weeping of our sisters, I seated myself by a window and, to comfort myself in this my great sorrow, drew out your letter and read it. Never in my life had I received such consolation. It seemed as though you had divined all that was passing in my soul, so that I wept and laughed both at once and became quite resolved to depart for the greater glory of God, for in truth it was as if you constrained me thereto.[3]

[1] Champagnot, p. 102. [2] Beauvais, pp. 83–4. [3] Champagnot, p. 75.

Quintanadoine's tracts took wing for the most unexpected places. "Several of them were written for the ladies and maids of the Royal Court of the Kingdom of Congo in Africa, under cover to Brascorrea, the black King's confessor and preacher, to distribute as he thought fit." Brascorrea "translated and read them from the pulpit amid the general applause of the assembly."[1]

Many of these jottings, most perhaps, were written at first for the author's own personal use, as a continuation of his private prayers. But this shy, tongue-tied man did not mind even these being read by friends. Imagine Pascal sending the *Mystère de Jésus* to Mlle. Roannez or to M. Singlin. The comparison is not so bizarre as it seems. Except in genius, which in these matters is unimportant, they have the same grave and tender ardour, the same depth of sentiment, even the same dramatic form. Read, for instance, the following touching page written during the siege of Rouen.

S. Martin's Day, Nov. 11, 1591. A man asked God to preserve the people of Rouen. The Lord commanded him to rise at five in the morning for love of Him, and to spend the time till seven o'clock in prayer.

He asked Him again to take pity on the kingdom and not suffer so many souls therein to be lost. The Lord granted him this and commanded him to do his utmost to further the introduction of the Carmel into France and that he should likewise aid the Society of Jesus in their need of the moment.

He said again: "Lord, have pity on my father, my brethren, and my house." The Lord granted this too, and said: "Serve thy father and thy brothers, negotiate thy business, that I may see how diligent thou wilt be in Mine. For how couldst thou accomplish My affairs, didst thou acquit thyself badly in thine own?"

He asked a third time: "Sooth, Lord, for the love of Thy beloved Son and for love of me, Thy great sinner, manifest Thy glory to-day to all the souls in Purgatory." The Lord granted it and said to him: "Thou shalt confess and communicate and say a hundred Paters and Aves upon thy blessed beads and cause four Masses to be said for them."

Again he besought and said: "Lord, have pity on those who are in mortal sin. In truth, for love of Thy Son and of me, great sinner that I am, needs must that Thou draw a thousand out of sin." Yet once again he asked and said: "Lord, cause that Carmelites be brought to France through me." And the Lord granted it.[2]

[1] Champagnot, p. 73.

[2] Champagnot, pp. 95–8.

In this long prayer, he forgets himself wholly, of so little worth was he in his own eyes. Here is a letter, more personal and more sorrowful, written later to one of the first French Carmelites. The original text, " one of the jewels " of the Rouen archives, to quote a scholar, is in Spanish.

" Mother Marie de la Trinité. Pontoise. Jesus! To whom shall I write, my God and my Saviour, to whom address my tears? On whom shall I repose, O ye my compassionate friends, for my pain is great.

" O Lord, meseems that earth and Heaven are shut to me."

" Jean, self-love is great in thee, it may be that thou art afflicted for thyself and not from pure love."

" O Lord, I am full of self-love and of a thousand sins."

" Jean, thou receivest the chastisement of thy faults, because thus thou losest time and performest thy works ill and imperfectly. Thou art like one who should enter into the King's treasury filled with silver, gold, precious stones great and small, and to whom the King should say: ' Take what thou wouldst and canst, while the clock strikes; all is thine.'

" Ah, how diligent would be the man in gorging himself with riches, how he would speedily load himself with diamonds, rather than that which is of small value. So shouldest thou do, in this thine hour of life."

" Lord, I regret the time past. . . ."

" Well then, from now out employ it worthily."

" O Lord, may I do so! . . . ."

" Jean, thou dost but waste time. . . ."

" O Lord, what a loss not to serve Thee! Ah, what loss! That I may serve Thee, O my God! "

" Well, what hinders thee in serving Me? "

" I hinder myself. . . . O Lord, long since I have offered Thee soul and body, since this belongs to Thee, take it. . . ."

" Jean, since it belongs to Me and Thou hast given it Me, I take and accept it as Mine. Now I give it thee anew, no longer thine, but Mine."

" O Lord . . . give me Thy grace, and I shall live, no longer mine, but as Thine and for Thee. . . ."

These very simple lines, which would seem almost banal from another pen, touch us by their genuine sincerity. One feels, and can scarce tell how, that here the dialogue is no literary device or sickly fiction. Whether we like it or not, the real persons are present,

Jean and Another; the Other is not to be revealed by mere eloquence, but we recognise Him in the stammerings of the lowly Quintanadoine as clearly as in the sublime prose of Pascal.

However, "a suitable marriage from the point of view of money and family" presenting itself, Quintanadoine bravely accepted his father's choice, only requesting permission to go to Spain beforehand, in order to arrange the matter of the Carmelites. There was no Machiavellianism in these final procrastinations. He agreed to celebrate the betrothal before his departure and presented his *fiancée* with a pearl necklace. Yet in his heart there lurked the desire that at the eleventh hour something unexpected should restore him his freedom. He could not have foreseen that his absence would last for two years (1592–4). So once again he was on Spanish highways, going from Carmel to Carmel, preaching his crusade and received everywhere with transports of joy. "The greater number of the Carmelites," he wrote, "entreated so earnestly to be enrolled in the holy expedition that, had they been taken at their word, the greater part of the Spanish convents must have been depopulated."[1] The Fathers showed, however, less ardour, and Philip II and his councillors still less. The times were, in fact, badly chosen for a project of the kind. What reception would the France of the *Satire menippée*[2] give the victorious Spaniards? After two years' entreaties, tired of the struggle, Quintanadoine sadly retook the road to Normandy; he was feverish, and the illness grew worse during the journey. He reached Rouen at length, but so ill that all deemed him near his end. Nothing can be refused to a dying man. His father had no heart to speak to him about his marriage and himself proposed his son's Ordination. The long looked-for miracle had come at last, Heaven had revealed its will, and the sick man soon recovered. He placed himself under the direction of M. Gallemant, one of the most saintly men of the time, and was ordained subdeacon in 1596, priest in 1598.

During all these changes he never abandoned his cherished design; fifty years of disappointment would not have shaken him. Suddenly a simple method occurred to him. France knew nothing as yet of S. Teresa, so he would reveal her to his adopted country. On one

[1] *Mémoire sur la fondation, le gouvernement et l'observance des carmelites dechaussées*, I. 528.

[2] [A satire which appeared in 1593 against the *Ligue*. Tr.]

of his Spanish journeys, learning that Mother Anne de Jésus was engaged "on the publication of the works of the saintly Mother, drawn from the keeping of the Inquisition," he had left with her a considerable sum to defray the expenses of the first edition, which appeared in 1588. He now began to translate the saint's life into French, aided in the task by Père du Chèvre, prior of the Carthusian monastery of Bourgfontaine (1601). He also had engraved the portrait of S. Teresa in copperplate, which "soon was spread throughout France together with her works, by means of which people of all sorts and conditions were attracted to the interior life and a multitude of maidens from the leading towns of the kingdom desired to join that Order."[1]

Thus ends the first chapter of this wonderful history, but the rôle of Jean de Quintanadoine was not yet finished. More zealous than ever, he effaced himself more and more behind the great foundress and the first superiors of the French Carmel—Mme Acarie, Bérulle, Duval, Gallemant. But the triumphant work remained his doing. In the words of the venerable Mother de Saint-Barthélemy: "Among all the Frenchmen who laboured to plant the reform of S. Teresa on French soil, God bestowed the palm on Jean de Quintanadoine: *Entre todos Dios le dio la Ventaja*."[2]

III. M. Duval must be allowed to tell us the chain of circumstances by which Mme Acarie was led to undertake the foundation of the French Carmel.

The works of the holy Mother Teresa together with her life . . . having been translated from the Spanish into French, were sold in Paris and read by the devout, some of whom, frequenting the house of Mme Acarie, so praised them to her, that the blessed one desired them to read her some chapters; she could not read them herself, from fear of being rapt into ecstasy. She listened attentively, yet was not much struck at the first, and wondered that the saintly Mother had been able to found so great an Order in the Church. It was doubtless the devil, who, foreseeing what was to happen, inspired this distaste and coldness, for as a rule at the least word of God or of Holy Scripture she would go into ecstasy. Some days later, when she was at prayer, lo, the holy Mother Teresa herself appeared to her visibly, warning

[1] Cf. *Mémoire*, I. 543.

[2] *Autobiographie de la vénérable mère Anne de Saint-Barthélemy*, translated by M. Bouix, Paris, 1869, pp. 93–4.

her that it was the Will of God that she should found in France convents of the Carmelite Order. Whether this vision was intellectual or sensible we cannot decide, for her director, Père Dom Beaucousin, being dead, there is no means of knowing; but it remained so present with her and so profoundly impressed on her soul, that she felt the necessity, despite inward repugnance, of begging the good Father to lay the matter before God. This he did fervently . . . (and) was of opinion that she should hold a meeting to consider means for the successful carrying out of the project, since he was assured that it was the Will of God.

They accordingly prayed M. Gallemant and M. de Brétigny, who were then in Normandy, to come to Paris, since these were known to be greatly set on the establishment of this Order. The meeting took place (in the Chartreuse at Paris) in the cell of Dom Beaucousin, Père de Bérulle and myself being present. The business was discussed, and so many difficulties were encountered that it was declared impossible, and the blessed one was bidden put it out of her mind, at least till God should have removed the great obstacles then existing.

It was in 1601, with the *Ligue* just ended. The great difficulty, we can readily understand, was to make the King and the country consent to a Spanish invasion. Mme Acarie, continues Duval,

was quite calm and determined to think no more of the business. But, seven or eight months later, the holy Mother appeared to her the second time, commanding her, more imperatively and forcibly than the first time, to bring the matter again under consideration and assuring her that . . . she would succeed. This second revelation being communicated to the Carthusian Father, he assembled once more the same persons who had attended the first meeting, together with M. de Sales, Bishop of Geneva, who was at that time gaining great reputation by preaching in Paris.

At this meeting . . . the affair was practically decided on, and it only remained to consider means of bringing it about. After deliberation, it was agreed that the first house should be established at Paris . . . that town being the capital of the kingdom and the meeting-place of all people of quality, whence the Order would readily spread through all the provinces. . . . And as in the establishment of an Order it is needful to understand its living spirit . . . it was next decided not to rest content with the book of the Rule and the Constitutions . . . but that someone should go to Spain to ask for Sisters. Thirdly, although the Order was already established and recognised by the Church in

Spain and Italy, yet, before introducing it into France, it was resolved to resort to the Holy Father the Pope, since there was no greater evil than lack of full powers. . . . Plainly also the Convent must be founded by some person of quality.

At the request of Mme Acarie, the Princesse de Longueville willingly lent her name and promised to endeavour to interest the King, whose consent was necessary. "She carried out her promise and obtained the letters of foundation, which were given by Henri IV, on July 18, 1602, and registered at once by the Parlement." As for the site of the monastery "they found it more convenient . . . to have it in the Faubourg Saint-Jacques, on the site of a former Benedictine Priory called Notre-Dame-des Champs, where, according to ancient Paris tradition, S. Denis, the apostle of France, had dwelt when he proclaimed the Catholic Faith to the Parisians."[1] To gain so precious a spot was not easy, but the calm will and perseverance of Mme Acarie carried the day. As yet there was neither approbation from Rome nor had the Spanish sisters responded. Yet, sure that she would not be disappointed in either quarter, this strong soul set to work, fashioning with her own hand the first stones of the French foundation, that is to say the young maids and matrons grouped around her, and actively superintending the building of the monastery. The future chancellor, Michel de Marillac, lent her his great credit and his business experience. He, too, had come under the spell of the life of S. Teresa and, getting wind of Mme Acarie's plans, put himself at her disposal. Princes of the blood, doctors of the Sorbonne, high magistrates, heroic women of all ranks from the highest to the humblest, all France joined together in the foundation of the French Carmel.

On March 21, 1603, the keys of the Priory of Notre-Dame-des-Champs were placed in the hands of M. de Marillac, acting for the

[1] Duval, *ibid.*, pp. 120–6. Cf. on the subject of the Priory the excellent works of M. l'Abbé Grente, *Une paroisse de Paris sous l'ancien régime, S. Jacques du Haut-Pas*, Paris, 1897, and the *Notice historique sur Notre-Dame-des-Champs*, Paris, 1885. This last, dedicated to the present and very modern parish of the name, recalls very happily memories of the ancient Priory, as well as of the Carmel later occupying its site. After the entrance into possession of the latter, the name of Notre-Dame-des-Champs disappears from the map of mystical Paris, and, "despite its glorious memories, must have fallen into oblivion had it not in the eighteenth century been bestowed on a street near the Luxembourg. But no church in Paris bore the name until it was given to a new parish, in the quarter of Mont-Parnasse, in 1858."

Princesse de Longueville. The workmen took possession at once, and all went forward on the lines traced by S. Teresa herself for the convents of Spain. On March 24, the Duchesse de Nemours, representing Queen Marie de Medicis, who had accepted the title of first foundress, laid the first stone of the cloisters; the Princesse de Longueville and her sister the Princesse d'Estouteville, as second foundresses, laid the second. The ceremony was attended with great pomp amidst an assembly numerous and brilliant as were all assemblies of this kind in those days. Some days later, M. de Bérulle and M. de Marillac laid the first stone of the choir. Mme Acarie had descended with them and the architect into the foundation trench. Lost in recollection during the ceremony, she remarked at the end to M. de Bérulle: "You will be the spiritual foundation of this edifice!" and turning towards M. de Marillac, added: "And you the temporal!" Both sayings were fulfilled to the letter, M. de Bérulle being till his death the director of the new convent, and M. de Marillac not only giving large sums for its establishment, but for many years acting as its honorary man of business.[1]

Some months after, the good news came from Rome that Clement VIII had granted the bull of institution in terms entirely satisfactory to the founders. Only the Spanish Carmelites were wanting, but would they ever come?[2]

IV. The Carmelites following the Teresian Rule lived at that time in Spain under the jurisdiction of the Discalced Carmelite Fathers, that is to say, that branch which had accepted the Reform of S. Teresa, and to which the saint's dearest friends, Jerome Gratian and John of the Cross, belonged. "At this moment," wrote the great reformer one day, "houses of the primitive rule are being founded for the friars of the Order, on the model of those which I have established for my nuns and where will prevail a like spirit of devotion and mortification; and it is to these monasteries that we shall be subordinated."[3] This general direction is entirely just and natural, but it must not be supposed that the saint had made a hard-and-fast ruling for all time, of this submission of her Daughters to the Discalced Fathers. She herself,

[1] Prince Emmanuel de Broglie, *La bienheureuse Marie de l'Incarnation*, Paris, 1913, pp. 111–13.

[2] I have summed up and abridged a chapter of endless detail. Those desiring to study the subject more at length have only to turn to the first Vol. of M. Houssaye's *M. de Bérulle et les carmélites de France*, but especially to the admirable *Mémoire sur la fondation*, etc., closely adhered to in the following pages.

[3] *Lettres de Sainte Thérèse*, Bouix, I. 84.

when circumstances demanded it, did not hesitate to put her houses under an authority outside the Order. Thus for long years the Avila foundation had no other superior than the Bishop of that town, Don Alvaro de Mendoza. The question is of less importance than an outsider might imagine. The canonical superior of a religious house directs it from a distance, leaving a good deal of initiative to the abbess or prioress, and only intervening in certain cases clearly defined by the custom and rules of the Church. He has no right to modify as he likes the internal organisation, essential tradition, or local spirit of the convent in his charge, nor would he have any means of doing so. To-day, for instance, studying the various religious congregations of a diocese, each with its own peculiarities, who would imagine that all had in reality but one Superior, the diocesan bishop? I emphasise these elementary principles, because everything depends on them in studying the delicate subject in hand. Whether Nuns of Carmel are governed by the Fathers of the Order or by bishops or by any other delegates of the pontifical authority, they remain none the less Carmelites, This was plainly contemplated by Pope Clement VIII when in his bull founding the French Carmel he placed the future sisterhood under the authority, not of the Discalced Fathers, who were not yet introduced into France, but of three ecclesiastics, Bérulle, Gallemant, and Duval. This triumvirate certainly never claimed a mission to create a new Order, or even to change an ancient one by adapting it to fit French conditions, but merely that of maintaining on French soil with scrupulous exactness the very spirit of S. Teresa.

From another point of view, no longer concerning the official government of the monasteries, but that of the private direction of the nuns, the saint had no desire to subordinate her daughters or herself to the ruling of any single Order. She freely consulted secular priests and religious of every habit, the Jesuit Alvarez, for instance, the Dominican Bañes, the Franciscan Peter of Alcantara; and she grants the same liberty to her Carmelites.

People persuade themselves (she writes with her keen and lofty wisdom) that it is a great gain in Religion to have to do with but one confessor, and the devil often ensnares souls thus. . . . If in their distress, the sisters request another confessor, it appears to convulse the whole cause of religion, and if this confessor be of another Order, were he even a S. Jerome, the mere idea is an insult to their own foundation. Give God the thanks then, my daughters, for the liberty you enjoy; for, without having recourse to a multitude of confessors, it is permitted to you beside the usual ones, to have spiritual relations with others capable of illuminating you in all things.[1]

In any case, the union between the Carmelite Fathers and the Sisters was naturally very close. They had much to bring them together—the same rule, the same spirit, the same heroic memories of struggles for reform, the same tender veneration of a common Mother. The breaking of this union could not but be very painful on both sides, yet it was the sacrifice demanded both of the Spanish Carmelites chosen for the French foundation and of the Discalced Fathers. The latter, it is true, had formerly accepted the proposals of Quintanadoine, but on condition that the summons should be extended to them also and that the French Carmelites should remain under their direction. This condition was now out of the question. The nuns chosen for this exodus—and assuredly they would be taken from the very best—must go alone. The Bidassoa once crossed, neither they nor their future novices would remain under the authority of their spiritual kindred. It was a sacrifice on both sides. In the enthusiasm of departure, doubtless the Spanish ladies saw nothing save the beauty of their mission, but with lengthening exile in a country strange in custom and speech, under the direction of priests doubly strangers to them, since they were neither Carmelites nor Spaniards, all, or at least the greater number, would regret their country, would mourn their absent family. The possible consequences, the dismay that actually ensued, may be judged from a supposed vision, absurd but significant, of one of the Carmelites, by no means the least. Mère Anne de Saint-Barthélemy sees, or believes she sees, S. Teresa in tears, and crying:

"See, my daughter, these sisters who separate themselves from the Order," and she showed me a great number (the French Carmelites?) assembled in a parlour and conversing with outsiders (Bérulle, Duval, Gallemant, Père Coton?)—seculars, ecclesiastics and religious of other Orders than ours. The sisters, thus conversing, became black as crows, and while the strangers had horns, the sisters had beaks, like veritable crows.[2]

[1] *Way of Perfection*, Chap. VIII; for similar passages cf. *Mémoire*, I. 295.

[2] *Mémoire*, I. 189.

To this must be added another reason, childish to our minds, but one which foreigners, and especially Spaniards, found plausible. I have already remarked that they believed France lost, its churches in the power of the Huguenots, and our priests and bishops unsound, to say the least, in the faith. If, thought the Carmelite Fathers, they were not with their spiritual daughters to accompany them to martyrdom, what might not be in store for them? Then again, these grave Spaniards were inclined to think that the splendid zeal of the French would soon die down like a fire of straw, till the tenacious Bérulle and others convinced them of their error. "Later," relates the secretary of Quintanadoine, M. Jean Navet, "I heard Père Joseph, provincial of the province of Castile, say, *ahora veo no es furia francesa*—I see now it is no French madness."[1]

It is easily foreseen therefore that the Discalced Fathers would obstinately oppose the ambassadors of Mme Acarie. In all probability, left to their own resources, both the good but timid Quintanadoine, at first entrusted with this mission, and his successor the strong-minded and more genial Bérulle, would probably have failed. Happily they were backed by a more important personage than even the General of the Carmelite Order, namely, the Pope, who was bent on the success of their enterprise; besides the bull of foundation, the envoys of Mme Acarie were furnished with a pontifical brief, called *bref de jussion*, ordering the Carmelite Fathers to submit, under penalty of grave censure. The French only had recourse to this letter after having exhausted all other means of overcoming subtle and stout resistance. The General yielded *malgré lui*, in his own words, but he did yield.

There is no need to say anything more here about these painful things, which doubtless we ought to know, but which need not distract us from calmer observations. A narrative with innumerable actors is never uniformly good and saintly, but, thank God, sublime, touching, or simply picturesque episodes far outnumber all others in this poem of history which concerns us. That nothing may be wanting to our pleasure, this great adventure is recorded by the actors themselves, Jean Navet, Quintanadoine's steward, and, still better, by a really brilliant woman, Mme. Jourdain.

This lady, widow of a Parisian *bourgeois*, had withdrawn from the world after her husband's death, and was preparing, under the direction

[1] *Mémoire*, I. 714.

of Mme Acarie, to enter the Carmelite Order. A longer introduction is needless, since all unconsciously she paints herself in her piquant and charming memoirs.

The work of building the first convent of the Carmelites (writes Boucher) had already been in progress for six months and the bull which would authorize its foundation was about to be granted at Rome. However, there was still little prospect of getting from Spain the nuns asked for in order to begin the establishment. For nearly a year M. de Brétigny (Quintanadoine) wrote letters . . . to the General of the Spanish Congregation of the reformed Carmelites . . . and always received discouraging replies. . . . Such was the state of things when M. de Brétigny went to treat in person with the Spanish Carmelites. It was Mme Jourdain . . . who was responsible for this journey. "If we cannot have the French Carmelites, we shall have to content ourselves with the Constitutions of the Order in forming our novices!" said Mme Acarie one day, depressed by the refusal of the Spanish General. "If you have not the sisters, the constitutions will avail you nothing!" replied Mme Jourdain. "Who will go and get them?" said the saint. "I will!" said the young widow. The words were as a flash of light for Mme Acarie . . . it was decided on the spot that M. de Brétigny should go to Spain to fetch the Carmelites, taking with him some French ladies to furnish an escort for the promised sisters.

Notice how apposite this suggestion was, that some ladies of quality should go with Quintanadoine. A journey is always a serious undertaking for enclosed religious. Companions of their own sex could not fail to smooth the way for the Spanish nuns, a consideration which had never occurred to Quintanadoine when he set off before with his valet and a chaplain. "Also," as Père Jerome Gratian, one of the most faithful partisans of the French project, wrote, "a rare example of virtue and edification will be afforded when ladies of quality from a distant country come to a strange land to seek so eagerly for something the world recks little of, and thus French devotion will be accredited."[1]

Mme Acarie's biographer continues the narrative.

Mme Jourdain, who had offered to go to Spain, was the first to be chosen. Then came Mme de Pucheuil, a relative of M. de Brétigny (and mother of one of the future Carmelites), herself of Spanish origin and bearing the name Quesada. As a maid for the journey, a member of the little congregation of Ste.-Geneviève, one

[1] *Mémoire*, I. 647.

Rose Lesgue, was chosen, who herself subsequently took the veil. M. Gauthier (councillor of State) went too. At the request of the Duchesse de Longueville, Henri IV sent him to ask in the King's name for some reformed Carmelites . . . to that end providing him with letters for his ambassador at Madrid and for King Philip III.

In order to keep the journey secret, Mme Acarie changed the names of all the travellers, fearing lest, should the Spanish Carmelite Fathers get wind of the enterprise, before ever their country was reached they might checkmate the plan by raising new difficulties. M. de Brétigny set off first by Normandy with his servant Navet . . . the others followed by the ordinary route on September 26, 1603, leaving Paris so secretly that Mme Jourdain did not even take farewell of her children.[1]

Before departure, Quintanadoine had written this last appeal to the General of the Carmelites.

In all humility and reverence I write these few lines, entreating you to receive them graciously for the love of Our Lord. I would remind you of the intention and its accomplishment granted by God to the saintly Mother Teresa . . . when she founded her first monasteries, having heard of the great number of souls being lost through heresy in France, to assist in some measure in remedying so great an evil, she assembled her daughters and bade them apply themselves to devotion and penitence, that God would be pleased to inspire preachers and defenders of the Church. Recollect likewise that Jesus Christ told the holy Mother to found as many convents as she could and to refuse no opportunity.

I beseech you, reverend Father, to consider these two points and to show yourself heir and successor of this saint, and in her spirit to procure the remedy for so many souls on the brink of destruction, that is, the foundation of many of these monasteries in which God delighteth. . . . See the Divine goodness which causes the very country for the welfare of which your reform was instituted, to come and ask for some of your sisters to found convents there. . . . Can your paternal heart refuse your daughters to populate this kingdom, redeemed by the Blood of the Son of God?

You hold the place of Jesus Christ in this holy Order, you are successor of the saintly foundress Teresa, do what the Lord Himself and the saintly woman would do at this crisis. Listen to the humble supplications that we make you to send your sisters, true portraits of their holy mother, who shall implant her rule and manner of good living in this kingdom.

[1] Boucher, pp. 249–52.

You will rejoice, my reverend Father, at the fruits that shall grow on those plants and for ever accrue to your glory, and in proportion to their temporal growth will be the measure of your eternal joy. Valogne, September 30, 1603.[1]

The travellers were to have embarked from Nantes, but for six weeks were delayed by contrary winds. They were obliged therefore to stay at S. Nazaire or Pouliguen, where Quintanadoine, accustomed to such nomad cloister-life, installed his companions in a wretched little house by the sea, drew up a rule, composed and distributed his spiritual papers, and presided at the common exercises. This first trial was soon followed by a more serious one. M. Gauthier, the prudent and experienced layman, councillor of State to Henri IV, left them.

Every evening after supper (writes Champagnot) the venerable Jean wrote on slips of paper the names of as many saints as were people present, adding on each a virtue to be practised with a prayer . . . to entreat a favourable wind and a prosperous journey. Then each of the company drew out one at random. As the time drew on to S. Martin's Day, one of these slips, whose virtue was to keep silence, fell to M. Gauthier. He obeyed so carefully that he passed the whole day (in November!) upon a rock which was only to be reached at low tide. In the evening he left this solitude and rejoined his companions, announcing without much preface that he found himself obliged to return to Paris.[2]

We shall never know his reasons! I may add that the plague was at Nantes and M. Gauthier's servant had died of it. "Was it his concern at this event or the conviction that M. de Brétigny, in spite of his eminent virtues, would, if left to himself, never succeed in the coming delicate negotiations?"[3] Or was it some crisis of nervous depression, caused all at once by the nearness of the pestilence, the delay, and the *ennui* of unaccustomed discipline? A little jealousy may be suspected; he said with some acidity, that Jean de Quintanadoine in his quality of priest "took upon himself the office of leader, although his proper part was only that of paymaster."[4] In any case he cuts a poor figure enough. Later he turns up again with Bérulle and renders good service. He translated some excellent books from

[1] *Mémoire*, I. 652–3.
[2] Champagnot, p. 158.
[3] Houssaye, I. 285.
[4] *Ibid.*, I. 285.

Spanish into French, *Fleur des Saints* by Ribadeneira and the *Life of Balthazar Alverez* by Père Dupont. Nevertheless it is hard to pardon his desertion. One takes an unkind pleasure in picturing him, a pathetic form perched on a dripping rock, legs dangling, morose eyes demanding from the inconstant waters a counsel of cowardice.

At last on the tenth of November sails were hoisted and ten days later, not without having encountered divers tempests, the party disembarked at the Biscayan village Larodo, where the inquisitors, searching according to custom the effects and books of the travellers, treated them with all deference. . . . After a few days' rest they set off on mules (by way of Burgos and Valladolid); they had great difficulty in crossing mountains, and traversing the precipices that marked the way. Looking down into yawning abysses Mme. Jourdain cried gaily: "I should only fall into the arms of God!"[1] Not till the thirtieth of December was Valladolid reached, where Mme. Jourdain and her party stayed till they left Spain. They led a retired life and went (practically) nowhere save to the Carmelites of the town, to whom they paid frequent visits to be instructed in the rules and customs of the Order.[2]

Some delightful notes of Mme. Jourdain on this Valladolid sojourn have been preserved.

One day (she writes) having gone to hear Mass at the Carmelite Church, the French communicated as usual, after which the Mother Prioress (Casilde de Saints-Anges) begged them to remain, having observed them in prayer and wishing to know somewhat of their inner life. "Verily, ladies," she said, "you seem most enviable to me, recalling the days of the Primitive Church by being so much at prayer and always upon your knees! Tell me, I pray, what is your method of prayer?" Each in turn replied, but the last—evidently Mme. Jourdain herself—answered all questions and especially those she found awkward by saying that she could not well explain because of her ignorance of Spanish. They talked for a long time of the Divine workings in the soul and the divers kinds of prayer. . . . Then said . . . the Mother: "Sooth, I praise God in seeing His Spirit poured out in all parts and upon all creatures, as here among ourselves. My one fear is that our holy Mother Teresa may transfer her spirit to France."[3]

[1] *Mémoire*, I. 661–2. [2] Boucher, *ibid.*, p. 252. [3] *Mémoire*, I. 670.

That was already done. But what an inspiring scene: Spain at her holiest and best, watching and contemplating the mysticism of France and humbling herself before it.

In their own way, peacefully but very effectually, the ladies aided the diplomatic negotiations of Bérulle and Quintanadoine. Philip III was frequently at Valladolid, and Mesdames Jourdain and du Pucheuil, "much admired in their French dresses," went "for several hours each day to various Court ladies, to interest them in their business, and to increase their already great reputation. For all these ladies were friendly and showed them much kindness. Since the object of their coming won general approval and gave them an entry everywhere. . . . Even the queen showed affection and helped them."[1]

Even so, however, the affair made but slow progress, "the good Carmelite Fathers," in the phrase of Bérulle's earliest biographer, Habert de Cérisay, "continuing to defend at the sword's point the approaches of the convents." It was therefore decided to despatch reinforcements to Quintanadoine, and Bérulle departed from Paris on February 9, 1604, in company with M. Gauthier; on arrival he at once began his own manœuvres. But the monotonous ebb and flow of negotiations need not be followed in detail. Bérulle has been reproached, in my opinion unjustly, for not having invariably followed the rules of Evangelical simplicity. But as the modern Carmelites, to whom we owe a conclusive work on all these problems, ask, "Why be astonished if he used diplomatic weapons? Was he not justified in so doing when confronted by the General acting in an identical manner?"[2] He held his ground with a saintly acumen and gentle obstinacy that greatly impressed the Spaniards, Mother Anne de Jésus remarking admiringly: "That little Don Pedro had more strength and vigour than all the rest!" doubtless more than the Carmel Fathers and the good-natured Quintanadoine. "Our holy Mother," she adds, "would have loved him well."[3] The General, finally forced to yield on the main matter, tried to take a petty revenge by granting permission only to Carmelites who had no outstanding virtues and had not been trained by S. Teresa. But Bérulle had made his choice. "They teach me to be obstinate here," he wrote to Mme Acarie; "I am resolved to return to France without nuns, rather

[1] *Mémoire*, I. 698–9. [2] *Mémoire*, I. 732; cf. Houssaye, pp. 541–7.
[3] *Ibid.*, I. 751.

than with mediocre ones!"[1] Finally the Nuncio applied the "last remedy," which was to deliver to the General of the Carmelites, "by special embassy major excommunication and removal from office, unless he at once delivered to the bearer the obediences," that is to say, formal leave to depart, for the six Carmelites demanded by Bérulle.[2] The battle, which had lasted six months (December, 1603 to August 12, 1604), was won.

"The little Don Pedro," guided by his Spanish friends, had chosen well, culling relentlessly, I had almost said unwisely, the rarest blossoms of the mystic garden which the formal orders of the Pope had opened to him. "Were S. Teresa living now," he wrote to Mme. Acarie, "she could not give France better Carmelites, unless she should come herself!" The Mother Anne de Jésus, Superior of the colony, was regarded by her contemporaries as a prodigy of holiness and wisdom. Entering the Order in 1570 at the age of twenty-five, she had almost immediately been entrusted by S. Teresa with the most important charges. "One Provincial called her the Captain of Prioresses after Teresa of Ahumada, and the saint herself said frankly: "Anne does the work and I get the credit!"—as later Bossuet would say of another Carmelite, Mme de Vallière, "I have laid the foundations of the building, but she has raised it and kept it in repair."[3]

My daughter and my crown (wrote S. Teresa once to Anne), I cannot sufficiently thank God for His grace done to me in calling you to this Order; for, as He brought the children of Israel out of their captivity in Egypt, making a pillar of fire to guide and enlighten them during the night, and protect them against the sun by day, so has He to-day stretched out His mighty Arm over our Order; you, dearest daughter, are this pillar of fire to guide, enlighten, defend us. It is clear that God dwells in your soul, since you impart so much grace and devotion to all that you do.[4]

S. John of the Cross called Anne a seraph. Dominique Bañes "said that Anne was in no wise inferior to her Mother in supernatural gifts and surpassed her in natural qualities."[5] In short, all praised her without measure, so it is not to be wondered at that the

[1] Boucher, p. 238.
[2] Houssaye, I. 544.
[3] Boucher, *ibid.*, pp. 261 ff. (note by P. Bouix).
[4] *Mémoire*, I. 32.
[5] Boucher, pp. 265–6.

Fathers should have fought desperately to withhold from Bérulle such a prize.

But we must speak plainly with the liberty of the historian and in the light of the events that followed. Though France witnessed the ecstasies of Anne de Jésus, it did not witness that "grace" which S. Teresa attributed to her, or that unique combination of "natural qualities" which Bañes admired. Perfection is not to be found in this world, but often the imperfections of the saints are lovable. Those of Anne de Jésus were not. Her dignified, glacial, sometimes bad-tempered stiffness, her Spanish prejudices, and other peculiarities, entailed suffering on the early French Carmelites, and even imperilled the work of Mme. Acarie. True, she did not come to France until the autumn of her life, but even in the heroism of her springtime there were as many thorns as flowers. Nevertheless she was a great saint and an outstanding glory to our Carmel.

After Anne de Jésus, Anne de Saint-Barthélemy holds the first place in this history. A humble peasant, she had been received in 1568 into the convent of Avila, to perform the humble offices of the sisters of the white veil (lay sisters). During long years till the death of S. Teresa, "she had the privilege of never quitting her day or night, lavishing care upon her, preparing her food, washing her linen, dressing her, for the arm thrice broken was entirely useless, taking care of all that concerned her physically."[1] "The day of her death," she says in her *Autobiography*, "I put on her fresh body-linen, sleeves, cap, and all; she was well pleased to see herself in such nice order and, turning her eyes towards me, looked at me with a smile and showed her gratitude by signs."[2] How can we speak of the writer without tenderness? She hardly belonged to this world. Her life is one long succession of visions and ecstasies. On arriving in France, she was raised to the rank of the other sisters and given the black veil. With God's help, she accomplished great things, though she lacked the intellectual power and indomitable character of Anne de Jésus. "Timid and simple, ignorant of business, easily upset and quick to change her opinion, her loving sweet nature, undeveloped by education, felt keenly and sometimes exaggerated the coldness of which she fancied herself the object." So modern Carmelites judge her, but,

[1] *Autobiographie de la V. M. Anne de Saint-Barthélemy*, Bouix, p. viii.
[2] *Autobiographie*, p. ix.

whatever were her foibles, all that was rarest in France surrendered itself with joy to the direction of this humble woman in whose eyes seemed still reflected the supreme ecstasies of S. Teresa. The four other nuns, Eléonore de Saint-Bernard, Isabelle de Saint-Paul, Isabelle des Agnes and Beatrix de la Conception, less striking, but not less illuminating, appear altogether lovable. They have more "finesse" and judgment than Anne de Saint-Barthélemy, more flexibility and humanity than Anne de Jésus. The eldest of this select company, Anne de Jésus, was then fifty-nine, the youngest, Eléonore de Saint-Bernard, twenty-seven.

V. "No victors brought back the trophies of conquest, or divided the spoils of the vanquished, with such joy as our French embassy returning from their battlefield. What richer booty indeed could be imagined than to have brought from Spain the seraphic spirit of the holy Mother Teresa, and this without Spain being deprived!" So M. Navet, and continues for a long time in the same strain. "What can be said," writes Mme Jourdain, "to describe the joy of all our French travellers at last, after so much toil and trouble, bearing away the living stones of the building they desired to construct, all fashioned and prepared by the hand of the Almighty and of His dear friend and servant, the blessed S. Teresa de Jésus!"[1]

Leaving Valladolid on August 14, 1604, they directed their course first of all to Salamanca, to take up Mother Anne de Jésus and two other Sisters, then to Avila, the dwelling of Anne de Saint-Barthélemy. The General of the Carmelites had chosen the latter convent in which to take farewell of his daughters. The scene was most moving.

The religious showed by their tears how much they would regret their spiritual father; although eager to go to France, to establish their Order there, they would not remain less attached in heart to the government of the Spanish Fathers. The General confided them to the care of the Provincial of Castile and to another Father of the Reformed Carmelites, who should escort them to Paris. They left Avila on August 29 and proceeded to Burgos to pick up (the rest of the chosen Sisters). On arrival at Burgos, the Provincial raised a difficulty which threatened to delay their departure for a long time. He demanded security of two thousand gold crowns to defray the return expenses of the Carmelites, should they remain under two

[1] *Mémoire*, I. 753.

years in France; M. de Bretigny, whose own purse was exhausted but who had credit in Burgos, . . . furnished the required security.[1]

From Mère Anne de Saint-Barthélemy we get a description of the *cortège* and her own travel impressions.

Two religious of our Order, notable servants of God, two French priests (Bérulle and Quintanadoine), and M. René Gauthier, with three Frenchmen on horseback, accompanied us. The three French ladies were alone in one coach, and we six Sisters in another, reuniting at the hostelries. The French ladies instructed us in their tongue, but it must be owned we made no great progress, with difficulty managing to say a few phrases. Our Lord desired thus to mortify us and I believe that it was wholesome, for it was as well that we should speak little—each nation has its own customs (an odd remark!). Think what poor women must suffer on so long a journey; what then must it have meant to religious, not indeed to be obliged to walk often, but to exposc themselves to people's gaze and to accept any chance help to extricate themselves from dizzy heights or deep mires? I cannot think of so many dangers without a shudder.

I cannot sufficiently praise the Frenchmen, both for their constant care of us and the goodness they displayed. They treated us with great consideration, and their behaviour towards us was so perfect . . . that we were amazed. During the whole long journey they never spoke an unbecoming or impatient word; they even refrained from the light discourse by which one naturally seeks to relieve the tedium and fatigue of the way.[2]

All this consideration did not prevent the Mothers " from a good deal of suffering when it was necessary to walk in rain and mud for long distances shod only in their *alpargates* or cord sandals. M. de

[1] Boucher, *ibid.*, pp. 262–79. This last shift and the reasons given for it make an unpleasant episode, auguring badly. It was one of many endeavours to implant in the minds and hearts of the Spanish Carmelites the desire and hope of one day returning to their country or, at least, under the jurisdiction of their own Fathers. The idea was constantly cherished by some of them, especially Anne de Jésus; and, at the first opportunity of returning to their countrymen and spiritual Fathers, they fled from France, with the exception of the brave and highminded Mère Isabelle des Anges, who declared: " Our Lord and the Blessed Virgin have given me France for my portion and I will never leave it!" (Boucher, p. 284.) It is true that, the work of foundation once accomplished, the foundresses could be spared. Things could get on very well without them, but by their departure they risked certain shallow thinkers conceiving the false idea that the French Carmelites, henceforth presided over by strangers to Spain, were not in a regular position, were in fact not truly Carmelite. This gave rise to many trying and even grave irregularities.

[2] *Autobiographie*, pp. 119–21.

Bérulle never failed, with his usual kindness, to step up to support them (offering his arm). But the good Mothers refused his help and were surprised, for such a thing was entirely contrary to Spanish custom."[1]

One of the two Carmelite Fathers was "by nature churlish and contrary. This, remarks Mme Jourdain, did not accord with the French disposition, but God overruled it. . . . The very animals seemed to cross him, for he often made his mule to go alongside the coach of the Mothers, that he might converse privately with them, when he saw M. de Bérulle there. But as soon as the good Father began to talk the coach-horses would set off at full gallop, leaving the Father behind. This happened so often as to annoy him extremely, especially as it never occurred when it was M. de Bérulle. The difference was so marked that the French ladies in the next coach remarked it. The good Father would often insist on short journeys, for when he saw it was getting late for dinner, he would not let them go on."[2] So, as always, human foibles and pettiness diminish the glory of God's work.

"At last a little river was reached—its name was not yet famous—which separates France from Spain. They crossed it in boats. As she set foot upon French soil, Mère Anne de Jésus cried out: '*Ahora io son madre* (Now at length I am a mother)'." So radiant is she when she abandons herself to grace. But, "just as there are twelve hours in the day," so, our chronicle tells us, the radiance was at times overcast. Scarce had he disembarked than "the worthy M. Gauthier knelt down, raised his hands to Heaven, kissing French soil and crying aloud the words of the royal prophet, *Laudate Dominum omnes gentes . . . Laqueus contritus est et nos liberati sumus.*" The two Carmelite Fathers no doubt affected not to comprehend this Biblical allusion to broken snares and liberated doves.

The narrative, of course, does not lack miracles. Anne de Jésus carried a flask of holy water, to exorcise the demons she saw clinging to the coachwheels. The French ladies, too, had their visions, but more alluring ones. "The pious travellers, reaching Saint-Jean-de-Luz, the first village on the French side, sought a church to hear Mass." Coming out, Mme de Jourdain (she tells the story without mentioning her name) "detected a very sweet and pleasant fragrance,

[1] *Mémoire*, I. 763. [2] *Ibid.*, I. 763.

which helped her to a state of unusual recollection. She mentioned the fragrance only to the Mothers." One of them remarked, "It is our blessed Mother Teresa of Jesus, who is bearing us company." The Sisters also perceived this devout fragrance, which "showed," they said, "that the saint was welcoming them into France."[1] "The fragrance only" was avowed by this rare nature, a gentle gift meant to be shared by her companions; she said nothing about the ecstasy. This is France's way, when she is mystical, even when she is simply Christian. She keeps her secret. So the world sees us as frivolous if not worse. Should war break out one day between us and Germany, Catholic Spain will pray for our enemies.

Bérulle and M. Gauthier had gone ahead "to prepare the lodging at Bayonne and to announce the arrival of the Mothers to the Comte de Grammont, governor of the province. He received them courteously and, at their request, gave orders that the city gates should be left open for the arrival of the travellers. Meanwhile these were journeying on, and at nightfall found themselves no more than a quarter-league from the town, when a violent storm overtook them and the drivers refused to proceed. The party were forced to spend the night on the road. The mules were unharnessed, and the French ladies joined the Mothers in their coach to leave their own to the gentlemen, and so the Spaniards passed their first night in France." "This misfortune fell conveniently on a fast day," says M. Navet, "for on any other they must have eaten 'maigre' willy-nilly!" But one of the Carmelite Fathers, that Père Joseph whose adventures in the saddle Mme Jourdain had watched with mischievous eyes, took the thing tragically. "This is not taking the Sisters to found anything, but to kill them!" he exclaimed indignantly.

Within the town, M. de Bérulle and M. Gauthier were a prey to the greatest uneasiness. Fearing that their party must have strayed . . . they caused fires to be lighted on the walls, to serve as beacon lights. . . . At daybreak they sent out in quest of the travellers a man who soon found them and conducted them happily into Bayonne. This was S. Matthew's Day, September 21."[2]

Next came four days, often on foot, across the Landes. The good Spaniards' heads had been stuffed with the most sinister ideas of

[1] *Mémoire*, I. 773–4.

[2] Houssaye, I. 352–4.

France. Martyrdom did not frighten them; rather they were astonished that the hour tarried. "Our holy nuns, with the idea of confessing Jesus Christ openly and gaining the inestimable happiness of martyrdom . . . held their crucifixes and rosaries out of the coach window for the people to see!"[1] The austere Anne de Jésus, writing to her Spanish sisters of the villages traversed between Bayonne and Paris, said: "Nearly all the inhabitants were heretics; that could be seen by their faces—truly they looked like lost souls." And again, the bishops of France "are not all Catholics."[2]

At Bordeaux Bérulle left them, to hasten to the King and prepare for their arrival in Paris, which they reached on October 15. Whether with some devotional purpose or because the convent of the Faubourg Saint-Jacques was not ready for them, it was decided to push on to Saint-Denis. "On the other side of Paris, at Petit-Châtelet, two carriages were there to meet them, one with the Princesses de Longueville, the foundresses of the new convent, and the other containing Mme Acarie, her three daughters and some other ladies. There, too, was M. de Bérulle, so well equipped and mounted that he seemed some great prelate. All turned round and accompanied the Mothers as far as the Gate of S. Denis, and a little further; then they stopped and alighted and all saluted one another with unspeakable joy and satisfaction."[3] The basilica and its treasures astonished the Spaniards.

> These holy places (writes Mother Anne de Jésus) are so richly ornamented that all one sees at the Escorial is a bagatelle compared with the treasure of relics here. The temple is so magnificent as to compare with that of Solomon, for not the walls only, but the very ground underfoot, is worked in gold; down to such vases as the Queen of Sheba brought from Jerusalem. All this is confided to the care of a monastery of three hundred Benedictines, not of the Reform, although they perpetually chant in choir.[4]

Prepared for the worst, she found nothing but edification in all the religious houses she visited during the journey; France, after all, was not so bad.

The next day was even better. Marie de Beauvilliers and her Benedictines, among whom was the daughter of Mme Jourdain,

[1] *Mémoire*, I. 778.
[2] *Ibid.*, II. 19–22.
[3] *Ibid.*, p. 2.
[4] *Ibid.*, II. 21.

received them at Montmartre; "holy women," notes Anne de Jésus, "for, thanks to the writings of our blessed Mother, they embraced the Reform two years ago, so that in many ways one might imagine them Discalced."[1]

Later, when she had got to know this Babylon that had been painted so black, she wrote:

> The rulers of this country show us much goodwill . . . asking through Père Coton for our prayers. The King has much need for them, although they assure me he is a good Catholic and that his need of prayers does not concern matters of the Faith. In some parts of France there is indeed little of this, but in Paris, a world of its own, there are abundant signs of religion, the frequenting of the Sacraments recalls that of the Primitive Church; in fact, they are surprised not to see us communicate oftener.[2]

October 17 found the Spanish nuns established in the Priory of Notre-Dame-des-Champs, and before the end of the same year, 1604, the seven first French Carmelites had taken the habit.

VI. These were: Andrée Levoix, Mme Acarie's maid, a lay sister who yet took precedence of the others till her holy death at the end of a few months; Mlle. d'Hannival (Marie de la Trinité), 1576-1647; Mme Jourdain (Louise de Jésus), 1569-1628; Mlle. de Fontaines-Maran (Madeline de Saint-Joseph), 1578-1637; Mlle. Deschamps (Aimée de Jésus), died 1634; Mme du Coudray (Marie de la Trinité), daughter of the President Sevin, 1571-1657; Charlotte de Harlay de Sancy, Marquise de Bréauté (Marie de Jésus) 1579-1652—all of them girls or young matrons aged twenty-three to thirty-three, trained by Mme Acarie and worthy of immortal fame. Among their Spanish Carmelites Anne de Jésus and the rest had never witnessed more saintliness or more of those human qualities rated so highly by S. Teresa, good sense, intelligence, and graciousness.

After the long months passed in the community of Ste. Geneviève they were more than simple novices; yet they had to be docile learners in the school of the Spanish nuns, and to model themselves on their pattern as regards the customs and rites that give each Community its distinctive colour. The apprenticeship may have been mortifying in some ways, but upon the whole it was easy and pleasant. Without

[1] *Mémoire*, II. 21. [2] *Ibid.*, II. 24.

having left Paris, they found themselves cloistered in a Spanish convent of the days of S. Teresa. The six Carmelites brought from so far continued before their eyes with renewed care the life of the Avila or Salamanca houses, which it was their mission to implant here. The thousand and one details of pious routine, so alarming to outsiders, are easily learnt and transmitted from generation to generation. Our French Carmelite convents to-day still observe, with hardly any change, the detailed programme, the "*point d'exaction*," brought by the Spanish Mothers into France.[1]

Such "*point d'exaction*," however, when conceived in the letter and not animated by the spirit, is a poor thing enough.

> The perfection with which our holy Mother founded her houses (wrote Mother Casilde, prioress of Valladolid, to Quintanadoine) cannot be written in a rule or a book; it consists rather in that which has been graven in the hearts of those who saw her at work and conversed with her. Something divinely infused into their own souls, to perpetuate a manner of life so excellent and outstanding, the principle of which was a close and perfect union with God and detachment from all created things. All this, I tell you, cannot be embodied in constitutions, and our rules are very short, consisting rather of spirit than of ceremonies.[2]

This living tradition, this treasury of impressions and reminiscences, was what above all had been sought from the Spanish Carmelites. Our French received it reverently at their hands.

Their initiation was the work of a master hand. The prioress Anne de Jésus "had a superior genius" and was born to rule. She was fundamentally kind, we are assured, but distant, cold, inexorably firm, and rigorous to a degree beyond reason.[3] Further, she was stubbornly fixed in her national memories and prejudices, and incapable of finding full satisfaction in anything French. Her letters have always a note of dissatisfaction. "Send me," she writes to her Spanish sisters, "some picture of the Nativity, for those made here do not please me," or again: "Some perfumes for our church, for there are none to be obtained here, and the supply brought by me from Spain is nearly exhausted."[4] She found her French daughters "refined,

[1] Cf. *Regularités ou Point d'exaction tiré de celui que les Mères espagnoles ont apporté en France.* Agen, 1883.

[2] *Mémoire,* I. 642–3. [3] *Ibid.,* II. 12–15. [4] *Ibid.,* II. 25.

but was persuaded that they were inclined to be less hard upon themselves than the Spaniards."[1]

Nevertheless we have a beautiful letter of hers about the great work then in train which was to have such consequences for the history of French Mysticism.

From the moment of their taking the habit their minds seem to be renewed in a method of prayer strange to them. I am careful that they meditate on and imitate Our Lord Jesus Christ, for He is often forgotten here. All devotion is concentrated on the abstract idea of God: I do not know how it is done. Since the coming of the glorious S. Denis, author of the Mystic Theology, everyone has practised a method of devotion rather passive than active (*suspension plutôt qu'imitation*). It is a strange affair. I can as little comprehend it as the language in which they seek to explain it; nay, I am unable even to read it.[2]

This letter is characteristic of Anne; she exaggerates and generalises far too much from such observations as she has been able to make in a few months. Neither the Catholic France of the past, nor the disciples of Mme Acarie and of Bérulle, needed the lesson of Mère Anne de Jésus to teach them the contemplation and imitation of Christ. Yet what wonderful insight is shown here in a woman, who does not know French, and guesses at, rather than understands, the confidences made to her; with what skill she has realized that danger of Quietism which has so often assailed French, and still more German and Flemish, spirituality, a too liberal devotion to the writings of the pseudo-Dionysius. She opposes the Latin and Teresian mysticism, the necessity of works and of a constant return to the Incarnate Word, to the other mysticism with its neo-Platonic elements, which in truth the labour and skill of great saints have rendered orthodox, but which retains nevertheless a leaven of pantheism and moral indifference under the formidable obscurity of its terms. The question will come up again in the fourth volume of this work, in which we shall try to explain the anti-mystical reaction that dominated the second half of the seventeenth century; it was fundamentally unjust and still more disastrous, but none the less was in a measure justified by undeniable excesses. For the moment it is sufficient to remark the extreme vigilance displayed by Anne de Jésus in the dawn of this splendid

[1] *Mémoire*, II. 15.

[2] *Ibid.*, II. 23.

movement, and the youthful adaptability of the Frenchwomen, who, as so competent and severe a judge admitted, understood and assimilated the Teresian tradition in its original purity. At the end of a few months they were Carmelites in every respect. "Their mind seems renewed in a method of prayer strange to them"; less change was necessary than the ardent Spaniard fancied. At any rate they soon received the Divine Touch still needed for their training. Daughters of prayer, they walked in the mystic garden with assured and easy step, ripe already for that mission to the country which France required of them.

In 1605, less than a year after the first foundation, the expansion began with the convents of Pontoise and Dijon. Next came Amiens, 1606; Tours, 1608; Rouen, 1609; Bordeaux and Châlons, 1610; Besançon, 1614; Dieppe, 1615. In 1644, the year of the death of the last Spanish Carmelite left in France, Isabelle des Anges, the French Carmelites counted no less than fifty-five convents, each of which shed its influence far and wide. Thus, for instance, Mère Elizabeth de Quatrebarbes went forth from the convent of Tours to that of Beaune, "to lead in the way of holiness" Marguerite du Saint-Sacrament, who in turn would one day direct a multitude of eminent followers, notably M. de Renty. Thus again the holy Père Surin attached himself to the convent of Bordeaux founded by Isabelle des Anges. "When scarcely ten years of age . . . he would often visit the Carmelites. . . . Several times in their church he received singular graces which influenced his whole life. Mère Isabelle took pleasure in initiating him into the interior life and teaching him the way of prayer."[1] I could enlarge this chapter indefinitely, but must confine myself to Dijon, a foundation which interests us especially.

Urged, we are told, by a prophetic inspiration, Anne de Jésus had set her mind on this foundation in spite of the objections raised by Bérulle and others. She took charge of it herself, deserting the Paris convent, and taking with her two other Spaniards, Isabelle des Anges and Marie de la Conception, as well as some French sisters, among them Marie de la Trinité (d'Hannivel). Quintanadoine and M. Gallemant also accompanied the party. They went out of their way a little to pray in the ruins of Clairvaux. They arrived in the last

[1] *Mémoire*, II. 144.

days of September, and before the end of October had given the habit to three Burgundians. "This ceremony," relates our chronicler, "caused so great a delight to the Spanish Mothers that, unable to contain the holy joy that enraptured them, they expressed it in action-songs, accompanied by declamation in the mode of Spain that added much to the effect. But the French mind is not worthy to understand it (why not?) and the French tongue cannot reproduce its force." The poetry opened with these words:

> Here behold cicadas three,
> Touched with love from God they be.

The refrain was more ordinary:

> Who perfection would require
> Dijon's daughters must admire.[1]

Away from Bérulle, who may have overawed her somewhat, Anne de Jésus expanded in these more homely surroundings. She seems to have been much attached to this house of Dijon, where, moreover, she had the companionship of an exquisite French soul, Sœur Thérèse de Jésus, who, to please her, had learnt Spanish. One day in recreation, Sœur Thérèse

> sang . . . in her angelic voice, some verses with the refrain:
>
> > O angels glorious,
> > Come ye, to the heavens bear my soul.
>
> These words so touched Mère Anne de Jésus that she forthwith led all her daughters to the Blessed Sacrament, where in such transports as those of David before the Ark, this venerable Mother, more like a seraph than a mortal creature, passed in rhythmic dance along the choir, singing and clapping her hands after the Spanish manner, but with such a majesty, sweetness, and gravity that all, filled with respectful awe, were deeply touched and raised heavenwards. The French, although less used to these devotional demonstrations, were not less edified than the rest.[2]

The great glory of the convent of Dijon, however, is that it revealed the Baronne de Chantal to herself, thus completing the initiation into Mysticism begun by François de Sales. The young widow, still

[1] *Mémoire*, II. 73–4.

[2] *Ibid.*, II. 75. I do not know the other name of Thérèse de Jésus.

hesitating whether to follow the Divine call to the interior life, came often to the Carmelite parlour, listened to Mère Anne de Jésus, and formed a tender friendship with Mère Marie de la Trinité. Long after, when the foundress of the Visitandines was passing through Troyes, " M. Duval permitted her to enter the convent; and, to leave Mère Marie de la Trinité, then prioress, a token of her affection, she presented her with a picture which S. François de Sales had given her on her birthday, representing the Child Jesus in a rose. The saint herself had fastened on the back of the picture two lines sent her at the same time by the holy bishop:

Mother mine, this wondrous rose
All our life doth safe enclose.

In making the gift to her friend Ste. Chantal added: ' I give you the thing I love best, for you are the Mother I cherish most! ' "[1]

VII. Since the complete success of the work to which he consecrated his life, we have hardly mentioned Jean de Quintanadoine. But three others, the Canonical Superiors of the French Carmelites, Bérulle, Gallemant and Duval, have fared little better. The silence is deliberate, not only because we can but touch the fringe of so vast a subject, but for a more important reason, which must be clearly understood. Carmel, whether governed by Fathers of its own Order or by secular priests, or by Bishops, still remains Carmel. It has an independent life of its own, which no doubt superiors can more or less either aid or thwart, but which no exterior authority can modify to any appreciable extent. Here the distinguished biographer of Cardinal de Bérulle seems to me grievously at fault; he allots to his hero the first *rôle* in a business, to which Bérulle no doubt was of much service, but as a subordinate. " Called to the preliminary conferences of the Carthusians (at which the foundation of our Carmelites was decided upon) . . . his voice is merged in those of the holy men who unanimously decided upon the foundation in accordance with the primitive constitutions and spirit, and with the express approbation of the Holy See. He was chosen by the blessed one (Mme Acarie) as spiritual director of the postulants gathered together by her . . . he busies himself in the negotiations with Rome, not alone but only in company with Mme Acarie and M. de Brétigny, on the

[1] Boucher, *ibid.*, p. 381 (note by P. Bouix).

lines mapped out by the Carthusians. . . . In Spain, though he may conceive his plans in solitude and communicate them only to few, he yet confides them unreservedly to Mme. Acarie; and his firm stand in the choice of the sisters is due to the express terms of the commission, charging him to select Carmelite contemporaries of S. Teresa, and in this choice he follows less his own lights than the pressing recommendations of the blessed one and the judgement of the most celebrated theologians. . . . Finally, he concludes the whole affair by a Papal brief, as he had been advised to do, even from Spain, when M. de Brétigny was alone concerned with the negotiations. . . . History teaches us what M. Bérulle did to found the primitive Carmelite Order in France; we look in vain for anything he did to found a (Bérullian or) national Order," as M. Houssaye would have it that he did.[1]

Nor, the Order once founded, is Bérulle the only one to direct it. He is more in the popular eye than Gallemant or Duval, as being more concerned with the convent in Paris, but his two colleagues, however, have no less authority than he over the growing work. On occasion they do not hesitate to reverse his decisions. In general, however, the three act harmoniously as one, as is fitting. No new foundation is started without their approbation and their choosing of Foundresses; they decide even on details of discipline. Whether as confessors or directors, they watch and aid the progress of the divine work in the souls opened to them. At this point their activity stops; in other respects, and especially as regards the reciprocal influence between the superiors and the Carmelites, it may be maintained that the latter received much less than they bestowed. The Carmelites were pupils of S. Teresa and Divine grace: Gallemant, Duval, and up to a point Bérulle himself, pupils of the Carmelites.

They were quite aware of this. We have already defined the attitude of Duval towards Mme Acarie. The new Carmelites confided to his care enraptured him. "Without belittling other religious," he ranked these over all, when he could speak freely. "Some," he said, "glow with miracles, . . . as if God, who always imparts His graces upon good Orders, rained them as it were in buckets upon these when they were at their first dawn. . . . That is why the primitive

[1] *Mémoire*, I. 705–6.

spirit of the Orders is of such importance and must be carefully preserved, for where it persists, great things are done."[1] Gallemant, who was more mystical by temperament and seems to me to have absorbed more simply and purely than the other two the Carmelite spirit, was of the same opinion. That he might more effectively direct the visionaries, he had received a measure of their grace. "It was when God gave him the authority of a superior over them that he was caught into that state of devotion in which the soul passively receives impressions from the Divine; this rendered him . . . apt to comprehend and guide the souls called to attain the heights of the spiritual life."[2] Far from leading them, he was raised to their level. Bérulle appears more independent, and less detached from his own ideas; he plays the master more, yet even he is directed as much as he directs. The visions of Mère Anne de S. Barthélemy move him deeply, Madeleine de S. Joseph, Catherine de Jésus, Marguérite du Saint-Sacrament, all three very docile and very loving, exercise an influence over him. The same is true of the superiors who followed this Triumvirate, Père Gibieuf, for instance. Assuredly the Oratory has its special type of mysticism, which is not that of S. Teresa, and we shall show its special sublimity later. But even in the development of this mysticism the Carmelite influence may be easily recognized.

Quintanadoine, as prompt to return to obscurity as he had been prompt to come forward when required, remained to the end the devoted servitor of the Carmelites. In 1605, at the moment of the foundation of the Dijon house, a period of trial had begun for him. During the journey, he tells us, he was once "so tormented by the spirits of darkness that M. Gallemant, who slept in the same room, rose early to commend him to the prayers of the sisters, for it seemed as though all the forces of hell had arrayed themselves against him. . . . Soon after, a messenger came express from Rouen to announce to him a heavy loss to the wealth of his family, so that he was obliged to depart in haste, to regulate his affairs. . . . His mental anguish continued to increase so greatly that he believed himself forsaken of God. At that time it was only because M. Mass, curé of his parish, served when he said his Mass that he was able to face the distress it cost him. . . . When he was not at the Altar, he would throw

[1] *Mémoire*, II. 607–19. [2] *Ibid.*, II. 606.

himself continually upon his knees, crying, *Deus, Deus meus, Deus, Deus meus, ut quid dereliquisti me?*" In February 1606 he wrote to a Carmelite nun in Spain: "I have almost entirely lost my interior gifts and (am) for my sins become all earthy, and I know not how to endure myself. Nought is left to me save a shred of hope in the goodness of God."[1] However, a new mission awaited him, almost more important than the first, although in some respects less pleasing. Quintanadoine, who had in a measure given the Carmelites of Spain to France, was now, in the innocence of his soul, to take them away again.

The Infanta Isabella, Governess of the Low Countries, being desirous to establish the Carmelites at Brussels, wrote in 1606 to Quintanadoine, who gladly undertook the new negotiations. The princess was very anxious that Mother Anne de Jésus should be the first prioress of the nunnery she was going to establish. Neither Bérulle nor the other superiors offered more than a purely formal opposition to this project. They gave Mother Anne full permission to take with her what nuns she thought best fitted to help her, and assigned to Quintanadoine all needful powers for the foundation. Clearly the enterprise was important, for, once established at Brussels, the Carmelite Order would speedily spread to the other towns of Flanders, a perspective vast enough to kindle the enthusiasm of the followers of S. Teresa. Yet we cannot help being surprised at the ready assent of France to the departure of that Anne de Jésus who, two years ago, had been so ardently desired and procured with so much difficulty, the more so as several of the sisters accompanied her, and it needed no great foresight to augur that most of the others would soon follow her, which did actually occur. The only explanation is that they were thought to have done their work amongst us so, that, in their presence or absence, the flame lit by them would never be extinguished. As for the Mothers themselves, the reasons for their prompt decision are evident. Flanders under the Spanish rule had received the Discalced Fathers and there they would return to the jurisdiction and direction of their own Order. Further, Brussels was for them on the way home, and they wished to die in their own country. This pathetic desire, which never left them, was

[1] *Mémoire*, II. 65.

destined to be fulfilled only in the case of Mother Beatrix de Jésus.[1]

Mme Acarie had foreseen this disappointing *dénouement*. On the day of the inauguration of the first Paris Carmel, she alone, her biographer relates, "failed to share the general rejoicings . . . (or at least) could not prevent an unaccountable depression in herself. Afterwards she confided to the Marquise de Bréauté that Our Lord had revealed to her then that the Spanish Carmelites, sought for with so much toil and cost, would begin the edifice of the French Order, but would not complete it. . . . In fact four of them left France within three years and after 1611 only Mère Isabelle des Anges remained. So we may say with truth that the Spanish Carmelites, having given birth to their Order in France, deserted it in the cradle, and that the French Carmelites gave it its youthful growth and the stability of maturity by founding most of the dependent houses."[2]

The responsibility for these memorable decisions in no way rested on Quintanadoine's feeble shoulders. Although he was nominated superior of the foundations contemplated in Flanders, he remained almost wholly the courier, the man-of-all-work, or, in the phrase of one who knew him there, the "porter" of the Carmelite Order.

He set out from France for Belgium in December 1606 with Anne de Jésus, full of goodwill but hampered by the difficulties, worldly or ecclesiastical, attendant on the foundation of a monastery. His calmness, even more than his blunders, irritated the ardent Spaniard. She wrote from Brussels:

> Oh, if you could see what I have to bear from the serenity of Señor Don Juan! When I tell him of my trials, he replies, "Speak not thus, my mother, we shall die here." And he does nothing at all but porter's work![3]

It was a rigorous winter, and the venerable Mother declares that she "has to shake icicles from her pen." Of course Quintanadoine is to blame.

[1] The greater number of the sisters, it seems, did not abandon France without reluctance, Beatrix de Jésus among them. But on the one hand the decision had been made over their heads, and, on the other, they would not have wished to separate themselves from the two great leaders, Anne de Jésus and Anne de S. Barthélemy, both on their part eager to return to the jurisdiction of their own Fathers.

[2] Boucher, pp. 294–5.

[3] *Mémoire*, II. 342.

As for Don Juan, he rejoices at everything. . . . I told him to-day he has not a father's heart. It is a bath of rosewater to him when he sees us suffer. Navet (the secretary) and he are very comfortable with the ecclesiastics who requested permission from me to accommodate them. You cannot imagine how cold it is.[1]

Bravo! We need no longer complain that she lacks humanity. She is jesting here, no doubt, yet when upon another expedition the question of lodging for Quintanadoine came up, "wishing him some little experience doubtless," says the chronicler, "she added sweetly: 'Do not trouble about it beforehand, let him suffer some inconvenience.'"[2]

These few strokes finish our picture of "Señor Don Juan." After Brussels, Louvain, Mons and Antwerp, he returned to France, and realized one of his earliest wishes by giving a Carmelite convent to his dear town of Rouen; after which we find him, always on the same errand, in Franche-Comté and Beaune. These peaceable, deliberate men have time for everything. In the midst of so many adventures he kept up a regular correspondence with the King, the Queen and Princesses, and the missionaries of the Congo, the beautiful country in which to the last he hoped to establish a convent. "Haste, haste," they write to him from thence, "haste to whiten these negresses for whom our sweet Jesus has given His life."[3] Other missionaries, Discalced Fathers and Jesuits, were to be sent with the Carmelites. The preliminary negotiations not proving successful, he set out for Rome in 1612 and placed in the hands of Paul V the following touching appeal:

These poor people demand the bread of the Gospel and there is none to break it for them. I avow, Holy Father, that I have not the talents needful for such high functions, yet God bestows upon me in my advanced age (he was fifty-six) the desire to act as escort and *servant* to the zealous ministers whom you will send there, so long as life may last me. I promise Your Holiness to devote to this good work fifteen hundred gold crowns for the voyage, and to establish at Lisbon a yearly income of a hundred crowns towards the expenses of the missionaries. I venture to make this offer to Your Holiness of all that I possess in the world.[4]

[1] *Mémoire*, II. 314. [2] *Ibid.*, II. 314. [3] Champagnot, p. 209.
[4] Beauvais, pp. 309–10. The text has been certainly touched up.

At Rome, "to get him to eat, it was necessary to talk to him of the negroes; when sad, the thought of the voyage to the Congo would cheer him. He would say: 'How happy should I be if God vouchsafed me the grace to die there embracing one little negro converted to the faith.'"[1]

Spain refused to entertain the project, and Quintanadoine returned to his native town, which he was hardly ever again to leave, and where he daily visited and exhorted his Carmelites. A few days before his death he had himself carried to them for the last time, and said Mass, assisted by two ecclesiastics who held him up, and "after speaking to the sisters gathered at the gates of the choir . . . like the ancient patriarchs, he gave them all his benediction and recommended himself to their prayers." He died on July 8, 1634, aged seventy-eight. His heart was given to the Carmelites of Beaune. His body was interred before the High Altar of the convent in Rouen and upon the choir screen two black marble slabs were placed on which was engraved this epitaph:

To the honour and glory of God and to the memory of the noble and venerable Jean de Quintanadoine, priest; first founder of this convent, seigneur of Brétigny, of Saint-Denis de Bost-Guerard and of Saint-Leonard, the first translator of the works of S. Teresa from Spanish into French, and the means of the establishment of the Order of Discalced Carmelite sisters in France, Burgundy and Flanders. Alphonse de Quintanadoine, sieur de Brétigny, his brother and heir, erected this epitaph together with his tomb in the year 1634.[2]

3. *Madeleine de Saint-Joseph and the two Carmels of Paris.*

I. During the Lent of 1603, M. de Bérulle went to Tours to negotiate with the Benedictines of Marmoutiers for the Priory of Notre-Dame-des-Champs, wanted for the future Carmelites. A meeting took place which was to have as splendid results as the famous meeting next year, 1604, between François de Sales and the Baronne de Chantal. On the outskirts of Tours there dwelt at that time "a great gentleman, Antoine du Bois, seigneur de Fontaines (of Plessis-Barbe, Maran in Touraine, and various other estates), formerly

[1] Champagnot, p. 219.

[2] Père de Beauvais says of this epitaph: "It still exists to-day, but the language is too antiquated to find place here" (p. 331). One can scarcely believe one's eyes.

ambassador in Flanders. For many years past he had withdrawn from the political world, with the consent of his wife, Marie Prudhomme, sister-in-law of the Chancellor of Sillery. The office of Secretary of State, pressed upon him by Henri III, had not tempted him back to the world. Living in retirement on his Fontaines property, he set there a rare example of a life devoted to God and the service of the poor. The death of Mme de Fontaines deepened his taste for solitude, and he only left home to come into Tours for the great occasions of the Church's life. On this occasion the Lent sermons had drawn him. There are supernatural as there are natural instincts. M. de Bérulle, learning that he was in the town, went to visit him at his *hôtel*, and found him in company with his daughter Madeleine.

Mlle de Fontaines (born in Paris, May 17, 1579, in the house of the President de Saint-Mesmin near the Hôtel de Guise) was then twenty-two years old. From childhood she showed signs of good judgement and great intellectual power. . . . "A pretty child," family friends used to exclaim, "but what a dreamer!" She did not dream, she thought. Already her thoughts were stamped with courage and originality. She was firm without being rigid, and dignified without being proud; sweetness tempered her vivacity; her face was a faithful index of the vigorous beauty of her soul; truly Heaven had bestowed upon her one of those rare natures in which delicacy is wedded to strength, and which seem born to rule and to be beloved in ruling. On such a rich foundation grace had worked freely, and the result was truly admirable.[1]

So speaks Bérulle's biographer, whose words I use the more willingly in that personally I find Mère Madeleine hard to visualize. Doubtless she is, with Mme. Acarie, the greatest glory of the French Carmelites. Both Spaniards and French, indeed a multitude of contemporaries outstanding for intellect and holiness, agree in representing her as a second Teresa. All readers of her Life, said a great Jesuit of those days, "are struck with the likeness in grace and mind between the great reformer and her daughter of France . . . one stream, drawn from the same fountain and poured into two vessels."[2]

All use the same language and such unanimity leaves no room for doubting the unique beauty of this amazing woman. Nor do I find

[1] Houssaye, I. 272–3. [2] *Mémoire*, II. 598.

myself reduced to accepting her solely by act of faith. Under the thick veil which hides her from us, we see marvels of nature and grace and the most attractive holiness. But she has not written much, and such letters as have been preserved are less revealing than one could wish. And then her Life has been written by a writer of undoubted merit, Père Senault, but eloquent, Balsacian, academic, in a word uninterested in those graphic touches which give life to a portrait. Still, Mère Madeleine remains infinitely precious. Though the Church has never given her a higher rank than "Venerable," our hearts acclaim her a saint.

There are between souls (continues Abbé Houssaye) mysterious affinities more profound and ancient than any are aware, and which at the moment willed by God suddenly declare themselves. M. de Bérulle and Mlle de Fontaines were meeting for the first time; yet hardly had they exchanged a few words than their souls recognized each other. They felt with what close bonds they were linked in the love of Jesus Christ. Mutual confidence opened their hearts. Their first interview lasted seven hours, so absorbing them that, although they were in a room through which people were continually passing, nothing interrupted their discourse.[1]

From that moment the young girl's vocation was decided; Mlle de Fontaines would be a Carmelite.

She took the habit among the first (in November 1604). A year later she was considered to have so fully absorbed the spirit of the Order as to be made novice-mistress. Had there not been such material at hand the superiors might have less lightly consented to the departure of the Spaniards. She was elected prioress in 1608, in 1617 she founded a second Paris convent, in the Rue Chapon;[2] after that date until her death in 1637 she was almost always at the head of one or other convent and never left Paris save for some short missions in the provinces. With the eyes of Paris upon her, not merely the nuns, but the superiors and especially Bérulle, hearkening to her as to an oracle, Madeleine exercised upon the destinies of the

[1] Houssaye, I. 274.

[2] So less than five years after the coming of the Order to France both banks of the Seine and both great centres of Paris life had their Carmelites. The first convent, that of the Faubourg Saint-Jacques, was called indifferently *Monastère de l'Incarnation, Grand couvent, Grandes Carmélites;* the other, in the Rue Chapon, *Monastère de la Mère de Dieu or Petit Couvent.*

French Order an all-important and decisive influence. It is incorrect to assert that she stamped it with her own individuality and more or less modified the primitive traditions, but it is certain that she wrought more efficaciously and brilliantly than any other to maintain and diffuse, whether among the Carmelites themselves or outside their ranks, the true spirit of S. Teresa.

Marillac had been a true prophet; the Carmelite convent in Paris would be first an interesting and exciting sensation, then a home of grace. Writing to Bérulle in Spain, to insist upon the necessity of careful selection among the Spanish sisters, "You know," he said, "what kind of spirit is needful for those of us who are dedicated to devotion and what kind to attract the world . . . for those who come will be called on to speak to the King and Queen and everyone will flock to see them."[1] The worldly and the devout were equally attracted by the French Carmelites.

These great and lovable religious left too much trace of their passage through the world to be quickly forgotten. The world felt its need of them too strongly not to try to take possession of them, and opportunities were not lacking. Rigorous though their enclosure was, the door must needs be opened to the Queen, and the Queen did not enter alone; her ladies always accompanied her. What a strange vision for young women, slaves of their own caprices and of fashion—the refectory with its rigorous abstinence, the austerity of the bare cells; the texts on the walls speaking only of penitence, death and eternity; sisters gliding gravely and noiselessly through the cloisters, always in silence except for the hour of recreation. . . . And when, at a word from the Prioress, a religious, leaving her companions in the group . . . and raising her veil, showed the Queen the features, once so often admired formerly at Court, of a Charlotte de Sancy, an Anne de Viole, a Marie d'Hannivel, emaciated now perhaps yet transfigured, one realizes what must have been the emotions of women themselves still slaves to the world as they realized "a life so serene and so free, free with triumphant freedom,"[2] lived by those who had renounced the world. Thus by these lowly religious the Gospel . . . was spread abroad in the heart of society and society grew used to the spectacle. . . . Worldly souls bowed before the doctrine of sacrifice set forth by women whose clear reason and incorruptible sincerity were known to them. Their fear of it

[1] Houssaye, I. 513.

[2] Houssaye quotes a line from Montalembert's *Moines d'Occident*, Introduction, p. lxxxi.

lessened when they saw the austere but incomparable joys tasted by the brides of Jesus Christ at the foot of the Cross. . . .

They had to reply to the Queen and her ladies. They had to win at the grille the kindred of the young girls to whose hearts God had spoken. Doubtless all did not profit from these grave and penetrating discourses. When Sœur Catherine de Jésus said to one young and brilliant maid-of-honour: "What profit is it to you, Madame, to be beautiful in your own eyes and not in those of Divine Majesty?" perhaps her words did not go home at once. Yet the seed was sown, and sooner or later it would bear fruit. When the hour of disenchantment and of secret bitterness had struck for these daughters of pleasure, they would recollect all at once that they could find a refuge in penitence and guides in the Carmelites.

For these daughters of S. Teresa . . . matched their celestial impulses, generous and daring zeal, and heroic detachment with a certain sanity and order; a gentle and discerning charity that reassured those whom such lofty virtues might have frightened or discouraged. . . . The women who came knocking at the gate (of the convent) found there women dead to the world, yet alive to every noble vibration of mind and heart. Drawn by holiness so sublime, ideas so large, so much liberty of thought and delight in things lovely, visitors came in ever-increasing numbers; and when they left the convent it was with minds determined to struggle against themselves and to give God the victory.

Thus the Carmelites worked in obscurity, tenderly but deeply implanting Jesus Christ in hearts. They did not address themselves to the crowd, but to souls prepared by sorrow or urged by charity, Divine election preceding in every case. Among these, whether belonging to the Court, the magistracy or financial circles which frequented their convents, the Carmelites carried on a great work.[1]

These fine pages of the Abbé Houssaye, in spite of a certain nerveless elegance, give a fairly accurate description of the Carmelite Order of that date in its relations with the world. I cannot improve on them. The special charm of a convent of Carmelites defies analysis. It is unique; those privileged to experience it will try in vain to define it. They will only say that no convent bell is sweeter, no grille less repelling; even a giddy child may feel its atmosphere and be astonished at a later day to find the impression as fresh as ever and more luminous. Deaf to more imperious voices, rebellious to less kindly discipline, after some moments of intercourse with

[1] Houssaye, I. 513–17.

women unseen behind their grating, he will lay down his intolerance, his pride, the bitterness of lifelong disappointment, even the doubts of longest standing, eased of the burden which no doubt he will soon take up again but henceforward will find lightened and, as it were, transfigured. To that Church whose title deeds seemed to him doubtful the Carmelites submitted absolutely; the world invisible, to him hardly more than a name, to these creatures of flesh and blood stood for supreme Reality. He exclaims, he cries out, with one of the Fathers of Humanism: Aflame with love of finding love, we have sought love, we have found it: *Amore incensi inveniendi Amoris, Amorem quæsivimus et invenimus.*[1]

These Carmelites were also true ardent Frenchwomen, passionately interested even in the temporal affairs of the kingdom. "Public affairs," says the biographer of Madeleine de Fontaines, "were of such importance to her that during her country's wars her prayers and penances were endless . . . having heard that the English were advancing on the Ile de Ré upon S. Magdalene's Day, she and her community passed the whole night before the Most Holy Sacrament, bringing there the picture of the saint and praying that she might be the advocate of France."[2] This mystical intervention was not disdained by the politicians of the day. Richelieu, who was more a man of the Middle Ages than is generally thought, entreated the Carmelites not only to pray for his undertakings but even to reveal to him the secrets of God. In a letter of November 16, 1627, Bérulle "promised him on the authority of a person whose name he did not divulge—Mère Marguerite du Saint Sacrament—a fresh victory over the English and final triumph." From November 23 Richelieu was pressing for the date of the victory and discussing means of hastening it. "They (the Carmelites) continue to pray in good hopes," was Bérulle's answer, "and in my opinion the time cannot now be long, but these things cannot be exactly specified. . . . God's power is as great as in the past which you rightly consider miraculous." But Richelieu, with the imperious perseverance of his stamp of genius, returned to the charge, and wished to know beforehand the day when La Rochelle would open her gates to him.[3] He

[1] Marsilio Ficino, quoted by Burton in his *Anatomy of Melancholy*, Sect. III. Preface.

[2] *La vie de la Mère Madeleine de S. Joseph, par un prêtre de l'Oratoire*, Paris, 1645, p. 240.

[3] Houssaye, III. 273–4.

wanted to have prophetesses of State! His mysticism was not of a high type, still, in his own way, Richelieu, like all Paris, bows before the prestige of the Carmelites; he knows that in those houses dwells the power of God.

II. Without meaning to do any such thing, Mère Madeleine has let us see the sublimity of her supernatural gifts, the wisdom and sweetness of her direction, and even her natural vivacity, in a small book which does not bear her name, but which only a saint and a genius could have written. This is the Life of one of her Carmelites, Catherine de Jésus, published in 1631 " by command of the Queen Mother," with a masterly preface by Cardinal de Bérulle. Several times reprinted during the seventeenth century, it rapidly fell into oblivion, like so many other remarkable works. Never, I believe, have the secrets of the higher Mysticism been more felicitously presented. The private papers of Catherine de Jésus, which are quoted at length, and the narrative itself with its short explanations, are both stamped with celestial simplicity and sincerity, and with extraordinary transparency. There is not a drop of that unctuous sweetness which too often irritates us in books of this nature, not a suspicion of pious rhetoric; it embodies the idea of perfection as conceived by the great masters.

Would you see, Philothée (writes the doctor of the Sorbonne who has approved the book), a Carmelite, spotless in innocence, stripped of all that is not God that she may live absorbed in Him, transmuted into pure spirit, . . . merged and plunged in the Eternal Uncreate, by dint of going out of herself and entering into supernatural and superessential Union, read at your leisure this collection of the private writings of Mère Catherine de Jésus. . . . I the undersigned (he continues with an enthusiasm and precision that do him credit)—Doctor of the Faculty of Theology and Professor of Sacred Letters at the Sorbonne, hold that it is impossible to treat of the Sacred Movements of the Spirit of God, the occult and inscrutable ways in which He reveals Himself to elect souls, the mysterious intercourse between the Beloved and the Spouse of the Canticles . . . in a more Catholic and lofty manner, and in a style more clear and intelligible and suited to the dignity of the subject than this little miracle of grace has done. As for the sketch of her life . . . it is clearly by one of her sisters, but as I read it and meditate on it I seem to find once more the pen and spirit of the deceased.[1]

[1] *La vie de Sœur Catherine de Jésus, avec un recueil de ses lettres et pieux écrits*, Paris, 1631. I quote from the third edition of 1631, the first being of 1628.

It is all this and still more; Madeleine could not so admirably have understood and described the graces of Catherine had she not herself received the same and even higher gifts.

Bérulle's preface—a letter to the Queen Mother—although slightly laboured and redundant, is nevertheless worthy of the book.

The Greatest of all great ones has made both great and small, as says the Divine Wisdom. . . . I speak to your Majesty of littleness, in honour of this little soul, the account of whose life is here dedicated to you. . . .

The Queen was well aware that this lowly soul had been housed in a body much below the middle height.

There is a passage in which it seems as if the Son of God desired to emphasize the triumph of littleness and to confound the pride of earth and heaven. It is in S. Luke, 9, *complexus illum . . . statuit illum secus se.* It seems in this action as though the Son of God wishes, in the sight of heaven and earth, to lodge littleness in His Bosom as upon the throne of His Love, and by this sweet, tender and familiar union pronounce His oracles in favour of littleness, and subject the greatest of His kingdom to it.

Great and sweet is it to behold Jesus, in Whom is the fulness of Divinity and of Eternal Wisdom, united to a little child and it to Him; happy child to be so close to the Heart where dwells and triumphs the Trinity itself. But if this thought is sweet and great, though the meaning to which it leads us is strong and severe, its result is mighty and its end seems strange. For Jesus, by act and word, not only abases the great of this earth, that would be a small thing, but also the great of His Divine and Celestial dwelling-place, by the formidable negation, the searching pronouncement: *Nisi efficiamini sicut parvuli, non intrabitis in regnum cœlorum.* This oracle should arrest us, this spectacle draw tears from our eyes, should melt pride by the sweetness of Jesus and cast down for ever the highest cedars of Lebanon at the Feet of Jesus and those of the little ones of Jesus upon earth.

These are not empty words. Himself a cedar of Lebanon, founder of the Oratory, confidant of two queens, the head of a great political party, Bérulle has put himself at the feet of this lowly creature, to whose life he writes the preface. As director of Catherine de Jésus, he always approached the young mystic with profound veneration, as one in whom was " the Greatest of all great ones " with all the treasures of "Divine Wisdom." What he has seen in her, he says, is too beautiful for human words, and the record of her life "is far inferior to the graces of her soul." What he recalls of his relations with Catherine de Jésus "transcends all that is here written."[1] Even the little here written is beyond his powers. He could not have written it, whereas the mysteries of this life hid in God seemed to Mère Madeleine as limpid and natural as the light of day. "I have written of these marvels," she says, "only the shadow of what I know of them."[2]

Catherine de Jésus—her other name is unknown—was born at Bordeaux on April 5, 1589. When about "seven or eight, she found a book of S. Catherine of Siena, and on reading it received the first touches of grace. . . . She felt in herself the Divine Majesty drawing her to seek Him and to flee from men; in her innocence she took the flight from men literally and would never leave her home except to go to church . . . nor even allow her writing-master to guide her hand." The discipline she practised henceforward "arrested her growth and made her so weak that she was very small all her life."[3] She was clearly predestined to the higher life, and the religious who directed her were thinking of sending her to the Feuillantines, when Bérulle's cousin, M. de Gourgues, subsequently first president of the Bordeaux *Parlement*, "obtained her a place" in the Carmelite convent of the Faubourg S. Jacques. She arrived in Paris in August 1606, making a short stay with Mme. Acarie, during which she was under the direction of Père Coton. She took the habit, without having brought "any dowry, being provided with much more estimable goods."[4] Mère Madeleine had just been nominated Prioress of the Great Convent, and when, four years later, she was summoned to found that of the Rue Chapon, she took Catherine with her. Their daily intimacy never ceased till the death of the latter in 1623.

Early in life the young Carmelite had perceived, though very vaguely, what God was preparing for her. "For several years," she said, "I threw myself into God as into a deep abyss, so that He might work in me things without limit or end." In a note written by her on the threshold, so to speak, of the mystic zone, she said:

[1] *La Vie*, prefatory letter.
[2] *Ibid.*, p. 66.
[3] *Ibid.*, pp. 3–4.
[4] *Ibid.*, p. 20.

To be lost in God ought to suffice me. God is my wisdom, my knowledge, my power. It suffices me that God is sufficient for Himself.[1]

When about twenty, during the Christmas feast, she felt herself greatly "occupied by God." "She was unaware of being upon earth, although she performed all her ordinary actions, but thought herself in Heaven, and was amazed at finding herself among us!"[2] She resumed for a short time only that life which "the animal-man" calls real; at twenty-two, continues Mère Madeleine, who observed each step of this ascending life,

God showed her another path and raised her into an interior life so high and withdrawn that but little can be said of it, since the greatest things are hidden, God not willing to reveal to the world the secrets He confides to His saints. . . . I will say that at this time Jesus Christ . . . drew her to Himself and took possession of her, marking her with His stamp that she might be His from that moment. In saying that she was marked with His stamp I am using her own words, and I cannot explain what it was, except that it was a working of God in the soul, manifested to her as a stamp or seal imprinted on her most secret depths, as something seized and set apart for His Divine Majesty. And this working was of Jesus, Who, as a child Himself, took her to Himself as a child to initiate her into the mystery of His Infancy, with all else in Him. . . . So He took possession of this soul and, as I believe, dwelled in her by presence and effects to her last breath of life.[3]

Union most marvellous with God, in the depths of the soul, through the intermediary of Christ, as is required by Catholic, and more particularly by Teresian, Mysticism; union, moreover, effected "by Jesus as a child," as is required by seventeenth-century Mysticism and especially by that of Bérulle, as we shall show later. Another characteristic of the same epoch is to be noticed: S. Mary Magdalene, "the seraphic Madeleine," as Catherine de Jésus called her, seemed to them, next to the Blessed Virgin, the most perfect example of this union. Speaking of the moment of the Magdalene's conversion—

O moment (she cries) that I can never weary of naming or magnifying, so lovely art thou! . . . In a single instant Jesus rent this holy

[1] *La Vie*, pp. 23–24. [2] *Ibid.*, p. 40. [3] *Ibid.*, pp. 45–7.

soul with His Love. Ah, what marvels did she see and feel! For being at the moment almost out of herself, without hearing, speech, or feeling, O, how must she have been filled (*occupée*) with Jesus!—

Then addressing herself to the saint:

At the instant that you heard the word of Jesus Christ, love swept you out of yourself and Jesus Christ took possession.[1]

Every word, *occuper*, for instance, has its full sense and even more. The young ecstatic explained herself "as best she could and with great difficulty in very brief and ordinary language, but full of meaning and dealing with sublimely high and holy things."[2] Of the two women, it is not Mlle de Fontaines, but the humble Bordelaise who writes the better. Both are equally lucid, yet the latter enraptures me by the luminous depth and supple rhythm of these notes which she certainly wrote only for private use.[3] The two writers, however, are both trying to describe the ineffable, I mean the long and persevering effort by which souls are emptied of themselves and filled with God.

In one of her notes Catherine writes: "I feel the operation of God in such penetration and strength that it is as if it consumes my soul and my spirit." "God wished to destroy self in her, to produce results secret and divine, so that this poor soul was no longer conscious of existence or of the operations of God, unless when the spirit dwelling within her gave her some breathing space that she might know herself and God in her. God's Will was to hide herself from herself as from others, so far as concerned at least the larger part of what passed within her."[4] She had but little light, yet it was sufficient for her to feel or divine or catch a glimpse of the marvels of this hidden life.

It seems to me that, when I am in this state, God takes all my consciousness and draws it to Himself, in order that I should have no knowledge of some especial thing that God wishes to effect in me.[5]

[1] *La Vie*, pp. 36–7.
[2] *Ibid.*, pp. 67–8.

[3] According to a scholar not given to speak at random, if the life of Mère Catherine is "by Mère Madeleine . . . the arrangement and general style belong to Nicolas le Fèvre, sieur de Lézeau, councillor of State" and a great friend of the Carmelites. Cf. the unpublished notes of Mercier de Saint-Leger Bertrand, *Mélanges de biographie et d'histoire*, p. 356. It may be so, of course, but I do not believe that Lézeau did much to touch up the prose of S. Catherine.

[4] *La Vie*, p. 49.
[5] *Ibid.*, p. 58.

What need had she of further knowledge? "Did I see what passes in me," she said, "I should be distracted from God, and that must not be; all must be occupied with suffering and love."[1]

I feel that all the powers of my soul are strained beyond themselves and are at work without my knowing anything of what is going on, and this deprives me of all desire and memory of anything; yet in the midst of this my impotence, I understand one great thing, which still remains only a small part, for that what is being wrought in me without my knowledge is continually on the increase. As for myself, I cannot think or say how I am. I know no desire in earth or in heaven, so that I can do nothing by myself, and sometimes I find myself speaking of something, when inwardly I am far away.[2]

Doubtless these fine passages teach nothing new to those who have studied the works of Catherine of Genoa, of Teresa, of John of the Cross. We should do wrong to represent the grace of Catherine de Jésus as exceptional. Rather, to a degree impossible to define, it is the grace common to all these exceptional beings. All true mystics would feel at home in these luminous confessions. But for one thing, Catherine describes this experience, ancient yet ever new, with the simplicity of a child, and thus imparts to her "little papers" an indefinable colour of reality; and for another, she limits herself to telling her impressions just as she feels and tries to understand them, with no hint of the reflections or emotions that preceded or followed her ecstasies.

A little paper of hers has been found with these words: "I see that my soul ought to be nought save an assent to God." She meant: I see that all must be annihilated in me, except an act of submission to the Will of God. . . . Very often she would begin several times to do a thing without having the power to finish it, or to say a word and not be able to bring out the second or third. And so this soul would speak and act according to the Will of God, or rather God's Will in her, for this Divine Majesty so possessed her that there was nought of herself left in her, according to ordinary modes of speech and action, and she often repeated: "I have nought, I am nought, a power greater than myself possesses and holds me—all of me."[3]

This good sister one day felt the power of God so strongly that it forced her to speak: one day she was in the garden for an hour, in an arbour of vines, pacing up and down and saying: "God puts His

[1] *La Vie*, pp. 52–3. [2] *Ibid.*, pp. 65–6. [3] *Ibid.*, pp. 67–8.

Power into me, God puts His Power into me, God puts His Wisdom and Knowledge into me"—continually repeating the same words, while subjected to experiences within for which she could find no words. Even when she related this to the Mother Prioress (Madeleine), it was with some questioning as to what it might mean, saying that she had done all she could to stop this happening, but it was beyond her power. Thus it may be seen that the excellence of her grace was partially concealed from her, that she might remain in the lowliness and abasement of life on earth.[1]

That the void within her might be the more complete and painful, it seemed that after having emptied her of herself, God chose from time to time to deprive her of Himself.

He imprinted in her something of that abandonment by the Eternal Father that He endured on the Cross . . . producing in her so immense and extreme a sensation that she deemed herself returning to nothingness, expressing her torment sometimes by the term annihilation, but oftener by that of privation, thinking that God was making her bear a withdrawal of Him insupportable to her, not that she saw God withdrawing from her as regards the grace necessary to salvation or any other kind of grace, but rather it was a kind of privation to which she was subjected and a trial and torment . . . inexplicable . . . save that He Who is All-Powerful had thus willed and wrought.[2]

The father of a family (said she) turns his house upside down to find a piece of silver, and God ransacks His creature to find the soul absorbed and lost in self and its own workings.[3]

Mère Madeleine skilfully proportions the different heads of her narrative.

As for the temptations of the evil one, I shall only say that of which God gives me memory and what I deem expedient, knowing that the greater part of that which passes in souls of God ought but to be known in Heaven. (Had this royal discretion been invariably copied, how many evils would have been avoided!) It pleased God many times to let this soul see the pains of Hell . . . so moving and appalling her as to cause her to lose consciousness for a couple of hours, during which she neither heard, saw nor felt anything, but lay on the ground wherever she might be. Nevertheless this never befell her save when she was alone, or in company with the Mother Prioress, or at most with one other sister. And in regard to this much hap-

[1] *La Vie*, p. 147. [2] *Ibid.*, pp. 107–8. [3] *Ibid.*, p. 146.

pened . . . which neither should nor can be uttered, nor even as to the extent God suffered the evil spirits to assault her.[1]

What splendid reticence! And with what complacency others would have dilated on the painful story!

She was an unimportant figure in the convent, but all loved her. "Her behaviour was so devout that all the sisters liked to be near her, and to look at her, even when she did not speak a word, as very often she was unable to do." Yet, whenever she mingled a little in conversation, she spoke "so naïvely and sweetly that it was like hearing a little angel."[2] The more she was "emptied" of self the more humbly she deemed of herself. She had "a very great love for all God's works." Once in the time of the last wars against the rebellious heretics, God showed her that He burdened her with the needs of France, bidding her to charge herself with them. This she accepted, saying to Our Lord: Yes, my God, I shall care for France and Thy people, and Thou wilt care for me. "And verily, all the length of the war, she told the Prioress that she had asked nothing of God for herself, nor had she anything in mind save the state of public affairs. She often asked Mère Madeleine: How are things going? Have they taken such and such a town or made such and such an advance?"[3]

I see, she would say, the Fulness of God in all things, even down to an ant, so that my soul is led to magnify God everywhere and in all.[4]

She was never occupied in tracing the divine work accomplishing itself in her, "not being attracted towards such things," and having docilely surrendered the care of her inner life to those charged with her direction. She revealed the secrets of her soul unreservedly either to Bérulle or to Mère Madeleine, "but they only followed what God was putting there."[5] She found some difficulty in confiding to Bérulle. On one occasion she wrote to him:

I find myself tongue-tied and timid when I speak to you, I do not know whether you have perceived this. It is strange and hindering to me. I surrender my will to you, for you to give it to God.[6]

[1] *La Vie*, pp. 54–55. [2] *Ibid.*, p. 98. [3] *Ibid.*, pp. 90–1.
[4] *Ibid.*, p. 116. [5] *Ibid.*, p. 109.
[6] *Ibid.*, pp. 172–3. Mère Madeleine does not name the recipient of the letters she publishes, but I believe most were addressed to Bérulle.

Pen in hand, she feels more free, yet days come when all communication is impossible.

I am such a captive that I cannot write a word, save to tell you that I wished for you to-day, for I had great facility in speaking of God, a rare thing with me, who am generally in a state of privation and weakness. I know not where I am, nor wish to know unless it is God's Will. . . . I have oft tried to write to you, but it was impossible for us.[1]

The "we" or "us" preferred by the Carmelites to the pride of "I" somewhat disturbs this naïve spontaneity.

Pray do not fear that *our* little sufferings will hinder *us* from remembering you before God. *I* entreat you to believe that I should sooner forget *myself*, so dear is your soul to *us* before Him.[2]

I am under so great obligations to you that *I* can repay them in no wise, save by remembering you before God.[3]

The writings of certain eminent mystics do not always appeal to us, but here we have a charming simplicity and refinement. Bérulle having told her of some of his own scruples, she answers:

The good Jesus has already forgotten all in which you fear to have failed, and I offer myself to Him to bear your penance.[4]

Or again:

Do not trouble yourself over the drowsiness you complain of, it is nothing. I feel the same sometimes.[5]

This delicate flame of life in her was quenched on January 19, 1623. "She said to me several times during her illness: I see the little Virgins . . . they call me to go with them!"[6] The sweet body, so light to carry, was borne in a coach to the monastery of the Faubourg S. Jacques. The Marquise de Maignelais accompanied it from one convent to the other, and the representative of the Sorbonne, André Duval, recited the last prayers over her grave. Such was the life which I cannot praise as I should, but which shines with its own light. In the course of our studies we shall meet more brilliant saints captivating us by the ardour of their sentiments, the greatness

[1] *La Vie*, p. 202. [2] *Ibid.*, pp. 226–7. [3] *Ibid.*, p. 186.
[4] *Ibid.*, p. 182. [5] *Ibid.*, p. 187. [6] *Ibid.*, pp. 120–1.

of their natural gifts, or the merit of their works, but I know none more exquisite, nor better fitted to make the mystic union real to us, in its simple and sublime truth.

III. An essential part of this long chapter would be missing if I did not devote at least some pages to the second of the three daughters of Mme Acarie—all three Carmelites—Marguerite du Saint-Sacrement. To make room for her I must omit the charming Marquise de Bréauté, Marie de Jésus (of whom Cousin has written at length) and many others.

For reasons which it would take too long to explain, we give the preference to Marguerite. She is a very original figure and at the same time thoroughly representative. She did not live like her mother in a continual ecstasy; God did not keep her for Himself alone, nor set a seal upon her lips, as He did for Catherine de Jésus. She is less majestic, less obviously outstanding, than Madeleine de S. Joseph, of whom it was said that "she would be distinguished among fifty religious by a certain unction of grace diffused by her presence."[1] Marguerite, on the contrary, readily merges with the rank and file. Small in stature and by inclination as far as possible from solemnity, she does not strike us at first. There is no aureole on the brow of this vivacious Parisian, brisk, downright, always direct and simple in speech. A nun trembling at the idea of meeting her for the first time, because "she expected to see a very serious and grave-looking person, was astonished at beholding her gay face, lively manner, and utterly unaffected bearing."[2] Far from affecting grandeur, she sought rather to put people off the scent by pretending to be silly or even worse. By dark hints about herself, she even took in her mother, the penetrating Mme Acarie, who confided to the other Carmelites of S. Jacques "the fears in which she is that her daughter's inner life is in a deplorable condition."[3] Another time, Mme Acarie asked her what she ought to do for her own spiritual advancement. "You must mortify self," replied Marguerite, "for, though you have taught others so much, you have always followed your own inclinations, and, good though they are, there is too much of your own judgement in

[1] *Mémoire*, II. 592.

[2] *La Vie de la V. M. Marguerite Acarie*, by M. T. D. C (Tronson de Chenvière), Paris, 1689, p. 145.

[3] *Ibid.*, p. 70.

your actions, and that is what you must let die within you!" Slightly surprised, yet edified, Mme Acarie repeated this to "some sisters, one of whom declared to Mère Marguerite her surprise that she should have spoken to her mother with such severity, saying with a smile, 'What behaviour!' to which our young religious only answered: 'Then why did she ask me when she knows me to be nothing but a giddy ass! I could not say anything else but what I thought.'"[1]

Such freedom of speech and manner deceived no one; all agree in representing her as a woman of extraordinary piety. "She will go further than her mother," said Père Binet. An incident unprecedented in processes of this kind occurred when "the Marquise de Maignelais, giving evidence for the beatification of the mother, put in a plea on behalf of the daughter, although she was still living. "Mme Acarie," she said, "was holy, but her daughter, Mère Marguerite, is still more so"; the actual words reported by M. de Lézeau according to the written deposition of the clerk of the court.[2] A number of charming miracles are told of her, performed without her conscious intervention, and, *a fortiori*, without her claiming to work miracles. With all this she was very intelligent, quick to make up her mind, incomparable in the direction of souls. The spiritual guide subsequently compiled from her letters and private papers is one of the best books of direction I know.[3] She was very human, kind, "courteous and caressing,"[4] but uncompromising in her resistance to all insipidity. For my part, if I had to pick out among the great religious of the past the ideal Carmelite, the one which corresponds best to the picture I have formed of a French daughter of S. Teresa, I should name almost without hesitation Marguerite du Saint-Sacrement.

She was born in Paris on March 6, 1590. The Marquise de Maignelais, herself a Gondi and aunt of Cardinal de Retz, told Vincent de Paul among several others, "that, visiting Mme Acarie shortly after Marguerite's birth, she was shown into a room where the cradle had been placed and was much amazed to see it as if on fire, but was reassured by an inward voice of a good angel saying: 'These flames are a figure of the celestial fire that will inflame this soul!'"[5]

[1] *La Vie*, pp. 71–2.

[2] *Conduite chrétienne et religieuse selon les sentiments de la V. M. Marguerite*, by Père J. M. de Vernon, Paris, 2nd edition, 1691.

[3] *La Vie*, p. 234. [4] *Ibid.*, pp. 10–11. [5] *Ibid.*, pp. 10–11.

We know our *Hôtel* Acarie. In this hothouse the piety of the young girl ripened rapidly, yet we have an impression that the precocious development was in no way forced. Always mistress of herself and incapable of pose, docile no doubt but independent, she yields herself to the influences that fitted her spiritual capacity and lets the others go. Though deeply humble and prompt to despise herself, she was not born to be a disciple of others. She venerated the holiness of her mother's friends and held them to be worthy servants of God, she modelled herself on none of them. As a Carmelite, she used no books save the *Imitation* and the writings of S. Teresa. Possibly she never even opened the works of Bérulle, her beloved director. We have several of her letters to the grave Marillac, who was, perhaps, even dearer to her. Though deferential to him, she was clearly as little dominated by him as by her mother, and nothing stronger can be said. Had a woman of her make been at the head of Port-Royal, Saint-Cyran himself must have beaten a retreat.

Among the visitors at the *Hôtel* Acarie, she had come into touch with Quintanadoine and sometimes asked his advice. This is how she writes to him when " she was no more than twelve or thirteen," as he assures us.

Monsieur and most revered Father in Our Lord Jesus,

The peace of Our Lord be yours in this my humble greeting. I pray you excuse my boldness in writing to you to tell you of the disposition in which I have been since I spoke to you about prayer. I have used the book you lent me and thank you most humbly for it, but since I spoke to M. de Bérulle, he told me to use the book of Jean Gerson, and it seems to me useful, for it does not pique my curiosity so much as that of your loan, where there is much that is too high for me, especially about the creation of the world and the angels. My mind wanders therein, and is much more speculative than when I spoke to you, and therefore I do not use it any more. But through God's grace my spirit is calmer the last three or four days than for a fortnight before. I beg of you to be so kind as to send me a scapular to give to a good soul who much desires to have one, and also I would entreat you to send me a hair shirt for myself. I have need of it, but it would take too long to write to you on this subject, I could say it better by word of mouth. Pray send it to me with the scapular, and I beseech you to pray God for me.[1]

[1] *La Vie*, pp. 30–1.

Somewhat later, but before she was fifteen, she wrote another surprising note to Mère Anne de Saint-Barthélemy.

My virtues are only imaginary, in reality I have not one. . . . What is worse, my temper is so quick and hasty that at the least contradiction I get carried away without meaning it. When I come to pray, I find myself unable to concentrate or apply my thoughts to God, and before I have soothed and tranquillized my spirit, much time is lost. And my soul is as arid as possible.[1]

These letters, so far in advance of her years, do not contain a hint of the irritating self-sufficiency of an infant prodigy. She neither likes to hear herself talking nor admires herself. Doubtless she is very mature, and expert in self-knowledge and appreciations of spiritual values, but still more is she naïve and genuine; she says frankly what she thinks at the moment, and uses each word in its true sense. What is remarkable is that one of the most subtle lessons of the mystical life, the *relinque curiosa*, has been already understood by this child. How firmly she holds the reins of her soul! She chooses freely between the too "speculative" book proposed by Quintanadoine and the *Imitation* advised by Bérulle. It would be delightful to follow the development of this young and vigorous wisdom. She became a Carmelite at fifteen, and soon Prioress, at first in the provinces, then at the Little Convent in the Rue Chapon. Never ceasing to grow along the first lines of her development, she remained full of vigour, sincerity and independence, not the independence, the fruit of pride, that adds to our fetters, but the independence which is but a form of self-forgetfulness.

Practise simplicity of spirit (she would say) in all things superfluous and nothing worth, even in your spiritual condict. . . . S. Teresa excelled in such simplification of spirit.[2]

The programme of the interior life and of Mysticism was for her comprised in a few words.

We must forget ourselves for the Love of God, so that He can raise our soul out of ourselves, to be wholly His, for it is easy to see that there is not much room for Him in us, if we are continually taken up with ourselves.[3]

[2] *La Vie*, p. 32. [2] *Conduite chrétienne*, p. 379. [3] *Ibid.*, p. 19.

To help us in "raising our soul out of ourselves" unto God is the sole object of direction; over-much occupation with the director is only a subtle mode of being taken up with self.

Tender and sensitive natures need a well-balanced direction if they are not to be ruined and lost by too long listening to their complaints. Spiritual daughters have a certain joy in having something to say in converse with their spiritual fathers. I confess that I should prefer to have nothing to say, so great is my aversion to wasting time in this fashion. It is far better to be occupied as little as possible with self.

We must give ourselves in our good moments to God . . . and accustom ourselves to be out of ourselves. . . . It amazes me that there is so much need for conversation with directors, for as a rule it is the same thing every time, and advice carefully acted upon would give enough to do.[1]

"Many put themselves into the hands of another for their own pleasure and ease; wherein they are mightily deceived"; doubly, first because the director's aim should be nought but to make us die to self, and secondly, because, after all, they can do so little! The aid for which we hope from them

in no wise draws us to God, if God Himself does not extend the arms of His goodness. Human efforts are so mingled with weakness and ignorance that I do not know how we dare regard them as infallible and holy. . . . If an angel made it his business to reply to us as we in our multitudinous fancies and our self-love desire, he would rather injure than assist us. . . .[2] As for creatures, however holy, it is but emptiness for us to seek after them, who have much in common with ourselves and the Deceiver; for a being revered by us may be, although all unknown, a devil, since having its portion in visible things of earth we are attracted by earthly reputation and the use for our sanctification can be only on the surface. Let us imitate the holy Magdalen, who stays not for angels but leaves them at the sepulchre, to seek out her Master.[3]

"Her Master," the interior Master Who excels all others, by the side of Whom the most skilful director is worth so little, or rather, before Whom the most skilful director effaces himself the most, this is the principle I should like to emphasize, nay, I must emphasize, as the spiritual keynote of the present work.

[1] *Conduite chrétienne*, p. 18. [2] *Ibid.*, pp. 14–15. [3] *Ibid.*, pp. 147–8.

Mère Marguerite continues:

But all this should not prevent us receiving direction or assuming it for others. . . . The illumination received from directors avails much.[1]

On the death of Bérulle in 1629 Marguerite wrote to a Benedictine Abbess among her friends a characteristic letter revealing the real woman, at once eagerly submissive and totally detached, in her relation with this man of God who had been the one most heeded of all her directors.

If we placed our hope of perfection and salvation in men we should have disquietude; but going hand in hand with God we have only to retire into Him, and to make use of the saints whom He has given in our own establishing. That which I desire for you and all your house is so to receive grace as to profit by it when left alone, when death removes what it has pleased God to give you. (The allusion is doubtless to the then director of the Abbey.) It is an unspeakable repose to be in God at all times, and no more in the creature. Since all passes away, and the best of created things must fade, it would not make us better, or more holy than others, if our privileges were fixed and assured to us in this life. May God have mercy upon me in the next! He has given to me that which I desired of Him, which was to enter religion in the time of saints and great personalities, to be as it were born among them. Well foreseeing the storms that time might bring upon all around,[2] I am indebted to God for granting me this grace. . . . It is good to accustom oneself early to love none but God, that He may be to us all things.[3]

One might wish more feeling on such an occasion, yet after all I am not sure that she does lack the tenderness which is so touching

[1] *Conduite chrétienne*, pp. 248, 123. She adds wisely: "It is often beyond our power to discern whether the outpouring of our troubles and our condition to a director arises from necessity or egotism. This is why it is better to abandon ourselves simply and without analysis to the impulse of the moment. Silence, it is true, is sometimes best, but restraint too rigorously imposed on ourselves gives the devil opportunity to afflict and torment us dangerously." In this manner she resolves beforehand the scruples that would beset a holy soul in the over-refinement of the *Maximes*.

[2] It is strange that when so young, and even before entering religion, she should have foreseen the conflict that broke out among the Carmelites when the Fathers of that Order, introduced into France, attempted to substitute their jurisdiction for that of the ecclesiastical superiors nominated by the Pope. Happily we need not enter into details of the sad and disgraceful history. All necessary information will be found in the *Mémoire* of the Carmelites already quoted several times and in the *Courte réponse* of M. Houssaye: *Les Carmélites de France et le Cardinal de Bérulle*, Paris, 1873.

[3] *La Vie*, pp. 196–7.

in the letters of Ste. Chantal. The " saints and holy personalities " of whom she speaks, Bérulle especially, may have had more virtue and prestige than human charm. On the other hand, our lively Parisienne, with her supple and sweet energy, soon attained a complete poise, which regulated according to her will both her sentiments and their expression. " Violence is not of God," she would reflect. " We must therefore have none of it."[1] Her illusions were few, whatever the subject. " We shall find Paradise something quite new," she said, " having found so little of it on earth."[2] " We have to put up with many failings in ourselves and others, for it is earth's way to lack fervour."[3] " The inner life is silence, suffering and patience."[4] Yet she herself was neither cold nor dry, but on the contrary sweet in looks and words; her firm touch healed the sick, her sane lips drove out evil spirits.

Nor was there any aridity in her mind. Her style has something real, intense, discreetly passionate about it that carries conviction to every soul. The following passage may be taken as an example of her vigorous and rigorous manner.

If our inner life be without confidence in God we are reduced to the most painful and miserable condition. This is why it is easy for the devil, having power to work in us and to bring us low as regards this most essential support to a sinful soul, to overwhelm us in a moment, though not to destroy Divine truth, which moors our souls to the belief that He is our God, Our Father and our entire salvation.

This truth, which the devil cannot take away, enrages the devil against the soul. He troubles it and darkens it as far as in him lies, which God permits, for our testing. Never let us say or think at such a time that we are wholly separated from God. I know that our souls merit it only too well, but as long as we live we must adore, implore and hope for the mercies of God; only in hell is it impossible to receive them. *Therefore, because this is truth*, let us never receive the lying suggestion dishonouring to God that there is no mercy for us.[5]

She is mistress of her thoughts and pen as of her soul. We may say of her direction what she says of the interior life: it " is sparing in words but has wide horizons towards God."[6]

As might be expected, her direction was much sought after. She

[1] *Conduite*, p. 17. [2] *Ibid.*, pp. 25–6. [3] *Ibid.*, p. 23.
[4] *Ibid.*, p. 130. [5] *Ibid.*, pp. 135–6. [6] *Ibid.*, p. 130.

was remarkably quick in intuition, and it was commonly believed that the secrets of hearts were revealed to her by celestial illumination. When she arrived as Prioress at the Convent de Saintes, so one of her nuns records naïvely,

I had been there four months. I said to myself: since our Mother is such a penitent, she will be very serious, and I had better appear as much so as possible. We all received her and her following of four nuns at the door. She embraced us all, six in number, and when she came to me she said: "This is Sœur Anne du Saint-Sacrement," which surprised me much, as I never had the pleasure of seeing her. But I was far more surprised when, stroking my face, she added: "Pride, pride, do not hold yourself so straight, walk in the humility of Jesus Christ. What matter if we are looked on as mad? There is no sin in that, but there may be in a haughty carriage. Be natural!" I was so inwardly rejoiced in hearing her thus speak that I wished always to be with her.[1]

Bérulle, who had known her from her birth, believed her divinely inspired. Perhaps he was too eager for the miraculous; he was mainly relying on the word of Mère Marguerite when he urged Richelieu to besiege La Rochelle, declaring that it was the Will of God that the King should take the town. I do not deny that it was so, why should I? Nevertheless, as the Church in such matters leaves us our liberty, I suspend judgement with regard to the wonder. Bérulle was sincere, but he may have impressed his own ideas on this Carmelite. One sees easily how it may have happened. He is in distress at the progress of the Huguenots. As often when in trouble, he goes to the parlour in the Rue Chapon, asks to see the Prioress, and pours out his anguish in view of the great misery of France. What is to be done? Why not advise the Cardinal to lay siege to the stronghold of the rebels, smoke the beast out of his hole? Marguerite, knowing little of these things, approves the strategy laid before her, as we did in the spring of 1915 when the journalists sketched out the general offensive. Whatever the means—they matter little and she is no judge—the Carmelite is quite sure that God will never fail Catholic France. Bérulle joins this conviction to the thread of his own idea, and assures Richelieu of the Divine Will. All, I repeat,

[1] *La Vie*, pp. 130–2. When she arrived at Saintes, Mère Marguerite had with her a daughter of Séguier, Mère Marie de Jésus-Christ.

in perfect good faith; it is the way of humanity, and especially of Bérulle. "He consulted her often," we are told, "on important affairs, and followed her advice with much success. He even told a famous Abbess that when he was anxious over the conversion of someone he would affect to treat it indifferently when talking it over with Mère Marguerite, and by *the tone* of her wise and penetrating replies could not doubt that she was the instrument used by the Holy Spirit to reveal to him the Will of God."[1]

Mère Marguerite's own views on the siege of La Rochelle are preserved in a letter "to a person of singular virtue who followed the King on this celebrated expedition," and who seems to have taken a direct part, either as soldier or Councillor of State, in the enterprise. After saying that she had no hopes in the "power of man," she goes on:

You ask me what I think, and I will tell it to you alone.[2] I hope for God's aid through His extraordinary mercies and the efforts of His servants. I cease not to fear and to pray. You know that our thoughts (her own) are so light and weak that you must look for consolation only in the courage that God will give you in these extremities.[3]

That this humble soul so skilful in hiding her own merits and so little esteeming her "light and weak" thoughts, would have ordered the Cardinal, as from God, to besiege La Rochelle, I find it hard to believe. The following letter with its magnificent exordium was written to the same correspondent.

We are more present in your labours and with the King's army than you yourself. I hope trembling for a happy issue, and the hope seems surer and more solid than fear. Nevertheless fear occupies us and works upon us though we were without hope. God works His wonders from moment to moment without giving us any light as to what is ahead. You have laboured in our affairs (probably the Carmelite troubles) for four years in ignorance and darkness; now you must labour for the State and for Religion in these straits set about with perils. It is this same State, however, that gives me certain hope of victory, for her knowledge, intelligence and power are of God,

[1] *La Vie*, pp. 34–5.

[2] If she confides her thought to him alone it is not that she attaches a divine importance to it, but on the contrary from a desire to avoid putting herself forward.

[3] *La Vie*, p. 182.

and men are as nought, overwhelmed with their ignorance and weakness, throwing themselves into peril without an idea how to extricate themselves. In a word, monsieur, the more you belong to the State under the mighty Hand of God, the more He is yours, and you are the instruments to work His wonders.[1]

See how she speaks to a friend from whom she will hide nothing. "You ask me what I think, and I will tell it to you alone." Was she more explicit with Bérulle? I doubt it. The matter is of small importance, but it is well to grasp the fatal transformation which the words of a mystic may undergo when reported by a prejudiced director.

In any case, public opinion ascribed to Mère Marguerite the gift both of prophecy and of miracles. In a memoir drawn up by Cardinal de Retz about the famous Carmelite with whom his own family had so many links, he writes:

I could fill a volume did I record all that I have heard from irreproachable sources about Sister Marguerite du Saint-Sacrement, but I will content myself with saying here what I know from my own family, which was so detailed and convincing as in my opinion to leave no loophole for doubting it. I have several times heard my late father (Philippe Emanuel de Gondi) say that some years before he entered the Congregation of the Oratory, and while he was yet engaged in the intrigues and pleasures of the Court, my late mother was wont to urge him to go to see Mère Marguerite. This he for long refused to do. Yielding at last from sheer complaisance, he found there the late Cardinal de Bérulle, a stranger to him, whom Mère Marguerite introduced in these words: "This, monsieur, is the R. P. de Bérulle, whom as yet you know not, but whom you will know some day, as the most efficacious instrument which God will use for your salvation. You scoff at me now, but one day you will see that I speak the truth." Even in my infancy I can remember my father telling this story, while yet Mme. de Gondi was living.[2]

But why go beyond the Convent of the Mère de Dieu for proofs

[1] *La Vie*, p. 183.

[2] *Ibid.*, pp. 169–70. Cf. Chantelauze, *Saint Vincent de Paul et les Gondi*, Paris, 1882, pp. 178–9. The biographer of Marguerite also gives (pp. 171–3), from the witness of the Archbishop of Sens, O. de Bellegarde, another version, more detailed and probably in some points more exact, of this event. According to Bellegarde, who heard the matter from the Père de Gondi himself, it was not till after several visits that Marguerite revealed to the Superintendent of Galleys the future in store for him. Cf. also Batterel, *Mémoires domestiques pour servir à l'histoire de l'Oratoire*, I. 340, Paris, 1902.

of this extraordinary gift bestowed upon Mère Marguerite du Saint-Sacrement? . . . The cases are numberless when, on being asked about those ill within its walls, she predicted roundly that such and such a sister would die, such an one recover, such an one suffer long, all of which turned out as she had said, to the great astonishment of the physicians, who had often themselves held quite contrary opinions. But it is important to remark that her humility usually hindered her knowing that she possessed this gift, often not believing that she had spoken so plainly till her words were explained to herself; and when others would have put her in mind of her predictions she would respond brusquely enough: " Heavens, what matter? Half the time I do not know what I am saying! "

There follows a famous scene which grates upon us a little, but is fundamentally noble and affecting, as well as picturesque and very characteristic. It is concerned with " what happened between her and Mme. de Chantal when, about July 1641, the latter came to the convent of Mère de Dieu "—we note in passing how faithful the saint, now in her seventieth year, is in her love for the Carmelites.

The Rev. Mother Anne des Anges, being Prioress, wishing to testify the esteem in which this lady was held by all and to show proper respect, led her Community to greet her in the parlour. Mère Marguerite . . . instead of going with the others, retired to a remote corner and betook herself to prayer. The saintly foundress of the *Filles de Sainte Marie* looked for her among them all and, not beholding her, enquired about her. The Mother and another Carmelite went immediately in search of her to make her come, and having found her at her prayers, spent some time in begging her to come to the parlour. She tried to excuse herself on the plea that she feared she might be impertinent, or say something foolish. But when the Mother Prioress told her positively that she must come, she obeyed.

We must understand her motives before we condemn her conduct. Her reputation as a wonder-worker and these parlour showings-off, at which so many unwise admirers had wearied her by rapt gazes and consulting her as an oracle, had become intolerable. Having resigned the office of Prioress, she had a right to escape these visits, which wasted her time and appeared to her in a ludicrous light. A *tête-à-tête* with the spiritual daughter of the Bishop of Geneva, and the friend, almost the novice, of the Carmel of Dijon, indeed with a saint, she would have enjoyed. But the idea of the company with its gaping faces and its ears pricked up to catch some Sibylline utterance irritated her.

As soon as these holy women met face to face they fell on their knees to salute one another, and as Mme. de Chantal seemed to find a difficulty in rising, Mère Marguerite spoke first, saying: "I am rejoiced to have an opportunity of recommending myself to your prayers, for you are shortly about to enjoy the vision of God in Heaven." On this the illustrious widow cried several times: "Ah, good news!" But the *Filles de Marie* who had accompanied her could not control their grief at these words. One of them, thinking at the moment more of the spiritual loss to their Community than of the Will of God announced through the lips of that incomparable woman, could not help saying: "Ah, Mother, we still have need of our dear Mother, let us hope that God will spare her!" To which Marguerite replied: "My sister, when God wills, His creatures avail nothing, He asks not your leave but acts without you!" and forthwith left the parlour, leaving all who heard her much amazed.

Soon after this incident Mme. de Chantal died, and those *Filles de Marie* who were present at the interview did not forget to report it to the Bishop of Evreux, then contemplating her biography. He went to the Convent of the Rue Chapon to examine the matter in detail. He even discussed it with Mère Marguerite herself . . . but her humility, which drew down on her such extraordinary graces, led her to entreat him not to mention it. "Refrain, Monseigneur, from putting those words of mine into your book, they would but injure it. I spoke without reflection!" But this learned prelate, naturally enough, did not "refrain."[1]

She was equally plain in her relations with the two "most serene queens," Anne of Austria and Marie de Médicis, assiduous visitors to the Carmel, and, truth to tell, somewhat in the way. Marguerite knew too well "the luxury and pomp which generally follow crowned heads; she feared with reason lest . . . such worldly pomp might make (on the Carmelites of the *Petit Couvent*) an impression similar to that made on the Israelites by the recollection of the flesh-pots of Egypt, and that they might remember with regret the enslavement to the corruptible in which the majority of the world is so lamentably held." She decided to contend against this abuse to the best of her power. In Marie de Medicis's case she was quickly and dexterously

[1] *La Vie*, pp. 264–8.

successful. "This illustrious Queen, being aware of the Court intrigues against herself, came several times to the Rue Chapon to see Mère Marguerite . . . desiring that she should foretell what the future held for her." She too wanted a prophecy.

> But the prudent nun, judging very wisely that she ought not to be mixed up with such things, managed adroitly always to escape having to talk to her. Her Majesty abandoned hope of learning her sentiments at first hand, and was obliged to employ confidential agents. These were very insistent that she should speak explicitly, but Marguerite said: "What can I say to her? There is nothing left for her upon earth save trials and afflictions!" following up her words in a few days by sending the Queen a crucifix with a letter announcing that all her earthly portion in future would be the Cross.[1]

The Queen never came again.

It was even easier to rid herself of the good-natured Anne of Austria.

> This august Queen having come to the convent one day with a numerous suite . . . the Community assembled where they were wont to receive her, but Mère Marguerite hid herself behind some taller sisters. The Queen, not beholding her, asked where she was, and the nuns were forced to draw apart and reveal her, at which the Queen said: "Have you not a word for me, Mère Marguerite?" Then this true daughter of the Carmel approached her and said: "Did I dare, Madame, I should ask a favour of Her Majesty, who does us so much honour in coming to visit us here. But did she know the effect that her visits have upon us, and how long it is before we recover from the distraction, I am sure that she would have the kindness to leave us to our solitude!" The Queen, not being accustomed to this sort of address in religious houses, . . . nevertheless graciously consented . . . to come no more to that convent.

Some time afterwards, "Her Majesty, hearing from where she sat some people speaking of Mère Marguerite, . . . remarked, 'She does not like my going to see her; but she is a saint.'"[2]

[1] *La Vie*, pp. 186–9.

[2] *Ibid.*, pp. 276–7. Compare in this same book (pp. 278–9) the piquant story of Frère Antoine, a holy peasant of Dauphiné, who had been brought to Paris and whom many at Court considered to be a prophet. The Marquise de Maignelais wished him to have an interview with the Mère Marguerite, but when it took place the Carmelite told him that the air of the Court would do him no good, and that the best thing he could do was to return as quickly as possible to Dauphiné. The excellent man was astonished at her wisdom and obeyed her forthwith.

Shortly before her death Marguerite was taken with "one of those terrible colics usually termed *miserere*." Other remedies being tried in vain, the doctors "agreed to try incision," at which the Prioress was much embarrassed, "persuading herself that the modesty (of Mère Marguerite) would oppose the operation." But doubly heroic in her courage and good sense, the saintly woman showed neither surprise nor repugnance. While the surgeons were making their arrangements, a stupid chatterbox of a doctor "drew near her bed and spoke of the pain which modesty might cause on this occasion." She answered with her usual straightforwardness, cutting short the absurd homily. Needless to say she did not flinch. We have the testimony of another physician, M. de Lorme, an old friend of Marguerite's to this. "I was so faint at the sight of her cruel sufferings that they were obliged to throw water on my face and give me vinegar. . . . I confess that nothing in my life, seen with my eyes or heard in any sermon, ever touched me so deeply as the behaviour of this holy virgin, bearing all without affectation, airs or grimaces, in a manner which I shall never forget, and which confirmed me in the opinion of her saintliness, held by all alike.[1]

"Without affectation, airs or grimaces" exactly explains the especial charm both of Mère Marguerite and of the Carmelites. It is remarkable—and in saying this I speak from experience—that these contemplatives, whom we consider so eminent, should almost always show, alike in their attitude, speech or writings, such frank, natural and perfect simplicity. Mysticism, like literature and science, has its scholars of primary grade, devout persons, self-conscious in their piety, anxious to attract notice, intoxicated by the sublime truths with which they are so pat on all occasions—small defects to which the Divine indulgence is less severe than are we, but which make sanctity less attractive. But the Carmelite convents as a whole, whether those found in the pages of history or those which I have had the intimate joy of seeing with my own eyes, have no such primary scholars. That doubtless is why a tender tradition holds Marguerite Acarie more particularly dear in the hearts of the French Carmelites. She was a woman of prayer, but her method has remained God's secret to this day.

[1] *La Vie*, pp. 337–42. Probably this Dr. de Lorme was the savant of that name, physician to three kings.

As one of her spiritual daughters remarked: " Her inner life was a sealed book to us, but we knew it to be very stable and exalted." " It seemed indeed as if God regarded the secret of her heart as a treasure of such extraordinary price that men could not conceive its value, and that He so jealously reserved it for Himself, that He allowed most of those to whom she revealed it to die before her. Without doubt M. de Bérulle, who knew her best of all, shared this view when he said ' that she had been set apart by God, among the number of those saints whose graces were at once eminent and hidden.' "[1]

Among the clauses of the *Testament of the Holy Virgin Mary against the Day of her Assumption*—a pious meditation drawn up by Mère Marguerite—there is the following passage:

> I bequeath to you the silence observed by me as to the grace and lights I received from God, leaving the understanding of these mysteries to Divine Providence, the better to magnify His Majesty. . . . Learn to imitate this silence of humility, . . . speak not of high things, but of homely ones, that thou mayest escape vainglory of spirit.[2]

In this first foundation, where the splendid manifestations of heavenly favours abounded, in this nunnery of the Rue Chapon, where Madeleine de Saint-Joseph, Catherine de Jésus, and many others lived between earth and heaven, many efforts were made to surprise the daughter of Mme. Acarie in ecstasy, but none was successful.

[1] *La Vie*, pp. 57–8. [2] *Conduite chrétienne*, pp. 344–5.

CHAPTER V

JEAN DE SAINT-SAMSON

I. "IT is related of S. Louis that, returning from the Holy Land, he was overtaken by a terrible storm off Mount Carmel. In his extremity he addressed himself to august Mary, held in especial honour upon that holy mountain, and vowed, should he escape his peril, to visit her shrine there. The tempest calmed, and the pious King kept his vow. He climbed the slopes of Carmel, prayed at the altar of the Virgin, conversed with the religious, and, being both comforted and edified by their words and their life, he took six of them, French by birth and no doubt old Crusaders, back with him to Paris (1254). On his return to France he gave the six Fathers who had followed him a house, which was abandoned some years later, to escape the inundations of the Seine, as also to be nearer the University. So *Les Carmes* in 1309 bought a house called 'of the Lion,' in the Rue de la Montagne-Ste.-Geneviève. It was this house which, enlarged several times, developed into the immense and beautiful monastery of the Place Maubert, famous for the learning of its professors and for the great number of students sent by it to the University."[1]

[1] *Vie du vénérable frère Jean de Saint-Samson*, by R. P. Sernin-Marie de S. André, Discalced Carmelite, Paris, 1881, pp. 25–6. Whatever may be the pre-Christian origin of the Carmelite Order, "the epoch of the Crusades, by introducing a Latin element, meant for it the beginning of a new life. Europeans of all nationalities, but more especially French, Italian, and English, attracted by its piety and the charm of Scriptural associations, threw in their lot with the Carmelites. From 1142 two Frenchmen were consecutively called to govern the Order. As regards the first migrations of the Order westwards it is difficult to say where legend ends and history begins. Certain foundations apparently preceded by some years the one ascribed to S. Louis. Thus Carmelites seem to have been established from 1244 at the Aygalades near Marseilles, a well-chosen spot for their hermitage. It is worthy of mention that the poet de la Cépède, mentioned in the first volume, with his savings rebuilt this house of Aygalades and in 1622 was interred in its chapel. The house of the Place Maubert was demolished by order of Napoleon in 1811, art. 5 of the decree running: "The existing market of the Place Maubert shall be transferred to the site of the ancient monastery of the Carmelites, of which we make gift to our good town of Paris." This is no doubt the covered market which to-day confronts the statue of Etienne Dolet from the other side of the boulevard S.-Germain. Cf. *Vie*, pp. 63, 353–4.

Among the students which the various houses of the Order sent to the seminary of the Place Maubert there was in the first years of the seventeenth century a young Breton Carmelite from the monastery of Dol, Frère Mathieu Pinault. He was a sincere and even fervent religious, but without spiritual training and too ready to accept both the recognized modifications of primitive austerity, introduced from time immemorial, and the abuses—properly so called—brought about by the evils of the times. It cannot be sufficiently emphasized that the reform of the ancient monasteries did not present as many difficulties as might be imagined. There was no lack of goodwill. Reports of the spiritual renewal following on the Council of Trent in Italy, Spain, and some parts of France roused in certain quarters the desire and the hope of speedy reform. Men of initiative are always rare enough, but in compensation there were then in France in fair numbers good men of the secondary order, from whom the great reformers recruited their first disciples and without whom the best plans for reform would have remained a dead letter. To this class Mathieu Pinault belonged; the day of grace found him ready. He was destined to be a good workman in the highly interesting reform soon to be instituted by Père Philippe Thibaut in one of the richest provinces of the Order of Carmel. His part in our religious history was to be important though not brilliant. A train of happy accidents linked his name with that of one of the most eminent mystics of France; humanly speaking it was through Mathieu Pinault that Jean de Saint-Samson came to the Carmelites.

On his arrival in Paris, he had many times remarked, picking his way through the mire of the Place Maubert or playing the organ in one of the churches of the Quartier Latin, a blind youth with something celestial about him, who, they told him, was named Jean du Moulin. This Jean du Moulin, Père Pinault records, "lodged at a grocer's hard by the Carmelite convent; a little lad would bring him at six o'clock in the morning to the Carmelite Church in the Place Maubert, where he generally remained till the afternoon, praying near the High Altar, where he communicated nearly every day and sometimes confessed to a Carmelite Father, by name Père Jacques." This is the way of the world: the supernatural confronts us; spellbound we pause a moment, then hurry on again. Had Jean du Moulin not made advances, Mathieu, his studies finished, would have returned to Brittany to pursue an ordinary existence to the end. Himself a musician, or at least an amateur, Pinault held the post of organist to his monastery. Perhaps his music revealed to the blind listener's ear the possibilities of grace latent within him. One S. Agnes Day the young Carmelite, seated at his keyboard, was already preparing to accompany the conventual Mass when Jean approached and begged as a favour to be allowed for once to take his place. It was the beginning of a friendship.

Gradually the friends came to speak of spiritual experiences. Jean "believed himself authorized to speak of the spiritual life and of devotion and to question the young monk as to his condition as regards these. He was told that they practised devotional reading in books of little doctrinal value, and that they were conscientious in vocal prayer, but as for mental prayer the term meant absolutely nothing to them—a sad testimony to the inner life of an Order whose original purpose was contemplation. Jean . . . began by putting into Pinault's hands the works of Louis of Granada, Arias, and other similar spiritual authors, and, since the fruit of devotional reading depends entirely upon the manner in which it is performed, begged him to read aloud a few pages from these mystics every day. . . . The reading was deliberate, and when they came to a passage specially affecting or profound they read it over twice or even thrice. . . . Jean also taught his pupil how to meditate . . . often, in their spiritual conversations, he spoke to him of the future, and thus, by enlarging the other's vision towards the horizons of the country of the soul, he strove to excite his enthusiasm and increase his desire for reform."[1]

Gradually other friars joined these readings, and Jean found himself insensibly drawn into the monastery. He had already stripped himself of his fortune, retaining only enough for bare necessities. The Carmelites offered him a cell and his scanty board in return for certain music-lessons. There was no question of receiving him into the Order, nor did he himself dream of requesting such a favour. Some years

[1] Sernin, *ibid.*, pp. 26–8. This excellent book is the best of the few written on this subject. I can give but a brief summary, but it is to be regretted that the author substitutes his own account for the documents consulted, the original text of which would be more to the purpose. Père Sernin, however, enjoys the great advantage of an initiation by personal experience into the mysteries of the mystical life. His style is a little too flowery and poetical for my taste.

passed in this manner. Finally, when P. Mathieu Pinault, having finished his studies, prepared to return to Brittany, Jean declared that he would not be parted from him; God was calling him also to take the habit and work with Père Pinault for reform. The plan did not seem feasible, but nevertheless it came to pass; the monastery of Dol accepted this singular vocation, and the two set off in the course of 1606. Our novice was then thirty-five; he kept his beautiful name of Jean, to which was added that of S. Samson, first Bishop of Dol and patron of the Cathedral Church.

He left many sincere regrets behind him. Several of the monks resolved to follow his example and embrace reform . . . and one of those who used to read to him, the son of an attorney, joined them in their noble design. The frequenters of the monastery church likewise long regretted the good blind man, who had edified them by his recollectedness, his prayers and the angelic piety with which he approached the Holy Table. That supernatural phenomenon so often admired in the saints was apparent in him; his beautiful soul shone through its earthly covering and transformed it. . . . An eminent priest, M. de Morlencourt, beloved for his learning and piety at the Court both of Henri III and Henri IV, observing him bidding farewell to the monks, could not refrain from crying out in wonder at the rapt expression on his ascetic face.[1]

Jean du Moulin was born at Sens in 1571, of Pierre du Moulin, controller of poll-taxes, and Marie d'Aiz his wife. Practically nothing is known of his parents, who were worthy bourgeois and apparently well-to-do. Of Jean's two brothers, the eldest, " a brilliant cavalier " in the service of Henri IV, " died valiantly, sword in hand, defending the town of Corbeil against the Spaniards." The second, by name Jean-Baptiste, had a somewhat remarkable youth, which our documents pass over too quickly. " After serious studies," so we learn, " he passed some time at Rome where he rendered himself esteemed and loved, and returned to France in the suite of Marie de Médicis (we long to know details), to marry in Paris the daughter of one M. Douet, acting-treasurer of the French gendarmerie, an office to which the son-in-law eventually succeeded, and died at Lyons in 1601."[2] These scraps of information throw some scanty light on the exterior history of Jean du Moulin. He was born to the position and

[1] Sernin, *ibid.*, p. 36.

[2] *Ibid.*, pp. 6, 12–13.

advantages of a man of good family, although in early manhood he gave up his possessions and chose for his portion the humiliations of poverty.

This, I think, explains why he was so readily accepted by the Carmelite Fathers, although he could render no other service than playing the organ at the Offices. He could not aspire to more than lay brotherhood, on account of his infirmity, although his education was at least as good as that of the majority of his brothers in religion. We must beware of identifying him with the host of mystics who owe their reputation solely to some celestial sign hovering over them.

Blind from the age of three, and soon after that losing both father and mother, he " came under the roof of his maternal uncle, Zacharie d'Aiz, who had become his guardian. His uncle took charge of the child's education, even having him taught Latin by M. Garnier, curé de S. Pierre-le-Rond. The boy made such rapid progress that, according to the documents dealing with this period of his life, he was soon able to understand Latin when read. But his uncle's special care was his musical instruction. Jean learned to play on the spinet, viol, mandore, lute, harp and flute, but his preference was for the organ, and so remarkable was his success in studying that instrument that at the age of twelve he was already organist of the Dominican church in his birthplace."

Already, it would seem, inclined to piety, but with a soul for the beautiful in all its forms, " he loved to be read to and spent his money in buying books." Later he told Père Pinault that " in his youth his relations and friends had read all kinds of books to him, especially historians and French poets, and that the style and phraseology of the poet Ronsard had so impressed his imagination that he used to write sonnets and other kinds of verse in imitation of him." " He reproached himself for having once composed some love-poetry, at the entreaty of a relative."

He was, I think, about twenty when the crisis began which was to detach him from " the fascination of vanity." " His beloved art, which had brought him such merited applause, gradually became a source of vexation. The world, always ready to ensnare the innocent, endeavoured to inspire him with a taste for false pleasures, inviting him to its festivals, appealing to his musical skill, and finding accomplices in those who should have been its adversaries, for his guardian and others of his family, instead of warding off dangers, rather by their advice lured him into a path that could not have failed to lead him to perdition. He then formed one of those resolutions which betray the strong soul predestined to great things. Seeing that perils lurked for him in his guardian's house, Jean did not hesitate to leave it."[1] He sought out a retreat, where he would be free to follow his growing attraction towards the spiritual life. At the end of five or six years a further inspiration led him to Paris, where we have already seen him.

"The monastery of Dol, . . . was not yet reformed, although soon to be so, and the abuses induced by the decadence of monastic discipline were to some extent found there. . . . We do not believe that it ever sank to the depths of licence, far from it. . . . Piety reigned within its walls, and in the place of strict regularity at least there were good intentions. It enjoyed popular esteem; the sick and the infirm frequented the church because of numerous miracles wrought in the Chapel of the Virgin, and every day sailors escaped from tempest came to make acts of thanksgiving. However, a breath of decadence had passed over it." That is the impression gained from our too scanty documents. Like many others of the time, it must have resembled those religious houses of Italy of to-day, which a law, cruel rather than merciful, has refrained from closing and which drag out a pitiable existence in sordid poverty. Five or six aged monks, fitter for a hospital of incurables, keep watch over long echoing galleries, deserted cells, a lonely chapel, and a thorn-grown garden. When the last of these veterans is dead the State will take possession of the poor building and instal schools or factories.

Jean's brethren at Dol were no Thélémites. Poor folk hardly knowing where to turn for the morrow's meal, most of them mechanically followed ancient routine; yet in some the sacred flame was still alive, ready to leap up at the touch of the strong soul bringing reform.

The novitiate of Jean de Saint-Samson in the monastery of Dol opens with a scene at once horrible and sublime, a fitting pendant to the *Lepers of the city of Aosta*. Soon after his arrival

the plague broke out in the town . . . one of the monks was soon infected and died in a few days. The brethren trembled, and when

[1] Sernin, *ibid.*, pp. 9–13.

a novice, nephew of the Superior, was struck down in his turn, they resolved to quit the house, leaving therein one young monk named Olivier, not yet priested, with a lay servant. . . . Jean de Saint-Samson did not follow his community's example; his blindness, which in itself might appear a hindrance to the care of the sick, did not seem to him a sufficient excuse for flight; he preferred to stay with the plague-stricken. One day he came upon the sick man in an access of delirium about to throw himself out of the window. He stopped him, and, having called his two companions, who from fear of infection had retired to the end of the garden, carried him to his bed. Sitting by his side, Jean prayed God to give the sick man the use of his reason and to grant him the grace of a peaceful death with the consolations of religion. He had the happiness to see the fulfilment of his prayer, for the patient came to himself at that very moment. The Superior having come for news, Jean forthwith took the plague-tainted victim in his arms and brought him to the Superior to make his confession. A few minutes more and the sick man, now back in bed again, passed to a better life. The holy man prayed beside the infected corpse and helped to bury it. The monk who had remained in the monastery with him was in his turn attacked and nursed with equal devotion. . . . Jean did the best he could and won from God the monk's recovery. Then he himself was attacked. There was near the town a place called Champ de Saint-James, reserved for victims of the pestilence. . . . Jean was taken to this place and gave new proofs of his charity; he tenderly encouraged the sick, giving them confidence by his holy conversation, and inspired the dying with such fervour and charity that they passed away in quietness and confidence. At last the terrible scourge ceased, and the religious returned to their monastery (Jean with them).[1]

II. About the same time a Carmelite from Anjou, affiliated to the province of Touraine, one of the most important houses of the Order, Père Philippe Thibaut, sub-Prior and soon to be Prior of the house at Rennes, gave a decisive impulse to the cause of Reform. This eminent leader—he is already the subject of many volumes, but we cannot here follow him in the details of his work and life—attached himself to that great centre in Paris which stimulated most of the Reformist movements and supervised the revival of Mysticism through France. As a young religious, after a preliminary stage at the Place Maubert, Thibaut had himself elected, as it would seem,

[1] Sernin, *ibid.*, pp. 39–40.

to finish his studies under the direction of the Jesuits, in the University of Pont-à-Mousson, which shortly before his time had trained three other reformers of note, S. Pierre Fourier, Servais de Lairuels and Didier de la Cour. The decadence into which he saw his Order fallen affected him profoundly, and not yet believing in the possibility of reform, he, with five of his companions who had similar aspirations, dreamed either of withdrawing into some Chartreuse or else of joining those Italian Carmelites who had adopted the Teresian reform. He was, however, detained in Paris, where he had for director the Carthusian Beaucousin, and for friends Bérulle, Duval and several Jesuits. We note the catholicity of his tastes. This catholicity was the great happiness of this too brief period, the living source of its strength, the secret of its conquests. Never was *l'union sacrée* better understood or accepted more sincerely. However, Père Thibaut's intercourse with so many saintly souls rendered the inertia of his own brethren increasingly distasteful to him. At the height of his discouragement he was about to set out for the Grande Chartreuse when a ray of light broke upon him. His Superiors summoned him to the house at Rennes, and promised him a free hand there. At the beginning of 1602 he departed from Paris on foot for Brittany, where full success awaited him.

The Reform which he introduced into the province of Touraine was conceived on broad and wise lines. It was, first of all, mystical and interior, and therefore interests us particularly. When drawing up his constitutions he put himself to school not only with S. Teresa but also with S. Ignatius, endeavouring to "marry" the spirit of the Society "to that of the Carmelites, as far as was possible in view of the main object of the two Orders." One of the monks of this Reform wrote later in a controversial work addressed to the Jesuits: "We know that our humble reform, which, under God's blessing, has been propagated in France, the Low Countries, Germany, Poland and even in the New World began its fortunate career in Brittany, through the zeal and by the direction of V. Philippe Thibaut, who was assisted by your counsels and accommodated our constitutions to those of the Society, as far as the poor and solitary spirit of Elijah would allow."[1] The import of such an avowal as this is apparent. It is often upheld that the principal and even sole object

[1] Sernin, *ibid.*, p. 82.

of many of the monastic reforms which at this time renewed the face of the Church was a return pure and simple to primitive discipline. Nothing could be less well-founded than this impression. The movement as a whole went far deeper than that and the transformation was more radical. A return to Primitivism would have been in vain, the past can never be brought to life again. Without in any way repudiating the spirit of their founders, on the contrary with a view of realizing it more fully, the elder Orders have found themselves more or less obliged to borrow from later ones, adapting their institutions to the present inspirations of grace and the particular requirements of a new world. We shall return to this point when we study the great abbesses and the Benedictine reform. But we have already seen a noted reformer, Père Thibaut, deliberately "accommodating" his constitutions to those of the Jesuits, moulding according to the innovations of the youngest of all the Orders the discipline and spirit of the religious family which boasts of having for founder a prophet of the ancient Law.

What (asks a Carmelite Father) was the spirit of these institutions, and in what precisely did the reform of the province of Touraine consist? When Père Philippe Thibaut wished to give definite laws to his reform, friends, more zealous than enlightened, counselled a return pure and simple to the primitive rule; but as a practical man, aware of the delicate nature of his ground and of the difficulties which would inevitably arise if his methods were too idealistic, he firmly resisted their solicitations. To enforce the letter of the ancient use would have been to discourage many excellent souls. . . . Père Thibaut, rightly in our opinion, considered it the part of wisdom to aim lower (than S. Teresa and John of the Cross); he believed that, without deserting the edifice weakened by mitigation, it was possible to repair it and find therein a sure refuge. . . . To continue in the mitigated branch of the Order but to instil new life was his aim. . . . He returned to severe poverty, abolished privileges, re-established the reign of humility and religious equality; and, having thus reconstituted the very essence of all monastic life, sought to sustain it by practices of interior life and penitence, especially those of fasting, mortification, retreat, silence, mental prayer and the midnight recital of mattins. It was a veritable return to the spirit of Mount Carmel; the reform of the province of Touraine, although less severe than that of S. Teresa, singularly approached the spirit of its elder sister.[1]

[1] Sernin, *ibid.*, pp. 82–3.

It could not be better expressed. The great originality of S. Teresa consists not in her having restored the austerities of the ancient observance, but on having based the restoration itself on the interior life and on prayer. The same is true of S. Ignatius and the other great leaders of the Counter-Reformation. They restored discipline, emphasized the authority of superiors, whether regular or secular, extolled the virtue of obedience, but in all this they never lost sight of the higher aim of establishing the kingdom of God in souls. They fettered wills but only to liberate grace. In a word, their crusade was fundamentally a mystical one. Of the two books of S. Ignatius, the *Exercises spirituels* and the *Constitutions de la Compagnie de Jésus*, the first was, in the author's opinion, infinitely more important than the second. Before deciding to impose rules on his brethren this rigid Spaniard, who, to so many, stands for authority and formalism, hesitated for years, persuaded, so he writes, " that the inward law of love and charity which the Holy Spirit is accustomed to write and engrave in the heart " would contribute more effectively " than written constitutions " to the maintenance and progress of the new Order.

Jean de Saint-Samson was the principal collaborator of Père Thibaut. Summoned in 1612 to Rennes, where, save for a short mission of reform at the monastery of Dol, he remained till his death in 1636, " his eminent virtues and the supernatural graces bestowed upon him created for him an exceptional position. . . . He became adviser, not only of the ordinary religious, but also of the Superiors. The latter consulted him as to the spirit which should inspire the new reform; the former laid bare their interior life to him, received his advice, submitted themselves to his direction." " God destined him to be the brightest flame in our little company as regards spiritual things," wrote his first biographer. To this influence of word and example " must be added that of his writings. It is no exaggeration to say that in this respect he was the S. John of the Cross of the new reform." In his *Vrai esprit du Carmel* " he proves that contemplation is the essential feature of the Order and gives rules for assimilating this spirit and elevating the soul to the sublimest heights of the mystic life."

Our rule (he writes in the preface of this book) being exceedingly concentrated and concise, and rather dealing with the inner things of the spirit than with outward expression, we must meditate on the need of being spiritual, that we may at least live in the practice of it, in a state of strict purity, and that we may follow its rules, which are to move towards God with all our powers, in good order and along the direct way by our constant activity.[1]

I am anxious to reach the mystical works of the blind saint and must not delay over the scanty record of his long years in the religious life. Even outside the monastery of Rennes his authority was great. Many pious souls and even such great figures as the friend of François de Sales, Mgr. de Révol, Bishop of Dol, came frequently to consult him. Marie de Médicis—always hoping for some miraculous turn of fortune's wheel—sought his counsels through Père Philippe Thibaut, of whom she was very fond. He writes to the possessed at Loudun to console them in their evil plight. One would like to know the exact quality—tenderness, pity, or awe—of the veneration in which he was held. He appears to have been completely good, wandering as it were between earth and heaven, ingenuously determined to speak only of God. This perhaps explains the annoyances, doubtless trifling, which he had to suffer at the hands of some of his brethren. "They found fault with his writings and his teachings, questioned the genuineness of his mortification and jested at his speech and gestures. Not only did they refuse the veneration due to him on so many counts, but they pushed their disrespect to the point of mockery which 'he felt only,' says his first biographer, 'to rejoice in it. But I resented it for him so hotly that I once complained of it to my Superior, who was well aware of it and repeated those words of Our Lord upon the Cross, *Nesciunt quid faciunt*.'"

"The artist was no more spared than the saint. Jean de Saint-Samson was the organist of the monastery chapel, but his playing was not to the taste of some young religious, whose ignorance of chant and music . . . might have made them more modest. When the organ was rebuilt, by dint of entreaties and criticisms they succeeded in obtaining another organist and shelving Jean."[2] This sacrifice, certainly one of the hardest that could have been devised for him, he accepted with genuine joy. Perhaps on those heights of contemplation which he had already attained, earth's sweetest melodies had

[1] Sernin, pp. 90–1.

[2] *Ibid.*, p. 263.

lost their attraction. He continued, however, at times to play the manichord. "When it was time to leave off, God warned him by a tap on the base of the instrument, heard distinctly." According to one of his intimate friends, warnings of the kind were frequently given to him.

One day when he was in conference with his confessor, both after some time heard a rap on the table. Brother Jean, as though at a familiar bidding, rose at once, saying to his confessor that God made known to him by this rapping . . . that he had spoken enough and must now depart. On the next day he reaffirmed this, saying that had he not instantly obeyed they would have heard the sound again; indeed it has been heard a number of times by several of our brethren, so that his hours seemed divinely regulated.[1]

Yet there was nothing of the seer either in his talk or bearing. "Those who did not know the saintliness of his life would have taken him for the most ordinary person possible." As for "those who did know it, those whom he directed and in whom he confided, the simple and the novices, it was marvellous to see him talking to them about God . . . it was indeed Paradise on earth, for the true lovers of God, for he would talk for hours on end spontaneously and with such mystic abandonment that he inflamed with divine love the hearts prepared to receive it."[2]

III. Nothing is known of the mystic initiation of Jean de Saint-Samson. When at the age of twenty-six or twenty-seven he came to Paris he had already passed beyond ordinary prayer and the first steps of the contemplative life, and had reached the heights. It is possible, probable even, though not certain, that at Sens or Paris he had revealed his experiences to some spiritual expert. It may be that Divine Grace, in combination with the old books which explained to him the workings of this grace, was sufficient. His disciples were many, but no one stands out by the side of him as a master. Hence, perhaps, his independence and uniqueness, a little strange and remote, which isolate him from the mystics of his time.

From a literary standpoint he derives in our opinion from the same sources as Benoit de Canfeld, the famous Franciscan, like himself saturated with the works of Tauler, Harphius and the pseudo-Diony-

[1] Sernin, pp. 305–6. [2] *Ibid.*, p. 273.

sius. But Canfeld was formed by that living tradition which illumines the teaching of the ancients and modernizes it, he has conferred with the masters of his day on his own spiritual life and on speculative problems of Mysticism. Jean de Saint-Samson developed alone. Reading him, one might judge him as a contemporary, not of François de Sales or even of S. Teresa, but of Ruysbroek; but competent judges do not hesitate to place him among the mystics of the first flight, some are even ready to hail him as the John of the Cross of the French Carmel. For my part I have neither the power nor the wish to pass such judgements.

Before leaving this layman full liberty to initiate the religious of the Rennes monastery into the utmost secrets of perfection, Père Philippe Thibaut had submitted the "states" of Jean de Saint-Samson to rigorous scrutiny. "Feigning to doubt that a simple lay brother could have attained so high a pitch of contemplation in a non-reformed monastery, like that of Dol, he desired Frère Jean to draw up a short summary of his method of devotion. In obedience to this order Jean dictated the first pages of an admirable treatise, which he subsequently finished, entitled *De la consommation du Sujet en son Objet*. These sheets were submitted to the Discalced Carmelites (recently established in France), assembled in provincial chapter; they were then communicated to the Capuchin Fathers, also in provincial chapter, under the conductorship of their Superior-General; to the Jesuit Fathers at Rennes; to a learned doctor of the Sorbonne, M. Gibbius,[1] and finally to M. Duval. All united in finding the work filled with manifest tokens of Divine grace and in approving the methods and spirit of the devout blind man. The Discalced Fathers wrote to Père Thibaut, entreating him affectionately to allow the designs of God full scope in this fervent soul, adding the Apostle's words, "Quench not the Spirit, *spiritum nolite extinguere*."

We hail once more the great Council, this federation of all the spiritual forces of the country—Carmelites, Capuchins, Jesuits, Oratorians, Doctors of the Sorbonne. Of such splendid and fruitful unanimity we shall too soon have to say: *Sed hæc prius fuere*.

[1] Père Sernin here, perhaps, misread his authorities or was misled by a faulty copy. Must not this *Gibbius* be the famous Oratorian Gibieuf (Gibiefus) who had just entered the Oratory and whom Bérulle in all probability would have recommended to his friend Père Thibaut?

Père Thibaut continued to test Jean de Saint-Samson by redoubling his severity as director. At last he desisted, sure of the holiness of his junior, his mind at rest as regards the spirit which was leading him, and ordained that he should edify his brethren by converse on the spiritual life and by dictating to them what the Spirit of God should inspire.[1]

The order was scrupulously obeyed. We have already remarked the conversations. The dictations by the time of Jean's death were enormous in bulk: *Cabinet mystique ; Méditations ; De la souveraine consommation de l'âme en Dieu par amour ; Le Miroir et les flammes de l'Amour divin ; Contemplations et divers soliloques*, and many others.

One of his friends relates that

it was marvellous to see him dictating without hesitation or pause, so that his scribes were fairly exhausted, for close attention was needed to remember what he said and quickness of hand to write it down. . . . Again, it is remarkable, as I myself remarked several times, that when the writer failed to recall a sentence and begged him to repeat it, when he stopped to reflect, he could not remember what he had said at first and repeated it in less apt terms, an evident token that the Spirit of God was at work in him and that his words were unpremeditated. He assured me several times, after finishing a treatise, that he did not know what he had said until it was read aloud to him.[2]

Towards the middle of the seventeenth century Père Donatien de Saint-Nicolas published some of these writings, at first separately, then in a collected folio edition of two volumes, entitled *Les œuvres spirituelles et mystiques du divin contemplatif et mystique, Jean de Saint-Samson.* But this edition is not only incomplete, "omitting whole books and including only a part of some selections from others," but, a more serious matter, continues the same monk, who had had the originals in his hands,

the aforesaid Père Donatien in his editions altered many words and even entire sentences (not respecting the poems themselves), thus doing away with much of the simplicity, piety, and austerity of the style . . . (fearing no doubt) that a language and spirit so abstract and other-worldly might not be to the taste of everyone. But I give this information only to advanced mystics, in order that they may

[1] Sernin, pp. 102–3. [2] *Ibid.*, p. 117.

have recourse to the originals, should they desire them in their full purity and truth. . . . Mystics of high degree will be much more satisfied with the originals.[1]

Alas! we may agree, but this treasure, if it exists to-day, cannot be found. The printed copies themselves are extremely rare, which seems to prove that, before the end of the seventeenth century, Jean de Saint-Samson had ceased to count. Passionately loyal to her moralists, the Gallican Jerusalem forgets her prophets. I have seen hundreds of Nicole's *Essais*, tiny volumes which seemed doomed to speedy oblivion. I have only once handled the folios of the "divine contemplative and mystic, Jean de Saint-Samson."[2]

It must be acknowledged that these works are only intended for "mystics of high degree," I cannot quote them at length. They have been called obscure, but that means nothing—is not every mystic obscure to the ordinary reader? Some of them, gifted with intelligence more subtle or imagination more vivid than their fellows, illumine and adorn the winding avenues that lead to the mystery of the Divine Union. Like the poets and philosophers of earth, they fascinate us, and by similar methods. But when they come to the mystery itself we do not understand them. Jean de Saint-Samson had no lack of genius, "reading his works one is impressed and feels oneself in the presence of a giant." But he was not, strictly speaking, either a professional philosopher or a poet. His thought, elsewhere so concrete, now appears terribly abstract.

Underlying his expression there is often a singular energy, but he never seeks to adorn his thought, and he seldom employs comparison to render his lofty conceptions intelligible; his palette has few colours. This may be due, not to disdain of such methods, but because, prevented by his infirmity from coming in contact with exterior nature,

[1] Sernin, pp. 345–6.

[2] Père Sernin is very vague as to both printed editions and MSS. He seems to have examined personally only the folio manuscript containing the poetical works of Jean de Saint-Samson preserved, so he tells us, in the departmental archives of Ille et Vilaine (pp. 120–1). But he quotes them in the text of Père Donatien. "Looking through this manuscript," he says, "the reader will perceive that Père Donatien has only published a very small number of pieces, as also that he has corrected the text, especially as regards literary form, which here is a graver matter than in the rest of the works of the blind saint. These corrections are indeed generally intelligent and in keeping with the progress of poetical language, but he does not seem clearly to understand the duties of an editor." The verses quoted by Père Sernin seem to me mediocre.

he found it impossible to make his imagination vivid and concrete. The same infirmity prevented his acquiring the intellectual discipline which comes from close and methodical study, and is so remarkable in the writings of S. John of the Cross.[1]

Nor must it be forgotten that the text of Jean de Saint-Samson, as given to us, has been retouched, rationalized and "banalized," in short, altered to suit the taste of an age doubly conventional, both in literature and in the things of Love.

The memoir, written at command of Père Thibaut to explain the blind brother's method of devotion, begins thus:

My exercise consists in an elevation of spirit above all sensible and created objects, by which I am firmly fixed within, steadily regarding God, Who raises my soul into simplicity and nakedness of spirit. This is called simple inactivity, in which I am passively rapt beyond sense into repose, and I continue in this state even though there may be movement within or without, prompted by reason and reflection. This is all that I can say for my interior. My state is simple, bare, obscure, and without knowledge even of God; a nudity and obscurity of spirit, raised above all inferior light to this condition. In this way I cannot use my inward faculties, which are all with one accord arrested by the power of the unique and simple species, which nakedly and simply arrests them, above sight and essence, at the highest point of the spirit, beyond the spirit I mean, in the nakedness and obscurity of the height all is incomprehensible because of its obscurity. There all that is sensible, specific or created merges into unity of spirit, nay, rather into simplicity of essence and of spirit.

In my ignorance I copy blindly for fear of omitting some important word. I do not pride myself on full understanding of it, still less on my failure to understand. What would be said of a blind man who should take Chateaubriand for a visionary or of a schoolmaster declaring a page of Aristotle or of S. Thomas to be meaningless? Besides, my aim is not to explain mysticism, but merely to indicate these mysterious regions, saying, like the ancient map-makers, *hic sunt leones*; my point is that, in the seventeenth century, there were numbers of men and women capable of recognizing their own experience in such a picture. Let us finish; I believe the end will be less dark.

[1] Sernin, pp. 180–2.

The faculties are there in arrested condition, all fixed upon God, Who draws them all equally to such contemplation. He it is Who ravishes and absorbs them simply by the operation of His continual gaze, His gaze at the Soul and the Soul's at Him. In this state there is neither creature nor created, neither knowledge nor ignorance, neither all nor nothing, neither limit, nor name, nor kind, nor wonder, no difference between past, future or even present, not even the eternal now. All is merged, confounded in that cloudy haze diffused by God, Who thus has His pleasure in those souls, within whom it pleases Him to work this noble operation.[1]

These are matters, remarks a theologian, and we readily believe him, "touching the highest point of mystic theology." God led this "soul to that state of consummated union in which it thinks divinely, enjoys divinely, and is one with Him. The Object has taken possession of the Subject, transformed it into itself; the Subject, through suffering, stripping itself of self, surmounting all the mystic tests, has flowed into the beatific Object, and is now united to Him in peace, in light, in quiescence of its powers."[2]

It would be easy to prove, as a recent biographer of Jean de Saint-Samson effectively does, from a maze of official documents, that this mystic is not to be suspected either of quietism or pantheism. His formulas are sometimes disconcerting in their audacity. A pupil of the pseudo-Dionysius and of the German mystics, he had already developed his characteristic bent when, late enough, he made acquaintance with the Spanish school. Although he never actually says so, we feel that the divine moderation of John of the Cross was to him timidity. But the few verbal indiscretions which may be laid to his charge merely serve to throw into relief the fundamental and profound wisdom of this great "*illuminé*." "Notwithstanding," he says once, "that we may be God Himself, none the less we differ infinitely from this super-essential super-essence . . . our created being remaining always with us, for to believe otherwise would be strange and absurd." Again, sublimely vigorous in his ponderous autodidactic logic, he says:

In God there is only God, only His Essential Being in Its super-essentiality; and there will never be, as there never has been, any

[1] Sernin, pp. 104–5.

[2] Sernin, pp. 106–7. The book of the R. P. Sernin de Saint-André has been approved by the General of the Discalced Carmelites and by the Cardinal (then Mgr.) de Cabrières.

created being which, even with all the comprehensive joy that it has from Him, in Him, by Him, can be united with Him save from an infinite distance. For if it were or could be otherwise, such a created being would be a substance divine and uncreate. Were it, to suppose the impossible, possible for created substance to approach by exceeding passion to joyous union beyond the bounds and limits of its created capacity, whether by excessive receptivity or excessive privation reaching to the very depths of spirit, such created substance would be in that instant annihilated.[1]

The " passivity " or " quietude " of which he makes frequent mention is, as may be seen in what he calls the " war or conflict of love," intensely active.

O my Sweet Life, I have not told Thee fully all the means by which I shall revenge myself on Thee, in the sweet and amorous war which Thou dost make on me in the perpetuity of love. This then will I do. If Thou, dear Life of me, in the acts of Thy deepest love art pleased to come continually to me, I will for the love I bear Thee come as frequently and incessantly to Thee; and so shall there be a continual and mutual meeting of spirit with spirit, until one of us sinks weary—but what say I? O my Love, pardon me this excess —until, I would say, my action, my power, my strength, quickened by Thy Love, succumbs to Thine, and I be wholly vanquished, moved and possessed by Thee henceforth, with no possible resistance from me.

In this war

all is spirit, transport, rapture, ecstasy suspension; all is intoxication, fire, heat, the glow and inexpressible ardour of love. Nought in it but is pleasure, delight, languor, union, transformation of the soul into God. . . . It is nought but forgetfulness of one's own life and self for the life and the joys of love in Love Supreme. It is nought but breadth, length, height. It is nought but unity, eternity, loss of and alienation from all things, including self.[2]

The violence of this love " was wont to send our devout contemplative into pure ecstasy. Not the ordinary ecstasy, which, by depriving the persons thus affected of the use of their senses, generally proves that they are still novices in the higher ways of the spirit, and is therefore a symptom of comparative weakness; . . . the ecstasy here in

[1] Sernin, pp. 188–9.

[2] *Ibid.*, pp. 161–2. Cf. the parallel passages of Ruysbroek quoted by Sernin, pp. 199 ff.

question operates in the noblest region of the soul and is sustained unflinchingly. 'The soul,' said Jean de Saint-Samson, 'is divine in proportion as she sustains in her the workings of the fire of love, without receiving hurt or weakening as regards its exterior bodily nature.'" He describes such an ecstasy as follows:

Although the creature may not be wholly ravished from the body by the immensity of this fire of love, as are those who are operated on by an ardour of love in an active state, yet she is nevertheless out of herself in proportion to the strength and absorbing might of this fire: the soul, being thus oblivious of sense and its workings, remains wholly spirit through its own very substance, since, impregnated and penetrated by this glory of flame, it has no other life than the life of that flame. Thus all intellectual qualities and created forms are as thoroughly annihilated as though they had never been. In the enjoyment of this state of ecstasy, the soul does nought save rest and contemplate her Object in His infinite fruition, and even should it fall out that reason commands bodily action of the members, the ecstatic spirit only loses itself the more in the abyss of its Infinite Object Beatific.[1]

Thus "the transports he experienced never crossed the threshold of his soul, so that, while the inner man was rapt in an inebriation of sweetness, the exterior man remained humble and calm, allowing none to suspect the mystery within. Yet at times the light which irradiated his spirit, the flames that consume his heart, betrayed themselves by a certain splendour, visible to all." Père Donatien tells us that "in these extraordinary states his face was frequently beheld to be divinely radiant, resplendent with as it were some luminous ray, as I myself and other very trustworthy brothers have witnessed."[2]

IV. Such a light, sometimes sensible but more often entirely spiritual, illumined several generations of young Carmelites. That is why this life, otherwise elusive, interests us so much. Sublime though he appears to us, Jean de Saint-Samson is not a solitary figure. As we said above, those writings, which dazzle and oppress rather than charm us, were comprehended, approved of, boundlessly admired by a kind of Gallican Council in which sat spiritual leaders of every order. "Beware of quenching this torch," wrote the Dis-

[1] Sernin, pp. 164–5. [2] *Ibid.*, p. 108.

calced Carmelites to the Superior of the Touraine reform. It was not quenched. For nearly thirty years Jean de Saint-Samson kept a school of mysticism, not in an obscure corner, but in the very centre of one of the most famous reforms of an epoch famous for reform. Among the religious then associated with the monastery of Rennes, many assuredly must have totally failed to grasp the message of the blind saint. What would those, for instance, who laughed at the musician, have made of the mystic? Some no doubt, although respecting what they could not understand, justly concluded that such teaching was not for them. Yet he trained a band of disciples—fifty, twenty, ten, perhaps, the number matters little—who in their turn became masters. Thus are born and spread the movements, small or great, which sustain and renew the highest life of the Church.

After Père Mathieu Pinault, of whom we spoke at the outset, another young Breton, Dominique de Saint-Albert (Vincent Leschart), who was born at Fougères in 1596 and died at Nantes in 1634, appears to have been the favourite disciple of Jean. Some illuminating letters of his have been preserved. "He had been appointed a professor of theology, but speculative instruction, for which he had a peculiar aptitude, was contrary to his inclinations, because it filled his mind with images distracting to the pure regard of his contemplation."[1]

The exercise of speculation (he wrote to Jean de Saint-Samson) is the deepest death that a loving spirit can suffer. I have lately experienced this, for having had a truce from it for fifteen days, I felt as if I were in Paradise. But, returning to my study, and embracing my speculations with alert mind, as it behoved me to do, I felt beside myself and like to die with heaviness. Had I not forced myself to hide my depression, the brethren would have deemed me seriously ill. Yet I am content in this death, for truly I consider it to be better than life.

He wrote again on the same subject:

I am lecturing on two treatises on love, that of *Grace* and that of the *Incarnation*. I prize the inward knowledge God has bestowed upon me infinitely more than that gathered from books. The one is mine, the others another's, the one is wisdom, the other learning: *hæc sapientia, illa scientia*. You, my brother, appreciate what is true theology, and I, although unworthy, appreciate in part, not through my books, but by communication of Our Lord.[2]

[1] Sernin, p. 208. [2] *Ibid.*, pp. 208–9.

Père Dominique died all too young. In his stead, another Breton Carmelite, Père Léon de Saint-Jean, devoted himself, throughout a long and brilliant career as orator and writer, to the spreading of the teachings of the mystic of Rennes.

In our study of Devout Humanism we have already met this figure, to-day forgotten but deservedly famous in his time.[1] He died at Paris in 1671. Coming to occupy the highest offices in his Order, he was, after Père Thibaut, one of the sturdiest pillars of the Carmelite reform. Richelieu esteemed him highly and made his last confession to him. As preacher-in-ordinary to Louis XIII and Louis XIV, his frequent lapses in taste must not prevent our recognizing the stamp of genius in his eloquence. Many of his pages remind me of Lacordaire, while his folios, both in French and Latin, are by no means negligible. He was of original and powerful intellect, although, perhaps, too little concentrated and more speculative than befits a true contemplative. Père Léon never lost the first stamp of his master, that "great soul," as he was wont to term him. He wrote much on mysticism, which in his opinion was an important factor in the education of every good man. One of his best works is entitled, *Jésus-Christ en son trône établissant la vraie religion, la morale chrétienne et la théologie mystique*,[2] in which in a curious manner he finds much in common between mystic experience and ordinary religious sentiment.

> Religion (he writes, in quite a modern style) is innate in man; it consists in a sentiment or secret instinct, in the knowledge and love of God. The maxims of mystic theology give the preference to love over knowledge, in that it is nearer to that spiritual and occult sentiment which forms the first concept, that is, the essence of religion.[3]

Contemplation is only the supreme development of this first seed, a development less rare than is commonly imagined. In a series of sermons preached at Montmartre during the octave of S. Denis, Père Léon expands this subject with singular clearness and conviction.

[1] His name in the world was Jean de Macé; born at Rheims in 1600, died in Paris in 1671.

[2] Illuminating remarks upon mystic indifference are to be found in his *Religionis christianæ liber primus, de numinis natura ac moribus, deque rerum omnium conditione*, Paris, 1643. This book won the warm approbation of J. P. Camus. In our first volume his *Studium sapientiæ universalis* has already been quoted. He had, it will be seen, a turn for great encyclopædic works. His style is very quaint. On all grounds he deserves study.

[3] *L'économie de la religion chrétienne, catholique, dévote, par un raisonnement natural, moral, politique*, Paris, 1643, II. 7. Note this lengthy and pregnant title.

There is no Christian, whatever may be urged, who, by the duties of his profession at the baptismal font, is not required both to study and practise mystical theology. . . . All those beautiful sentiments now almost wholly appropriated to the monastic life belong, originally and literally, to every Christian. "Ye are no longer of this world." "Ye are dead and your life is hid with God." To whom, O my master, dost thou pronounce these great oracles? To the cloister? Nay, not primarily; rather for the whole Church. To whom and of whom speak you, O great S. Paul? To the solitaries, to the nuns, to the Benedictines, to the Dionysiennes of Montmartre?[1] Not at all! To whom then? Why, to the baptized, the faithful, the Christians. And you, ye French, you, Parisian people, you, the children and disciples of S. Denis, are you not the more obliged to hearken to his teachings and to practise his doctrine?[2]

In consequence he does not shrink from dedicating a long panegyric to "the divine writings of S. Denis," following the Areopagite boldly into the thickest gloom of "true mystic obscurity."

Having attained the consecrated shades, he (S. Denis) banishes all scientific reasonings or discourse; henceforth he belongs neither to others nor to himself. Thus he enters upon a divine cessation of all awareness, a blissful repose, since he is united, by the pure and innermost point of the soul, to Him Who is above all. There he sees and knows all things, even while he sees and is conscious of nothing.[3]

This may sound hard, absurd even. Beware nevertheless of the logical consequences of your lofty contempt.

Reproaches cannot be directed against any science that will not include its master. And in all mysticism there is nothing so sublimely obscure which, not to speak of the Apocalypse or the vision of Ezekiel, is not be to found in the divine epistles of the Apostle of the third Heaven.[4]

Let us not be hindered by appearances.

This path, so lofty, so sublime . . . if we were but faithful to grace, is the most simple thing in the world. Consider three proofs

[1] Tradition places at Montmartre, in the very precincts of the Benedictine Abbey, the first Christian Temple erected by the first apostle of Paris. Thence the word "Dionysienne" as applied to the Benedictines. Père Léon in a preceding sermon had discussed the criticisms passed on this legend. "Mon Dieu," he cried, "why cannot they leave the world alone when it is not ill?" *La France convertie . . . octave à l'honneur du B. S. Denys l'Aréopagite*, by R. P. Léon, Paris, 1661, p. 180.

[2] *Ibid.*, pp. 305–6.

[3] *Ibid.*, p. 304.

[4] *Ibid.*, p. 316.

which seem to me convincing: can anything be imagined more easy then to despoil oneself, to be ignorant, and to love?

(*a*) Every man cannot enrich himself, but every man can make himself poor.

(*b*) *Melius jungimur ignoto.*

To sacrifice to an unknown God, to approach this Sovereign by the way of humility, the surest as it is the easiest way, one need not be a Cicero or an Aristotle.

(*c*) Finally, love God. There you are spiritual and mystical both.

Nevertheless I dare not deny that all great undertakings have their danger.

It must be understood that Père Léon's real end in such utterances is not to initiate the faithful in a science which God alone can teach, but rather to confound the enemies of this science,

those who, plunged in a life grossly animal or purely rational or addicted to the sensuous side of devotion, dispose of all mysticism as ideas and chimeras of Plato, likely to bring forth beautiful illusions and agreeable imaginings, but at bottom indolent, sterile, and full of dangers.

In the following notable passage, a veritable manifesto, every word counts.

Verily I can excuse atheists and heretics, libertines and vain scholars for such sentiments, because one can only judge of what he knows and not meddle where he is ignorant, but it is insupportable when those who have the golden reed in their very hand to measure the Temple of Jerusalem, should take their measurements so badly in all that concerns the sanctuary. To hear them, S. Denis and all the mystics fly too high, their writings are incoherent, their style is unintelligible, or at best their high-flown words contain nothing but ordinary things, disguised and twisted. What! do they not desire that God should be God, inaccessible, inconceivable, ineffable? *Tu es Deus vincens scientiam nostram.* Do they wish to limit His Sacred plenitude, to restrain the sacred might of His Spirit Which bloweth where, when, and as He listeth? Would they rob the sanctuary of the soul of those holy experiences transcending all that is sensible? *Est quidam tactus Divinitatis omni cognitione melior.* Wherefore, since it is allowed to everyone to speak his native language and to use the terms of his profession, must Love have his tongue cut out and those who love be forbidden their native accents? *Lingua amoris*, said the second S. Denis of our France, *non amanti barbara*. Let us leave to God His Majesty, to S. Denis his flights, to mysticism its own language, and let us content ourselves with revering that which it is not given to us to understand.[1]

When the old disciple of Jean de Saint-Samson spoke thus in the latter years of his life (1661) he was not fighting with shadows. Already from all quarters storms of disdain and even hate were rolling up against the mystics. Later we shall have to trace the origin of this hate and follow its ravages.

[1] *La France convertie*, pp. 313–15.

CHAPTER VI

THE GREAT ABBESSES

1. *The Reform*

I. BETWEEN the years 1570 and 1670 France witnessed the birth, supremacy and death of many splendid Abbesses, who in less than thirty years had re-established in every quarter of the kingdom the nearly vanished prestige of the Order of S. Benedict. Such a miracle is more wonderful than those already described or those that still await us, since the creation of a new Order is surely less inexplicable a phenomenon than the resurrection of one already dead. Unfortunately, this miracle to some extent baffles the historian of the religious renaissance of the seventeenth century, if this historian remains faithful to his methods of preferring living details to dry statistics. So far we have had to depict groups relatively few or at least concentrated in limited areas. Now what a difference! Marie de Beauvillier, Abbess of Montmartre; Madeleine de Sourdis, Abbess of S. Paul-les-Beauvais; Louise de l'Hospital, Abbess of Montivilliers; Anne-Bathilde de Harlay, Abbess of Notre-Dame-de-Sens; Claude de Choiseul-Praslin, Abbess of Notre-Dame de Troyes; Laurence de Budos, Abbess of Sainte-Trinité de Caen; Marie de Lorraine and Madeleine de la Porte, Abbesses of Chelles; Renée de Lorraine and Marguerite of Kirkcaldy, Abbesses of S. Pierre de Rheims; Anne de Plas and Françoise de la Châtre, Abbesses of Faremoustier; Charlotte-Flandrine de Nassau, Abbess of Sainte-Croix de Poitiers; Marie de Laubépine, Abbess of S. Laurent de Bourges; Marguerite d'Angennes, Abbess of S. Sulpice; Françoise de Foix, Abbess of Saintes—and many more whom I pass over—in truth there are too many of them! Each of these women, moreover, has her own particular setting, her following of disciples, directors, friends and foes; ten big volumes would not exhaust their history in detail. Remember, too, that this story is more closely associated with our national life than that of the Carmelites, Capuchins and even the Jesuits, all of them new-comers and without roots in French soil. The Abbeys of this period themselves rise transformed; they concentrate on the interior life and are in process of isolating themselves as far as possible from the world, but while they endeavour to be convents and nothing else, they do not as yet succeed. So in their chronicles we come across hundreds of picturesque, piquant, sometimes tragic incidents, with which mysticism has nothing to do, but which a historian finds it hard to sacrifice. Sainte-Beuve could testify to the difficulty of getting out of an abbey, and that far from being the most remarkable, once the threshold has been crossed. It is necessary then to restrain ourselves and resist temptations, however seductive, and to leave most of these Abbesses to hagiographers, and the real history of Benedictine Reform to a writer free to devote himself to this vast subject. This book must confine itself to a careful study of a few nuns, prefaced by a panoramic view of the Reform.

To guide the student, there exist a multitude of contemporary notices and funeral orations, and especially the *Éloges* of the Mère de Blémur, a work of the first importance. Through rare good fortune, denied to the Benedictines of S. Maur, as to the Capuchins, Jesuits, Carmelites and many others, the great reforming Frenchwomen of the Order of S. Benedict at the outset of the seventeenth century found a historian worthy of them, one whom we may boldly rank with the delightful artist to whom we owe the life of Ste. Chantal and the chronicle of the newly founded Order of the Visitation.

Madeleine de Chaugy and Jacqueline Bouëtte de Blémur: the Convent and the Abbey! The Benedictine is less fresh, less suave, less graceful than the Visitandine. She writes with a hand worthy to bear the abbatial crozier, recounting with serene gravity and without surprise the most recent achievements of an Order venerable above all others. She eschews solemnity, but displays a certain majesty, simple and smiling, and often relieved with a light touch of humour. Madeleine de Chaugy is more flowery and full of colour; her book takes the reader into a sweet spring garden, Jacqueline de Blémur's into a forest of oaks. If the one has more unction, the other has more religion, using the word in its most august sense; again she loves books and knows them better. Scripture, the Fathers, all the Christian past is familiar to Jacqueline de Blémur. She excels, as we shall soon see, in those biblical allusions which lend a dignity to the most ordinary events. Speaking of an Abbess who, in the midst of the task of reconstructing her burnt-down Abbey, died leaving many debts, she writes: "Her buildings were not those of Solomon. No David had gathered stones, wood, marble for her. Hers were rather the painful building of the Maccabees."[1] She has no fear of the concrete, and her touches are often telling, as when she remarks of another Abbess that she never passed the statues of the saints "without genuflecting, although hindered by her prodigious corpulency."[2] Here is a vignette of the same sufferer on the eve of death.

> It was proposed to substitute a feather-bed (she never slept save on a board), and she, weary of contesting it, agreed to what they wished; but, once laid upon it, finding no firm support, she sank into a hollow whence she could not raise herself. She bore this in silence, as she did all her discomforts, but seeing the alarm of her poor daughters, she said: "Dear children, do not be frightened, but let me be slipped to the ground." This done, she could not get up again, but she seemed satisfied with this lowly posture.[3]

Jacqueline de Blémur is very human in spite of her sublimity; she understands instinctively, and enters into the feelings she delineates. Here is another quotation from the same record, dealing with the Abbess of Saintes, Françoise de Foix.

> Her unrequited tenderness caused her worst sufferings. She had given her friendship to a certain woman on whom she relied much. She even said to her sometimes, speaking of the inconstancy of another: "I should be much to be pitied were you to be faithless as this creature of whom I speak!" Yet this befell her. She was asked a certain thing which she could not grant, conceiving it unjust, although her refusal cost her many vigils and tears. A hundred times she cried with groans at the feet of her crucifix: "Dear God, to what case hast Thou brought me, to be unable to appease the bitterness of heart of one so dear to me, without displeasing Thee! . . ." From that time her health was practically gone, the violence she had done herself in trying to hide her distress having absolutely changed her constitu-

[1] *Éloge de Mme. Françoise de Foix . . . abbesse de Saintes, seconde du nom*, by M. de Blémur, p. 23. The bibliography of M. de Blémur is complicated. Most of the *éloges* that I shall quote are found in a collection in two quarto volumes which I shall call "Blémur I; Blémur II." But I have also consulted separate *éloges* which I shall indicate by their titles, as in the case of Françoise de Foix and Anne d'Aligre.

[2] *Ibid.*, p. 32.

[3] *Ibid.*, pp. 34–5.

tion. Her heart could not yield in the matter, since it was contrary to God's Will, but as little could it relinquish its affection for one she had loved for many years.[1]

With all this she had the wisdom and practical good sense of a Madame de Maintenon.

Born in 1618 and dying in 1696, Mère de Blémur hesitated for a while between the two spiritual currents which share the century between them. When she began to edit her *éloges*, she was somewhat out of sympathy with things mystical. Some unexplained trait in her makes her shrug her shoulders over discussions of the most sublime forms of devotion; she suspects lurking illusion or verbiage. Yet by degrees she surrenders, and ends by learning, loving, and writing with a rare mastery the mystic language, becoming thus one of the most important witnesses to this mystic renaissance. Jacqueline as a rule does little more, I imagine, than revise, cut down, and embellish after her own fashion, which seems to me easily recognizable, the memoirs sent to her from other abbeys. Her entire Order, or rather the lettered *élite* of that Order, speaks through her, and since the history which we write is above all else literary, and we are trying to detect the religious movement in contemporary writings, we have every reason to leave this *pléïade* of hagiographers to speak for themselves as often as possible.[2]

Everyone agrees that towards the end of the religious wars our Benedictine Abbeys were in a lamentable condition. To quote from the funeral oration preached by the Jesuit Père Polla in 1675 on Marguerite de Quibly, reforming Abbess of the Déserte de Lyon:

Since such things are in our time, it would be unseemly to refuse credence to that seen and witnessed by so many. It is certain then, gentlemen, that all the arches of this church were crumbling, that the ancient building was uninhabitable, that the rents, estates, and rights of the Abbey were lost. As for the spiritual side, I learn from the brief of Urban VIII, that no evidence existed that the Dames de la Déserte had ever been subject to any of the Rules approved by the Church; that they had either ever lived in community or practised

[1] *Éloge de Mme de Foix*, pp. 33–4.

[2] Jacqueline lived to form one of the second generation of Benedictine reformers, together with Elizabeth de Brême and Catherine de Bar. Here, however, she chiefly concerns us in connection with the abbeys newly reformed, in which the mystic harvest of the succeeding years was beginning to appear.

enclosure; that the habit affected by them was in any wise unlike those of the day; that there was any distinguishing mark by which it could be known whether they were religious women or secular. All the observance practised by these ladies consisted in meeting in this church at their pleasure and without being separated from the congregation, to chant what they would of the canonical office. To describe their conduct in detail would be easy enough but would require dark colours. I do not wish to disturb the ashes of her whose portrait I draw to-day, for throughout her life I know her mortal aversion to aught that could tarnish a reputation or sully a memory. I will but add then that the religious of whom we speak, or rather of whom I prefer not to speak, were their own mistresses in all things, the young as much as the old, the novice as much as the professed.[1]

I have chosen this passage because it is picturesque and illustrates well the Benedictine decadence towards the end of the sixteenth century. Biographers and panegyrists, Mère de Blémur among the number, all tell the same story. Clearly we must accept their testimony, but, I maintain, with reserve. Our authors' judgement is not invariably well-balanced, and they are given to declamation. Thus the grave biographer of Mère de Ponçonas assures us with perfect seriousness that his heroine, when a novice in the Abbey of Aies, " drank like the rest the cup of iniquity, and intoxicated herself with the subtle and deadly wine of the world." These swelling words merely mean that the young girl took pains " to say neat things . . . to relate an incident agreeably." Another crime—that, deformed from birth, she " endeavoured to win by wit the admiration she desired and which her physical deformity denied her." The " manifest prevarication " and the " crimes " of this Abbey are deplored, but it is a relief to learn that " the affectation of having beautiful furniture " was " not the least of these crimes."[2] So it is necessary to read with caution, checking their eloquent assertions by the instances they give, and especially taking care not to fill in the details by unworthy imaginings.

With very rare exceptions these Abbeys had not become haunts of pleasure, for the excellent reason that many of them were utterly poverty-stricken. Soldiers and Huguenots had passed by alike, and

[1] *Oraison funèbre de Mme. Marguerite de Quibly*, Lyon, 1675, pp. 8–10.

[2] *La Vie de la Mère de Ponçonas, institutrice de la Congrégation des bernardines réformées*, Lyons, 1675, pp. 35–7.

with them had come pillage and burning. The young no longer flocked to these houses, now in perpetual danger. In a lamentable state themselves, the occupants of these lamentable ruins would have been hard put to it to enjoy the pleasures of life. We shall see presently that the Reformers had great difficulty in reconciling the proprietary instinct of the old Sisters with the demands of holy poverty. The lessons of greed and avarice taught by the evil days still so recent in memory may be pleaded in excuse. They were painfully and carefully restoring their lost property, grain by grain, like ants, bringing together the wherewithal of existence. I grant, some Sisters were not so old, those of La Pommeraye near Sens, for example, who "scrupled not to dress up as shepherdesses and go in this dress to country merrymakings and dance at weddings."[1] Such butterflies were, however, the exception. That there had been grave disorders, including some to which a Benedictine Sister could not allude save in veiled words, is clear, but there was no universal corruption. The bar of enclosure once removed, the door was open to scandal. In the Life of Laurence de Budos we read: "One day a gentleman of her acquaintance, as he sat over the fire with her, let slip a phrase of gallantry, so enraging her that as her sole comment on his impertinence, she flung the knob of the firedog at his head. . . . She banished from her house all those with tarnished reputations, and had much to endure in consequence, and were it permissible to particularize on this point, I should praise her still more highly. But prudence and charity impose silence."[2] The impudence of the gentleman and the indignant surprise of the young Abbess sufficiently indicate the just proportions of good and evil in the abbeys. We see also that they could rid themselves, although with difficulty, of black sheep.

Henri IV's character resembled that of the gentleman just mentioned. Our Abbesses could not use a brass knob on him and had to devise other measures to keep him at a distance. Renée de Lorraine, "having learnt that King Henri IV was preparing for a journey to Rheims, begged her mother to be of the party as she feared to be alone with the monarch. (The King), who did not care for such untamed virtue, nevertheless declared that for goodness and dignity the Abbess of S. Pierre ranked before all the others in

[1] Blémur, II. 256. [2] *Ibid.*, II. 119.

France."[1] Marie de Lorraine, Abbess of Chelles, did better still, if possible. She received the King, "accompanied by her whole Community."[2]

It seems, too, that, whether by few or many, badly or well, the Divine Office was still sung, even in half-burnt churches. In spite of innumerable troubles the monastic life continued, weak and lukewarm to outward appearance, but ready to burst into new life. Thus at S. Pierre de Rheims, even before the reform, the Abbess Renée de Lorraine (second of that name) and her nuns "wore shifts of coarse serge, and during the wars of religion, while experiencing all the hardships inseparable from such times, they neither relaxed this austerity nor the diligent recital of the Office night and day. Enclosure and community of linen might be laid aside, seculars might have liberty to enter the nunnery, but modesty always reigned among them. These flowers of the field and lilies of the valley retained the fragrance and white purity of those who are always enclosed with hedges or dwell in walled gardens. One must give this testimony to their virtue."[3] In many other places these nuns, whether wise or foolish, had still a little oil left in their lamps. There were many good souls, we suspect with good reason, who only asked to be allowed to resume a stricter life. As an old historian tells us: "The Providence which takes particular care of religious houses that have special claim to divine protection, scarcely ever leaves them without some seed of benediction, some Jacob who studies wisdom in the tents of peace while the Esaus range the countryside, a-hunting and taking their pleasures."[4] As for the foolish virgins, they were generally foolish rather than wicked. After all, it was in these surroundings that the idea of reform sprang up spontaneously throughout the kingdom, and since so few years sufficed to achieve so great a work, we have the right to conclude that a rich and lofty life still stirred in all these slumbering hives.

This is illustrated by an affecting and typical incident taken from the history of Florence de Werquignœul, first Abbess of Paix-Notre-Dame at Douai. Florence had made her profession at the Abbey of Flines and had there won seven or eight nuns to the idea of reform.

[1] Blémur, I. 152. [2] *Ibid.*, II. 491. [3] *Ibid.*, I. 196.

[4] *La Vie du Reverendissime évêque Claude de Granger*, by R. P. B. Constantine, Lyon, 1640, p. 24.

As Flines would not change its ways, they decided to found another house. Just before departure the reformed

> made a general and public confession of all their breaches of the Rule and craved pardon of the whole Community. . . . After the Chapter, the other religious followed their example with many tears and such tenderness that they could hardly cease embracing one another, those who had seemed most stiffnecked now showing themselves the most humble and affectionate, asserting that all they had said or done had proceeded from resentment at their separation rather than from want of affection. The day passed in these sad yet sweet explanations. The Abbess-elect led her little flock all over the buildings, particularly to the parts occupied by the old nuns, who received them with much sincerity and affection, admonishing them to persevere in their generous enterprise, but assuring them that if the demands of reform proved over hard for them there need be no hesitation in returning to Flines, where the usual kindliness would receive them.
>
> On the morrow, having heard Mass very early, they proceeded to eat a mouthful at Madame's table. Then the religious crowded together for a last adieu, with renewed askings of pardon amid tears. They could not be separated, their hearts were torn and filled with tenderness and love.
>
> Finally the venerable Abbess of Flines, who, with the Prioress and some others, was to conduct them, started off in a chariot, followed by another containing our reformers. Each chariot held seven, so that there were seven to remain, seven to return. As it was yet night, the moon at her full lighted the little procession, as the Star of the East the three Magi.[1]

This Memling-like sketch is perfect in its sweet colour and penetrating humanity as in feeling. " If it is too hard, come back to us," said the old to the young setting out in quest of a more austere perfection. They would have liked to go too, but they were too old and the unknown terrified them. Never did the *ancien régime* bid a more tender and noble farewell to a young generation leaving it behind and soon to eclipse it.

II. Indeed, the story of the Benedictine renaissance celebrates the triumph of youth, for these reforming Abbesses at the outset of their undertaking were one and all girls, almost children. Of one we are

[1] *La Vie de noble Dame Florence de Werquignœul*, Douai, 1733. This edition is, I think, the republication of an older text.

told that, when she began the reform, her strongest passion was sleep. "The Sisters charged with awakening her for Mattins deprecated the violence they had to use, very often lifting her out of bed fast asleep and dressing her without her wakening."[1] Most of them were under twenty. They were doubly young in a sense, for they knew nothing of the world. The Abbey had received them as babies, some even with their nurses, on whom they were still dependent. Renée de Lorraine, daughter of Henri, third Duc de Guise, and Catherine of Cleves, "was but six weeks old when she was taken to the Abbey of S. Pierre to be confided to Madame her aunt for her whole education." Six years later the little one received the religious habit. "Could anyone have imagined," writes Mère de Blémur, "that at such a tender age this blessed child would begin her novitiate? I am sure this will seem a paradox. It is certain nevertheless that, from the day of her clothing, she slept in a cell of the dormitory adjoining that of Madame her aunt."[2] Anne de Plas was handed over, two months after her baptism, to her aunt, Mme de la Châtre, Abbess of Faremoutier, a severe aunt, who waged war on mirrors. "Knowing that her niece was one of the most beautiful girls of her time, she allowed none to see her, and once, when the Queen-Mother came to the Abbey, shut the child up in her room." Anne had a charming voice, and on a Christmas night was chosen to sing the *Parvulus*, whereupon "they rushed from all sides to hear her," which did not suit the worthy Abbess at all! For ten years, however, Anne de Plas had at Faremoutier a little companion, one day to become the Princess Palatine. Their "favourite recreation was reading the Lives of the Desert Fathers with which they were regaled. They resolved to imitate these examples" by camping with three rolls of bread in an old shed in the courtyard.[3] Bossuet might have used this incident in his funeral oration on the Palatine! The terrible aunt, Madame de la Châtre, herself had been only six when her parents brought her to the Priory of Glatigny in Berry; Claude de Choiseul-Praslin at four had been confided to her aunt, Mme. de Dinteville, Abbess of Notre-Dame de Troyes; Marie de Châteauneuf was hardly born before it was decided "to place her in the royal Abbey of S. Laurent de Bourges as soon as she should be weaned."[4] Such was the system

[1] Blémur, II. 124.
[2] *Ibid.*, II. 145–6.
[3] *Ibid.*, II. 155–6.
[4] *Ibid.*, I. 292.

then in vogue, and, whatever judgement we pass on it, it must be admitted that these children knew each smallest detail of their little kingdoms, when the deaths of their Abbess-Aunts placed them in possession.

The maternal instinct of most of the nuns, the officious zeal of some, made this Abbess' niece, that *dauphine*, destined one day to carry the crozier, dear and precious to them. Besides, were not these innocent children a good influence, counteracting the unhealthy suggestions that came from elsewhere? When they left those too accessible parlours, not without regret, it must have been good for more than one nun to bend over a cradle, or to encounter in tree-shaded gardens little girls playing at being saints.

How did the desire come to these girls to change the order of things in the midst of which they had grown up happy and not so much spoiled after all? This phenomenon will appear less inexplicable when we remember the treasures of integrity, generosity and faith that were the heritage of many of these children, as also the heroism then in the air. We have just seen Anne de Plas and Anne de Gonzague fascinated by the Lives of the Desert Fathers. More recent and still living examples of virtue were to impress these ardent natures even more. Already there was talk of the new Orders springing up around, of many holy women the admiration alike of city and court. Their own Abbeys had more than once afforded hospitality to the conquering mystics. The first Carmelites from Spain had halted at Sainte-Croix de Poitiers: Madeleine de S.-Joseph, on her way to found the Carmelite convent at Lyons, had stayed at Notre-Dame de Troyes, the future reformer of which, Claude de Choiseul, with the little sister destined to succeed her as Abbess, had been so enraptured with the saint that they had longed to follow her as Carmelites.

The panegyrist of Claude de Choiseul comments on this incident very happily. From the moment she became a novice, Claude

began to lament . . . like the Spouse of the Canticles, that instead of the Bridegroom whom she sought in this solitude, she found only the shadow of the forest; that having separated her from the world by one road they had led her back there by another, the more dangerous that it had the aspect of the Narrow Way; and judging aright even at that age that Jesus Christ was not to be found in the softness of a lax mode of life, nor in the dense darkness of ignorance that filled the house, she formed a design in advance of her years. . . . Divine Providence had revealed to France the rich valleys of Mount Carmel, where, since its re-establishment by the illustrious Teresa, religious discipline had flourished in its pristine vigour and purity. Claude hastened to these illumined heights, to knock at every convent door there to be found. *Adjuro vos, filiæ Jerusalem, si inveneritis dilectum meum ut nuntietis ei quia amore langueo:* happy inmates of this Jerusalem, which is without doubt the veritable abode of my Bridegroom, if ye possess Him, inform Him of the aspirations of a soul that, like yourselves, seeks and sighs after none but Him. Addressing herself to the wise Cardinal, her director (Bérulle), she laid her crozier and her Abbey at his feet, protesting that she would prefer the wallet of a poor Carmelite to all the tokens of the honours laid upon her. But the response of the Beloved in the Canticles was much what she received in return, *Si ignoras te, abi post vestigia gregum et pasce hædos tuos:* my daughter, if you know not God's design for you, know that He wills you to take again your crook, to return and direct your flock, and bring the wandering sheep back to the paths whence they have strayed.[1]

Stimulating examples were not wanting elsewhere. The idea of reform was already at work in the religious houses; it was vaguely felt that things could not continue as they were. The less austere life, to which they had gradually become accustomed, had its disadvantages even for the less fervent, for the material interests of an Abbey always depend to some extent on its prestige. Here and there nuns and abbesses were suffering in silence, hoping for better days. When Mère Anne de Jésus was on the way to found the Carmelite convent at Dijon,

she sojourned several days at Troyes, where Mme de Dinteville, Abbess of Notre-Dame and aunt to our little one (Claude de Choiseul), received her with all possible esteem. She spoke to Mère Anne in confidence of her desire to reform her Abbey, and of the apprehended difficulty of such an undertaking, to which the other replied: "Do not be afflicted, madame, if I assure you that God accepts your good-will and that you will not have the consolation of establishing the reform among your daughters." Then taking in her arms Mlle de Praslin, then only a year and a half old, she added: "This child will accomplish this great work. God expressly destines her for it, and He wills of you that you shall with matchless pains rear her in devotion.[2]

[1] *Oraison funèbre de Madame Claude de Choiseul-Praslain*, by a priest of the Oratory, 1667, pp. 12–13.

[2] Blémur, II. 347.

There was then a kind of obscure and timorous conspiracy, each nun keeping her secret humiliation and hope to herself. Had they known their strength they would have begun sooner and not left the honour of the liberating decision to a number of girls. When Marie de Beauvillier revived one of the most degraded Abbeys in France, and the flame leaped up on the hill of Montmartre, it was immediately answered by beacon fires on all sides.

Sudden as the reform was and coming like a thunderclap, needless to say it was not accomplished automatically and without lively resistance. The reforming Abbesses knew their ground too well to have any illusion on this point, but happily the odds between their youth and the bulk of the opposition were not equal. It was a conflict between dawn and darkness. It would be difficult to exaggerate the ignorance and folly of these old religious, fighting desperately for their traditions of ease, coquetry and sloth. Mère de Blémur, a book-lover herself, mentions with pride that her heroines were well educated. Françoise de la Châtre, Abbess of Faremoutier, "spoke Latin, Spanish, and Italian like her mother-tongue . . . she loved Gregorian chants and was so learned therein that she even composed the special Offices of her convent."[1] Claude de Choiseul, from her fourth year, "learned to read both French and Latin perfectly, and found such satisfaction in books that she would not hear of other recreations."[2] The future reformer of Montivillier, Louise de l'Hospital, brought up in the monastery of Poissy, "learned Latin, Spanish and Italian." Subsequently, even during her labours at reform, we find her much occupied "with reading in the originals Luis de Granada and the Fathers who wrote on religious perfection."[3] Marguerite d'Arbouze was no sooner professed at S.-Pierre de Lyons, about 1599, than, so her biographer, Claude Fleury, relates, "she began to learn Italian and Spanish, in order to understand such spiritual works in those tongues as had not yet been translated into French."[4] When Madeleine de Clermont-Tonnerre was novice-mistress, her great-aunt Madeleine de Sourdis, so the Oratorian Malinghen records, "made her write the history of the Abbey of S. Paul, the said history being sent to the author of the chronicles of the Order, who inserted it in his work as it stood, with high praise. It was exceedingly well

[1] Blémur, I. 326. [2] *Ibid.*, I. 347. [3] *Ibid.*, II. 189, 192.
[4] *La Vie de . . . M. d'Arbouze*, by M. Cl. Fleury, Paris, 1865, p. 5.

done, being full of piety and sincerity. Her solid intellect was not easily caught napping, and she was able to penetrate the obscurities of history with much illumination and discernment. The work had been considered so difficult that none before her had attempted it, yet she accomplished it at a time when she did not lack other occupation."[1] From a host of other such examples one more must be selected, the coadjutrix of S.-Cyr, Anne d'Aligre, granddaughter to the Chancellor and daughter of the French Ambassador to Venice—a "book-worm," and for some years in the bad sense of the word. When still a child at the Abbey of Bellomer, Anne "was wont to shut herself into her little cell" and "devour books"; notwithstanding, she grew up frivolous and eager to quit the Abbey. "Her great ardour for knowledge helped to distract Mme d'Aligre . . . she studied history, sacred and secular, the map and the globes. The report of her tastes brought a certain priest to see her, out of curiosity and in hopes of establishing a connection with her. He offered to initiate her into the secrets of astrology, thinking that this would often procure him admission to the grille, but she dismissed him coldly, saying that she had no wish to pass for a lunatic."[2] She continued to read everything, save medical books in which she did not believe, and heretical ones which she felt she might believe too much. For she was fundamentally Christian and her entire conversion was not long delayed. Afterwards, Jacqueline de Blémur tells us in a curious passage, "she suffered most violent temptations to unbelief, her great intelligence and strength of reasoning causing her inexplicable difficulties. She saw the most venerable features in our holy religion as pure dreams and human inventions; she doubted everything, and in these years of distress all the practices of the religious life seemed to her ridiculous."[3] Possibly in the period of her intellectual hunger, when "her brothers furnished her with all the books that might divert her,"[4] Anne might have been in touch with the sceptical authors of the day; at any rate, even after conversion, she always remained of the school of Balzac. It is true that

[1] *La vie de Madame Madeleine de Clermont-Tonnerre*, Paris, 1704. There were two Madeleines de Clermont-Tonnerre, Abbesses of S. Paul-les-Beauvais; the first niece, the second, here in question, great-niece of M. de Sourdis.

[2] *Éloge de feue Madame Anne d'Aligre*, Blémur, p. 591.

[3] *Ibid.*, p. 612.

[4] *Ibid.*, p. 593.

finer shades of style did not commend themselves to her, she being wont to say that literary uncouthness could not conceal truth and that she herself had frequently discovered incomparable things in old manuscripts. She nevertheless loved new books and good writing, her appreciation being so just and keen that she sometimes pointed out important blemishes in pages which all were admiring . . . she would not criticize in public, as that would have been contrary to charity and modesty, but she did not conceal her sentiments from certain intimates, capable like herself of appraising things at their true value.[1]

I trust the reader will note the humanism of these last words.

Our Abbesses had other weapons more spectacular and more formidable. Mère de Blémur, in her *éloge* of Françoise de la Châtre, records that " one day the Comtesse de S.-Paul requested to see the Community, and when they were assembled demanded of Mme de la Châtre whether they were all of noble birth? " ' Yes, Madame,' replied Abbess Françoise, ' they are all daughters of a great King and brides of Jesus Christ! ' "[2] Well done, Mme de la Châtre! But facts are facts, and Jacqueline de Blémur, with all her dislike of ostentation, recounts them with an emotion she does not trouble to hide. There is hardly one of my heroines, she practically says in her preface, who is not of noble birth, and she begins each notice with a genealogy that vies in splendour with its neighbours. The Abbess of Saintes, Françoise de Foix, for instance, " was related in the third degree to the Queen-Mother, Anne of Austria, cousin through Candale and through France with the royal line of England, allied to that of France through the house of Valois, in particular triply to Louis the Just, once through the Medici family and twice through the house of Foix itself."[3] It is the same, more or less, with the others, so that all the glories of old France pass before us in procession in Mère de Blémur's introductions. The same proud story is told in the funeral orations spoken over our Abbesses, and though the orators might begin with the conventional " You will not expect, gentlemen," and the rest of it, yet the concession once made to the Christian principle that admits no nobility save virtue and no low estate save sin, they return to the panegyric of armorial bearings which they have forsworn. The funeral oration of Henriette de Lorraine d'Elbœuf, Abbess of

[1] *Éloge de feue Madame Anne d'Aligre*, Blémur, p. 621.

[2] Blémur, I. 327.

[3] *Ibid.*, I. 558.

Notre-Dame de Soissons, pronounced on March 12, 1669, by the Abbé du Pille, is a rare specimen of such rhetoric; the exordium is specially choice.

> Behold the end of human greatness! Lo, the goal of high birth! A slight remembrance in a few generous or grateful souls, even all the fame possible, what can such be fairly called? Nothing! We must appear before the dread tribunal of the severe Judge . . . the Church makes fervent prayers, but they are uncertain in effect and she cannot be certain of the issue. . . .
>
> In preaching the funeral oration of the great, I think that it hardly befits the preacher of the gospel of Jesus humiliated, to dwell on the lengthy and proud histories of the vanity of mankind. But here are no such pitfalls to avoid. . . . If (our princess) had remained in the world, I should announce: "I am pronouncing the eulogy of the very high and mighty princess, Mme Henriette de Lorraine." To this great name would be linked great titles, of duchies, of principalities, perhaps of kingdoms, for her condition warranted aspirations to all that is highest in this world. These great titles, these superb dignities, these exalted qualities are at hand to embellish a discourse. But, verily, is it not sweeter to a Christian preacher to say simply: Hearken to some of the virtues of a humble religious, of an Abbess who, we may well believe, now beholds God! These are the titles it is easy to speak about and suitable for the pulpit.[1]

Would anyone believe, after so Christian and touching a beginning, that a good half of the ensuing harangue would be dedicated to the fame, the "light," the "gentleness" of the house of Lorraine? Yet, perhaps, after all it was as well not to separate what history has linked so closely, the aristocracy of France and the reform of the Benedictine Abbeys. The French *noblesse* had indeed their full share of responsibility for the decadence of those Abbeys, but, under God, they had nearly all the honour of their renaissance. Since the monasteries were for them almost so many hereditary fiefs, reform could not have been accomplished against or even without them, they alone could carry it by assault.

We can easily imagine what the prestige of these noble girls, born to command, must have been among the nuns of that time. Listen to Père Marc Donfrère in his funeral oration on Catherine de Montluc de Balagny, Abbesse of Origny.

[1] *Oraison funèbre de feue Madame Henriette de Lorraine d'Elbœuf*, by the Abbé du Pille, Soissons, 1669, pp. 3–5.

Our young princess who had the attractive mien and noble pride of her father (nephew of Blaise) and the disposition and high courage of her mother (Renée d'Amboise, great-niece of the two cardinals), had likewise inherited from both, that greatness of soul which renders men masters and sovereigns of others, and fits them for rule and empire.

On her father's side she was a wolf, continued the good Father, who will have his little jest:

To be a wolf and to be a Montluc are the same thing, for λύκος signifies "wolf" in our tongue.

If in later life she proved herself a lamb, that could not have been due to Renée d'Amboise, whose warlike feats are well known.

The princess her mother had given her the education of an amazon. The harsh and severe reprimand which she received when four or five years old, because she had shown fright at a cannon-ball piercing the room in which she was, had taught her once for all to tremble at nothing.[1]

Luce de Luxe bore a milder name, but she also sprang from a race which knew how to make itself obeyed. "She used no force in any of her regulations, but contented herself with stating her wishes and adding that true Benedictines did this and that. Her sweetness and her tact did the rest. It is true nevertheless that, with it all, she had a certain air of firm resolve, which made her daughters abandon all thought of resistance."[2] So the biographer of Louise d'Humières, Abbess of Mouchy, notes "a certain air of gravity which always hung about her, and augmented the veneration inspired by her virtue, possibly also made her a little feared."[3]

Père Bouhours, writing of Mère de Bellefont, remarks: "The slightest sign, I will not say of indignation, but of dissatisfaction, seemed like a thunderclap . . . her *grand air* at once dazzled and inspired fear."[4]

That this "certain air," whether at Saint-Ausone d'Angôuleme, where Luce de Luxe reigned, or elsewhere, was an important factor

[1] *Oraison funèbre de Mme Marie C. de Montluc de Balagny*, by P. M. Donfrère, Saint-Quentin, 1666, pp. 21, 31–2.

[2] Blémur, I. 8.

[3] *La vie de Madame d'Humières* (Félibien), Paris, 1711.

[4] *La Vie de Madame de Bellefont, supérieure et fondatrice du monastère . . . de Rouen*, Paris, 1691, p. 90.

of Benedictine reform seems certain and need not disturb us. Just because authority came naturally to these young girls, it never dazzled them—it is notorious that the rule of *parvenus* is apt to be harsh. It is a joy to discover them unconsciously queening it, as for example in the fine scene recorded by Mère de Blémur in the story of Laurence de Budos, Abbess of the Trinité of Caen.

The following incident must not be neglected if one wishes to understand the character of our worthy Abbess. She found (on arriving there) in a granary an old coffer filled with the most important papers relating to the house. She wished to examine what they were about, and having discovered this for herself, she took possession of the principal ones and carried them off in her robe. Descending the ladder, she met the *intendant* who had served Madame her predecessor. Seeing her thus laden, he would have relieved her, but she said firmly: " I am surprised, Monsieur, that a man of your understanding and, as I hope, probity, should have had so little care of the most valuable things in this Abbey! " The *intendant* in confusion replied that she certainly merited the royal appointment, since she had begun so soon to exercise her functions. Our own eyes have witnessed (Jacqueline de Blémur was a professed sister of Caen) the incomparable order into which she brought all things when years had fortified her good inclinations, and I believe that in no other house could the papers be in better order than in hers when death snatched her from us.[1]

With all this,—I do not say in spite of this—most of these Abbesses knew likewise how to make themselves loved. To quote again Mère de Blémur, this time on Guyonne de Médavy, Abbess of Saint-Nicolas de Verneuil.

I will say in passing that her goodness entered into all the needs of her daughters, as may be shown by this characteristic incident. She had an admirable voice and kept all the choir going in their antiphonal singing. Further, when some sister had to sing a solo, and was overcome with nervousness, as happened fairly often, she would look towards her Abbess, who would forthwith approach, reassuring her by her presence, sustaining her when her voice trembled, and even joining in if she judged it needful. At these times she used to sign to the Community to be seated, contrary to custom when the Abbess was standing, but she would have none inconvenienced for her, and opposed obedience to respect, in order that all should be at ease.[2]

[1] Blémur, II. 116.

[2] *Ibid.*, II. 386.

To humble her natural pride, and in order not to crush on the spot any sister who failed in due respect, Françoise de Foix used to practise self-repression to such an extent that she

invariably paid for it . . . by a double tertian fever. She began the conflict young. Her high birth seemed to justify a natural love of grandeur, and she was obliged to make many efforts to humble herself as much as she did.

The result was great gentleness and tender affection. Another Superior, not a Benedictine, Mère Galiote de Gourdon, was remembered by one of her nuns, "as accustomed to weep with us, when she saw us weeping as we confessed our failures."[1]

To these natural gifts must be added another which the saintly Mère de Blémur herself takes pleasure in mentioning. Our Abbesses, at least according to their biographers, were almost all beautiful. When Marguerite of Kirkcaldy, arriving from Scotland in circumstances unknown to us, was sent to the Abbey of Saint-Pierre of Rheims, "she was forthwith known as . . . *la belle écossaise*, and it was fitting that this lovely lily should be placed in a garden enclosed." Since the enclosure was not yet authorised,

our little dove hid herself in outbuildings and clefts of the rocks, she fled into the cellars when any visitors of note came to the house, knowing that they would instantly demand to see *la belle écossaise*.[2]

As for Marie-Françoise Lescuyer, Abbess of Lys,

none would believe her affliction at knowing herself beautiful nor the pains that she took to spoil her complexion, washing her face and then exposing it to the hottest beams of the sun, in hopes that she might become weather-beaten and ugly. All in vain, her humility was ever baulked; Our Lord loved her as He had made her, and would not spoil that which He had made. If at times she said with the Spouse: I delight in Thy beauty, My Beloved! He replied: Thou art fair to My eyes, My sister, My dove, perfect art thou, without blemish![3]

"One might have found more regular beauty" than that of Marie Granger, foundress of Montargis, "but her charm made her distinguished in nearly all companies."[4] So we see them, one after another,

[1] *Histoire de la vie et des vertus de la Vénérable Mère Galiote de Gourdon*, by P. F. Thomas d'Aquin de Saint-Joseph, Paris, 1633.

[2] Blémur, II. 538–9. [3] *Ibid.*, II. 305. [4] *Ibid.*, I. 185.

beautiful, majestic, or dainty in fragile grace. The foot of Anne d'Aligre would have left no imprint on the grass. "She was so delicate in build that her stiff coarse habit held her up, and when sometimes the wind whirled under her skirts when she was walking in procession, she was blown down."[1] How could one have helped loving her? Laurence de Budos was small too, but less white and frail, "beautiful of face" and "very healthy." Such was her appearance when she had interviewed Henri IV on behalf of the rights of the Abbey. "The King heard her not only with patience but with pleasure, for she was charming and could not have spoken more gracefully. And when the justice of her cause made her blush, the prince would have liked the remonstrance to be longer."[2] This illustrates the wit and sanity of outlook found in a book written by a nun in 1669 to edify and delight our Abbeys!

III. Behind our young Abbesses we find François de Sales, Pierre Coton, Canfeld, Bérulle, Asseline, Condren, and others, in short all those famous spiritual masters whose influence, discreetly used but very effective, inspired, sustained, and guided to success all the religious enterprises of the dawning seventeenth century. This is in accord with one of the invariable laws governing the great movement we are describing. From the King down to obscure village saints, the whole country had its share in this truly national movement, the chiefs of which, to whatever Order they belonged—Capuchins, Jesuits, Oratorians, Feuillants, and Reformed Benedictines—worked together in a common brotherhood. More than one reforming Abbess had received the divine spark or had come to rekindle her zeal in the *cénacle* of Mme Acarie. Louise de l'Hospital, who was naturally devout and on her nomination as Abbess in 1596 had entered the good town of Montvilliers with bare feet, "treading on the sharp little pebbles," was sometimes known to make her appearance in the capital under conditions less suggestive of mortification. Happily she was put into touch with Père de Bérulle, the Carthusian Dom Auger, Mme Acarie, Gamache, and Gallemant, the last of whom helped her to begin her reform. Marie de Beauvillier, whom we shall study later in detail, had the constant support of the same group, and God knows the poor girl needed support. Among her usual admirers I find two Capuchins, two Benedictines and two

[1] *Éloge de feue Madame Anne d'Aligre*, pp. 589–90. [2] Blémur, II. 114–17.

Jesuits. "The Jesuits Pères Gontier and de Montigny worked (at the reform of Montmartre) with Père Potier (Benedictine), conspiring together to establish the reign of Jesus Christ."[1]

Père de Salin and Père Lallemant, with other Jesuits of Bourges, directed Marie de Châteauneuf, Abbess of S. Laurent. Laurence de Budos maintained correspondence with Condren, as well as with Oratorians and Jesuits. Thirty years later the encounter of these two Orders in the same parlour would have inspired some wicked epigram, but at that time the little chapels gave way to the greater. Down to the early Port-Royal Jesuits, Capuchins, and Feuillants were consulted indiscriminately. Quite a Council was gathered together by Madeleine de Sourdis at S.-Paul-les-Beauvais; the Cardinal de Sourdis and the Bishop of Maillezais; Gallemant and Duval; several Benedictines from Saint-Vanne; and four Capuchins, Ange de Joyeuse, Honoré de Champigny, Benoit de Canfeld and Archange of Pembroke. The work was important enough to justify the assembling of all these eminent men. But was there not reason to fear that these helpers, by their very eminence and the diversity of their origin, might to some extent divert the Benedictine reform from its aim? The mind of Mère de Blémur, at once acute and wedded to tradition, was disturbed by this delicate question.

> The Benedictine Fathers, more than any others, have the right to inspire the spirit of the Order; none can give what he has not got. . . . Other religious may form in souls the sentiments of goodness in general, but not those of S. Benedict in particular, not having studied his maxims.[2]

This somewhat radical declaration is just, and gives the first signal of an extremely curious phenomenon, with which we shall soon be concerned, namely the complete transformation that was taking place in the greater number of these Abbeys. Such transformation was inevitable. These old houses needed a reformation, and the Benedictine monks, who were only just beginning to reform themselves, were not yet numerous enough to undertake the reformation of their Sisters singlehanded; it was therefore imperative that the reform should be brought about in a more modern spirit and by younger hands. In vain did Oratorians, Capuchins and Jesuits try to steep

[1] Blémur, II. 164.

[2] *Ibid.*, I. 149.

themselves in the Rule of S. Benedict, in the renovation of which they worked hard; they remained to the core modern men, post-Tridentine religious. Consequently our Abbeys, without losing the essential features of their primitive originality, received a new impress. The Order of S. Benedict had meditated long before the Council of Trent or the birth of S. Ignatius. It seems, however, that this reform within the reform, if the phrase be allowed, introduced into the Abbeys an interior life more systematic and orderly, and more resembling that of newer congregations, in a word, more conformed to the Ignatian *Exercises*. The reformers were not content to return to the regularity of old days, enclosure, poverty, liturgical splendour; they endeavoured, besides all this, to mould the Benedictines by methods and practices unknown to the first centuries of the Order. We shall demonstrate this presently in detail; for the moment let us return to our Abbesses, their struggles for reform and their triumph.[1]

IV. In some places, whether because the majority of the nuns were already anxious for reform, or because the reformer had displayed charm or genius above the average, the battle was won immediately. At Chelles, Mère de Blémur notes, " that which elsewhere cost much trouble was effected here with inconceivable peace ";[2] and at S.-Pierre de Rheims the nuns, far from murmuring at the re-establishment of the enclosure, " testified a lively joy and avowed that they had long desired such separation from the world."[3] At Beauvais they were in such haste to return to the old observances, that they were fain to turn out their Abbess, Madeleine de Sourdis, who was indeed well disposed towards reform but much too young to undertake it. She was not yet old enough to be professed and she wished to wait for her bulls and the abbatial benediction. " Certain nuns, meaning well but disregarding wise counsels, impatient of the delay and wishing to see prompt reform in their house, resolved to demand from the King another Abbess, older and able to act with decision."[4] I should not have commented on this detail had it not been well to recall that there was a certain amount of intrigue and exaggeration

[1] The Abbess of Montmartre " arranged " for her nuns an *Exercice religieux* (Paris, 1620), a volume in which she did little more than include sundry treatises written to herself " at various times by several deeply religious persons." Some certainly of these papers, if not all, were written by Jesuits or under their dictation, as for instance " the formula and instruction for self-examination," on pp. 193–5.

[2] Blémur, II. 488.

[3] *Ibid.*, I. 147.

[4] *Ibid.*, I. 507.

in the camp of Reform. On the other side, nothing is purer, simpler, and more delightful than the story of the reform of Saintes.

Françoise de Foix, one of the most attractive of our heroines, who had been Abbess since 1606, had gone unobtrusively to study the exact observance in the Abbeys already reformed in her neighbourhood, the Trinité, and the Sainte-Croix of Poitiers (1610, 1611). This novitiate lasted six months.

On her return she assembled the Community and spoke to them, as if she had been an angel, on the obligations of religious souls, on the true peace found in the crucified life, and on other truths, so affectingly as to win over her little flock. They began by depriving themselves of all secular intercourse, sending away all persons whose visits seemed useless or likely to excite suspicion. Parlours were built, the door was shut, and the convent surrounded with strong and high walls. The house became the garden enclosed of the Beloved, the fountain sealed, the vine defended by a hedge from the wild boar; the Beloved was welcomed in secret and His divine caresses were enjoyed, in a way, according to S. Bernard, impossible in public. It must be owned that the hand of God worked mightily through this incomparable girl, since in less than eight days she accomplished all which others achieved only after long years of effort and patience. For her indeed were highways smoothed and mountains brought low. For more than two hundred years personal property had been allowed among the nuns, each lived to herself, spending as she chose her portion from the convent. Such disorder, although not only tolerated, but regulated personally by former Abbesses, seemed appalling to Mme. de Foix. . . . She told her daughters of her great wish to establish a common table and (to) relieve them of the cares of housekeeping, assuring them nevertheless that she desired to force nobody, being sure that, having been professed without understanding, God would pardon their ignorance. Her gentleness was crowned with victory; several yielded on the spot, and the rest in less than a week. They laid all that they had at the feet of their Mother, keeping nothing back and abandoning themselves absolutely to her care and charity. On Maundy Thursday, 1611, community life was re-instituted, and a common table set for those who would, the old nuns being free to use it as they liked. Such graciousness drew them, like a magnet according to the word: I will draw them by the cords of Adam, by the bonds of love.[1]

[1] Blémur, I. 561–2.

When Mère Gautron decided on reform in her Priory of Saumur, "she prayed Père Letard and some other priests (of the Oratory) to come and give moving and powerful instructions. . . . The community was stirred thereby much as are towns during some celebrated Mission." The simile is peculiarly happy for the whole of this history. Mère Gautron herself one day spoke to her nuns "so strongly concerning converse with seculars, that all requested linen screens should be put up in the parlour, behind which conversation might be carried on. The Abbess promptly provided light frames, to which the Sisters nailed the canvas, the foundress of the house, Mère de Lézé, herself hammering the first nail, and each doing her share."[1] Thus God can use all things, even the attraction of novelty and the delight of pleasant activity.

As may be guessed, the ordinary tactics employed were an appeal to enthusiasm. The younger professed, naturally more ardent and less rooted in abuses, were gained first, then organized and equipped. The elder nuns, if recalcitrant, were simply left alone, free to continue their petty semi-secular lives. Many among these, whom unhappily no Blémur has immortalized and who never thought of writing their own memoirs, were good women, narrow rather than vicious. Their opposition was not without excuse, since they were disturbed in their vested rights, in the practice of the Abbeys at the time when they made their own professions. Naturally enough they looked black at these young heroines, who were sometimes, perhaps, a little tormenting or inclined to mockery, and however sweet and humble, by their behaviour censured venerable traditions. The life of Anne d'Aligre, the *intellectuelle* whom we have already met, contains an amusing anecdote on this point.

The first time that Anne was cellaress she found that several aged Mothers, professed long before the Reform, had retained the right of choosing what they would for meals, but, as their tastes all varied, the Sisters in the kitchen had their hands full to satisfy everyone. Mme la Coadjutrice, desiring to call them to a sense of their duty, devised an amusing stratagem. When all were assembled in recreation she appeared with paper and ink to write down the names of the dainty ones and below them the dishes which each would not eat, although served to the rest. She began with the Prioress, explaining that, being

[1] *La vie de la R. M. Madeleine Gautron, prieure de Saumur.* Saumur, 1689, pp. 38–40.

unable to remember each item and wishing to please everyone, she had hit on the idea of this register, which should be hung up in the kitchen. This was a great surprise to the malcontents, especially the old Prioress, who was an Israelite indeed without guile, and was so horrified at the idea that she said to our Mother, whose name was Saint-Louis: " Madame Saint-Louis, sweet one, in the name of God do not put me down on your paper; I will eat anything just as it comes." She kept her word, being very virtuous, and the rest likewise had no mind that their names should be pilloried in the kitchen.[1]

Some may possibly think that the youthful coadjutrice took a base advantage and was unmerciful. Sometimes, however, the hostile army had leaders more formidable than these poor and pious old Sisters. Some Abbeys could produce veritable megaeras, bristling against reform. We shall meet some of them soon at Montmartre, which was one of their chief strongholds. The old nuns of Rheims for a long while sorely tried Margaret of Kirkcaldy, " saying to her things to relate which would make my paper blush."[2] It is Mère de Blémur speaking, who is herself free and downright enough. Anne de Harlay was at Chelles under Marie de Lorraine when she was appointed by the King, Abbess of Notre-Dame de la Pommeraye, near Sens. The poor girl, knowing what to expect from the degradation of her Abbey, took three years to resolve to leave Chelles, and when at last, on September 30, 1633, she set out to take possession of La Pommeraye, " she no sooner beheld the top of the belfry than she shed a torrent of tears. Her bitterness of soul was much increased when she realized the character of her nuns, who quarrelled in the middle of the ceremony, as to who should first sign the deed of taking possession, and waxed so warm that they nearly came to blows. . . . When it came to the question of establishing some kind of regular life among them, God alone knew how much the pious Abbess had to suffer."[3] When, after incredible difficulties, the noble sweet woman had transported her community to Sens and acclimatized the reform among them, two formidable veterans were there to recall perpetually her former purgatory. " Their talk was all of climbing over the walls, they threw over them letters filled with complaints and invectives, they shrieked through the cloister insults to their Abbess." One day

[1] *Éloge de feue Mme. d'Aligre*, pp. 624–5.

[2] Blémur, II. 541.

[3] *Ibid.*, II. 257.

"she was told that one of these old ladies was in such a state of frantic excitement that the doctor believed she could not live more than two or three hours. The Abbess was taken to her room where she sat alone with her, but scarcely had she watched by her for a half hour before she recognized that the illness was feigned and that a drug had been used to blacken the tongue." Wanting to hinder reform by exhausting the household, the malcontent had found no better plan than simulating a terrible illness. As for the other rebel, "she has been seen to raise her hand to strike the good Abbess," and during the Office, before a full church, "she made an outcry which terrified the seculars."[1]

Incredible as it sounds, cried Père Polla in the funeral oration over Marguerite de Quibly, one of the mutineers of the Abbey of La Déserte "armed herself one day with a firebrand to set alight the place where her Abbess was, in order to burn her alive." Sometimes young intriguers associated themselves with these old fiends—one novice "would readily have passed over a burning bridge to seat herself on the throne."[2]

At S.-Paul-les-Beauvais a nun played the part of antipope; by a farcical election she had been made Abbess, and Madeleine de Sourdis had for a long time to tolerate her absurd claims. When the beautiful Marie Lescuyer came to the Abbey of Lys she found there, according to Mère de Blémur,

> an old Abbess who had resigned her charge . . . after many adventures that need not be related here. When the beautiful postulant entered the convent, this good lady, charmed with her looks, so far from approving her zeal for the religious life, did her best to alter the girl's intention and marry her to one of her own relatives.[3]

It must be confessed that this anti-reformist Old Guard sometimes secured unexpected reinforcements. When Claude de Choiseul decided to enforce the rule of lowered veils in the convent parlour, the town of Troyes was furious at the news of this reform.

> On the Day of the Assumption of the Queen of Heaven it was customary for the canons of the Cathedral Church of Troyes to come to the Abbey Notre-Dame to sing Teerce and preach, leaving three of their number, together with three priests and two choir-boys, for the

[1] Blémur, pp. 262–6. [2] *Ibid.*, I. 209. [3] *Ibid.*, II. 307.

celebration of High Mass. The dean, finding the veils of the nuns lowered during the conference, burst into furious invectives against the pious Abbess. She listened calmly, and, when he had ceased speaking, said that as S. Paul had ordained women to veil themselves in church because of the angels, she was obeying the precept, knowing that the ministers of Jesus Christ were in sooth angels.[1]

Claude de Choiseul clearly had more sense of humour than this Canon, who appears to us less odious than ridiculous, but what humour, sense and supple firmness must have been necessary when, for one reason or another, episcopal authority objected to the reform, as sometimes happened! Also, and very frequently, lesser powers had to be reckoned with, the ordinary confessors of the Abbeys, disarranged in their ways by these outbreaks of austerity and strongly inclined to range themselves with the older nuns on the side of tradition. To this coalition may be added the families and friends of the nuns and Abbesses, in themselves a little world interested for obvious reasons in the maintenance of the old order.

Sainte-Beuve has described in the sublime manner the heroic day of the *guichet*, when Angélique Arnauld, inflexibly decided on integral reform, closed the door of Port-Royal to her own father. Analogous scenes are not lacking in the chronicles of our Abbesses. Here is one, doubly interesting from the rank of the persons concerned and the eloquence of the panegyrist who tells the tale. It is found in the "funeral oration on Mme Claude de Choiseul de Praslin, Abbess-Reformer of the royal Abbey of Notre-Dame at Nonnains of Troyes," preached on September 13, 1667, by an Oratorian.

Understand then, gentlemen, that the greatest obstacle to be overcome by her was the love of a father (the Maréchal) whose power in the province rendered aught against his will impossible and whose tenderness for his daughter caused him to agree with all the opposition to the life of austerity she would fain embrace. When he had devoted her to religion, he had felt none of the pangs and sorrow which this sacrifice causes in the soul of most fathers and mothers. Not that martial pride had extinguished in him the sentiments of nature—his heart, steeled to all else, had indeed the weak spot common to all true fathers—but because the religious life, as it then was, would

[1] Blémur, II. 354.

separate his child only in part from him, and the repute of the Abbey would afford her retreat some semblance of her former condition, so that he could persuade himself that, while belonging to God and quitting the world only to this degree, she would still remain his. But when he saw her take resolutions to give herself wholly to the one and to quit the other, it was then that this great hero for the first time became aware that he was weak and sensitive like other men, that in him was being fulfilled the prophecy of the Son of God, Who came into the world to put asunder father and daughter. It might have been imagined that, in this innocent war, paternal tenderness would have inspired the Maréchal with all the skill and courage he showed in battle or in the assault of an enemy town. . . . What lightnings, what thunders did he not launch when, notwithstanding all his opposition, he found the seals of the enclosure on all doors of the convent, and the very doors he had used the day before sealed up, and learned that he would no longer be permitted to see his daughter save through a grating in the wall of that which she had made a voluntary prison. But as at times it chances that a great storm is shattered by a furious thunderclap, the impetuosity of which scatters afar rain and clouds, unveiling the heavens and spreading an unexpected calm over the heads of those it terrified, so the ragings of this storm of love were incontinently followed by a sudden change, a wholly unexpected calm. Is it permitted here to unveil the weakness of so great a hero? May I say, without tarnishing his fame, that the conqueror of cities, the victor of many a battle, was vanquished in this encounter, that the anger which had so oft caused armies to tremble, could not shake the constancy of a daughter, and that recognizing the temper of his own blood in her, he was constrained to yield the field.[1]

Mère de Blémur recounts more calmly a scene of the same kind, perhaps even more painful. When Laurence de Budos informed her brother that she intended re-establishing enclosure in the convent of the Trinité at Caen, he

warned her that *Madame sa mère* would be much displeased thereat, and that she should beware of thus grieving her, since she would risk never seeing her mother again—which indeed was but too true. But our courageous Abbess . . . persevered in her saintly resolve . . . in their presence and without heeding their counsels, she re-established the enclosure on Palm Sunday, and on the morrow her mother departed without bidding her farewell and never saw her again in this life.[2]

[1] *Oraison funèbre*, pp. 13–15. [2] Blémur, II. 118–19.

Re-establishment of enclosure was nevertheless not the critical point of reform, as masculine imagination and modern students are disposed to believe. The women of that time were strange creatures, generous enough to accept courageously the hardest sacrifices, such as the *grille* or the midnight Office, yet sufficiently childish to cling desperately to trifles, the colour of a habit or the lace trimming of a surplice. It seems in fact that, in the catalogue of sacrifices imposed by the reform, the two articles which in the majority of Abbeys inspired the most dramatic resistance were the return to, in Benedictine language, " the community " and to the ancient habit.

Benedictine " poverty," like that of many other Orders, especially the Jesuits, is less thorny, but no less exacting than Franciscan. The religious possesses nothing of his own, being dependent on his Superior for all his needs. At the time in question this fundamental article of the rule was in Abbeys only a distant memory, like baptism by immersion or Communion in both kinds with us. The nuns, in accordance with a toleration universally admitted, held property; they laid out their income, great or small, purchasing their own linen, books, objects of devotion, plate, and everything else; even, when their means permitted, enjoying in their own apartment regular and supplementary meals, chosen and paid for by themselves.

A curious passage in Mère de Blémur helps us to realize this state of things. After Laurence de Budos

> had begun the reform of her monastery by restoring the enclosure, she carried on the work by gradually introducing the rest of the observances, such as the community of linen, the common supper-table, at least on fast days—this last reform was especially difficult and only to be accomplished by degrees, for as each religious had means of her own, they were not supplied from the convent with half the things necessary to sustain life, for which reason beginning was made with fast days—it having been custom that those who desired to fare better ate in their own cells with their chosen friends. Madame put a stop to this abuse, preferring the greater expense caused by her daughters taking their repasts in the refectory, where she herself was always the first to appear.[1]

So the Abbey itself, for economy's sake, used to invite the nuns to look after themselves. Other abuses more or less similar were

[1] Blémur, I. 119.

established elsewhere. This *régime* of individualism had many attractions, especially for women, but one realizes, to say nothing of many inconveniences more or less serious, what daily anxiety and humiliation it must have involved for nuns who lacked money or "good friends." It is certain that the dissatisfaction of these unfortunates must have been a strong factor in facilitating reform. Mère de Blémur says as much in her abstract and Biblical way.

Formerly they were constrained to a thousand meannesses, to obtain the wherewithal to furnish themselves with necessaries. Time was passed in useless talk and the Prince of this world held sway over them, governing them through the agency of his subjects; while now, since the breaking of their chains and their assent to the precious nakedness of which the Apostle speaks, they no longer groan nor do they beg for the alms of Egypt or Babylon.[1]

This fine imagery conceals definite realities, often sordid and distressing, that need not be described here. The property, generally very humble but all the dearer on that account, which the nuns kept jealously in their cells, was given up with little difficulty. Often a touching exhortation or an infectious impulse of generosity precipitated the sacrifice.

The ravages of the wars having injured in part the revenues of the Abbey (S.-Paul-les-Beauvais), the religious sought alleviation by appealing to their relatives, and instead of kissing the hand which had despoiled them in order to enrich them with the treasures of grace, they renounced poverty of spirit, hardly enduring that to which they had been reduced by the vicissitudes of human life. Thus the door was opened to a hundred petty licences. . . . Individuals received pensions of which they disposed at will; they received gifts for themselves—she who was thus most favoured receiving the applause of which the Psalmist said: *They have said, Blessed are the people who possess the riches of the land:* but they had no part in the rest of the verse, for the Lord was not their God, their lot, nor their heritage. Our admirable Abbess (Mme de Sourdis) induced the reverend Fathers, Honoré de Champigny and Benoit de Canfeld, to hold some conferences on this point, which they did so efficiently that on June 8, 1607, in full Chapter, all the Sisters of their own freewill renounced all private possessions, in convincing proof of which they brought that very hour their silver and all else in their cells to the Mother, leaving their necessities, present and future, to her charity.[2]

[1] Blémur, I. 522.

[2] *Ibid.*, 521–2.

A similar touching, picturesque, even amusing scene, appealing to the reader's imagination, was witnessed at Notre-Dame in Troyes, where the charming Abbess, Claude de Choiseul, who herself bore the whole burden of responsibility, used the Vigil of S. Benedict to speak the "hard word" to her daughters.

At the end of her discourse, she said that she would not establish the reform by violent means, but would assure all who desired to live the life of community that they should be treated as herself. . . . She then quitted the Chapter, leaving the company as amazed as though a thunderbolt had fallen on their heads. They went to sing Compline, and the (morrow's) festival passed in silence, but not without fruit . . . for the next day about four in the morning all the nuns laid at their Mother's feet whatever they possessed of money, linen, ornaments and plate, in fact all superfluities, with a joy which could only proceed from the Holy Spirit. It is true that there were some among them, less sincere than the rest, who kept something back, but these were punished in this world (by tragic remorse) like Ananias and Sapphira. . . . Madame de Notre-Dame had six great silver-gilt chandeliers for the high altar made out of the plate which her sister and the other nuns had brought.[1]

Hardest of all, perhaps, everywhere was the renunciation of the white habit which for long years had replaced the black. Although this change "may appear a trifle," yet it cost these Abbesses, Laurence de Budos for instance, many difficulties with the Sisters.

They were so attached to their white habit that the proposal to take to the black was odious. The Spouse appeared not comely to the innocent shepherdesses of whom Solomon speaks, because she was tanned, and yet it resulted from the sun's looking upon her, hiding some great thing beneath this darkening. So these good Mothers, believing themselves children of the day, held that a colour not symbolizing light was not suitable to their condition, and they appealed to everyone to take their part, down to a confessor who declared himself for them, against Madame (L. de Budos). For a whole year after she had caused the habits to be made she endured this petty revolt. For myself, I am sure that the more reasonable among them must have been ashamed of having so long disputed about leaving off a habit so little suitable to the Sisters of S. Benedict, not so much as regards the colour, which he leaves open in the holy rule, but in the fashion and the quality of the stuffs. For, instead of some cheap material as he

[1] Blémur, II. 353–4.

ordains, they had not only robes of fine serge, but also surplices of delicate linen pleated and starched with cunning fingers, so that the most elaborate were most prized. There were jealousies as to who should have the most beautiful rosary, or the greatest number of ornaments, in the belief that such things would draw attention and make the wearers pass for ladies of condition.[1]

This obstinacy, for or against white, is explained by the ornaments and frills which were added to the habit and perhaps went better with white. Doubtless, too, some saw in this change from day to night an impressive symbol of the radical transformation then taking place. At Beauvais war had to be waged on black, not on white.

Instead of their church habits, (the nuns of S. Paul) wore a surplice of black linen introduced, they believed, into the house by Madeleine de Clermont, who had been a religious of Fontevrault. It is hard to explain the difficulty over suppressing this ridiculous vestment. The enclosure, it is true, did not give so much trouble (to Mme de Sourdis), only one of the Sisters for fifteen days holding out against her; but when it came to the surplice, even the most reasonable of the Sisters refused to hear a word of abandoning it, declaring that, having received it at their profession, they would wear it till their death.[2]

A little revolution broke out in the convent, the party which had submitted in sullen silence to the other reforms availing themselves of the chance to rally some better spirits to their side on the question of white against black, and the Bishop of the town, Augustin Potier, unwisely ranking himself with them. It is all childish enough, but have we not seen the question of a flag kindling political passions and dividing France? Again, reform was a whole, each part of which supported and involved the rest. As a panegyrist says, eulogizing Marie de Montluc for having changed the white robe for the black: "It would appear from the great and happy results of this substitution that at times it is good to feel anxiety and take thought for raiment."[3]

V. All the stages recorded above had been already tested in the numerous Benedictine reforms of preceding centuries. It could hardly have been otherwise, since the common programme of all such reforms was a return to the purity of primitive observance as it stood in the written Rule of S. Benedict, and since weak places and

[1] Blémur, II. 119–20. [2] *Ibid.*, I. 526.
[3] *Oraison funèbre de Mme Marie de Montluc*, p. 76.

dangerous cracks had practically always appeared at the same points of the monastic rampart. Nevertheless, as has been pointed out, the reform we are considering had its own characteristics. Undertaken at a time when all Catholic France felt the need of interior renewal, it had been directed by new men, strangers as a rule to the old Benedictine family, men who, although convinced of the necessity of religious observances, were pre-eminently contemplatives, mystics and, at least in several instances, sublime souls. It was unavoidable that such men should fashion the Reform to their own image, more or less adapting the Benedictine Rule to their own experiences, pious habits, and temper of mind. To lay undue stress on the contrast between the Benedictines and those religious who conceived and carried out Counter-Reform would be unscientific ; it would be absurd to attribute to the latter any monopoly of the interior life, as though their predecessors, only half-Christianized, had confined their religion to the material observance of a Rule. The religious orders, like the Church herself, live only by the spirit, and if there have been always, among ancient and modern alike, certain formalists and even Pharisees, it is self-evident that there have also always been spiritual and mystic souls. It must be allowed that the moderns, though they may not have practised more heartily, yet taught more explicitly and methodically, possibly more insistently, the more intimate exercises of the devout life. It is a curious and suggestive thing that the moderns appear to have applied to the inner life, the regular and rigorous discipline reserved in earlier ages for the outward life, I mean the common and public life of the Abbeys. The Rule of S. Benedict ordains meditation, but leaves the religious freedom to meditate as he pleases so far as times and method go. The Rule of S. Ignatius defines times and method with the utmost precision. I shall be told that this spirit is peculiar to the Jesuits. This is saying a good deal, considering their number and importance, but where did the Jesuits come from? Were they not, like everyone else, children of their own time, on which they left their mark, but not until they had first been marked by it? However this may be, it is impossible not to recognize their teaching and influence or that of those closely akin to them, in the regular daily meditations and annual retreats of eight or ten days, imposed on the reformed Abbeys by our Abbesses.

Yet it must not be thought that these Abbeys became merely

feminine " extensions " of the Society of Jesus, like the Sacré-Cœur of Mme Barat or the many Congregations of the nineteenth century which follow the Rule of S. Ignatius. There are very interesting reasons against such a view. To begin with, the Jesuits were not the sole directors of our Abbesses; by their side we have already seen Feuillants, Capuchins, Oratorians and seculars of note. It is true that these various influences had a common aim, the expansion of the meditative and contemplative life, but they did not all take the same way. Prayer with the Oratorians allowed more scope for speculation than with the Jesuits, with whom it seems less spontaneous, less warm, perhaps, certainly more methodical than that of the Capuchins.

Disciples in turn of such masters as Condren, Jacquinot, and Canfeld, our Abbeys received all that was richest and choicest in these great traditions, from which, in the light of their own traditions, they will have picked out what suited them best. As water takes the shape of the vessel into which it is poured, so the Carmelites, their intimate relations with the Oratorians notwithstanding, did not change the spirit of S. Teresa for that of Bérulle, and our Abbeys generally adapted the outside teaching they now received to the exigencies of the Benedictine life.

Mère de Blémur has described from personal recollection, and with all her quaint Biblical charm, the laborious and naïve initiation of a whole reformed Abbey, the Trinité of Caen, into those spiritual exercises, which were then a mysterious novelty.

At the time of which I write the very name of mental prayer was so unknown to our religious that they had great fear of it, and, like to the Israelites, preferred that God should not speak to them lest they might die. Madame (Laurence de Budos) was scarce more enlightened in this matter than the rest, yet she resolved to try it for a time in order to judge of its utility. She communicated this design to Mère de Blémur, her *chapelaine*, honoured by her with special favour, and to put it into practice, when all the Sisters had retired to the dormitory, the two at nine o'clock betook themselves to the church to study this noble lesson and, like Nicodemus of old, to confer with Jesus by night. For a whole year this went on, she who had been instituted sentinel of her Israel keeping vigil at the gate of Wisdom while her daughters slept in security. It is in sooth probable that she penetrated into the treasure-house, since His promise (of the Divine Wisdom) was plighted: *Those that seek me early shall find me.* Her great fidelity through her whole life in this divine exercise testified to the favours bestowed on her by Our Lord. After this first year of practice she incited her beloved daughters to apply themselves as she had done to this devotion, and caused them to receive instruction thereon from a great servant of God, a Father of the Society of Jesus. . . . As soon as this pious usage had been introduced into the community and communication with God had rendered her nuns capable of interior exercises, Madame established the ten days' retreat, first practising it herself before inculcating it on others. . . . It was in consequence of these exercises that the Sacraments began to be frequented, which before had been a rare thing.[1]

The last remark is significant, in view of the fact that the Abbey had already accepted reform when they began mental prayer, and so were led on to frequent the Sacraments. The order is curious, and reminds us that the Reform in the strict sense of the word, that is, the return to the original rule, was no more than a beginning. Without affirming that the same order was followed in all convents, it is certain that the majority accepted daily meditation at fixed hours—generally half an hour morning and evening—and the yearly ten days' retreat. This innovation, although in the nature of things not raising such storms as the enclosure, community of goods, and the change of the habit, nevertheless tried more than one youthful nun, such as the artless young Sister of whom Mère de Blémur tells in her notice of Mme de Châteauneuf, Abbess of S.-Laurent of Bourges. The Abbess

never missed the time of common prayer twice a day. . . . Did it chance that any religious found herself in difficulties during the holy exercise, she would place herself beside her good Abbess, that the latter from time to time might say a word to encourage her. Several times has a young Sister been seen to nudge her three or four times during prayers, that she might hold a light to her steps.[2]

They were still children in the religious life, but their hearts were wholly opened to the Divine action, and many sacrifices prepared them for higher graces. Like all religious movements of the period, the renaissance of the interior life which succeeded Benedictine reform promised to the older Order of the Gertrudes and Mechtildes a fresh blossoming of mystics. In the following volumes we shall

[1] Blémur, II. 121–2. [2] *Ibid.*, I. 306.

meet numbers of the rare souls of the generations following the reform, but at the outset of this Reform there was an impression abroad that the age of miracles was about to dawn once more, nay, that it had dawned already.

2. *Marie de Beauvillier and the Mystics of Montmartre*

Marie de Beauvillier, even during her life, was aureoled; the incense offered her so lavishly might have intoxicated a less well-balanced mind. " Great Abbess, who hast had the glory of re-establishing the foremost of the convents of our age in the purity of past ages!" said a preacher, apostrophizing her from the pulpit. Another, Père Nicolas Caussin, said:

The most august of the emperors said that he had found a Rome of brick and had left it of marble. But you may say, with all humility, that having found a Mount of the Martyrs of mire and dung, you have caused it to shine forth in gold and azure. You have builded, adorned, enriched the house of God with material and spiritual jewels. Your zeal has effaced the blot cast by the past dissolution on the ashes of the Martyrs, has given light to things of darkness, rule to the unregulated, firmness to the unstable, devotion to the lukewarm, new life to the old, authority to the new, order and grace to all connected with your Order.[1]

The eulogy was not in reality exaggerated, although Marie de Beauvillier must not be ranked higher than her daughters or sisters in religion. Many of the noble women already mentioned in these pages surmounted no fewer difficulties, and some had possibly greater charm than she. Placed, however, on a more exalted stage than any of the others, and seconded by the most eminent spiritual leaders of her time, she certainly accomplished great things in building up Montmartre, giving the veil to 227 nuns, and sending out more than fifty to reform and found daughter-houses. With all this she was, if not the actual soul—this is beyond my knowledge and in any case I doubt it—at least the centre of a very important group of mystics which, whether rightly or wrongly, interests me more than the Abbess herself.

[1] *Les devoirs funèbres rendus à l'heureuse mémoire de Mme de Beauvillier, coadjutrice de Mme l'Abbess de Montmartre.* In spite of the emphatic apostrophe of this extract, this funeral oration, spoken over one of the nieces of Marie de Beauvillier, contains beautiful passages.

History is made up of simplifications and symbols which are sometimes hard to explain, and is disposed to concentrate all the glory of a period in the one outstanding figure. As a rule the choice of these dominant and absorbing presentments is not dictated by caprice, and it is always rash, if not sacrilegious, to tamper with official classifications. Our audacity stops short of that, and so here nothing more will be said than that in Marie de Beauvillier a magnificent life is presented to our gaze, but our description of it must remain superficial.

According to our chief authority, Mère de Blémur, Marie de Beauvillier came into the world in 1574 "at the Château de la Ferté-Hubert, in Sologne, between Orléans and Cléry, belonging to her father, M. le Comte de Sainte-Aignan." This family has made its mark in the history of mysticism. The eminent Anne-Berthe de Béthune (1637–1689), Abbess of Beaumont-les-Tours, was one of the nieces of the Abbess of Montmartre, the latter's sister Anne-Marie having married a nephew of Sully; and Paul de Beauvillier (1648–1714), the governor of the Duke of Burgundy, friend of Fénélon and disciple, although a prudent one, of Mme Guyon, was one of Marie's great-nephews; Marie de Beauvillier herself was a disciple of Benoit de Canfeld. Perhaps these facts have little significance, but they form curious connecting links between the three periods which we can distinguish in the history of French mysticism in the seventeenth century.

Towards her tenth year, Marie de Beauvillier became a novice in Beaumont-les-Tours, where her aunt, Anne Babou de la Bourdaisière, was Abbess.[1] Some time subsequently

having gone to Mme de la Bourdaisière (sister to the Abbess) to name one of her daughters (the youthful Marie), unfortunately encountered there a gentleman, who, struck with her beauty, regretted that so many charms should be hidden in a cloister. Nor did he fail to paint her own portrait for her in glowing colours, assuring her that a girl of her quality, with such advantages, was without doubt fit mate

[1] Claude de Beauvillier, Count of Saint-Aignan, had married Marie Babou de la Bourdaisière, sister of the Abbess of Beaumont. The latter, who was much attached to her niece and, as we shall see did all that was possible to prevent her acceptance of Montmartre, had her nominated coadjutrix of Beaumont. At the death of her aunt in 1613, Marie, Abbess of Montmartre and Beaumont, had to choose between them. She did not hesitate, but obtained Beaumont for her first cousin, Anne Babou, the second of the name. Cf. the excellent work of Canon Boissonnot: *La Lydwine de Touraine, Anne-Berthe de Béthune*, Paris, 1912.

for a prince. It was the poisonous breath of the serpent hoping to blight this delicate flower. She returned to Beaumont in a melancholy mood, and for long was tempted to resist her vocation, although her confessor has borne witness that she suffered without sinning.

At sixteen she took her vows (1590).

Beaumont at that time seems to have been a good example of those easygoing Abbeys nearly ripe for reform, which we mentioned above. Too limited, it seems, for new undertakings, the Abbess was religious and strict enough, maintaining fit order in her household. It is, however, difficult to explain how this cold, gray, well-meaning environment should have developed the two illustrious cousins, Marie de Beauvillier and Madeleine de Sourdis, who were there at the same time, and had hardly left Beaumont before they had to lead the movement of reform, one at Montmartre, the other at S.-Paul-les-Beauvais. The convent confessor was a downright fool; we do not know if there were any higher influences to counteract his. I am inclined to believe that Marie de Beauvillier, so resolute and quietly energetic by nature, was aided by none in her interior development. Her aunt, the Abbess, perhaps alarmed by the somewhat " pensive " silence and the " incomparable beauty " of the young girl, laid the humblest and hardest tasks on her, and much approved of her remaining invisible whenever Queen Louise, widow of Henri III, came over from Tours to Beaumont and asked for " the beautiful Madame de S.-Aignan."

However, the brother-in-law of the young girl, Pierre Forget de Fresne, Secretary of State, had obtained the Abbey of Montmartre for her, and Marie de Beauvillier consented to this, to the great anger and scandal of the Abbess of Beaumont, who was anxious to hand over her own Abbey to her niece. In vain she declared, on the word of a Minim Father, sent to the capital for this express purpose, that Montmartre " was a scandalous house, the mere entering of which was unlawful for good people."[1] The opposition was so strong that the confessor of the convent, won over by the Abbess, for three months refused absolution to the guiltless girl. In this time of perplexity she " had a mysterious dream, the meaning of which became clear some time afterwards. She seemed on the edge of a precipice, almost ready to fall over, and a Capuchin, giving her his hand, supported her." Whatever its precise meaning, this dream, which she

[1] Blémur, II. 148.

herself must have recounted later on, promised the help of Benoit de Canfeld. Similarly, a few years later, Jeanne de Chantal when anxious and perplexed had a vision, but far more definite, of François de Sales. Anyhow, after a long and painful delay, during which she had need of all her calm tenacity to resist the pressure of her aunt and the confessor, Marie de Beauvillier, having at last obtained her bulls, left Beaumont for Montmartre in the course of January 1598. Her aunt having pitilessly refused the two or three nuns whom she had wished to take with her and needed so urgently, she departed alone, " save for a poor village girl who desired much to be a nun (and who was) of a sublime devotion." All honour to this humble disciple. Such women were a feature of this age.

There is no need to dwell on the disorders which made the reform of Montmartre more urgent and more difficult than that of many other religious houses. Such details are outside my subject and would demand minute erudition. Indeed all these incidents were already more than fifty years old when Mère de Blémur began to describe them, and she could only have known them through the traditions, already more or less legendary, of the victorious reformers: so this chronicler, elsewhere probity itself, cannot here be wholly relied upon. The nuns of Montmartre, for instance, have been accused of various attempts to poison their Abbess; this is possible, probable if you like, but not certain. As to the licentious adventures hinted at by this pious pen, at once pure and audacious, we cannot call them in question, but one would like to know how far they represented an average state of things. There were at Montmartre thirty-three nuns. That five or six of them were lost to all sense of shame no doubt was sufficient to explain the retrospective horror of the reformers as they relate the sad story, but that tells us next to nothing of the other sisters who, being neither saints nor perverts, attracted no notice, and yet in all probability formed the majority of the community, commonplace enough, but at least fairly decent. It would be harsh even to pronounce them accomplices in that they silently accepted the scandals; how do we know that they were aware of what went on? Besides, what protest could be made when the culprits possessed more prestige and influence than the rest? How, for example, could the poor nuns of Maubuisson have opposed the pleasure of their Abbess, Jacqueline d'Estrées?

Montmartre indeed did not equal Maubuisson in licence. Mère de Blémur herself relates that the Archbishop of Paris, Henri de Gondi, was in ignorance of nearly all the abuses, but on learning them, he deplored and certainly endeavoured to suppress them, without, however, pronouncing for Marie de Beauvillier against the original community. Like the reformers, these others had their party in Court and city, and among them were irreproachable Christians.

All this makes us reflect. Did not the imagination of the reformers gradually combine the misdeeds of their adversaries, I mean the actual scandals in the lives of some and the obstinate resistance to reform on the part of others? As the events, some of which were difficult for pure minds to handle, receded into the past, the victorious party may have bestowed the same reprobation on lukewarm and sinners alike. But it does not matter. Religious history is neither a novel nor a melodrama; scandals neither frighten nor interest us. When we meet them in our documents we mention them, but without investing them with more importance than they deserve. We reserve our curiosity for phenomena more interior and less obtrusive.

To support her against the original nuns, foolish or otherwise, of Montmartre, Marie de Beauvillier had only four, but all four singularly attractive characters. The first was that village mystic whom she had taken from Touraine. The second reminds us a little of Jules Lemaître's "Serenus," dying a martyr for the Gospel in which he did not believe. "God," writes Mère de Blémur, "gave her (Marie de Beauvillier) a Sister of good morals who served her diligently in temporal matters, but without wishing to hear of reform. She loved her Abbess . . . (and showed it) by scrupulous devotion to the good of the house, and confined herself to that, so that it might be said that the Mother had found a good trustee in an indifferent nun." After the attempts, real or imaginary, at poisoning, this excellent creature took care that nothing should be offered the Abbess "which she herself had not first tasted, loving her so tenderly as to be willing to lay down her life for her sake."[1] This instance of independence of thought in a place soon to be the scene of the loftiest mysticism deserves attention.

The Abbey possessed also two genuinely holy nuns from Paris,

[1] Blémur, II. 151–5.

Catherine and Marie Alvequin, who had long groaned over the spiritual misery of the house and from the first day rallied to Marie de Beauvillier. Both had been in religion from about twenty years of age, the younger, Marie, having been received at Montmartre about 1578. According to her biographer the decadence of the Abbey had only set in after the civil wars which convulsed France and Paris during the closing years of the century. If this be true it would confirm our indulgent verdict. As elsewhere, the material ruin of Montmartre was the chief factor in the laxity of its poor daughters. The nuns suffered from dire poverty, and their chief preoccupation was to procure enough to eat. It is hard to realize their tribulations. Reduced to such privations and destitute of almost all spiritual succour, the Alvequin Sisters wondered whether it might not be their duty to flee.

In this uncertainty they had recourse to a holy man, by name Frère Jean, then living on Mont Valérien in the odour of sanctity. . . . This great man often had holy inspirations, and his mind, penetrated with illuminations from Heaven, perceived the designs of Providence, to declare them in all humility to those consulting him. Our two good Sisters, having extreme confidence in this servitor of God, wrote to him sometimes, discovering their innermost thoughts.[1]

They confided to him their project of fleeing to Flanders and entering some reformed convent there. The pious hermit after some time sent word to them that God was about to send to Montmartre an Abbess full of grace and courage, and that He had reserved both of them to aid her in the reform of the Abbey. So Marie de Beauvillier found them at her disposal; she confided to them the most important tasks and leaned on them constantly.

These valuable helpers nevertheless yield in importance to the eminent man who, during the first years of the heroic campaign, was the illumination and the strength of the young Abbess—Père Benoit de Canfeld. On the advice of Cardinal de Sourdis, Marie de Beauvillier took him as her director, soon recognizing in him the Capuchin of her mysterious dream. We have already described this man, one of the most important of the age. A rapid survey of his relations with the Abbess of Montmartre is enough to display him in all his

[1] *La vie et les actions de la V. M. Marie Alvequin*, by M. H. de Lacout, Sieur de Marivaut. Paris, 1687, pp. 46–7.

greatness and originality. One can picture the pair in the parlour or the confessional, she alternately eager to act or be cast down before insurmountable obstacles, he calm, detached, apart in God, seemingly forgetful of this mutinous Abbey, where delegates from the Bishop of Paris have been hooted, where the shame of recent scandals still broods, or perhaps assassination is being plotted. At need, the mystic knew well how to direct the energy of the Abbess towards some decisive initiative, but his real preoccupation does not lie there. He hardly troubles about the formidable Old Guard who have sworn to prevent reform. He sees only a single soul, which he treats as if it were the only soul in the world, as if it belonged to some unknown nun, hidden in a regular and holy community. Mère de Blémur remarks finely:

Père Benoit de Canfeld never failed her, but his care was not so much to remedy exterior disorders as to train her inwardly to bear all crosses in submission to the commands of God. He composed an exercise on the Divine Will—this mystic *chef d'œuvre* is known to us as the *Règle de perfection*—which proved of great use to Madame de Montmarte, because she practised it fervently, confessing her lightest failure therein to the Father, so that she advanced with long strides in the paths of grace, gradually surmounting the difficulties which had caused her many pains in the beginning, but the efforts (of both) entirely concerned matters which would advance the glory of Our Lord. . . . Sometimes, when conversing with her, Canfeld would suddenly fall into ecstasy, for some time rapt out of himself, without speech or movement; then, coming out of his vision, he resumed his conversation on themes so holy and elevated as to be of marvellous consolation to her.[1]

The mystic accomplished his work, and men of action took the stage. Benoit de Canfeld, on his departure from France, laid it on Père Ange de Joyeuse "to act as protector to Madame de Montmartre, which he did with great zeal." Père Honoré de Champigny also was a frequent visitor, but the honour of converting the stalwarts of Montmartre chiefly, as is but natural, belongs to the Capuchin best trained in the arts of diplomacy and war.

Pére de Joyeuse reaped a larger harvest in the community than the rest, gaining the younger nuns over by his gentleness, so that shortly

[1] Blémur, II. 156–7.

there remained but eight of the old faction living according to their private pleasure, refusing to submit to the regular observances and always opposing everything ordained by their Superior.[1]

There was still, however, much to do, and many trials remained for Marie to endure; in these she was supported by François de Sales, Père Coton, P. Gonthier, and all Madame Acarie's group. But from 1600 or 1601 the reform was accepted as a principle, and the young recruits needed for the total renovation of the old convent began to appear. After all, the real battle had lasted for no more than three years!

Montmartre presents the first example in the seventeenth century, at least in France, of a reformed Abbey of Benedictine nuns. News travelled fast in those days as in ours, and the triumph of Marie de Beauvillier was speedily the talk of the kingdom. Montmartre became, and for over fifty years remained, the sacred mount of reform, the fountain whence flowed the pure spirit of S. Benedict, the perfect model for other Abbeys. Women with a vocation flocked thither from the most distant provinces; as has been already said, the great Abbess gave the veil to more than two hundred. We see also many Abbesses sitting for long months at her feet, learning how best to conduct reform in their convents. From the mother-hive the daughters of Montmartre went forth in all directions to reform old Abbeys or found new ones. As for Marie herself, we can only call her very great and very holy, though we are unable to fill in the picture suggested by these vague epithets with any life-like strokes.

It is evident that so prodigious and long-continued a success could not be the work of an ordinary woman, but we do not know, or at least I do not know, what she really looked like. She appears to have been physically frail, which makes her tenacity and indomitable energy the more amazing; if, as is asserted, she was incomparably beautiful, I suspect she was a little aloof and forbidding. Perhaps she was a trifle selfish and less generous than we could have wished towards the most eminent of her daughters, Marguerite d'Arbouze for instance, to whom she caused suffering. With all this she remains magnificent and resplendent, for all the spiritual experts of her time bowed before her, and three generations of nuns canonised her.

[1] Blémur, II. 158.

Benoit de Canfeld after a few meetings judged her worthy of being guided into the royal road of absolute abnegation and pure love.[1] This is worth all the panegyrics. So let us be content to view her from afar, imposing, seated like a priestess on the Abbess's throne, behind clouds of incense. To give the finishing touch to her majesty, she is seen growing old at her post, seeing one after another die in turn, not only the last of the older nuns who in the end had all submitted to her, but a throng of younger ones, among them the two coadjutrices appointed by her, her niece Marie de Beauvillier and her young cousin Henriette de Sourdis. A princess of the superb House of Lorraine, Madame de Guise, a nun of S.-Pierre de Reims, was her last coadjutrix. The great Abbess died herself on April 21, 1657, at the age of eighty-three. Born two years after the massacre of S. Bartholomew, she had lived long enough to behold Louis XIV.

II. It can scarcely be doubted that so long and full a life, triumphant and splendid, was divinely ordained, not merely for the suppression of certain scandals and abuses, but also and before all for the spiritual and mystical enrichment of several generations of nuns, as indeed was assuredly the case with various other Abbesses of Reform. To all this story of Benedictine reform, as indeed to all great religious movements, we apply boldly, with a word altered, the words of S. Paul, *Omnia propter mysticos.* If, on the one hand, the intention of the workman must be judged by the finished results of his labour, it is certain on the other hand that whatever renews the interior life and spirit of prayer in any religious group tends normally to liberate grace, to encourage, force as it were, the mystic faculties of the elect few, who are, however, more numerous than is generally supposed. We say *normally*, since this law is at times suspended by the exterior or interior influence of anti-mystic prejudice, hampering divine action in souls truly holy. If all Christian effort in some wise prepares for the development of the mystic, it is no less certain that the mystics

[1] Her writings testify that she was far advanced in mystic ways. Her *Exercise divin ou pratique de la conformité de notre volonté à celle de Dieu* . . . (by R. M. D. B., Paris, 1631) is an elementary but pertinent adaptation of the teachings of Canfeld and of the pseudo-Dionysius. Here is a characteristic passage: "While speech is a human, love is a divine thing, and frequently the speech of understanding is neither perfection nor true contemplation, sometimes indeed it is contrary and hurtful to perfection. S. Denis counsels his disciple Timothy to cut short and suspend the operation of understanding" (pp. 149–50). This is the common lesson, but well put; it is strange to find the Abbess imparting this piece of high mysticism to the general body of nuns.

return with interest what they have received from us; they live no less for us than we for them. The Church universal receives of their fullness, and this is the theme of every page of our book.

The Montmartre of this period must not be thought of as a special school of mysticism under Marie de Beauvillier's direction. "School" is always an awkward word in these matters, but while there may be schools of spirituality, as for instance those of S. Ignatius or Bérulle, there can be none, strictly speaking, of mysticism. Certainly the word would be entirely inapplicable to the mystics who lived, more or less simultaneously, under Marie de Beauvillier. There were notable differences between them; there is nothing to show that all had the same director in this immense community, where each nun, it seems, had full liberty to address herself to any spiritual father she pleased. Further, I question whether the Abbess exercised a direct influence on the spiritual development of this mystic cluster. If they resembled one another, it was not in being nuns of Montmartre, but as daughters of S. Benedict, with a certain ripeness and gravity about them, a solemn religious sentiment doubtless generated and coloured by the liturgical life, the frequent readings of the Old Testament and the Fathers, the majestic Benedictine tradition. It is not the spirit of fear, nor is it quite the childlike spirit. Mère de Blémur said of one of them, Geneviève Granger, that "she belonged in a measure to the Ancient Law," even "reverencing circumcision." Some of the others give the same impression. If these views, which deserve a more attractive presentation, are fundamentally sound, these mystics of Montmartre would seem to herald the victim Abbesses, Catherine de Bar, Anne de Béthune, and their sisters of sorrow, dealt with in the following volumes. But all we know of the mystics about whom I am going to speak is little enough, and there were certainly others, probably many, totally unknown to us.

With Marguerite d'Arbouze, to be studied by herself later, the oldest of the Montmartre mystics was Marie Alvequin, whom we have already seen struggling with her sister and Marie de Beauvillier in the early days of the Reform. Her Life has been written passably by a certain Sieur de Marivaut. In 1616, accompanied by seven others, among them Adrienne Colbert, aunt of the future minister, Marie quitted her Abbey, to reform the old convent of S. Magloire, inhabited since 1572 by the Augustines Pénitentes of Paris. Marivaut reminds us very properly that we must not identify penitence and repentance, and gives a number of interesting details about the foundation of these Penitents under Charles VIII and Alexander VI. Their first house was so commodious and beautiful that Catherine de Médicis took it from them in 1572 to make it the seat of her Court. Even towards the close of the seventeenth century their Church of S. Magloire preserved "venerable relics of antiquity . . . and its figures, some immense in size, clad as penitents, casque on head, and loaded with iron chains, or others like charmingly modelled children."[1] Marivaut further relates that the Augustines enjoyed special royal favour from Charles VIII and Louis XII down to Henri IV, who "honoured these Religious by visiting them first after his entry into Paris."[2] The royal favour presently fell on Val-de-Grâce, a few steps from S. Magloire.

The reform of the Augustinians was carried through as successfully and speedily as that of Montmartre itself. We shall not describe it, but merely note the Christian *élite* of the day passing through the parlour, eager to approach the friends of God. One of Marie Alvequin's supernatural gifts at least is known to us—she could read the depths of souls, whether near her in the flesh or otherwise. She would "seek out, during the night, Sisters in their cells at the crisis of their struggles and ready to sink under the violence of the demonic assaults."[3] There is nothing to astonish us here; I find it harder to understand the rapidity with which the Paris of that day grasped that a new seer had risen in its midst.

This spirit of penetration did not limit itself to the cloister. The character of grace is to diffuse itself like an emanation of sovereign good, and it fell upon all who had the fortune to approach our incomparable Mother. Those of eminent sanctity and rare merit who most frequently sought her, and all who came to confer with her touching their conscience, were obliged to avow, after the illuminations and consolations derived from their conferences, that the Spirit of God abode in her heart. (The) greatest men of the age found sweet consolation in communing with her and sharing in her illuminations, the reverend father *Gontrand* (Condren), M. l'Abbé de Soluëres . . .

[1] Marivaut, pp. 147–8. I call attention to these curious details to remind scholars of the many points of interest in these religious works, so long neglected by the custodians of public libraries and likely to be found soon only in American collections.

[2] *Ibid.*, p. 94.

[3] *Ibid.*, pp. 166–7.

M. Charton the Grand Penitentiary, M. de Gamache, his first cousin, a doctor of the Sorbonne, Mme Zacharie (Acarie), finally M. de Bérulle and an infinity of others (all anxious to profit by) that gift of penetration by which were unveiled to them hidden and individual things in their daily lives.[1]

Anne of Austria herself was among Mère Alvequin's friends and besought her many times, as she did all the saints of her acquaintance, to obtain for her, for Louis XIII, and for France, the miracle so long and passionately desired by innumerable monasteries. On this subject Marivaut has a characteristic phrase which deserves to be remembered, one which later was to be plagiarized by Victor Hugo writing of the birth of the King of Rome.

I venture to say that, although other holy souls likewise solicited Heaven by their sighs and swelled by their tears that fortunate cloud which would presently rain down that rare gift from the heavens, Louis XIV . . . she (Marie Alvequin), by the ardour of her prayers and the fervour of her devotions, hastened the birth of the Dauphin.[2]

Another less usual trait of this mystic was her love of sacred images. On the top story of the convent rebuilt by her was a great gallery "convenient for the nuns to walk in at the hours permitted." "At one end of this promenade" the Abbess had constructed, either of bronze or stone, "a grotto of the Magdalene representing her pouring forth torrents of tears . . . at the other end, Bethany, with Magdalene at the feet of a figure of Our Lord." In another part of the house she had placed the Risen Christ forbidding Magdalene to touch Him, "as though she would not that the Resurrection Joy should blunt the nail-prints" of the Passion.[3]

Of a higher type certainly than Marie Alvequin was Marie Granger, novice-mistress at Montmartre where she had come in 1617, and from 1630 to 1636 foundress and Superior of the Abbey of Montargis. During her short life she made more impression on her contemporaries by the exterior manifestations of her grace. Mère de Blémur wrote her Life with especial fervour and the reputation of this

[1] Marivaut, pp. 168–71. It is interesting to note that as the Benedictines at Montmartre had for many years their "lay brothers" so the Augustinian Pénitentes had their begging brethren, living outside the convent, and taking their vows at the grille before the Abbess and the Convent confessor.

[2] *Ibid.*, pp. 185–6.

[3] *Ibid.*, pp. 133–8.

now forgotten mystic must have been great for them to think of using her relics to touch the brows of the possessed of Loudun. She was a delicate, suffering creature, tormented by terrible maladies and, like so many other mystics, had often been the object of dread, of contempt, or of cruelty.

Before she was Superior she was regarded as an epileptic, and this mortification, keen though it was, rejoiced her, seeing herself abandoned by all her world, everyone fearing the contagion of so dreadful an evil. She then would adore the cruel dereliction of her Bridegroom, treated by His Father as a leper, and she could mourn with Him when her friends stood far from her. She bore all such approbrium without a murmur, knowing that the sinner is a spiritual epileptic. As long as she ruled, she endured perpetual opposition; her extraordinary graces were condemned and those who reverenced her sanctity were told that she was deluded. What especially tormented her was that, being convinced of her nothingness, she held with her own enemies that it was possibly true that her lights were but illusions. In this state all was a terror to her and she even feared herself.[1]

In one of the too few writings of hers preserved she cries:

I am tormented with blasphemies, I hear a crying in the ears of my soul that I am a fool and demented to run after a God Who flees from me, to seek a Beloved Who has no love for me.[2]

Sometimes at night " she would cast herself on the ground, no longer being able to endure her bed and crying in the words of the most afflicted of men, ' Who will show me favour to finish what He has begun to destroy; let Him not spare me in my sorrows, let me not disprove the words of the Saint, It is time, my God, that sin should make an end! ' " How deep and true all this rings!

Nevertheless if Thou hast vowed my ruin, I accept this decree, submit to Thine ordinance. Yet at least grant that I take not my sins with me. Suffering is not so insupportable to me as any stain, and the fires of hell would be well pleasing did I but burn there as a victim, who has not fallen out of grace.[3]

What a fine passage! I should say, if such thoughts were permissible in the face of such anguish. All unheeded by herself, she

[1] Blémur, I. 210–11. [2] *Ibid.*, I. 224. [3] *Ibid.*, I. 225.

developed visible graces which roused in her circle either devotion or jealousy.

When she could not resist the compelling drawings of God, and her transports could no longer be hidden, her confusion was great, and to conceal the divine workings she wished them to believe her swooning. If it chanced that she was rapt into ecstasy in the parlour . . . the nun who was in her secret would bring her wine, feigning that she had fainted. Thus this excellent being hid all that would have made her shine in men's eyes, even scratching her arms till they bled to prevent trances. She desired to feel the thorns that crowned her Master, but she did not wish them to take even the shape of a diadem. The shadow of glory was sufficient to terrify her.[1]

This desire of guarding their divine secret is indeed a feature of all true mystics. A sort of modesty, a profound humility, and the fear always more or less haunting them that they may be the victims of illusion make it intolerable that they should be held up as a spectacle, as is often the case, to a world always inquisitive about the supernatural, even when it pretends not to believe. Since a mysterious incident during her first years at Montmartre, Marie Granger found herself particularly the object of this curiosity, the more painful to sensitive natures for its so often being coarse and morbid.

Her charity so increased that it dilated her heart, which could no longer contain it, so violently as to raise two ribs, which for a couple of years remained two fingers higher than the others, and through life continued to rise and fall according to the movements of her love. How great it must have been thus to enlarge the heart, raise the chest, and produce a miracle unexampled in previous ages! Several of the nuns, eye-witnesses of this fact, attest it.[2]

Marie Granger's director, Père Rabasse, a Franciscan friar of rare sanctity, attached perhaps too much importance to this miracle, at least spoke about it more than he should have done. For the Queen-Mother, passing through Montargis, where was Marie Granger, formerly known to her as Montmartre,

came to the convent and heard Mass in choir, then commanding her ladies to leave her, entered the parlour to confer with Père Rabasse in the presence of the good Superior. The servant of God had no sooner begun to speak of the spiritual life than the Mother fell into ecstasy,

[1] Blémur, I. 201. [2] *Ibid.*, I. 202.

which gave Père Rabasse opportunity to relate to her Majesty the extraordinary graces bestowed by Our Lord on this soul, in particular the elevation of her ribs. The Queen wished to touch them but could not through the thick habit. The Abbess came to herself, unconscious of what had been passing, and for two hours talked with our august princess . . . (who) promised her protection and commanded her to apply to herself in all things where royal authority might be required. And in fact when subsequently Madame de Montmartre was minded to withdraw the nuns (whom she had lent for the foundation of Montargis) the Queen had the goodness to acquaint her by letter that she would do her a favour by leaving them with Mère Granger.[1]

I have kept the last lines, which give a vivid description of one of the numerous occasions on which the Abbesses were indebted to the Court. Otherwise the story embarrasses me a little. Blessings on the thick habit which checked the joint indiscretion of Père Rabasse and the Queen! Marie Granger, doubtless more embarrassed than we, hid herself as best she could from human eyes.

While she yet dwelt at Montmartre, the Cave of S. Denis was the scene of her retreats and ecstasies, where she would remain for four or five hours . . . and would have often passed the whole night had not some nuns in her confidence taken care to fetch her away. After she had won from God the boon that these abstractions should not be outwardly visible, she was nightly visited by Our Lord, and when all human voices were silent she had communion with Him.[2]

One could not learn precisely what she saw in her ecstasies . . . (unless it were by a word that once fell from her that) when beholding sacred things . . . she could not but pity the ignorance of the artists who copied so badly originals so perfect.[3]

When she returned to earth she lived but to suffer.

She did things impossible to describe: enough to say that for a long time she drank out of a skull, and when very thirsty was content to look at the water without swallowing a drop, in order to increase her thirst. Fruit being dangerous in her state of health, she sought to look on it, and offer the privation to Our Lord. (Severe on herself and on others), she had scruples about smelling a flower, and seeing a nun pause before one could not refrain from reproving her.[4]

[1] Blémur, I. 211.
[2] *Ibid.*, I. 221.
[3] *Ibid.*, I. 221.
[4] *Ibid.*, I. 230.

Finally, on her death-bed, she encountered a trial of which even her ingenuity in self-tormenting had not conceived. The confessor of this death-hour

> was a man so coarse and ignorant as to be fitter to chagrin souls than to inspire them with sentiments of piety. It is true that a Father of the Society of Jesus, who was preaching in the town, was brought to her, but, as he was a stranger to her, she had not the comfort she could have wished. She was fated to die in dereliction, and thus to honour by her own condition the abandonment of the Son of God.[1]

Marie Granger is to be reckoned among the precursors and precise anticipators of that devotion to the Heart of Jesus which a Visitandine of Paray-le-Monial, Marguerite-Marie Alacoque, was to preach towards the end of the seventeenth century. About 1630—Mère de Blémur writes in 1679—

> our Divine Saviour appeared to her, holding a cross in His hand, with a heart pierced with three nails and a crown of thorns; it was as though this heart dropped blood. "My daughter," said Our Lord, "I give you this coat of arms, and desire you never to take another. By the Cross you will triumph." The servant of God accepting it in gratitude caused a seal to be cut, still in use to-day among the religious of Montargis.[2]

As we remarked above, the boundaries of the Montmartre group are not clearly marked, and so we may rightly speak of Geneviève Granger here, though she never belonged to Montmartre. She had been professed in the Abbey of Hautbruyère, belonging to the Order of Fontevrault; in 1630 she came to her sister at Montargis, to take her place worthily from 1636 to 1674. Equally devoted to both sisters, who obviously have a special fascination for her, Mère de Blémur has perhaps more comprehension for the second, whose interior life was less miraculous.

I have already said that this exquisite chronicler of the Benedictine mystics feels, or pretends to feel, a curious embarrassment, when in her progress she meets pure mysticism. Had Jacqueline de Blémur never personally known these sublimities of devotion? or did her eminently well-poised temper fear to paint the special graces under too favourable colours, which might dazzle young readers? or did she share or simply not wish to provoke the almost universal suspicion

[1] Blémur, I. 234. [2] *Ibid.*, I. 204–5.

of such things at the time she wrote? In any case, it is a pleasure to follow her excursion into such sealed gardens, hesitating, curious, eager in spite of herself. And we must study attentively the luminous page she wrote on the " States " of Geneviève Granger.

Geneviève, like many others, was a mystic in spite of herself. This doubtless explains, at least in part, why she is such a favourite of Mère de Blémur. Rather alarmed than attracted by the poignant example of her sister Marie, but irresistibly drawn to graces of the same kind, she " sometimes said that she had had great reluctance to surrender herself and that she thought there had never been a soul more stubbornly set against entering the paths of the interior life."[1] For her there was no question of, like Marie, avoiding too startling favours from Heaven, on the contrary she was to allow herself to be conducted in a passivity and apparent darkness which must have been especially trying to this clear, vivid and resolute soul. Mère de Blémur has described this immobility and twilight of the soul with sure pen.

Those who knew the state of grace of this Blessed Mother testified that she possessed God in a manner incomprehensible to herself, and that the more He dwelt in her, the more she felt her nakedness and the impurity of the creature. She had a treasure and yet felt herself poor. . . . This saintly virgin had not sufficient light to recognize the graces planted within her by God. . . . The workings of God tended to kill all else in her soul and to place her in the attitude of a victim always prepared for sacrifice and destruction. She arrived at that blessed passivity when the soul simply leaves God to act, without seeing or knowing what is passing within it. . . . The purity of God deprived her of all things, taking from her even the consciousness of her own deprivation. She was not aware of her own condition nor of the holy use she was making of it. All took place in her soul without her noticing it. She believed that prayer and the presence of God were not for her. Darkness hid the interior way from her and helped her to lose herself entirely in God.[2]

I could wish no other words than these to bring home to the most prejudiced minds the reality and excellence of the mystical gift. " The purity of God deprived her of all things "—I know only too well, we can hardly give a meaning to these splendid words; but we feel instinctively that this is no bombast, and if studying them patiently we try to illuminate them by the light of our own most sacred experi-

[1] Blémur, II. 441.

[2] *Ibid.*, II. 439–40.

ences, we feel also that, far from becoming estranged from humanity by this mysterious dereliction, the mystics are rather drawn nearer and shown the extreme possibilities of experience. What beauty, even of the material kind, that does not in a sense demand that the gazer empty himself in order to receive it better and model himself on it? The incredulous reader must forgive quotations which at first seem to him strange, even absurd. All our mystics have shared Geneviève Granger's feelings and they have striven, each in his own fashion, to formulate them, using a host of subtle turns to bend our language to express what is at once most human and most divine in our hearts. Now let Geneviève tell us again, this time with an arch appreciation which so far I have not found in her.

In July 1666 (she was then aged sixty-six) it was whispered in the ear of her heart that as yet she had not holy liberty in God. She was shown in detail what retarded her progress. All ordinary practices were forbidden—meditations, desires, aspirations; only morning and evening prayers were left, and they in a very short form. Thus stripped bare, she laughed at herself saying gaily to a close friend: "Have you ever seen anything like this? I am not allowed to think of the saints except as hidden in God." Some time after this she openly confessed to the same friend that, having passed many days without doing aught but lose all in God, she became aware of a notable progress and that assuredly He was doing all in her soul, which in pursuing this method willed to do nothing of itself, and that one moment of the Divine operation was worth more than a lifetime of creaturely activity.[1]

All this is pure crystal. A few touches of the pastel and the portrait will be finished to perfection. Thus stripped of all, even of herself,

she had, however, the sense not to plunge the Community into such a state, which was beyond their capacity of grace, knowing that, as the saying goes, one must not try to be good beyond one's powers. . . . She rejoiced when others aspired to this happiness, but forced none to try it. . . . "I endeavour to preserve peace in their souls" (was a favourite saying of hers).[2]

In these words the high-water mark of direction and religious rule is reached. To show once more the stages and vicissitudes of the mystic tradition, we add that for more than twenty years (1652–74) Mère Granger had under her guidance that very attractive and lofty,

[1] Blémur, II. 440–1.

[2] *Ibid.*, II. 439.

but disquieting, person who, as Mme Guyon, was to cause such a stir one day.[1]

III. Among all the mystics of Montmartre, at least those who are known to us, Charlotte Le Sergent (1604–1677) may be considered, next to Marguerite d'Arbouze, the most sublime. Here again we owe the outline of her life to Jacqueline de Blémur, who merely quotes and summarises from the private papers of Charlotte Le Sergent, and consequently is able to break more boldly the seal of reserve which she generally respects in these delicate matters. Her little book, unfortunately now very rare, is one of the pearls of French religious literature, deserving to rank beside the Life of Catherine de Jésus by Mère Madeleine de S.-Joseph. Save for the ill-omened date of its publication, 1685, it is hard to understand why such a work only excited the interest of a select few, and soon sank into an oblivion so complete that even the name of Charlotte Le Sergent is absent from the recent and otherwise very erudite biography of one of her most illustrious scholars, Anne-Berthe de Béthune, Abbess of Beaumont-les-Tours. Nevertheless I believe that anyone with an inquiring mind who loved the light would read at a sitting this limpid book, transparent as a Dialogue of Berkeley. For once Mère de Blémur's pen has forsworn its eloquence; there is no trace of lyrical flights of devotion, *à la* Bossuet; I was going to say not a drop of unction. The region in which Charlotte Le Sergent dwelt, and would have liked to root her disciples, was the barest and most despoiled of which anyone could dream; the centre or the point of the soul, the apex of that abyss where God trysts with His creature. In this rare atmosphere, imagination and sensibility and the reasonings of reason are motionless, save for imperceptible pulsations immediately repressed. Only the spirit of the spirit, the soul of the soul, there moves freely, dilates, and realizes itself. Let men debate these experiences as much as they like, let them say that at this altitude, or in these depths, the mystics find only themselves, that at this rendezvous assigned, as they are firmly convinced, to them by God, they descend or soar merely to converse with their own image—they are wrong, I believe, but in any case the experience remains real, magnificent, and worthy to arouse deep

[1] Born at Montargis in 1648, Jeanne-Marie Bouvier de la Motte was placed at the age of four in the charge of the Benedictines. As a girl, and then as a young wife, she remained in intimate relations with the Abbess.

interest in anyone who claims Terence's *homo sum* as his own. Whether or no Mère Charlotte Le Sergent penetrated further than others in such experiences, she describes them with extraordinary clearness. Her whole interior life consisted in this entire self-abnegation, all her religious activity in heroic struggles against our surface activities and the methods that govern them. In other respects her portrait lacks colour and her story picturesque incidents. But this does not seem to matter, so fascinated are we by the depths of this transparent soul. Let us be content to record that she was born in Paris in 1594, and died at Montmartre in 1677, after carrying out confidential missions in several houses of her Order. She had much intellectual power and good sense, gaiety, vigour, energy, and vivacity. She had tasted the world and found it pleasant. When she was quite young, she tells us, "God pressed her closely, and she on her side was frantically impatient at this, being even tempted to blaspheme and to such violent evil that she almost resolved to do her worst, that the Divine Lover might withdraw Himself and leave her to live at her ease."

She was not quite fifteen when she began to yield to the Heavenly promptings.

> Being one day in the church of S.-Jean-en-Grève, she perceived a poor charcoal-burner kneeling before the crucifix with his eyes full of tears. Accustomed to get amusement from passers-by, her sense of humour was tickled by the blackness of this man, but God gave a turn to her thoughts, touching her with emotion at the tears of this poor artisan and guiding her own gaze to the image of the Crucified. It seemed to her as though a voice spoke to her soul in accents imperative as sweet, bidding her contemplate the Divine sufferings and forsake her miserable condition. At that moment . . . she received a gift of lofty devotion with so keen an impression of the pains of Our Lord, as to penetrate her whole being.[1]

Some time afterwards, "she was told . . . jestingly, that it was the fashion to go to the Jesuits, to a certain confessor who was skilled in discovering the thoughts of hearts. She wished to test him as did others," but such an attempt complicated matters in this strange child of Paris, torn between the amusement she still sought and the grace that possessed her and was already beginning its work of simplifica-

[1] *Abrégé de la vie de la V. M. Charlotte Le Sergent*, Paris, 1685, pp. 10–12.

tion. The Jesuit quickly perceived that he had to do with an uncommon soul, but he either could not discover her vocation or judged it too precocious. He applied the Ignatian method with her, directing her expecially "to examine with care the depths of her soul; she shuddered thereat, fearing the sight of her portrait," but as her ardent nature rendered full obedience, "she experienced inconceivable hells and mental tortures, and, instead of the holy freedom of Our Lord's service, felt herself in slavery. She undertook at first to analyse all that was passing within her, jotting down on paper every thought," and re-living "every past temptation with increased wretchedness, because having a faint inclination to the inner life of devotion she felt herself drawn to that side in the interior of her soul, while all the rest of her was still in revolt," through these laborious and discouraging exercises.[1]

This experience, several times to be repeated in Charlotte's life, is very significant. If I am not mistaken, Mère de Blémur insists on it with obvious satisfaction. She herself, though never speaking in the *éloges* of the Jesuits without sincere respect, rarely misses an opportunity of showing her dislike for over-regulated prayer. Filled with the Benedictine spirit, she favoured "holy liberty" in all pious exercises outside the liturgical office. Charlotte, at any rate, having endeavoured about this time "to use a complicated method in a book . . . found no results but obscurity and no interior unction."[2] Here is another precious testimony; this great mystic in the making, would come later to understand that God willed "to be her director in the stead of any creature."[3] Her sufferings during her first years in the convent enlightened her on that point.

She herself wished to enter the Carmelite Order, but her parents insisted upon Montmartre which, although reformed, appealed more to the ambitions and social vanity of the important Le Sergent family. The young girl obeyed. "She was still so simple as to assure herself that, if the Lord did not approve of the change, He would cause her to be borne away by angels to Carmel."[4] The angels did not come; yet it is evident that her special gifts would have caused less astonishment and roused less resistance among the Carmelites than among the daughters of S. Benedict. The latter, indeed, were very severe on

[1] *Abrégé*, pp. 14–16.
[2] *Ibid.*, pp. 20–1.
[3] *Ibid.*, p. 33.
[4] *Ibid.*, p. 34.

their new novice, who struck them as difficult and more or less fantastic. She was very young for her age when she took the veil, and ignorant of almost everything in the religious life. But she was already drawn towards the heights of prayer and loved solitude; her one gift was the rare faculty of recollection. The routine of the convent fatigued her and actually seemed odious. This bad disposition, continues Mère de Blémur, went so far as to inspire in her distaste for the holiest and most delightful things, such as the plain-chant of the church and sacred ceremonies. Everyone knows the universal attraction of the Divine Offices at Montmartre, how people run together from all parts and how all are charmed, but our postulant could not endure them. She requested indeed to be received as lay-sister in order to escape the obligations of the Divine Office on the choir Sisters, but this was refused her.[1]

So the lively child sowed her spiritual wild oats, disturbing all around, including the Mother Abbess, who did not spare rebukes. They certainly did right in making this innocent rebel obey all the requirements of the Rule. The wild shoots of mysticism must be unrelentingly pruned even on the most promising stems, and much unhappiness would have been avoided had Mme Guyon, sixty years later, been subjected to similar constraints. But to stifle a soul is not to train it. The very exaggerations of Charlotte Le Sergent sufficiently indicated the Will of God for the development of this novice, and the necessity of more insight and elasticity in training her. They required " that she should pray by method, and solely on the heads of meditation read to the novices. . . . It was Greek to her. The captivity in which her novice-mistress held her, as regards devotional exercises, was for her a species of tyranny; the more they tried to impart illumination to her the denser waxed her ignorance."[2] Such obvious incapacity did not spring either from lack of mortification or from caprice. Surely it was grace itself resisting " methods." They were rending this young conscience needlessly, in forcing it to choose between an irresistible drawing and those who gave orders in God's name. The trial was so severe that Charlotte began to fear she would " lose her wits " and " to avoid such disgrace she sought distraction in exterior things." But with her, as with many others, these diversions were no more successful than the efforts she had made to

[1] *Abrégé*, pp. 30, 31. [2] *Ibid.*, pp. 30–2.

get used to the ordinary methods and thus to shake off the divine constraint. She was anxious not to spoil her life.

Her inclination for the Carmelites reviving more strongly than ever, she found happiness only in her sleep, because she dreamed every night that she was among those holy virgins. But the pleasanter the dream the sadder she was that it was so soon over.[1]

This delightful childishness reassures us as to Charlotte's destiny; like all genuine mystics, she possessed that soft obstinacy before which sooner or later all resistance must yield.

To follow the stages of her development one by one would take too long. "This virgin who was one day to conduct so many in the paths of grace passed through every degree of the spiritual life in order that no secret of it should be unrevealed to her." A mighty Hand paralysed her, "cutting her short," when curiosity or natural eagerness would have swept her along too fast or too far. From the outset "she was led to a strong and tender love for the sacred Humanity"; then the time came

that she was swallowed up in God. It is true that, at intervals, she would be rapt towards the sacred soul of Jesus Christ . . . that as it were overflowed its holy floods into her own, thus bringing about that annihilation so necessary for persons who aspire towards true perfection. Her condition was then an interior detachment and a great conformity to Jesus Christ's suffering, but, although it was so high, at last even this sensible occupation, in which the superior powers of her soul had little enough light, was taken from her. Her understanding was suddenly translated into a vast landscape so luminous as to delight her, (where) secret mysteries were explained to her with such clarity and certainty that it was impossible for her to conceive a doubt.[2]

So she gradually left the surface of her soul behind; but she was yet far from the supreme simplification towards which she was unwittingly moving. "She herself confessed that there was much impurity in this way, as yet unrecognized by her, so greatly was she absorbed in her illuminations. 'The curiosity and vanity of my mind,' said this humble creature, 'the support and attachment which I found in my lights, left my will cold and sluggish.'"[3] This is clear enough, but how it comes about that these "lights" are stimulating rather

[1] *Abrégé*, p. 34. [2] *Ibid.*, pp. 43, 54–5. [3] *Ibid.*, pp. 59–60.

than nourishing, and that this atmosphere is cold and sterile, Charlotte must try to explain to us herself.

We have seen the point to which the preceding stages had led her, namely such a detachment from all images and everything sensible, that contemplation of the Gospel scenes was only at intervals permissible and beneficial to her. At this point the "luminous landscape" opened out before her. I cannot describe this region, but assuredly it must not be identified with the *templa serena* of the philosophers nor even with the more devout regions where Malebranche heard the Word, for it is a region at once intellectual and mystical in the proper sense of the word. The Divine Presence, to come in the closest possible contact with which is the whole of mysticism, is here more directly and concretely, if the expression be allowed, than in the contemplation of the Gospel, yet it is as yet veiled by the intellectual speculations provoked by itself. Hence the first joy of Charlotte is quickly followed by a feeling of exhaustion and coldness, as the Divine movement brusquely brings night upon a soul still too curious, too full of self-love.

It was then in fact that the Uncreated Wisdom, wishing her to enter on a way of simple intelligence, drew a curtain through which she might only behold in a simple gaze the divine realities; that this impression might kindle in her heart an ardent desire for the possession of God and that it might please Him to remove the obstacles hindering His purest operations in her soul.

This fresh condition was not one of entire darkness, and indeed many mysteries were then rendered more intelligible to her, but

she regarded as a temptation this eagerness to know these things by her own lights, at a time when this new approach of God and her sudden response were ineffably impressed on her soul. (But soon) the curtain grew too thick for any perception. She was as though relegated to deep and dim caverns, with interior terrors of meeting there some object of death or annihilation.[1]

The like experiences are to be found in most mystics, but this descent of the soul into the depths of itself has never been portrayed with so sure and touching a stroke.

By what tokens the Montmartre community perceived Charlotte's

[1] *Abrégé*, pp. 60–1.

interior progress is not recorded, but such souls shed rays around them, attracting some, irritating others, and inevitably raising up both persecutors and disciples.

She had already composed exercises and meditations which proved helpful to several. She conferred with some Sisters and in all simplicity revealed her thoughts to them. These innocent conferences were like Joseph's dreams. The convent took alarm and a whole Visitation was devoted to the matter. During the storm the servant of God was placed in an infirmary cell under the charge of the infirmarian with orders that none should speak with her. They were not so strictly observed, that some Sisters were not adroit enough to keep her informed of what was going on. The Visitor had given express commands that all the papers of this poor Mother should be placed in his hands, a sore humiliation for her, who had never meant that her private outpourings should see the light. At everything else she laughed. Finally she was summoned before him. They wished to prove to her . . . that she was badly deluded

as regards dogma, but she defended herself with ease, and the Visitor, not as terrible as he wished to appear, got out of the difficulty by a compromise in the Italian manner, scolding the poor nun in full Chapter, " though in private he had sufficient prudence not to discredit her and to permit those whom she had aided to continue to use her help."[1] It must be owned that in all this, as well as in other persecutions endured by Charlotte Le Sergent at Montmartre, the Abbess Marie de Beauvillier does not show to advantage. Perhaps the pressure of certain jealous and spiteful nuns, who had already incited their own directors against the gentle mystic, was too much for her; perhaps she herself objected to a too marked elevation above the common level. Yet she was an upright and godly woman, and when she understood that in this instance she was opposing the divine operation, if she did not encourage Charlotte, she at least left her free to act and even to influence others within and without the Abbey.

It cannot be repeated too often, that even the worst annoyances are as nothing for the mystics, compared with their interior torments that end in detaching them from the creature and from self. Charlotte's " natural temper had a horror of the passive state." " What," she said, " do nothing, have no sentiments or affections, renounce all

[1] *Abrégé*, pp. 68–70.

connection, all knowledge, walk blindfold through darkness and the shadow of death!" Mère de Blémur resumes with excellent good sense:

The depths of her soul found ineffable delights in such deprivation, repugnant though it was to her senses. . . . A certain director who told her to beware of remaining idle in the precious times of devotion nearly succeeded in doing lasting harm, for, endeavouring to obey, she multiplied acts of prayer, while God on His side revealed to her the beauty of a soul desirous to be nought save pure capacity for Divine operation. She suffered much and at last sought a Capuchin Father, who made her see that God called her to the prayer of simple regard, and that she was in great error in opposing the impurity of human acts to the divine work. This word for her was as the breaking of a sun through the fogs of her spirit. From that moment she put herself under this Father's direction.

Benoit de Canfeld had directed the reform at Montmartre, and it was left to another religious of the same Order to liberate the great mystic of this Abbey. It was only a coincidence, but worth noting. Under the direction of this Father—they ought to have told us his name—Charlotte

after six months of exercises continually broken by the eagerness of her natural temper with its tendency to desire to understand all things, resolved finally to annihilate all that opposed the drawings of grace . . . and forthwith seemed to feel in her inmost soul a very secret and certain approach to God. . . . God made a void in her soul, as when one sweeps with a besom all impurities from a room. Indeed she felt so lightened that she could breathe freely and without fear.[1]

This strenuous apprenticeship had probably lasted several years, but perhaps not so long as Mère de Blémur's detailed analysis seems to imply.

As novice-mistress at Montmartre and Prioress elsewhere, Charlotte Le Sergent seems to have ruled over a number of disciples worthy of herself. Marguerite Guérin, for instance, was exalted to "the highest stage of passive contemplation, though she knew it not, calling the effect simply 'loss of consciousness.'"[2] Marie Pavin "used to be advised in sleep of what she should do on the morrow (and) was never mistaken."[3] Catherine Guiette, who belonged to

[1] *Abrégé*, pp. 71–5. [2] *Ibid.*, p. 175. [3] *Ibid.*, p. 192.

Mme Acarie's group, and Anne-Berthe de Béthune, were others. It would take too long to enumerate them all. I must also, to my regret, make only a passing mention of Charlotte's brother, who joined the Minims of the Place Royale when still very young, and whose Life she wrote. He was less subtle than Charlotte, but had almost the same grace. He said of himself:

Certain gifts have been bestowed upon me, which make me see without seeing and taste without tasting that which has not name nor taste nor savour nor colour. It is a thing above all intelligence and being and beyond power of words. A curtain is drawn aside and I behold so many beauties, truth and rarities that I apprehend more in a moment than I should in ten years of study. When reading I oft break off to kneel, lost in my nothingness before the contemplation of God present with me.

He beheld himself gradually consumed like a sacrifice, losing something each day of his natural being, bearing patiently, however painful to the outward man, the workings of grace. He said sometimes to his sister that he was made to walk a path unknown to him, blindfold, knowing no other thing than that God was all his desire and everything else pure nothingness. . . . Some years before his death he has lost sight of self, God was all his vision. All else might be taken from him without his expending a sigh on his own deprivation.[1]

We have some of the letters written by Charlotte Le Sergent to the many who consulted her on spiritual things, containing much that is beautiful and instructive, no doubt dictated from memories of the personal experiences described above. A Superior having asked "her opinion concerning a remarkable nun under her authority," Charlotte replies:

You are laughing at me, my very dear daughter, to submit such a proposition to me. . . . I know only that all creaturely operation is impurity and that it is for God to glorify Himself. . . . But alas! this is language little comprehended by the poor intelligence of His slave! Let him hear, who can! (a favourite expression of hers). It is true that the soul may be as though lost without knowing when she is or what is passing within her. She dares not so much as move. . . . (As to her in question) there are persons for whom one cannot lay down rules, but rather abandon them to the laws of love and leave love to whatever empire it pleases him to assume over them. . . . It

[1] *Abrégé*, pp. 157–9.

seems to me as though she had not yet lost sight of her spiritual interests, which is an error in the way of nothingness; lead her, my dear daughter . . . in no wise to depend on her illuminations.[1]

To a monk who appears to have styled her his directress, she replies in noble style:

The title which your charity imposed upon me in your last letter, Reverend Father, would silence me for ever, were I not pressed to praise our good God for His manner of manifestation to your soul, with which I own that mine is closely linked, *in the Heart of Jesus Christ*. But, my Father, I conjure you not to reverse the established order of the Church, by thus speaking to a simple, ignorant nun such as myself, as though I merited any high rank in your estimation. I will indeed tell you my thoughts, but not in anyway claim authority. May God preserve me from such presumption so contrary to His spirit! Certain souls He brings together to aid each other in mutual love, without authority other than this union of grace.[2]

How firmly and well these women write! The exceptional importance of M. de Bernières-Louvigny in the history of French mysticism is generally recognized. When we meet him again, as we shall before long, let us remember that he was one more of Charlotte's disciples.

Everyone was acquainted with the extraordinary merits of the late M. de Bernières, of whom it may be said without exaggeration that the fame of his goodness had flown overseas. Nevertheless this man, consulted as an oracle by all and so divinely illumined, did not scruple to submit his revelations to the judgement of our venerable Mother. In an answer to one of his letters she remarks: " My soul is not only humbled, but annihilated, in receiving your dear letter." Nevertheless she answers him, incapable as she feels of doing so: " It seems to me as if your soul *stoops too much* in contemplating itself and the divine workings within it. In my opinion it ought to be more simple, to attach itself solely to the Author of these workings and not to their effects. . . . I know what I wish to say better than I can explain it. I desire solely that you should let all good gifts flow back into the source of good, without pausing over even the most remarkable. . . . One must practise a bare faith raised above all sense-aid, this virtue having the power to fix the soul in God, above all the *tintamarre* (riot) of the senses, permitted by the Divine Wisdom in order that each may recognize his own weakness, were he left to himself. Such contemplation is the preservative against a secret self-esteem prone

[1] *Abrégé*, pp. 109–12. [2] *Ibid.*, pp. 132–3.

to form itself in the human soul. . . . If the soul wills to act by itself, it opposes its low and debasing action to that of God. This desire to act is a remnant of those bygone desires which must needs be annihilated and lost in God to leave the soul free."[1]

Unweariedly she enjoins him "to concentrate less on himself and not even to think of his spiritual interests." In another letter "she congratulates him on his spiritual lethargy and rejoices at the captivity of his powers."[2] Yet it must not be imagined that this direction never touched earth. In her, as in all these mystics, heavenly wisdom and common sense went hand in hand. Influenced by an impetuous director and certain rather dramatic aspirations, Bernières, who was very rich, contemplated renouncing all that he had and turning mendicant. Charlotte neither approves nor disapproves this fine plan, but advises riper consideration.

One must not, my dear brother, depend on the advice of one director, whose guidance is apt to be more ardent than well-balanced. I believe him to be a very good man, but too inclined to lean on his individual illuminations, and favourable to hasty and unexamined execution of them.[3]

But, of all the pupils of Charlotte Le Sergent, Catherine de Bar was dearest to her, and most nearly moulded in her own likeness. Charlotte had known beforehand the particular vocation of this future "victim," whose genius and apostolate we shall study with admiration in the sequel.

Being in prayer this morning (she wrote) I beheld you in the arms of Jesus Christ, like a victim offered by Him to His Father for Himself, in such wise that your soul was motionless, suffering in all simplicity His workings within it. . . . You have nought to fear, the something which will separate you from all sweetness is, I think, the simplest and surest step on your path. . . . I say to you that which was laid upon me without comprehending it, being in a state wherein I have nothing, nothing, nothing, save a certain desire which wills that which God wills and is ready for all.[4]

Catherine de Bar, or, to call her by her name in religion, Mechtilde du Saint-Sacrement, had been driven from her Abbey of Rambervillers by the war and taken refuge for some time at Montmartre in

[1] *Abrégé*, pp. 136–41.
[2] *Ibid.*, pp. 150–1.
[3] *Ibid.*, p. 145.
[4] *Ibid.*, pp. 116–18.

1641. Here she was especially drawn to the youthful Anne-Berthe de Béthune and especially to Mère Le Sergent, and after her departure she did not cease to correspond with them. Montmartre, its great Abbess and the other Sisters, left on her ineffaceable recollections. "If there be a Paradise on earth," she wrote to Elizabeth de Brême, "I say that it is Montmartre." She goes on to add somewhat surprisingly:

I know that you have an idea that reform had not touched it; I can assure you that it is so strictly practised by the holy religious there that their fervour would enrapture you.[1]

To a nun of Montmartre, probably Charlotte herself, she wrote:

Try my heart and see whether it could be base enough to fail you. Aye, I ask as a token of your goodness that you would treat me as a rag under your feet, for I am more at your service than any rag could be.[2]

Charlotte on her side declares:

My soul had this morning some little intelligence of (God's) guidance of you. I saw your whole being absorbed in a light, before which your own vanished, and I saw in that luminous region a light without shadows in which the creature was no more and God was all. The soul remained in the arms of its Lord, without knowing or perceiving it. . . . Ah, God, how great a desire have I to be with you, that we might talk a little in our own language about all of which I have no words to write.[3]

It was with Mère Le Sergent's support and counsel that Catherine de Bar founded in 1653 that *Institut de l'adoration perpétuelle* where later Jacqueline de Blémur came to learn of her. Thus all these high souls are linked together, and Charlotte Le Sergent's voice echoes for the reader in the pages of her biographer. We end with a scene delightful in its colour and harmony, which Mère de Blémur tells appropriately in the epic manner.

After she had directed many eminent people and had been consulted by those who were themselves experts in the interior paths; after she had ruled as Prioress for long years, it fell out that the

[1] *Vie de la vénérable Mère Catherine de Bar*, Nancy, 1775 (Abbé Duquesne), p. 113.
[2] Boissonnot. *La Lydwine de Touraine*, A. B. de Béthune.
[3] *Abrégé*, pp. 127–8.

parlour-Sisters wearied of superintending for three hours on end every morning the little pupils of Montmartre at their music-lessons. The venerable Mère (Le Sergent) was therefore installed in their post, on the ground that the occupation was very good for her. She agreed without a murmur.[1]

The picture of this class on the holy hill, the little Parisiennes, the awkward scales on the clavecins, the aloof and morose nuns shrinking from the discords, the sweet aged saint who has seen God, and continues to see Him, calm and attentive amidst the chatter of the little girls, is enough in itself to prove the truth of Mère de Blémur's words, that the spirituality of Charlotte "has never been appreciated as it ought to have been, with its supernatural heroism." Unknown, persecuted, forgotten, even during her lifetime, by those whose glory she was—such a life is none the less the most beautiful flower of the Benedictine reform.

3. *Marguerite d'Arbouze*

I. Whenever Anne of Austria, as was her frequent custom, visited Val-de-Grâce, "the Abbess was wont to lead her before the Holy Sacrament (the present church was not yet built) to the spot where rested the body of Mère d'Arbouze, before which the Queen would long remain in prayer, often saying: 'If she obtains me a child, I will have her canonised!'" This promise, natural enough from a woman and a Queen, although for some reason or another it was never fulfilled, would have astonished none who knew Marguerite d'Arbouze, for all regarded her as a very great saint. She was a saint without doubt, and so great, so perfectly lovable, that in placing her portrait by the side of Marie de Beauvillier's I fear I may be inviting a comparison between the two Abbesses not flattering to the latter. Marie de Beauvillier interests us exceedingly; Marguerite d'Arbouze thrills us. We cannot fail to love her. She is at once more out of reach and closer to us. She was a reformer too, no less energetic than the other and only seeming less heroic because she was more tactful and tender. She won all hearts; her daughters seem to us more simply and truly united among themselves than the nuns of Montmartre. She is indeed the ideal Abbess. True, we find a diffi-

[1] *Abrégé*, pp. 221–2.

culty in making her life and work real to modern minds, though they are involved in a striking and often picturesque way with the general history of her time. Leave out some proper names and forget some dates and Marguerite seems a contemporary of the great mediæval mystics. But we know the cause, or one of the causes, of the strange reaction which the figure of this saint arouses in our mind. Marguerite d'Arbouze belongs to her time, like everyone else, and represents it very well, but her biographer was a kind of Joinville, naïve, suave and learned, who, whether we like it or not, paralyses our historic sense by the delightfully archaic touches with which he depicts his heroine.[1]

Jacques Ferraige, or Ferrage, "*cozeranois*" (*fils du* Couserans), doctor of theology, had been Marguerite's ordinary director, and her collaborator in every step of the reform of Val-de-Grâce. This is enough in his praise, for the saint, with clearer insight than Marie de Beauvillier, never bestowed her confidence save on priests of the highest type. Ferraige was wholly devoted to her, hanging on her lips, and almost as much fascinated by her amazing learning as by her saintliness. When not in her presence he sought her and naturally enough found her in books, as he compared the words and acts of this living saint with the lives of others in the past and with all that theologians had written on sanctity. To take one example out of many, Anne of Austria, he tells us, "just as King Clotaire found all the letters and communications of the Benedictine S. Columbanus much to his taste, took in excellent part all that came from our Mother."[2] The whole book is along these lines, and the author gradually accustoms us to these delightful wanderings in far countries. The various incidents of Marguerite's life are found prefigured in the notices of the Benedictine menology, and the Abbess of Val-de-Grâce reproduces the character of S. Gertrude. He is always comparing them and hardly distinguishes one from the other. During an illness almost fatal to Marguerite he had vowed, if she recovered, to translate into French the works of S. Gertrude. This translation happily still exists, but if it did not its spirit and atmosphere would be preserved

[1] *La Vie admirable . . . de la B. Mère Marguerite d'Arbouze*, by M. Jacques Ferraige, Paris, 1628.

[2] Ferraige, *ibid.*, I. 233. The book is curiously paged, being divided into five books each with its own system, except for Books I and II, the pages of which run consecutively from 1 to 716.

in the *Vie admirable et digne d'une fidèle imitation de la bienheureuse Mère Marguerite d'Arbouze, dite de sainte Gertrude, dediée à sa Majesté.*

In instituting such parallels, Ferraige was not solely influenced by his erudite fancy or by his desire to exalt the pearl of the Val-de-Grâce. The personal development of Marguerite suggested and commanded this pleasurable task, for from the moment that she recognized her reforming mission, her one object was to conform to Benedictine history as also to Christian antiquity, in which she rightly saw the source of the spirit of S. Benedict. We must note carefully this conscious and tenacious effort of the young nun, which shows that her mind was moving on the same plane of thought as Bossuet's and Newman's.

Nearly all the mystics dealt with in these pages attached themselves directly and more or less exclusively to the spiritual leaders of the Counter-Reformation—S. Ignatius, S. Teresa, S. John of the Cross, and others. The step was natural in those belonging, as members or disciples, to the new Congregations. Certainly the Christian Past was dear to them all; some of them were well grounded in it, the Counter-Reformation having revived the study of ecclesiastical history and Patristic study. Yet as a whole the general and principal inspiration of these mystics is of later origin. Nor at first did Marguerite d'Arbouze show signs of a different orientation. She had learnt Spanish and Italian in order to read in the originals the mystics of these countries; she owed much to the Jesuits, Père Jacquinot especially; the Carmelites so attracted her that she would certainly have joined them had not that been impossible for the professed of any other Order. Her devotion to S. Teresa went so far that she has at times been taken for a Carmelite in disguise. It was from duty and at the cost of persevering effort that, a Benedictine a little *malgré elle*, she resolved to become one in real earnest, moulding herself with all her might on the pattern of that Benedictine spirit, the perfect incarnation of which she gradually became. Not that she was foolish enough to break away from the traditions of the more modern mysticism which she had already proved so helpful. On the contrary, to the end of her days she remained faithful to them, and especially to the *Exercises* of S. Ignatius, which she both followed herself and imposed on her nuns; but from the time that the Rule of S. Benedict became her supreme ideal, she assiduously set herself to seek the footprints of the old masters, profiting from their teachings so greatly, that her own history resembles a chronicle of the Middle Ages. In thought and devotion she was one with the great Abbesses of old.

All this is so important in my opinion, that I must quote almost in its entirety Ferraige's fine chapter on the learning and devotional reading of Marguerite d'Arbouze. It is rather long, for when he begins on the subject of books there is no stopping him.

Her learning, not acquired by study, rather infused by holy inspiration into our blessed Mother, since she had never attended the schools,[1] was so well assimilated by her excellent mind that for some years back she could read, understand and explain all manner of Latin books. Meseems that it was on the Feast of Pentecost or in its octave that she received this gift. . . . The R. P. Dom Eustache (Asseline), worthy Visitor of the Val-de-Grâce, recognizing the grace in this daughter of his, who doubted whether she should read the Fathers, so humble was she, and afraid of vanity, bid her do so. . . . Of these good works she most read and admired . . . the Angelical Doctor S. Thomas, saying that she marvelled that all theologians were not all saints, seeing that S. Thomas had prepared them the richest, most sublime and elevated subjects of meditation possible. . . . In Advent and Lent she generally furnished subjects of meditation suitable for the season to her daughters. In Advent, the third part of the *Summa* of S. Thomas afforded her so much wealth and her spirit availed itself thereof so well as to move her virgins to admiration and the pursuit of perfection. . . . O God Eternal, how she embellished all her matter with the multitude of her varied thoughts. Would to God that she had written all down. . . . For Lent, the conclusion of the same part of the *Summa* furnished her with subjects, together with high mystic thoughts drawn from the works of S. Augustine, pre-eminently the treatises on S. John in the ninth tome. She availed herself of S. Dionysius the Areopagite, S. Bernard, S. Chrysologus, and the Homilies of Origen on the holy Magdalene and the Canticles. And to reform herself and those committed to her she read S. Gregory the Great, S. Bonaventura, Blosius, Dacrianus, Harphius, and Jean Gerson's Imitation of Jesus Christ. But, above all, she read the Scriptures, both Old and New Testaments, and rare was it to find her without a New Testament and her Rule by her, like another S. Cecilia. For when folk talked long to her in the parlours, she was wont to read, spin, or sew, and if

[1] Our doctor means that she had not graduated.

ever distaff or sewing were laid aside, she had some portion of Holy Writ open before her, though she would listen and answer those addressing her. Certain passages of S. Dionysius and S. Augustine were difficult to me, and I asked how she understood them. She forthwith explained them most clearly. For she was plain in speech, clear in mind, and quick of comprehension. This did not come from study or natural genius, rich though hers was, but from God's gift, as in the case of SS. Gertrude, Mathilde, Hildegarde and many other holy daughters of the sacred Order of S. Benedict, who had received from God the gift of infused knowledge; or like Abbé Uvalric, who from a shepherd rose to be a learned and pious Benedictine. A man of piety and scholarship has said to me, what I too have proved by my own experience, that her discourse and learning were more profitable to learned men than to nuns, although they were profitable to all.[1]

The inner life of Marguerite d'Arbouze, however, assuredly did not confine itself to such traditional, laborious and erudite devotion, which cannot be called mystic in the true sense of the word. With her, as with many others, dogmatic and pious speculations were often a prelude to a less intellectual and more detached devotion, of which the learned Ferraige, with his devotion to scholarship, has said too little. Marguerite appears in these things to have been reserved, almost diffident, so that she was a little isolated among her contemporaries. Père Binet remarks with a tinge of humour:

Her devotion was stamped with extreme simplicity. No affectation, no parade, no high-sounding words or phrases to demonstrate her eminence or illumination. In sooth I believe that she did what others talked about and that her acts of devotion were the substance of what others said, as it is to be hoped they also did. To my knowledge she anxiously avoided discoursing on transcendent spirituality, fearing that in such flights there might be peril of windiness and secret vanity. I call to mind a confidential conversation with myself one day on this subject, but it is not expedient to put it down here, since her frank speech might possibly wound the feelings of some who would readily believe the packet addressed to themselves, and that is inadvisable.[2]

Père Binet was one of those persons, so numerous in the history of Christian thought, whose irony, through long use upon illuminates and religious charlatans, sometimes bespatters genuine saints.

[1] Ferraige, I. 608–15.

[2] *Ibid.*, I. 523–4.

Marguerite d'Arbouze was a mystic who, as Binet agreed, did what others talked about, but doubtless she would have thought that in saying so, he singled her out unduly. However, his criticism deserves to be remembered. We already know, and shall have more to say about it in the sequel, that this criticism touched very real evils, which later would provoke a violent reaction. I do not mean that such as Madeleine de S. Joseph, Bernières, or any of our friends, ever approved of the poses and braggings of so-called mystics. But there were some, even among the great, and naturally more among the small, who too often lacked prudence and perhaps modesty. They talked too much, wrote too much. There was too great a readiness to accept candidates for the mystic way. Wise with an admirable secular wisdom, the Abbess of the Val-de-Grâce, who re-read the *Summa* of S. Thomas between two ecstasies, saw and judged the peril as S. Gregory the Great himself would have done. That is why she tried to moderate in her community that passion for direction which threatened to develop into mania. She would have shrunk from hindering souls, but as one of her biographers, Claude Fleury, says:

she could not endure a Father to be disturbed in his prayers, his studies and his silence, to satisfy the curiosity of a nun who, on her side, broke in on the hours of regular observances and while continually talking to her director did not become more exact in her Rule or more charitable and obliging towards her Sisters. "I would sooner," she said, "that these nuns were less vigilant, for those who talk too much seldom amend. In the convent where directors abound there is usually much knowledge, but little observance."[1]

These are admirable sentiments, but we must not applaud them unthinkingly. They are only inoffensive when the Superior inspired by them is a large-minded and great-hearted woman like Marguerite d'Arbouze. The system by which the door was closed to all directors other than the regular one was much more open to abuses than that to the contrary. S. Teresa at least was of this opinion and, without the open door, our Abbeys would never have been reformed. But this is a digression, and since we now see the reformer of Val-de-Grâce in her slightly archaic originality, let us tell her story, or rather let the most candid and devout of her disciples tell it—Jacques Ferraige.

[1] *La Vie de la V. M. Marguerite d'Arbouze*, by Claude Fleury, Paris, 1685, pp. 91–2.

His book contains more than 1200 pages, not all of which are readable. There are in this exasperating jumble three elements of unequal value; the chronicle *à la* Joinville, a very string of pearls; the memoirs supplied by other friends of Marguerite at Ferraige's request, containing much of value; finally an immense litter of reflections, effusions, and theological phraseology uniformly intolerable. When the doctor makes his own contribution he deserves to be muzzled. But when he records and interprets faithfully what he had seen and heard he is so perfect that no man of taste would ever try to rewrite the story of Marguerite d'Arbouze. One might, rather one should, burn 800 or 900 pages of Ferraige, and add to the rest the historical proofs and references about which he is so careless, but the actual chronicle could not be better done. This was clearly understood by the great historian Claude Fleury, the wise, learned and delightful writer whose friends included Fénelon and Bossuet, and who, about 1684, was commissioned by the nuns of Val-de-Grâce to write a Life of Marguerite d'Arbouze less "gothic" in style, shorter and more in accord with contemporary fashion. Fleury's book is a masterpiece in its way, and a comparison of the two writers who treated the same subject with fifty years' interval between them, whether from the literary or from the moral and religious point of view, is of great interest. Fleury has retained all the charm of Ferraige enshrined therein, with a little smoothing and modernizing here and there. The chapter dealing with certain miracles, too artless no doubt for the contemporaries of Richard Simon, is the only exception. He most frequently quotes the passages he retains without changing anything, merely supplying the needful and always very brief links. Whenever the impersonal tone which he thinks suitable prevents him from reproducing Ferraige's confidences as they stand, he turns them into indirect speech, keeping nearly all the words. Those interested in such matters will like to surprise this skilled workman at his task. The passage chosen, which deals with a semi-miracle performed by Marguerite, is interesting for its own sake.

Ferraige.	*Claude Fleury.*
Several sick folk of the town came to the convent and pressed me that I should entreat her to	Several sick folk of the town came to the Abbey and entreated M. Ferraige to oblige Mère

pronounce a blessing over them, when she was in the church. I spoke to her of it, but that annoyed her, being desirous of no *éclat*. I commanded her twice to give it. One invalid thereupon recovered, and I have never seen the other since. (I. 427–8.)

d'Arbouze to pronounce a blessing over them, when she should be in the church. He spoke of it to her. This proposition annoyed her, for she desired no *éclat* : he, however, used his authority and commanded her twice to give her blessing. One invalid thereupon recovered, and nothing further was heard of the other (pp. 229–30).

The concluding phrase, charming in both versions, is better in the first. Much of the original rhythm has been preserved, and it is interesting to note a master like Fleury sensible to the points of so rustic a writer. He allows the good Ferraige and Marguerite d'Arbouze to write in their own way and refrains from giving them lessons in style. Thus he finds in certain letters of Marguerite to an Abbess with whom she had to find fault, " a mixture of love and respect which makes an agreeable impression." " Here we see a good friend opening her heart. . . . Generally speaking, all these letters have about them a love and tenderness which cannot be imagined. The heart is speaking, not the mind. It is the language of S. Teresa, of the Apostles, above all of S. Paul. In such a style we need not look for studied method or exact construction; charity is not bound by these rules."[1] He appreciated " proportionately " the same qualities in Ferraige's book, and was himself a sufficiently great artist to fashion himself on the humble and affecting model. Even when he supplements Ferraige, he writes in the same style and does not try to patch the chronicler's homespun with the academic purple of the age of Louis XIV. Such treatment is rare and deserves to be emphasized because the Fleury-Ferraige style enables us to put our finger on the native flexibility and essential simplicity of French prose. This book, recalling, not by turns, but all at once, Joinville, Fontanelle, Voltaire and even Anatole France, comes from a serious ecclesiastic writing at the literary *apogée* of the *grand siècle*. The spirit of Voltaire is different, alas, from that of Ferraige, but the prose is hardly changed

[1] Fleury, *ibid.*, pp. 214–6.

at all. "*Un malade s'en trouva bien. L'autre, je ne l'ai jamais plus vu,*" or better, "*l'autre, on n'en a pas su de nouvelles*"—this is the author of *Candide* speaking. It is not the artistic writing of La Bruyère and our contemporaries, but something perhaps finer. This is too secular a digression; but it will explain why in the following pages I make more use of Ferraige than of Claude Fleury. However, Fleury is indispensable for all that concerns the relations, sometimes very strained, between Marguerite d'Arbouze and the Abbess of Montmartre. Marie de Beauvillier was still alive when Ferraige's book appeared, and in any case he was not the kind of man to mention such incidents.

II. Those who are struck with admiration at sight of the buildings of Val-de-Grâce (so Fleury begins) are for the most part content to hear that they witness to the piety and magnificence of Anne of Austria, and never ask the reasons which led the princess to honour this convent with such marks of special affection. Nevertheless, her motives are more noble even than her gifts, for it is more beautiful in a great Queen to have loved a religious house because of the perfect regularity of its atmosphere, than to have adorned it with stately edifices. It was Mère d'Arbouze who both attracted the royal favour and established the regular observance.[1]

Marguerite d'Arbouze was born in Auvergne at the château of Villemont on August 15, 1580. Her father was Gilbert de Veni d'Arbouze, her mother Jeanne de Pinac, daughter of a *lieutenant du roi* in Burgundy; her grandmother on the mother's side was Perronnelle de Marillac, being cousin-german to the future Keeper of the Seals. It is a characteristic touch that Marguerite to the end loved her name with its meaning of flower and pearl. Her piety also delighted in the sweet associations that her father's name had with the Bible—de Veni d'Arbouze: *Veni columba mea.*

In 1589 she was sent to the Abbey of S.-Pierre de Lyon, where ten years later she was professed, having as Abbess the sister of the Montmartre reformer, Françoise de Beauvillier. Although the rigour of the observance had been relaxed, S.-Pierre was a house in good repute. The recent achievements of Marie de Beauvillier must have been well-known there. Marguerite soon sighed for a holier Rule. Being debarred, as a professed Benedictine, from joining either

[1] Fleury, pp. 1–2.

the Clares or the Carmelites as she would have wished, she obtained, not without difficulty and chiefly through Jesuit intervention, leave to transfer herself to Montmartre, which she entered as a novice in 1611 at the age of thirty-one. The regular life was easy to her.

Her habit alone cost her a sacrifice. It was black and plainer than that of Montmartre, which then was white with a surplice like that of canonesses. M. de Marillac, after having spoken to her of it several times, said one day: "Well, my cousin, you have not yet asked for the habit!" She began to cry and confessed her repugnance to it. "Oh well," he said, "I beg you, ask for it at once!" She did so and received it with entire humility. But at the end of five or six months the Abbess and all the community resolved to adopt the black habit of the reform. Thus she had the joy of making new vows, in a black habit, and even of seeing the one she had brought from Lyons serve as model for the rest.[1]

In 1613 the Princess de Longueville and her sister d'Estouteville, having founded the priory of Notre-Dame-de-Grâce at Ville-l'Évêque near the Faubourg S.-Honoré, offered it to Marie de Beauvillier, who temporarily took up her residence there with a little colony from Montmartre. Among these Sisters was Marguerite, then sufficiently esteemed by her Abbess to be appointed novice-mistress and subsequently Prioress, when after some months, in the spring of 1614, Mère de Beauvillier left on a long journey.

It is always the same story, but none the less each time it begins again I am filled with fresh surprise. In a very short time this unknown Prioress, from Auvergne and Lyons, is receiving great ladies, who have already lost their hearts to her.

Madame de Sévry, formerly governess and now lady-in-waiting to Françoise de Lorraine, Mlle de Mercœur, who had married the Duc de Vendôme . . . often brought Mlle de Vendôme to see Mère d'Arbouze . . . (whom) Mlle de Vendôme found so attractive that in her turn she brought the young Queen Anne of Austria and the princesses, Madame Elizabeth, who became Queen of Spain; Madame Henriette, later Queen of England; and Madame Christine, subsequently Duchess of Savoy.[2]

Madame de Maignelais came too, and all the influences that were to be at Marguerite's disposal when the moment came for them to be wanted, were already beginning to work.

[1] Fleury, pp. 12–13.

[2] *Ibid.*, p. 20.

When at the end of six months Marie de Beauvillier returned to Ville-l'Évêque she found all these friendships flourishing, and the young Marguerite in high repute. Though a saint she remained a woman, and she was not heroic enough to rejoice at such unexpected progress. Everything was out of joint. The buildings, begun by her on a modest scale, had been hurried on during her absence, thanks to the princely gifts showered upon the Priory, and were too magnificent. The Abbess promptly suppressed this zeal, and when, the visit over, she returned to Montmartre, her sentiments towards Marguerite were wholly changed. Conflict between these two natures, so different in character but alike in possessing strong and marked personalities, could not be long delayed. It was a right royal battle in which the tougher was destined to be vanquished.

New difficulties presently arose, in which Marie de Beauvillier played a noble enough part.

For a long time Mère d'Arbouze had ardently desired to observe the Rule in all its primitive strictness, more perfectly than was customary at Montmartre, where there was still some relaxation, and various great people encouraged her in this project. (Possibly Marillac, certainly the newly reformed Benedictines.) As the Priory of La Ville-Levesque possessed but a few nuns, all of whom were devoted to her, she easily won them over to her ideas, and they presented to the Abbess an address signed by all. (After a more than natural resistance) the Abbess yielded and ratified the petition.[1]

Thus did the mother and mistress of all the reformers publicly recognize the incompleteness of her own work, from which she had gained so much glory. The memory of this generous action will suggest indulgence and fair judgement if the subsequent conduct of Marie de Beauvillier towards one whom she appeared to see in the light of a rival, is in danger of irritating us.

The prestige of Marguerite was daily increasing. One of her nuns, the one who is never lacking in such cases, kept the Abbess informed of everything and persuaded her that Marguerite was preparing a *coup d'état*, that is, " desiring to render the Priory independent of Montmartre. . . . A monk whom the Abbess consulted made matters worse, and the building which had been so much accelerated during her absence continued to stick in her throat."

[1] Fleury, pp. 24-5.

Whether before or after the gathering of these new storm-clouds, Marguerite, justifiedly uneasy and supported in her alarms by one of the Court confessors, Père Suffren, " ardently hoped never to be forced away from La Ville-Levesque, declaring frankly in a letter to Cardinal de Retz, Bishop of Paris, her terrible apprehensions of being made to return to Montmartre." Whatever we may think of this significant request, it was not a beginning of revolt, as the sequel shows. Retz intervened as she had wished, but the Abbess purposely did not open his letter until after she had gone in person to see to Marguerite's removal (*enlèvement*). I have not invented the word. The Abbess, says Fleury, " resolved to remove (*enlever*) her promptly . . . and to depose her as seditious." This was in 1617.[1]

Mère d'Arbouze, having been brought back to Montmartre, was kept there in the straitest confinement. It was a kind of excommunication (Fleury certainly does not mince his words!). All communication with the outside world was forbidden her and the nuns themselves were not allowed to speak to her. The Abbess of Montmartre acted according to her prejudices, believing her seditious and presumptuous, but she could not hinder the young Queen and the royal princesses entering the convent to visit her, and ladies who were her friends often availed themselves of this to persuade the princesses to take them to Montmartre. . . . When these ladies could not see her, they at least would send their pages to enquire of her health and how she was treated, to which she always replied that she lacked nothing.[2]

Marguerite's story is always picturesque, from the Queen's pages in the parlour inquiring for her health, to the cupola of Val-de-Grâce that shaded her tomb. This lasted nearly a year, and Marguerite learned to her cost what an Abbess, even upright and godly, could make her subjects endure. She was tried in every conceivable way and made to pay dearly for the royal visits that could not be stopped.

In a serious illness that befell her (Marie de Beauvillier) she insisted on Mère d'Arbouze's serving her night and day, without any repose, so that she was fifteen days or three weeks without taking off her clothes. While she was being thus treated the Queen was ardently

[1] Both in life and death Marguerite had the last word. In 1647, thirty years later, after twenty years of similar struggles, the Abbess of Montmartre had to consent to the complete independence of the Priory.

[2] Fleury, pp. 28–31.

desirous to assign her an Abbey, as the only means of rescuing her from such tyranny. She often urged M. de Villesavin to find her one, to which he would respond laughingly that, short of killing some Abbess, there was nothing for it but to await a vacancy. At last tidings came that the Abbey of the Val-de-Grâce was vacant, at the end of October 1618.

All the necessary business, usually tedious, attending these promotions was raced through, and Marguerite was appointed Abbess of Val-de-Grâce in January 1619. Marie de Beauvillier, who had so long "checked" the Queen, was, strangely enough, "surprised and enraged at this news, her vexation obliging Mère d'Arbouze to quit Montmartre at the earliest possible moment, without having even received her bulls."[1] She fled then on January 30, taking shelter, while she waited for her bulls and transacted all necessary business, with the Augustinian Pénitentes, then under the sway of Marie Alvequin, another daughter of Montmartre, whom we have already met.[2]

The bulls at last arriving, Charles Miron, Bishop of Angers, gave her the abbatial benediction in the chapel of the Carmelites, March 21, 1619. The Queen was present, and the next day took the new Abbess in her coach to Val-de-Grâce, three leagues distant from Paris in the valley of the Bièvre. During the journey, Anne of Austria "amused herself by frightening her about the King, who that day was hunting in the neighbourhood. At the slightest noise the Queen said to Mère d'Arbouze: 'The King's coming!' The Abbess, aware that she would have to raise her veil in his presence, was seriously alarmed. . . . 'Heavens, Madame, what will become

[1] Fleury, pp. 33–42.

[2] [*Translator's Note.* One wonders how much and how honestly was self-examination practised by such as Marie de Beauvillier? The eternal feminine does not suffer loss even in the sanctified atmosphere of a convent; anywhere among a number of women jealousies, petty spites, and "cattishness" are inevitably to be looked for, and their outbreakings on the very pilgrim-way are to the full as dangerous, because less recognised, as the cloister-peril of *accidie.* The remedy might seem to be, not the sterilization of all human affections, but the cultivation of the charity that esteems "other better than themselves." Omission is the besetting sin of the confessional, but it is hard to understand how one of the Beauvillier's numerous confessors, in view of her acts towards Marguerite d'Arbouze and Charlotte Le Sergent, should not have proposed to her a meditation on S. James iii. 14–8. It is disappointing that no record should exist of any contrition for her treatment of her saintly companions, which it is to be hoped that Mme de Montmartre felt before the end of the life which had won so great a reputation of holiness.]

of me?' She was terrified."[1] On arriving at the Abbey she found the nuns in most extravagant costumes. The hem of the Benedictine habit worn by them under lace rochets afforded glimpses of sumptuous petticoats. Their shoes and head-dresses followed the prevailing fashion as nearly as possible. The Queen and her ladies, with the Abbess and her black-robed following, passed between these startling figures. That same evening the reform began.

When the Queen had gone, Marguerite harangued these poor nuns. She had not come to force them to be saints, and she would not demand more of them than the essentials of their Rule. As for the rest, matters of rising, retiring, silence and meals, they should be left undisturbed, provided in return that they would promise not to hinder the work of reform, which was offered to all, and would be imposed on all new-comers. Her speech ended, the old nuns "conducted her to a chamber hung with tapestry, beds covered with silks and broideries, tables with damask cloths, chairs well stuffed." This was the apartment of the Abbess. Marguerite forthwith "demanded a ladder and with her own following of Sisters unhooked the tapestries, dismantled beds, removed chairs, tables and carpets, and put all away for the service of the Church. . . . The old prioress who was there, gazing at the ruin and the *débris* of vanity, said to our good Mother: 'Will this state of things be for long?' and was told: 'As long as we are good Benedictines!'"[2] The old nuns resisted, the Abbess was patient and won the day. This summarises the story, the reader can imagine the details. It is enough to say that the Abbey of Val-de-Grâce was already a model when, two years later, for various reasons, it was decided to move to a suburb of Paris.

The Queen's choice for the move had at first fallen on S.-Honoré, because of its neighbourhood to the Louvre, but this had proved impossible, and the nuns had to content themselves with the house in the Faubourg Saint-Jacques, where Bérulle had assembled the first Oratorians, almost opposite the Carmelites.

This house . . . in olden times called the fief of Valois, later became known as Le Petit-Bourbon, from belonging to the princes of that family. After the disgrace and death of the Constable, Charles de Bourbon. . . . Louise of Savoy obtained permission from her son François I to transfer from this confiscated succession up to the

[1] Fleury, p. 48. [2] *Ibid.*, pp. 106–7.

value of 12,000 livres annually, and bestowed Le Petit-Bourbon with its dependencies in 1528 on her physician Jean Chapelain, whose descendants possess it to this day. In 1611 Père de Bérulle rented it . . . and for four years it was occupied by the Fathers of the Oratory (till they migrated to the Rue S.-Honoré); finally it was bought with its dependencies in the name of the Abbey of Val-de-Grâce, May 7, 1621. The Queen paying down 36,000 livres as purchase-money became foundress of this convent, and the King bestowed on it all the seigneurial rights.[1]

But the old donjon was not designed for a religious community, and was gradually replaced by new buildings, the first stone of which the Queen laid in 1624. Marguerite did not live to see these buildings finished. They in their turn were succeeded by the finer church and convent still existing, which were inaugurated in March 1665, a few months before the death of the Queen-Mother, so long devoutly faithful to the memory of Marguerite d'Arbouze.

III. When she took possession of this new home, Marguerite had no more than five years to live. It is remarkable that in so short a time she was able to win the veneration of Catholic France. Marie de Beauvillier, an Abbess for half a century, had no more prestige, at least in Paris, and was forgotten sooner. Indeed her star must have set before the end of the century for Fleury to have spoken with such freedom as the quotations already given show. Needless to say the friendship of the Queen for Marguerite showed the way to Val-de-Grâce to many admirers who would not have been influenced merely by the sanctity of a nun. Anne of Austria

usually resorted there two days a week. Friday was one, and on that day she dined in the refectory with the Sisters, who continued the ordinary convent penances and humiliations in her presence. When they had to kiss the feet, this being one of their practices, they began with the Queen, whom Marguerite had induced to submit to this. At the great festivals she would spend several days at Val-de-Grâce, the better to perform her devotions and to have religious conversation with Mère d'Arbouze. She always went there for prayers on the feasts of Our Lady, and on Christmas Eve she laid the image of the Christ-Child in the *Crèche* with her own hands.[2]

There are no signs that these royal visits interfered in the least with the regular observance of the Abbey; their very frequency

[1] Fleury, pp. 109–10. [2] *Ibid.*, pp. 143–4.

rendered them less distracting. The Abbess was too good a ruler not to train her nuns against all emergencies, and she had both independence and tact. She dexterously avoided the inconvenient pressure sometimes put on her by the Court, if I have rightly filled in the gaps left by our discreet historians. Behind the Queen, in the parlour of Val-de-Grâce, we see one of the most unpleasant features of the period. Ferraige makes more than one almost transparent allusion to it; so does Père Binet. Piety being in fashion, many people used it, either to make themselves conspicuous or to give scope for the emotional side of their nature. They were not exactly hypocrites, but restless, busybodies—religious, priests and laity alike. The type still exists, but to-day is less interested in the interior life. Under Louis XIII they stormed the convents, harassing with their advice any saint they could get hold of, especially if she was a woman. The moment they heard of a contemplated reform, they would swoop down on their prey, declaring the Rule too easy here, too severe there. At the news that the Abbess of Val-de-Grâce was imposing two hours of meditation daily on her daughters, they dared the marshes of the Bièvre in order to restrain her. In Paris it was still worse.

Everyone claimed her attention (groans worthy Ferraige), and if she had not been strong-minded it would have befallen her as it did Theletias, the Grecian youth of antiquity, who, having gained the prize at the Pythian games, was torn in pieces instead of being crowned as he deserved by the peoples who claimed him, declaring, "He is ours!"[1]

Père Binet echoes him.

As she had a very good intelligence, and saw clearly how the land lay, she avoided taking the advice of any, because when she perceived one too impetuous . . . or another with some interested motive, or not conversant with religious matters, she did not desist from holding these persons in all honour, but would say that she could hardly follow the counsels of those without special knowledge of the matter.[2]

It is easy enough to guess the names of some of these persons. They hurried from Val-de-Grâce to Montmartre and back again to the Faubourg S.-Antoine to descend upon the Jesuits and Visitandines. Meeting them constantly one comes to know them, but as I have

[1] Ferraige, I. 195–6. [2] *Ibid.*, I. 519.

not set out to write their history, I content myself with a passing mention, as indeed Marguerite d'Arbouze's biographers invite us to do.

The leading mystics of Paris, whom we have already met, also passed through the parlour of Val-de-Grâce, where they met for discussions of difficult problems, as for instance the question of the two hours' meditation, on which point Honoré de Champigny, André Duval and Don Eustache Asseline firmly supported the daring innovation of the Abbess. To Val-de-Grâce came also Dom Auger, a Carthusian; the Benedictine Père Tenière and several others of the Reform; the Minim Père d'Attichy, Marguerite's cousin and subsequently Bishop of Autun; M. le Clerc, professor of theology; two of the Court confessors, P. Suffren and P. Arnoux; finally two other Jesuits, P. Granger and P. Etienne Binet. Together with Dom Eustache, the canonical Visitor, Père Binet appears to have been the counsellor most trusted and beloved by Mère d'Arbouze. The choice is significant, for Binet, Jesuit if ever there was one, favoured exclusively the solid virtues and never excused weakness in his penitents. He delighted in Marguerite,

> who had a masculine mind, keen and clear, with a great and happy discernment of spirits, detachment from the creature, and strength of purpose to execute what needed to be done.

According to him, the Abbess strongly resembled or, in his own words, " symbolized greatly " Mme Acarie.

> Whatever befell, she never lost her peace of soul. What was more precious, she was a woman of quiet, penetrating and noble temper, naturally active and prompt (we see here the qualities he prizes) and all the more sensible on that account. . . . But she generally said to me after some unpleasant experience (when she had been insulted by some visitor, which was by no means rare): " My Father, alas! how much more do my sins deserve, so if the good God is glorified thereby . . . I do not mind." " Yes," I said, " yet it has made you ill and then you tell me you do not mind." " I cannot help my temperament or constitution, and my body is good for nought save to perish . . . but I hope, God helping me, that neither by this nor by anything in the world will my soul or my aspirations be affected."

She was perfectly submissive and obedient to him, like the true daughter of S. Benedict that she was—and of S. Ignatius, thought

Père Binet privately. "Only once to my knowledge," he says, "did she take sides against me." He concludes his *Mémoire* thus:

I do not think that any could have loved our Society more tenderly. . . . Whenever a storm arose against us, which often enough befell us in the infinite mercy of God, her heart was rent . . . and when I demanded how it affected her, seeing that others of the same profession as herself were not much concerned . . . she replied in words worthy of her loving heart, but too flattering towards the Society for modesty to permit me to write them down. So I will but note that she was wont to say that she had infinite obligations to the Society, and that its spirit was entirely one with hers and that she admired its solidity more than its brilliance.[1]

The passage is amusing. Binet no sooner realizes that his penitent is a Benedictine than he has a sly thrust at other religious of this Order—witty perhaps, but hardly magnanimous. He certainly does not misrepresent Marguerite's sentiments, for she thought very highly of the Jesuits, and owed much to them. Only instead of saying that their spirit was "entirely one with hers," Fleury's tacit correction, "one with hers to a remarkable extent," would have been better. Filled as she was with the true Benedictine spirit, Marguerite had little difficulty in adding to it the excellences of the other Orders. To a great heart and royal soul she joined, in the words of Ferraige,

the œcumenical and universal spirit . . . (she) loved good wherever she met with it, without a thought of envy. She was amazed when she saw envy in others, especially in spiritual things. She was wont to say that the greatest sign that there could be of a small mind, without the spirit of God, was when it was contracted and stunted so as to love only certain good and certain persons and not the general good. As if all did not bear the living image of the august and adorable Trinity, and as if in universal good the individual were not included.[2]

We should like to see her when she leaves the parlour and lifts her veil, in her cell or among her daughters. But neither Ferraige nor Fleury troubles to enlighten us. All they say of her can be said of many other Abbesses. The only clear view we shall get of her will be when she leaves Val-de-Grâce to die among strangers.

[1] Ferraige, pp. 518–27.

[2] *Ibid.*, I. 200–1.

Inclined, with "certain ancients," to see "in beauty of body an infallible assurance of nobility and dignity of soul," Ferraige tells us that "nature had been at pains to preserve in her the exact proportions and dimensions requisite to create a body of rare beauty, with divine grace and demeanour." This theological pastel does not help us much. Much clearer, though a little overpowering, is the avalanche of details he gives us when he describes the richness and flexibility of her mind.

A religious from the age of nine, . . . nevertheless she knew, though apart from the world, how business ought to be carried on. . . . I used to marvel at hearing her speak of things in general. . . . She understood architectural plans and designs, façades, courtyards, and would correct the plans, both masonry and woodwork. She understood music, sang melodiously, was expert in medicine, a clever economist, ordering and regulating all things without confusion, foreseeing all emergencies, as her constitutions prove. She had a perfect grasp of ethics, knew how to draw the full sense from passages of Scripture, grasped and explained metaphysical definitions and abstractions and could use them with ease when required, wrote clearly or dictated skilfully pious discourses and well-composed letters. . . . Sometimes, though rarely, making verses for some great festival at which she was greatly affected by the mystery commemorated, and if she did not know much of quantities, measures and rhymes she did her best, and she certainly knew how to lead souls to Heaven.[1]

On this last point Fleury says almost all that requires saying—"She was gentle with herself."[2] When a true saint is sufficiently human and reasonable to resign herself to her own weaknesses she will have nothing but firm tenderness for the failures of her spiritual children. Marguerite is depicted as majestic, but also simple and vivid. She disliked fine postures and fine words. One might almost say that her most eminent quality was common sense, did not the dull colours suggested by the phrase go badly with her personality. Rich in the rarest gifts of mind, heart and grace, she governed herself with the sense of fitness, that in another order of perfection marks the great artist.

One day, during the Mass of Our Lady of Compassion, it struck her during the Gradual in praise of the Blessed Virgin that *lacerans*

[1] Ferraige, *ibid.*, pp. 573, 612–13. [2] p. 156.

vultus et pectora signified that Our Lady, in her sorrow at seeing her Son crucified, tore her face and breast; whereupon she made them substitute another Gradual, saying that this Mass had never been made by the Church nor seen nor approved, and that the Blessed Virgin had ever been constant, patient and resigned to the will of God.[1]

A tiny detail no doubt, but the vivacity and serene sense of fitness of this noble spirit shine out in it. After these additional touches to the portrait of Marguerite d'Arbouze let us return to her history.

IV. She had restored the right of election in her convent, Louis XIII having renounced in her favour the right of nomination which he had at Val-de-Grâce. She inaugurated this reform, in a sense the boldest of all, by unexpectedly divesting herself of the title of Abbess, which the new statute allowed her to keep and which the unanimous choice of her nuns would have accorded her, had she been willing to receive it. The monastic world was surprised and greatly impressed, for few among the reformers had gone so far. Marguerite in sacrificing the irremovable character of her post had also lost for it its quasi-heredity. Even the most saintly Abbesses had always managed to persuade themselves that no such excellent coadjutrices could be found as in their own families; once coadjutrices their nieces succeeded them without difficulty. Thus for a century S.-Paul-les-Beauvais was, fortunately for itself, a fief of the Sourdis and the Clermont-Tonnerre families, while various La Bourdaisières and Béthunes reigned indefinitely over Beaumont-les-Tours. Such deliberate nepotism distresses us as does also the partial insincerity which it imposed both on the nuns themselves and on the historians and panegyrists who vied with one another in seeing God's finger in these successions. Mère d'Arbouze not only chose to become once more a simple nun, she also, instead of guiding the votes of her daughters towards either of her two nieces already in the Order, caused the election of one of the nuns of Montmartre who had accompanied her to Val-de-Grâce, Mère Louise de Milley.

Up to 1626, the year that witnessed her laying down of office and her death, the reformer of Val-de-Grâce had steadily refused all proposals for further foundations. Influence as she understood it should be deep rather than wide. Now, back again in the ranks,

[1] Ferraige, *ibid.*, pp. 586–7.

she changed her mind and consented to found a daughter-house, perhaps less drawn by the holy ambition of extending her conquests than from a wish to leave the new Abbess of Val-de-Grâce entirely free. A little group of nuns, who had left the Abbey of Charenton-en-Bourbonnais to live in strict observance, under the provisional government of one of themselves, Mme de la Rochechouard de Jars, had for some time been awaiting her at La Charité-sur-Loire. "All La Charité wanted her, in order to have a religious house in which to receive such of the countryside as should have vocations. The diocesan Bishop, that is, the Bishop of Auxerre," Gilles de Souvré, consented with all his heart. "M. de Broc du Nozet, a neighbouring gentleman, offered some land for the foundation of the new convent, which his daughters wished to enter"; and at last the bulls sanctioning building were ready, creating "in the town of La Charité a new convent of Daughters of S. Benedict, following the constitutions of Val-de-Grâce," and to bear the name of the Mont-de-Pitié.

Mère d'Arbouze left Paris on April 28, 1626; on May 3 she inaugurated her house of Mont-de-Pitié, and remained two months at La Charité-sur-Loire. On July 2 she started for Charenton-en-Bourbonnais, where she wished to sow the first seeds of reform. At the end of three weeks she felt very ill and desired to return to La Charité, dying on the way home on August 16, 1626. These sad dates are landmarks in the most beautiful chapter in the Golden Legend of the seventeenth century. The garden of the Beloved is enclosed by a thick hedge from the secular gaze, a triple grille forbids too near an approach to the greater number of our mystics. But the main road belongs to us all, and when by good fortune the saints use it they cannot hide from us. They are made in the same way as we, and the road which at first alarmed them soon stimulates them and increases their gaiety. They think of the sallies of the Word Eternal, leaping like a giant from heaven to earth and from earth to heaven; of the Virgin hasting towards Elizabeth so fleetly that the mountain grasses scarce bent beneath her footprints; of the barque on the Lake of Gennesareth, of the Roman roads which witnessed the passing of S. Peter and S. Paul; of the pilgrimages of S. Louis; of the Church's name of pilgrim for the faithful on earth. All this applies to our Marguerite during the last months of her life, which were one long journey. The good Ferraige was with her, more eager than ever to note all his saint said or did. I wish I could reproduce his pages exactly as they stand, all divine and moistened with so many tears.

The year of grace 1626, on April 28 our blessed Mother went forth from the convent of Val-de-Grâce in the Faubourg S.-Jacques-lez-Paris to go to the town of La Charité-sur-Loire, with the R.M. sub-Prioress of Val-de-Grâce, Sœur Marie de Burges (daughter of Mme de Séry), Sœur Catherine Compans . . . Sœur Marguerite du Four . . . choir-sisters, and Sœur Thomasse le Queux . . . lay-sister. But before describing this journey let us witness the dolorous adieu and the tears there shed. (She was as much moved as her daughters and too human to harden herself at such a moment.) " At times we attach ourselves," she said in this last exhortation, " to a certain visible presence of the creature, which hinders us belonging perfectly to God. Not that in this I wish to condemn your sentiments and mine, but mother-love constrains me to call you my dear children, and announce in the words of Jesus to His apostles: If I go not away, you will not receive the Holy Ghost; not in the same measure as did the apostles but in some small proportion according to our attachment to one another visibly, as were the apostles to the visible Presence of Jesus Christ. And as they received the Holy Ghost, losing the visible Presence of Jesus, so God will bestow upon us much increase of virtues and graces through this parting, stripping and separation undertaken by us for the love of Jesus, and to sacrifice in eternal homage all that we are. Set apart from one another by distance, let us not fail to be more purely, perfectly and spiritually united in the holy and sacred wounds of Our Lord Jesus Christ, true refuge and abiding-place for His brides." And with a heart animated by maternal and filial love after this long and loving discourse . . . she prostrated herself at the feet of her Abbess and entreated her benediction. The Reverend Mother raised and embraced her, clasping her in Jesus Christ and giving her the last kiss. Thus did all her nuns, and then she received the permission to leave the convent for another from Monseigneur, the illustrious and reverend Archbishop of Paris, and that of the Reverend Mother, and was given a great crucifix which she always carried, and, getting into the coach, departed with the said company of nuns, an ecclesiastic, a secular lady and a servant.

The ecclesiastic was Ferraige. He and his servant followed on horseback and for the first stage were accompanied by the other convent-confessor, M. Fiant. The secular lady was Mme Langlois.

This blessed Mother, finding herself on a journey, suddenly bethought her that she could not do better than conform her journey to that of Jesus . . . going into Egypt to cast down the idols there; or to that of S. Benedict, going to Monte Cassino to deliver the hermit . . . or else to that of the Benedictine S. Hildegarde, on her way to Saint-Disibode to reform the Bernardines. . . . She then borrowed an alarm-clock in order to keep the Office-hours exactly, as once was done by a certain S. Leger, a Bishop, as well as the hours of devotion, conference, reading and silence.[1] She had also taken a little bell, to ring at these hours. At Essone, where they dined the first day, M. Fiant, to his great regret, must quit the party. "Taking leave of her," he wrote subsequently, "I saw her face marvellously beautiful, so illumined with majesty and radiance that it was impossible to contemplate her without awe and a greater respect even than was ordinary, nevertheless it was impossible for me to resign myself not to look after her and follow the coach with my eyes, as long as I could distinguish her, though my companions urged me to turn my horse, saying: 'Come, you must lose sight of that carriage, it will be late enough ere we can return to Paris.' Nevertheless we were there before sunset."[2]

This good priest is an affecting figure as he stands motionless in the road, deaf to the urgent voices of his companions, his eyes fixed on the coach already disappearing in the dust of the highway, with utter sincerity, for no one could suspect him of striving after literary effect. So Marguerite enchanted all with whom she had to do, from the humblest of her servants to the Queen of France. Ferraige proceeds to depict what he naïvely but aptly terms "this travelling Devotion."

Those on horseback in their company (that is, Ferraige and his servant) sometimes recited the rosary, sometimes the hours, litanies and other vocal and mental prayers. We sang canticles, hymns, or psalms, to which the nightingales seemed to invite us. But when it was the turn of the exposition (doubtless the company would halt and descend from coach or saddle), O God Eternal! how would this blessed soul, animated by the fires of divine love, and raised to heaven, incite us to leave all things and strip ourselves of all, even of self. For if our soul is attached and bound to nothing, it will in obedience to divine attraction soar to the Lover Jesus with a true impulse, though the less sensible in proportion as it is beyond sense. Writing her words, it seems to me as though I read the colloquies of

[1] Ferraige, I. 341–2.

[2] *Ibid.*, I. 570.

S. Benedict and S. Scholastica, or of S. Francis and S. Clare. Often I drew her out on the Canticles or the Gospels, on which she would speak marvellously. God grant that I may remember all she said in her own words, for they were clear, powerful and energetic! I said to her that the Spouse was very bold in daring to demand of Sovereign Majesty a kiss from His lips. She replied: "When the Spouse said these words . . . love having transported her, she no longer dreamed of fearing, but of loving, holding and clasping the Heart of her heart and the centre of her love, Jesus." . . . The Mothers and I admiring these replies which entered so profoundly into the spirit of the Scriptures, I said to her: "But of what flavour spake the Spouse when she cries: *meliora sunt ubera tua vino?*"—"Meseems," she said, "that God conducted this Spouse by the degrees of love . . . and she is not yet capable of tasting them all at once. He, having given her the sacred kiss of peace, first makes her savour the sweetness and fire of His love, better than wine, being not yet sufficiently enlarged to be able to comprehend the heights and depths and length and breadth which the wine would represent. For when the soul has arrived at the point of exterior mortification and interior annihilation, and nought else lives or reigns in the kingdom of her heart, than Jesus with His cross, passion, nails, scourge and thorns, all is as well with her as when her beloved Lover and Bridegroom comes to her with every attribute of His Divinity. When the soul savours, as much as a creature can savour, divine attributes in general, not preferring one attribute to another, seeing them all in God essentially one and the same. . . . And the Spouse adores her Bridegroom and cherishes Him as much in the sweetness of the breasts as in the fervency of the wine. For the living God, flowing into the Spouse, is as much Himself when He flows like milk or water or ointment as when He flows like wine." . . .

O Eternal God, while I marvel at these words, how I adore Thy Wisdom and am amazed to see this holy virgin's knowledge of so many truths of Scripture. There is no pleasure greater than in penetrating and savouring these truths, therefore may I say that I think I have never received more delight than in the discourses of this divine journey and should esteem myself unfortunate did I forget them. Never had I so strongly experienced desire to live stripped of all things than when I thus beheld and heard her speak of the Sacred Scriptures.[1]

I have quoted this effusion on the Canticles at length because I seem to see in it not only, as Ferraige suggests, a pious and skilful

[1] Ferraige, I. 352–6.

paraphrase, but also something of a valuable personal confidence. In places, notably when she speaks of the exterior and interior annihilation of the soul, Marguerite is clearly describing the higher states of the mystic life too vividly not to have herself experienced them. We shall therefore be right not to take too literally Père Binet's words recorded at the beginning of the chapter. In the *conférence* just read there is certainly no " affectation " or " parade," but if the terms used by the mystic of Val-de-Grâce are less transcendent than certain others, the realities of which she speaks are absolute. Moreover, these words have a double sense, the one sublime, as Marguerite employs them, the other more humble, accessible and profitable to the rank and file of faithful souls, and that is the sense in which Jacques Ferraige understands them. This involves misunderstanding between those who have not received exactly the same measure of grace, but the misunderstanding is fraught with blessing, since it enables mystics to shed their influence over the whole Church.[1]

One question exhausted, Dr. Ferraige passes on to another, for his devout curiosity is untiring.

> I eagerly brought up a number of passages, in order to learn their secrets and comprehend their marvels. I said to her: " Why does the Bride say . . . *Introduxit me Rex in cellam vinariam*—why does she call Him King, and not Goodness, Love, Spouse, etc.? " " Ah," she said, " the soul being beside herself . . . being nothing either to herself or to the world, was absorbed in her Bridegroom who lived and reigned . . . in her heart, in a peaceful kingdom, in the quietude of sense . . . in the abyss of light, in the transport of love, where the Bridegroom was all the Bride's and the Bride all the Bridegroom's. So she said: *Dilectus meus mihi et ego illi.* It seems to me that it was for this, that she should savour Him as King and not as Flower, Wisdom, etc."
>
> Now at this time (just before May) the woods were full of flowers excellent in beauty and fragrance, uncultivated by human hand, which the Maker of flowers had called forth and watered with His showers. Some of them were handed into the coach, she took them with delight and wove them all about a great crucifix which was always in her arms, putting crowns on the head and posies on the pierced hands and feet. Then she said: *Ego flos campi et lilium convallium.* . . . I asked her why field flowers, and not blossoms of

[1] We shall go further into this when we come to analyse the correspondence of François de Sales and Jeanne de Chantal.

some parterre cultivated by the skill of the gardener, were named in this passage. She said: "Jesus is the flower of the field and the lily of the valleys, for various reasons. The Word, begotten in the bosom of the Eternal Father, is a flower of this essential flower, begotten through knowledge without being cultivated; and when making Himself the flower of Jesse in the womb of a virgin, He is again brought forth without being cultivated, either by angels or by men . . . and having taken our flesh in the womb of a maiden, the Blessed Virgin, this flower of the fields, adored in the wide fields of heaven, in the bosom of the Eternal Father, and trodden under feet of passers-by, the Jews, heedless of His Beauty surpassing all beauties, or of His fragrance, sweeter than all perfumes!" . . . "But, Mother," I interrupted, "it is not clear in this passage whether this flower be the Bridegroom or the Bride. . . ."

She replied again and again in her divine fashion, but finally hesitated and stopped, the worthy Ferraige having involuntarily betrayed that he was adroitly drawing her out.

She had been brought red and white flowers. To make her speak of these sacred mysteries of which she had such excellent and deep understanding, I said: *Candidus et rubicundus, electus ex millibus.* "Yes," she said, "the Bridegroom of souls." Then I said: "Say, my Bridegroom." And she: "That is not for me to say, I am too great a sinner. White and red is His livery, to make me know myself, whether I am white in purity and red in love in Him; whether I mount above all participated purity and communicated charity, to Him Who is essential purity and love. Whether I have the spirit to know in truth that He is Himself not merely all beautiful, all good . . . but rather Beauty, Goodness, Power themselves. . . . *Electus in millibus*, the chosen one among thousands, for, in making a choice, if one does not wish to show oneself a fool . . . one must choose the best. Now Jesus . . . is the very Best. One must then choose Him." Said I then: "I believe that those who endeavour to make themselves like to Him do make that choice. Now there is nought so like this Bridegroom white and red than the marguerite. You have chosen well then!" At this one of her nuns said, "Mother, it is true, you have turned quite red!" Seeing that she was spoken of, she said abruptly, "What is my dear . . . Abbess of Val-de-Grâce doing? Ah, I love her well. She is good, simple, sincere, large-hearted. . . . Ah, how her tears flow. I pray God that He Who is called Paraclete may be her consolation!" She said this that she might distract our thoughts and hide herself interiorly.

The charm was broken for a few moments only. Seeing Marguerite sink back into the semi-ecstasy which his allusions had disturbed, Ferraige resumes his questions.

"What support," I said, "had the Spouse in those languors of love when she longed to be stayed with flowers and comforted with apples?" (But the fruits of autumn were far away; Marguerite was "stayed" on her red and white anemones.) "Such sacred languors," she said, "are healed by the flowers of that Flower of Jesse, Jesus Christ, blossoming at His Nativity, beaten down at the Column, withering upon the Cross, resuming His radiance and fragrance at the Resurrection. In love He blossomed, in love was He beaten down, withered, cast on the earth, in love He sprang up again on the Morn of Resurrection. Therefore the bringing of this Flower to the flower of the Spouse, in amorous union, stays the Spouse in her languors, and these flowers not being sterile . . . bear apples, fruits of unifying love, which satisfy the Spouse, yet leave her a-hungering for more love . . ."

The interview breaks off at this point, and Ferraige, the humble Ferraige who, when irradiated by the light of his saint, ranks with the greatest of French geniuses, ends with these magnificent words:

Would to God that I could remember more. It would be a holy and profitable communication, enkindling souls to entire renunciation, perfect nothingness, in order to fill them with Him Who was emptied, poured out and made nought in the fullness of time, to fill us to overflowing with God.[1]

I need not quote the speeches that greeted her arrival at La Charité, whether delivered by the Vicar-General—"Do not expect of me, gentlemen . . ." or by the sheriff (*échevin*) of the town—"Madame, we present ourselves before you in order to assure you of the unspeakable rejoicing . . ." Ferraige asked the orators for their manuscripts and transcribed the speeches into his great book. For two months Marguerite d'Arbouze settled down in her new house. It is touching to see how her heart was still at Val-de-Grâce, whither she wrote constantly, receiving in turn many affectionate letters, both in prose and verse. These tender simple notes would be more informing to us of to-day than the speeches, but they are probably not now to be found. We have already seen that a little group of nuns, anxious to take part in the Reform, awaited Mère d'Arbouze at La Charité.

[1] Ferraige, I. 41–63.

We learn from Fleury some things about them which illustrate the pious customs and whims of this epoch.

These worthy daughters had founded themselves far more upon the Devotion of the Slavery than on the Rule of S. Benedict, which was scarcely known to them. This so-called devotion consisted of a vow of slavery to the Blessed Virgin, by virtue of which they wore chains, practised sundry special exercises, and celebrated festivals neither ordained nor approved by the Church. Mère d'Arbouze gently examined the spirit of this devotion and recognized that they considered this the essential and looked on their Rule as only accessory. She considered it right to use her authority as Superior, to declare these superstitious vows null and void and to forbid all such practices, although she would not do so without consulting M. Ferraige and several Fathers, who were all of her opinion. These nuns, who had only erred through ignorance and simplicity, and whose intention was right, obeyed, and Mère d'Arbouze made them comprehend that no innovations should be introduced into the Church of God, and that such novelties, even though they may be well enough in themselves, are always mischievous as the cause of distraction. She exhorted them to seek after perfection by the means prescribed in their ancient and authorised Rule, ranking the observance of the ancient Institutions with the ancient interpretations of Scripture bequeathed us by the Fathers.[1]

When Fleury talks like this, with the somewhat rigid and inflexible wisdom of his contemporaries, I fancy he forces, or at least manipulates a little, the ideas of Marguerite d'Arbouze. In any case the reasons he alleges, whoever is responsible for them, are only half convincing. Taken literally, they prove too much. A new devotion need not be incompatible with the rightful demands of an ancient rule, nor even too distracting, for the Church was soon to approve, not only the devotion of the Sacred Heart, but also that of "the Slavery," as adapted by Blessed Grignion de Montfort. It is curious that both these new devotions should have taken root in Benedictine soil. We have seen this happening as regards the second; so also as regards devotion to the Sacred Heart, which will be met again in the chapter on Marguerite-Marie Alacoque.[2]

[1] Fleury, pp. 207–8.

[2] The devotion of "the Slavery" at this period was, however, known in other Orders. Agnès de Langeac, disciple of M. Olier, "took the chain in token of servitude at the age of eight, in 1611." Cf. an interesting note on this subject in *La vie de la V. M. Agnès de Jésus*, by M. de Lantages, new edition by M. l'Abbé Lucot, Paris, 1863. I. 271–4.

At that time Cluny had a Priory at La Charité, several members of which, including Dom Jean Passelége and Dom Robert Mauvielle, were eager for reform, but without the courage to make a start. Like many other devout people from the neighbourhood, these two religious often visited Mère d'Arbouze. She soon succeeded in making up their minds, and led her own brother, Dom Pierre d'Arbouze, Prior and Seigneur of Ris in Auvergne, to a similar resolution. Indeed she was irresistible. She "changed . . . my weakness into strength, my lukewarmness into fervour," wrote Dom Mauvielle.[1] A priest once came to visit her who was prevented from preaching by an incurable timidity; but a word from her restored his speech.

Yet her strength was failing, and it is hard to understand the permission given her to undertake a new enterprise. The Abbess of Charenton-en-Bourbonnais, Anne de Montigny, had for some time been entreating her to come and help her in pacifying her convent, in which reformers and anti-reformers were at daggers drawn. The wise Ferraige was against her going and Marguerite herself hesitated, but the local Superiors showed less prudence, and the journey was decided upon. "Pray for me, my children," wrote Mère d'Arbouze to Val-de-Grâce, "one must abandon oneself to the will of God, unknown though it be in this affair, for, according to human insight, there is neither rhyme nor reason in it."[2] Her farewells to her daughters at La Charité show clearly that she never expected to enter it again alive. The party set out on July 2. Save for two nuns left behind, the little group was the same as that which left Val-de-Grâce. But la Mère d'Arbouze was ravaged by fever, and there was no more gaiety in the hearts of her companions, no more anemones by the wayside.

There is nothing to be said of the journey, save that everything went wrong. The worst roads in the world, the most ignorant driver, horses tired out, everyone depressed with no desire to go on. . . . (Near Montfaucon) the coach stuck between two rocks. We were forced to unharness . . . it rained hard and we were well soaked. We stopped there for dinner. It was not possible to get a fresh egg. Our blessed Mother felt very ill and wrote as much to Paris, to Val-de-Grâce. . . . We went on then with no pleasure. Nearing Néronde the coach was smashed passing under a great

[1] Ferraige, I. 532.

[2] Fleury, p. 221.

branch of a walnut tree, and in the fields there was no way of mending it. The blessed Mother descended with her crucifix, as calmly as if nothing had happened. We endeavoured to tie the coach together with cords and arrived at Néronde. . . . There fever set in on her, or rather increased, all night. On the morrow I asked how she was, and whether she had slept? They told me that she had been very ill . . . and, being about to say the Holy Mass, I said to her: "Mother, your illness gains ground, the fever increases, let us return to La Charité and thence to Paris." "Courage," she replied. "Jesus gave birth to His children in the throes of a painful cross, a sinner as I am must not spare herself. Let us go on and die with Him." After celebrating the Mass and communicating her and her daughters, as she was still ill, I said to her: "For God's sake, good Mother, let us return to La Charité." "I will do whatever you will," she said, "but the will of God is that we should go on where we are summoned." "Let us go then," said I with great sadness at my heart, which I could not suppress as she well knew, and sought to console us. . . . On the road there were such jerks, ups and downs, stones and roots of trees, that she was sorely shaken and I pitied her greatly, for I could bring no remedy. . . . She repeated to me often that she was dying . . . that the houses would get on better after her death. I replied that I could not believe that, for it was the same humility that always made her say, "I spoil all." She insisted that it was the pure truth. O God Eternal! it is truth that her words have been accomplished; the houses have prospered to this day. . . . So we came to Charenton on July 3. She entered into the convent, as of old S. Hildegarde, the Benedictine, made her entry into S. Disibode, to reform the Bernardine nuns.[1]

Was this only a preliminary visit to pave the way for reform, or did illness compel Marguerite to remain at Charenton as short a time as possible? We cannot say, but she set out again for La Charité in less than three weeks. It was the vigil of S. Mary Magdalene, and the day was spent in talking of the saint.

Our blessed Mother, as she abounded in pain from her bodily swellings, abounded and superabounded in knowledge and love . . . she told us marvellous things. Seeing in her as it were a seraph, I asked her what S. Augustine meant by those words, *Accessit ad Dominum . . . confessa, ut rediret professa?* (She thus explained them: Magdalene had become professed in perfect love.) I frequently asked her how she was. She signed to me that she was very

[1] Ferraige, pp. 412–17.

ill and that the keen pain grew worse, which she concealed from the others in order to spare them affliction. For throughout her life, even as a child, she sought to please and support all, refreshing and consoling them. . . . I cannot write these things without showing what I feel at having lost so perfect a model.[1]

That evening they arrived at the Château de Séry, belonging to the Maréchale de Montigny, mother, or perhaps sister, of the Abbess of Charenton; here she was to die. Ferraige's pen trembles as the last hour approaches.

Reader, I confess that I have shrunk as long as I could from writing this chapter. So did S. Jerome shrink and procrastinate when he came to describe the death-bed of a saint. In writing the other acts of our blessed Mother I feel that she is not dead, but when I write this chapter I am forced to see her die over again.

His great sorrow had had its reward. After three centuries of forgetfulness, should I ever have succeeded in interesting my readers in Marguerite d'Arbouze if Jacques Ferraige had not loved this saint and told us how he loved her?

The best physicians of the neighbourhood were summoned.

Seeing that nothing was gained thereby, they had recourse to vows, pilgrimages to Notre-Dame de Liesse et de Consolation, near Bourges, to Ste-Solange, Ste-Jeanne, etc. . . . to the discipline, fasting and devotions of the Forty Hours, but all in vain. Our blessed Mother said to me: "You are taking so many vows, and what if you gain nought?" "I hope in the prayers of the Holy Virgin," said I. "You will see," said she, "in this octave of the Blessed Virgin what you would fain not see," thus assuring me that she would die then. They brought a number of relics from Val-de-Grâce, among others the finger of S. Benedict. I made her kiss them. She was aware of varied and sweet odours from them, and said to me: "There is no need to place artificial perfume around the relics of the saints, the fragrance that they have of themselves is incomparable."

Another time, when they bore her to the chapel to hear Mass, they beheld her marvellous in beauty, of great and radiant majesty. From that time I thought that she was no longer ours, that her words to me, that I should never bring her back alive to Paris, would come true, that she would soon be with the saints and that the fragrance of Jesus Christ would lure her from us. The thought was so

[1] Ferraige, I. 428–34.

present to me, wherever I was, and the sense of the coming separation so keen, that all I did was watered with my tears and I would willingly have ended my life to prolong hers.

He still continued to suggest to her theological or Biblical problems, no more indeed from curiosity, for he would have given all the knowledge in the world to see her cured, but solely to distract her. Thus, on the Vigil of the Assumption, he questioned in her presence, "What angel was it who announced to the holy Mother of God that she was about to die?" feigning to believe that it was S. Michael, and not S. Gabriel, as the dying woman held. "Am I right? uphold me, assure me," she said to another priest present, M. Chabanes, "for I cannot persuade myself that it was another than S. Gabriel." "Of which we were all agreed," adds Ferraige, "but I was glad to refresh her in these mysteries and to make her speak of them, for she became so absorbed in them . . . that she felt not half the pain."

Two days after, on August 16, he gave her extreme unction. Then,

seeing her on the point of departure, I . . . bade her say "Jesus," and she said it with all her heart, and as she said it her soul took flight, as though following the sigh with which she had uttered the Name. She died about noon, the hour at which this Bride, like the one of the Canticles, demanded of her Bridegroom: "Show me where Thou feedest and reposest, and there make Thy Bride feed and repose, in the noontide of Thy sacred affection," a place of peace and eternal union, whither she fled without giving further sign of suffering . . . for neither head, eyes, lips, nor hands so much as moved. . . . Thus died the blessed Mère Marguerite . . . as once of old the heart of S. Catherine of Siena who, oppressed with grief, died of love.[1]

The body of Marguerite d'Arbouze was first taken from Séry to La Charité, where it was embalmed, then onwards to Val-de-Grâce. Perhaps we ought not to follow her now she is dead, but such tender scenes accompanied her dear relics that I have not the heart to end my long chapter yet.

Dom Mauvielle was one of those who accompanied Marguerite to the gates of La Charité on May 17; two days after her death he went with the procession as far as they could along the road to Paris.

[1] Ferraige, I. 453-61.

In the memoir he wrote soon afterwards at the request of Jacques Ferraige, he says:

> At daybreak, the body having been carried to the bridge over the Loire, all La Charité, that is to say the ecclesiastics, justiciaries, sheriffs and others in great numbers, met it to assist in this solemn procession. But as soon as I perceived the hearse with you on one side and the R.M. sub-Prioress (Marie de Burges) and Sœur de Ste-Cecile clasping the coffin itself, sorrow choked my voice, rendering me unable to utter a word.
>
> The four religious of our Observance detailed by me to bear the corpse being, as I thought, not strong enough, I placed myself at its head and with singular joy helped to carry it as far as our church . . . which she had promised to enter on her return, assured that the Reform would have been already established there, which indeed was the case.

After this touching halt among the Benedictines who owed their reform to Marguerite's exhortations, the procession went on to the Mont-du-Piété, where for two days the body was exposed to the veneration of the faithful, who, Ferraige tells us, treated it "as in olden times the bodies of S. Hugues, Bishop, and S. Charles were treated." They would have liked to prevent the departure of the saint's relics, and Mauvielle reminds Ferraige:

> I myself was of this opinion, but on confessing as much to you, you said firmly: "I will bring her back dead to those who entrusted her to me living, it will be an indescribable sorrow to them."

Dom Mauvielle still hoped that at least the heart of the saint, which had been embalmed separately, might be left with him, and he was distressed to see it "put into the hands of the sub-Prioress, who was already in the carriage beside the body; she took it with intense affection and pressed it . . . close to her own." When they arrived at Pouilly, where they were to halt for the night, Dom Mauvielle tried once more to get hold of the heart which fascinated him. I thought, he said,

> that at the descent from the coach, at least I should have the comfort of receiving it in my hands, though only to bear it as far as the church to the spot destined for it that night, but I was fated to receive a second disappointment. For when I stretched out my arms to the said sub-Prioress to receive it, she quickly withdrew it and showed by her

action that she would not part with it for any cause whatsoever. This refusal increased my sorrow, and caused the resentment of which I allowed you to become aware. But then, *consolationes tuæ lætificaverunt animam meam.* For, being conducted to behold that sacred body, its face still uncovered and very fair, I received in my hands (thanks doubtless to the intervention of Ferraige) that holy heart which had been a sacred altar.[1]

Will the modern reader be more severe than we are to the tender infatuation of Dom Mauvielle or to the ungraciousness of Marie de Burges? French taste is so capricious and sometimes so unreasonable that the question must remain unanswered. I must recall nevertheless that these beautiful details did not find favour with Fleury, who merely summarises Mauvielle's narrative. "Dom Robert Mauvielle followed as far as Pouilly and was solicitous to remove everything touched by Mère d'Arbouze, down to the mat of rushes on which she had lain."[2] For all the next month the mat gave out a sweet odour. "The tears flowed from my eyes, although I am little given to sentiment . . . and I cried involuntarily: *Odor Margaritæ.*"[3] These last words do not occur in Fleury's book. Whether or not he appreciated such beautiful human traits, he should have kept them if only from a historian's interest in details, for they show how the saints make themselves loved and how they bestow on those who love them a measure of their own poetry and tenderness.[4]

Another Benedictine of the Reform, Dom Athanase de Mousin, subsequently addressed a letter to Ferraige, some quotations from which may fitly close this account of Marguerite d'Arbouze.

Pax Christi.—Here are a few thoughts concerning our worthy Sister whom I always bear within my heart. The first is a great regret at having so seldom seen and conversed with her, having been hindered by my continual avocations at the College. When I planned to resign my mastership in order to be able to visit her according to the desires of us both, I was sent to the monastery of Corbie to teach

[1] Ferraige, I. 544–50. [2] *Ibid.*, p. 243. [3] *Ibid.*, I. 552.

[4] The delicacy of the closing seventeenth century had standards of its own, to judge from Fleury's own story of a miracle wrought by the roses from the tomb of Marguerite d'Arbouze on behalf of the Duc d'Alluin, which, to say the least, is remarkably outspoken. These variations of taste in matters of literature and morality, and, especially from the secular standpoint, the difference between the hagiographical schools of Ferraige (1626) and Fleury (1683) afford opportunity for much interesting discussion.

theology. . . . My regrets make me say at times *Revertere, revertere, Sulamitis, ut intueamur te.*

The second is a lively sentiment of the celestial perfume spread abroad by her graces in the hearts of those who visited her. I have had much familiar intercourse with several persons of eminent sanctity, who have been conducted in the paths of especial grace by various leaders at Paris and elsewhere, more often than with our blessed one. Nevertheless I can in truth assure you that *odor unguentorum illius* . . . "the fragrance of her balms was above all other ointments." Her devotion has more effectually spurred me on in the exact observance of our Rule than that of any other known to me. I never visited her without returning greatly comforted. Her piety was full of the Divine unction and wealth of the spirit of God, which she diffused in simple words with no high-sounding phrases, no affectation or pose of devotion, but flowing naturally from her pure breast and lips. To me this was ever in truth an evidence of her maternal fecundity, such as the Bridegroom desired in the fourth of the Canticles: *Emissiones tuæ paradisus malorum punicorum cum pomorum fructibus ejus.*[1]

"Return, return, O Shulamite, that we may see thee again."

All the intimates of Marguerite d'Arbouze, inspired by the same love, uttered the same prayer to the saint of Val-de-Grâce.

Anne of Austria heard of the death of her friend when travelling in Languedoc with the King.

She was so afflicted thereby that for some days she thought never to return to Val-de-Grâce, having lost the one who attracted her thither. But later on she decided that she would testify better to the friendship which she had had for Mère d'Arbouze, by continuing after her death to give proofs of it to her nuns and her house, which she did ever after so long as she survived her, that is to say, during nearly forty years.[2]

At first Mère de S. Etienne (Louise de Milley) was much embarrassed at having to converse with the Queen and said to her: "You will find, Madame, much difference between the conversation of our Blessed Mother and the poor patois of a rough provincial like me!" The Queen, however, would not be discouraged from liking and trusting her, and this pious intercourse lasted more than ten years until finally, innocent though it was, it drew a great persecution upon the Abbess.

[1] Ferraige, II. 75-7.

[2] Fleury, p. 244.

For the Queen being Spanish and the Abbess, born in the Comté de Bourgogne (Burgundy), having all her relations in the service of the King of Spain, it was not hard to persuade Cardinal Richelieu that the Spanish were availing themselves of this religious to win the Queen to their interests.

On August 13, 1637, about eight in the morning, therefore, the Archbishop of Paris and the Chancellor Séguier made a descent upon Val-de-Grâce. They ransacked all the drawers but found nothing suspicious. Nevertheless the Abbess was exiled, at first to La Charité, then to Nevers, and was replaced by Marie de Burges. But at least the Cardinal assigned her a small pension, a detail which other ministers, not Churchmen, have sometimes neglected to attend to in similar cases. Fleury, who is much amused by it all, goes on:

Cardinal Richelieu being dead and the King dying soon after, on May 14, 1643, on the same day two hours after his death the Queen said to the Presidente Le Bailleul who was in attendance: "We must think of bringing back our good Mother of Val-de-Grâce." They told her that she was ill. "No matter," said the Queen, "living or dead, I wish to see her again." And, desiring her first equerry, the Comte d'Orval, to be summoned, she commanded him to send her best litter and a coach to Nevers to bring back Mère de S. Etienne. This was done so promptly that those escorting this equipage had had no time to assume mourning and throughout the journey bore the liveries of the Queen. This called forth much remark, and all who met them demanded the reason. Cardinal Alphonse de Richelieu, Archbishop of Lyons, doing likewise, the Prior of S. Pierre-le-Moutier, who was in the coach, replied, "Monseigneur, the Queen-Regent is causing the Mother of Val-de-Grâce to be brought back, whom your brother the Cardinal banished!" (The faithful companion of the exiled Abbess) Mère de Gaboury could not refrain from saying to Mère de S. Étienne that this reply had delighted her and had aroused some resentment against the defunct Cardinal, but Mère de S. Etienne answered: "Well, Sister, for your penance you will say your rosary for his intention." (On June 3, 1643, they arrived at Val-de-Grâce.) The Queen, who was still keeping the forty days after the King's death and should not have appeared in public, went *incognita* in the coach of Madame La Princesse who accompanied her, together with Mme. de Vendôme and some other ladies.

The meeting after these ten years of separation was the more touching in that Mère de S. Etienne, who was dangerously ill, could not leave her bed. Mme la Princesse said to the Queen:

"Madame, here is your Majesty's martyr!"[1] The Queen's Martyr did not long survive such emotion, dying on June 18, after thus doubly experiencing the dangers of the friendship of the great.

Of the three religious of Montmartre who had left Marie de Beauvillier in 1619 for Val-de-Grâce, only one now survived, Marie de Burges, for the last ten years Abbess in her turn, whom we have seen travelling in the coach that bore the coffin of Marguerite d'Arbouze, and during all that sad triumphal procession often "touching her heart with that of the saint" which she cherished in her hands.[2] Anne of Austria was also much attached to Marie, and when on coming to Val-de-Grâce she found her in bed, "she ate in the same room where she lay, causing the table to be placed close to the invalid."[3] Marie de Burges put the great influence which she had with the Queen at the service of Benedictine Reform, which had not yet triumphed everywhere and was often in need of royal protection. The reform of S. Maur owed much to her. She also engaged more directly in the great work, sending her own nuns to Abbeys desirous of reform, for example, to the Abbey of Estival, near Mans (1648).[4] The Queen generally had these missionaries of Val-de-Grâce conveyed in her own carriages.

On April 1, 1645, the young Louis XIV laid the first stone of the new church of Val-de-Grâce, but the work, suspended for a considerable interval, was not completed till 1665. From 1661, however, divine service was celebrated in the choir, where Bossuet preached in Lent 1663. The inauguration of the church and convent took place on March 21, 1665, in the presence of both Queens. Much has been written on the architecture and decoration of this church, the great artist of which knew how

By mingling the shadows and lights of the whole,
To clothe stones with flesh and give colour a soul.

[1] Fleury, pp. 265–8. [2] Ferraige, II. 493–4. [3] Fleury, p. 269.

[4] *Ibid.*, pp. 282–3. The Priory of La Celle, near Brignoles, on which M. A. Hallays has written one of his most charming sketches, is connected, like so many others, with the history of Val-de-Grâce. In 1657, Mazarin, who was Abbot of S. Victor, and on whom the Priory of La Celle was dependent, made Marie de Croze, a nun of that Priory, enter Val-de-Grâce to equip herself for the task of reformer. She remained three years, leaving in 1660 with two nuns to reform her own Priory, which was soon transferred to Aix. Anne of Austria, being at Aix at the time of this move, "favoured it . . . by her presence."

In 1662 Anne of Austria had promised the nuns that the hearts of the royal princes and princesses of France should be deposited in their church. The first was that Anne-Elizabeth of France, eldest daughter of Louis XIV, who died on December 30, 1662, aged six weeks and a day, the forty-fifth, and last, heart was that of Louis-Joseph-Xavier-François de France, the seven-year-old Dauphin, who died at the Château of Meudon, June 4, 1789.[1]

In 1792 the dust in those forty-five hearts of silver-gilt was scattered to the winds, and the silver-gilt itself taken to the Hôtel des Monnaies (Mint). On July 31, 1793, the Convention "through its *comité d'aliénation* (board of confiscations) authorized the Ministry of War to turn the national property of Val-de-Grâce into a military hospital."[2]

[1] There were only five exceptions. The Dauphin Louis, son of Louis XV, and Marie-Josephe of Saxony his wife (1765–7), having been interred in the cathedral of Sens, their hearts were taken to S. Denis; that of Marie Leczinska at her own desire was given to the Bon-Secours at Nancy (1768). Louis XV was buried, heart and all, at S. Denis, and Louise of France in her convent in 1787.

[2] Cf. the *Notice sur la monastère du Val-de-Grâce*, by M. l'Abbé H. de Bertrand de Beuvron, Paris, 1873.

CHAPTER VII

FRANÇOIS DE SALES AND JEANNE DE CHANTAL

I. NOT the author of *Philothée*, the master of devout humanism, but the author of the *Traité de l'Amour de Dieu*, the master of the higher mysticism, is our subject here. A friend of several of the contemplatives we have been studying, François de Sales, like them, aspired to transcendent heights and actively continued their propaganda. His appearance is an epoch in the history of mysticism. No spiritual master of the time has more weight than he. His intervention, gentle but firm, reassured the timid, paralysed by fear of quietism or illusion; it disciplined the indiscreet and rash who failed to see that, without "the ecstasy of works," the most sublime raptures only foster spiritual pride; it consecrated the progress made in this first period of Renaissance and accelerated the magnificent development that was to follow.

In the inner history of the *Traité de l'Amour de Dieu*, Ste. Chantal occupies a large space. It was for her and near her that this book was written; what is more, it is of her and the first Visitandines that it tells. The historical and analytical method pursued in these volumes makes it therefore necessary to study these two souls together as they scale the heights of mysticism, each assisting the other in the ascent.[1]

Until the death of her husband from a hunting accident in 1601, Jeanne-Françoise Frémyot, Baronne de Rabutin-Chantal, had led a pious and Christian life, but without a hint of the sanctity to which she was one day to attain. "This blessed Mother," we read in the *Mémoires* of Madeleine de Chaugy, "has admitted in confidence that whenever M. de Chantal absented himself her heart and all her

[1] Jeanne Frémyot, daughter of the advocate-general, Bénigne Frémyot—subsequently royal Councillor and President of the Burgundy Parlement—and of Marguerite de Berbisey his wife, was born at Dijon on January 23, 1572. At twenty she married Christophe de Rabutin-Chantal, by whom she had several children, among them a daughter, destined to wed a brother of François de Sales, and Celse Bénigne, one day to be the father of the future Marquise de Sevigné. Mme de Chantal died at the Visitation de Moulins on Dec. 13, 1641.

affections turned towards Our Lord." Even at that time she seemed very devout. "When I no longer saw my husband," she would say, "I felt great longing to be altogether devoted to God; but alas, I knew not how to profit by or even recognize the grace God was offering me, nearly all my thoughts and prayers being limited to the preservation and return of M. de Chantal." On the return of this dear husband, the perfect contentment which the blessed one had in him made her forget her previous devotion, and she would no longer spend so much time in prayer to God. The rush of occupations and society (visits, amusements, hunting-parties) came back with him, and among their distractions she went on as before until the year 1601.[1]

As we have seen, the first assaults of God, when He wishes to win the secret depths of the soul, sometimes resemble a sudden, silent, but violent blow. Sure of its garrison, the town has gone to sleep in perfect tranquillity; dawn finds it in the hands of a new master already installed there and settling in with the imperiousness of a conqueror. So it is with the soul upon whom grace has swooped. It awakes, astonished, bruised, anxious, in a paralysing grip that affects every part. After the sudden blow comes the state of siege and martial law. It feels itself mercilessly deprived of all—the serenity of a faith untroubled by sophisms, the easy sweetness of prayer, the simple and plain sense of duty, the tranquillity of conscience. In spite of the noble summons which sustains it and which it deliberately purposes to follow, it seems to be sinking, engulfed in evil. Assuredly it would submit with joy to the worst consequences of defeat, if it knew the name of the conqueror. But he reigns, as he has conquered, in darkness, and when for a moment, repenting, as it were, of his ruthlessness, he lets the light of his countenance shine forth, the light falls unexpectedly on eyes that so much darkness has rendered timid, and dazzles and terrifies instead of consoling.

This was exactly the experience of the Baronne de Chantal, from her widowhood to the fortunate day when she met François de Sales, and even long after. There was an agonizing transition between the two passions which in turn ravished and absorbed the saint. The

[1] *Mémoires de la M. de Chaugy.* These *Mémoires* form the first volume of Ste. Chantal's *Œuvres*, published by Plon. All the quotations not supplied with references are taken from this book.

Baron de Chantal disappeared, and though God almost immediately entered by the cruel breach, He could be neither seized nor touched. This soul doubly desolate was enveloped in a cloud, which hid her from herself. She was a mother. So when the sobs of a fortnight's mourning were stifled her four little ones saw her smiling as usual. She was generous to every form of need; the sick and the poor felt her kinder, if possible, and more compassionate than ever. Decorous and moderate in sorrow as in joy, she took up, with the gravity that her bereavement demanded, her daily life; her tact and charm were soon to soften the morose solitude of her father-in-law, old Guy de Rabutin; and François de Sales would before long be blaming her excessive display of laces. She tried, but without success, to deceive her friends and the members of her household. Her women knew that some nights she forgot to go to bed and that frequently she would "walk alone in a little wood . . . to weep to her heart's content. All the ladies of the neighbourhood, who loved her well, were assiduous in visiting her; her aunts and cousins from Dijon came to stay with her in turn . . . thinking it a great kindness to distract her." They meant to bring consolation, but their visits were a martyrdom to her. But fussy and powerless to help, they watched the transformation which was taking place within her. They did not know that God was besieging her and lacerating her. Nor did she, for she was too profoundly humble to believe herself the object of exceptional favours, and as yet too ignorant of the mystic way to recognize the strange shores on which she had been cast up by an irresistible wave.

The saint has left us only vague information about the temptations endured in those years of trial, which were fated to return towards the end of her life with fresh sharpness and subtlety. Faith and consequently hope, it would seem, suffered the worst assaults. A certain modern philosopher thinks he can detect her engaged in a struggle with grosser temptations. In my opinion nothing authorizes this conjecture, and everything disproves it. Of the graces which sometimes sustained her in her perplexity more is known. One especially should not be passed over here.

One day, when she was at prayer, God gave her so pressing a desire to have a director who should instruct her in perfection and the Divine

Will, that henceforth she demanded it incessantly. "Alas!" she said, writing to our first Mothers, "I desired a director and asked for what I knew not. For though I had been reared by virtuous persons and had always associated with the good, nevertheless I had never heard of directors or spiritual masters or anything approaching thereto. Nevertheless God put this desire so before my heart, and the inspiration bidding me ask for this director was so strong that I made this prayer with such fervour and force as never before."

We must try to understand the hidden work by which God prepared her to formulate so definite a prayer and one so little expected by her. Little by little out of the depth of her distress light began to appear; a feeling of certainty had arisen, fixed and serene, if as yet not grasped. God was permitting all which was passing within her, to fashion her for some great work. She must hold herself in readiness, and such indeed was her attitude during the years of waiting which were to follow. But her good sense, humility, natural docility, in fact grace in her, told her that no voice would sound from heaven to reveal to her the programme of these mysterious designs. A man of God would come, and her part would be to obey him. Only, once again, how was she to disentangle the contradictory movements at work in her? how know, once for all, whether she should shun as delusions or accept with simple gratitude the intangible clear shinings that took possession of her soul and led her to believe that God was there? Here also she needed the clear responses and authoritative councils of a man of God.

To Jeanne de Chantal at the age of thirty, director and direction might have been Hebrew for all she understood of them. A heavenly inspiration was needed to explain them—an illuminating fact sufficient in itself to show the originality of her interior life. With her direct experience preceded knowledge. God took her in hand fresh, artless, hardly richer at thirty than she had been at twelve years old in abstract ideas of the spiritual life. Her devotional library would appear childish to Christians of to-day. No matter, she is in herself a living book written by the Spirit of God.

In this state of mind, eager but ignorant, it is not surprising that she accepted the yoke of a priest met by chance who offered his direction; no doubt a worthy man, but too rigid, dense and tyrannical. The poor woman let herself be bound by this pastor, who rejoiced to have so saintly a sheep in his hands, and attached her to his direction by four vows: first, that she should obey him; secondly, that she should never change her director; thirdly, that she should keep all that he said to her secret; fourthly, that she should speak of her interior life to none but him.

This priest may be pardoned for not recognizing the saint's interior qualities, but not for having abused her docility and innocent ignorance; for having imprisoned her, when she was already tormented by so many scruples, in those "tiresome nets" which for two years were to hold "her soul cramped and captive." No doubt instinct often warned her that this man deluded himself and her, but

this truly obedient woman was like a statue in the hands of her director, without resistance or will of her own. She never departed from any of his counsels (orders rather), contrary though she felt them to be to the inclinations and instincts of her heart. He loaded her soul with quantities of prayers, meditations, speculations, acts, methods and divers observances, and extremely laborious considerations and ratiocinations. He likewise ordered midnight prayers and numerous fastings, disciplines and other macerations.[1]

II. François de Sales and the Baronne de Chantal saw one another for the first time on March 5, 1604, in the Sainte-Chapelle of Dijon, where the Bishop of Geneva was preaching the Lenten Course, and where, with at least two of her children, she had come to hear a preacher highly praised by President Frémyot. At that time S. François was thirty-seven and she thirty-two.

They recognized each other from the first: she with obvious alacrity, he with subtle prudence. "From the moment that I had the honour to know him, I called him a saint in the depths of my heart," she wrote later. That was all—those few words, but her heart was on fire. For the rest of her life so she spoke and wrote of him and saw him. That Lent she caused

her chair to be placed opposite the pulpit, in order to see and hear the preacher at her ease. The holy prelate on his side, intent on his discourse though he was, speedily remarked this widow among the others. He had a holy curiosity to know who she was, and by a happy chance addressed himself to Mgr. de Bourges (André Frémyot,

[1] *Œuvres de Ste. Chantal*, II. 227.

her brother), saying, "Tell me, I beg, who is that young lady, the fair brunette in widow's weeds, who sits opposite me during the sermon and hearkens so attentively to the words of truth?" Mgr. de Bourges, smiling, was able to reply to the question.

Soon the Bishop beheld her more closely and freely at the President's or the Archbishop's, where "he frequently went to a meal." The baroness never missed a chance of meeting him. Wherever he preached she was sure to be there. "She followed him everywhere, whenever possible." From the first instant he had won her fully and for ever.

In his writings François de Sales is inexhaustible. He loves to let his pen run on, very sure of himself, but always on his guard. In public, on the contrary, even with his intimate friends, he was very silent, observing and listening with an air of smiling and dignified benevolence, speaking only now and then. This young widow, the fair-brown creature, at once so vivacious and so thoughtful, must have appeared something of a mystery. The Savoyard had seen many Frenchwomen in his time, both in Paris and at Dijon, but never one after this pattern—lively and serious, friendly and reserved, ardent and timid, simple, but finished and extremely elegant, with nothing of the devotee about her. In the *salons* only commonplaces were possible, and her lips were sealed to any intimate conversation. "I never spoke to any of private matters except with great fear," she tells us, "although the holy kindliness of this blessed one sometimes invited me to do it, and moreover I longed to do so," had it not been for the luckless promise binding her to a jealous director.

Reduced to snatches of cautious conversation, the holy Bishop was quietly taking his bearings. Once he "asked her if she meant to marry again, and on her saying 'No,' 'Well then,' he replied, 'one should haul down the ensign.' She understood his meaning, she was wearing certain adornments permitted to ladies of quality after their second mourning; but on the next day she removed them, a mark of docility which pleased our blessed Father immensely. At dinner, remarking some little silken laces in her crape trimmings, he said: 'Madame, if those laces were not there, would you not still be neat?' It was enough; that same night, when undressing, she unpicked them herself."

While they were still so near and yet so far from one another, a more "furious attack" of her usual temptations, fortunately coming in the absence of her director, put the Baroness in the happy necessity of breaking a silence already too long kept. On Wednesday in Holy Week she timidly laid open her soul "to the holy prelate, and left his presence so reassured that it seemed as if an angel had spoken to her." "Although," she says, "scruples from my vow to speak of my interior life only to my first director so weighed on me that I only said half to this blessed prelate."

Four months of anguish followed. François de Sales was already master of the situation, and he knew it. At a word from him the last scruples would give way, the jealous director would have to withdraw, whether he liked it or not, and the saint would see the gates of her stifling prison open. But he (François de Sales) hesitated, tacked, withdrew himself. At the height of the crisis an eminent priest, Père de Villars, rector of the Jesuits of Dijon, was consulted. He replied with fine vigour and perhaps with some courage that the tyrannical pretentions of such a director were unjustifiable and this unnatural yoke entirely contrary to the spirit of God and of the Church must be shaken off. Another religious agreed. It was clear to all that it was the Divine pleasure to bring so rare a soul under the guidance of M. de Genève. Nevertheless the latter did not modify his cautious methods, his letters of that period are marvellous in their subtlety, advancing, retiring, and always in the end eluding our grasp. I am surprised at anyone's thinking them simple. What opening for doubt remained? Certainly he had no theological scruple as to the validity of the vow that linked her to another director. But he wished no human element to enter into a decision the extreme importance of which he foresaw. I imagine that his hesitation was quite genuine, that he himself had hardly made up his mind. This soul wanting his direction both attracted and alarmed him. Her brow and eyes betokened heroism. She was set apart at once by the rarity of her natural gifts and by the mysterious signs of grace already at work in her. Let her find a spiritual guide worthy of her, worthy especially to further within her the divine operations, and she will go far. Is he this predestined master? That, so it seems, is the question his humility on the one hand and his clear and uncompromising judgement on the other were asking. Further, if one day he must say "Yes," as doubtless he foresaw, why not begin already to mould her in his own way, by checking and bridling that impetuous directness, that heart and brain, that would never wait, but always run to the destination by the shortest road? Thus, from the dawn of their intimacy, the contrast is sharply defined between this daughter of France and this gentleman-prelate, naturally serious and slow-moving, whose smiling *finesse* had been sharpened by his Italian experiences, and who as the neighbour of an intriguing court and subject of a suspicious prince had been jealously eyed by many and had learned at an early date to trust few men and to be very careful in his relations with all.

Along this wandering way described for us by S. François himself, we reach at last the great day, August 22, 1604, a stern and majestic gateway at the entrance of the new life on which the saint was entering. From the close of the previous Lent it had been settled that the Bishop of Geneva, in company with his mother Mme de Boisy and his sister Jeanne de Sales, should meet during the following summer the chief among the new friends made at Dijon, the Presidente Brulart, the Abbess of the Puits d'Orbe and the Baronne de Chantal, at the tomb of S. Claude, half-way between Savoy and Burgundy. Always cautious, the Bishop had arranged everything with care; neither he nor the baroness came alone. At the last moment his intense preoccupation became manifest. The Burgundians arrived towards evening, it seems, awaited by the others, who were interested and excited, and perhaps somewhat shy—Annecy at that time was not French and by the side of Dijon considered itself as a mere village. When they had been introduced to one another "almost on the first greeting," Mère de Chaugy expressly notes, François de Sales dexterously manœuvred the rest into his mother's company and

as for himself, took his dear spiritual daughter aside and made her tell him all that had passed within her, which she did with such precision, simplicity and candour as to forget nothing. The holy Bishop listened most attentively, but without answering a single word, and so they separated. On the morrow (August 22) at an early hour he came to find her. He seemed weary and exhausted. "Let us sit down," he said, "I am tired and I have not slept; I have been in travail all night concerning you. In truth it is the will of God that I should charge myself with your spiritual guidance and that you should follow my counsels." After this the holy man remained silent for a little, then, turning his eyes towards heaven: "Madame, shall I say it to you? Needs must, since it is the will of God. All these your former vows have but availed save to destroy peace of conscience. Wonder not at my long delay in giving you my decision, I wished to be assured of the will of God, and that there was nothing in this affair that was not from Him." Our blessed Mother recalled: "I listened to the holy prelate, as if a voice from heaven had spoken. He seemed as though in a trance, so great was his state of recollection, and brought forth his words hesitatingly as if scarcely able to speak." That same morning she made her general confession to our blessed Father.

A noble scene truly! The sleeplessness, the final hesitation, the solemn and laborious slowness, the few heavy words interspersed by intervals of silence—all these details raise us to supernatural heights and put us once for all in an atmosphere of sanctity.

S. François' future direction of Ste. Chantal can be summed up in one word, and is not that word the true definition of direction? He *liberated* at one and the same time both her soul and the grace to which till then she either dared not or knew not how to abandon herself, thus speeding her further on the mystic way than he could have done by even a personal intervention. "O God," wrote the saint, recalling her interview at S. Claude, "what a happy day for me! It seemed as if my soul turned about and emerged from the interior captivity in which the counsel of my first director had bound me hitherto." In the witness that she bore later to this unique director the word liberty keeps on recurring.

He was altogether admirable and incomparable in training souls according to their capacity without ever straining them, thus bestowing, and imprinting on the heart, a certain liberty which set free from all scruple or difficulty.

He preferred to leave the spirit of God to act in the soul with all liberty, following himself the lead of that divine spirit and leading the soul in accordance with the divine inspirations rather than by his particular instinct. I recognize that by my own experience.[1]

This method, which he always followed in dealing with souls truly spiritual, he imposed on himself more than ever, if possible, when confronted with the woman who surprised him so much and whom

[1] *Œuvres*, II. pp. 200–1. Cf. *Literary History*, I. pp. 98–99.

he could leave with so much confidence to the movements of grace. This does not mean that he directed her with a feeble hand or that even with her he did not always speak as master.

I have already shown in the preceding volume[1] that the soul can only remain humble and become supple if it recognizes a spiritual master; but this director himself must obey Him Whom he represents, curbing or relaxing the reins at the will of the Spirit that bloweth where it listeth. S. François then was very firm, very precise and inflexible when he thought it necessary, but still more was he discreet, prudent, forgetful, even disdainful of himself to an unusual degree, and he certainly never abused the docility of Ste. Chantal in any way. Ste. Chantal writes:

"Often I was troubled at his not commanding me sufficiently."[2] When he did give orders he wished them to be accepted and followed "without fuss"—"broadly and simply, *à la vieille Française*, in good faith, *grosso modo*."[3]

This respect for souls and the divine in them, this distrust of self and readiness to efface himself before the workings of grace, appeared to still better advantage when viewed at close quarters, as Ste. Chantal was able to view it.

> The manner and speech of this blessed one were most majestic and grave, yet he was always the humblest, sweetest and simplest one had ever seen. . . . He spoke low, gravely, sedately, sweetly and wisely.[4]
>
> Never did this blessed one make quick replies.[5]

Needless to say this slowness in answering, at first surprising in a man of such brilliant parts, this fear of harming souls by imperious personal direction, had nothing affected about it. He would not play the oracle, like some who mask their intellectual poverty under airs of majesty, or their dominating instincts under a pretence of fumbling for words. His faith, even more alert than his intellect, lingered in reverence on the threshold of the mystery of the spiritual life. Perhaps no one has realized the *Song of Songs*, his favourite book, as he did. In this divine idyll, by a favour which amazes and abashes him, he is assigned a secondary rôle. He is the poor servitor of the

[1] *Literary History*, I. pp. 83–84
[2] *Œuvres*, II. 201.
[3] *Œuvres de S. François de Sales*, XIII. 392.
[4] *Œuvres*, II. 221–2.
[5] *Ibid.*, II. 136.

Bridegroom and the Bride; he does not raise his voice, nor give commands except when the Bride wanders in her quest. Effacing himself with joy, he stands in silence to admire her when her feet are set on the path leading to the Beloved.

Our incomparable director never obeyed his watchwords of caution, patient waiting and effacement more strictly than in his dealings with Ste. Chantal. He had only a very confused idea of the mysterious designs that grace seemed to be forming for her. When the young Bishop undertook the task of directing her, he had not yet attained those lofty heights of which he would later write with such ease in the *Traité de l'Amour de Dieu.* He still trod most frequently the " low valleys " of the Christian life, as distinguished from the mystic life, and did not generally leave the sweet region of bees and doves. When he was summoned in his turn to mount the heights, his natural prudence, his humility and his habits of prayer, which was nearly always graceful and fluent, on the one hand bade him to fear " the high seas " which " make our head swim and fill us with convulsive terrors," and on the other hand endeared to him the " earth to earth," the " little virtues fit for our littleness." " A little buyer has a little basket! " he writes;[1] the humble posy of the flower-girl Glycera was enough for him. He practised, but " with extraordinary fervour and perfection, the ordinary exercises of the Christian."[2]

It must not, however, be fancied that, during this first stage of his ascent, François de Sales was altogether ignorant of the regions which he would one day reach in the track of Ste. Chantal. It is a nice question where the " low valleys " of the devout life end and the high mountains begin. Between the frontiers of these two worlds is there not a debatable land, in which the sweet breezes of the first begin to mingle with the mighty winds of the second? That between 1604 and 1610 the saint traversed this zone and even penetrated to the mystic ways beyond, appears certain, although he himself may not have been conscious of the change which was being sketched out or prepared within. His heart had no doubt outstripped his mind, and that mind itself, so clear-sighted and detached, so calm, was shielded from those restless wanderings and vain curiosities with which grace has nothing to do, but which rather hinder it. Anyhow, he has

[1] *Œuvres de S. François de Sales*, XII. 205.
[2] *Traité de l'Amour de Dieu*, VIII. Chap. XII.

told us himself, in the preface to the *Traité de l'Amour de Dieu*, that he had at that time much to learn and much to unlearn. Must we blush for him? Or need we be surprised that before becoming one of the masters of mysticism he had to serve his apprenticeship? I shall presently quote passages to support these conjectures. If my analysis goes astray, it can easily be corrected.

Let us try to realize the Baroness as she then appeared to her director. God was at work in her, to unite her more closely to himself. Did God's work disconcert S. François? Surely not. He knew well that on the Divine side all is unsounded mystery. For the rash man who tries to define them, the commonest graces, flashes of supernatural impulse, are not less enigmas than the rapture of S. Paul. When God encounters us, darkness goes before Him, enshrouds Him, hides His departure and covers His retreating steps. But when it comes to mystic graces, the nights of man, if the expression be allowed, reinforce the Nights of God. They are graces doubly mysterious, travelling from deep to deep, cleaving, so it seems, new depths in the soul that receives them. Hence the agonizing of the elect victim. The richer the natural gifts, the sharper the resistance to the mysterious pressure away from human things, paltry and worthless in themselves but precious as the material whence such gifts derive value. The more he resists and tries to climb back again, the greater his distress. From such struggles come incessant doubts, giddiness of the soul, temptations to despair, fear of foundering in the hell of unreason and blasphemy. But thence also, at times, when resistance weakens, when reflection ceases and the eyes of imagination close, when sensitiveness no longer reacts, then arise mighty impressions of peace, light, strength, coming from regions which the mystics themselves cannot describe. They have passed the frontier of earth's language. Metaphors which to them are luminous and infinitely sweet, but obscure and meaningless to our weak flesh, flow from their pens with an insistence which is in itself revealing. They go towards "their centre," towards "the extreme point of their spirit." Thither God invites them, thither He bears them and there He awaits them.

But listen to Ste. Chantal herself.

At daybreak God made me aware, but almost imperceptibly, of a spark of light in the highest supreme point of my spirit. All the rest of my soul and its faculties were untouched thereby; but it endured about half an *Ave Maria.*[1]

There are certain souls, she writes in another place, among those whom God leads by this way of simplicity, whom His divine Goodness strips in such extraordinary wise of all satisfaction, desire and feeling that they can scarce endure or express themselves, because what is passing within them is so slight, delicate and imperceptible, being wholly centred in the extreme point of the spirit, that they cannot speak of it.[2]

A longer extract follows, remarkably lucid, like everything else this saint wrote, and chosen from a thousand more or less similar passages, partly because it brings us to S. François de Sales and partly because it shows Ste. Chantal at the outset of her pilgrimage. Writing in 1637 she says:

I remember that, when it pleased Our Lord to afford me the beginnings of consolation in the heavy temptations under which I had laboured for so many years, since the taking of my vow (the vow of obedience to her first director), His Goodness bestowed upon me this method of devotion consisting in a simple beholding and realizing of His divine presence, in which I felt utterly lost, absorbed, and at rest in Him. And this grace has been continued to me, although by my unfaithfulnesses I have opposed it much; permitting entrance into my mind, of fears of being useless in this condition, so that desiring to do somewhat on my part, I spoiled all. And yet ofttimes am I attacked by this very fear, not in this devotion but in my other exercises, where I would ever be active and multiply acts, although well aware that I thus draw myself from my centre; above all, I see that this unique and simple looking towards God is my only remedy and sole consolation. And, certainly, did I follow my inclination, I should do nought but this without exception. For when I think to fortify my soul with thoughts and discourse, resignations and acts, I expose myself to new temptations and difficulties, and can only do it by a violent effort which leaves me dry. So it behoves me to return promptly to this simple abandonment, conceiving that God thus wills me to understand that He desires a total curbing of the sallies of my spirit and of its workings along these lines. And the activity of my spirit is so great that I need ever to be consoled and comforted for such (curbing of mental effort). Ah, how oft has my blessed Father said thus to me! . . . While on this subject, I remember that some days ago Our Lord bestowed upon me such clearness on this point that it

[1] *Œuvres,* I. 21.

[2] *Ibid.*, II. 337–8.

was as if it had become visible to me: that I must no longer regard myself but walk with closed eyes leaning upon my Beloved, without desiring to see or know the way by which He will conduct me, nor to have care for aught whatsoever, not even for asking anything of Him, but simply remaining as though lost and at rest in Him. If . . . I do not express myself well, . . . no doubt you will not fail to comprehend me.[1]

"How oft has my blessed Father said thus to me." Deeply attached as he was to "the little customs of our predecessors," that is in the exercises of the devout life, he nevertheless not only respected but aided the mystical development of Mme de Chantal. If as yet they were not fully upon the same spiritual plane, at least they understood one another admirably, and the words of the saintly man met the present needs of the saintly woman perfectly. If they did not as yet see it from the same point of view, and if also they did not reach it simultaneously, yet one reality, differently comprehended but none the less essentially one, was the object of both, namely to know the love of God; the devout life and the mystical alike have no other aim than this. And as the sole object is attained on both sides by following the same discipline, by entire detachment and self-abandonment, there is no cause to be afraid that the very severe direction of S. François will impede the progress of his pupil. If he as yet does not realize the presence of God "in the supreme point of the spirit" or the absolute detachment which is the condition and the necessary result of such grace, if even the confidences which he receives on this subject from Ste. Chantal leave him perplexed, his direction none the less goes on its way unfaltering to help forward this twofold mystery. Such direction brings both peace and deprivation. It means an entire yielding to God's purposes without resistance or unrest, but a becoming detached from self. "The whole teaching of our blessed Father," wrote Ste. Chantal later, "aimed at complete deprivation of self."[2] The sublimest mystics have nothing else to teach.

III. During her numerous sojourns with President Frémyot at Dijon the Baroness frequently visited the Carmelite nuns, recently installed in that town, repeating her visit as often as she could down to the eve of her departure for Annecy. It is delightful to think of this meeting of S. Teresa and Ste. Chantal, of Carmel with the

[1] *Œuvres*, IV. 735–7.

[2] *Ibid.*, I. 352.

Visitation soon to be born. There was never any danger of the one influencing the other unduly, of a wind from Avila carrying away the tender seed which God and François de Sales were keeping from another garden. The saintly man is there between the two saintly women, strong enough if need arise to keep his hold on the one, humble and enlightened enough to feel that he needs the teachings of the other and to seize with joy the chance of penetrating into the spirit of S. Teresa through the medium of Ste. Chantal.

Besides her confessors—between 1604 and 1610 she made her confession to S. François only four or five times—the Baroness eagerly consulted every expert in devotional and doctrinal matters who crossed her path. Thus we see the Rector of the Jesuits coming at her request to meet her at the house of President Frémyot and the future Cardinal de Bérulle engaged in conference with her. For the present then, that is for four years, she is closely associated with the Carmelites. But why all these conversations? Was not S. François enough? No, he was far away. Letters were slow and unsatisfactory. When the snow came Annecy was cut off for weeks at a time. Besides, we must remember the temptations and scruples which tormented this beginner and her utter inexperience in the spiritual life. Even if François de Sales had been near her, she would have had no reason to live in seclusion; on the contrary, she would have had every reason to visit her friends, that new world of saints still so novel and delightful to her. Her director was not jealous. He knew her to be supremely frank and docile; no important decision would ever be taken without him. A word from him would amend or efface any counsels of which he did not approve. He was kept fully conversant with those visits to the Carmelites; Ste. Chantal, breathless with awe, told him—whom else should she tell?—all the details of the secret of S. Teresa. Besides, she did not go alone. Another of the Salesian *Philothées*, the Présidente Brulart, was wont to accompany her, and she too wrote letters to her director. We can only refer in passing to this beautiful picture, the two beloved daughters of François de Sales welcomed by Anne de Jésus, the dear companion of S. Teresa. All Dijon crowded round them, but the Carmelites were quick to perceive the quality of these two visitors, and to make much of them. The Baroness looks, asks questions, abandons herself to the atmosphere, feels herself at home. God does not mean her to be a Carmelite, but He does mean the Visitation to resemble Carmel.

Nevertheless all was not clear in the teaching of S. Teresa, as it came to her, although everything seemed an answer to the obscure cravings of her soul. But she knew no Spanish and most of the Carmelites knew no French. Mère Marie de la Trinité, herself a Frenchwoman and sufficiently illumined to be able to impart teaching of her own, was the interpreter. Naturally one subject alone occupied these interviews, that interior life which the Carmelites had learned in a good school and on which the ardent Baroness desired more light. She was as yet very "rustic," to use her own word, in these delicate questions. , But not excessively so. Maybe the Carmelites, finding her so quick of apprehension and of so generous a temper, yielded quickly to that impetuosity which S. François de Sales himself found it hard enough to hold in check. I cannot be sure of this, and I have reasons for thinking that she understood even then the sublime teachings which she received and hastened to submit to her own director. But as yet she did not formulate them with the necessary precision. As she presented it, the teaching of Mère Marie de la Trinité unquestionably justified the wise reservations which, as will be seen, S. François de Sales opposed to it. The teaching in itself, whatever certain critics may have said, is thoroughly good, and not only did S. François never condemn it, but later he made it his own.

After all, why make so much of this? According to some biographers, Mère de la Trinité foolishly transported her youthful novice to the highest tower of the mystical castle. Nothing could be less exact. To her was opened, on the contrary, no more than the first ward, raised but a few steps above the level of common life, that which later S. François and Ste. Chantal would reckon as the ordinary abode of the daughters of the Visitation. And, in fact, even these outer precincts were not opened to the saint; it was merely revealed to her that she already dwelt there. "The prayer practised by Mme de Chantal," writes one of her biographers, "seemed (to Mère de la Trinité) too simple and ordinary for one of such eminent holiness . . . she desired that Mme de Chantal should advance from the first grade of prayer to the second." As much as to say that this fine flower of the Carmelites knew less of her business than any scatterbrain of a postulant! Mère de la Trinité assuredly neither thought nor desired anything of the sort. She never said to Philothée: "Endeavour to be Théotime, abandon all these exercises of the devout life." Rather she said to one who saw herself, as S. François de Sales saw her, as Philothée: "You are already Théotime; if such and such posies of the devout life distract or weary you, if they hamper in you the workings of the divine, throw down, without scruple, the flower-girl Glycera's little basket." What folly to speak of "illusive attractions," which an "imprudent" zeal suggested to Ste. Chantal! Those drawings towards a form of devotion more elevated, more abstract, less in accordance with the laws of ordinary prayer, had been not only long felt by our saint, but even gropingly followed, with the approbation of François de Sales, as we have seen above. What did both of them lack then, save the full satisfaction and perfect security imparted by a definite doctrine, supported by the tradition and experience of the saints? Is there anything wonderful in Mère Marie de la Trinité's possessing such a doctrine, or, possessing it, is she to be reproached for having imparted it to Ste. Chantal?

Thus, it seems to me, we may justify, admire and love both the voices—Annecy and Dijon—that guided Ste. Chantal during these fruitful years (1606–10): the voice that showed her boldly the heights to which God was calling; and the more hesitating voice which tried, not to establish her for ever in the valleys of ordinary life, but to keep her there a little longer. The two voices were not hostile. Marie de la Trinité and François de Sales were not disputing for her. On different lines, but in harmony, they were striving to liberate and develop her gift of grace. Again, S. François need only have lifted his hand and Mme de Chantal would never again have crossed the Carmelite threshold. That he refrained, says all to one who remembers how precious this soul was to him. Everything that came from the Carmelites, through Ste. Chantal or Présidente Brulart, was received, weighed and discussed by the Bishop with singular consideration. If a point surprised him or appeared exaggerated, or if a direction seemed premature, he said as much, but without setting up as the master. Indeed he was disciple rather than master, for he was practising the Carmelite counsels in his present devotional life.

There are some fine passages which will help us to understand this initiation to which he was submitting so modestly and cautiously. In 1606 he replied thus to a question of Ste. Chantal:

According to this good Mother (Marie de la Trinité or Anne de Jésus or both), it is not necessary to avail oneself of one's imagination in realizing the sacred Humanity of the Saviour. Not, *perhaps*, for those who are already far advanced up the mount of perfection, but for *us others* who are *yet* in the valleys. . . . I think that it is expedient to use all our powers.[1]

The words in italics are essential. There are two groups; the Carmelites are one; the other consists of the Baronne de Chantal, the Présidente Brulart and the Bishop of Geneva—the infant class as it were standing on tiptoe to peep in at the windows of the great class-room. The saint is careful not to burn his boats. His "yet" protects the present and reserves the future. Nor is his "perhaps" less admirable. Summed up and simplified by the inexperience of Ste. Chantal, the doctrine of Mère Marie de la Trinité suggested danger of a kind that had never occurred to the Carmelite, but which would, at the outset, have prejudiced a less prudent director. S. François de Sales proves by that "perhaps," not merely that he has been struck by that false interpretation, but that he has not taken alarm, feeling secure that Marie de la Trinité was not a Quietist and that Ste. Chantal was in no danger of becoming one. He did not clearly comprehend what the daughter of S. Teresa really meant, but he had confidence in so enlightened a soul. The day would come when, master in his turn, he himself would fearlessly formulate the same doctrine, and write in the *Traité de l'Amour de Dieu*:

The soul recollected in God needs not to make use of either memory or understanding, for she so sweetly beholds her Beloved present that memory would be useless and superfluous . . . neither has she need of imagination, for what need is there to represent to ourselves an image, be it exterior or interior, of Him Whose Presence is being enjoyed?[2]

The Carmelites were not alone in divining the mystic vocation of Ste. Chantal. At this period M. Gallemant, a man of rare gifts whom we already know, met her while himself visiting the Dijon Carmelites, had long interviews with her, and gave her precisely the same counsels as Marie de la Trinité had done. S. François could

[1] *Œuvres de S. François de Sales*, XIII. 162.

[2] Book VI. Chap. IX.

not neglect such indications, but he was never precipitate. Translating into his own language the words of another Order which Mme de Chantal communicated to him, with gentle wisdom he opposed certain directions which appeared to him imprudent, and were so in the sense in which he understood them. In a letter to the Présidente Brulart he says:

As regards devotion I should approve of your still going slow. . . . Now I well know that when by good fortune the soul encounters God, it is good to pause to behold Him and rest in Him; but, my dear daughter, always to expect to meet Him suddenly, without preparation, is not, in my opinion, good for us who are yet novices.[1]

This is very true. He is speaking here of the movements of sensible devotion, of the vivid illuminations that come unawares upon pious souls, superseding the normal preparation that must precede ordinary devotional exercises. To wait for such inspirations with folded arms before beginning prayer would indeed be sloth or folly. The Carmelites spoke of something different, of that more profound recollection which does not depend on human effort. To attempt by oneself and by the use of "all our powers" to attain the mystic Union would be equally foolish. S. François de Sales is as wise as S. Teresa. Let us be patient and they will soon both say the same thing.

(Mystic) recollection is not brought about by the command (or the preparations) of love, but by love itself, that is to say we cannot accomplish it ourselves at will, in so far as it is not in our power to have it when we would, for it depends not on our effort. . . . So said the blessed Mother Teresa de Jésus—who has written that the prayer of recollection resembles a hedgehog or tortoise withdrawing into itself, and said well save for this difference, that these creatures withdraw at their pleasure; while recollection lies not in our will, but befalls us when it pleases God to bestow such grace.[2]

Some words written by S. François to Ste. Chantal in 1607 (chosen from twenty similar passages) remind us that the heart had far more share than the mind in the mysterious initiation taking place within him. The manifest progress of his two spiritual daughters, the influence of the distant Carmel, the presentiment of the great things God was preparing, all stimulated him to a new fervour.

[1] *Œuvres de S. François de Sales*, XIII. 290.
[2] *Traité de l'Amour de Dieu*, VI. Chap. VII.

I can now say, better than formerly (he writes to Ste. Chantal), that I exercise myself in mental prayer, since not a day passes without that. . . . God at times gives me strength to rise before daybreak for this. . . . I seem to have a great affection for it and would gladly practise it twice a day.[1]

So things went on, peacefully and slowly but without any setbacks, until the day when Ste. Chantal, leaving Burgundy for Annecy, must bid the Carmelites farewell; henceforth it would be in the parlour of the Visitation and by word of mouth that the lowly Bishop would complete his initiation and Ste. Chantal's training. He has already learned and unlearned much. Some difficulties remain, soon to be cleared up. We are about to reunite the two founders, but first we must enjoy the fairest page of our whole chapter. Before leaving the school in which she—and he too—has received so much illumination, François de Sales wishes the Baronne de Chantal to ask the Carmelites several vital questions.

For the present I will say nothing concerning those precepts of devotion which you have received from the good Mother Prioress (Louise de Jésus): I only entreat you to learn all you can about the foundations of all that, for, to speak plainly, although two or three times last summer, having placed myself in the Presence of God without preparation or design, I felt it well indeed with myself before His Majesty, with but a very simple but very steadfast sentiment of love that, though almost imperceptible, was yet of great sweetness, yet I should not dare to leave the highroad to reduce this to an everyday occurrence. I know not; I love the ways of the saints that have gone before and of the simple souls; I say not that when after making preparation one is instead drawn to this sort of devotion, it behoves one not to go; but to take as a method that of not preparing oneself, seems to me rather strong. . . . Nevertheless (I speak before Our Lord and to you to whom I can only speak purely and frankly) I am not so assured of knowledge as not to be very glad, I say advisedly very glad, to lay aside my conviction and follow that of those who must by every reason know more than I, and this I say not solely of this good Mother, but of one far lesser than she. Learn then thoroughly all her ideas on this without a fuss and in such wise that she may not suspect that you are playing the inquisitor.[2]

To see in the second part of this letter merely protestations of humility seems to me to be not taking it seriously. Note the adverbs

[1] *Œuvres de S. François de Sales*, XIII. 318. [2] *Ibid.*, XIV. 266.

and parentheses. If S. François did not mean to express with all earnestness his own very sincere and fervent desire to learn, we had better say frankly that he does not know how to write. The same strange exegesis is applied to the first part of the letter. "The saint," we are told, "does not wish Mme de Chantal to abandon the preparation for prayer." The text does not say so, it is a simple exchange of views in which the authority of the director is hardly felt. Here again we must choose: either the saint is perplexed, hesitating, expectant, or he cannot write. If he had clearly taken up his position, would he say he is ready to change his views? In other ways the passage is very curious. For the saint himself the mystical life has begun already, it seems, yet he still applies the rules of ordinary prayer to this higher prayer. He has no wish, he says, "to reduce this to an everyday occurrence," indeed, how could he, for it did not depend on him. As for "the ways of the saints that have gone before," the *Traité de l'Amour de Dieu* deals amply with this difficulty.

If we read this letter attentively, trying to forget that it is addressed to Ste. Chantal, what impression does it make on us? It sounds like a young scholar who, having followed the teaching of an illustrious professor by means of a friend's notebooks, sends his friend on a deputation to their common master to obtain additional information on some points that still remain obscure. The two disciples are themselves masters. They are in a position to discuss freely and examine anew the doctrine brought before them, though they are as yet distrustful of their newly won light. The letter testifies to the highest appreciation and unlimited confidence. The upshot of this obvious and sure line of interpretation is clear. In 1610 the mystical development of Ste. Chantal was accomplished. François de Sales had entrusted her as a novice to S. Teresa. She returned to him fully professed.

IV. "Towards Pentecost of the year 1607" Mme de Chantal had gone to Annecy to learn finally the plans her director had formed for her.

Speaking of this journey . . . she said: "I went to see the blessed prelate with the greatest detachment possible to me. . . . I came to this holy Father of my soul four or five days before Pentecost, during which time he spoke much with me, making me give account of all that had passed and was passing in me, without revealing anything of his plans.

We saw a similar scene above. At Annecy there are the same preparations, the same vague soundings of the soul, the same silences, the same slow and dramatic solemnity.

The blessed Father (continues Mère de Chaugy) left her in this condition till the morrow of Pentecost. . . . Having taken her apart after the holy Mass, he said to her with a grave and serious countenance and the air of one swallowed up in God: " Well, my daughter, I have decided what use I shall make of you." " And I," said she, " Monseigneur and my Father, am resolved to obey you." With that she fell on her knees. The blessed one left her thus, and standing two paces off, answered, " Look now, you must become a Poor Clare." " My Father," she said, " I am all ready." " Nay," said he, " you are not robust enough, you must be a sister at the Hospital of Beaune." " Anything you please." " That is not really what I want," said he, " you must be a Carmelite." " I am ready to obey," she replied. After that he proposed several other Orders the better to test her, and found that here was wax softened by divine warmth, ready to receive the imprint of whatever form of the religious life it should please him to impose upon her.

" With a grave and serious countenance "—please remember this. There is no suspicion of a smile on his face. This last hesitation is perfectly serious. Had he seen the imperceptible start of resistance for which he watched in the eyes of this kneeling woman, he would no doubt have been surprised, but not disturbed. He was made like this. The root of the unique sweetness that was his characteristic was bitter. None perhaps among the saints and moralists has been more convinced than he of human nothingness.

Finally, he . . . declared to her most amply the design conceived by him of our dear *Institut*,

of that new religious order one day to be called the Visitation Sainte-Marie. He expected it to take six or seven years, but in three years his design had taken tangible shape (May 1607–June 1610).

The circumstances which hastened this decision need not be here recorded. Nor need the tragic scene of farewell be dwelt upon, young Celse-Bénigne de Rabutin-Chantal—the future father of the

Marquise de Sevigné—flinging himself down on the threshold to hinder his mother's departure, and the mother, all tears, going where God would have her go. Besides, Celse-Bénigne had already outgrown the maternal tutelage and taken his first steps in the world. As to her daughters, the eldest, Marie-Aimée, was married to a brother of François de Sales, the Baron de Thorens; in leaving Dijon for Annecy, the mother was coming nearer to her. The two younger girls were to remain at the Visitation till their marriage. Charlotte died very soon. There remained the little Françoise, Françon, as she was called. She was far more fortunate than Celse-Bénigne. The veil does not produce the same impression inside the convent as outside. Seen close at hand every day, her mother never appeared changed to her. The humble dwelling at the edge of the lake, of the young community in the making, had not the air of a convent; no *pensionnaire* was ever so petted, cared for, caressed as she. In the Golden Legend of the Visitation her name flits to and fro, together with that of Marie-Aimée, a graver and more remote figure, oftener there than at her own home. Of a morning when Ste. Chantal went to the chapel, the little Baroness, tumbling out of bed and opening the door of her tiny chamber, would salute the saint, who only smiled at her, it being still the Great Silence. The shadow of the cross worn by their mother was sweet for both daughters of Ste. Chantal.

The Visitation, as an introduction to the life of perfection, was conceived by François de Sales in the same spirit as the *Introduction à la vie dévote*. The dominant idea of that immortal book is well known. *Philothée* has a husband, children, a thousand cares which did not permit of more than a short morning Mass and left her desolated by the thought that the devout life was not for her.

> It is an error, even a heresy (replied her director), to banish the devout life from the company of soldiers, the workshop of artisans, the prince's court, the household of married couples.

All the rules of the Visitation say the same. It is an error, a heresy, to think to banish the perfect life from the company of those of delicate health. *Philothée* has lost her husband; her children, happily established, no longer need her, and she is desolated whenever she hears the bell of the Carmelites. The world is no longer anything to her; and she would so willingly tear herself from it! Contemplation attracts her; she longs to consecrate herself to it! Cruel longings! At Carmel, weakling that she is, she would faint in the night offices; after three days of fast and discipline she could not longer stand upright. Console yourself, *Philothée*. Night offices, fasts and the discipline are not indispensable to that all-holy life for which you sigh, to which God invites you. A new Order is about to be founded expressly for you and your like; to-morrow there will be a Carmel for the weak, a Carmel for all. It will be called the Visitation.

This congregation (wrote the founder) has been started with the intent that no great severity shall prevent the feeble and the weak from joining it, there to devote themselves to the perfection of the divine love.[1]

The novel idea amused many. The celebrated Père Ignace Armand wrote to S. François de Sales in a splendid letter:

True, they say that you are establishing a hospital rather than a devout company, but who would not laugh with you, my most honoured Seigneur, at the foolish wit of the children of this world? . . . When formerly we had nuns leading a life so austere as to debar them from receiving any infirm or of frail constitutions, the world . . . taxed them with indiscreet rigour. You, Monseigneur . . . have found the key and the secret, in your Visitation, not too mild for the strong or too harsh for the weak. . . . Alas! who would not pity a virgin, who, having her lamp well trimmed and filled with good oil, yet cannot enter a cloister there to celebrate the marriage of the Lamb, for lack of shoulders strong enough to wear a robe woven of camel's hair . . . or a digestion sufficiently robust to fast half the year and digest roots.[2]

The last lines indicate what S. François de Sales understood by "weak." Illness in the strict sense was not needed to qualify for the Visitation; it was no hospital, but its infirmary would soon be crowded, if all the Sisters practised the austerities of the Carmelites. This is readily intelligible and reminds us in passing what to think of Ste. Chantal's alleged severity. Had she been of a less tender nature, would François de Sales have placed her at the head of so gentle an Order?

[1] For a long and important note, cf. *Mémoires de la Mère de Chaugy*, p. 159.

[2] *Mémoires de la Mère de Chaugy*, pp. 145–6.

The second clause of the Visitandine formula—"to devote themselves to the perfection of the divine love"—is as lucid as the first. Whatever form it had taken at its beginning or would take in the future, this religious community belongs to the family of contemplative Orders. The evidence is conclusive. In 1610, as in 1615, the Visitation aimed essentially at the development of the interior life, devotion, and all the exercises which lead to the "perfection of the divine love." "Our foundation . . . is entirely based on the interior life," Ste. Chantal formally announces, "to give to God *daughters of prayer* . . . leaving the great Orders . . . to honour Our Lord by excelling in great exercises and striking virtues."[1]

It is true that before 1615 the Visitandines visited the sick and that after that date, for reasons which need not here be discussed, they ceased to do so, but it is not less true that it is entirely wrong to compare them in this respect with Sisters of Charity, Little Sisters of the Poor, or any other community of the kind. It would be as much off the point to compare the toilsome day of the Trappist with the few minutes spent by the Carthusian over his garden. Pious distraction, recreation, and charitable works held a subordinate place in the programme of the early Visitandines, and the life and the special grace of the Visitandines tended to reduce them more and more, even before the interventions which compelled François de Sales to modify the primitive Rule. Grace and Life are imperious mistresses which remodel even the plans of genius—especially those of genius—and once more S. François, not without surprise, but with cheerful gaiety, received their biddings. Once out of his hands, his work showed him what he wanted to do, or rather what God wanted to do through him. Later Ste. Chantal wrote to one of the saint's biographers:

> It is the truth that rare and excellent virtues, mortifications and charities were practised during this opening period, and this lasted with unequalled fervour for about five years. There were none but the earliest professed employed on outside errands, never the novices, but all at once we found everyone changed and desirous of enclosure.[2]

We can understand this "all at once," which is characteristic of the writer. The internal and irresistible development summed up in these lines was no abrupt change, but had begun at once. In 1615

[1] *Œuvres*, I. 305–6. [2] *Ibid.*, II. 306.

the Visitandines found "everyone changed and desirous of enclosure" and solely anxious "to devote themselves to the perfection of the divine love"; that is, after five years of life and a thousand imperceptible changes their supernatural evolution was complete. In 1610, though contemplation was henceforward their principal work, they left it more or less often for works of charity. At first we see them Martha and Mary by turns. Then charitable errands interest them less and less, contemplation more and more till finally, in 1615, Martha has disappeared, Mary alone remains.

Once again we must marvel at S. François de Sales in his school of grace and of souls. Assuredly he did not anticipate the marvellous transformation related above. The Visitandine of his first schemes might be Mary much more than Martha, and remain Mary even while fulfilling the tasks of Martha, but still, whether little or much, there would be something of Martha in her. At the outset he did not visualize her as a Sister of Charity, but dividing her time, "giving a good portion to the exterior works of charity and the greater part to the interior work of contemplation."[1] So he sketched a plan in his mind; well aware that another than he would fill in the portrait. The experiences to come were like a field open to influences from on high, wide enough for grace to have free play, its boundaries sufficiently undefined for grace to modify or contract them.

His mission was to give rules to this growing Community. As a whole and in detail his ideas would have the force of law, so long at least as God Himself did not intervene. Such divine intervention would be manifested to the founder by the Visitandines themselves, not by word, but by the lives lived out under his eyes. A learner at the moment when he most appeared to be master, he daily observed them with that intensity of affection and clairvoyance which amounted to genius in him, noting the rhythm of those souls which believed themselves pulsing in time with his, pondering the smallest indications of that supernatural growth slowly appearing before his gaze.[2] Seen in this light, the beginnings of the Visitation are among the most memorable experiences handed down in the history of sainthood.

[1] *Œuvres de S. François de Sales*, XIII. 311, 318.

[2] "Our first Mothers and Sisters," says Ste. Chantal, "never wanted to speak of anything but prayer; they insisted on this perpetually to our blessed Father, and *were not altogether pleased* because he was wont to reply briefly, dwelling on the exercises of true virtue." *Œuvres diverses*, I. 359.

In this humble little Annecy the mystic idyll, old and ever young, one and yet manifold, takes shape before the wondering eyes of the discreet Bishop. The violets of Philothée pale before the glow of blossoms more splendid: *novas frondes, non sua poma.* In other words, these lowly women insensibly turn more and more towards their centre, "that supreme point" where God awaits them. A fine passage of Mère de Chaugy allows us to follow this imperceptible transformation step by step.

Our blessed Father had desired, for the sake of humility, that the Sisters should by turns perform the cooking and all domestic offices. . . . Our blessed Mother never dispensed herself, save for illness, from being cook in her turn. . . . As the house . . . had a large orchard, and there was much need of milk for the little children of the poor, our Mother likewise persisted in her turn there, and found much sweetness in such low and domestic exercises.

What beautiful symbols of heavenly realities—all these Marys clinging, so to speak, to the menial tasks of Martha—the kitchen, the orchard, the low valleys. All in vain, God willed for them "the better part," which will open another world to us.

It is very true that her principal care and dearest endeavours were to ground her daughters in the true interior and spiritual life, to which all were strongly drawn, so that they sought only mortification, recollection, silence and retreat in God, Who by His immense goodness gratified these dear souls with supernatural favours. By such grace divine several speedily enjoyed the prayer of quiet, the loving sleep of the soul, and a very lofty union; others had extraordinary illuminations on the divine mysteries, in which they were piously absorbed. Others again had frequent raptures and holy ecstasies in which they were caught up as it were into the felicity of God, receiving thus great gifts and graces by His divine liberality. Our blessed Father, in his preface to *L'Amour de Dieu*, says that this holy book "formed part of what had passed between him and our first Mothers and Sisters, whose purity and piety had drawn him to hold forth to them on the most delicate points of the spiritual life, far surpassing what he could say to Philothée."

Thus we see there was no catastrophe, no revolution, no visible change. The Visitation changed as everything living must change, when placed in an atmosphere and under conditions favourable to its growth, as the frail sapling becomes an oak, or the child becomes a man. Further, we see that this change was not and could not have been the personal work of S. François de Sales; but had he been less flexible in spirit, less humble, more jealous of his creation, he would have paralysed the divine workings. His glory is to have forwarded it, and no less to have surrendered and adapted himself with the same flexibility to the interior movement which without his assistance completed his own ideas, thus revealing him to himself.

This splendid history is all of a piece—the Visitation, Ste. Chantal, and the Bishop of Geneva. It will be remembered that we left him in 1610 more and more dazzled by the mystical radiance of the saint, yet still withheld by some final doubts and perplexities. Full light came between 1610 and 1615, with his observation of the birth, progress and character of this higher life, not merely in one or two souls, but throughout an entire community. The Visitation in its early days was for him an Academy of Pure Love. There one by one he traced the many studies which resulted in the definite portrait of Théotime, there the author of *L'Introduction à la vie dévote* was made capable of writing the *Traité de l'Amour de Dieu.*[1] What we owe to these few women, Jeanne de Chantal, Charlotte de Bréchard, Marie Péronne de Châtel and the rest, can never be fully appraised. The purest flame of French mysticism has been lighted by them. and of their fullness we have all received. Their history is contained in the *Traité de l'Amour de Dieu*, more worthily than even in the immortal chronicles of Mère de Chaugy. Whole chapters of the book are filled with Ste. Chantal, but her first daughters also find their place there, great or small. As to the author himself, spirit, heart and pen are so closely moulded to his subject that it is impossible to tell where the observations of the director and moralist end and the personal confidences of the saintly Bishop begin. One thing at least is certain: many of the marvellous favours there described, he had received likewise himself.

Five or six years before his decease (Ste. Chantal writes), speaking of prayer, he told me that he had no sensible appreciations, that what God brought about in him was by illuminations and sentiments in the highest part of his soul, the lower portion being untouched by them. Another time he told me that he had certain good thoughts,

[1] The first edition of this book was in 1616. On the above see the *aperçu historique* of Dom Mackey in *Œuvres de S. François de Sales*, IV. viii ff.

but rather in a manner of a flowing of his heart into eternity and the Eternal than by words. . . . Sometimes he wrote to me that I should remind him to tell me what God had given him in holy devotion, and when I saw him I would do so. He replied: These things are so simple and delicate that one can say nothing when they are past.[1]

These "sensible appreciations," "discourses," imaginations, devout reflections, are they not all part of S. François himself? Who has tasted the sweetness of prayer more truly than he and described it more lovingly? True, this was the first stage of grace, but he too had to go up higher.

Such was the beginning of the Visitation and such it remained until the death of Ste. Chantal. A technical definition of the prayer of these "daughters of prayer" is outside our scope. It need only be added that the first years of the Order fully confirmed the experience of its beginnings. Ste. Chantal, writing of one of her nuns who was crowned with mystic graces, observes:

Such a soul is worth a hundred others, yet it must never be paraded; for such a treasure should be hid, and by skilful management she must be kept ignorant and persuaded that it is the usual course of the Daughters of the Visitation, several of whom are truly drawn that way. . . . To rest in the spirit of God is the most useful occupation that the Daughters of the Visitation could have. They should not take heed of the considerations, conceptions, imaginations and speculations of others, although they should honour them as gifts of God and conducting to God.[2]

Here there is no room for fear that so lucid a mind, by nature almost too "reflective," should incline in any manner towards quietism, thus putting the Visitation on a dangerous slope. She knows better than any that acts of prayers are made continually.

I believe that those who declare that they never make any at any time do not understand what they mean, (I) believe even our Sister N. makes them without knowing it, at any rate I require her to make exterior ones.[3]

Again he says:

They deceive themselves by the idea that they are incapable of con-

[1] *Œuvres*, II. 172–3. [2] *Ibid.*, I. 341. [3] *Ibid.*, I. 504–5.

siderations; and perhaps they desire to place themselves in this mode of prayer of themselves, which one ought never to do. . . .

adding, however, immediately:

neither should they be drawn away from it and hindered from walking therein when God draws them, for that would be a great evil.[1]

"Those who are not led by this road find it strange" when they consider this guidance of the nuns of the Visitation by God. Hence come frequent difficulties with various persons without, well-intentioned otherwise, but "in general highly opposed" to this leading.[2] Strengthened by the authority of S. François de Sales as well as by her own personal experience, and judging the tree by its fruits of rare abnegation and sanctity, the foundress of the Visitation reiterated to all objections: "God wills us thus." Let us conclude with a final passage more decisive and solemn than the others.

I tell you (in the *Réponses*) I have recognized that the almost universal leading of the Daughters of the Visitation is a very simple presence of God, through an entire abandonment of themselves to the holy Providence. I thought of not putting in the word "almost," for truly I have recognized that all those who have from the beginning applied themselves to prayer as is meet, and who did their duty in mortifying themselves and practising virtues, alike reached this point. Several were drawn to it from the first, and it seems as though God availed Himself of this sole road to bring us to our end and to the perfect union of our souls with Him. Finally, I hold that this method of devotion is essential to our little congregation, the which is a great gift of God to Whom is due an infinite gratitude.[3]

It is abundantly evident that, if the saint were here speaking of prayer common to all Christians, she would not employ such language. Let us leave her then with her nuns and S. François in the mystery which veils them from our profane gaze. It is enough to know that the Bishop of Geneva, when founding the Visitation, had for his essential aim to give God "daughters of prayer," mystics, and he succeeded beyond his utmost hopes.

[1] *Œuvres*, IV. 513.

[2] *Ibid.*, III. 537.

[3] *Ibid.*, II. 337. She says elsewhere: "The great method of prayer is to have none. If in going to prayer one can form in oneself a pure capacity for receiving the spirit of God, that will suffice for all method. Prayer should be accomplished by grace and not by artifice." *Ibid.*, p. 260.

V. Although far too little read nowadays, the *Traité de l'Amour de Dieu* nevertheless remains one of the finest books of religious philosophy come down to us from the seventeenth century, perhaps the finest.[1] We need not examine it here from this point of view and it is sufficient to emphasize the historical significance of this *chef d'œuvre*. It would be in fact hard to exaggerate the importance of the conspicuously public adhesion of the wisest and most authoritative theologian and director of the period, to the great mystic movement now appearing everywhere and disturbing certain pious souls. We have seen the author of *Philothée* once half tempted to contend with the influence of Carmel over his spiritual daughters; now he publishes a work in which he follows, step by step, the example and the teaching of S. Teresa. Before 1610, pressed by grace, simultaneously with Mme. de Chantal, to rise above the common level of prayer, he hesitated, not daring to "step aside from the highway"; he preferred to follow "in the ways of the saints gone before and of the simple." In 1616, after the experiences we have described, he reveals boldly "the secret of the King," in a book sure to be read by the majority of the innumerable readers of the *Vie dévote*. He wisely remarks, speaking of the more abstruse chapters: "This treatise is difficult, especially to him who is not an expert in prayer," but he says likewise, and with justice, that "in the most difficult passages of these discourses" prevails "a good and lovely clarity." He fears lest "this little work should not succeed so well as the preceding one, from its being rather more nervous and strong," but he has worked very hard to bring his book within the scope of all. "I have tried to soften and avoid the difficult features," and, in the words of Dom Mackey's conclusion, "we see him recommending the *Traité de l'Amour de Dieu* to men of the world and to courtiers."[2] "What he did for devotion he did also for the mystic life; he showed it as lovable, simple, desirable, even easy."[3] "It is an error, even a heresy," he

[1] See the articles of R. P. Desjardins: *S. François de Sales docteur de l'Eglise* (*Etudes*, 1877), and especially the Introduction of Dom Mackey (*Œuvres de S. François de Sales*, IV. i–xciii), a wholly remarkable piece of work, in spite of some errors of facts in the quietist controversy. Cf. too the capricious and most interesting analysis of M. Strowski: *S. François de Sales: introduction à l'histoire du sentiment religieux*, Paris, 1898.

[2] *Œuvres de S. François de Sales*, IV. xxxv.

[3] I had nearly said "natural", in the sense which Dom Mackey has excellently defined. "S. François de Sales," he remarks, "brings the human heart into the presence of infinite Good, towards Whom it is doubly drawn by the might of grace and a natural instinct which

said, "to wish to exclude from the higher experience of prayer the soldier in his regiment, the artizan in his workshop, the prince in his court, the married couple in their household."

There is a danger that the originality and boldness of such an enterprise may be insufficiently realized. The spiritual leaders of the Salesian school, and of kindred schools such as the Jesuits, generally shrink from discussing mystical subjects. They prefer to ignore them, fearing, and not without reason, that some souls, dazzled by the perspective of a life above the common level, should excite themselves in the pursuit of a chimerical ideal and view with distaste the humble practice of Christian duty. On this subject we may quote one of the great friends of both François de Sales and Jeanne de Chantal, the General of the Feuillants, Dom Sans de Ste-Catherine. In a work addressed to religious, he writes:

The kingdom of God does not consist in words and secret lore of acquired knowledge, but in the spirit of virtue, of truth, of life. . . . Therefore I have not given a place (in my book) to the heights of the contemplative life, for this said life, although of a surety good, is gravely perilous if it be not founded upon mortification and the acquirement of virtues. . . . Rather let us read Thomas à Kempis . . . the Epistles of S. Jerome, S. John Climacus, Cassian, Pinelli and other like books which humiliate and tend to self-examination, than Harphius, Ruysbroeck, Tauler and others, excellent contemplatives though they be.[1]

Ste. Chantal was in full agreement with this author. She writes to a Visitandine:

I well believe, child, that you do not know how to answer those daughters of yours who demand what difference is there between union and contemplation. O, *vrai Dieu*, how can my sister the Superior, and you in her absence, permit this! *Bon Jésus*, where is humility? This must be put a stop to; give them books and discourses dealing with the practice of the virtues and say to them that they

original sin has not totally destroyed. To make this point plainer, he shows us in the effects of human passions the correlative of these ardours, these "wounds," these liquefactions "which are the extraordinary manifestations of divine love." Down to the "supreme effect of active love . . . the death of the lovers! there is no result which has not been produced at one time or another by the insensate transports of profane love." Mackey, *ibid.*, p. xlix. The ideas of S. François de Sales were indeed at opposite poles to those of Jansenism.

[1] *Œuvres spirituelles de R. P. D. Sans de Sainte-Catherine*, Paris, 1650, Preface and p. 497. After S. François, Dom Sans was Ste. Chantal's favourite author.

must try to acquire them and afterwards they may speak of these high matters. . . . When they become angels they will know the angelic speech.[1]

Such an attitude is fundamentally Salesian. Nevertheless the *Traité de l'Amour de Dieu* which was meant for all convents, which S. François recommends even to men of the world, far from limiting itself to simple considerations on "the practice of virtues," speaks "in angelic speech" of "high" matters, and devotes whole chapters to supernatural workings of sublime mysteries.[2]

Its daring and originality will not be denied, but it was a daring calculated and regulated by the wisest of directors and by a writer whose pen is marvellously sure. Here indeed the *Traité* almost attains the miraculous. One finds no single line running any risk of encouraging illuminism or failing to emphasize the necessity of "mortification and the acquisition of virtues." Its sublimity is so continuous and calm, its terms are chosen with such consummate dexterity, its progress towards the heights so gradual, in fact the method of initiation so prudent, that worthy souls have been deceived and have seen in this work of high mysticism only a humble sequel, a second volume of the *Introduction à la vie dévote.* "François de Sales," writes a learned Jesuit,

was not a mystic like Bernard, Bonaventura, above all like Teresa or John of the Cross. He sowed the rough paths of devotion with flowers, but without leaving the beaten tracks. His proper place . . . then is between S. Alphonse the moralist, and S. Bernard, or the seraphic Bonaventura, those princes of the mystic life. The domain of which he holds the sceptre is asceticism in the proper sense of the word.[3]

This is a curious commentary on the decree of Pius IX placing François de Sales in the ranks of the doctors of the Church: *in mystica theologia mirabilis Salesii doctrina refulget.* But if this error raises a smile nowadays, it has a certain significance. Even when he approaches the heights of contemplation, François de Sales scarcely seems to leave the "beaten tracks." He avoids the extraordinary words affected by so many spiritual experts, which hypnotize beginners. As for the consecrated terms which he feels he must retain, he removes from them that atmosphere of mystery which excites the

[1] *Œuvres*, I. 136. [2] Cf. Dom Mackey, *ibid.*, pp. liii–lv.
[3] R. P. Desjardins, *S. François de Sales, docteur de l'Eglise*, *Etudes*, 1877, April 3.

curiosity of some and feeds the vanity of many others. He avoids obscurity and needless complication: he does not insist on the distinguishing shades of mystic states. Contemplatives find all necessary illumination in him, but he never causes spiritual vertigo to those who have not received the call to leave the highway. Finally and above all he

places the exercises of humility and the solid virtues far above "deifying unions" and the "supereminent life." . . . Describing the sublimest workings of grace, (he) constantly recalls that they are neither the irrefutable proof nor the necessary recompense of sanctity. For him, as for S. Teresa and all genuine mystics, charity and the practice of all the moral virtues derived therefrom are preferable to contemplation.[1]

Ste. Chantal somewhere remarks, "All the teaching of our blessed Father tended to the perfect stripping of self."[2] The *Traité*, as well as all else written by him, bears her out, but notice how the glow, the mystic charm, pervades its sternest pages. Where the properly ascetic part ends and the mystic begins no one has ever discovered. These elements, elsewhere so distinct, seem to unite and are in fact united by François de Sales. All the seduction, without the perils, of contemplative works is in this book. Also, and this is my point, it is adopted by directors least of all suspected of encouraging illusion, and sanctioned by the most vigilant Orders, without the slightest hesitation. "They consider it useful to all pious souls," writes Dom Mackey, "as also to those trying to become pious. S. Vincent de Paul terms it 'immortal and very noble,' and gives it to his Congregation of Mission Priests, not merely to serve 'as a ladder to aspirants towards perfection,' but also as 'universal remedy for the weak and spur for the indolent.'" In a letter to a Carmelite nun, Ste. Jeanne-Françoise declares that it solves all the difficulties of the spiritual life; and adds elsewhere: "Humble souls . . . find therein all that they can need for their practical guide towards perfect union with God." The testimony of the celebrated Pierre Berger, canon of Notre-Dame in Paris, is still more explicit.

"God bestowed (on the saint) the grace of expounding the deepest and most mysterious secrets of sacred love, with so much clarity and

[1] Dom Mackey, *ibid.*, pp. l–li. [2] *Œuvres*, I. 352.

ease that what till then had been held impenetrable by far the greater number of men, is to-day understood and practised with much delight by a goodly number of both sexes, who are not versed either in letters or philosophy.[1]

It is still better and more important testimony that the Jesuits themselves, usually severe towards all spiritual adventures beyond "the beaten tracks," have received with ardour this mystical book, in which their old pupil after a fashion recognizes their Society. And what important consequences this adoption was to have for the future. . . . Together with the Oratorians and the Capuchins, the Jesuits have remained the leaders in direction; they hear confessions in a multitude of towns, they preach and write; few convents are closed to them; visions, revelations, supernatural states are all submitted to them when difficulties arise. They are to be the judges, to some extent, of this movement in the outcome of which we are so much interested; they are the great power to check and develop at will. Once rallied to François de Sales and permeated by his spirit, far from hindering this renaissance they will forward it, as we shall see, please God, in the next volume.

Bishops, secular priests, Oratorians, Capuchins, Jesuits and others were all conquered by the same influence and swept into the same current. About 1604 none would have been more astonished than François de Sales had he heard it predicted that some day he would write upon the higher ways of prayer. He had indeed long before "planned to write something on Sacred Love," but, in his own words, his "plan was not comparable to that which 'Providence' made me write."[2] He had dreamed of another *Philothée*, he gave us *Théotime*, and yielded thus, not without long resistance, to the great wave of mysticism that carried away the *élite* of French Catholicism. In his *Traité*, François de Sales does not submit his own theories or reasonings, he contents himself with bearing witness of that which he had seen and felt and handled of the work of God. He relates and describes rather than preaches; his story is that of his own soul and of the souls of Ste. Chantal and the first Visitandines. "The book of *L'Amour de Dieu*," he wrote to Jeanne de Chantal, "is written expressly for you."[3] "For you," however, scarcely expressed his

[1] Dom Mackey, p. xxxvi.
[2] *Œuvres*, IV. x–xi.
[3] *Œuvres de Ste. Chantal*, I. 44–5.

intention. "From you, listening to you, raising myself little by little to the level on which I watched you live," was rather what he should have said, did, in fact, say many times. In January 1614, announcing to Ste. Chantal a speedy visit on the subject of the book then on the stocks, he wrote: "To-morrow I have to confer with her (your soul) on the things of divine love and decide on the line (to be taken)."[1] Another time, still dealing with what had become the dearest preoccupation of both, and summing up for Ste. Chantal one of the most beautiful chapters, he said:

I am working at your ninth book of the Love of God, and to-day, praying before my Crucifix, God showed me your soul and condition by the comparison of an excellent musician.[2]

And Mme. de Chantal on her side, directing one of the first biographers of the saint, writes:

If your reverence desires to see clearly the condition of this holiest soul . . . read the three or four last chapters of the ninth book of *L'Amour divin.*[3]

So with the other Visitandines of this Golden Age, Mères Favre, de Bréchard, de Châtel, de Blonay and de la Roche. All alike sincerely told their saintly director the divine favours which crowned them, thus witnessing themselves to the mystic phenomena recorded in his admirable *Traité.* The life of Mère Anne-Marie Rosset especially was an uninterrupted series of experiences of the most sublime order. Speaking of this religious, Bossuet did not hesitate to declare her spiritual condition a foretaste of the joys of the Blessed. Mère de Chaugy wrote of her: "Our holy founder had her in mind during the composition of several chapters of the sixth, seventh and eighth books of *L'Amour de Dieu.*"[4]

What has here been said of S. François de Sales is no less true of the other directors, spiritual writers and hagiographers of whom we have spoken or whose words we have quoted in this volume. They all give evidence to, and affirm the progress of, a divine enterprise, that Coming of Mysticism which we have endeavoured to describe. The *Traité de l'Amour de Dieu* puts the seal upon all these testimonies; it sums up and closes in magnificent fashion the first period of this history.

[1] *Œuvres de S. François de Sales*, XVI. 144.
[2] *Œuvres*, XVI. 128–9.
[3] *Ibid.*, II. 250.
[4] Dom Mackey, p. lv.

APPENDIX

NOTES ON MYSTICISM[1]

A. *The Mystic Experience*

"TO a superficial observer," writes Père Maréchal, "the mystic state is a Proteus of multiple and varying forms, slenderly linked to one another by a vague pathological religiosity. Further, as manifestations of this condition, the rather short-sighted view of Pamphleteers, doctors with a materialistic outlook on psychology, or ill-instructed pietists, has too often seen only bodily phenomena, religious eccentricities and the crudely miraculous. Thank God, our day seems to witness an agreement among serious investigators to make a careful distinction between the essential and the accessory in mysticism. In the delicate tracing out of this frontier-line, authors of the most different tendencies are learning to approach one another. . . .

"Père Poulain, for instance, declares of 'mystic states', that 'their real difference from the recollection of ordinary devotion is that, in the mystic state, God no longer contents Himself with helping us to think of Him and putting us in mind of His Presence, but that He imparts to us *an experimental intellectual knowledge of that Presence*.'[2] This indeed is the fundamental mystical phenomenon—the direct consciousness of the presence of God, *the intuition of God's Presence*. All the rest—physical ecstasies, suspension of sense, visions sensible or imaginary, words heard interiorly, levitations, prodigies, clairvoyance, etc.—are pure accessories which may or may not accompany the fundamental state, and of which the immediate cause may vary.

"M. Boutroux sounds the same judicious note: 'The essential phe-

[1] Cf. *A propos du sentiment de présence chez les profanes et chez les mystiques*, by J. R. M(aréchal), S.J., extract from the *Revue des questions scientifiques* (1908–9, Louvain, 1909); *Science empirique et psychologie religeuse, notes critiques*, extract from *Recherches de science religieuse*, 1912 (No. 1, Paris); *Sur quelques traits distinctifs de la mystique chrétienne*, *Revue de Philosophie*, Sept.–Oct., 1912. To save space I shall quote these articles as Maréchal I, II, III. The views of Père Maréchal have been discussed by M. Pacheu in *Les mystiques interprétés par les mystiques*, (*Revue de Philosophie*, May–July, 1913), and on the other hand very faithfully reproduced in the articles of R. P. L. de Grandmaison, *La Religion personelle*, *Études*, Feb.–May, 1913. When in a note I give de Grandmaison without addition, I shall always refer to the last article (May 5) of this valuable series.

[2] *Les grâces d'oraison*, p. 66.

nomenon of Mysticism is what is termed ecstasy, a condition in which all communication with the exterior world is broken, and the soul has *consciousness that she is in communication* with an interior object that is the Infinite Being, God.' "[1]

This is also the point of view of William James. These phenomena, he writes, " hallucinations, verbal and graphic automatisms, and such marvels as levitation, stigmatization and the healing of disease . . . which mystics have often presented (or are believed to have presented), have no essential mystical significance, for they occur with no consciousness of illumination whatever, when they occur, as they often do, in persons of non-mystical mind. Consciousness of illumination is for us the essential mark of mystical states."[2]

" It would be easy to multiply quotations on this point, easy also, even more instructive, but alas, too lengthy a process, to appeal to the uniform witness of the mystics themselves. We are then on solid ground (in the study of mystic states) when we take as centre of perspective the culminating point of such states, *the consciousness of the immediate Presence of a transcendent Being*."[3]

Let us not say: What have such exceptional mortals to do with us? Leave them to enjoy by themselves their immeasurable privileges, the mere description of which makes the night to which we are condemned darker and more stifling! This is a wrong attitude of mind and heart. Out of reach though the mystic experience appears to us, it neither disconcerts nor repels as might a chimera, rather it attracts us like a promise. Instead of supposing the mystics superhuman, we are rather disposed to open the mystic career to all mankind. The fallen divinity remembers heaven and is not surprised when certain brothers and sisters of his find their way to the lost Paradise. If mortal intelligence cannot directly and immediately attain to the Supreme Being, yet it may aim thereat, and from the moment it stirs to action it affirms His Presence. " It is," observes Père Maréchal, following S. Thomas, " an activity orientated in its secret depths towards a definite object, the sole one which could completely absorb it, the Absolute Being, Absolute Truth. The Absolute has set His stamp on the fundamental inclination of our intelligence." It aspires towards God before knowing Him by Name, it cannot rest save in His possession. In short, it is not possible to ignore the mystics without disowning one's self. Is it then surprising that human nature understands in a manner, respects and envies those whose ecstasies attain " for an instant the aim which calls forth and directs its movements "?[4]

There is no need to demonstrate scientifically the value of the testimony

[1] *La psychologie du mysticisme*, Paris, 1902, p. 6. Père Maréchal does not agree with identifying the mystic state and definite ecstasy in so limited a sense. He adds that " several mystics declare that mystical communication can be experienced without breaking communication with the outside world."

[2] *The Varieties of Religious Experience*, London, 1904, p. 408, note 2.

[3] Maréchal, I. 72, 74.

[4] *Ibid.*, I. 68.

of the mystics.[1] Their history is sufficient to assure me that in the mass they cannot be either impostors or visionaries. Although never banal, all nevertheless translate, each in his own manner, a common experience. Each one may be ignorant of the rest, yet they all seem to copy from each other. This perhaps is the most moving feature of their history. The differences of so many witnesses " only renders more striking " the harmony of their witness; " Italians, English, Flemings, Germans, Spanish, or French; monks or seculars; theologians or unlearned; contemporaries of S. Bernard or of Philip II . . . born writers or almost illiterate peasants details vary . . . but the main lines stand out, always the same. Difficulties meet the mystics and the fine dust of psychological observations settles always on the same points. The same phrases recur spontaneously in order to characterize the stages of the spiritual ascent. On the essentials . . . there is agreement."[2]

This essential has already received a scholarly definition, but let Père de Grandmaison summarise it in carefully phrased but glowing language.

1. There are moments, fleeting and unforeseen, during which the soul has the consciousness of entering, not by an effort, but by a call, into immediate contact, without image or speech, but not without insight, with Infinite Goodness.

2. This quasi-experimental perception of God, very variable in intensity and splendour, this experience poignant and exquisite, it may be both at once sometimes—is ineffable. The least defective approximations are those for which the terms of sense are borrowed—taste, savour, sight and touch . . . but no term avails to convey an impression so novel, so special, so mighty. . . . The experience involves often doubts and anxieties . . . not as to its reality, but concerning the interpretation to be given and the causes to be assigned to it. Complete security can but revive with the reviving impression, it then becomes absolute, only to be shaken again by new vicissitudes.

3. The knowledge which results from this is not less *sui generis* than the savour itself. It is usually general, poor in elements of direct instruction, in details. . . . It is rather an assurance bestowed, a ray falling on a living reality and revealing its depths.

4. This generality notwithstanding, the mystic knowledge habitually possesses an affective richness and an incomparable force of penetration and inward light. For the dry and banal abstract knowledge, is substituted a sort of immediate evidence, indisputable, imposed from without.

5. These features of the mystic life justify the language instinctively employed in the greater number of writings of this *genre*. . . . How is the impression to be conveyed? Its power, unexpectedness, originality, drive the mystics to have recourse to the most startling expressions. . . . When

[1] To reject *a priori*, as impossible, what the mystics tell us of their extraordinary intercourse with God is not, properly speaking, heretical—the Church having given no ruling on this point—but it is rash, being opposed to the general teaching of the doctors. The theologians " give no absolute guarantee of the supernatural character of the states and revelations of individual mystics. The approval given by the Church to certain writings of contemplatives carries with it, as Benedict XIV said, no such guarantee." Maréchal, II. 57.

[2] Grandmaison, pp. 323–4.

speaking of a unitive knowledge they naturally take their terms of comparison from the closest of human unions—when speaking of direct perceptions, immediate or appearing to be so, the mystics resort to metaphors drawn from the operations of sense . . . a whole organism of spiritual meanings seems thus to be at their disposal; . . . finally, when speaking of an extreme act, shaking the human instrument to its inmost depths and demanding of it an extraordinary tension, the mystics prefer antitheses, and opposed, even contradictory, terms. This defiance of language emphasizes and pleads their inability to say all.

6. One final and important feature unites all Christian mystics, although awkward and incomplete descriptions—still more an ignorant hagiography—may at times have suggested the contrary. This is, that the core of the state of "infused contemplation" consists in the sole act described above . . . (that is to say, according to those who have experienced it) the joy of immediate contact with Primal Love. Where this consciousness of immediate Presence is lacking, there is not, where it exists there is, Mystic Contemplation.[1] The mystic experience must be always for us "the active, not symbolic, presentation of God to the Soul, with its psychological correlative, the immediate intuition of God by the Soul."[2] Immediate as far as is possible on earth, this experience has several names; it is called indifferently "Contemplation," "Prayer," "Mystic knowledge," "Mystic union" or "Union," "Ecstasy," etc. We employ these various names, according to the exigencies of the subject, or merely for euphony, but usually we say "Ecstasy." Like the others, this term is equivocal. It must then be thoroughly understood that "Ecstasy" and "Immediate intuition of God" are for us the same thing.[3]

B. *Visions and Revelations*

In spite of this name "Contemplation," so frequently bestowed upon it, which may lend itself to misconception, Mystical Experience properly so-called—of which alone we speak here—must not be confused with visions, accompanied or not by explanatory words, with, for instance, the voices of Jeanne d'Arc or with the apparitions of Lourdes. Such doubtless are mystic facts, but differing profoundly from those just described. S. Teresa had visions and ecstasies, and formally distinguishes between these two experiences. This is obvious, since every vision implies an intermediary, plainly perceived, between the Soul and the object of vision. There is no vision without images; no revelation which does not offer to the mind clearly defined conceptions.

[1] Grandmaison, pp. 324–8.

[2] Maréchal, III. 478. Cf. the definition given by M. Pacheu: "The irruption within of the personal consciousness of an intervention strange to it, which by its effect avers itself divine" (*Revue de Phil.*, May–July, 1913, p. 643), or that of M. l'Abbé de la Croix, "a higher knowledge of God with an intense love in will, both of them infused, both of them *special* fruits of the gifts of the Holy Spirit." (*Ascétique et Mystique*, Paris, 1912, p. 50.) The independent psychologists, M. Delacroix for instance, accept the Maréchal definition, depriving it of all its dogmatic connotations.

[3] So S. François, *Œuvres*, V. 20 ff.

In short, " Visions, of whatever nature, by no means express the essence of Mysticism, they are no more than showy episodes of the secondary order and often debatable. They may aid the mystic life (or rather the devout life) by the comfort or the stimulus they bring ; but the most eminent among their recipients unanimously repeat with S. Paul—*Æmulamini charismata meliora*. There exists a loftier contemplation which is not excited by the idea of any tangible yield, even the noblest (or of an enrichment of knowledge), but which is joined with the fundamental tendency, intellectual and loving, of the soul towards God.[1] Plain historians as we are, we are not called on to discuss the visions of our Mystics ; if we do relate some, it will always be from an historical, psychological, or literary point of view. All the contemplatives we have studied, lived docilely in communion with the Church, and their confidences merit our respect ; it is for competent judges to weigh their writings in more exacting scales.

C. *The Borderlands of the Mystic Life*

" Contemplation is sometimes preceded and very often accompanied or followed by noticeable physical or mental phenomena, more striking for onlookers, and certainly more extraordinary than the act of contemplation itself. Certain human faculties are put aside and for a time suspended. Imagination, memory, intelligence lose their activity, passing into silence and as it were slumber ; all life concentrates on the point of union between spirit and spirit. But far from such ecstatic phenomena constituting—as the vulgar believe—the essential of the mystic state, or calling forth our admiration, they are but the concomitants, the effects, the price paid. They are due to the weakness, imperfection, inadequate spiritualization of the human instrument and they will diminish as it progresses. Ecstasy (I restrict this term at present to the phenomena of inhibition, temporary insensibility, immobility and contraction, subsequent exhaustion, partial immunity from the laws of gravity, automatic speech and action) is neither a distinction nor a faculty ; it is a tribute paid by the mystics to human fragility. Therefore it is possible to imitate it, or rather produce it by all sorts of methods. There are natural swoons due to physical weakness or overstrained concentration of thought, in excessive efforts after Divine Union : there are also diabolic ecstasies, simulated and pathological, the morbid fruits of fraud, hysteria, and even the assimilation of certain poisons, such as valerian."[2]

This explains the little space we give to descriptions of these " somatic " phenomena ; here and there, however, facts are mentioned which for one reason or another appear to possess a particular interest.

[1] Maréchal, III. 441. Père Poulain pronounces as follows on the nature of the greater number of Visions or Revelations. " Practically, one may without imprudence admit that as regards those who have not attained to high saintliness, three-quarters of their revelations are illusions," *ibid.*, p. 317. Further, it is not wise always to take literally the " I saw " or " It was shown to me " so frequent in mystic literature. " In many cases the writers only meant to describe their devout and more or less vivid imaginations."

[2] Grandmaison, pp. 328–9.

D. *Mystical Knowledge*

Mystical Knowledge is unlike the common stock of doctrinal knowledge which is formed by the acquisition and successive elaboration of a certain number of concepts and judgements—both sharply defined—and therefore presents " teachable " matter. It is a veritable knowledge, since by it human intelligence assimilates a spiritual object, the God present; but it is not either science or speculative theology. God does not act at the centre of the mystical soul like a master enunciating and explaining a series of theorems. We ourselves invariably tend to see Him in this guise when we try to realize the mystical lesson. In truth, God does much better than speak to this soul, He inhabits it, takes His place in the centre, not merely as He abides in the centre of all things, but allowing this Presence to be directly experienced. With ordinary knowledge, as for instance in the recital of the Nicene Creed, we collect and detail a series of affirmations and negations, each a text for a long discourse by theologian or catechist. Mystical knowledge is not like this, built up gropingly, precise, fragmentary, and progressive, it comes suddenly, apprehended as a whole and at once. Its object (the Infinite !) it seizes, embraces, envelops, as a closed fist might imprison a tiny creature, or rather, it is itself seized, embraced and enveloped by its object, as we are by the air we breathe. Its object is the Supreme Being. The mystic's capture is truly magnificent above all captures, but it is Truth rather than truths, Light rather than lights, a Presence rather than a doctrine. The Truth is the source of all truths, the Light is the central heart of all lights, the Presence radiates out doctrine, but the mystic contemplates directly the Source and not the streams, the Fire and not the Flames, the Sun and not its rays. From such contemplation all individual consideration is necessarily excluded, the soul, forgetting all, cannot contemplate itself. Père de Grandmaison, speaking of this mystic knowledge as " commonly general, poor in teachable elements, in details," is condemned like all of us to use deceptive approximations. " General," although employed by S. John of the Cross, too much implies an abstract knowledge ; " poor in teachable elements "—elements of instruction—at once says too little and too much. Strictly speaking, in this connection there can be neither " elements " nor " teaching." From this point of view there is pure indigence, but, on the other hand, there is something far better than elements or teaching—there is Presence, full, perfect, in some way totally possessed and contemplated, massive, if such a term may be allowed ; all the Divine Being and all His riches. All the *Credo* is there, all the treatises of the theologians, come to life, not a succession of judgements husked and parcelled out ; *patrem—omnipotentem—factorem*— but God Himself.

What do we know ? Of ourselves, nothing, but we docilely accept and endeavour to explain what has been told us by the only experimenters who have revealed to us this mysterious manner of knowing. " The mystic," writes the pseudo-Dionysius, is " raised to the supernatural radius of the divine darkness," above " all that is sensible and intelligible." Again he writes, " If in beholding God one knows what is beheld, it is not God who is contemplated but one of the things coming from Him and capable of being known by us." And S. John of the Cross: "Contemplation imparts but a general and obscure knowledge, by which the understanding cannot avail to know distinctly that which is shown."[1]

These remarks may disconcert those—alas, too numerous—who hold the works of the mystics to be divinely dictated, and make only a nebulous distinction between the contemplation of the ecstatic and the inspiration of the sacred writer. But is there a trace in these works of any communication which has added to the doctrinal treasure of the Church? Do we owe them, I do not say a single dogma, but anything beyond either the theological teaching already known before their day, or the possibilities of Christian knowledge? Not that ecstasy is an empty thing, God forbid! S. Teresa said: "In the length of a *Credo* we receive without words more light than we could acquire in many years by all our terrestrial industry."[2] But this superabounding light is, so to speak, supra-doctrinal. S. François Xavier, on coming out of his ecstasies, cried: "*O beata Trinitas!* This does not mean that ecstasy had communicated any new theological explanations of the dogma. That would be revelation, quite possible, but not simple ecstasy. What he had received is far more sublime; he had directly found himself in the immediate Presence of God, One in Three Persons. Theologians may or could *know* as much as he, but what they taught, the saint *felt and realized.* The real knowledge which was his of the Trinity—wholly spirit to spirit—resembles, in a manner, sensible knowledge; there is the same solidity and security of grasp, the same burning fullness of contact, of envelopment, of acuteness. It is no more ordinary vision, *per speculum, in ænigmate;* for some moments it is already almost the vision of heaven.

When the mystic returns to himself he not only thinks, imagines, desires and feels like the rest of us, but he even preserves, in the different activities by which alone he is known to us, his individual tendencies, whether hereditary or acquired.[3] Thus the mystic life helps him to become perfect, but each after his kind, thinning out but not wholly eradicating the old tares. S. Jerome as a contemplative remains rougher than François de Sales. This is equally true and for our purpose more interesting, when applied to the intellectual and literary faculties, the gifts proper of the writer. All contemplatives have not the genius of S. Teresa, nor the depth and doctrinal soundness of S. Thomas. Many of the rank and file, fully receptive of the mystic grace, would be certainly tedious and often startling if they took pen in hand. They seem to think that, provided they confine themselves to telling their experiences, they deserve attention and forget that for this introspective work qualities of clear vision and delicacy are necessary, which mystical grace may

[1] Quoted by Maréchal, I. 97–8, III. 460–1.

[2] *Œuvres Complètes*, I. 160.

[3] Hence the constant relation, too often neglected, between devotional and mystical literature. The greater number of mystics have been formed by purely devotional books, hence the interest of our first volume on Devout Humanism, relative to its successors; hence, finally, the place reserved in these for certain schools of lofty devotional metaphysics, such as the Oratory, and M. Olier.

polish but cannot give. Four-fifths of such writings are almost valueless. "I would," says Père Guilloré, that they "contained only veritable lights and solid sentiments. For usually one is apt to say more on paper than has taken place in the soul. It is so natural to put all concerning oneself in the best light, to describe it in such well-chosen terms that it comes out quite different from what really occurred; for there is no lack of mysterious words in which to tell what after all was no great thing. Is it not thus that directors, judging a soul by its writings, often form a much higher estimate of it than its actual favours and divine workings warrant?"[1]

As to the doctrinal considerations which they add to their autobiography, as to the *lights* of the mystics, they are equivalent, not to their ecstasy, but to their genius and their sanctity—for sanctity, too, is luminous, and much more so than ecstasy.

In a word, it should never be forgotten that the mystics, as mystics, do not belong to the teaching Church. Their "confused" light, the only one that properly belongs to them, is not the aureole of the doctors. It is sometimes deemed surprising that authority should judge or condemn them, but is it not quite natural? What has passed in the centre of their souls the Pope himself cannot know directly, but once they open their lips or take the pen, they are reduced to the level and lot of ordinary writers; no longer mystics, but theologians, philosophers, or poets, good or bad, exposed accordingly to admiration, pity, or censure. Let us, however, beware of condemning them too speedily. He who thinks them absurd often betrays his own poverty and the innate meanness of that "animal man," which comprehends nothing of the things of God.

E. *Pure Love*

If the mystic experience is knowledge—in the limited sense assigned to it above—it is also union, love. There is no need to distinguish ontologically between the different aspects of one great, but marvellously simple, reality. This knowledge is loving, and this love knowing. One sole activity perceives the Divine Presence and surrenders itself to that Presence, perceiving in surrender, surrendering in perceiving. If one of these two aspects could be more necessary, more essential than the other (though that is impossible), it would be love.[2]

[1] Guilloré, *Maximes spirituelles pour la conduite des âmes*, Chap. VI., Max. IX., ch. ii.

[2] To follow this out in detail would call for nice metaphysical definitions outside our province. It could, for instance, be demonstrated that of the two equally unfit names given to the mystic experience—"union" and "contemplation"—the latter is the more unfit, since, if all our reasoning faculties have a mystical tendency (as Père Maréchal has demonstrated for the intelligence), this tendency is much more direct, and less likely to meet with hindrances in the will. All union of love is attached either to the centre of the soul (as in the mystic union) or else to the region nearest to it. As Hugh of S. Victor and many Schoolmen after him say, "*Plus diligitur quam intelligitur et intrat dilectio et appropinquat ubi scientia foris est.*" (*Exposit. in hierarch. cœlest. Dyon.*, I. 7.) It often happens "that, knowledge having produced sacred love, that love passes the bounds of the knowledge

We must understand the relation of knowledge and love. Knowledge does not hold first place, as in the common affective life. Pragmatism need no longer be feared; the maxim of the Schoolmen, *nil volitum nisi præcognitum*, does not apply when the centre of the soul is in question, which gives an impulse to all our faculties, and which is in itself more lucid than intelligence, more free than the will. It is even more imperative to put aside the phantom of sensible sweetness, those "consolations" which usually accompany the impulses of human love and piety. The mystic union may react on the feelings and even on the senses, and these, both alike, are subjected to terrible dearth and atrocious sufferings, but its loving joy is not "sensible" nor its light outwardly radiant. Ecstasy neither delights nor instructs—it unites. We do not doubt that it is frequently—perhaps normally—accompanied or followed by devout delights; we simply say that those delights are not the ecstasy.

This is so true that, according to the mystics, "It is a special grace to the soul that loves (ecstatically) when it does not feel the fires of its love . . . and even doubts if it loves at all. For then neither feeling nor sight nor assurance can afford a channel for aught impure." "It will sometimes chance," we are told again, "that your heart loves in truth, when at the same time you will feel that it does not love. Be not then surprised, these two things agree very well, it is but pride and corruption when the human heart reposes in its love and not in the object of its love; when, by a faithless return upon itself, it rests and takes comfort in the sacred fire which burns it, and not in Him Who has enkindled it; truly, this is to extinguish the divine flame, and to have only a bastard glow, lit and heaped up only by self-love."[1] Whether or no such "faithless returns" are dangerous, they all necessarily hinder ecstatic love; when human faculties succeed—not in adding to or enjoining this love—but in freely exercising their reflective activities, ecstasy, so to speak, cedes the field and vanishes.

Happily there is no need of a grace of Mystic Union to love God with disinterested love. Many worthy souls imagine that the Church, in condemning the *Maximes des Saints*, has with that condemned Pure Love. As well say that it condemns the Decalogue and the Gospel; "Pure Love," properly speaking, is as much a pleonasm as a universal panacea. Acts of disinterested love—do we not all perform them when we love our friends without thinking what service they can render us? Is not the Act of Love, which the Church

which is understanding, and advances far beyond it," *Œuvres de S. François de Sales*, IV. 52, 314–15. This brushing aside all intellectual representations to attain intimate union with God beyond the region of imagery, marks the progress of loving activity towards the depths or the centre of the soul. There is the zone of the normal will, close to that of the mystical, while the intelligence remains fettered to the borders of the sensible world, chained to the windows of the senses where it awaits the images for which it craves.

That union is consummated in the centre of the soul is so evident to the contemplative, that in any description of his "states" he does not dream of "placing" his ecstatic love Union always takes place at the centre of the soul, or near the centre. Acts of intelligence happen differently and the mystic always asserts that ecstatic knowledge is produced in a particular region, the apex of the spirit.

[1] Guilloré, *Les progrès de la vie spirituelle*, Lyons, 1687, pp. 525–8.

ordains, shall be recited by all the faithful, in itself an Act of Pure Love? Some extracts may be given from the clear catechism on this subject drawn up by Père de Caussade:

Q. What is that love of God which is termed disinterested and of pure goodwill?

A. It is that by which God is loved for Himself alone, without thought of oneself.

Q. What is interested love?

A. It is that love of Christian hope by which we love God in relation to ourselves, as our Sovereign Good and our future Sovereign Beatitude.

Q. What was the error of the new mystics on this head?

A. It was admitting Pure Love only in a certain stage of so-called perfection; whereas it may be practised even by beginners.

Q. But if this love is common to all, what difference can exist between the just and the perfect (that is, non-mystics and mystics)?

A. The difference is that the latter love God more perfectly, with the same love of pure goodwill, *since there are not two kinds of love*.

Q. But in what does this perfection of love consist?

A. To quote Bossuet, "In a more habitual, continuous, dominating exercise of the love common to all."

Q. What difference is there then between Love and Pure Love?

A. None but in degree, for all true love is so essentially disinterested that none can exist which is not pure, according to the words of S. Paul: "Charity seeketh not her own."[1]

Since Pure Love is to be met at the two poles of the inner life, in the practice of the simple faithful and in the Mystic Union, it may well be asked why theologians should impart an air of mystery to the subject, and why so many battles—the Quietist controversy for instance—have been fought on the question of Pure Love? The reason is that, in a life already on a high spiritual level, unconsciously advancing towards the mystic experience, the "more habitual, continuous, dominating exercise of the love common to all," to quote Bossuet, is subjected to a special discipline, subtle and infinitely mysterious, which startles the superficial observers, puzzles and wearies many directors, and reduces the contemplative himself to an obscure distress. One of the longest and most delicate chapters of mystic theology deals with those strange probations which, as it were, form the apprenticeship of ecstasy. Whither do such "probations" tend, if not to the progressive "purification" of love? A harsh and dark reverse side of the sublime grace at once communicated and veiled by them, they implacably strip the future contemplative of all his too human ties, of all that yesterday made his joy and strength, sometimes his pride, delights of prayer and ease in practising virtue. They dislodge the adversary of pure love, that is to say, self-love, from its last fortress, by mortifying the will, dimming the intelligence, and attenuating the "little

[1] Père de Caussade, *Instructions spirituelles en forme de dialogues sur les divers états d'oraison, suivant le doctrine de M. Bossuet*, Perpignan, 1741, pp. 128–30. See also my *Apologie pour Fénelon: La revanche du pur amour*, pp. 433–77.

thread of natural life which is hardly ever broken because it is too great a renunciation to sacrifice irrevocably all individual impulse of heart and mind."[1] They harass in twenty other fashions their victim and they empty him little by little of himself, or rather of what he believes to be himself, driving him back, naked, desolate, and terrified towards some unseen abyss—to find it no gulf of nothingness or even hell, but in reality the blessed centre of the soul, in which, all probations terminated, will be consummated the mystic union, the coronation of Pure Love. In this awful Night but one light remains, the certainty—battered, panting, heroic—that not ecstasy, nor even heaven is beyond, but that it is imperative to leave all to the cruel Craftsman rending the soul, to abandon oneself to the Divine Will. This abandonment, to which the mystics return so insistently, is the last stage reached by Pure Love before it passes into Ecstatic Love. Yet "abandonment" is an equivocal term, it can be translated into the "Live as you will" of the Quietists or else into the "Let God work in you" of the saints.[2]

Need we add that neither in the thought nor in the practice of true mystics has the school of Pure Love and abandonment ever been one of ease. How have the souls of the contemplatives been rendered "so supple and pliable in God's hands?" asks Père de Caussade, and replies: "For this it has been necessary that all their wills, through the holiest use of the powers, should have been a hundred times crossed, broken, tamed and captured under the sole will of God; that a great emptiness of the spirit, often and for long periods experienced, should have almost entirely stifled their natural activity; that long and terrible inabilities to accomplish the smallest act decided on or distinctly perceived, should have driven them to seek in the higher regions of the soul alone the direct acts of their simple resolutions, and taught them to be contented when it pleases God thus to reduce a soul to the utmost poverty and nudity of spirit. Others again have been called to pass through many other trials, a hundred interior agonies (such as) impressions of terror as of one again and again on the point of death . . . which here happens every time when, by a special grace, but without visible light or conscious perception, they are inwardly impelled to abandon themselves to God in the darkest depths of faith, where there would seem to be no interior support to sustain the agonizing soul in sight of the fearful gulfs of such terrible abandonment; for it seems to them in those moments that they are about to be precipitated, swallowed up, and lost in some unspeakable abyss, even wiped out of existence by an invisible hand: the terror thus inspired being like that of a man from whose grip, in the midst of a vast ocean, is plucked the plank which alone sustains him as a last resource."[3]

[1] Caussade, *ibid.*, p. 387.

[2] "As for my condition," wrote Ste. Chantal, "it seems a simple waiting for that which it may please God to work in me. I have neither desires nor intentions nor aught but the will to let God act; as yet I do not see it clearly, but it seems to be in the depth of my soul" (*Œuvres*, III. 599).

[3] This passage sufficiently explains those "impossible suppositions" which scandalized Bossuet so much that he would only allow them much against the grain to even the greatest mystics. Without entering into such depths, it is well to remark that these trials doubly

This striking passage, in which nothing is written for literary effect and which sums up countless testimonies, explains the instinctive opposition that mysticism inevitably arouses in a multitude of spirits otherwise excellent and devout. Pure love, abandonment, quietude, passivity, almost complete cessation of the common acts of Christian practice—what else is all this but scandalous indolence, camouflaged by mysterious names which disguise the poison and make it all the more dangerous? No doubt illusion and the hypocritical exploiting of holy things are always to be feared. False mystics will always find in this doctrine grounds for vanity and self-indulgence, a ready-made excuse for weakness either in avoiding evil or practising the good. But these imaginary or counterfeit ecstatics betray themselves almost invariably to any practised observer. The indolence of their habitual conduct reveals and condemns the illusory quietude of their devotion. As for the true mystics, their obedience to the Church, their zeal and mortification, in a word their holiness, sufficiently vindicate them. Those scandalized by their apparent inertia in devotion fail to perceive that there is nothing more active than ecstasy, less passive than the global act of being that enters into union with God. Even the faculties momentarily exhausted by an experience that draws forth all the forces of the soul, gain through the very discipline which has humiliated them, and find impulses and power hitherto unknown to them, a very magnificence of expansion, accruing to them in their period of inaction.

F. *Quietism*

Quietism despises and neglects the ordinary practices of the Christian life, such as vocal prayers and meditations, frequent use of the Sacraments, and the practice of Christian virtues, substituting for these an indolent abandonment to the mystic work of grace in certain elect souls. According to the Quietists, the perfect will be raised into a state of bliss in which mystic contemplation will be easy and constant, if not altogether uninterrupted—a crying absurdity. Ecstasy is their normal and daily element, and therefore they logically claim for every hour that which the mystics have affirmed of the moments of their sublime experiences, namely, that during the concentrated and transitory activity in the centre of the soul the effort of the faculties becomes useless and even hurtful. Therefore religion should resolve itself into absolute repose of intelligence and will, untroubled by any too precise devotion to the Divine attributes or to the Person of Christ; since all concentration on definite objects must darken the divine twilight of contemplation. No need to do good, no anxiety to avoid evil. Ecstasy suffices.

belong to the state of mysticism: (1) because by means of them God prepares the soul for ecstasy; (2) because they already in some wise belong to the mystic consciousness; the Mystic Union beatifying, although obscurely and insensibly, the summit of the soul, while the active surface is subject to this anguish. "God," writes Guilloré, "draws you to this nudity in order that you may be suffering, dead, and detached in this condition. So much for your part (understand by this the part of our ordinary activities, intelligence, etc.), while, on His side, he is filling the soul and working in it marvels of grace beyond all conceptions."

When this doctrine has been first fairly understood, there ensues a species of stupefaction, varying according to temperament. "One is horrified," cries Père Poulain, "to see that in the seventeenth century so many follies could be admitted and admired by theologians and sensible people."[1] Père de Caussade is equally disquieted, but for another reason: "If the suspicion of Quietism were such a stigma, no doubt right-minded people would make it a matter of conscience neither to nourish nor spread such suspicions without strong proofs. How comes it then that a few half-comprehended words in a book, a letter, a discourse, should be enough to raise a hasty outcry of 'This is Quietism, he speaks, or he writes as a Quietist!'"[2] It was but too easy for Caussade to answer his own question, and in truth who could believe that a doctrine even more idiotic than scandalous could have been approved by saints and scholars, by Benoit de Canfeld who directed the loftiest souls of his age, by Bernières, or by Fénelon?

Nevertheless it is evident that various mystics were not always able to foresee the interpretations, ridiculous or dangerous, occasionally, perhaps frequently, given to their works by some of the faithful. The best souls understood them aright, but outside their scanty number how many weak wills and feeble spirits! If Nicole failed altogether to understand the Jesuit Guilloré, one of those suspected of Quietism, many a little woman, ignorant and vain, may have fancied she had discovered in those high and beautiful writings all manner of fine excuses for sloth or illuminism. Such was the common lot of many writers, sufficiently justifying the Church's severity towards them, but it would be injustice to suspect them of Quietism, either in thought or word. The whole system indeed is in itself but a synthesis of exposition and of battle-cries; and in such a form no true Christian, so far as I know, has ever taught it. But the tendencies which the system traced back to their dogmatic principles, that is to say the spirit of Quietism, certainly infested Catholic Europe throughout the whole seventeenth century. Before the birth of Bossuet the mystics had already given the alarm, as we shall often have occasion to recall, and although it is sadly true that too often party spirit exploited the accusation of Quietism, to destroy the innocent, yet the peril was no imaginary one. It called on spiritual writers to exercise reserve and precaution, and sometimes called in vain.[3]

[1] Caussade, *ibid.*, p. 491.

[2] *Ibid.*, pp. 205–8.

[3] Part at least of the evil was due to the mystical terminology, notably the neo-Platonic term "passive" or "passivity." Popularized though it has been by the orthodox, it yet lends itself to difficulties. By "passive," it seems to me that the most philosophical of the mystics, in describing their experience, desire to imply the idea of "infused" or "given," that this experience presents; of passivity, in the common sense, there is nothing in ecstasy. Certain contemplatives think and say that God alone acts within them. He assuredly acts, in all our actions, but it is by stimulating the contemplative's own activity, although in another manner, more efficacious and direct, than in the daily life. Nor do we believe that the faculties which are rendered less active either by the approach of ecstasy or the ecstasy proper, can be spoken of as "passive"; their energy but suffices for an act of abandonment to the divine will which mortifies and desires to suspend them, but such abandonment is heroically active. Nor is this less true of similar acts practised in ordinary life.

All that has been said of Quietism can be repeated on the subject of Pantheism. He can

G. *The Mystic Life*

In condemning ourselves, as we must, to isolate the so-called mystic phenomenon from the living *milieu* in which it is embedded, the strange experiences which strike across it, and the activities which it prolongs and which are prolonged in their turn by it, we have fatally mutilated and even falsified it. It is the same with all anatomical dissections and moral analyses, for instance, of the self-absorbed man in La Bruyère, or the egoist in the *Maximes.* Classification is necessary, but dangerous when we forget that true analysis defies analysis, and dictionaries are too earthbound when things of the other-world come to be described. A pure mystic, a being whose every movement is mystical, never will exist. It is necessary to remember firmly that devotion is not ecstasy, and to distinguish the new element, *sui generis*, added by ecstasy to devotion : to bear in mind also that the two states enrich one another, interpenetrate and conduce to the harmonious development of one and the same sanctity. This new element which is the mystic experience, we must not think of as possessing an independent and parasitic life of its own, nor must we see it present in the moral organism of the mystic like a bullet embedded in the flesh, nor again must we compare it to the fabulous river which kept its waters sweet indefinitely.

Whence then comes this absolute separation ? From God Himself as object of mystic consciousness and goal of mystic union ? Does God then alter Himself in order to be known and possessed in a more intimate fashion ? From the soul, perhaps ? But is not the soul, whether before or during ecstasy, always one single and marvellously simple creature ? No doubt, using and abusing a convenient metaphor, we have spoken of a surface and a centre in this soul, but nowhere has it been asserted that such centre is to be regarded as an accumulator of electricity encased in glass. No, all the spiritual fluids which animate the surface rise from and return to this centre. Add to this that the theologians, if they cannot explain how the mystic grace grafts itself on the sanctifying grace which already in a manner deifies the simple faithful, all hold that the first of these graces depends upon the second. By what right then shall we make a gulf between mystic experience and devotion ?

Further, who shall exactly define where devotion ends and ecstasy begins ? A modern theologian, Père Poulain, affirms, in the face of countless authorities, that the devotion of Ste. Chantal or of the author of the *Imitation* was not mystical. One might wish this were so, but it must be recognized that from devotion already so lofty, to another form of devotion still loftier, the distance is quickly covered, and the point of transition is imperceptible to us. It is plain that devotion tends towards mysticism as its normal development, and consequently that interior affinities link the one to the other. Without

comprehend nothing of the mystical life, who could fear that any true mystic could ever make shipwreck on that reef. The mystic realizes himself, as a person, distinct from the universe and from God, so intensely that it never occurs to him that anyone could doubt it. Hence the daring freedom of certain expressions in mystic writers.

asserting that devotion entails ecstasy, as sanctifying grace, duly cherished, entails the Beatific Vision, we may say with S. Teresa that if a devotedly holy soul did not obtain that supreme crown there would be a flaw in the mystic code.[1] The mystic and the faithful, without precisely speaking the same language, nevertheless understand each other admirably. If the one does not penetrate so deeply as the other, yet they are both concerned with one and the same reality, the knowledge of God; one and the same path conducts them to that aim, namely detachment from self and the sanctifying exercises of Pure Love. That is why the *Imitation of Christ* or the *Traité de l'Amour de Dieu* appears to some simply devotional, to others properly mystical.

Devotion is the flower, the Mystic Union the fruit; but, while the flower does not survive the fruit which is its completion, devotion derives from the Union a new vitality, in fact carries it on, exploits it, if the term were not too vulgar. As the most humble of these gifts takes rank with the sublime, so the most sublime takes rank with the humblest. From the mystic experience, "poor in elements of instruction" and in acts, are derived abundant and detailed graces in the pious intelligence, new forces in the will, new impulses of tenderness in the heart. This dim hearth irradiates a whole literature, from this death springs the *Acta* of the saints. Nor is this all; for Devotion thus renewed will in turn lead to or provoke fresh ecstasy, that ecstasy a fresh rush of devotion, and so on, at least so long as the soul continues loyal to grace.

If it be difficult to say where mystic experience begins, it is no less so to decide where it finishes. It is true, in a sense which is true when rightly understood, to say that it never finishes. For even when that special mode of union with God lapses, the union itself remains. It is unthinkable that the mystic, on returning to himself, is deserted by God, or that these immolations—often so crucifying—which present the reverse side of ecstasy, should, once consummated, be lost for ever, as though in the Celestial design they had no other end than to bring about an ephemeral and unfruitful transformation. No, such graces do not fade away. Interrupted and suspended, they continue to shine forth.[2]

Intelligence, imagination, heart and will, in short all the faculties of the mystic, remain transfigured by the mysterious union which has been consummated beyond them and without their aid; such transitory inaction healing them of their natural feverishness, their covetousness, egoism and unrest. Henceforth the actions produced by these faculties will be, as S. François de Sales says, "tested and distilled by *la pointe de l'esprit*." Thus we achieve the

[1] I sum up here the very interesting remarks of a Spanish Jesuit, quoted by the Abbé Jean de la Croix in his valuable pamphlet, *Ascétique et Mystique*, Paris, 1912, pp. 56–7.

[2] "Since that time," writes the Venerable Mère Marie de l'Incarnation (Mme Martin), "my soul has abided in its centre, God. That centre is within itself, and it is there above all consciousness. This is so simple and delicate a thing that I cannot express it. *It is possible to speak of anything, to read, to write, to work*, to do all that one will, without distraction from this occupation or without ceasing to be united to God." *Vie de la V. M. Marie de l'Incarnation*, by Père de Charlevoix, p. 112.

most enduring, the most perfect and surest of ecstasies, that "of work and life," as the same theologian, careless of our abstractions and analytical geometry, has said elsewhere. "So that henceforth we do not live merely an honest, respectable and Christian life, but one that is supernatural, spiritual, devoted and ecstatic, that is to say a life in every way free and lifted above our natural condition."

INDEX

Secular names printed thus: Beauvillier, Marie de.
Names in religion thus: Marie de la Trinité.

C

D

The Mayflower Press, Plymouth. William Brendon & Son, Ltd.